LAW AND THE INTERNET

This successful book offers students and practitioners an up-to-date overview of developments in Internet law and practice. The editors have once again assembled a team of expert authors to write about those aspects of Internet law which are of special importance in the global regulation of the Internet and focused around three principal themes—e-commerce, intellectual property, and privacy, data protection and cyber-crime with, in addition, a major contribution on Internet Governance. This edition incorporates for the first time areas such as data protection, privacy and electronic surveillance, cyber-crime and cyber security, jurisdiction and dispute resolution online. The section on IP contains a clear and comprehensive analysis of the ways in which IP and the Internet intersect including coverage of open source licenses and the IP problems around search engines. The new edition also takes account of all current cases and legislation, including the draft revised EC Telecoms Package and the Audio Visual Media Services Directive.

Law and the Internet
Third Edition

Edited by
Lilian Edwards and Charlotte Waelde

·HART·
PUBLISHING
OXFORD AND PORTLAND, OREGON
2009

Published in North America (US and Canada) by
Hart Publishing
c/o International Specialized Book Services
920 NE 58th Avenue, Suite 300
Portland, OR 97213-3786
USA
Tel: +1 503 287 3093 or toll-free: (1) 800 944 6190
Fax: +1 503 280 8832
E-mail: orders@isbs.com
Website: http://www.isbs.com

Hart Publishing Ltd, 16C Worcester Place, Oxford, OX1 2JW
Telephone: +44 (0)1865 517530 Fax: +44 (0)1865 510710
E-mail: mail@hartpub.co.uk
Website: http://www.hartpub.co.uk

British Library Cataloguing in Publication Data
Data Available

ISBN: 978-1-84113-815-2

Typeset by Forewords, Oxon
Printed and bound in Great Britain by
TJ International Ltd, Padstow, Cornwall

For Thomas
für immer vermisst
Charlotte

Preface to the Third Edition

The last edition of this book appeared nine years ago in the year 2000. In Internet years, rather as with dog years, that is a very long time. Notwithstanding that some chapters were in essence updated and revised for the intervening collection, L Edwards (ed), *The New Legal Framework for E-Commerce in Europe* (Oxford, Hart Publishing, 2005), this is substantially a new volume, and, indeed, almost twice as long as its millennial predecessor. This remarkable increase in length can, the authors assert, be fairly laid on the sheer exponential volume of increase of the topic, rather than the logorrhoea of the contributors. Internet law has become a field where you can hardly take your eyes off the cursor for a moment without missing (at least) two vital developments before breakfast (and probably a few new consultations on file-sharing). This pace of development makes the field both infuriatingly difficult to follow and addictively fascinating to study, and has required the virtual (*sic*) rewriting of parts of this text several times as events overtook it. The contributors have in the end stated the law formally as of 1 May 2009, but in many places it has been possible to take into account much later developments, right up to mid-August when the book went to press.

So what is new since the last edition in 2000? Skipping the kneejerk response "almost everything", the most obvious influence on this volume has been the unavoidable rise of the so-called "Web 2.0". This much contested portmanteau phrase, coined by IT guru Tim O'Reilly, denotes such themes as

- the advent of user-generated content (UGC) sites, such as Facebook, YouTube, MySpace, Flickr, Wikipedia and eBay;
- the connected boom in social networking, and the rise of the advertising rather than subscription or sale business model for monetising information; and
- the distribution of the dissemination, publication, tagging and editing of content as well as its authorship – see, for example, the peer-to-peer (P2P) file-sharing revolution; the online multi-hands-edited encyclopaedia, Wikipedia; online resource-sharing projects such as SETI@Home; collective tagging sites such as Digg and delic.io.us; etc.

Arguably "Web 2.0" also embraces the rise of sophisticated search algorithms as the vital pathfinders through information overload, even though such were already in development back in the old days of Web 1.0. A final strand of technological development which heavily pervades the book relates to the diversification of digital technologies away from mundane personal computers. A generation of young users are now probably as likely to access the Internet via mobile phones, games consoles or cable TV sets as via their laptops and desktops. Furthermore the population routinely interacts with, and is tracked by, digital sensors that now form part of the "real" rather than virtual world – RFID (radio frequency identification) tags and similar sensors embedded in everything from supermarket groceries, clothing and library books, to cars, pets, transport smart cards and roads. This concept of the "Internet of Things" is most influential in this book in the section on privacy, surveillance and data collection, but its implications will be profound generally for citizen and consumer involvement with e-commerce and the information society.

If we turn to the law and regulatory structures explored in the book at hand, the effects of this disruptive batch of innovative technologies and approaches are everywhere to be seen. Perhaps most notably, in the e-commerce section, the uncontroversial idea in 2000 that online intermediaries, such as Internet service providers (ISPs), should be immune from liability for the content they distributed or hosted has become savagely controversial in a world of pirated music and film, P2P distribution, collapsing business models, UGC sites, news aggregation, RSS feeds and dozens of other innovations (see chapter 1, 20 and *passim*). When we turn to intellectual property (IP), in 2000 we still spoke worriedly of the possible "death of copyright"; in 2009, we speak more of the death of digital rights management (DRM) and pay-per-copy business models, and the rise instead of levies, streaming and online services and open source/open access alternatives (see chapters 5, 6, 11 and 12 especially). Once domain names and how to stop cybersquatting (see chapter 9) were the key infrastructural problems associated with the Internet and IP; now much more debate revolves around how the laws of both copyright and trade marks may need to be amended to provide protection for the vital search engines which keep the Internet manageable (see chapters 7 and 8).

In the world of privacy, traditional data protection law has been brought to its knees by Web 2.0 and its world of millions of data controllers (see chapter 14); and the new technologies for data collection, tracking and surveillance, such as RFID mentioned above, as well as distributed production of data, threaten to make our world a "transparent society" whether we like it or not (see chapters 15–19). In cybercrime too, the distributed world has lead to the "professionalisation" of cybercrime, as botnets and malware as the foundation of cybercrime activity have replaced the old paradigm of the mad, sad, but not that bad, hacker. Modern cybercrime, largely perpetrated from networks of computers captured and enslaved by viruses, is big and routinised business, and fast becoming an integral part of both the underworld economy, and potentially, cyber warfare and cyber terrorism (chapter 21). In light of the remarkable relevance and tremendous growth of these two areas of law, the coverage of both in this volume has been considerably expanded.

Some legal problems never go away though, however much they are transformed by new technologies, and the reader will still find in these pages, as in previous volumes, considerable discussion of the nuts and bolts of, for example, e-contracting (chapter 2), online jurisdiction and dispute resolution (chapter 3), online defamation (chapter 1), protection of computer software (chapter 10) and (sadly) online pornography (chapter 20). We are also very happy to have added brand new specialist chapters by Richard Jones looking at the criminological analysis of cybercrime, Abbe Brown on IP rights, human rights and competition, and Elizabeth Newman on the EC Audio-Visual Media Services Directive.

What next? As the production of this volume draws to a close, the law continues to develop in almost every area discussed. We still wait on tenterhooks for the final acts in the long running saga of the revision of the EC Telecoms Package, one of the largest pieces of digital reform ever. The process of revising Europe's old warhorse, the Data Protection Directive, has finally, if a little reluctantly, begun in the European Commission. It cannot be forever before the same is true of the Electronic Commerce Directive, parts of which are already under severe judicial attack throughout Europe. The judiciary (in both domestic and supranational courts) will undoubtedly continue to adjudicate on all aspects of IP as it affects the Internet, with crucial consequences for stakeholders. Yet more initiatives will almost certainly be unleashed by regulators in desperate protection of the rightsholders of the music, games and video industries. Rather more to be welcomed, Europe (and the world) will, we hope, begin to wake up to the need to safeguard human rights online as much as offline, especially in relation to key liberties such as privacy and freedom of expression. The European' Parliament's "Recommendation on Security and Fundamental Freedoms on the Internet" adopted in March 2009 is an excellent step along this road.

But, as ever, the next big thing to happen to Internet law will probably be, as with Napster, Facebook, Phorm and the botnet economy, something that lawyers had never anticipated and do not quite understand to start with. This unpredictable direction of Internet law may be a curse to editors, but it is also why this field remains almost uniquely intriguing to its students and teachers. (Future developments can at least be accessed via a myriad of online sources, including (plug) Lilian Edwards's blog *Pangloss,* available at http://blogscript.blogspot.com/ and *ipkat,* available at http://www.ipkat.com.) It is also why a book of this kind requires a large cast of contributors, whose expertise can reach from copyright to crime and back again; to all of those who gave so generously of their time and expertise in this volume, our thanks.

Lilian Edwards and Charlotte Waelde
August 2009

Contents

List of Contributors

Tobias Bednarz, Research Associate and PhD student, SCRIPT, the Arts and Humanities Research Council (AHRC) Centre for Intellectual Property and Technology Law, School of Law, University of Edinburgh.

Abbe Brown, Lecturer in Information Technology Law and Associate, SCRIPT.

Ian Brown, Senior Research Fellow, Oxford Internet Institute, University of Oxford.

Lilian Edwards, Professor of Internet Law at Sheffield University; Associate Director, and co-founder, of SCRIPT.

Andrés Guadamuz, Co-Director SCRIPT and IT Lecturer, School of Law, University of Edinburgh.

Jordan S Hatcher, JD, LLM. IP/IT lawyer and strategy consultant (www.jordanhatcher.com).

Julia Hörnle, Senior Lecturer in Internet Law, Queen Mary School of Law, University of London.

Richard Jones, Lecturer in Criminology, School of Law, University of Edinburgh.

Arne Kolb, solicitor and research associate with SCRIPT. Since 2005 he is also lead cellist with Broken Records.

Hector MacQueen, Professor of Private Law and co-director, SCRIPT, Law Faculty, University of Edinburgh.

Christopher T Marsden, Senior Lecturer in Communications Law and Director of the LLM in IT Media E-Commerce (ITME) Law, University of Essex Law School

Elizabeth Newman, Editor in the IPIT & Communications service at Practical Law Company.

Judith Rauhofer, Research Fellow in Law, Information & Converging Technologies, Centre for Law, Information & Converging Technologies, University of Central Lancashire; and Editor, IPIT & Communications, Practical Law Company.

Christine Riefa, teacher of consumer law and intellectual property law at Brunel University (West London).

Antony Taubman, Director, Intellectual Property Division, World Trade Organisation, formerly Director, Global IP Issues Division, World Intellectual Property Organisation.

Charlotte Waelde, Professor of Intellectual Property Law, and co-director, SCRIPT, Law Faculty, University of Edinburgh.

Caroline Wilson, Lecturer in Intellectual Property Law, University of Southampton, School of Law. ILAWS (Institute of Law & The Web at Southampton).

Table of Cases

Table of Legal Instruments

International/Bilateral Instruments

Bilateral Agreements

Council of Europe

National Legislation

Australia

Belgium

France

Germany

Part I
Introduction: Governance

Introduction

International Governance and the Internet

ANTONY TAUBMAN[1]

Give a laptop. Change the world.[2]

Everyone, everywhere should have the opportunity to participate and no one should be excluded from the benefits the Information Society offers.[3]

The important ingredients are the whimsy, the nerds, the 'let's just try it out and see what uptake it gets' . . . you can find nerds everywhere, that's the hope of the One Laptop Per Child project and others like it. . . . I don't see it as a digital divide thing, I think that nerds can come up everywhere . . . people willing to devote some passion and some brain cycles to these problems.

I don't buy the 'global Internet community' in sense [of] ICANN. . . . At the formation of ICANN, I was on the membership advisory committee. And we were there talking about . . . how do we have the last Sherpa in Afghanistan be represented in ICANN because everybody has a stake in it even if they don't know it yet. And you end up realizing that while you're waiting on the votes to come in from all corners, to decide on some essentially top-down scheme that you say is bottom-up because you have to get consensus from everybody, it just fades away. That's my worry about that kind of process.[4]

I. 'INTERNATIONAL' GOVERNANCE AND THE INTERNET?

WE START WITH a confronting question: does it make sense to talk about the 'international law' or 'international governance' of the Internet at all? Is there anything special, truly distinctive about the Internet

---

[1] Written prior to his current appointment, this chapter expresses the personal views of the author only and has no association with the author's official capacities; no opinions or interpretations in this chapter should be attributed to the World Intellectual Property Organization or the World Trade Organization.

[2] http://laptop.org/en.

[3] WSIS, Geneva Declaration of Principles, Doc. WSIS-03/GENEVA/DOC/4-E, Dec. 12, 2003, available at http://www.itu.int/dms_pub/itu-s/md/03/wsis/doc/S03-WSIS-DOC-0004!!PDF-E.pdf.

[4] J Zittrain, 'The Future of the Internet—and How to Stop It', Princeton University UChannel Podcast, 26 March 2008 (from 1 May 2009).

that makes it a useful subject for study at the international level? Or, once you strip away the hyperbole about cyberspace and the headline-grabbing topicality of Internet issues, is the Internet, at core, no different from any other medium of international communication and exchange, without any distinctive legal characteristics and without distinct challenges for international law and international institutions? Is the international governance of the Internet just the international system on steroids— exemplifying, accentuating, intensifying existing international trends that would nonetheless be present in an age of globalisation and increasing commercial exchange and cultural interaction across national borders? Alternatively, to take the opposite extreme, is 'cyberspace' a separate legal domain, for which new rules (if any) are needed and the old rules are useless, inappropriate, or self-defeating?

The early years of the Internet saw, on the part of some advocates at least, a brave vision of cyberspace as a lawless anarchic frontier, free of the deadening hand of the lawyer and the industry monopolist, in no need of the laws and regulations that tie us down in the physical world. Prompted in part by perceived heavy-handed attempts at national regulation of the Internet, John Perry Barlow penned 'A Declaration of the Independence of Cyberspace' which argued for national sovereignty to be kept at bay:

> Governments of the Industrial World, you weary giants of flesh and steel, I come from Cyberspace, the new home of Mind. On behalf of the future, I ask you of the past to leave us alone. You are not welcome among us. You have no sovereignty where we gather.
>
> We have no elected government, nor are we likely to have one, so I address you with no greater authority than that with which liberty itself always speaks. I declare the global social space we are building to be naturally independent of the tyrannies you seek to impose on us. You have no moral right to rule us nor do you possess any methods of enforcement we have true reason to fear.[5]

Yet the years since the first popularisation of the Internet have seen a steady assertion of national jurisdiction over cyberspace[6] and the application of existing legal doctrines to Internet transactions. The increasingly mundane and routine practice of law and regulation in cyberspace[7] can lead some to question whether there is anything *legally* new about the Internet at all.[8] To what extent does the Internet define a distinct regulatory space, all to itself,

[5] JP Barlow, A Declaration of the Independence of Cyberspace, at http://homes.eff.org/~barlow/Declaration-Final.html.
[6] J Goldsmith and T Wu, *Who Controls the Internet?: Illusions of a Borderless World* (Oxford, Oxford University Press, 2006).
[7] Regarding defamation, for instance, see *Dow Jones & Co. Inc v Gutnick* [2002] HCA 56: 'Existing principles of defamation law are that legal proceedings should be undertaken in the place where the communication is received, not where the communication is sent from. This applies equally to Internet communications, despite the new nature of the technology.'
[8] For the classic discussion, see D Koepsell, *The Ontology of Cyberspace: Law, Philosophy, and the Future of Intellectual Property* (Chicago, Open Court, 2000).

where the rules are different, where conventional law simply fails to reach; and to what extent is it merely a mildly exotic setting for established legal doctrine and legal practice? Does the Internet need actively to be defended against those who would impose upon it the tired doctrines of the bricks-and-mortar world, choking off its vitality and its distinctive, unbounded, adaptive, generative quality? Or, less dramatically, has the rise of the Internet more or less validated the broad principles of the law, even if there are some practical wrinkles in applying them in the online environment?

And, internationally, the rise of the Internet posed the question of whether greater interconnectivity is effectively abolishing national boundaries, or whether national jurisdictions have reached out, amoeba-like, to envelop, contain and absorb cyberspace. Are some stretches of cyberspace truly international in character—like the international legal status of the high seas,[9] the moon,[10] or non-cyber (actual) 'space',[11] for that matter; or is the regulation of cyberspace ultimately reducible to national jurisdictions, without any distinct or separate international layer. On a practical plane, perhaps the essential international legal issues raised by the Internet concern the resolution of conflicts between domestic laws, to be settled by the rules of private international law—questions such as whether you can defame someone or breach censorship laws in a third country when publishing on the Internet, and in which jurisdiction you enter into a contract (and in which jurisdiction any dispute might be resolved) when you are trading on the Internet.

These questions suggest that the study of 'Internet governance' at the international level may turn out to be more valuable for the insights it offers into the nature of international governance in general, into the character of international regulatory institutions, international legal structures and doctrines, as they come under increasing conceptual, political and technological pressure from the growth of the Internet; and also for insights into the limits of international law and intergovernmental institutions, and how they interplay with domestic law and national regulatory authorities. The advent of the Internet and its permeation into many aspects of international law and its administration have helped to isolate and accentuate the essence of the truly *international* layer of law—as distinct from how national laws interact in cyberspace.

---

[9] United Nations Convention on the Law of the Sea (UNCLOS), entered into force on 16 November 1994.

[10] Agreement Governing the Activities of States on the Moon and Other Celestial Bodies, entered into force, July 1984.

[11] Treaty on Principles Governing the Activities of States in the Exploration and Use of Outer Space, including the Moon and Other Celestial Bodies (the 'Outer Space Treaty', adopted by the General Assembly in its resolution 2222 (XXI)), opened for signature on 27 January 1967, entered into force on 10 October 1967.

Hence, in studying international Internet governance issues, we may ultimately learn more about the nature of international law and regulation, and about its limitations, than about the Internet as such. The Internet may, on analysis, turn out to be a distillation of existing trends and existing tensions in the international system, rather than a discrete new regulatory domain in itself defining an entirely new category of challenges for public international law. So the Internet can perform an unexpectedly useful service—serving as a kind of laboratory rat for scholars of international law and governance, intergovernmental institutions, and the role of governments and non-state actors in shaping those laws and institutions.

Despite a profusion of international initiatives and international norm-setting processes addressing the Internet, it is now apparent that the Internet has not, for the most part, carved out a distinct regulatory domain—a separate cyber-jurisdiction—to be studied and managed in strict isolation. The Internet accentuates some central dilemmas of international law and policymaking, and both accelerates and epitomises existing trends towards borderless social, economic and intellectual domains. This is what makes it an indispensible heuristic tool for exploring the nature of international law. Yet it certainly does not break free from the mainstream of international law and governance.

To be sure, there are some distinct regulatory issues thrown up by the Internet, closely connected to its technical character and its practical operation—the most important being the question of who should manage the essential backbone and architecture of the Internet, in particular the Domain Name System (DNS), particularly Generic Top Level Domains (gTLDs), and the allocation of Internet Protocol (IP) addresses. Root servers function, in effect, as the central switchboards of the Internet, reliably converting requests for access to Uniform Resource Locators (URLs) into IP addresses. It is a fundamental regulatory need, if the Internet is to function effectively, for root servers to contain unique and authentic information about the specific IP addresses that domain names refer to; inaccuracy or ambiguity in this information would render the Internet unworkable. This is a distinct and fundamental regulatory challenge peculiar to the Internet, and already the subject of some controversy—the debate ranging along a spectrum between pragmatism and informality, on the one hand, and intergovernmental structure and political legitimacy acquired through consultative processes and demonstrably inclusive procedures. Jonathan Zittrain cogently captures the difficulties of traversing these challenges in the opening quotation. One pragmatic way of measuring the legitimacy of Internet governance mechanisms has been simply to see whether it works in practice. The original progenitor of the Internet, the US government, has laid emphasis on the need for a practical, private-sector-driven approach, and has been wary of any movement towards a fully intergovernmental governance structure, continuing actively to propound a private-sector governance model.[12]

Other governments maintain an interest in having a more active and direct role in Internet governance, through a formal international approach that would give national governments a direct say over such issues as the creation and management of new gTLDs and more direct guidance on policy formulation. Accordingly, a vigorous debate over Internet governance continued throughout the proceedings of the United Nations World Summit on the Information Society (WSIS), a key policy process that unfolded between 2003 and 2005 (discussed in more detail below). The technicalities of Internet governance provoke wider concerns over economic, political and cultural ramifications, concerns that are reflected in a debate over whether the Internet should be governed through genuinely international structures with distinct legal personality under international law, or whether the legal roots of the Internet should remain embedded in the fertile soil from where it was first cultivated, in the domestic jurisdiction of the US.

This fascinating debate has many dimensions—pitching the perspectives of technical experts against those of multilateral diplomats, the public interest against private interests, advocacy of active intervention to promote the development dimension against a laissez-faire approach, and a private, contractual legal structure against a public law approach. The form of the debate illustrates not only how norms are developed and applied in a politically important and contested domain, but also shed light on how a wide range of practical legal mechanisms can give effect to diverse policy objectives and general legal norms.

---

[12] First propounded, in response to a direction from President Clinton to the US Secretary of Commerce to 'privatize, increase competition in, and promote international participation in the domain name system', Department of Commerce National Telecommunications and Information Administration, Improvement of Technical Management of Internet Names and Addresses; Proposed Rule, Federal Register: 20 February 1998 (Vol 63, No 34), 8825 (available at wais.access.gpo.gov [DOCID:fr20fe98-24]), identifying 'pressures for change . . . [in DNS administration] coming from many different quarters', and observing that 'from its origins as a US-based research vehicle, the Internet is rapidly becoming an international medium for commerce, education and communication.' The Proposed Rule identified as 'shared principles [that] have emerged from our discussions with Internet stakeholders': stability, competition ('the Internet succeeds in great measure because it is a decentralized system that encourages innovation and maximizes individual freedom'), private, bottom-up co-ordination ('a private coordinating process is likely to be more flexible than government and to move rapidly enough to meet the changing needs of the Internet and of Internet users. The private process should, as far as possible, reflect the bottom-up governance that has characterized development of the Internet to date') and representation ('technical management of the Internet should reflect the diversity of its users and their needs. Mechanisms should be established to ensure international input in decision making'). For discussion on domain names, see ch 9.

II. INTERNET GOVERNANCE AND GLOBAL PUBLIC POLICY

One emerging aspect of international law and the Internet is the growing tendency to look to the Internet as a means of fulfilling broader public policy goals, including the objectives of multilateral treaties and the fundamental, bed-rock principles of international law such as human rights. The Geneva Declaration of Principles[13] was adopted at the first phase of the WSIS process as an authoritative policy document expressing a shared political vision for the Internet (rather than a binding legal instrument). The Declaration sets international co-operation on information and communication technology (ICT) firmly in the context of public policy and the fulfilment of human rights. It expresses a

> common desire and commitment to build a people-centred, inclusive and development-oriented Information Society, where everyone can create, access, utilize and share information and knowledge, enabling individuals, communities and peoples to achieve their full potential in promoting their sustainable development and improving their quality of life, premised on the purposes and principles of the Charter of the United Nations and respecting fully and upholding the Universal Declaration of Human Rights.[14]

According to the Declaration, ICT can

> promote the development goals of the Millennium Declaration, namely the eradication of extreme poverty and hunger; achievement of universal primary education; promotion of gender equality and empowerment of women; reduction of child mortality; improvement of maternal health; to combat HIV/AIDS, malaria and other diseases; ensuring environmental sustainability; and development of global partnerships for development for the attainment of a more peaceful, just and prosperous world.

It invokes Article 19 of the Universal Declaration of Human Rights (UDHR)[15] in reaffirming the right of freedom of opinion and expression as an essential foundation of the information society and sounding a universalist note:

> [T]his right includes freedom to hold opinions without interference and to seek, receive and impart information and ideas through any media and regardless of frontiers. Communication is a fundamental social process, a basic human need and the foundation of all social organisation. It is central to the Information Society. Everyone, everywhere should have the opportunity to participate and no one should be excluded from the benefits the Information Society offers.

The Declaration draws further guidance for Internet governance from Article 29 of the UDHR, which concerns the duties everyone has to the

---

13 WSIS, Geneva Declaration of Principles (above n 2).
14 Ibid.
15 Adopted and proclaimed by General Assembly resolution 217 A (III) of 10 December 1948.

community 'in which alone the free and full development of their personality is possible'; and the proviso that

> in the exercise of their rights and freedoms, everyone shall be subject only to
> such limitations as are determined by law solely for the purpose of securing due
> recognition and respect for the rights and freedoms of others and of meeting the
> just requirements of morality, public order and the general welfare in a
> democratic society.

This proviso offers a justification for the continuing regulation of the
Internet in the interests of such policy objectives as countering terrorism,
suppressing child pornography and dealing with other obvious social ills;
but also, more controversially, it may also justify state intervention to limit
use of the Internet considered to be prejudicial to public order and welfare
in areas where the legitimacy of such constraints may be challenged, such as
in regulating political discourse.

Changes in objective, factual circumstances, in particular the advance of
technologies, can in turn provoke a recalibration of what we perceive as
being just, fair and equitable. For example, before audio recording
technology existed, vocal performers had no need of an intangible 'right'
over their performances; technological advances mean that a performance
can now be easily appropriated and commercialised by third parties, a
change in the factual background that led to the formulation of a distinct
performer's right first in national laws, and ultimately in binding international law as well.[16] Similarly, modern ICT, and the Internet especially,
have sparked this evolution from technological progress to a new sense of
equity and entitlement, showing how fundamental ideas of fairness and
equity respond to changed technological circumstances. Despite its recent
advent for the bulk of humanity, the practical importance of the Internet
as a practical tool for fulfilling human rights has introduced notions of
justice into debates about Internet governance—if in the contemporary
world, Internet access is considered important for participating effectively
in democratic processes,[17] expressing one's beliefs,[18] obtaining an adequate
education,[19] enjoying the benefits of scientific progress, and even securing
the highest attainable standard of health,[20] then does access to the
Internet itself evolve into a stand-alone 'right'—a right to access Internet

---

[16] This trajectory—from technological innovation, to claim for equitable rebalancing, to international law—is described in AS Taubman, 'Nobility of Interpretation: Equity, Retrospectivity
and Collectivity in Implementing New Norms for Performers' Rights' (2005) 12 *Journal of
Intellectual Property Law* 351.

[17] UDHR Art 21 and Universal Covenant on Civil and Political Rights (UNCCPR) Art 25.

[18] UDHR Art 18 and UNCCPR Art 19.

[19] UDHR Art 26 and ICESCR Art 13; see also W McGeveran and WW Fisher 'The Digital
Learning Challenge: Obstacles to Educational Uses of Copyrighted Material in the Digital
Age' (August 2006). Berkman Center Research Publication No 2006-09. Available at SSRN:
http://ssrn.com/abstract=923465.

[20] UDHR Art 25 and ICESCR Art 12.

infrastucture, to access and to share content over the Internet?[21] Policy-makers draw attention to the 'digital divide' both within and between nations—originally concerned with disparities in access to computer technology in general, this 'divide' increasingly refers to the gap between those who enjoy Internet access and broadband access in particular, and those who lack access. Bridging the divide is ultimately a practical question of deploying the needed resources, of infrastructure development, and of initiatives such as the One Laptop Per Child project.[22] Yet the rapid emergence of the Internet as an essential public resource—as the WSIS Tunis Agenda for the information society puts it, evolving 'from a research and academic facility into a global facility available to the public'[23]—brings with it normative expectations, expressed in terms of justice, equity and fundamental rights, sometimes difficult to mesh with the technicalities of establishing and financing a national broadband infrastructure.

This rich palette of human rights and public policy considerations means that broader concepts of equity and fairness, and inclusiveness and partici-pation, flow back into expectations of how the core structure of the Internet is to be managed, forging a distinct international perspective on Internet governance. The Tunis Agenda defines 'Internet governance' as 'the development and application by governments, the private sector and civil society, in their respective roles, of shared principles, norms, rules, decision-making procedures, and programmes that shape the evolution and use of the Internet'.[24] Addressing Internet governance for the first time as a fully international and multilateral issue, the WSIS Geneva Declaration and Tunis Agenda stipulate that

> international management of the Internet should be multilateral, transparent and democratic, with the full involvement of governments, the private sector, civil society and international organisations. It should ensure an equitable distribution of resources, facilitate access for all and ensure a stable and secure functioning of the Internet, taking into account multilingualism.

This is a remarkable normative development, and a far-reaching assertion of claims for fairness and equity in Internet governance, considering that for much of its short life the Internet was seen as an academic and research

---

21 Amidst a dense literature, see the recent commentary in E Pfanner, 'Is Internet Access a Human Right? Debate Over What to Do with Copyright Pirates Raises a Basic Question' *International Herald Tribune*, 13 April 2009; see, also for a discussion under national law, C Crawford 'Cyberplace: Defining a Right to Internet Access Through Public Accommodation Law' (2003) 76 *Temple Law Review* 225–76. Available at SSRN: http://ssrn.com/abstract= 518525.

22 http://laptop.org/en.

23 At 30; cf also the contrast between 'its origins as a US-based research vehicle' and 'the Internet . . . rapidly becoming an international medium for commerce, education and communi-cation' in the Proposed Rule, n 11 above.

24 Tunis Agenda, para 34.

tool, and largely as the province of researchers and technicians, of no interest to the broader sweep of humanity.

III. SETTING THE BOUNDS TO INTERNET GOVERNANCE

This account of the normative context of the Internet as a means of promoting the common goals of humanity at such a fundamental level of international law and policymaking contrasts with an earlier utopian view of the Internet which had a more liberal, libertarian or even anarchist hue, an outlook contrasting significantly with the more structured and legalised international account: broadly speaking, setting top-down and bottom-up strategies at odds with one another, albeit within the same technological structure. The deflating observation that the Internet has not, on the whole, carved out a separate legal domain runs flatly contrary to widespread perceptions in the early period of popularisation of the Internet, in the early 1990s, when there was a strong, utopian expectation that many of the laws and regulations, the national boundaries and jurisdictional issues, that clutter regular exchange and discourse would not apply to cyberspace.[25] Early hopes were that the fresh space of discourse, exchange of information and social interaction defined by the Internet ('cyberspace') would continue to flourish in an anarchic, lawless environment, freed of the shackles of government, and unconstrained by national boundaries and jurisdictions. The argument was made, for example, that no use of trade marks on the Internet should fall within the rights enjoyed by trade mark owners, and that domain names should not be considered to have trade mark significance.[26] Whatever their appeal or feasibility, these hopes of keeping the Internet disengaged from conventional law have, it has to be said, been comprehensively disappointed, as the body of domestic case-law applied to the Internet builds up and the use of the Internet and its governance increasingly interact with key areas of international law.

IV. IDENTIFYING THE ISSUES FOR INTERNATIONAL GOVERNANCE

The Internet does nonetheless still offer freedoms and capacities to avoid the reach of specific national jurisdictions that can confound national

---

[25] See above, n 4.

[26] For a colourful account of an early encounter between a trade mark lawyer and the central actors in early Internet governance, see DW Maher, 'Reporting to God', Chicago Literary Club Paper, 9 January 2006, at http://icannwiki.org/Reporting_to_God. The tenor of the time is caught in this exchange: 'I saw that he was close to apoplectic. He said—perhaps not his exact words—"How dare you come out here and tell us how to run the Internet?" I was, of course, quite flustered and tried to make the best of it, mostly to the effect that I was really trying to help, and trying to keep the Internet from getting tangled up in legal complications.' See the discussion in ch 9.

regulators and that stimulate demands for some forms of international governance of actions undertaken on the Internet: we will review the kind of power struggles over control of the Internet that these concerns have provoked, and the conundrums that confront regulators when they bring to a virtual domain in which information is profuse and abundant, a bricks-and-mortar mentality and an assumption that power flows from constraints on information rather than effective use of it. And the Internet did, and still does, in itself pose unique questions of governance, with an unavoidable international dimension that results from the apparent detachment from the physical world of the flow of information and the flow of commerce. Partly these governance issues concern the very backbone of the Internet itself, a question we explore in more detail. But there are also many practical questions for public and private international law and its practice and administration. Consider, for instance:

(i) the difficulty in determining the geographical location, and the applicable national law, of acts undertaken on the Internet, say the formation of a contract, an act of libel,[27] or an act of copyright infringement:

   • creating a new challenge for the conflict of laws—the body of law that determines which national jurisdiction should apply to acts with an international dimension; considering how to apply existing principles in practice in the on-line environment, and how these may have to be adapted to resolve practical problems posed by commercial exchanges and claimed infringement of intellectual property (IP) on the Internet;

   • can you escape the reach of copyright law by simply relocating your server, or yourself, or your company, to a physical location in a country that is not party to international copyright treaties?

   • what obligations do states owe one another to enforce copyright and other IP rights in the digital domain, and to facilitate their enforcement in other jurisdiction, such as through extradition in cases of IP infringement?[28]

   • how should other trade-related commitments between states be interpreted when the rise of Internet-based commerce potentially

---

[27] Gutnick case, n 6 above. See also ch 3.

[28] In the Drink Or Die case, Hew Raymond Griffiths was extradited from Australia and convicted in the US for copyright infringement under US law, despite having been located in Australia throughout the time of the offence: 'Extradited Australian Ringleader Gets 51 Months for Software Piracy 6/22/07 (Alexandria, VA): Hew Raymond Griffiths was sentenced to 51 months in prison for crimes committed as leader of one of the oldest and most renowned Internet software piracy groups worldwide. From his home in Australia, Griffiths violated the criminal copyright laws of the US as the leader of an organised criminal group known as DrinkOrDie, which caused the illegal reproduction and distribution of more than $50 million worth of pirated software, movies, games and music. This was one of the first ever extraditions for an intellectual property offense', US Department of Justice, at www.usdoj.gov/usao/vae/Pressreleases/02-FebruaryPDFArchive/07/20070220griffithsnr.pdf.

changes the balance of interests represented in existing trade commitments, and confronts existing regulatory mechanisms? For instance, if a state has agreed to open up its services market to foreign firms in a particular sector, assuming that those services would be delivered in person, do such access commitments extend to services delivered via the Internet? If so, where are the services considered to be provided—at the actual physical location where the consumer is accessing the Internet, or where the service provider's server is located?[29] In other words, when using a foreign-based gambling site or telemedicine provider, is the consumer effectively 'visiting' that country, or is the service provider effectively making a 'house call' to the consumer's location? This kind of classification issue may appear to be nitpicking and legalistic but an actual international dispute over classification of trade in internet services (gambling) led to a claim for compensation of US$3.443 billion.[30]

(ii) the ease of creating personal identities that hover above or beside the legal categories defined under national and international laws:
   • how anonymous can you manage to be on the Internet; can you legitimately construct an entirely fictional persona? How does your privacy conflict with the public interest? And how to hold individuals responsible for culpable acts undertaken under the cover of an internet persona?
   • do you have enforceable rights in your personal name against its registration as a domain name?[31]
   • does your Second Life avatar have individual entitlements to legal protection, rights that are acquired second hand from you?

(iii) the creation and adoption of signs and addresses that appeared to lose any fixed national character altogether, to slip loose from the relatively sure referential framework of any one linguistic community, and to operate in a global or even universal realm:

---

[29] Under the WTO General Agreement on Trade in Services (GATS), Members of the WTO can give different levels of commitments for market access to services, depending on whether they are provided to the consumer across the border ('Mode I') or consumed abroad ('Mode II'). So the physical location where a service provided over the Internet is considered to be provided can have significant implications for the resolution of trade disputes (see discussion below).

[30] The actual award was, however, US$21 million annually: Decision by the Arbitrator, Recourse to Arbitration by the United States under Art 22.6 of the DSU, United States—Measures Affecting the Cross-Border Supply of Gambling and Betting Services (hereafter *US—Gambling*), WTO Document WT/DS285/ARB, 21 December 2007.

[31] WIPO Arbitration and Mediation Center, Administrative Panel Decision, *Julia Fiona Roberts v Russell Boyd*, Case No D2000-0210 (<juliaroberts.com>); the registration of a responsible cabinet minister's personal name, according to press speculation at the time, spurred a stronger interest in the regulation of domain names (see eg A Camphuisen, 'Minister Urges WIPO Anti-Squatting Policy', *Internet News*, 23 June 2000, at http://www.Internetnews.com/bus-news/article.php/6_401271,.

- it can be tough enough within the one national jurisdiction and within the one linguistic community for a judge to assess the full import of a sign (including questions such as whether 'linoleum' is a trade mark or a descriptive term; whether 'champagne' denotes a particular location or is a generic description), and to adjudicate on the multiple references and cultural resonances of a term such as 'Madonna';[32] but when these references are used on a borderless Internet, or are used as domain names not linked to any particular national jurisdiction (at least in the mind of members of the public browsing the Internet), and can potentially be seen across the globe—which linguistic community or communities should prevail when the signification of a word, sign or symbol is assessed?

(iv) the rise in trade in digital products, valuable goods and services that were ordered, delivered and paid for entirely through packets of data sent through the Internet.

- When paying for a track on iTunes, you essentially part with money to have the logical contents of your hard drive reorganised, but in concluding the sale, what are you actually 'buying'—the song itself? Are you paying for a kind of cultural service? Or simply acquiring a license to use a certain sequence of bits in a limited way? Where, in what jurisdiction, does the transaction take place? How do the international rules regarding, say, tariffs on the equivalent physical goods apply to digital products traded internationally? If you see the downloaded music as a 'product', is it essentially the same as the purchase of a physical CD for the very same music? Should it be taxed and regulated the same way, or is the download an altogether different thing from the physical product?

This chapter suggests that there is nothing about these questions that is truly unique to the Internet, or totally unprecedented before the Internet; rather, that the Internet simply distils and intensifies issues that have always been present in international governance, and have come to the fore since the Internet has entered the mainstream of human interchanges and commerce.

Public and Private International Law: What's the Difference? Does it Matter?

The difficulty in nailing down the international legal characteristics of the Internet actually mirrors a long-running theoretical question about the character of international law. Public international law—or the 'law of

---

[32] WIPO Arbitration and Mediation Center, Administrative Panel Decision, *Madonna Ciccone, p/k/a Madonna v Dan Parisi and "Madonna.com"*, Case No D2000-0847 (<madonna.com>).

nations'—is the law that governs relationships between states, and that governs intergovernmental organisations such as the United Nations: it includes the international law of human rights (eg the International Covenant on Economic, Social and Cultural Rights) and international environmental law (eg the Kyoto protocol under the United Nations Framework Convention on Climate Change (UNFCCC)), as well as more functional matters such as the operation of the international postal and telecommunications networks. It covers both substantive commitments states make to one another, as well as how their relations are conducted. For example, the mutual obligations agreed between members of the World Trade Organization (WTO) create substantive obligations (such as not to discriminate unreasonably between foreign firms and local firms, the principle of 'national treatment' that was the subject of the recent dispute over regulation of online gambling in the US[33]), as well as the agreed means of resolving covered trade disputes and dealing with trade retaliation, through procedures laid out in the WTO Dispute Settlement Understanding (these procedures were used in the dispute over regulation of foreign gambling websites, resulting in a quasi-judicial decision[34] finding US regulations to be partly inconsistent with obligations assumed under the WTO's General Agreement on Trade in Services (GATS), and a subsequent arbitrator's assessment of the level of trade damage caused by the non-compliant regulations[35]).

Public international law questions touching on the Internet include the human rights to take part in cultural life and to enjoy the benefits of scientific progress,[36] as well as international governance of the infra-structure for telecommunications.[37]

Private international law, or the rules concerning conflict of laws (ie resolving the conflicting overlapping reach of the national or municipal

---

[33] *US—Gambling*, WTO Dispute DS285.

[34] Appellate Body Report, *US-Gambling*, WT/DS285/AB/R, 7 April 2005.

[35] Award of the Arbitrator, *US-Gambling*, n 29 above.

[36] As discussed above. See ICESC, Art 15(a) and (b).

[37] Principally through the International Telecommunications Union (ITU), one of the first intergovernmental organisations, established in 1865 with the adoption of the International Telegraph Convention. It describes its role in these terms 'Every time someone picks up a telephone and dials a number, answers a call on a mobile, sends a fax or receives an e-mail, takes a plane or a ship, listens to the radio or watches a favourite television programme, they benefit from the universal telecommunication and ICT frameworks put in place by the [ITU]. ITU has been at the cutting edge of information and communication technologies, defining and adopting the globally agreed technical standards that have allowed industry to interconnect people and equipment seamlessly around the world. It has also successfully regulated worldwide use of the radio-frequency spectrum, ensuring all international wireless communications remain interference-free to ensure the relay of vital information and economic data around the world. Spearheading telecommunications development on a global scale, ITU also fosters the deploy-ment of telecommunications in developing countries by advising on development policies, regulatory frameworks and strategies, and by providing specialized technical assistance in the areas of technology transfer, cybersecurity, management, financing, installation and mainten-ance of networks, disaster mitigation, and capacity building.'

laws of different countries), is generally distinguished from public international law. For example, public international law questions are mainly resolved by international institutions or tribunals, most notably the International Court of Justice, whereas the rules of private international law are generally considered by domestic tribunals (eg a court in your country may need to consider conflict of laws issues in considering whether you can sue me in that court's jurisdiction when I breach a contract with you which we concluded over the Internet).

In a globalised world, sometimes the boundaries between public and private international law can be difficult to discern. That is perhaps the greatest conundrum posed by international governance of the Internet. There is a long-running controversy over whether the main architecture of the Internet should be governed directly by international organisations, or whether it should remain under the control and direction of national governments. For example, does my registration of a domain name in a gTLD give me a kind of global trade mark right that can or should be governed by international institutions, or is it a kind of imprint of trade mark rights that really only exist under national jurisdictions? This debate is a real, tangible one, with important implications. Consider three recent submissions to the consultations on Improving Institutional Confidence conducted by the Internet Corporation for Assigned Names and Numbers (ICANN), the body responsible for managing the main identifiers on the Internet, notably domain names and Internet protocol addresses (ICANN is not an international organisation, but a not-for-profit corporation established under Californian law):

> Internationalizing ICANN: ICANN's current operation *is* international, and bylaws amendments are not required to achieve this. We are gratified by the firm statement by the PSC that ICANN's status as a California-based not-for-profit corporation will not change. Further, we support the establishment of satellite ICANN offices in other countries where there is a demonstrated advantage or need for this. . . . We do not, however, understand the proposal for 'global legal presences,' and we would oppose the establishment of additional legal entities in other countries.[38]

> In an ideal world, a global transnational and multi-stakeholder public good organisation such as ICANN would not be legally based in any country, or, if it were, it would have a specific agreement with that country so to exempt it from local laws for what regards its mission. Such agreements are in place, for example, for United Nations agencies, in whatever country they are located. Such an instrument is the standard way for setting up an international organisation and would seem fit for ICANN's case as well. Unfortunately, it looks like

---

[38] Submission of the American Intellectual Property Law Association (AIPLA), AIPLA Preliminary Comments on the Transition Action Plan, Improving Institutional Confidence in ICANN and FAQ prepared by the ICANN President's Strategy Committee, filed 31 July 2008.

this solution is made impossible by the US Government's refusal to renounce to its present role in any way, or to accept any kind of diplomatic immunity for ICANN's actions.[39]

The critical importance of the domain name system, and the historic role of the United States in creating and fostering that system, dictates that the interests of the US government (and by extension its citizens) be protected to a greater extent. . . . ICANN has mentioned its desire to consider a change of its corporate status, which it perceives could contribute to a more 'internationalized' image. As lawyers, we urge the Department of Commerce to recognize that the United States has one of the most highly developed legal systems and body of laws in the world, including especially intellectual property protections. ICANN's registry and registrar contracts are governed by US law and, we believe, it is essential that this continue through 2009 and beyond.[40]

The US government has stated its intention to 'maintain its historic role in authorizing changes or modifications to the authoritative root zone file'[41] even while remaining 'open to operational efficiency measures that address governments' legitimate public policy and sovereignty concerns with respect to the management of their ccTLD'.[42] This has led to clashing views in international fora, which in turn reflects the issues of power and sovereignty that underlie the formal overlay of international law:

The United States and Europe clashed . . . in one of their sharpest public disagreements in months, after European Union negotiators proposed stripping the Americans of their effective control of the Internet. The European decision to back the rest of the world in demanding the creation of a new international body to govern the Internet clearly caught the Americans off balance and left them largely isolated at talks designed to come up with a new way of regulating the digital traffic of the 21st century. 'It's a very shocking and profound change of the EU's position,' said David Gross, the State Department official in charge of America's international communications policy. 'The EU's proposal seems to represent an historic shift in the regulatory approach to the Internet from one that is based on private sector leadership to a government, top-down control of the Internet.'[43]

[39] Comments of Vittorio Bertola, ICANN Improving Institutional Confidence consultation, 31 July 2008 at http://forum.icann.org/lists/iic-consultation/msg00006.html.
[40] AIPLA Comments on the progress achieved by ICANN on the goals in the Joint Project Agreement between NTIA and ICANN, filed 13 February 2008 available at http://www.ntia.doc.gov/ntiahome/domainname/jpacomments2007/jpacomment_110.pdf.
[41] Domain Names: US Principles on the Internet's Domain Name and Addressing System (30 June 2005), at http://www.ntia.doc.gov/ntiahome/domainname/USDNSprinciples_06302005.htm.
[42] Letter of MA Baker, Acting Assistant Secretary for Communications and Information (30 July 2008), to Mr P Dengate-Thrush, Chairman of the Board of Directors of ICANN, at http://www.ntia.doc.gov/comments/2008/ICANN_080730.html.
[43] T Wright, 'EU and US Clash Over Control of Net' *International Herald Tribune*, 30 September 2005.

> We will continue throughout this chapter to examine these distinct legal mechanisms, and the contrasting views of regulatory effectiveness and the comparative virtues of private, contractual law and public international law.

V. THE INTERNET AS A BORDERLESS, GLOBAL DOMAIN

You would think there is nothing *more* 'international' than the Internet; and all sorts of international organisations, groupings and initiatives have embraced the Internet—many were forged by the Internet or even now survive by it. A generation of diplomats, scholars and activists cannot now conceive of operating without using the Internet, to organise, access documentation, report and develop positions: part of the research for this chapter was undertaken in an isolated part of Meghalaya, in north-east India, where official records of recent debates in numerous international fora were instantly available online. Even bearing in mind the serious (if, thankfully, progressively diminishing) disparities in access to the Internet experienced by many communities, the very possibility of universal availability of documentation on international law and on governance processes would have been unthinkable a little over a decade ago; affordable and more widely distributed ICT, the spread of Internet access, and an increasing norm and expectation of public access to information converge as mutually reinforcing trends to put unprecedented quantities of information in the hands of the global public. The significance of this huge leap in accessibility and transparency, and its implications for international governance, should never be taken for granted.

Although the Internet was conceived and crafted in the context of a national defence programme during the Cold War,[44] and the US continues to assert national authority over the main components of Internet architecture,[45] conceptually it was born global: and in practice, it is famously blind to national boundaries, confronting assumptions about the reach and effect of national legal jurisdictions. The private international law of the Internet is difficult enough—where does your online purchase of a song download take place? But there is also an emerging body of *public* international law touching on the Internet—in its first session in 1946, the UN General Assembly declared that 'freedom of information is a fundamental human right and is the touchstone of all the freedoms to which the United Nations is consecrated',[46] and as we have noted, the Internet is now inter-

---

[44] J Abbate, 'White Heat and Cold War: The Origins and Meanings of Packet Switching', *Inventing the Internet*, (Cambridge, MA, MIT Press, 1999) ch 1.

[45] US Principles on the Internet's Domain Name and Addressing System, at http://www.ntia. doc.gov/ntiahome/domainname/USDNSprinciples_06302005.htm.

[46] UN General Assembly Resolution 59(I), Calling of an International Conference on Freedom of Information, 1946.

twined with the achievement of the right of access to information, the right to receive an education,[47] and rights to take part in cultural life and to enjoy the benefits of scientific progress and its applications.[48]

The greatest impact of the Internet, however, may turn out to be its transformative effect on international norm-setting and the practice of international governance work in many fields well beyond the scope of telecommunications as such. For many, the Internet has transformed the international system, the way people interact, the way opinions are formed and asserted, and the way treaties and other norms are negotiated, implemented and monitored. And this has happened only since the mid-1990s, when the Internet very swiftly entered the international mainstream (despite the unresolved challenges and inequities of the digital divide, and the fact that the majority of humanity remain effectively digitally excluded). The examples are legion, fully mapping the entire international legal landscape from human rights, across issues such as the environment[49] and climate change,[50] to the nuts-and-bolts work of the UN specialised agencies maintaining international infrastructure.[51] Consider a few examples:

- In 1998, the Organisation for Economic Co-operation and Development (OECD) suspended its negotiations on a Multilateral Agreement on Investment (MAI). The Internet was a key factor in the failure of this process: a draft treaty was leaked onto the Internet and a widespread coalition of non-governmental organisations (NGOs) worked together to render it politically unsustainable. According to a European parliamentarian reporting on the process:

  [T]he development of the Internet has shaken up the environment of the negotiations. It allows the instant diffusion of the texts under discussion, whose confidentiality becomes more and more theoretical. It permits, beyond

---

[47] The UN Committee on Economic, Social and Cultural Rights, in its General Comment on the right to education (Art 13 of the International Covenant on Economic, Social and Cultural Rights), document E/C.12/1999/10 (8 December 1999), observes that the right to receive an education requires some educational facilities to have 'a library, computer facilities and information technology'.

[48] See Art 15 of the International Covenant on Economic, Social and Cultural Rights. States are required to take necessary steps 'for the conservation, the development and the diffusion of science and culture'.

[49] Eg The Clearing-House Mechanism (CHM) of the Convention on Biological Diversity at http://www.cbd.int/chm/.

[50] Eg Greenhouse Gas Inventory Data, at http://unfccc.int/ghg_data/items/3800.php.

[51] From meteorology (see http://worldweather.wmo.int/) to the postal system: 'The Universal Postal Union, the specialized agency of the United Nations responsible for postal services, places the information society at the heart of its current strategy and actions . . . new technologies are impelling postal operators to adapt and upgrade their services. The postal sector of the future will thus be capable of contributing to economic development, to the strengthening of social cohesion and to the narrowing of the digital divide.' E Dayan, Director General of the Universal Postal Union, World Summit on the Information Society, Tunis (Tunisia), Plenary (7th session), 18 November 2005.

national boundaries, the sharing of knowledge and expertise. On a subject which is highly technical, the representatives of civil society seemed to us perfectly well informed, and their criticisms well argued on a legal level.[52]

- The WTO agreed in 2005 on an amendment to the Agreement on Trade-Related Aspects of Intellectual Property Rights[53] in order to facilitate the use of compulsory licenses to leverage access to pharmaceuticals for countries with limited manufacturing capacity, the only amendment so far to the wide-ranging package of WTO Agreements that had been adopted a decade earlier. Hard-wired into the design of this important new legal mechanism was a provision for transparency; and this mechanism positively requires that all notifications be posted on the Internet, as a distinct international legal obligation and as an official means of notification.

- The Internet has transformed the custodianship of the very backbone of the international legal system—the vast network of international treaties. The UN Charter (Article 102) requires registration with and publication by the Secretariat of 'every treaty and every international agreement' that any UN Member State enters. The UN Secretariat, the principal custodian of international legal texts, maintains the UN treaty collection (comprising over 158,000 treaties and related actions) as part of its formal obligation under the Charter. In line with the General Assembly resolution on the UN Decade of International Law,[54] and the policy of legal information institutes that 'public legal information . . . is *digital* common property',[55] the General Assembly approved an online business model[56] to fund this service and to disseminate this vital legal information, with tiered payment for online access compensating for lost revenues from past sales of hard copies and using legal and technological constraints on access to cross-subsidise preferential public sector, educational and developing country access.

- Wholly new forms of international governance have emerged to deal with the regulatory challenges directly posed by the Internet and the way its core architecture is managed. For instance, ICANN is a private, non-

---

[52] C Lalumière, *Report on the Multilateral Agreement on Investment, Intermediary Report*, September 1998.

[53] WTO General Council, document WT/L/641 (dated 8 December 2005), Amendment of the TRIPS Agreement, Decision of 6 December 2005.

[54] UNGA Resolution 44/23 of 17 November 1989.

[55] Declaration on Free Access to Law, World Legal Information Institute, Montreal, 2007 at http://www.worldlii.org/worldlii/declaration/ (emphasis added).

[56] A/RES/51/158, A/RES/52/153 and A/RES/53/100: 'the United Nations Treaty Series involve high costs and additional costs which result from the need to maintain, update and improve the service; the revenues generated from hard copy sales are inadequate to cover these costs and will increase as a result of their on-line availability; accordingly, it will be appropriate to charge a fee from users of the on-line version to generate revenues to fund at least the maintenance and improvement of the service.'

profit corporation established under US law, evolving from the Internet Assigned Numbers Authority (IANA) and other entities which were contracted by the US government to manage key parts of the Internet architecture—notably allocating IP address space, managing generic and country code top-level domain names, and managing the root server system (the repository of all IP addresses). ICANN has a strong international character, functions as a private–public partnership, and puts strong emphasis on broad-based consultation (despite the quizzical note sounded by Jonathan Zittrain, above). Failure to manage these issues would lead to radical uncertainty in the Internet, and perhaps its effective collapse, with dramatic impact on international commerce, communications, governance and even national security—a reminder of how quickly the world has come to depend on the stability of the Internet, in the space of only a decade or so. Yet these functions are kept outside the hands of governments and of international organisations, as attempts have been rebuffed to 'regularise' Internet governance by vesting it in an international, intergovernmental organisation—such as the International Telecommunications Union (ITU), which administers, for instance, the country codes for the international telephone system and which by one conventional reading of international governance would naturally take charge of Internet architecture.

- As legislators and the courts wrestle with the seeming irrelevance of national borders to activities on the Internet in fields such as libel, copyright infringement and the significance of trade marks, all of which have been defined by national jurisdiction, a novel form of international governance has been developed to deal with the trade mark significance of domain names. The Uniform Dispute Resolution Policy (UDRP) adopted by ICANN in 1999[57] created a distinctive kind of legal regime to deal with disputes over abusive registrations of domain names (so called 'cybersquatting' or 'cyberpiracy'—the bad faith registration of a domain name in conflict with another's trade mark[58]). The UDRP formally had a tenuous international legal footing at the level of principle—it is essentially based on contracts between applicants for domain name registration and registrars (who are often located in different countries from one another). You agree to have disputes settled this way when applying for a .com domain name, for instance. In the first instance, remedies are enforced not by the courts or by the legal

---

[57] http://www.icann.org/dndr/udrp/policy.htm. See ch 9.

[58] The UDRP requires a domain name registrant to submit to a mandatory administrative proceeding when a complainant asserts that '(i) [the] domain name is identical or confusingly similar to a trade mark or service mark in which the complainant has rights; and (ii) [the registrant has] no rights or legitimate interests in respect of the domain name; and (iii) [the] domain name has been registered and is being used in bad faith.'

system but by the technical gatekeeper function of the registrars (if you lose the case, your domain name will simply be transferred to the opponent). Yet the system has been very effective in settling many thousands of disputes,[59] has created a distinct and well-documented body of jurisprudence,[60] and has become a major area of international intellectual property practice. Illustrating how it is effectively detached from the international treaty system, the UDRP system has so far not implemented elements of the Paris Convention, the foundational international treaty on industrial property, despite recommendations by the General Assembly of the World Intellectual Property Organisation (WIPO), that it should do so.[61]

- The Internet has spawned, or at least massively facilitated, a new form of international commerce: trade in bits rather than atoms.[62] Software, music, films and books were traded on surrogate physical platforms that were shipped across borders and counted as trade in goods—even though what really matters is the information content, not the physical medium that stores and transports it. Now these 'digital products' can be downloaded directly, without passing through customs and without registering on international trade statistics. This has posed a real, practical conceptual dilemma for international trade law, discussed in depth below—if trade negotiators hammer out deals over the terms of trade in goods, including commitments on tariffs, do these apply when the 'same' goods are then traded online, passing from hard drive to hard drive, without ever taking on discrete physical form? The emergence of such 'pure' trade in bits is perhaps the most distinctive challenge for international law posed by the Internet. The approach so far has been to agree at a political level to freeze any specific measures to impose further tariffs on such trade. The issue of taxation on e-products is a tantalising

---

[59] To 10 May 2004, reportedly 7,790 decisions had been handed down under the UDRP concerning 13,311 domain names (http://www.icann.org/en/udrp/proceedings-stat.htm); to the end of 2008, one dispute resolution service provider, the WIPO Arbitration and Mediation Center, had dealt with 14,663 cases (http://www.wipo.int/amc/en/domains/statistics/cases.jsp).

[60] See eg WIPO Overview of WIPO Panel Views on Selected UDRP Questions, at http://www.wipo.int/amc/en/domains/search/overview/.

[61] The WIPO General Assembly recommendations included the proposal (from which the US dissociated itself) that the UDRP be modified to allow Intergovernmental Organisation to file complaints in respect of the abusive registration of their protected names and acronyms, on the basis of the Paris Convention for the Protection of Industrial Property (which under Art 6*ter*1(b) of provides for direct protection of 'armorial bearings, flags, other emblems, abbreviations, and names, of international intergovernmental organisations'). In view of the privileges and immunities enjoyed by international intergovernmental organisations in international law, the recommendation included a proposal for a special appeal procedure by way of de novo arbitration should be available to any party wishing to contest a decision made under a UDRP complaint. See WIPO document 'Internet Domain Names' (WO/GA/28/3) and Report of the WIPO General Assembly, October 2002 (WO/GA/28/7, paras 57–81), transmitted to ICANN by WIPO in February 2003.

[62] N Negroponte, 'Bits not Atoms', *Wired*, 1 January 1995.

one, raising questions about the nature of international trade, creating possible anomalies in national regulation of commerce and taxation,[63] creating potential digital loopholes,[64] and posing questions about the very character of trade as such—if I purchase software or a song by digital download, am I purchasing a good and acquiring ownership over something, or am I just getting a license to use something that someone else still owns? This has significant legal implications at the national level and international levels (see discussion below on e-products).

VI. 'DIPLOMACY . . . IN THE PUBLIC VIEW'

Perhaps the most dramatic impact of the Internet on international governance is the unprecedented transparency it has enabled. We now take for granted very ready online access, free of charge and effectively free of cost, to official documents and working texts. Yet this possibility has largely come into practical effect for most international organisations just within the past decade. When the multilateral system of governance was conceived in the aftermath of the First World War, transparency was the first of President Wilson's Fourteen Points: '[O]pen covenants of peace, openly arrived at, after which there shall be no private international understandings of any kind but diplomacy shall proceed always frankly and in the public view'.[65] But only now is this expectation being fully carried out in practice, thanks essentially to the technological possibilities of the Internet, and the public hunger for information this has stoked. As the MAI negotiators and delegates to the Seattle WTO Ministerial Conference discovered in practice, the Internet allowed both for rapid international diffusion of working documents but also unprecedented organising capacity on the part of civil society and non-governmental players. Numerous international governance processes now function through Internet commentary and web-based mechanisms for broad-based input and collective decision making, potentially broadening the base and the political legitimacy of norm-setting processes.

But the central importance of the Internet in international governance inevitably focused attention on those who were excluded from the Internet,

---

[63] See eg the UK rules at http://www.customsandrevenue.eu/vat/int-serv-abroad.htm which provide that, when assessing taxation purposes, the place of supply of digitised publications such as online newspapers, e-books and e-zines depends on their content: 'If a publication is largely fiction, such as a novel, the place of supply is always where the supplier belongs. If the content is non-fiction, it is treated as information, and special rules apply—the place of supply is where the customer belongs.'

[64] See eg R Watts, 'Apple to Exploit Guernsey Loophole', http://www.telegraph.co.uk/money/main.jhtml?xml=/money/2006/01/15/cnapple15.xml.

[65] Woodrow Wilson, speech to Congress, 18 January 1918, text available at http://en.wikipedia.org/wiki/Fourteen_Points.

many of whom were already marginalised in existing governance arrangements and disadvantaged in terms of access to infrastructure and other resources. The Internet, now a symbol of technological advantage, also keyed into long-standing differences of perspective between countries that are conveniently—if at times misleadingly—classed as the North and the global South. From the beginning of its global phase, when the Internet seized the attention of the public and of policymakers from the mid-1990s, the growth of the Internet and its increasing economic significance exacerbated existing international sensitivities that technology, and the benefits flowing from it, were unevenly and unfairly distributed around the globe. The Internet thus opened a new chapter in the long-running international debate over transfer of technology, a staple issue in the debate over the creation of the New International Economic Order in the 1970s, now expressed in terms of concern over the Digital Divide.[66] Yet the democratising, empowering quality of the Internet—its capacity to level distances, its possibilities for bringing the economically, socially marginalised to the heart of international trade and policymaking—has been perhaps the most significant impact of the Internet on global governance. But there has also been a significant shift in how developing countries perceive their economic interests under the Internet:

- early on in the explosive growth of the Internet, roughly in the late 1990s, there was a sense of pessimism and exclusion, epitomised by the cautious reaction of developing countries to the development of an Electronic Commerce program by the WTO, which reflected concerns that the infrastructure limitations of developing countries would impair their capacity to make use of the opportunities of the Internet for trade—the concern was that the Internet could exacerbate, not ease, existing global inequities in access to markets;[67]
- later on, by contrast, as developing countries began to leverage access to the Internet to give effect to their economic comparative advantage, a more confident view emerged,[68] as developing countries used increased connectivity to capitalise on their areas of comparative advantage, such as low-cost professional and customer support capacity (the software outsourcing and call-centre phenomena), culminating in the partially

---

[66] M Compaine (ed), *The Digital Divide: Facing a Crisis or Creating a Myth?* (Cambridge, MA,MIT Press, 2001).

[67] See eg Communication from the Delegation of Egypt, Electronic Commerce in Goods and Services, Committee on Trade and Development, WT/COMTD/W/38 (3 March 1998).

[68] 'Barbados, as well as many other developing countries, stands to gain much more by maintaining an environment for the growth and development of electronic commerce than by introducing new, cumbersome and restrictive measures to tax digital products and services.' Barbados Statement, Senator Goddard, WTO Seminar on 'Revenue Implications of E Commerce', Geneva, 22 April 2002

successful WTO challenge by Antigua of the laws of the US governing access to the market for online gambling services.

Electronic commerce has subsequently experienced massive growth in terms of overall scale, geographical breadth and reach, and range in the character of transactions. This growth has occurred for the most part in the absence of specific, dedicated new rules at the international level—in spite of various review processes concerning the applicability of existing rules, and initiatives to formulate new rules. Yet at the same time the growth in the quantity and diversity of electronic transactions has had major implications for the existing body of rules and has influenced how countries perceive and defend their commercial interests under those rules. Once again, the effect of the diffusion of Internet and its rapid uptake in commercial and cultural exchanges has been to shed light on the essential characteristics of international rules and of the institutions of international governance. To demonstrate this effect, this chapter will review some general themes in international governance of the Internet: the nature of international rules; the characteristics of electronic commerce; and the role of international institutions in governing the Internet.

The first theme is how rules operate to promote international exchanges and, paradoxically, how a backbone of rules-based harmonisation may provide a basis for diversity in cultural expression and diffusion of information. The Internet is a compelling case study of the nature of international rules and standards, and their role in creating the architecture of international co-operation and exchange. The Internet exemplifies the curious paradox of harmonisation: rules can allow freedoms; compliance with standards opens up pathways to diversity. Consider: what is the true essence of the Internet? It is not the fact that many computers are interlinked across the globe: ATMs can be accessed in many countries, but obviously do not offer the freedoms and flexibility of the Internet. And the Internet is blind to specific hardware platforms. Nor is it the fact that point-to-point communication is possible from any location to another remote location: you can do this by fax or telegraph. Surely the essence of the Internet is the fact that one rule, one protocol (Transmission Control/Internet Protocol (TCP/IP)) determines how data are to be packaged and transmitted, blind to both the content of the information and the actual physical route it takes to its destination address: the universal uniformity of this protocol is what makes it possible for information of any content, from images to telephony, to be transmitted across the Internet regardless of the route taken by specific data packets.

To this necessarily rigid, uniform protocol, you need to add a single, unambiguous set of addresses (the domain name system and the IP logical addresses to which domain names point), and you have a reliable system of exchanging and forwarding data to predictable addressees with confidence that the data will be intelligible to the recipient. The universality, the flexibility, the adaptability and openness of the Internet—what Zittrain calls a generative grid[69]—flows paradoxically from this rigid orthodoxy. The essence of the Internet is therefore a protocol, not any particular collection of hardware or network of data conduits—it is a rule rather than an assemblage of plumbing. This provides an instructive metaphor for the more general function of international rules as underpinning greater flows of information, cultural exchanges and trade:

> Electronic commerce presents major policy contradictions for many governments. On one hand, the creation of the Transmission Control/Internet Protocol (TCP/IP) as a harmonised protocol for data exchange sets the stage for explosive growth of Internet-based commerce in a virtual global community and marketplace. On the other hand, the trade policies and strategies of governments are embedded in notions of territoriality.
>
> Governments must avoid fragmentation of the emerging global online market because of incompatible approaches to rule making among nations. The best way to do this is through negotiating effective multilateral rules. In key respects, the TCP/IP is a metaphor for good rule making. Just as the TCP/IP is a set of rules which makes globalised data exchange possible, so good trade rules facilitate global commerce, including electronic commerce.[70]

It is not only trade policies of national governments that are 'embedded in notions of territoriality'—the same applies to many areas of law and regulation, and the same tension—between the need for interactivity, compatibility, seamless interaction, reduced transaction costs, economies of scale, pooling of regulatory resources, and so on, on the one hand, and the political and economic imperative for regulatory self-determination on the other—is felt in many other areas, ranging from the law of defamation and censorship, through telecommunications and broadcasting regulation, to intellectual property rights and exceptions. Take the public domain, a matter of intense current public policy interest. Legally, the public domain is a set of discrete bodies of material, defined and accessed according to the diverse rules of different national jurisdictions; the fact that a publication has fallen into the public domain in one country (or is not protected by copyright at all there) should not, normally, imply its public domain status elsewhere—so, in legal terms, there is not one single international public domain, but a congeries of public domains defined and regulated at national level.[71] But this does not square with the look and feel of the Internet, even though country-specific controls and constraints on the

---

[69] J Zittrain, 'The Generative Internet' (2006) 119 *Harvard Law Review* 1974.

[70] Department of Foreign Affairs and Trade, 'Driving Forces on the New Silk Road' (Canberra, 1999) 85.

[71] For an extended discussion, see A Taubman, 'The Public Domain and International Intellectual Property Law Treaties', in C Waelde and H MacQueen (eds), *Intellectual Property: The Many Faces of the Public Domain* (Cheltenham, Edward Elgar, 2007).

Internet are possible (and are actually implemented): the web—the *World Wide* Web, indeed—functions as a seamless network of information. Users are very likely unaware of the physical origin of the data their web browsers download, still less of the several legal jurisdictions through which the data may have travelled since, in principle at least, each individual packet may potentially take a different physical pathway and may traverse significantly different national regulatory systems. The growth of the Internet increasingly fuels a practical expectation, and bolsters a normative claim, that digital information should flow freely regardless of physical location; but it also facilitates transactions in tradeable digital products that do not pass through the conventional border controls that their physical analogues are subject to. In confronting territoriality in this way, do the advent and uptake of the Internet present a distinct new challenge for national sovereignty and the efficacy—even the foundational logic—of distinct and diverse efforts at domestic regulation.

The Treaty of Westphalia[72] is conventionally cited as the cornerstone or origin of the modern system of sovereign nation states. It effectively abolished the idea of an overarching hegemony of the Holy Roman Empire, gave formal recognition to the principle that discrete nation states enjoy sovereignty over domestic affairs (including matters of religion), and constructed a system of diplomatic relations and a distinct corpus of international law. The concept of sovereignty is dependent on territoriality, precisely because it concerns absolute or predominant authority of the sovereign powers within the territory of the state, exclusion of external authority and comity between states. Conventional notions of sovereignty are therefore dependent on the integrity of the capacity to exercise control within a well-defined territory.

If it is abolishing borders in practice, is the Internet therefore posing a threat to the very foundations of Westphalian sovereignty, dependent as it is on power exercised within defined physical territoriality? Or does it at least, along with Web 2.0, usher in Westphalia 2.0, a restructured system of sovereignties defined also by virtual borders? Again we are confronted with the question of whether the Internet presents a truly distinctive new set of issues, or simply accentuates and accelerates existing trends. The classical notion of sovereignty was already under threat, well before the advent of mass Internet usage, in a direct practical sense because of the rise of global business patterns[73] and globalised communication and cultural exchanges; as well as from a theoretical perspective.[74] Even the legal system exem-

---

[72] Peace Treaty between the Holy Roman Emperor and the King of France and their respective allies, done at Munster, Westphalia, 24 October 1648, English translation available at http://www.yale.edu/lawweb/avalon/westphal.htm.

[73] R Vernon, *Sovereignty at Bay* (New York, Basic Books, 1971).

[74] S Krasner, Sovereignty: Organized Hypocrisy (Princeton, NJ, Princeton University Press, 1999).

plified by the Treaty of Westphalia hardly precluded the exertion of influence beyond national boundaries, as real and virtual empires, and global systems of hard and soft influence, rose in the following centuries. Nor did Westphalia establish atomistic, discrete states, sealed off from one another: notably, the Treaty re-established liberalised international trade, and in terms reminiscent of the 1947 General Agreement on Trade and Tariffs (which was also, tellingly, concluded following a ruinous period of warfare) it provided that 'immoderate Expences and Charges of Posts, and other Obstacles to Commerce and Navigation introduc'd to its Prejudice, contrary to the Publick Benefit . . . shall be fully remov'd [. . . and t]here shall be a full Liberty of Commerce'.[75] The Treaty also applied to the domestic legal system a pivotal rule of contemporary trade law, the principle of national treatment, which continues to provide a safeguard against discrimination in the regulation of on-line trade today: 'the Magistrates, on the one side and on the other, shall be oblig'd to protect and defend [each one of the Vassals, Subjects, Inhabitants and Servants of the other side] . . . equally with their own Subjects'.[76] Hence, the recognition of state sovereignty, the loosening of restrictions on trade and other exchanges, and the assurance of non-discriminatory treatment formed part of the same integrated settlement, at the supposed dawn of the modern system of sovereign nation states, when the kind of exchanges enabled by the Internet were scarcely conceivable:[77] so the impact of the Internet, its dramatic effect of facilitating international exchanges and practically eliminating discrimination of access, seem less likely to threaten the essential idea of national sovereignty. In fact, in eroding away many of the contingent, non-essential physical constraints on exchanges and communication, the Internet helps clarify what are the indispensable, core elements of national sovereignty and the legal character of frontiers and linkages between nation states; and what is essentially accidental, a mere consequence of the current state of technology at any one time.

Even so, reflecting on the international order and the impact of the Internet, it is difficult to see a single pattern emerging. Rather, the impact

---

[75] Treaty of Westphalia, Art LXIX.

[76] Ibid, Art LXX.

[77] Almost. See Francis Bacon, *The New Atlantis* (1627), an extraordinary conception of the multimedia web: 'We have all means to convey sounds in trunks and pipes, in strange lines and distances.' And in practice services offering online streaming of live performances to subscribers were available in Paris, London (including coin-operated outlets in Earl's Court) and Budapest in the late 19th century (Marcel Proust was a noted fan of live theatre enjoyed through the Theatrophone); see P Collins, 'Theatrophone—The 19th-century iPod', *New Scientist*, 12 January 2008: 'On 22 March 1876, just 12 days after Alexander Graham Bell's momentous "Watson, come here, I want you" ushered in the telephone era, The New York Times was predicting a wired future where multichannel entertainment was a household utility like gas and water. "By means of this remarkable instrument, a man can have the Italian opera, the Federal Congress, and his favorite preacher laid on in his own house,' the paper proclaimed. "Fifty eminent preachers, of different denomination, can be kept constantly on draught."'

of the Internet has been to precipitate or at least to catalyse trends towards more diverse, hybrid forms of governance, which blend national and international layers of norms, and link public and private law. This hybrid character is exhibited, for example, in the evolving regime for governance of Internet names and addresses under the general direction of ICANN, and by the mechanism for settlement of disputes concerning domain name registrations—the UDRP,[78] introduced above. The essential legal character of the international governance of names and addresses, and of the UDRP as a dispute settlement policy, is difficult to situate within the established categories of public and private law, municipal and international law, and multilateral governance and self-regulation. ICANN itself is a non-profit corporation governed by the law of California, but it derived its original mandate and a degree of political legitimacy from the US Department of Commerce,[79] and has responded to demands that it should take on a more international character and should be representative of a wider spectrum of stakeholders base. The strong, residual interest of the US government in Internet governance stems both from its unique status as the original progenitor of the Internet, and from economic and political concerns. These interests have been manifested in a continued desire on the part of US policymakers to maintain the current governance model, with the management of Internet names and addresses still in private hands, but open to a broad base of stakeholder consultation and a degree of political influence.

An alternative vision, most clearly advocated by the European Union during the WSIS process, would see the key policy-level functions of Internet governance shift from this hybrid, but essentially private model towards a more structured, conventional multilateral system, directed by representatives of national governments within an intergovernmental structure. Indeed, the WSIS was in part a diplomatic initiative to remodel Internet governance, and to make a decisive shift towards a multilateral model that would set governance within a far broader normative and public policy framework and give the governments of the world in a more direct say over the fundamental principles that should apply.

The WSIS process, culminating in the 2005 Tunis Agenda for the Information Society,[80] is therefore of more fundamental interest in tracking both the evolution of institutional arrangements for international governance of the Internet, but also as a register of the distinct interests that different governments bring to the table, and the way those interests are played out in the multilateral environment.

---

[78] http://www.icann.org/dndr/udrp/policy.htm.

[79] Memorandum of Understanding between the US Department of Commerce and Internet Corporation for Assigned Names and Numbers, 25 November 1998, available at http://www.icann.org/general/icann-mou-25nov98.htm.

[80] WSIS-05/TUNIS/DOC/6(Rev 1)-E, 18 November 2005.

The ITU, as the UN Specialised Agency concerned with international co-operation and norm-setting on telecommunications, initiated the proposal for a World Summit under the aegis of the UN, in part to provide a forum to deal with different policy perspectives and interests in relation to the governance of Internet names and addresses.[81] This proposal was developed by the UN Secretary-General and endorsed by the UN General Assembly itself in 2001.[82] The WSIS was seen as a two-phase process, rather than as a stand-alone event, with an initial phase convened in Geneva in 2003 to shape the agenda and to establish a plan of action,[83] and the final phase convened in Tunis in 2005 to give effect to the plan of action and to reach agreement on some of the core governance issues ('to find solutions and reach agreements in the fields of Internet governance'[84]). The agenda of the WSIS was extremely broad and ranged well beyond the specific issue considered here, ie regulation of Internet names and addresses, but nonetheless that issue was both controversial in its own terms and illustrative of broader trends and interests overall on Internet governance issues. Generally speaking, the defining differences were between a top-down, essentially intergovernmental approach, and the more ad hoc, essentially private mechanisms that had defined Internet governance up to that time. On the one hand, it was indisputable that all governments and all nations had a legitimate interest in the healthy operation of the Internet, and ensuring reasonable access to it; and they retained core national interests such as security, censorship, fair trading and cultural policy, which the technical arrangements for management of the Internet could not be expected to trump. On the other hand, there was resistance against establishing a burdensome, politically charged and potentially unwieldy and inefficient new intergovernmental structure they would shift Internet governance away from its informal, pragmatic and more technically focused roots, and thus undercut its value as a global communications medium.

These competing interests were expressed in a key document from the Geneva summit, the 'Declaration of Principles: Building the Information Society: A Global Challenge in the New Millennium'.[85] On Internet governance, the declaration observed that 'the Internet has evolved into a global facility available to the public and its governance should constitute a core issue of the Information Society agenda' and provided that:

---

[81] International Telecomm Union, World Summit on the Information Society, ITU Plenipotentiary Conference (Minneapolis 1998) Res 73, http://www.itu.int/council/wsis/R73.html.

[82] GA Res 56/183, UN Doc A/RES/56/183 (31 January 2002).

[83] WSIS, 'Geneva Plan of Action', Doc WSIS-03/GENEVA/DOC/5-E, Dec. 12, 2003, available at http://www.itu.int/dms_pub/itu-s/md/03/wsis/doc/S03-WSIS-DOC-0005!!PDF-E.pdf.

[84] WSIS, Basic Information: About WSIS, http://www.itu.int/wsis/basic/about.html.

[85] Document WSIS-03/GENEVA/DOC/4-E of 12 December 2003.

The international management of the Internet should be multilateral, transparent and democratic, with the full involvement of governments, the private sector, civil society and international organisations. It should ensure an equitable distribution of resources, facilitate access for all and ensure a stable and secure functioning of the Internet, taking into account multilingualism.

The management of the Internet encompasses both technical and public policy issues and should involve all stakeholders and relevant intergovernmental and international organizations. In this respect it is recognized that:

- Policy authority for Internet-related public policy issues is the sovereign right of States. They have rights and responsibilities for international Internet-related public policy issues;

- The private sector has had and should continue to have an important role in the development of the Internet, both in the technical and economic fields;

- Civil society has also played an important role on Internet matters, especially at community level, and should continue to play such a role;

- Intergovernmental organizations have had and should continue to have a facilitating role in the coordination of Internet-related public policy issues;

- International organizations have also had and should continue to have an important role in the development of Internet-related technical standards and relevant policies.

This declaration of principles, and the Geneva plan of action, provided a normative framework within which to address issues such as the management of names and addresses, and possibly to institute more formal, more directly intergovernmental governance. As the diplomatic process moved close to its culmination in Tunis in late 2005, the EU put forward a major proposal that, among other things, went to the heart of the governance of names and addresses, essentially by formalising a set of principles that would determine how names and addresses were managed, and proposing direct multilateral oversight that would determine how an agency such as ICANN would carry out its more technical duties. Thus the EU proposal for a 'new model for international co-operation' would

> not replace existing mechanisms or institutions, but should build on the existing structures of Internet Governance, with a special emphasis on the complementarity between all the actors involved in this process, including governments, the private sector, civil society and international organisations each of them in its field of competence.

The role of governments would 'be mainly focused on principle issues of public policy, excluding any involvement in the day-to-day operations'. Critically, in the field of names and numbers, the proposed model would

> include the development and application of globally applicable public policy principles and provide an international government involvement at the level of principles over . . . naming, numbering and addressing-related matters . . . including (a) Provision for a global allocation system of IP number blocks, which

is equitable and efficient; (b) Procedures for changing the root zone file, specifically for the insertion of new top level domains in the root system and changes of
ccTLD managers.

Thus a new international body would set the normative framework and the
essential architecture of the Internet, and assume many of the broader
management and policy functions of the existing ICANN Board of
Directors.

The EU proposal did stress that it would give effect to the accepted
Geneva principles and would build upon, rather than replace, the existing
institutions of Internet governance (presumably a reassuring reference to
ICANN). These reassurances were not, however, enough to win the
support of the US, which did not accept this model and maintained its
long-standing resistance to the internationalisation of governance of the
core elements of the Internet—the allocation of names and addresses.[86]
Ultimately, when the concluding document, the Tunis Agenda for the Information Society, was negotiated it did not introduce a new mechanism for
Internet governance that would significantly alter the existing role of
ICANN, and the existing hybrid model centred on a not-for-profit corporation under US domestic law. The essential contribution of the Tunis
Agenda to Internet governance was the creation of a 'new forum for multi-
stakeholder policy dialogue',[87] to be termed the Internet Governance
Forum (IGF) and to be convened by the UN Secretary-General 'in an open
and inclusive process'.[88] The role of the IGF was clearly delineated and
distinguished from the actual governance of the Internet: it would 'have no
oversight function and would not replace existing arrangements, mechanisms, institutions or organizations. . . . It would be constituted as a neutral,
non-duplicative and non-binding process. It would have no involvement in
day-to-day or technical operations of the Internet.'[89] The essential legal
character of Internet governance was therefore unaltered by this outcome,

[86] See eg US Department of Commerce, Management of Internet Names and Addresses,
Docket Number: 980212036-8146-02 (National Telecommunications and Information
Administration (NTIA)), 5 June 1998: 'The US Government is committed to a transition that
will allow the private sector to take leadership for DNS [domain name system] management.
Most commenters shared this goal. While international organisations may provide specific
expertise or act as advisors to the new corporation, the US continues to believe, as do most
commenters, that neither national governments acting as sovereigns nor intergovernmental
organisations acting as representatives of governments should participate in management of
Internet names and addresses.' See also NTIA, 'US Principles on the Internet's Domain Name
and Addressing System', http://www.ntia.doc.gov/ntiahome/domainname/USDNSprinciples_
06302005.htm: 'While the United States recognizes that the current Internet system is working,
we encourage an ongoing dialogue with all stakeholders around the world in the various fora as a
way to facilitate discussion and to advance our shared interest in the ongoing robustness and
dynamism of the Internet. In these fora, the United States will continue to support market-based
approaches and private sector leadership in Internet development broadly.'
[87] Tunis Agenda, para 72.
[88] Ibid.
[89] Ibid, para 77.

even if the strong policy interest of the governments of the world was recognised and issues of fairness and global equity were acknowledged as central to the policy environment within which the managers of the Internet must operate. Yet as the opening quote from Zittrain exemplifies, tension remains between the overarching objectives of inclusiveness in policy dialogue and widespread stakeholder consultation, and the more direct legitimacy of practical initiatives that simply make the system work: with the unavoidable observation that many of the benefits of the Internet, for more open global diplomacy, for improved educational and cultural opportunities, and for the advancement of human rights in general, did not result from international institutions and from a conscious, collective normative impulse, but from the steady accumulation of practical initiatives and grass-roots activity, and in part also from private-sector activity such as the rollout of connectivity spurred by liberalisation of the telecommunications sector in many countries.

VII. INTERNATIONAL GOVERNANCE OF ELECTRONIC COMMERCE—FROM A TRADE IN ATOMS TO TRADE IN BITS

One largely unforeseen, but potentially momentous, consequence of the growth of the Internet, and especially the expansion of the functionality of the World Wide Web, has been the expansion of electronic commerce in the online environment. Electronic commerce is not necessarily linked with the Internet—e-commerce is typically defined in terms of commercial transactions facilitated in some way by the use of information or communications technology, covering a wide array of transactions in which ICT may be used to facilitate payment, ordering, customs formalities, as well as the actual delivery of a product. The WTO Work Programme on Electronic Commerce defines the term to mean 'the production, distribution, marketing, sale *or* delivery of goods and services by electronic means'.[90] It specifies that any or all of the three main stages of a commercial transaction—advertising and searching, ordering and payment, and delivery—'may be carried out electronically and may therefore be covered by the concept of "electronic commerce"'.[91]

E-commerce in its general sense includes facilitation of existing forms of trade—browsing and purchasing books, for instance, or delivering architectural services online. But it also includes a new category of trade altogether. From the point of view of international governance issues, this is the most interesting component of electronic commerce: the emergence of the digital product, or digitised product—the growing trade in 'bits', which

---

[90] WTO document WT/L/274, 30 September 1998. For discussion on e-contracts, see ch 2.
[91] Ibid.

Nicholas Negroponte contrasted with trade in atoms, in a series of influential articles in *Wired* magazine in the early 1990s.[92]

Prior to the widespread availability of digital networks as a channel for delivery of products direct to the consumer, many creative works and knowledge products were normally delivered on a physical medium—optical or vinyl disks, the printed page, etc—even though what mostly counted was the content. Digital networks now enable trade in pure content—eg direct digital downloads of music, and electronic versions of books and periodicals. The carrier medium can be dispensed with, and no physical containers or packages need be delivered; above all, from the governance perspective, no goods need pass across national borders and through customs clearance. From the point of view of the consumer, some digital downloads may be almost identical to the physical product—in practice, I may be entirely indifferent as to whether I download and install functional software, then burn a back-up disk; or purchase a disk and install the software from it. A music CD may be more appealing because of its distinctive packaging (and a collectible vinyl disk especially may be valued as a physical object in itself), but in general commerce the downloaded tracks (and cover art) may not be considered significantly different from the physical product.

Uncertainty shrouds the essential character of the commercial transaction undertaken when such content is acquired;[93] this leads to legal equivocation: an early decision considering the effect of the legend 'not licensed for radio broadcast' when applied to a sound recording concluded that this constraint was a reasonable 'equitable servitude on a chattel'[94]—in other words, enjoyment of the possession of a physical copy of the recording was subject to continuing liability to the originator of the sound recording. While debate continues over the legal nature of transactions in intangible content such as sound recordings and software,[95] the possibility of trade in pure content clears away some of the physical clutter and sheds light on the true nature of the transaction: when purchasing a music CD or software on a disk, one had never been essentially purchasing 'the song' or 'the program', but one had rather obtained a limited licence to use the content in certain specified ways. These limitations were mostly formalised through statutory intellectual property rights, which provided a consistent

---

[92] Collected in N Negroponte, *Being Digital* (1995), e-book version at http://archives. obs-us.com/obs/english/books/nn/bdintro.htm.

[93] In the information and entertainment industries, bits and atoms often are confused. Is the publisher of a book in the information delivery business (bits) or in the manufacturing business (atoms)? The historical answer is both, but that will change rapidly as information appliances become more ubiquitous and user-friendly. (Negroponte, 'Bits and Atoms', in *Being Digital*, above n 91).

[94] *Waring v WDAS Broad Station Inc*, 194 A 631, 638 (Pa 1937).

[95] MS Van Houweling, 'The New Servitudes', *Georgetown Law Journal*, forthcoming. Available at SSRN: http://ssrn.com/abstract=1028947, discussing the 'new servitudes' applied in click-wrap licenses on downloaded software.

legal framework informed by public policy. A purchase did confer owner-ship over a physical good—the disk, the book, etc—and this did give certain entitlements over the content (eg normally one could sell the original copy and thereby effectively transfer that license to use the content to the purchaser); but one could not do whatever one liked with the content—so full, unquestioned ownership of a legitimate DVD still does not confer the right to play the film it contains at a public gathering or to copy it in commercial quantities. Paring away the supporting medium and engaging in pure digital trade therefore spotlights the true nature of the transaction—effective access to content that is still 'owned' by the access provider, rather than a physical product changing hands.

Fascinating (perhaps). But why does this matter at the level of inter-national governance? In fact, the emergence of digital products has driven a long-running debate in the WTO, exposing deep divergences between national perspectives. Several major questions arise over how international rules should apply to digital products: essentially, how they are taxed, valued and classified, and whether differential treatment of digital trade amounts to discrimination. More broadly, as we will briefly see, the emergence of trade in 'pure' digital products opened up a new vein in several long-running tensions in the politics of trade—transatlantic differ-ences over the importance of cultural exceptions to trade liberalisation; and north–south concerns about disparities in access to international markets and the technological advantages enjoyed by developed economies. Trade in digital products—in effectively shrinking distance and abolishing trans-portation costs, challenging the effectiveness of border controls and the viability of import tariffs—offers a glimpse of 'free trade', and thus exacer-bates all the hopes and apprehensions that the idea of free trade provokes.

Perhaps inevitably, one key issue concerns taxation: when a CD passes through customs clearance, it is relatively straightforward to impose import duties. In the absence of 'free trade' internationally, a country does have the right to impose tariffs on goods such as packaged software, music CDs, DVDs and books. Trade in these physical media is governed by the GATT. Under the GATT, WTO members commit to keep tariffs on goods under certain agreed ceilings or 'tariff bindings', not to discriminate between goods imported from different countries (the 'most-favoured-nation' principle), and not to impose unreasonably different requirements on imported goods over domestically produced goods (the principle of 'national treatment').

Some governments continue to see customs tariffs as an important source of public revenue: in some developing countries, for instance, the infrastructure for raising revenue from the domestic economy can be less effective and tariffs may also be relied upon to protect emerging producers domestically. Customs officials may apply different tariff levels to media with recorded content as against blank media, and may value recorded media much more highly than blank material (given that packaged software on a disk may cost literally hundreds of times more than the blank disk). The international system for classifying goods for the purposes of tariffs, the Harmonised System, itself recognises the 'value-added' quality of content supplied on physical media. It has separate classifications for blank media and recorded media, a practical recognition that adding intangible content to a physical medium alters its character from a regulatory perspective.[96] But even this formal distinction conceals an unresolved dilemma about how the intangible content captured on a recorded medium should be valued, a dilemma neatly captured by Negroponte anecdotally:

> I recently visited the headquarters of one of America's top five integrated circuit manufacturers. I was asked to sign in and, in the process, was asked whether I had a laptop computer with me. Of course I did. The receptionist asked for the model and serial number and for its value. 'Roughly, between one and two million dollars,' I said. 'Oh, that cannot be, sir,' she replied. 'What do you mean? Let me see it.' I showed her my old PowerBook and she estimated its value at $2,000. She wrote down that amount and I was allowed to enter the premises. The point is that while the atoms were not worth that much, the bits were almost priceless.[97]

Concerning software, the same dilemma over valuation had arisen in a more formal setting, in the Tokyo Round of trade negotiations under the GATT; this led to a Decision on the valuation of carrier media bearing software for data-processing equipment,[98] adopted afresh by the newly constituted WTO Committee on Customs Valuation in 1995. This provided:

> Given the unique situation[99] with regard to data or instructions (software) recorded on carrier media for data processing equipment, and that some Parties

---

[96] The Harmonised Commodity Description and Coding System (HS) of tariff nomenclature is an internationally standardised system of names and numbers for classifying traded products developed and maintained by the World Customs Organization (WCO). Separate classifications apply for 'prepared unrecorded media (no film) for sound etc' including magnetic tapes, disks and other media (classification heading 8523) and for 'records, tapes & other recorded sound media etc computer software' (8524); a similar distinction is made between unexposed film (3702) and motion-picture film, exposed and developed (3706).

[97] Negroponte, 'Bits and Atoms, in The DNA of Information', *Being Digital*, above n 91.

[98] GATT document VAL/M/10, of 24 September 1984, para 7.

[99] This 'unique situation' was characterised in a statement made by the Chairman at the Meeting of the GATT Committee on Customs Valuation of 24 September 1984 as follows: 'In the case of imported carrier media bearing data or instructions for use in data processing equipment (software), it is essentially the carrier media itself, eg the tape or the magnetic disc, which is liable to duty under the Customs tariff. However, the importer is, in fact, interested in using the instructions or data; the carrier medium is incidental. Indeed, if the technical facilities are available to the Parties to the transaction, the software can be transmitted by wire or satellite, in which case the question of Customs duties does not arise. In addition, the carrier medium is usually a temporary means of storing the instructions or data; in order to use it, the buyer has to transfer or reproduce the data or instructions into the memory or data-base of his own system. 'Under the international Customs valuation practices which were superseded by the

have sought a different approach, it would also be consistent with the Agreement for those Parties which wish to do so to adopt the following practice: In determining the customs value of imported carrier media bearing data or instructions, only the cost or value of the carrier medium itself shall be taken into account. The customs value shall not, therefore, include the cost or value of the data or instructions, provided that this is distinguished from the cost or the value of the carrier medium. For the purpose of this Decision, the expression 'carrier medium' shall not be taken to include integrated circuits, semiconductors and similar devices or articles incorporating such circuits or devices; the expression 'data or instructions' shall not be taken to include sound, cinematic or video recordings.

In other words, the 'unique situation' concerning software means that the carrier medium will be valued for customs purposes, even though the user is interested in the content, noting that the user can in many cases obtain the same content by electronic transmissions. This did not apply to other copyright-protected content, such as sound or cinematic works. Even so, many countries continued to value imported software not on the basis of the value of the carrier medium, but the transaction value that takes account of the actual price paid for the content of the software.[100] In effect, the international rules left open the possibility of continuing to value on the basis of actual transaction costs, not the value of the carrier medium, bearing in mind that this will typically be a small fraction of the total value of most digital products. Concerning the gathering of statistics in trade in software, the UN[101] recommends that

> goods used as carriers of information and software, such as packaged sets containing diskettes or CD-ROMs with stored computer software and/or data

Agreement on Implementation of Article VII of the General Agreement on Tariffs and Trade (the Agreement), the value of the software was not, as a general rule, included when valuing the carrier medium. Following their adoption of the Agreement, those countries which followed the previous international practice have changed their rules for valuing carrier media bearing computer software or have maintained their previous practice.'

[100] See eg Australian Customs Notice, 2000/51, Tuesday, 1 August 2000 ('Valuation of Carrier Media Bearing Software'), at http://www.customs.gov.au/site/page.cfm?c=2199: 'some confusion may . . . have arisen following the [GATT] Customs Valuation Committee decision on the Valuation of Carrier Media Bearing Software for Data Processing Equipment in September 1984. This decision noted the application of normal valuation rules which provide for the customs value to include payments for both the software and the carrier media. However, in recognition of the fact that some countries wanted to continue their previous (pre-Customs Valuation Agreement) practice of excluding the value of software from the customs value, the decision also allowed Members to adopt that approach. Australia notified the Customs Valuation Committee that normal valuation rules would apply to carrier media bearing software, but that the software was free of customs duty. . . . notwithstanding the various changes to customs duty and sales tax in relation to software and carrier media, the normal principles of customs valuation . . . apply to carrier media bearing software and remain unchanged. The customs value of carrier media bearing software should therefore include the payments made, or to be made, for both the software and the carrier media.'

[101] UN Department of Economic and Social Affairs, Statistics Division, 'International Merchandise Trade Statistics—Concepts and Definitions,' document ST/ESA/STAT/SER.M/52/Rev.2.

developed for general or commercial use (not to order), be valued at the their full transaction value (not at the value of the empty diskettes or CD-ROMs, paper or other.[102]

By contrast, customised software (software developed to order) is to be treated as a service and excluded in principle from customs treatment as a good, even if shipped on a physical medium.

This dilemma now has major significance for the application of tariffs on imported products. What happens when the 'same' content is conveyed across the same border, but through electronic transmissions as a digital product? The packet switching technology and dispersed architecture of the Internet could mean that different elements of this content could pass undetected through many different jurisdictions. But no distinct package is presented to customs officials for clearance at a defined border. Is this the 'same' product from the point of view of import duties? Can the importing country impose tariffs (to the extent that such trade can be monitored and policed, and where *de minimis* and personal-use exceptions to imported goods do not apply)? Is the purchaser required in principle to pay tariffs, even if this is difficult to enforce in practice? And where does the imported product come from: given that countries can impose preferential tariffs on goods originating from certain countries (such as partners to a free trade agreement), is the product considered to originate from a server farm somewhere, or from the physical location of the supplying company? And do commitments on tariff levels for the product on physical media apply to the analogous product in digital form?

This uncertainty over the 'real-world' characteristics leads to the second question: that of classification of the trade in digital products. International trade law recognises a fundamental distinction between trade in goods and trade in services. Conventional trade law addressed trade in goods—stuff you can drop on your foot. Only recently, in 1994, upon the conclusion of the array of agreements constituting the WTO, did multilateral trade law and mutual commitments among trading partners extend to the so-called 'new' trade areas of services and intellectual property through the General Agreement on Trade in Services (GATS) and the TRIPS Agreement, respectively. This dramatic development in trade law coincided—fortuitously or otherwise—very closely with the rapid uptake of the Internet as a means not only of communication but of direct trade.

Trade in goods and trade in services are regulated differently within the trade law system administered by the WTO, meaning in effect trading partners make different commitments to each other over access to their markets for goods and for services. To characterise this difference very crudely, the GATT rules on trade in non-agricultural goods apply across the board, for instance prohibiting discrimination between goods of domestic

---

[102] Ibid, 48.

and foreign origin—a special tax or quota on imported CDs could not be sustained under WTO law; whereas for services a WTO member can elect which services are covered by its commitments under GATS—if a country did not nominate architectural services, for instance, it would not be obliged to grant access to foreign architects to its domestic market; or it could restrict the numbers permitted to practice. In the cultural domain, restrictions on foreign 'service providers', such as musicians or cinema directors, may be construed as a means of preserving a strong domestic cultural sector—indeed as having bearing on the conservation of cultural diversity[103] and providing a defence against cultural homogenisation.

So the GATS would ensure national treatment or market access for digital products only if a country had positively undertaken a commitment under GATS to allow access; a commitment need not provide for open-ended access but may include, for instance, exceptions to the non-discriminatory principle of 'most favoured nation'. Given that one high-profile WTO dispute has already turned on the question of whether a specific service was included under a GATS classification, some uncertainty could be expected as to whether digital products fall under existing scheduled GATS commitments.

The greater flexibility available under GATS compared with the GATT, and the perceived greater scope for protecting domestic cultural interests, is one factor driving a complex debate about the seemingly technical matter of how digital products should be classified—as goods or as services, as covered by GATT commitments or GATS commitments. What may once have appeared to be an interesting academic question is potentially a directly practical, even political, question, concerning billions of dollars of trade in an industry that remains relatively buoyant even in times of economic downturn.

The classification issue pivots on digital products, rather than the general provision of services over the Internet—so, along with web-based professional services and financial services, trade such as online gambling services are regulated by the GATS and subject to commitments under that agreement (provided a WTO member chooses to include such services under their commitments, a matter which was at issue in the WTO dispute *US-Gambling*). But the fuzzy conceptual boundaries that surround the provision of a digital product[104]—is it an intangible 'good', a service,

---

[103] UNESCO Convention on the Protection and Promotion of the Diversity of Cultural Expressions, 2005.

[104] Early in the WTO debate, one delegation pointed out that 'it was difficult to see how a distinction between "goods" and "services" could be handled in practice, even if agreed on in theory. As the transmitted bytes of data streams consisted only of one's and zeroes, the delegation raised the questions how it was possible to decide for each individual case whether a particular transmission was covered by goods or services disciplines?' (General Council, Interim review of progress in the implementation of the work programme on electronic commerce, Communication from the Chairman of the Council for Trade in Goods, WT/GC/24, 12 April 1999, 3).

altogether a distinct thing in its own class, or several of these options at once—open up considerable uncertainty over what commitments and legitimate expectations exist between trading partners. In turn, this uncertainty can impair the stability and predictability, as well as basic fairness and transparency, that international trade rules are intended to engender, and which are needed above all in those areas where commercial interests and broader public policy interests intersect (such as the interplay between the gambling industry and regulation of public order and public morals that was considered in *US-Gambling*).

On the classification of digitised products, Indonesia and Singapore put forward an interesting proposal, moving beyond the conventional divide between goods and services, in the context of the WTO programme on electronic commerce. In a joint submission, they discuss the need for legal certainty in classification, and raise the possibility of a third category of trade, that of trade in intellectual property as such, which would be consonant with the increasing attention given to the contents, rather than the platform on which the contents are delivered:

> In attempting to classify digitized products one possible criterion that has been raised is to consider whether the product has a tangible counterpart in the physical world. This criterion could then be applied to over-the-counter purchases of books, music and software even if such purchases were delivered as digitized products and not in terms of their physical counterparts.
>
> An alternative is to just consider the contents themselves. Books, music and software are not in themselves new commercial products. It is just that prior to the advent of e-commerce, they were treated as goods because they had to be delivered in the form of a carrier media, be it paper, cassettes or diskettes etc and those carrier media were classified as goods. Now that those forms of tangible carrier mediums are no longer necessary maybe what we need to consider is whether the software and music would continue to be classified as goods, or it might be more appropriate for them to be classified as services.
>
> It may also not be a coincidence that all these three examples, without a carrier medium are intangible goods considered under the ambit of intellectual property rights. Could such products than be simply considered as trade in intellectual property rights and not be classified as a good or a service?
>
> What is paramount though is that the criteria for classification should provide legal certainty on how the good, the service or the intellectual property right is to be treated.[105]

We have noted the continuing uncertainty over the classification of software, a highly valuable component of trade (and a significant proportion of the value of the physical package), which is not itself the subject

---

[105] WTO, Communication from Indonesia and Singapore, Preparations for the 1999 Ministerial Conference: Work Programme on Electronic Commerce, WT/GC/W/247, 9 July 1999, at paras 10–14.

[106] Ministerial Declaration on Trade in Information Technology Products, Singapore, WT/MIN(96)/16 13 December 1996 at www.wto.org/english/tratop_e/inftec_e/itadec_e.htm.

of a classification under the Harmonised System. The Information Technology Agreement,[106] an accord among a subset of WTO members (in WTO language, a 'plurilateral agreement'), aims to secure 'maximum freedom of world trade in information technology products' through eliminating 'customs duties and other duties and charges of any kind'[107] on IT products. Yet even this agreement does not mention software as such, despite its critical role in the information economy, and only refers to the carrier media through their Harmonised System headings (including those discussed above).

Nonetheless, the particular importance of software in modern economic infrastructure—increasingly for developing economies as much as for the developed world—has led to some expectations that a liberalised trade regime should be fostered, regardless of the precise classification issues. Thus the US has argued that

> [T]rade in electronically delivered software positively impacts both developing and developed countries. . . . The collaboration among many different countries on the development and creation of software that is then transmitted seamlessly across borders warrants a creative approach which builds on trade disciplines across the whole range of WTO agreements. It is inherently in the interests of all Members to pursue approaches, in all appropriate fora, that ensure liberal trade treatment for electronically transmitted software.[108]

The arguments for more liberal treatment of electronic trade in software have attracted broader consensus than when the same arguments are applied to audiovisual works or digital cultural works. Liberalised trade for audio-visual works is potentially more sensitive than for software, since it touches more directly on the overlap between trade and cultural policy (although the distinction between 'cultural' audio-visual works and software is breaking down—witness the increasing interrelationship between computer games and cultural works). The question of how digital products should be classified therefore plays directly into sensitivities over market access commitments for audio-visual and other cultural services, touching on long-running tensions over the 'cultural exception' to trade rules that were evident in the negotiations on the GATS during the Uruguay Round and help to spur, for example, negotiations on the UNESCO Convention on Cultural Diversity. The GATS does include audio-visual services under its general obligations—in other words, there is no blanket 'cultural exception' for audiovisual services—but many WTO Members elect not to include such services under their specific sectoral

---

[107] Such duties and charges are specified as being 'within the meaning of Article II:1(b) of the General Agreement on Tariffs and Trade 1994'; in other words, relating to importation as such—it does not preclude, for instance, non-discriminatory value added tax on such products.

[108] WTO General Council, Work Programme on Electronic Commerce, Communication from the United States, WT/GC/W/551, 28 October 2005.

commitments under GATS, as a means of preserving entitlements to protect domestic providers in the cultural sector.

Firmly classifying audio-visual digital products as goods, governed by GATT obligations, would restrict the legitimate scope for constraints on distribution of foreign cultural works, and for preferences and quotas for domestic works. This seemingly narrow technical issue resonates with the broader 'trade and culture' debate'; so it is not surprising that the debate over classification of digital products should take on a transatlantic, or more directly US–EU, dimension; and indeed, the US has been consistent in supporting the incorporation of digital products under GATT, whereas the EU has called for their incorporation as services under the GATS. This debate has continued, on and off, for almost a decade in the WTO (or longer than the original Uruguay Round negotiations on the entire WTO package of trade law), without any definitive resolution. Meanwhile, the trade in digital products has grown apace, suggesting either that no firm position is needed under international trade law, or that the question may ultimately be resolved in a more ad hoc way, through pragmatic negotiation or through dispute settlement. Already, WTO dispute settlement has effectively confirmed that services delivered over the Internet are indeed covered by GATS obligations, despite the positions taken by some governments in WTO policy discussions that either an express common understanding would be desirable, or specific, additional commitments concerning Internet-supplied services would be required before any obligations came into effect.[109]

A certain degree of pragmatism has been evident, also, in the way WTO members have dealt with the question of tariffs on electronically traded goods. The first substantial outcome from the WTO on Electronic Commerce was the moratorium on new tariffs, agreed among trade ministers at the ministerial conference in Geneva in 1998. Ministers issued a political declaration on Electronic Commerce which called on WTO members to 'continue their current practice of not imposing customs duties on electronic transmissions'.[110] In other words, trade ministers agreed on a general political understanding that new tariffs would not be imposed on cross-border electronic transmissions, regardless of the finer points of the classification debate. This moratorium has been supported by some WTO members as a kind of de facto trade liberalisation measure—inasmuch as digitally traded products would compete with products traded on physical carrier media, a moratorium on customs duties on electronic transmissions may induce liberalisation on trade in their physical counterparts. Equally,

---

[109] See the summary of the debate in S Wunsch-Vincent, 'The Internet, Cross-border Trade in Services, and the GATS—Lessons from US-Gambling' (2006) 5(3) *World Trade Review* 319–56, 323.

[110] WTO, Geneva Ministerial Declaration on Global Electronic Commerce, WT/MIN(98)/DEC/2 (20 May 1998).

however, the moratorium has been questioned because of concern about possible loss of revenue, especially for those developing countries that rely more on customs duties as a source of revenue given the comparative lack of domestic infrastructure for tax collection. Given the different trading interests, and negotiating strategies, that different countries bring to the table at the WTO, there may also be a tactical interest in bargaining over the extension of such a moratorium. Hence, the moratorium remains an informal understanding at the multilateral level, rather than a legally binding component of the trade law administered by the WTO.

Given that trading nations lay increasing emphasis on their economic interests in the appropriate governance of the online environment, and in the light of continuing uncertainty in the multilateral system, is perhaps inevitable that some governance issues would find their way into bilateral agreements, agreement that may pre-empt multilateral outcomes on key issues. For example, to take one such agreement among many, the free trade agreement reached between Singapore and the US touches already on several of the questions discussed above; concerning digital products, it precludes the application of 'customs duties or other duties, fees, or charges on or in connection with the importation or exportation of digital products by electronic transmission'.[111] It also settles the question of whether customs valuation will include the content ('bits') when digital products are imported on physical carrier mediums:

> [T]he customs value of an imported carrier medium bearing a digital product [shall be determined] according to the cost or value of the carrier medium alone, without regard to the cost or value of the digital product stored on the carrier medium.[112]

While such bilateral agreements are typically viewed in the context of relations with major economic powers, similar arrangements have been reached between middle level economies: so, for instance, the Comprehensive Economic Co-operation Agreement Between the Republic of India and the Republic of Singapore[113] contain similar provisions regarding digital products.[114] Interestingly, several bilateral agreements define 'digital products' as including computer programs, text, video, images, sound recordings and other products that are digitally encoded, regardless of whether they are fixed on a carrier medium or transmitted electronically. In other words, the primacy of the content, or the 'bits', is effectively asserted over the carrier medium, or 'atoms'. The norms, practices and interpretations of such bilateral agreements certainly do not automatically flow into the multilateral context, and cannot be regarded as authoritative readings

---

111 United States–Singapore Free Trade Agreement (Washington, 6 May 2003), Art 14.3.1.
112 Ibid, Art 14.3.2.
113 New Delhi, 29 June 2005.
114 See Arts 10.4.1 and 10.4.2.

of international standards, nor as binding other countries not party to such agreements. Even so, the steady accumulation of such bilateral norms, coupled with the mostly laissez-faire approach taken to the regulation of trade in electronic transmissions over the Internet (whether by conscious choice or by default), may be indicative of a general international trend towards governance of international commerce over the Internet, and may prefigure continuing liberalisation of trade in information products generally, regardless of carrier medium. A rough analogy could be drawn with the way in which the practical reality of large-scale file sharing over the Internet—legitimate or otherwise—precipitates new business models more suited to the online environment.

This observation returns us to the original dilemma we confronted regarding international governance of the Internet—how sovereign nations, asserting jurisdiction within physically defined boundaries, could ever effectively control behavior on the Internet; and the aspirations of earlier cyber-pioneers for cyberspace kept free of the dead hand of regulation. The transition of the Internet, in little more than a decade and a half, from a research and academic tool known to and used by a relatively small number of people, to a central means of political participation, communication, education, public diplomacy, multilateral governance and negotiation, and international commerce, makes it inevitable that issues of Internet governance will be taken up by domestic authorities and by multilateral organisations: too much is at stake, and the perceived pragmatic interests are too great, for these regulatory interests to remain disengaged— whatever theoretical or political preferences may be nurtured. However, the regulatory impact is far from one-way: just as national authorities and international/intergovernmental organisations may be seen as reaching out to incorporate the Internet within their respective areas of competence or jurisdiction, the impact of the Internet itself has been to transform the nature of governance. At the international level, this transformation is felt in a hitherto unprecedented transparency and accessibility of multilateral organisations and processes. Equally, the remarkable diffusion of new commercial opportunities presented by the Internet, including greater access to global markets for smaller enterprises and traders from the developing world, may in time have impact on the way sovereign nations perceive and pursue their economic interests, and the way in which rules governing international trading relations are construed and negotiated. In the end, studying the area of 'international governance and the Internet' may concern international governance *by* the Internet at least as much as international governance *of* the Internet. Over time, it may transpire that the Internet will transform international governance more than international institutions transform the Internet . . .

Part II
Electronic Commerce

1

The Fall and Rise of Intermediary Liability Online

LILIAN EDWARDS

I. INTRODUCTION AND HISTORICAL DEVELOPMENT

THE INTERNET IS a giant network of networks designed to carry, host and transmit information or 'content'. This information is distributed, hosted and located by online intermediaries, whose part in the entire enterprise of the information society is thus vital. Content often carries with it legal liability, which may be civil or criminal. A text (or a video or a song or a picture or an executable file) may be defamatory. It may contain illegal images of child sexual abuse. It may infringe the copyright of the owner thereof, if the host (or the publisher or the reader or listener) has made an unauthorised copy. It may incite racial hatred. It may infringe laws on truthful advertising, or reveal facts that are embargoed by laws of confidence or contempt of court rules. It may negligently give misleading advice to someone reliant on it. In all these (and many more) cases, an issue arises which is, to some extent, novel to the Internet: how far should online intermediaries be responsible for this content, or contrarily, how far should responsibility stay with the original content author or provider?

In relation to this, if the intermediary is deemed even partially responsible, what acts should the law demand it takes to remove this content, or perhaps even to prevent it being made available in the first place? Alternatively, if only the content provider, not the intermediary, is held responsible, will it be practical for the law to control the dissemination of the undesirable content (or abuse of legitimate content, as in the copyright example)? And finally, if liability *is* placed on online intermediaries, what will the impact be on their business models and economic survival, given their aforementioned importance to the Internet economy? These are all, as we shall see, crucial questions for the modern information age, and have become more so as a result of two key developments: the exponential rise in unauthorised downloading of digital music, film and video; and the

47

arrival of the so-called 'Web 2.0' (discussed in detail below) in particular, the rise of interactive user-generated content sites such as eBay, Facebook, etc.

The problem of liability of Internet intermediaries for content authored by third parties—known at first as the issue of 'ISP liability', but now of considerably wider scope—was in fact one of the earliest problems in the cyberspace environment to worry the fledgling Internet industry and demand the serious attention of lawyers.[1] Early cases mainly originated in the US and focused on the liability of the first Internet service providers (ISPs) such as AOL or CompuServe.[2] The problematic content might be content originated by a party with whom the ISP had a contractual relationship, ie an ISP subscriber; content provided by a third party with no contractual nexus with the ISP, eg where a newsgroup posting was transmitted by the ISP as part of its standard 'feed' to customers; or content originated by the ISP itself. The different issues of policy raised by these different classifications of authorship, responsibility, control and types of content were largely not teased out systematically in the early jurisprudence, leading to widely differing regimes being imposed both across different legal systems, and within the same legal system but in differing scenarios depending on the type of content or the type of 'publisher' or 'host'.

This lack of harmonisation in the emerging case-law led to calls from industry for some form of rescuing certainty in the form of special statutory regimes from as early as the mid-1990s. As discussed below, as the millennium approached and the dotcom boom came and went, the liability regime debate came to be seen, at least in Europe, less as tied to different types of content—libel, pornography, material infringing copyright—and more as a holistic problem of whether intermediaries on the Internet should in general be made responsible for the content they made accessible to the public, and more importantly, whether they could in practice take any steps to deal with such responsibility and avoid risk.

At the same time, the issue of liability for content became a major worry not just for the relatively small traditional ISP community, but also for a wider spectrum of Internet hosts, eg universities, traditional media organisations going 'digital' (eg the BBC, *The Times*), software providers like Microsoft and Sun, libraries and archives, chatrooms and 'webblog' sites,

---

1 *Cubby v CompuServe* 766 F Supp 135 (SDNY, 1991), for example (see discussion at n 27 below) was one of the earliest cyberlaw cases of any kind to be decided, in 1991. A Dutch prosecution of an ISP for hosting copyright material was also reported in 1991, see DTL Oosterbaan et al, 'eCommerce 2003: Netherlands' in *Getting the Deal Through: eCommerce 2003 in 25 Jurisdictions Worldwide* (Law Business Research Ltd, 2003).

2 For historical context, see earlier discussion of these issues by this writer in L Edwards, 'Defamation and the Internet' and 'Pornography and the Internet', in L Edwards and C Waelde (eds), *Law and the Internet: A Framework for Electronic Commerce* (Oxford, Hart Publishing, 2000). An even earlier version of the defamation chapter appeared in L Edwards and C Waelde, *Law and the Internet: Regulating Cyberspace* (Oxford, Hart Publishing, 1997).

individuals setting up personal Web 'home pages' and the emerging social networking sites. This issue also affected a wider range of Internet communications intermediaries than traditional telcos, such as Internet backbone providers, cable companies and mobile phone communications providers. The early sharp distinction drawn between Internet access providers (IAPs), who merely provided 'fundamental communications services such as access, information storage etc', and ISPs, who provided 'some additional service which facilitates a transaction between end users, eg identifying one of the parties, providing search facilities etc',[3] became less and less meaningful as the ISP sector expanded during the boom years of the Internet to provide portal services giving access to large amounts of both in-house and third party produced content, while providers of what might be seen as 'pure' telecommunications services, such as mobile phone companies, also became deeply involved in both the 'content business' and in providing 'value-added' services such as locational data handling. All this had serious implications for the development of an online intermediary liability regime that was practical, uniform, acceptable to industry, and yet protective of both consumer and citizen needs.

II. TYPES OF ONLINE INTERMEDIARY LIABILITY

The issue of intermediary liability is not a simple one. Issues arise around, most notably, hosting and transmission of child pornography and other types of obscene or criminal content; material that infringes intellectual property (IP) rights, especially copyright but also trade marks, patents and publicity rights; and libellous or defamatory material. The growth of concern around music and film piracy and peer-to-peer (P2P) networks in recent years has in particular exposed ISPs and hosts to potential risk[4] in a volume and manner quite different from that anticipated in the early cases on 'publication' liability for ISPs, and continues to reshape this area of law. In the US, a combination of historical accident[5] combined with domestic and international pressure to crack down on Internet piracy in music and films, led to the creation of two quite separate regimes of immunities for ISPs and hosts, one in respect of material infringing IP rights, especially copyright, and the other relating to all other types of liability. The first regime is found in the US Digital Millennium Copyright Act (DMCA), Title

---

[3] C Reed, *Internet Law: Text and Materials* (London, Butterworths, 2000) ch 4, 78.

[4] See discussion in MacQueen, below ch 6. Note that although sites such as the original Napster or KazAA/Grokster which support peer-to-peer (P2P) uploading and downloading might claim to be regarded as online intermediaries or information society service providers (ISSPs) with attendant immunities from liability, US case-law has so far found that a P2P software author itself does *not* benefit from ISP immunity under the DMCA—see discussion of P2P and intermediary liability below, 78.

[5] See discussion of the demise of the Communications Decency Act bar its provisions on service provider immunity, in ch 20 below.

512, which largely exempts ISPs from liability for hosting copyright-infringing material in a set of 'safe harbours', but only on certain terms, such as the disclosure of the identity of infringers on request, subscription to a detailed code of practice relating to notice, 'take-down' and 'put-back', and the banning of identified repeat infringers from access.[6] By contrast, section 230(C) of the Communications Decency Act (CDA) provides total immunity in respect of all kinds of liability bar that relating to IP,[7] so long as the content in question was provided by a party other than the ISP. In Europe, as we shall see, by contrast a harmonised regime exists in the E-Commerce Directive (ECD) for liability for all kinds of content.

Disputes have been reported across Europe and the globe concerning ISP or host liability for a wide range of material, including material in contempt of court;[8] to which privacy rights apply (eg the *Estelle Halliday* case in France[9]); material that is blasphemous;[10] relating to racist, anti-Semitic or hate speech;[11] and so on. Some of these topics are explored in detail elsewhere in this volume (eg copyright intermediary liability in chapter 6; pornography in chapter 20) but we shall deal with the third major area for ISP liability, defamation, in somewhat more detail here.

---

[6] See further below in this chapter, and MacQueen, ch 6 below.

[7] See detailed discussion of the very wide scope of this immunity in M Lemley, 'Rationalising Safe Harbors' (2007) 6 *Journal of Telecommunications and High Technology Law* 101, 102–05.

[8] But note *Mosley v News Group Newspapers* [2008] EWHC 687 (QB) at http://www.bailii.org/ew/cases/EWHC/QB/2008/687.html, where Eady J refused to grant an injunction preventing publication of an 'intrusive and demeaning' sex video of Max Mosley, head of the Fédération Internationale de l'Automobile (FIA), on the *News of the World* website, pending an action against said newspaper for invasion of privacy, since the material had already been widely published on the Internet, and as a result the plaintiff 'no longer has any reasonable expectation of privacy in respect of this now widely familiar material or . . . even if he has, it has entered the public domain to the extent that there is, in practical terms, no longer anything which the law can protect. The dam has effectively burst.' It is suggested that this precedent has probably substantially diminished the risk for ISPs and hosts of being held liable for contempt of court in cases where there is little they can do to stop circulation of material already 'out' on the Internet. See also *R v Barnardo* [1995] Ont CJ Lexis, where in 2001 the ISP Demon successfully asked the English courts to grant them an exemption from strict liability for contempt of court in advance: this arose in relation to their fear that they would inevitably be involved in illegal pre-trial publicity relating to the trial of Thompson and Venables for the murder of Jamie Bulger: see http://www.guardian.co.uk/Archive/Article/0,4273,4222156,00.html.

[9] Tribunal de Grande Instance de Paris, 9 June 1998. See also the *Martinez* case, noted below n 47.

[10] See unreported 1997 UK case involving gay poem found illegal as blasphemous in the UK courts; a host in the UK subsequently linked to that poem (which was hosted physically on a server abroad) and was reported to the police for so doing. A police investigation followed but no charges were, to this author's knowledge, ever brought. Details at http://www.xs4all.nl/~yaman/linkpoem.htm .

[11] See the much-discussed case of *LICRA and UEJF vs Yahoo!Inc and Yahoo! France*, Tribunal de Grande Instance de Paris (Superior Court of Paris), 22 May 2000 and TGI de Paris, Ordonnance de refere du 20 November 2000, discussed below at n 58.

A. Defamation

The topic of Internet defamation has played a more significant role than might be expected in shaping the legal debate around the liability of Internet intermediaries. Internet libel cases are regularly reported in the media, though few appear as a final reported opinion with most being settled or abandoned after a period of sabre-rattling. There are a number of key reasons for the volume of Internet libel.

Early Internet users (who were predominantly American, often of libertarian sympathy and conscious of their First Amendment rights) placed considerable emphasis on freedom of expression, and perhaps regarded protection of the reputation of others as a minor concern in comparison. 'Flaming'—robust discussion, sometimes verging on flagrant insults or outright aggression—was common and even applauded as character-building. Even when this early disdain for niceties such as politeness and the law of libel had receded somewhat, as the Internet became both commercialised, domesticated and ubiquitous, the medium retained a reputation as a place where irascible, hasty and unwise comments were often made. This characteristic of Internet communication, as in some ways nearer speech than written text in terms of forethought,[12] has persisted—especially, perhaps, in chatrooms, website comment threads, instant messaging (IM) sites and social networking sites, though decidedly not in commercial spheres, where businesses go to considerable lengths to restrain the riskiness of the medium.

The Internet also makes inadvertent defamation remarkably easy. Transmission of e-mail is virtually instantaneous and, once sent, usually irrevocable.[13] It is the work of a moment to repeat or forward the defamatory comments of others via e-mail, but in the libel law of most common law countries, a republisher is just as liable as the original publisher (bar the possibility of innocent dissemination defences, discussed below). Note, however, that sending an e-mail containing defamatory statements merely from person A to person B will in some legal systems not be regarded as 'publication' for the purposes of libel law, since there is no communication to the public but only to the specified recipient. This is true, for example,

---

[12] See 'It's All About Me: Why Are Emails So Easily Misunderstood', *Christian Science Monitor*, 15 May 2006, at http://www.csmonitor.com/2006/0515/p13s01-stct.html . See also *Smith v ADVN* [2008] EWHC 1797 (QB), where Eady J remarked that 'Bulletin board postings are rather like contributions to a casual conversation (the analogy sometimes being drawn with people chatting in a bar) . . . they are often uninhibited, casual and ill thought out. Those who participate know this and expect a certain amount of repartee or "give and take".' He concluded that communications of this kind were nearer to slanders than more permanent libels and thus less likely to give rise to lawsuits.

[13] Although Googlemail, in beta, have introduced a feature which allows the retraction of an e-mail, albeit sadly only within a few seconds: see Gmail Blog, 19 March 2009, at http://gmailblog.blogspot.com/2009/03/new-in-labs-undo-send.html.

of English law,[14] but not apparently, of Scottish law.[15] On a mailing list, it is very easy for a slightly careless user to think he is replying only to the maker of a particular comment, but actually send his reply to every member of the list. The embarrassment factor can be considerable, particularly where the members of the list form a small professional community within which the professional reputation of the person defamed can be severely damaged. It is not a coincidence that one of the earliest reported substantive cases on Internet libel, *Rindos v Hardwick*,[16] revolved around comments made on a mailing list for academic anthropologists which implied that Rindos, the Australian plaintiff, had been denied tenure because he was not a properly ethical researcher.

Internet libel is, significantly, a transnational phenomenon. Because the Internet provides a global audience at almost zero cost, the rules of private international law may need consideration in almost any potential defamation dispute.[17] In pre-Internet days, international publication would have been almost exclusively the preserve of a traditional publisher, such as a newspaper, television station or book publishing house, who would be likely to have both the resources to take legal advice, and the foresight to have a system of prior checking in place to head off legal risk; not so in the era of the blog. Even if care is taken, it is difficult to be sure where a communication will be posted or read: national indicators are often few, in an online world of credit cards, PayPal and English as *lingua franca*, and even a country code ending will not always give the game away (.com, for example, is used all over the globe).[18]

Furthermore, in English law, it has been held that for online publications, liability is effectively perpetual; the normal three-year rule does not time bar potential lawsuits, because each time an item online is read, a new time of publication is created.[19] Despite unsuccessful pleas to the European Court of Human Rights that such a rule effectively stifles freedom of speech online by creating unlimited risk,[20] especially for online newspaper

---

[14] *Pullman v Hill* [1891] 1 QB 524. It is possible, however, that e-mails might be regarded as inherently insecure and so as akin to postcards, which may be read by anyone in transit, in which case communication to a third party is not essential for publication even in English law: *Sadgrove v Hole* [1901] 1 KB 1 and see Napier, 'Logging on to Libel Laws' (1995) 92 *Law Society Gazette* 21.

[15] See K Norrie, *Defamation and Related Actions in Scots Law* (Edinburgh, Butterworths, 1995) 28.

[16] Unreported, Supreme Court of Western Australia, 31 March 1994.

[17] See detailed discussion on tort and private international law in ch 3, below, at 133ff. See in particular the discussion of *forum non conveniens* and the English libel courts' reluctance to accept this plea at 139.

[18] EU distance-selling law does, of course, theoretically require any business selling into the EU to make clear its name and registered place of business, but these rules of pre-contractual information are often ignored. See further Riefa and Hornle, ch 2 below.

[19] See *Loutchansky v Times Newspapers* [2001] EWCA Civ 1805, in which the Court of Appeal interpreted s 4A of the Limitation Act 1980 in the context of Internet publication.

[20] *Times Newspapers Ltd (Nos 1 and 2) v UK (Applications 3002/03 and 23676/03)*, ECHR, 10

archives, English law still doggedly resists any 'single publication' rule of the kind found in US states[21] which would state that a publication can only be sued for in one place,[22] and within a limited time from the date of original publication. This 'ceaseless liability' regime has come under strong criticism as being out of line with much of the globe,[23] and may be reviewed in the near future.[24]

Finally, Internet libel enticingly offers to victims, not one but two possible people to sue: not only the original author or 'content provider', but also the intermediary (ISP or host) who conveys the defamatory words to the world. Such intermediaries are often seen as a potentially lucrative target with 'deep pockets'—and the ISP is also likely to be locatable, with a registered place of business. By contrast, the original defamer might have vanished, acted under the cover of anonymity or pseudonymity,[25] be living in another country where judgements for damages are difficult or impossible to get recognised and enforced, or simply have no attachable assets. This in itself has clearly encouraged a fair amount of Internet litigation.[26]

B. Substantive Online Defamation Law

The role of ISPs as 'publishers' for the purposes of liability or immunity in respect of defamatory comments originated by third parties was thus extensively discussed in case and statute law in both the US and the UK in the mid to late 1990s, especially in the key US cases of *Compuserve v Cubby*[27] and *Stratton Oakmont v Prodigy*,[28] which, taken together, gave rise to a general rule of thumb that an ISP or host should exercise as little editorial control as possible over content provided by third parties, lest they be deemed a 'publisher' and held legally responsible for it. In the UK, the case of *Godfrey v Demon*[29] raised for the first time the issues of whether ISPs

March 2009, at http://cmiskp.echr.coe.int/tkp197/view.asp?item=1&portal=hbkm&action=html&highlight=Times%20%7C%202009&sessionid=23830644&skin=hudoc-en. Note the case went to the ECHR from the Court of Appeal as leave to appeal to the House of Lords was not given.

[21] Applied to web publications in the US case of *Firth v State of New York* (2002) NY Int 88. See criticism in L Edwards, 'Times for a Change: Loutchansky v Times Newspapers' [2002] *E-Law Review* 3-2, commenting on the first instance decision.

[22] See discussion in n 17 above.

[23] See S Robertson, 'Indefinite Liability for Libel Must End' [2008] *OUT-LAW News* 12 March, at http://www.out-law.com/page-9865.

[24] See UK Justice Minister Jack Straw's proposal to ask the Law Commission to look at reform in this area: see 'Straw Plans Crackdown on Internet Libel', at http://uk.news.yahoo.com/16/20090520/ttc-straw-plans-crackdown-on-internet-li-6315470.html

[25] This is true of many well-known Internet libel cases. See eg *Godfrey v Demon* [1999] 4 All ER 342 and in the US, *Zeran v AOL* 1997 US Dist Lexis 3429 (ED VA, 21 March 1997).

[26] See notably *Godfrey v Demon*, ibid, where the aggrieved plaintiff had toured the world suing a number of ISPs before arriving in the English courts.

[27] (1991) 766 F Supp 135.

[28] 1995 NY Misc LEXIS 229 (NY Sup Ct, Nassau Co, 1995).

[29] *Godfrey v Demon Internet*, above n 25.

should be treated differently from conventional publishers, and when Demon lost, both alarmed the Internet industry and stirred the civil liberties debate about how free speech should operate on the net. *Godfrey* was heard under the Defamation Act 1996, section 1, which introduced a special defence of innocent dissemination for ISPs in the area of defamation, but it is likely that future Internet intermediary libel cases in the UK will refer to both the 1996 Act and the subsequent more generic rules of the ECD, Articles 12–15.[30] We shall thus here elide discussion of the 1996 Act defence of innocent dissemination in favour of the more general discussion below.[31]

Surprisingly few Internet law cases in the UK have involved new points of substantive defamation law, with most reported case-law concentrated in the field of jurisdiction.[32] Web 2.0 and the arrival of user-generated content (UGC) have, however, brought some issues to the fore. It is now clear that legal liability can arise from 'blogging' (online web journalling or diary-keeping, often by unpaid amateurs) , and from comments or posts on social networking sites such as Facebook,[33] Twitter[34] or dedicated blog sites,[35] just as it can from more conventional journalism. In *Smith v Adven*,[36] Eady J noted, however, that just as in ordinary libel cases, some comments may not be deemed legally libellous if they are 'obviously, in their context, either vulgar abuse or fair comment'.[37] This will be of relief to some of the more outspoken citizen journalist contingent.

On this point, there has been considerable debate in some US states as to whether rights of 'journalist's privilege' in relation to disclosure of sources

---

[30] See eg *Bunt v Tilley* [2006] EWHC 407 (QB).

[31] But see a fuller discussion of s 1 of the 1996 Act in L Edwards, 'Defamation and the Internet' in *Law and the Internet*, 2nd edn (Oxford, Hart Publishing, 2000) 265–66.

[32] See discussion in Hornle, above n 17.

[33] See *Firsht v Raphael* [2008] EWHC 1781 (QB).

[34] See 'Love's Online Spat Sparks First Twitter Libel Suit' *The Independent*, 29 March 2009, at http://www.independent.co.uk/news/media/online/loves-online-spat-sparks-first-twitter-libel-su it-1656621.html. Note the suggestion by A Murray, 'Twittering Could Harm Your Wealth', *Guardian Comment Is Free*, 21 February 2009, at http://www.guardian.co.uk/commentisfree/ 2009/feb/20/twitter-internet, that persons impersonating celebrities by setting up Twitter accounts with their name (a common practice) might run the risk of defamation by imper-sonation, much as in *Firsht v Raphael*, above n 33.

[35] See eg *Carrie v Tolkien* [2009] EWHC 29 (QB) and the *Mumsnet* case noted below n 37.

[36] Above n 12.

[37] The defence of fair comment, or even truth, did not, however, appear to help the defendants in the 2007 *Mumsnet* case. In this case, Mumsnet, a site which provided advice to mothers on babycare, published comments from its users on a site bulletin board, critical of the methods of Gina Ford, a self-appointed childcare guru. Ms Ford sued and the site settled, though without admitting liability. The main issue appears to have been the period before disputed comments were removed (see discussion below on notice and take-down 'expeditiously') but these defences should also have been relevant. See account at *OUT-LAW*, at 11 May 2007, at http://www.out-law.com/page-8040 . Note that in the US, under the very different regime of the CDA s 230(c), moderators of bulletin boards have been held exempt from liability in respect of content provided by contributors, even where they exercise some minor editorial control—see *Batzel v Cremers* 333 F3d 1018, No 01-56380 (9th Cir, 24 June 2003).

apply to bloggers.[38] In the UK, there has been no such debate but similar problems of discrimination against the online journalist may be emerging in relation to defamation and the defence of 'qualified privilege'. Qualified privilege provides a complete defence to libel in circumstances where (briefly) publication is justified in the public interest, and although truth cannot be proven, the journalist has acted 'responsibly', eg consulting known accurate sources.[39] In *Loutchansky v Times*,[40] the English Court of Appeal held that rights of qualified privilege were not relevant to online publication in news archives, even where they might be if the same text was published in an ordinary 'hard copy' newspaper. This was because archives were 'stale news, and its publication cannot rank in importance with the dissemination of contemporary material'. The Court of Appeal suggested that 'where it is known that archive material is or may be defamatory, the attachment of an appropriate notice warning against treating it as the truth will normally remove any sting from the material'; this advice was reiterated by the European Court of Human Rights (ECHR) in *Times Newspapers (Nos 1 and 2) v UK*,[41] which found that such a requirement would not 'constitute a disproportionate interference with the right to freedom of expression'.

These decisions are justified, it seems, on two underlying grounds: firstly, that defences in respect of hard copy news publication, especially when it is immediate and electronic publication is archival, are more important to the public interest than those for online publication; and secondly, that since there is more time to get online archives 'right', and they will be a matter of historical record and less 'perishable', they should be absolutely truthful as far as is possible. While there is some value in the latter argument, the overall tone of both the English and the ECHR judgments seems worryingly to deprecate online publication as less important to freedom of expression than print on paper. This is an increasingly wrong and dangerous perception: as online and hard copy publication become simultaneous, the concept of 'archive' versus 'today's paper' disappears,[42] and even more so as hard copy itself begins to vanish. Finally, it is worth noting that the English and ECHR cases do not address whether qualified privilege could be claimed by an amateur blogger as opposed to a professional journalist:[43] in principle there seems no legal bar but the

---

[38] See eg AM Macrander, 'Bloggers as Newsmen: Expanding the Testimonial Privilege' (2008) 88 *Boston University Law Review* 1075.

[39] See *Reynolds v Times Newspapers* [2001] 2 AC 127.

[40] [2001] EWCA Civ 1805.

[41] Above n 20, para 47.

[42] Note also the rise of online aggregators reproducing online news headlines as 'today's news', eg Google News—and see one reaction from the traditional press in 'Google Dubbed Internet Parasite by WSJ Editor', *The Australian with Wall Street Journal*, 6 April 2009, at http://www.theaustralian.news.com.au/business/story/0,28124,25293711-7582,00.html.

[43] See also *Jameel v Wall Street Journal* [2003] EWCA Civ 1694.

stringencies of the *Reynolds* test may make it a difficult wall to climb for the amateur, despite the increasing importance of political and investigative blogging.

An interesting set of facts arose in one of the first reported cases on defamation on social networking sites, *Firsht v Raphael*.[44] Raphael created a false profile on the social networking site Facebook, plus a false group (entitled 'Has Mathew Firsht Lied To You?'), both of which alleged falsely that (inter alia) his former friend, Matthew Firsht, was gay, owed business associates money and had lied about paying it back. The court awarded Firsht £15,000 in damages for the libel and £2,000 for the invasion of his privacy. Firsht's company, Applause Stores, was awarded £5,000 for the libel. It is well known in libel law that impersonation and 'putting words into a person's mouth' can be interpreted as defamatory. Less conventional was the finding that the case gave rise to damages for invasion of privacy as well. The judge held:

> As far as the tort of misuse of private information is concerned, I accept Mr Firsht's evidence that it caused him, a very private person, great shock and upset. The information which has been conceded to be private, or which I have held in the private annex to this judgment to be private, related to his supposed sexual preferences, his relationship status (single or otherwise), his political and religious beliefs, and his date of birth. It seems to me that the most important information is that which relates to his supposed sexual preferences.

Although in *Firsht* the information that was regarded as private and wrongly disclosed was also, it seems, entirely false,[45] this leaves begging the question of whether an action for damages for breach of confidence might lie if the information disclosed was *true*, but still upsetting to reveal, as has been the case in many of the long string of actions for breach of confidence which have trooped through the English court since *Douglas v Hello!*.[46] What, for example, if Firsht was indeed gay, but had concealed that true fact all his life? Should damages still be claimable? In terms of the current development of privacy law, there seems no reason why not; but the implications for the free exchange of information on sites such as Facebook (and indeed, the liability of the owners of such sites[47]) are quite profound. It is

---

[44] Above n 33.

[45] It is hard to be exactly certain which material was proven to be false by the court, as their findings of fact were contained in an Appendix not made public with the court's opinion.

[46] See brief discussion of this very complicated jurisprudence in HL MacQueen et al, *Contemporary Intellectual Property* (Oxford, Oxford University Press, 2007) ch 18.

[47] Online intermediary hosts have been successfully sued for vicarious liability in respect of material which invaded privacy, in France and other European countries: see eg the *Martinez* case, reported in *OUT-LAW*, 10 April 2008, at http://www.out-law.com/default.aspx?page= 9038, in which Olivier Martinez sued a French news aggregator site Fuzz.fr for providing links to stories about his alleged romantic attachment with singer Kylie Monogue, which he argued violated his right to privacy. Both the site and the two bloggers were required to pay Martinez damages under Art 9 of the French Civil Code.

possible we may see a number of actions in future where damages are claimed under *either* defamation or privacy; whether the courts will wear this,[48] and whether defendants might install defences based on their rights of freedom of expression against the latter ground of claim, remains to be seen. Such pleas have been notably unsuccessful in 'traditional media' cases involving the kind of 'kiss and tell' journalism encouraged by the tabloid press, eg *McKennitt v Ash*;[49] however, it might be argued that bloggers and social networkers do not have the kind of resources traditional media have to check facts, and that a plethora of privacy as opposed to defamation actions (where even establishing the truth of the facts reported will not necessarily help) might have an unreasonable chilling effect on the rights of freedom of speech of the ordinary citizen. Given that the right to speak about your life, even if it is a 'shared experience' with others (the phrase used in *Ash*), is one of the basic building blocks of the UGC boom, and arguably more generally of trust on the Internet, there is a patent conflict between privacy and freedom of speech online brewing in the social networking sphere.[50] Of course, much will depend on the quality of the information disclosed; if there is no confidence to break, no damages will result, as was the case in *A v B plc*[51] where (truthful) details of a casual affair of footballer A, with a third party, were disclosed by B, but the court held the information did not have the requisite quality of confidence to be protected.

C. Forum Shopping and Other Abuses

Finally, it is worth noting steps recently taken by the courts to reduce the possible of frivolous or oppressive actions in relation to UGC in particular and defamation online in general. As discussed in more detail by Hornle in chapter 2, the English courts are generally willing to accept jurisdiction in defamation cases where the plaintiff has a reputation to defend in the forum, regardless of whether the case has little other factual connection to the jurisdiction and arguably greater connections to other countries, eg one or both parties resident abroad, and the principal readership outside the UK. This has created an undesirable reputation for the English courts as a magnet for forum shoppers in libel cases. However, in cases of minimal or unproven readership in England, the courts have developed a doctrine of abuse of process designed to forestall such claims.

---

[48] See, albeit in very different circumstances, *Quinton v Pierce* [2009] EWHC 912 (QB) where the court refused to accept a plea that data protection rights had been infringed, as an alternative to an apparently unproven claim for injurious falsehood.

[49] [2006] EWCA Civ 1714.

[50] See for further discussion of the problematic privacy issues around the social networking sites boom, ch 14 below, 476.

[51] [2003] QB 195.

In *Jameel v Wall Street Journal*,[52] the Court of Appeal held, first, that publication in England, ie readership by more than one or two people, could not be presumed simply because an article was available to the world online. In *Jameel*, it was shown that only five people in England had clicked on the offending comments, three of whom were lawyers or associates of the plaintiff. Since the damage to the reputation in the forum was thus minimal and damages would be nominal in comparison to the costs of the process, the case was thrown out as an abuse of process. Similar approaches were taken in *Al Amoudi v Brisard*,[53] where no clear proof was presented as to how many readers in England had downloaded the allegedly defamatory article, and in *Carrie v Tolkien*,[54] where the offending comment was only legally actionable for some four and a quarter hours and the number of page views (if any) was not proven. The lesson here for a libel plaintiff is that the courts want hard log statistics on the number of page views and downloads, will not presume a readership, and that even if the action is allowed, the level of damages will be crucially dependent on the number of readers.

Finally *Carrie v Tolkein* raised another interesting and rather unusual defence, that of consent to the defamation. Here, the allegedly defamatory comment was left on the plaintiff's blog, and was not removed in the 22 months leading up to the court hearing. The court firmly held that since it was within the plaintiff's power to remove the comment at any time, he had to be deemed to have consented to the publication. Only the very short period before his attention was drawn to the comment could be regarded as attracting legal liability, and as already noted, there was no evidence from which readership during that brief interval could be inferred.

Although the courts remain swift to assert that rejection of cases as abuses of process will remain exceptional,[55] it does seem that real attempts are being made to stop plaintiffs cashing in deliberately on the libel 'car-crash' that UGC sites represent, and where the real agenda does not seem to be vindication of reputation.

III. POLICY FACTORS AND THE DEVELOPMENT OF THE 'LIMITED LIABILITY' PARADIGM

As already noted, by virtue of their obvious role as the gatekeepers to Internet publication, the emerging industry sector of ISPs quickly became aware of their potential high-risk status in content liability cases sometime in the mid to early 1990s. As a result, ISPs pleaded a case for immunity

---

[52] [2005] QB 946. Note the appeal to the House of Lords concerned the point of qualified privilege, not publication.
[53] [2001] 1 WLR 113.
[54] [2009] EWHC 29 (QB).
[55] See eg *Steinberg v Pritchard Englefield* [2005] EWCA Civ 288.

from content liability around the world, which heavily informed the development of limited liability regimes in the US DMCA and the ECD.

This ISP plea rested mainly on three factors: lack of effective legal or actual control, the inequity of imposing liability upon a mere intermediary ('shooting the messenger'), and in Europe especially, consequences for the public interest if unlimited liability was, nonetheless, imposed.

On the first point, ISPs argued forcibly that they could not conceivably check manually the legality of all the material which passed through their servers, without impossible amounts of delay and expense,[56] nor was it desirable or possibly legal for them to do so without invading the privacy and confidentiality of their subscribers. Their aim was thus ideally to be classified legally not as publishers who carried the risk of the content they made available to the public but as common carriers, akin to the postal service and telephone companies in the US, institutions that carry no liability for content carried but do owe duties of confidentiality.[57] One way to circumvent the problem of filtering massive amounts of information was via automation, but content classification and filtering technologies, even in the late 1990s, were highly unsatisfactory and tended to radically under- and over-block. In areas such as libel, false advertising and hate speech, of course, where semantic meaning is hugely dependent on human interpretation, blocking was (and is) regarded as entirely impractical.

In the significant 2000 turning point of the *France v Yahoo!* case, however, the French court, presented with the defence that it was technically impossible for Yahoo! US to block access to pages on its site selling Nazi memorabilia items to *all persons from France*, remitted the question of automated filtering of requests from a particular *location* to a technical subcommittee to investigate. They reported back that, in fact, Yahoo! had the capacity (already used to serve up adverts in the relevant language to users from whatever country of origin) to identify and thus block access to

---

[56] BT Internet estimated in 1999 that just to effectively monitor newsgroup traffic alone, they would have to hire 1,500 new employees working 24 hours a day. See *WIPO Workshop on Service Provider Liability*, Geneva, 9–10 December 1999, paper by Janet Henderson, Rights Strategy Manager, BT Internet. One's mind boggles to think what the figure would be today.

[57] In fact the US courts took a middle way in two early decisions. See discussions in *Cubby v CompuServe* 766 F Supp 135 (SDNY, 1991), and *Stratton Oakmont Inc v Prodigy Services* LEXIS 229 (NY Sup Ct, Nassau Co, 1995). The former held in US law that the early ISP fitted best into the model of distributor rather than a carrier; the latter that an ISP which took some editorial decisions might nonetheless still be classed as a publisher with full liability for content published. Note that the common carrier doctrine also contains the idea of universal service, ie that any local user should be able to access the services of the carrier without discrimination. ISPs have never fitted into this part of the metaphor. Note also that *Prodigy* was in fact overruled by the US Supreme Court in a subsequent case, *Lunney v Prodigy Services Co*, on 5 February 2000 (available at http://www.courts.state.ny.us/ctapps/decisions/164opn.htm). However, by that time the force of the decision had been overtaken by the immunity provisions for ISPs introduced in the CDA. The case does, however, confirm that in US law an ISP is now officially regarded as not a publisher at common law.

90 per cent of French citizens.[58] Accordingly, Yahoo! were instructed to block access. This decision was unusual in some senses in that it related to location-based rather than content-based blocking, since Yahoo! already manually classified items for sale on its site. In cases of pure automated content classification, however, most informed opinion still agreed that online intermediaries could not yet successfully automate the process of sieving out unwanted material and stay in business.[59] Furthermore while conventional publishers, such as newspapers or book publishers, could limit their risk contractually, by, for example, issuing acceptability guidelines to its employees, or putting indemnity clauses into contracts with freelancers, ISPs and hosts were exposed to risk as a result of content authored by parties with whom they most often had no contractual nexus.

Secondly, ISPs argued that they were mere messengers not content providers, and thus that it would be inequitable to hold them liable.[60] The model typically contemplated at the time was probably that of a subscriber, business or domestic, who used his ISP, or an online host such as Geocities or Hotmail or a corporate server farm, to store his web pages, documents or e-mails; perhaps also of a university or school where large numbers of students stored files on central servers for free. In such a scenario, it is easy to see the host as both morally 'innocent' and factually devoid of actual or constructive knowledge of illegal or unwelcome content, unless specific notice is given. Although it can be argued that the business model of at least a consumer ISP is and was always partially dependent on users storing material which might conceivably be illegal or infringing (eg collections of pirate MP3s or of child pornography), in practice, a sense of 'common enterprise'[61] between the online intermediary and the user was not readily apparent at the stage of industry development which formed the backdrop to the drafting of the ECD. This lack of perception of the ISP industry as culpable collaborators was combated only by the music industry, the

[58] See *LICRA et UEJF vs Yahoo! Inc and Yahoo France* (20 November 2000, Tribunal de Grande Instance de Paris, Superior Court of Paris) 14. The country of origin of around 70 per cent of users could be established from IP address and the remaining 20 per cent or so could be made up by asking users to fill in a form declaring country of origin. Some degree of evasion would always be possible, however, because of use of foreign ISPs, proxy servers and anonymising services.

[59] ISPs do, of course, routinely filter e-mail for *spam* messages, and very successfully at that (some 90 per cent of email is now estimated to be spam—see further ch 15 below) and some have then questioned why classification of other types of content is so hard. However, the strategies involved are very different as spam is mainly detected not by its communicated content but first by the bulk in which it is sent, and second, by associated fraudulent practices, eg a mismatch between address from which it appears to come and address to which replies are directed. Filtering spam by actual content alone would be almost as difficult as filtering for copyright or pornographic content.

[60] See adoption of this metaphor in G Sutter, 'Don't Shoot the Messenger? The UK and Online Intermediary Liability' (2003) 17 *International Review of Law, Computers and Technology* 73

[61] A test proposed by C Reed, 'Policies for Internet Immunity' (2009) 19(6) *Computers and Law*, 20, available online in fuller version at http://www.scl.org/site.aspx?i=kc189.

business model of which was already under threat by 2000 from online piracy, and which was already militating for ISPs to take part of the blame. In particular, Jack Valenti, former President of the Motion Picture Industry Association of America, spearheaded an onslaught against ISPs in the hearings prior to the passing of the US DMCA, designed (successfully) to prevent them being granted total immunity in respect of downloadable infringing content.[62]

Finally the fledgling European ISP industry argued that their emergent business could not withstand the burden of full liability for content authored by others. Since the promotion of e-commerce and the information society in Europe depended on a reliable and expanding Internet infrastructure, an immunity regime was in the public interest. Without it, the ISP industry might rendered uneconomic or move outside of Europe, something that at the time seemed plausible, since servers were, after all, easily moveable, and the ISP industry had not yet been absorbed into the concentrated market of cross-media conglomerations that now dominate the modern Internet services market.[63]

From the mid-1990s, therefore, in the US, the UK and elsewhere, ISPs made vigorous and largely successful claims that they should be exempted from liability on the basis of some kind of 'innocent dissemination' defence, a term borrowed from the law of defamation. In the US the DMCA resulted in a series of 'safe harbours'. Against this plea in Europe, however, was the Commission's strong belief that ISPs, as the only effective gatekeepers, should take on the role of 'cleaning up the Internet', ie ridding it of pornography, spam, libel and other forms of undesirable content. This was a policy goal not only for the obvious reasons, such as child protection, but also as part of a general drive to improve public trust and confidence in the Internet as a safe space for economic activity.

By the year 2000 or so, therefore, a rough consensus had emerged in both Europe and the US that ISPs should in principle be left free from liability for content authored by third parties, *so long as* they were prepared to co-operate when asked to remove or block access to identified illegal or infringing content. Such a 'safe harbour', implemented in Europe in the ECD, and in the US in the DMCA (with respect to IP-infringing material only), was to prove of incalculable benefit to the ISP, e-commerce and fledgling UGC industries. Anderson, in the context of a threatened suit against YouTube for hosting a controversial video, describes it thus:

62 See in particular On-Line Copyright Liability Limitation Act and WIPO Copyright Treaties Implementation Act: Hearing on HR 2280 and HR 2281 Before the House Judiciary Committee, Courts and Intellectual Property Subcommittee, 105th Cong (1997) (statement of Jack Valenti, President, Motion Picture Industry Association of America). Famously Valenti described downloading as the ISP industry's 'dirty little secret', claiming that around 80 per cent of ISP bandwidth was devoted to P2P traffic.

63 In the UK, around 95 per cent of consumers access the Internet via one of six ISPs: Sky, Virgin Media, BT Internet, Tiscali, Orange and Carphone Warehouse.

For YouTube, the 'safe harbor' protections that it enjoys under current copyright law are aptly named. Outside the harbor, litigation dreadnoughts roam the waves, mixed with public interest skiffs and consumer dinghies. Every one of them could rake the SS YouTube with grapeshot and cannonballs should it leave the harbor, but the SS YouTube is perpetually moored beside a balmy dock, bobbing gently in the clear water, its crew drinking a heady grog called 'We Cannot Be Sued'.[64]

We shall examine this solution below, and then ask: how did these immunity regimes work out, and what happened next?

IV. THE EUROPEAN E-COMMERCE DIRECTIVE REGIME

A. ISSPs: Definition

Articles 12–15 of the EC ECD[65] introduced throughout Europe a harmonised regime on the liability of online intermediaries. The regime affects not just 'ISPs' but 'ISSPs', ie 'information society services providers'[66] or, as the title of section 4 of the ECD also calls them, 'intermediary service providers'. An 'information society service' is defined[67] as 'any service normally provided for remuneration, at a distance, by means of electronic equipment for the processing (including digital compression) and storage of data, and at the individual request of a recipient of a service'. 'Recipient of a service' is defined[68] as 'any natural or legal person who . . . uses an information society service'.

Thus, broadly, the ECD intermediary service provider liability regime covers not only the traditional ISP sector, but also a much wider range of actors who are involved in selling goods or services online (eg e-commerce sites such as Amazon and Ebay); offering online information or search tools for revenue (or not) (eg Google, BBC News website, MSN, LexisNexis); and 'pure' telecommunications, cable and mobile communications companies offering network access services. However, the requirement that an information society service be offered 'at the individual request of the recipient' means that television and radio broadcasters do not fall within the remit of the ECD liability regime, although sites which offer individ-

---

64 See N Anderson 'YouTube Sails Out of Safe Harbor to Reinstate Marriage Video', 14 May 2009, *Ars Technica*, at http://arstechnica.com/tech-policy/news/2009/05/youtube-sails-out-of-safe-harbor-to-reinstate-marriage-video.ars.

65 2000/31/EC, passed 8 June 2000. The ECD was implemented in the UK via the Electronic Commerce (EC Directive) Regulation 2002, SI 2002/2013 (hereafter the 'UK ECD Regs') largely taken verbatim from the European English text.

66 Art 2(b) ECD. These providers can be natural or juristic persons.

67 Art 2(a) ECD refers back to the definition in Art 1(2) Directive 98/34/EC as amended by Directive 98/48/EC. The definition is discussed further in Recs 17 and 18 of the ECD.

68 Art 2(d) ECD.

ually on-demand services such as video on-demand or e-mail are included. In particular spammers and other 'providers of commercial communications'[69] are included as providers of information society services.

Importantly, Recital 18 of the ECD notes explicitly that although a service may be free to the recipient, this does not mean the provider of that service need fall outside the scope of the ECD if the service broadly forms part of an 'economic activity': so, arguably, providing non-commercial services online, such as the delivery of e-government services by state departments, falls within the ECD regime if the state will be making economic gains out of the activity (eg, if they are cutting costs by putting service delivery online). Since the ISSP immunity regime is designed on the whole to benefit rather than burden the service provider, it seems right to argue it should be defined extensively. Given that one of the dominant successful models of e-business is to give away a major product or service but then make money out of it in lateral ways (eg Google, which gives away its search services but makes millions out of associated advertising), it would be foolish if the ECD definition of a service provider was to be interpreted in any more restrictive way.[70]

Some relationships are clearly excluded by Recital 18 as not provided wholly 'at a distance': an employer, for example, is not a provider of an 'information society service' in terms of his employment relationship with his workers, it seems (even if they work for him exclusively down a broadband line from home and were hired after a videoconferenced interview); a doctor is not a provider of such a service even if he bills his private clients and sends them their prescriptions by email, so long as his advice even partially requires the 'physical examination of a patient'. The ECD also excludes certain activities from its remit,[71] including taxation, competition law, the activities of notaries and gambling. Thus, online intermediaries in these domains do not fall within the ISSP immunity regime.

B. Limitation of Liability: The Notify and Take-down Approach

The ECD takes a horizontal approach to ISP liability. In other words, it deals with all kinds of content issues—intellectual property, criminal obscenity, libel and so on—rather than focusing on a single area, as the US

---

[69] See further Rec 18 ECD.

[70] See *obiter* discussion affirming this view in *Bunt v Tilley*, above n 30, paras 43–45 but suggesting that a distinction might be drawn between a service provider who makes money in a loosely connected way and one who actually acts gratis, eg a private fee-paying school offering Internet access as 'part of the package', and a state school doing the same but charging no fees. Note, however, that a French court has found Wikipedia, the free online encyclopedia, to be deserving of ISSP immunity: see *OUT-LAW* news report of 6 November 2007, at http://www.out-law.com/page-8615 .

[71] See Art 1(5).

DMCA does with copyright. Furthermore, rather than giving a blanket immunity to ISSPs in all circumstances, as the US CDA section 230(c) does, it takes a more subtle approach in which the various activities of ISPs are addressed separately.

Where ISSPs act as a *'mere conduit'*— ie as a relay station transmitting content originated by and destined for other parties—the ECD, in the form of Article 12, regards them as basically absolved from all liability. To maintain immunity, the ISP must not initiate the transmission, select the receiver of the transmission or modify the information contained in the transmission.[72] This is very much in line with the common law position in England developed for neutral carriers such as the Post Office and the telephone companies.[73]

Where ISPs *cache* material, they will not be liable for it subject to the same conditions as outlined in the previous paragraph above.[74] Caching is a ubiquitous technical process whereby local copies of remote web pages are made by hosts when requested, in order to speed up the delivery of those pages on subsequent request. It was initially uncertain if such activity would be construed as making unauthorised copies of copyright work. This has mainly been resolved by the Infosoc Directive, though some clashes between this Directive and the ECD may remain.[75] Since the effect of caching is to speed up the Web for all users, it is important that caching not be legally discouraged. As with the 'mere conduit' provision, immunity is subject to the requirement the information not be modified by the ISSP, and also that the cached copy be updated regularly according to industry practice. Immunity is also subject to the ISSP taking down cached copies once they obtain actual knowledge that the original source of the information has been removed or access to it disabled, or removal or blocking of

---

[72] Art 12. Transmission includes automatic, intermediate and transient storage. Presumably 'information' excludes header information which ISPs routinely and automatically add to through traffic they forward. Such header information is vital to the routing of packets through the Internet to their destination, but does not form part of the message information actually read by the recipient.

[73] This was confirmed in *Bunt v Tilley*, above n 30, paras 37ff, where the court held there was no binding authority at common law which deemed a 'passive mode of communication' such as an ISP acting as 'mere conduit' a publisher at common law.

[74] Art 13 ECD actually refers in full to 'automatic, intermediate and temporary storage of that information, performed for the sole purpose of making more efficient the information's onward transmission to other recipients of that service'.

[75] See in Europe, EC Copyright Directive 2001/29/EG of the European Parliament and the Council of 22 May 2001, Art 5(1) which includes as an exemption from the exclusive right of reproduction of the author, 'temporary acts of reproduction which are transient or incidental and part of a technological process whose sole purpose is to enable (a) a transmission in a network between third parties by an intermediary and (b) a lawful use of a work or other protected material)'. There are still doubts that the provisions of the EC Copyright Directive and the ECD on caching are entirely reconcilable: see C van der Net 'Civil Liability of Internet providers following the Directive on Electronic Commerce', in H Snijders and S Weatherill, *E-commerce Law* (Dordrecht, Kluwer, 2003) 53.

access has been ordered by a competent court or authority.[76] These ECD rules in Articles 12 and 13 are largely replicated verbatim in the UK ECD Regulations 17 and 18.

C. Hosting

The main controversy in the ECD regime has centred on the hosting provisions in Article 14, which deals with circumstances where ISSPs host or store more than transiently content originated by third parties. Under Article 14, ISSPs are exempt from criminal liability in respect of the 'storage' of information provided by a recipient of their services, so long as they have no 'actual knowledge' of 'illegal activity or information'; and are immune from civil liability as long as they have no such actual knowledge *and* are not aware of 'facts and circumstances from which the illegal activity or information is apparent'.

Article 15 furthermore provides that EU Member States are not to impose any general monitoring requirement on ISSPs, especially 'a general obligation actively to seek facts or circumstances indicating illegality' and this has generally been taken to mean that ISSPs cannot be instructed to proactively look for and filter out illegal content on an ongoing basis, since this would drive a coach and horses through the 'notice and take down' (NTD) limited liability paradigm. Recital 48 provides, however, that it is still possible for Member States to require ISSPs 'to apply duties of care which can reasonably be expected from them and which are specified by national law, in order to detect and prevent certain types of illegal activities'. So, for example, in the UK, ISPs might be (and indeed are) asked to monitor and intercept transmissions under the Regulation of Investigatory Powers Act 2000 for purposes of crime prevention and national security. The 'duties of care', however, it is argued,[77] should not be read as extending to duties under private rather than public or criminal law, since that would negate the point of Article 15 in the context of the Directive's hosting provisions generally. In practice, the main debate in the UK around

---

[76] See further discussion on NTD in relation to Art 14 below. Immunity for caching is most obviously relevant to content copied by an ISP prima facie in breach of copyright. However, it is conceivable that a cached copy of a page containing libellous or obscene material might be deemed to be 'published' by an ISP or host since it can still be retrieved by other subscribers to that ISP seeking that particular page until the cache is purged. In the US, cease-and-desist letters under the DMCA demanding 'take-down' of material infringing the copyright of the rights-holder are frequently received by the search engine Google, which maintains cached copies for a short period of material even after it has been removed from the original host site. See, as sample, report of such request for removal from cache from Church of Scientology to Google at http://chillingeffects.org/dmca512/notice.cgi?NoticeID=1352 and request for removal of a 'collection of recipes' from cache at http://chillingeffects.org/dmca512/notice.cgi?NoticeID=1327 (the last notable, since copyright rarely subsists in recipes).

[77] See R Bagshaw, 'Downloading Torts: An English Introduction to On-Line Torts', in Snijders and Weatherill, above n 75.

Articles 14 and 15 to date has concerned not constructive knowledge but *actual* knowledge and the effect of NTD on free speech; however, as we shall discuss below, this is likely soon to change.

V. PROBLEMS WITH THE ECD REGIME

A. 'Expeditious' Take-down

Article 14(1)(b) provides that so long as an ISSP 'acts expeditiously to remove or to disable access to the information' they host, immunity is retained, even after notice. No guidance is given in the Directive as to what 'expeditious' means, however, and whether it allows enough time, for example, to check facts, consult an in-house lawyer, find an external lawyer or request counsel's opinion. This vagueness can clearly be oppressive to defendants who wish to clarify their position before taking down. In the *Mumsnet* case,[78] for example, the defendants, who moderated an online childcare forum, were forced to settle even though they might well have had arguable defences to the claim of defamation, apparently because they were uncertain if removal of comments within 24 hours constituted 'expeditious' removal. This seems a ridiculously short time to provoke uncertainty: private research by the author in 2005–06 found that in a representative sample of UK ISPs and hosts, take-down periods varied hugely from 24 hours to about a week, depending on the type of content and the size of the organisation.[79] The UK implementation of the ECD gives no further guidance than the Directive, although the specialised Electronic Commerce Directive (Terrorism Act 2006) Regulations 2007, which provide specific immunities for ISPs from offences under the Terrorism Act 2006, do prescribe that take down must take place within two days.

In large ISSPs, it may take some time for a take-down request to find the appropriate employee, or for the appropriate page to be located on a large website (a problem aggravated by the lack of a statutory form of notice); while in small ISSPs it may be difficult to identify an employee responsible, especially in a non-profit-making or volunteer organisation; and how these indoor management issues affect 'expedience' remains unclear. Article 14, furthermore, seems to imply that once notice has been given and the expedient period of grace expired, liability is strict even if take-down presents technical or administrative problems. A better alternative might be, as the German Multimedia Act provides, for liability to arise only after

---

78 Above n 37.
79 See L Edwards, 'From Casual Censorship to Cartelisation? ISP Control of Illegal and Harmful Content', *3rd IDP Conference on Internet, Law, and Politics*, Barcelona, 2007 .

the ISSP has failed to take some kind of 'reasonable steps'. Reed suggests similarly that once an ISSP has received a take-down notice, its duty should not be simple removal but to 'to do what is reasonable to prevent further communication of that notified content'.[80]

B. Neutral Intermediary or Knowing Partner?

When the ECD was debated, as discussed above, the distinction between an online hosting service provider and a content provider was a fairly clear-cut one. In the world which has grown since the inception of the ECD, things are very different. We have seen the extraordinary growth and success of Web 2.0 and UGC sites such as eBay, Facebook, MySpace, YouTube, GoogleDocs and Flickr—all sites where, in essence, the platform owner derives revenue from encouraging subscribers to use platform facilities to publish and share their own UGC, and where although no joining fee is charged, revenue then comes from some variety of advertising[81] catering to this audience. The extraordinary growth of such sites (200 million users with Facebook accounts as of 2009;[82] 100 million video clips served on YouTube, per day, even back in 2006[83]) makes it far harder to say that the subscriber is the only content provider and the platform a mere innocent intermediary. It seems obvious to ask that if a site is making a financial or other benefit from the hosting of illegal or infringing content, should it not be at least jointly responsible for that content? Another way to look at it is to suggest that when a neutral intermediary bases a business model on hosting large amounts of UGC, some of which is anecdotally well known to be illegal or actionable, then surely it must have known of that illegality, even where no actual notice has been served: this is the 'constructive knowledge' which the ECD contemplates in relation to civil, though not criminal, liability in Article 14.

For some IP rights-holders, these issues have become crucial to their economic survival. For example, eBay is well known to have many thousands of listings which advertise counterfeit goods, usually 'ripping off' luxury brands such as Gucci, Tiffany, Jaeger, Harrods, etc. eBay can (and does) prescribe that sales of such counterfeit goods are forbidden under their acceptable use policy,[84] but enforcement of that policy given eBay's insistence on being regarded as a 'neutral intermediary' is often ineffectual. For the luxury trade mark holder, the first response is to

---

[80] See Reed, above n 61.
[81] The Web 2.0 business model, and in particular the growth of 'targeted advertising' on sites such as Google and eBay, is discussed in detail in ch 16 below.
[82] See http://www.facebook.com/press/info.php?statistics.
[83] See http://www.techcrunch.com/2006/07/17/youtube-serves-100m-videos-each-day/.
[84] See eBay's IP policy for sellers which excludes counterfeit goods, at http://pages.ebay.com/help/policies/intellectual-property-ov.html.

demand take-down of any listing which attempts to pass off a counterfeit good as a 'Gucci handbag' or the like. However, policing such an NTD policy takes endless vigilance by the brand's employees, who will also inevitably always be acting after the fact. eBay does already provide a 'priority' NTD service known as Verified Owner (VeRO), which allows brand owners to ask eBay to expedite the suspension of specific auctions of counterfeit goods.

For such businesses, a far more desirable solution would be to compel eBay to filter out ex ante listings containing infringing trade marks. The typical argument is that eBay must have some degree of knowledge of, and control over, its listings if only because its profits come from taking commission on specific listed sales, and because it provides software which facilitates automated categorisation of, and searches for, items. Thus arguably eBay has to have 'constructive knowledge' of infringement, disqualifying it for immunity under Article 14.

Accordingly, in *Louis Vuitton Moët Hennessy (LVMH) v eBay*,[85] a French court found, despite the immunity provisions of the ECD as implemented into French law, that eBay were responsible for failing to prevent the sale of counterfeit luxury goods on their site.[86] The French court found 'serious faults' in eBay's processes that led to auctions of counterfeit goods going ahead, damaging the reputation of the luxury brands in question. eBay was fined £31.5 million and ordered to forbid the sale of some luxury perfumes on its site.[87] By contrast, however, in a very similar dispute but in the US,[88] eBay won and Tiffany lost. The case was argued under the rather different rules of US trade mark and unfair competition law, and without reference to a generalised safe harbour law. Tiffany argued that eBay had turned a blind eye to the sale of fake Tiffany jewellery on its site, and that eBay's own programmes for IP rights-holders were inadequate to prevent fraud. The US District Court held, however, that ultimately it was 'the trade mark owner's burden to police its mark and companies like eBay cannot be held

---

[85] See account at *OUT-LAW*, 1 July 2008, available at http://www.out-law.com/page-9225. A L'Oréal spokesman previously said that 'EBay is not a victim because it gets a cut from each transaction and advertisement, real or fake', see report at *OUT-LAW*, 12 September 2007 at http://www.out-law.com/page-8463 .

[86] The matter was complicated by the fact that it is not clear in French law if eBay falls under the laws applying to 'offline' auctions, where liability is different from in ordinary sale of goods law. The proposed Draft EC Consumer Regulation may address this issue. See further ch 2 below.

[87] But note that a Paris court seems to have reached the reverse decision in a very similar action by L'Oréal against eBay in respect of sale of counterfeit perfumes, reported on 15 May 2009 at http://www.guardian.co.uk/technology/2009/may/13/ebay-loreal-court-paris-counterfeit.
French courts, of course, do not follow English rules of precedent, and the court here reportedly based its decision on the belief that 'eBay was meeting its obligations to combat the sale of fake products'. Similar actions, some of them successful, have been raised by other luxury giants such as L'Oréal and Hermès against eBay in countries such as France, Germany, Spain and Belgium. Note that eBay won in the suit raised in Belgium by L'Oréal, in 2008—see *OUT-LAW* report, 15 August 2008, at http://www.out-law.com/default.aspx?page=9354.

liable for traders based solely on their generalised knowledge that trade mark infringement might be occurring on their websites'. Tiffany's request for eBay to pre-emptively police listings of 'Tiffany' branded goods on its site was thus rejected. In the UK, eBay won yet another decision as this book went to press, but the merits of the case as far as ISSP liability goes were almost wholly not dealt with in detail pending a reference to the ECJ.[89]

Such arguments are in the end primarily economic, not moral or legal. Who should bear the cost of policing the sale of counterfeit or other infringing goods (such as bootleg recordings)? The most obvious answer is the IP owner, since they most proximately make profits from enforcement activity by maintaining the untarnished reputation of their brand. Yet the costs of enforcement might arguably be less for eBay who control listings access and search if—and it is a big if—automated filtering of counterfeit listings is possible, and not subject to too high an error rate (either positive or negative). A third consideration is that the costs of policing listings in advance will inevitably be passed on to consumers (eg in higher rates for listing items by eBay, or in higher prices for goods by Tiffany), thus producing a less competitive online marketplace, whoever bears the costs. Such arguments are almost impossible to resolve without empirical economic evidence that is rarely available.[90]

Yet another way to slice this argument is to argue that on UGC sites, the platform is really authorising the acts of the content provider who supplies the infringing or actionable content, and thus should be equally liable, since it provides the facilities for infringement, and also derives financial benefit therefrom (commission on eBay, and revenue on most other Web 2.0 sites). The ECD appears to allow for this 'vicarious liability' argument, albeit in rather minimalist form. Article 14(2) provides that content is not to be treated as originating from a third party if that recipient acts 'under the authority or control of the [ISSP]'. The qualifications for such liability have not, however, been defined so far in the case-law of the ECJ, or in the UK courts, but again, illustrative case-law may perhaps be drawn from an equivalent provision in the US DMCA.[91]

---

[88] *Tiffany (NJ) Inc v eBay* US District Court of NY (SDNY 14 July 2008), No 04 Civ 4607 (RJS).

[89] See *L'Oréal v eBay* [2009] EWHC 1094 (Ch) (22 May 2009).

[90] See a critical assessment of this suggestion of 'no safe harbour' for Web 2.0 sites, in Lemley above n 7, 112.

[91] But cf s 230(c) CDA, which confers absolute immunity on service providers in publication torts and where there is no exception for agency or authorisation. This has had unfortunate effects—see eg *Blumenthal v Drudge* 992 F Supp 44 (DDC 1998) where Drudge contributed an online gossip column which defamed Blumenthal, and for which AOL paid Drudge a considerable sum, as it drew audiences to their fora. Despite this financial gain by AOL, the US court found that AOL were not responsible for Drudge's defamatory comments and were immune from suit under s 230(c) as this was what Congress had intended to prevent stifling of free speech.

C. *Viacom v Google*

In 2007, Viacom, owner of the rights to numerous entertainment television programmes and films, sued Google, as owner of YouTube, for failing to police the widespread unauthorised posting of clips there from properties owned by Viacom (such as MTV videos, or television comedy clips).[92] According to Viacom, 160,000 clips owned by them had been viewed over 1.5 billion times on YouTube, and $1 billion damages were claimed. YouTube's business model was, it was said, 'based on building traffic and selling advertising off of unlicensed content, [and] is clearly illegal'. Google responded that take-down notices from Viacom were promptly dealt with and designated content removed. For example, in February 2007, YouTube had taken down 100,000 unauthorised Viacom-owned clips. Viacom's reply was that Google must know in a generalised way of constant widespread infringement, given Google's own search engine revealed extensive postings of Viacom-owned properties.[93] As with the *Tiffany* and *LVMH* cases, Viacom appeared prima facie to be looking for YouTube to shoulder the burden of policing the site by filtering ex ante, and protecting Viacom's IP rights.

The matter was complicated by the reality known to both parties, namely that Viacom's properties benefited from an enormous audience on YouTube, far more than might have been attracted either to Viacom's television programming or to a paying download site on Viacom's own websites. Indeed, negotiations between Viacom and YouTube for a blanket license from Viacom for plays of their properties on YouTube had only recently broken down. Many commentators thus speculated that the Viacom lawsuit was actually a smokescreen, simply designed to push YouTube into agreeing a revenue-sharing deal on advertising sold next to Viacom clips, but on better terms than first offered. YouTube for its part argued that it was on the threshold of developing an automated system, known then as 'Claim Your Content',[94] which would allow IP rights-holders to submit every item of content they wished protected to YouTube,

---

[92] See original complaint, *Viacom International v YouTube, Inc* No 1:2007-CV-02103 (SDNY 13 March 2007). See case documents at http://news.justia.com/cases/featured/new-york/nysdce/1:2007cv02103/302164/ .

[93] On 1 May 2007, for example, Viacom announced 'It is simply not credible that a company whose mission is to organise the world's information claims that it can't find what's on You Tube'. See Silicon.co, 1 May 2007, at http://management.silicon.com/government/0,39024677,39166945,00.htm. On the other hand, around the same time a Vidmeter survey, for December 2006–March 2007, sampled YouTube take-down notices and claimed that only 9.23 per cent of all videos on YouTube were removed on notice of copyright infringement, and views of videos removed made up less than 6 per cent of all YouTube video views. (However, of those removed for copyright infringement, 40 per cent did belong to Viacom.) See http://theutubeblog.com/2007/04/05/vidmeter-study-debunks-viacoms-copyright- lawsuit/.

[94] Later known as 'Video Identification'—see BBC News site, 16 October 2007 at http://news.bbc.co.uk/1/hi/technology/7046916.stm .

who would then turn it into a 'watermark' hash, against which user-supplied videos would be compared. If the content to be uploaded matched a known copyright item, then YouTube would reject it (presumably unless proof of rights-holder permission was shown). YouTube thus appeared to be about to offer in good faith the kind of pre-emptive filtering solution Tiffany had looked for in the eBay case; however, Viacom potentially had more to gain from a revenue-sharing solution than a filtering solution. Viacom asserted that YouTube was dictating the terms of copyright protection to Viacom, something YouTube as the infringer had no right to do. This standoff is still at time of writing embroiled in long-standing factual and legal hearings.[95] It is interesting, however, to look at what the relevant safe harbour laws might seem to say.

In US law, as a question of immunity in relation to IP rights, the DMCA, section 512(c)(i) applies, which holds a service provider immune from liability for copyright infringing content if (in words almost identical to the ECD) it does not have actual knowledge of such content, nor is aware of facts and circumstances from which such infringing activity is apparent. As in the ECD, immunity is provided subject to material being taken down or access blocked expeditiously—something that YouTube appeared to be able to demonstrate.[96]

However, under section 512(1)(B)—the DMCA's more detailed equivalent of Article 14(2) of the ECD—the service provider does not benefit from the safe harbour if it 'receive[s] a *financial* benefit directly attributable to the infringing activity in a case in which the service provider has the *right and ability* to control such activity' (italics added). Does this apply to YouTube? Only a court can say. Indubitably, however, such an assessment will be heavily affected by how many advertisements were shown alongside downloads of Viacom-owned video clips, and how much revenue YouTube made from them.[97]

D. Host or Publisher?

Turning back to Europe, continental courts have tended to avoid the immunity provisions of the ECD (as locally implemented) in contentious

[95] See above. For example, Viacom secured a court order on 3 July 2008 which forced YouTube to disclose the log of the viewing habits of every user who had ever watched a YouTube video clip. Privacy advocates responded with appropriate horror. See BBC News site at http://news.bbc.co.uk/1/hi/technology/7488009.stm .

[96] Note, however, that the DMCA, unlike the ECD, requires a service provider to have a system in place to bar repeat infringers. YouTube have not yet proven they can meet this requirement.

[97] Interestingly, YouTube only in fact began making money from adverts next to video clips on 22 August 2007—some time *after* the complaint was served on them by Viacom. See BBC News at http://news.bbc.co.uk/1/hi/business/6958103.stm. Revenues were earned from banner ads before that date.

Web 2.0 cases, not by bringing in ideas of 'agency' or vicarious liability, but by classifying a site as a 'publisher' not an 'intermediary'—a strategy quaintly reminiscent of that ancient warhorse of ISP liability law, *Prodigy v Stratton*.[98] In the French *MySpace* decision of 22 June 2007,[99] a French cartoonist whose sketches had been posted without his authorisation successfully sued MySpace for infringement of his author's rights and personality rights. The court found that MySpace should be classified as a 'publisher' not a host because it provided 'a presentation structure with frames, which is made available to its members' and significantly, 'broadcasts advertising upon each visit of the webpage, from which it profits'. As a result MySpace did not benefit from the hosting immunity as implemented in Article 6.I.2 of the French Law on Confidence in the Digital Economy.

Contrarily in another French case, *Dailymotion*, the French court found that DailyMotion, a French YouTube equivalent, was *not* a publisher.[100] Nonetheless the same result was reached. The court ruled that Daily-Motion, although classed as a hosting provider, was still liable for providing Internet users with the means to commit copyright infringement, because 'the success of Dailymotion's website depended upon the broadcast of famous works because . . . these works captured larger audiences and ensured greater advertising revenues'. The court also found that DailyMotion should have exerted prior restraint on giving access to copyright infringing works—in other words, installed effective filtering tools. Since they had not, they were liable.

As can be seen, such decisions from France and elsewhere are not exactly helping the cause of harmonised interpretation of the ECD across the Single Market (or even within France),[101] nor of global harmony between the EU and US systems. Instead we see a confused and splintered range of approaches. Where does the UK stand in this continuum? So far there have been no relevant reported opinions involving Web 2.0 and IP rights, or other forms of content liability except defamation, although there have been a number of threatened suits. One interesting case involved an attempted criminal prosecution of eBay UK by the UK's General Optical Council (GOC) for 'aiding and abetting' the illegal sale of contact lenses.[102] The basis of the complaint was that although eBay's official policies banned the sale of contact lens since they must be prescribed by a licensed practitioner, in fact listings of contact lens on the site could easily be found using eBay's own search facilities. The prosecution was, however, dropped on

---

[98] Above n 28.

[99] Translations of the extracts from reports in this case and *Dailymotion* below borrowed with thanks from *Bird & Bird IT and E-Commerce Law Bulletin*, October 2007, available at http://www.twobirds.com/english/publications/newsletters/upload/43288_1.htm.

[100] In a decision dated 13 July 2007 of the Tribunal de Grande Instance of Paris.

[101] See also the disparity between European cases raised by luxury manufacturers against eBay cited above p 67.

advice that eBay would be immune from liability under Article 14. Note that unlike the French and US cases, this involved criminal liability, and so claims of 'constructive' knowledge would not be allowable (though vicarious liability under Article 14(2) would still be applicable).

Frustratingly, in the UK and elsewhere, Web 2.0 litigation often simply does not happen, not because there may be no ground of liability, but because business sense points towards a negotiated settlement or even a blind eye. For example the owners of the rights to Scrabble in the US and the UK (respectively, Hasbro and Mattel) recently threatened action against the owners of a highly popular online game, Scrabulous,[103] which bore transparent resemblances to an online version of Scrabble playable on the Facebook platform. It was notable that although threats of legal action for trade mark and possibly copyright infringement were made against the Indian promoters of Scrabulous (and judgment obtained for the former in the courts of Delhi[104]), no action was ever taken against Facebook in any jurisdiction—even though they hosted the game, and reportedly made a great deal of advertising revenue from it, as it was one of the most popular draws of the site. However Mattel and Hasbro's end aim, of course, was to strike a deal with Facebook for a share of the advertising placed next to their own online Scrabble game, and/or a share of the advertising revenue from the infringing Scrabulous game (now renamed 'Lexulous'), and not to cut off their own access to a lucrative Web 2.0 platform. Accordingly, the interesting question of Facebook's liability was never raised.

VI. NOTICE AND TAKE-DOWN

In the 2005 version of this chapter, emphasis was placed on the controversy as to whether NTD in the EC regime exerted a potential stifling effect on freedom of speech. Since 2005, NTD has continued to attract criticism from free speech advocates, but the battleground has moved to debating whether ISPs should be compelled not just to take down after the fact but, as we have already begun to discuss, to filter ex ante. Pressures to mandate this are coming from places as diverse as the copyright industries, law enforcement action against child pornography and the fight to protect the Internet from the onslaught of malware. In this volume, much of the discussion around the free speech worries arising from a move from take-down to filtering has been incorporated into chapter 20, on pornography and censorship, pp 623ff.

NTD has so far only been explored to a very limited extent in UK

---

[102] See *OUT-LAW* report of 7 March 2006, at http://www.out-law.com/page-6708 .

[103] See *OUT-LAW* report of 29 July 2008, at http://www.out-law.com/default.aspx?page=9308.

[104] See *OUT-LAW* report of 24 September 2008, at http://www.out-law.com/page-9452.

case-law, the first reported case being *Godfrey v Demon Internet*,[105] a defamation decision which preceded implementation of the ECD but was dealt with under a similar set of rules in the UK Defamation Act 1996, section 1. The case involved allegations by a British physicist, Lawrence Godfrey, that an anonymous hoax message posted in a newsgroup, soc.culture.thai, in 1997, was libellous. Godfrey asked the ISP, Demon, which carried the newsgroup in question, to remove the offensive posting. When Demon did not comply, Godfrey sued them for libel as publishers. Demon pleaded section 1 of the Defamation Act 1996, which provided that an ISP was not liable if it 'did not know and had no reason to believe what [it] did contributed to the publication of a defamatory statement'.[106] Because Demon *had* been notified and not removed it, the judge held they clearly could not take advantage of the section 1 defence.[107]

The message forcibly sent by *Godfrey* to UK ISPs was that, in the interest of avoiding litigation or risk, they would be best served by removing or blocking access to any notified item of content without investigating it in detail. Cyber-liberties groups protested that this meant any crank caller or pressure group could now censor text posted on the Internet simply by complaining to the ISSP. ISSPs are thus arguably pushed into what has been termed 'privatised censorship' even though they do not have the authority of a court, nor always any knowledge of libel law.[108]

One factor that might deter an ISSP from taking-down might be the fear that unfounded take-down would lead to a claim for breach of contract from the content provider. In the US DMCA, when an ISSP takes down in good faith, it is protected it from any liability arising. No such protection exists in the ECD or in the UK rules implementing it (although as the Directive is a minimum harmonisation, there is no reason states cannot introduce such protection). It seems likely, though, that EU ISPs regard default take-down on demand as their safest and easiest option. Acceptable-use clauses in subscriber contracts can probably control the risk of breach of contract, and consumer-oriented ISPs may also rely on the inertia of consumers in relation to litigation, but police or industry law

---

[105] Above n 25.

[106] 1996 Act, s 1(1)(c).

[107] The case was subsequently settled. Demon originally publicly stated their intention to appeal on the s 1 defence point, but later dropped the appeal, ostensibly because they were anticipating legislative change, but probably because of the adverse publicity they received as at the time they were going through a takeover battle.

[108] See discussion in C Ahlert, C Marsden and C Yung, 'How Liberty Disappeared from Cyberspace: The Mystery Shopper Tests Internet Content Self-Regulation', cited at http:// pcmlp.socleg.ox.ac.uk/text/liberty.pdf. In a survey of Dutch ISPs, out of five who responded, none said they would involve a lawyer in examining take-down requests. The overall impression given is that ISPs regarded dealing with take-down requests as a time sink which did not contribute to their core business goals. In private research by Edwards (above n 79) of 17 ISPs and hosts responding to a questionnaire, only one used a legally trained person to deal with notice and take-down requests and the rest used technical or human resources professionals.

enforcement authorities (in respect of obscenity and copyright infringement, respectively) are less easily avoided.[109]

In research carried out at Oxford known as the 'Mystery Shopper'
test,[110] a major UK ISP was asked to take down a webpage alleged to be a
pirate copy. In fact the webpage contained an extract from Mill's *On
Liberty*, published in 1869 and long in the public domain. Nonetheless the
webpage was removed without demur.[111] The Oxford researchers concluded from this and other examples that 'the current regulatory settlement
has created an environment in which the incentive to take down content
from the Internet is higher than the potential costs of not taking it
down'.[112] Subsequent empirical evidence bears this conclusion out.
Looking at the roughly similar copyright NTD regime of the US DMCA,
Urban and Quilter found that almost a third of take-down requests made
by rights-holders were apparently flawed or unjustified, and that over half
the demands for link removal came from competitor companies.[113] The
project analysed all the take-down notices (876 in total) received by the
search engine Google between 2002 and 2005[114] and subsequently posted
on the Chilling Effects website.[115] Thirty per cent of take-down notices
received raised 'obvious' queries as to validity, which a court would have
been bound to consider before granting an injunctive remedy. These

[109] ISPs could theoretically also insure against potential risk, as other commercial operations
do; or could insert indemnity clauses into subscriber contracts to protect against risky content
originated by that subscriber. However, it seems the market has not developed support for either
suggestion. See *Rightswatch* report conducted by the MCPS-PRS Alliance, on behalf of the
European Community, November 2002–January 2003 (www.rightswatch.com), s 9.10 (on
insurance) and 9.2 (on indemnities). Consumer indemnity clauses might also be challengeable as
unfair under European and UK consumer protection legislation such as the EC Unfair Terms
Directive and the Unfair Contract Terms Directive 1977.

[110] See Ahlert et al, above n 108.

[111] Similar results were found in a similar experiment carried out subsequently by Sjoera Nas
at Bits of Freedom, a digital human rights group based in the Netherlands. Nas, posing as
copyright owner, asked 10 Dutch ISPs to remove works by a Dutch writer who died in 1860 and
hence was in the public domain. Seven providers took down the text without apparently
checking it out at all; one failed to respond to the complaint; one examined the text complained
of and noted it was in the public domain (xs4all, a small ISP with a history of digital rights
activism) and one forwarded the complaint to the website owner. Her 'take-down hit rate' was
thus 70 per cent.

[112] Ahlert et al, above n 108, 12.

[113] J Urban and L Quilter, 'Efficient Process or "Chilling Effects"? Takedown Notices Under
Section 512 of the Digital Millennium Copyright Act: Summary Report', available at
http://mylaw.usc.edu/documents/512Rep-ExecSum_out.pdf

[114] See discussion of the particular problem of search engine filtering in Edwards, ch 20. It is
to Google's credit that it delivers its take-down notices received to a public website, although
no equivalent site exists in the UK, partly due to fears of defamation claims by senders of notices.

[115] See 'Chilling Effects Clearinghouse' at http://www.chillingeffects.org/, a joint project of the
Electronic Frontier Foundation and the universities of Harvard, Stanford, Berkeley, University of
San Francisco, Maine, and the George Washington School of Law. The site hosts take down
notices voluntarily submitted by private parties and participating ISPs and sites such as Google.

included defences of fair use, claims over public domain material, and notices in unclear form. The authors commented:

> The surprising number of questionable takedowns we observed, taken in conjunction with the *ex ante* removal of content, the minimal remedies for abuse of process, and the lack of knowledge about the counter notice procedures, suggest that few are well served by [the NTD process].[116]

The DMCA does in fact build in a number of safeguards which could well be incorporated into the ECD regime to discourage arbitrary NTD. Nothing in the EC regime requires notification to the site whose content is taken down, and largely this would be a matter for each ISP's contractual rules and internal procedures. The requirement of 'expedient' take-down only encourages an ISP even further to take down now, and notify later, if at all.[117] However, in the US the DMCA provides that a take-down notice *must* be notified to the content provider, who then has the opportunity to protest that the material should not be removed, in which case it must be 'put back' by the ISP. If the original notifier then continues to dispute the legality of the content, and the content provider to assert it, the argument must be taken to the courts. While dispute is in progress, the ISP is given 'safe harbour' to keep the content up, free from liability, even if in the end a court does decide the content was illicit or actionable.

The DMCA also has strict rules that the person demanding take-down must properly identify themselves as the rights-holder with locus to demand take-down (using digital signature identification if requesting take-down by e-mail) and specifies details enabling offending content to be easily located. Both rules discourage spurious complaints and overbroad or unauthorised take-down. These DMCA rules might well be helpfully imported into any future revision of the ECD, or the UK implementation thereof. In the UK, Regulation 22 of the ECD Regulations merely provides that in determining if an ISSP has 'actual knowledge', the court shall take into account all matters that seem relevant to it, including whether a notice had been received, and the extent to which that notice adequately identified the complainant, the location of the information complained about, and the nature of the unlawful activity or information.[118]

---

[116] Interestingly from an EU perspective, 37 per cent of notices received by Google.com also referred to sites outside of the US and not subject to the DMCA jurisdiction.

[117] There are also concerns in areas such as child pornography that notice to the site concerned will warn it that the law enforcement authorities may intervene: this is why, eg, the IWF did not notify Wikipedia in their dispute over an alleged image of child sexual abuse on the Wikipedia site. See discussion of the Wikipedia case in ch 20 below, 651.

[118] Some guidance on the form of 'notice' was given in *Bunt v Tilley*, above n 30, para 72. In this case the mere incidental mention of allegedly defamatory content in an e-mail to an ISP requesting other information (the anonymous commentor's real identity) was not a valid notice.

VII. SEARCH ENGINES AND HYPERLINKERS

Another issue expressly dealt with by the DMCA but left out of the ECD is the question of linking liability. This is a particularly crucial matter to consider for search engine sites, which as their raison d'être create links to material over which the search engine has neither legal nor de facto control. 'Hosting' as dealt with in Article 14 requires storage, undefined in either the ECD or the UK Regulations, which seems to imply that merely making a hyperlink to content cannot constitute 'hosting'—therefore any liability that may arise in relation to a hyperlink under national law is not excluded by Article 14. The DMCA, by contrast, expressly grants immunity[119] under certain conditions where a link is made to infringing material.

Although the European Commission was specifically instructed to investigate linking liability on an ongoing basis by Article 21(2) of the ECD, so far only a few states have chosen to create special linking immunities, creating an unhelpful cross-Europe disharmony.[120] Linking is of ever greater significance as the Internet becomes manageable only via search engines and other linking intermediaries, eg tagging sites such as Digg[121] and delic.io.us. Since the drafting of the ECD, aggregators have also become important online intermediaries—sites which aggregate content from a variety of linked sites so that, say, a user can read the headlines and a few lines from multiple news sites conveniently on one page, or compare prices from a range of providers for utilities such as gas or water. 'RSS' aggregators provide text streams from multiple sources aggregated conveniently into one place, and so help prevent information becoming unmanageable—so, for example, I can read the blogs of several colleagues, physically hosted on numerous separate websites, in one place, using a reader such as Google Reader or Bloglines.[122] What all such aggregators are doing is in essence making links to a wide variety of 'upstream' content

---

[119] S 512 (d) Information Location Tools.

[120] See 'Consultation Document on the Electronic Commerce Directive: The Liability of Hyperlinkers, Location Tool Services and Content Aggregators—Government Response and Summary of Responses' (DTI, December 2006). See also the first UK case on search engine immunity for defamation, reported July 2009, *Metropolitan International Schools Ltd v Google and ors* [2009] EWHC 1765 (QB).

[121] See the controversy in 2007 over whether Digg were legally responsible for taking down on notice tags made by its users, linking to sites featuring a digital encryption key, which AACS were attempting to suppress since it assisted in DVD piracy. As *Boing-Boing* reported (2 May 2007, at http://www.boingboing.net/2007/05/02/digg-users-revolt-ov.html) 'Digg's users revolted at this stricture, and saw to it that every single item on the front page of Digg contained the forbidden number.'

[122] The ability of an RSS reader (aggregator) to remove one item from an entire 'feed' which contains allegedly illegal or actionable content is highly dependent on how the original content is arranged at source, ie its underlying XML structure. Although it will normally be possible to remove a single item, as a worst-case scenario, the entire feed might need disabled. Many users do set up RSS feeds against the wishes of the copyright owners, eg to syndicate cartoon strips and avoid 'home' site ads, so this is a live issue of risk for the platform providing RSS reading tools.

over which they have no editorial control, and where they may or may not
have technical control to remove individual items, depending on how the
software code is implemented. Aggregator sites, alongside search engines
and tagging sites, are generally seen as a public good in terms of promoting
access to knowledge, information management, consumer choice and
competition.[123] It would seem logical therefore, both for reduction of
business risk, harmonisation within Europe[124] and harmony with the US
DMCA scheme, to incorporate immunity from linking liability into the
ECD intermediary scheme in future.

A. The P2P Problem

Yet on the other hand linking is exactly (and merely) what the sites
currently under siege in the war against P2P downloading also do, as a
matter of simple technological fact. This controversial matter is dealt with
more fully in MacQueen, chapter 6, but is also highly relevant here. Once
upon a simpler time, a search-and-destroy exercise was launched by the
content industries against P2P software providers as 'evil intermediaries'
par excellence in the *Napster*[125] and *MGM v Grokster*[126] litigation. These
sites did not host infringing files, but did clearly point to such files held by
others: abetting unauthorised filesharing by providing, originally, a database index to files hosted by others, and latterly P2P client software which
helped locate these others. Modern decentralised protocols of the
BitTorrent generation and later make it impossible to find a critical central
chokepoint intermediary to sue, as was true in the days of Napster.
However, modern P2P networks do still depend on intermediary sites, such
as the notorious Pirate Bay,[127] which host files known as 'torrents'. Torrent
files are themselves merely small files which when installed into a P2P
software client point to other users using the same P2P client and network,
from whom parts of the desired file can be downloaded. So if I wish to
download, without authorisation, the song 'Thriller' by Michael Jackson, I
merely locate (using any search engine) and install the torrent file of that
name into an appropriate client, which then automatedly finds for me
uploaders who have made this file available. Clearly the war on P2P would

---

123 See eg F Pasquale, 'Copyright in an Era of Information Overload: Towards The Privileging
of Categorisers' (2007) 60 *Vanderbilt Law Review* 135.
124 A French court (the Tribunal de Grande Instance de Nanterre) is believed to be the only
European court to have found a website liable for reproducing an RSS feed of content which was
found to be in breach of privacy rights. The French court found that three websites, Planete Soft,
Aadsoft and Lespipoles, were liable for invasion of privacy because of articles published by
other people but available via RSS from their sites. See *OUT-LAW*, 18 April 2008 at
http://www.out-law.com/page-9058.
125 *A&M Records, Inc v Napster Inc*, 239 F 3d 1004 (9th Cir 2001).
126 *MGM v Grokster* 545 US 913 (2005).
127 See http://thepiratebay.org/.

be easier to wage if torrent hosts were declared to be contributory or secondary infringers of copyright (or some such formulation) and such a ruling occurred for the first time in a Swedish court, to great global excitement, in 2009. Yet arguably Pirate Bay merely makes links to offending files, and should benefit as much as search engines (the 'Google argument') from any available linking safe harbours.

The details of how the Swedish courts found the operators of Pirate Bay to have criminally infringed Swedish copyright law, and sentenced them to a year in jail and a £2.4 million fine, are not for this chapter.[128] However, the policy point that is relevant here is to ask what crucial conceptual bright line can be drawn between sites such as Pirate Bay and sites such as Google? It was noticeable in the weeks following the decision against Pirate Bay that some UGC sites made well-publicised efforts to remove links to Pirate Bay from their own site, for fear of linking liability.[129] Commentators pointed out, however, that identical links existed from wholly legitimate sites such as the BBC News webpages, and could of course be created from search engines such as Google at any time.[130]

Could the law separate 'good' hyperlinkers, deserving of ECD immunities, from 'bad' ones, which were not? Well, intuitively, of course; but on what basis is such a differentiation to be made? Does it lie in acts that can be objectively assessed; in revenue models (both Pirate Bay and Google make money, in essence from site advertising); or in pure intention? If the latter, then a qualitative scrutiny of evidence and motivations will be required to assess liability, something demanding considerable legal expertise and far from the bright lines of Articles 12–15. Such an examination is far closer in character to the scrutiny we have already discussed as to whether a UGC platform, such as eBay or You Tube, should be legally characterised as a complicit author or principal, rather than a mere intermediary or tool. Neither judgment would be easy for a commercial entrepreneur rather than a lawyer to second guess. Again, new technology, in this case the decentralised P2P protocol and its massive use for illegal activity, has blurred a central piece of dogma that helped shape the ECD—the assumed 'innocence' of the average online intermediary in respect of illegal behaviour by its users.

---

[128] *Sony and Ors v Neij*, Stockholm District Court, Division 5, Unit 52, Verdict B 13301-06, 17 April 2009 handed down in Stockholm, Case no B 13301-06. Unofficial English translation commissioned by the IFPI, available at http://www.ifpi.org/content/library/Pirate-Bay-verdict-English-translation.pdf .

[129] See the *OUT-LAW* report 'Facebook Blocks Pirate Bay Torrent Links', 9 April 2009, at http://www.out-law.com/page-9940 .

[130] See, amusingly, http://www.thepirategoogle.com/, a site deliberately created to demonstrate that: 'The intention of this site is to demonstrate the double standard that was exemplified in the recent Pirate Bay Trial. Sites such as Google offer much the same functionality as The Pirate Bay and other Bit Torrent sites but are not targeted by media conglomerates such as the IFPI as they have the political and legal clout to defend themselves unlike these small independent sites.'

Pirate Bay's functionality similarity to Google was strongly argued by the defendants, but both their 'awareness of illegality', and their acts, according to the Swedish court, were very different. The judge found that:

[A]ll the defendants were aware that a large number of the website's users were engaged in the unlawful disposal of copyright-protected material. By providing a website with advanced search functions and easy uploading and downloading facilities, and by putting individual file-sharers in touch with one other through the tracker linked to the site, the operation run via The Pirate Bay has, in the opinion of the District Court, facilitated and, consequently, aided and abetted these offences. (unofficial English translation)

Furthermore in terms of financial complicity, the Pirate Bay operators were not, as often portrayed, merely high-spirited anarchists, but, the court found, were making serious money from advertising on the site. The written evidence confirmed that at least SEK1.2 million had been paid to the defendants for advertising space on the website.[131] Significantly, in comparison to Google, furthermore, the majority of the files the Pirate Bay linked to were protected by copyright, implying that their business model was indeed substantially based on infringement.

The ECD exemptions for online hosts, as incorporated into Swedish law, were pleaded but rejected, just as the DMCA immunities for mere conduit and location tool had been similarly rejected in the US in the *Napster* and *Grokster* decisions. Since the Pirate Bay notoriously posted take-down letters sent in by copyright-owners on their own site to ridicule, they clearly had actual knowledge of copyright infringement. Thus in this case the court could, perhaps unusually for the future, rely on actual notice, without having to look for constructive knowledge.

In short, although the *Pirate Bay* case cannot be regarded as a precedent for the UK, it does show that courts can apparently find ways to distinguish between 'innocent' hyperlinkers and those that might be categorised as 'evil' and undeserving of immunity. But the plethora of evidence available here, of complicity with infringing users, business models obviously built on illegality, notice of illegality ignored, plus failure to co-operate with law enforcement or industry enforcers, may not all in future be present in such demonstrable style. The future looks grey for hyperlinkers.[132]

131 Although this did not match the claim made in the course of the trial that the Pirate Bay site made SEK10 million in revenue during one year. See report at EDRI-Gram, 11 March 2009, at http://www.edri.org/edri-gram/number7.5/pirate-bay-trial.
132 Compare also discussion of Google News, which makes hyperlinks to, and also quotes, substantial sections of, news stories posted by other authors on third-party websites, in the Belgian case of *Copiepresse v Google* [2007] ECDR 5, Brussels Court of First Instance (TGI), 13 February 2007, discussed in ch 7 below, 248.

VIII. FILTERING, ONLINE INTERMEDIARIES AND THE 'PERFECT STORM'

The final important trend that needs noted, if only in brief, before we attempt to reach some conclusions about the likely future of online intermediary law in Europe, is the desire of many powerful industry players to move from the currently prevalent NTD solution, where intermediaries are only obliged to remove illegal or actionable content post factum, to a filtering solution, where instead it must be removed ex ante. As we have seen in the earlier discussion of cases such as the continental eBay suits and *Viacom v Google*, IP rights-holders have already mounted litigation campaigns seeking such a solution. The *Pirate Bay* case, like its US predecessors, *Napster* and *Grokster*, also demonstrates that the entertainment industries will look to ISPs and intermediaries such as torrent sites, as 'chokepoints', and the natural place to throttle the dissemination of content by P2P and similar disruptive technologies. Accordingly there has been a series of attempts throughout Europe and elsewhere in the last few years, both via court cases[133] and legislation backed by content industry lobbyists,[134] to enrol ISPs as 'copyright cops',[135] who might take an active part in protecting the revenues of the copyright industries.

A variety of roles have been proposed for ISPs, such as disclosing the identities of filesharers, with[136] or without a court order; warning filesharers that their illegal downloading has been observed;[137] filtering out

---

[133] See, most notably, the Belgian case of *SABAM v SA Tiscali (Scarlet)* [2007] ECDR 19, District Court of Brussels (under appeal at time of writing), English translation available at http://www.cardozoaelj.net/issues/08/case001.pdf, where a Belgian ISP was compelled in July 2007 to implement technical measures in order to prohibit its users from illegally downloading music files; and the Irish case of *EMI v Eirecom*, High Court of Ireland 2008/1601 P, settled January 2009, in which the ISP Eircom agreed, as part settlement of a lawsuit brought by EMI, Sony, Universal and Warner which accused the ISP of knowingly facilitating copyright infringement, to implement a 'three strikes' system of notice and disconnection of alleged filesharers.

[134] See notably the French *Loi Olivennes*, or 'HADOPI' law, passed on second attempt by the French legislature on 13 May 2009: see BBC news report at http://news.bbc.co.uk/1/hi/technology/8046564.stm; the New Zealand Copyright Act 1994, ss 92A and B as amended in 2009 (amendments frozen indefinitely following public opposition—see http://www.nbr.co.nz/article/entire-copyright-act-be-scrapped-101820); and the amendments made in 2008–09 in the reform process of the EC Telecoms Package or 'La Quadrature'—see discussion below in main text and commentary at the site www.ipintegrity.com by Monica Horten.

[135] See L Edwards, 'Should ISPs Be Compelled To Become Copyright Cops?' (2009) 6 *Computers and Law* 29, also available at www.scl.com.

[136] See the important ECJ decision in *Promusicae v Telefonica* C-275/06 Judgment (OJ) OJ C64 of 08 March 2008, 9 in which the court asserted firmly that although copyright enforcement was a goal backed by EC law, it could nonetheless not overrule the rights to privacy of alleged filesharers, and instead a balance had to be struck according to human rights jurisprudence. The case itself concerned whether it was legitimate under EC law for a national Spanish court to demand that identifying data be handed over to rightsholders claiming infringement; in the UK, it is already clear this is possible via a *Norwich Pharmacal* order (see n 156 below for case-law, in relation to claims for identification in cases of defamation online.)

[137] This policy was trialled under a Memorandum of Understanding struck between the six

copyright material acquired via suspicious activity such as downloading from P2P sites; traffic management (ie slowing of traffic to a user, classified by type, volume or origin perhaps); and at the most draconian, operating a policy of 'notice and disconnection'.

The last of these was pioneered by the French government under the presidency of Sarkozy as a policy of 'graduated response', and has become known internationally as 'three strikes and you're out'.[138] The basic idea is that warnings that a subscriber is known to have illegally shared files, based on information collected by the music industry, are passed on to the subscriber by his ISP; when three (or however many) warnings are accumulated, the ISP disconnects the subscriber. All of these options are currently being canvassed, with varying degrees of enthusiasm and practicality, in the extensive 'Digital Britain' consultation underway in the UK,[139] which also proposed an 'industry-led' Digital Rights Agency. Its job would hypothetically be to police these various activities, as well as to look after consumer interests, and promote new business models for digital content. Subsequent policy documents seem however to have dropped the DRA idea.

Whether it is currently legal to impose ongoing filtering obligations on ISSPs in Europe is an uncertain question. Certainly, Article 15 of the ECD, as discussed earlier, forbids Member States from imposing 'a general obligation to monitor'. However Article 14(2) does allow a court or administrative authority to require an ISSP to terminate or prevent an infringement, and this preservation of injunctive relief is what appears to have been used in cases such as the Belgian *SABAM* case.[140] The EC Telecoms Package being debated in the European Council of Ministers at the time of writing may, within its labyrinthine complexities, also eventually contain provisions mandating filtering by ISPs and telecommunication providers in relation to obligations to clamp down on copyright infringement, illegal content such as pornography, and possibly to maintain the security of a network. Again, whether such obligations would clash with the ECD as it stands remains currently both uncertain and controversial.[141]

---

largest ISPs in the UK and the music industry, brokered by Ofcom and BERR (now BIS), for six months in 2008: see Memorandum and consultation at BERR 'Consultation on legislative options to address illicit P2P file-sharing', 24 July 2008, at www.berr.gov.uk/consultations/page47141.html.

[138] See HADOPI law, above n 134.

[139] See consultation document, 'Copyright In a Digital World: What Role for a Digital Rights Agency?' (BERR, 2009), available at http://www.ipo.gov.uk/digitalbritain.pdf . The consultation closed on 30 March 2009. A previous interim report on 'Digital Britain' was published on 29 January 2009—see http://www.culture.gov.uk/reference_library/media_releases/5783.aspx.

[140] Above n 133.

[141] One strand of the legality argument may depend on the most controversial part of the Electronic Communications package, namely whether sanctions can be imposed on filesharers without the involvement of a court or tribunal as required by the due process guarantees of the ECHR Art 6. At time of writing the Council of Ministers and European Parliament are still in

Moving on from copyright, elsewhere in this volume, we have also seen strong support for ISPs to be enrolled as a different kind of 'cop' with responsibilities to filter out online child pornography. In Chapter 20, this author traces the evolution of the UK Internet Watch Foundation (IWF), from a hotline designed to receive complaints about illegal images of child sexual abuse online, to the creator, updater and distributor of a filtering 'blocklist' of URLs and images, which is now taken by the vast majority of ISPs in the UK on a voluntary basis. The IWF blocklist/filtering solution has proved popular with policymakers in Europe, and is currently being examined with a view to implementation by, among others, governments in Sweden, Germany and Belgium.[142]

There are still more reasons why states and their law-enforcement agencies might want to compel ISPs to take a more active filtering and monitoring role. Western governments are more worried than ever before about terrorism and extreme Islamic activity, and this is yet another potential driver towards mandated upstream ISP filtering. The increasing sophistication of deep packet inspection (DPI) tools—which allow ISPs and 'mere conduits' to not just identify the type of packets they are distributing, but effectively to look inside them to their actual content[143]—makes this all the more desirable, as well, of course, as all the more privacy invasive.[144] Yet another area where ISPs are in a unique position to fix problems with the very infrastructure of the Internet is Internet insecurity. Internet hosts—especially domestic home computers—are often hacked by viruses or malware, and then used as 'zombie hosts' from which all kinds of evils can be perpetrated by remote control: deluges of spam and phishing emails, distributed denial of service (DDOS) attacks, the spreading of more viruses and malware, and even in the worst potential scenario, attacks on critical infrastructure as part of so-called 'cyber-warfare'.[145] Tackling this problem is a huge task, but one contribution to control of insecurity would be for ISPs to be made responsible for the security of the machines attached to its network, with obligations to quarantine and disinfect on notice. This

---

deadlock over this point and it is likely to go to a Conciliation stage. If court or 'judicial' involvement *is* required before any filtering requirement can be imposed on ISPs, it could conceivably be argued this is not any different from the process recognised as legal in *Promusicae* (above n 136) nor indeed, injunctive relief for specific wrongdoing.

[142] See detailed discussion in ch 20, 651.

[143] The Canadian Privacy Commissioner has expressed concern over the privacy implications of DPI and produced a collection of essays, available at http://dpi.priv.gc.ca/. See also P Ohm, 'The Rise and Fall of Invasive ISP Surveillance', forthcoming *University of Illinois Law Review*, available at http://papers.ssrn.com/sol3/papers.cfm?abstract_id=1261344#.

[144] For a full discussion of the problem of balancing interception of content in the public interest, with the privacy rights of users, see Rauhofer, ch 17.

[145] See ch 21 below and L Edwards and I Brown, *Macafee Virtual Criminology Report 2007*, passim, available at http://www.mcafee.com/us/research/criminology_report/default.html and the 2008 edition of the same report, available at http://www.mcafee.com/us/research/criminology_report/virtual_criminology_report/index.html.

solution was proposed in an influential report by the House of Lords in 2007[146] and has also been endorsed by ENISA, the European security agency.[147]

In each of the above cases, the bright line of the ECD regime, the starting point that the intermediary is prima facie not liable in respect of content supplied by, or the activities of, third parties, unless it has knowledge or complicity, is disregarded. Yet in each case, the practical advantages of putting responsibilities on to ISSPs, backed by the sanction of liability, are more than apparent. Marsden has suggested eloquently that what we are seeing is a 'perfect storm',[148] in which currents and tides from the worlds of copyright and child pornography and anti-terrorist activity, from industry and from law enforcement agencies, from those who 'think of the children' and those who think of their profits, are sweeping ISPs, hosts, aggregators and search engines (in declining order perhaps) away from any semblance of a neutral intermediary status and towards actively engaged agents, policed by a variety of private and public law obligations to achieve socially desirable goals, and increasingly mandated to use as an enforcement tool not just take-down after the fact, but proactive general filtering. How will and should the law respond to these overwhelming pressures? We discuss this in the concluding section.

IX. THE FALL AND RISE OF ONLINE INTERMEDIARY LIABILITY

Near the beginning of this chapter, we described the three factors which won the day for the emergent ISP industry in securing regimes of immunity from liability in Europe and North America. ISPs, it was claimed, could not exercise effective factual or legal control over the content or activities of others; were not morally responsible for the content or acts of others; and if they were held so liable, the consequences for the public interest in terms of access to the information society would be harmful in the extreme.

In 2009, it can be argued that the foundations of this narrative have been almost entirely deconstructed. Perhaps the greatest revolution has been a technological one, in relation to the claims that the volume of offending material on the Internet could never be successfully managed. As we saw in the discussion of *Viacom v YouTube*, in terms of IP rights at least, practical automation of filtering of at least some infringing material is finally visible on the horizon. Without the extensive co-operation of

---

[146] See House of Lords Science and Technology Committee, 'First Report on Personal Internet Security', HL, 10 August 2007, available .at http://www.publications.parliament.uk/pa/ld200607/ldselect/ldsctech/165/165i.pdf .

[147] See ENISA report, 'Security, Economics, and the Internal Market', March 2008, available at http://www.enisa.europa.eu/doc/pdf/report_sec_econ_&_int_mark_20080131.pdf.

[148] See C Marsden, *Network Neutrality: Towards a Co-Regulatory Solution* (London, Bloomsbury Academic, 2009).

rights-holders, as in YouTube's 'ClaimYour Content' solution, such technologies are still, however, either wildly demanding in terms of resources or likely to be highly error-prone (the forthcoming appeal in *SABAM v SA Tiscali (Scarlet)*[149] is likely to be instructive on these points). A similar revolution has arguably occurred in the field of blocking obscene content, although here, as discussed in chapter 20, it is asserted that the potential stifling impact on freedom of speech demands that the benefits, and accuracy, of blocking be demonstrated with a far higher degree of conviction than in the copyright field. In future, it seems that the question will be not whether intermediary filtering is possible or not, but *if* it is mandated, what degree of accuracy will be required, what costs can justifiably be imposed, and what trade-offs in terms of free speech, privacy, due process and restraints on access to knowledge are acceptable. It will still be important to remember that in areas such as defamation or hate speech, where filtering has to be based substantially on a human understanding of nuances of interpretation and intention, automated filtering will continue to be merely a science-fiction dream, and that even in areas such as copyright, defences of fair use and fair dealing are equally impossible for automated systems to recognise.

What of the moral argument that the intermediary *should* not be responsible for the wrongs of third parties? As we explored above in relation to the lawsuits against eBay and YouTube, etc, the decline of the simple access provider, the rise of the 'free services but ad-supported' business model, and the sense that many intermediaries are engaged in a 'common enterprise' with their infringing users, has diluted almost to nothingness the moral core of the adage not to 'shoot the messenger'. Yet this too flippant summary perhaps also ignores the plight of the many more traditional ISPs or hosts that still exist, the revenues of which come directly from delivering hosting services and giving Internet access, not from advertisements or listing fees. These actors include important industries such as server farms and the new service providers of 'cloud computing'. Any revised solution to ISSP immunity must take their needs into account too.

Finally, on the third and most instrumental point, it now seems rather unlikely that the information society in Europe would collapse if liability was to be imposed on ISSPs. The Internet service industries are now solidly established, multinationally based and often consolidated into larger business entities. Outsourcing is of course common (eg of customer helpdesks), but the resources and chief personnel of European telcos are now firmly based in Europe. Special 'start-up' immunities for ISSPs so they stay in Europe no longer seem relevant or necessary.

Having nibbled away at the three pillars of the ISSP justification for immunity, we have seen also that the incentives to place liability burdens on

---

[149] Above n 133.

ISSPs have become ever more enticing. In consequence, legislative controls asserting safe harbours are beginning to bend and break globally, as European and US courts attempt to find ways around them where they find the results unhelpful or inequitable. Even in the jurisprudence of the US CDA section 230(c), which unusually grants not limited but total immunity to online service providers in respect of publication torts,[150] a series of cases have begun to whittle away at this immunity, including in relation to UGC sites, *Grace v EBay*,[151] *Fair Housing Council v Room Mates*,[152] *Doe v Friendfinder*[153] and, most recently, *Barnes v Yahoo!*.[154]

In 2004, this author wrote:

> At the end of 2000, as the dust settled on Articles 12–15 of the ECD, the DMCA and the Australian government's climb down on the Broadcasting Services Act, it was a commonly held belief that global intermediary immunity had reached some kind of tentative harmony. In 2004, it now seems that this may only have been a momentary blip of consensus. . . . In the meantime, this writer would predict that ways of circumventing ISP immunity which are already allowed under the ECD—eg the seeking of injunctive relief[155] and demands to reveal the identity of anonymous or pseudonymous content providers[156]—will be utilised more and more by rights-holders and other 'victims'; that in terms of hosting liability, renewed attempts will be made to find ISSPs liable on the basis of 'constructive' as well as 'actual' knowledge; that pressure on non-traditional intermediaries such as credit card companies and banks to at least self-regulate to help control illicit content will increase[157]; and that technical methods of access prevention may be more and more put into operation by ISPs, again seeking to forestall leg-

---

[150] See above, p 50.

[151] 2004 WL 1632047 (Cal App 2nd Dist, 22 July 2004). eBay was sued for defamatory remarks made on its auction site by a disgruntled bidder in respect of another user of the site. But note that although eBay lost on CDA immunity, having been found not to be a publisher of information but a distributor, they still were held not liable because their contractual terms successfully excluded liability.

[152] *Fair Housing Council of San Fernando Valley, et al v Roommates.com LLC*, 489 F 3d 921, CV-03-09386-PA (9th Cir, 15 May 2007) aff'd en banc 2008 WL 879293 (9th Cir, 3 April 2008).

[153] *Doe v Friendfinder Network, Inc*, 540 F Supp 2d 288 (DNH 2008).

[154] See *Barnes v Yahoo!, Inc*, 2009 WL 1232367 (9th Cir, 7 May 2009). Interesting commentary can be found at Eric Goldman's blog, 13 May 2009, at http://blog.ericgoldman.org/archives/2009/05/ninth_circuit_m.htm. See also the controversy current in May 2009 as to whether Craigslist should be held responsible for its users offering 'erotic services' as online small ads: see eg AP 'Craigslist to Drop Erotic Services', 13 May 2009, at http://www.google.com/hostednews/ap/article/ALeqM5hCZLZQ3vY7SW071JNNl7cf0seq8wD985KPB00.

[155] Art 14(3).

[156] Nothing in the ECD provides a framework for when disclosure of the identity of a user of an ISSP is legal, although other EC legislation such as the Data Protection Directive is of course relevant. See further in the *UK, Totalise v Motley Fool* [2001] EMLR 29; *Sheffield Wednesday v Hargreaves* [2007] EWHC 2375 (QB); note also *Promusicae v Telefonica*, above, n 136.

[157] There has not been room herein to review the use of credit card intermediaries to police illegality online, but it is now well established, especially in relation to payments for pornography, and to control offshore gambling. See however ch 21 on the difficulties posed by the lack of control over new online payment mechanisms.

islative action requiring them to utilise such technologies.[158] [some footnotes added]

These predictions appear to have been broadly accurate. The immunity provisions of the ECD in Articles 12–15 now desperately need to be reviewed if there is to be any kind of harmony across the Single Market, yet the Commission shows no signs of wishing to initiate such a process, probably because it would indeed be highly controversial; in the meantime a number of references for clarity on Articles 12–15 are pending at the ECJ.[159]

This author's provisional conclusions in 2009 are that a bright line of no liability on intermediaries for content provided by third party content providers, unless or until notice is given to take down, can no longer be sustained. With or without supranational legislative intervention, we are seeing a move towards a new European system, driven by piecemeal European law-making by courts, national legislatures and industry sector regulators, which is likely to include the following features.

- The disassembling of the current horizontal scheme of immunities in the ECD to reflect the very different pressures in the fields of, notably, copyright, pornographic and pro-terrorist material, as opposed to defamatory or private material. Any future EC legislative regime might well be best expressed in more detailed terms, and as a maximum harmonisation, both to produce more predictability for businesses operating across the Single Market.

- A response to the increased blurring between the notions of 'intermediary' and 'content provider', especially in the world of UGC intermediaries such as eBay and YouTube, etc, by removing immunity from such hybrid intermediaries, or imposing extra obligations alongside it.

- In particular, an increased heavy reliance on looking at what *financial gain* an intermediary makes from hosting or linking activities, thus moving to a far more case-by case-assessment of immunity, which will be difficult to predict for intermediaries.

- Recognition of the increased demands of both IP rights-holders and law-enforcement agencies for pre-emptive filtering rather than post factum takedown, probably by taking advantage of the ECD's exemption of injunctive relief from the immunity provisions.

- Recognition that filtering obligations can only be practically imposed if

---

158 L Edwards, in L Edwards (ed), *The New Shape of European Electronic Commerce* (Oxford, Hart Publishing, 2005).

159 Note that in addition to the reference in *L'Oréal v eBay* noted above, n 87, a reference may yet be made from the UK case of *Interflora v Marks and Spencer* [2009] EWHC 1095 (Ch) in respect of Google's liability (if any) for trademark infringement by providing AdWords to competitors to trade mark holders. In both these cases, a number of ECJ references on Arts 12–15 from other EU courts are also noted.

they can be successfully automated, with a heated debate around what counts as 'success'.
- Recognition that search engines and other information management tools may need new distinct safe harbours in Europe to fulfil their critical role.

Finally, many of the above changes are likely, without further regulation, to lead to substantial incursions into fundamental values such as freedom of speech, privacy and due process. In particular, market forces alone are likely to lead to not just defensive or industry-required take-down but also to unregulated monitoring and surveillance, possibly via deep packet inspection, as well as filtering. This author hopes that courts, if not legislatures and regulators, will take a serious role in providing safeguards for these key values of the maturing information society.

2

The Changing Face of Electronic Consumer Contracts in the Twenty-first Century: Fit for Purpose?

CHRISTINE RIEFA and JULIA HÖRNLE[1]

The enormous success of eBay, Facebook, Google, Second Life or Amazon illustrates how consumers and businesses alike have embraced electronic commerce and the Internet in the last decade. Indeed, focusing on eBay alone, the site counts a staggering 86.9 million active users worldwide, 1 billion page views per day, and reports a net income in excess of $1.78 billion for 2008.[2] In the UK, figures demonstrate continued growth in the online shopping market. The figures released by the Office for National Statistics in November 2008 showed that sales by UK businesses rose to £163 billion in 2007, an increase of over 30 per cent on the previous year. The figures also revealed that 70.3 per cent of businesses had a website.[3] Whilst slowing penetration rates[4] and the economic downturn have affected growth, electronic commerce is here to stay and will continue to develop at a steady pace.[5] The 'Net economy', as it was

---

[1] The chapter was primarily written by Christine Riefa, with sections from Julia Hörnle on the postal rule and unfair contract terms. The authors wish also to thank Lilian Edwards for her useful contributions and skilful editing.

[2] Figures for the fourth quarter and full-year results 2008, available online: http://files. shareholder.com/downloads/ebay/593094761x0x266606/581a206a-78df-4c3c-81c4-4a8b57e 62440/eBay_FINALQ42008EarningsRelease.pdf (accessed 26 March 2009).

[3] Office for National Statistics, News Release, 'Internet Sales Rose by 30 per cent in 2007', 21 November 2008, available online: http://www.statistics.gov.uk/pdfdir/ecomnr1108.pdf (accessed 26 March 2009).

[4] In 2008, 65 per cent of Great Britain households had Internet access, a 7 per cent increase over 2007 figures, according to the Office for National Statistics, http://www.statistics.gov.uk/ cci/nugget.asp?id=8 (accessed 26 March 2009).

[5] eMarketer predicts a slight deep in electronic commerce sales in 2009, followed by a spending spike in 2010. Longer term, the US retail e-commerce sales are set to mature in 2013 at US$203.5 billion (note that these figures exclude travel, digital downloads and event ticketing).

once called, has become part of the fabric of our daily working and private lives. It follows that users have embraced the Internet, not just as a place for entertainment, but also as a tool to enter into legal relationships.

Electronic contracts (e-contracts) have rapidly evolved from contracts between businesses (B2B)[6] on closed private networks, to transactions on open networks, such as the Internet, between businesses and consumers (B2C) and amongst consumers (C2C).[7] Perhaps as a result of this rapid evolution of e-contracts, the legal regime applicable to them is not found in one single instrument but defined across a vast array of Directives and national legal instruments. The two main Directives which can be identified as the backbone of B2C electronic contract regulation are the Distance Selling Directive (DSD)[8] and the E-Commerce Directive (ECD).[9] The DSD and the ECD were implemented in the UK by the Consumer Protection (Distance Selling) Regulations 2000 (DSReg 2000)[10] and the Electronic Commerce (EC Directive) Regulations 2002 (ECReg 2002).[11]

The DSD is specifically targeted towards the protection of consumers. It gives consumers buying at a distance a number of rights, including:

- the right to receive clear information about goods and services before they buy and confirmation in writing;
- a right to withdraw from the contract for a period of seven days;
- protection against credit card fraud.

The ECD has a broader scope, covering many aspects of e-business and encompassing both B2B and B2C transactions.

Although much legislative progress has been made in the last 10 years on policing consumer e-contracts, new ways to deceive and rip off consumers have also emerged. This has done much to erode consumer confidence in e-commerce, despite the legal framework of the DSD and ECD which was intended to inspire such confidence. Furthermore, the application and interpretation of these texts remains unsatisfactory in many Member States.

For more online, see: http://www.emarketer.com/Article.aspx?id=1006963 (accessed 26 March 2009).

[6] Prior to the Internet, Electronic Data Interchange (EDI) was the main conduit for B2B e-commerce using a defined framework for online transactions.

[7] See R Ong, 'Consumer Based Electronic Commerce: A Comparative Analysis of the Position in Malaysia and Hong Kong' (2004) 12 *International Journal of Law and Information Technology* 101; C Reed and G Sutter, 'E-Commerce', in C Reed and J Angel (eds), *Computer Law*, 6th edn (Oxford, Oxford University Press, 2007) 220–27, no 4.4; C Ramberg, 'The E-Commerce Directive and Formation of Contract in a Comparative Perspective' (2001) 26(5) *Entertainment Law Review* 429–50.

[8] Directive 97/7/EC, of the European Parliament and of the Council of 20 May 1997, on the protection of consumers in respect of distance contracts, OJ L144/19, 04.06.1997.

[9] Directive 2000/31/EC of the European Parliament and of the Council of 8 June 2000, on certain legal aspects of information society services, in particular electronic commerce, in the Internal Market (Directive on electronic commerce), OJ L178/1, 17.07.2000.

[10] SI 2000, no 2334.

[11] SI 2002, no 2013.

Ambiguity remains on some key points of law such as the definition of e-contracts, their formation and the jurisdiction in which an e-contract is concluded.[12] The legislation does not address issues that have emerged as technology has changed, and e-commerce with it.[13] For example, the sale of music downloads is excluded from the scope of Directive 1999/44/EC on the sale of consumer goods because this Directive only covers tangible moveable items and not intangibles. As a result, consumers currently have no redress should a piece of music downloaded from the Internet not play satisfactorily on an MP3 player, or if the file is corrupted.[14] Furthermore, the purchaser of digital products is excluded from the right to withdraw from a distance contract. More problems arise with online auctions where consumers in different Member States receive differerent levels of protection.[15] The legal status of automated contracts (concluded by automated software), mobile contracts (m-contracts, ie contracts concluded using mobile phones) and 'virtual contracts' (contracts entered into in virtual environments such as Second Life) also remain problematic. Virtual contracts in particular are not as yet dealt with by any specific legislation.

Finally, the legislation in practice is often not well enforced. For example, a recent Office of Fair Trading (OFT) web sweep[16] revealed that nearly one-third of retail websites in the UK were breaking the aforementioned laws designed to protect shoppers.[17] In particular, the OFT survey revealed that 40 per cent of sites were not transparent about their pricing and many also did not provide all the required information. The European Commission also uncovered that almost 60 per cent of airline sites were breaking consumer law by providing misleading information about their pricing.[18]

Changes in the regulation of consumer e-contracts are, however, on the horizon. The proposal for a Directive on Consumer Rights (pDCR),[19]

[12] Jurisdiction and choice-of-law issues are discussed at length in ch 1 above.

[13] M Butler and A Darnley, 'Consumer Acquis: Proposed Reform of B2C Regulation to Promote Cross-border Trading' (2007) 13(4) *Computer and Telecommunications Law Review* 109–14.

[14] Ibid, n 15.

[15] We will address this issue in our developments on the right to withdraw, p 117.

[16] OFT, Web Sweep Analysis, March 2008, OFT982.

[17] Out-law.com, 'Third of Online Shops Undermine Consumer Rights, Says OFT', News 12 March 2008, available online http://www.out-law.com/page-8934 (accessed 11 March 2008).

[18] Out-law.com, 'One in Three Airline Sites Break Consumer Laws', News 13 May 2008, available online http://www.out-law.com/page-9113 (accessed 16 May 2008).

[19] COM(2008) 614 final. The proposal is the product of the Review of the Consumer Acquis launched in 2004 by the Commission with a view to modernise the existing consumer directives and simplify as well as improve the regulatory environment for both professionals and consumers. The review encompassed eight Directives protecting consumers. In 2007, the Commission issued a Green Paper (COM(2006) 744 final), identifying three main issues that needed to be addressed by new regulation: new market developments, fragmentation of rules and lack of confidence. The final proposal focuses on just four Directives: the Doorstep Selling Directive 85/577/EEC of 20 December 1985, the Unfair Terms in Consumer Contracts Directive 93/13/EEC, the DSD, and the Consumer Guarantees Directive 1999/44/EC.

published on 8 October 2008, suggests major alterations. At the time of writing, the pDCR is only at the first stage of the legislative process, and will no doubt be the object of fierce negotiations amongst Member States in the months to come. It is already clear that because of its wide-ranging scope (spanning four Directives), the pDCR will have an important impact on electronic consumer contracts.

Unfortunately, there seems less political will for a revision of the ECD. Indeed recent discussion of reform of the law in France implementing the ECD on the liability of intermediaries was not well received in Brussels, with the European Commission indicating that it did not consider it necessary to revise the ECD at present.[20] In the absence of changes to the ECD, the pDCR may still not prove sufficient to ensure that regulation of consumer e-contracts is fit for purpose in the twenty-first century.

In order to assess the changing face of B2C consumer contracts, we will first turn our attention to the current regulatory landscape and the viability of the fragmented model of regulation adopted in the EU. We will then look at the substantive rules applicable to consumer e-contracts, and see how those may need to be improved in order to adequately meet the objectives of consumer confidence, and the promotion of e-commerce, set by the European Commission.

I. A REGULATORY APPROACH TO CONSUMER E-CONTRACTS: FIT FOR PURPOSE?

Regulation of e-contracts in the EU is done piecemeal within the ECD. The European Commission opted for what can be described as 'contract law neutrality',[21] ie an instrument which instead of replacing national laws on contract formation, only provides supplementary rules. Unfortunately this approach was not based on sound policy decisions but rather on political strategy with, as we will see, important consequences.[22] Alongside the ECD, a number of Directives also form part of the e-commerce regulatory landscape; these include the Electronic Signatures Directive (E-sigD)[23] and a number of Directives on consumer protection, eg the Unfair Terms Directive,[24] and other more specialised instruments.[25]

---

20 As reported in 'Hébergeurs: Bruxelles s'inquiète d'une éventuelle réforme de la LCEN', ZDNet.fr, 19 September 2008, www.zdnet.fr/actualites/ (23 September 2008).

21 JK Winn and J Haubold, 'Electronic Promises: Contract Law Reform and e-Commerce in a Comparative Perspective' (2002) 27(5) *European Law Review* 574.

22 Winn and Haubold (ibid, 576) talk about 'a deliberate abstention of the drafters' in the light of the difficulties of European contract law harmonisation still in the project phase.

23 Directive 1999/93/EC of the European Parliament and of the Council of 13 December 1999, on a Community framework for electronic signatures, OJ 19.01.2000, L13/12.

24 97/7/EC.

25 Rec 11 ECD enumerates these further consumer Directives including misleading and comparative advertising, consumer credit, package travel and package holidays, indication of prices, general product safety directive, timeshare, injunction directive, liability for defective products, etc.

As a result of this fragmented approach to regulation, no single definition of either 'consumer' or 'electronic contract' exist. Instead, definitions
are tailored to the group that each regulatory instrument seeks to protect,
making navigating the regulatory landscape difficult at times. However, the
combination of the recognition of the validity of e-contracts (in Article 9
ECD), electronic signatures and the 'technology-neutral' approach used in
consumer protection regulation, has certainly improved the harmonisation
of e-contract regulation across Europe.

A. Absence of a Uniform Definition of Electronic Consumer Contracts

(i) Electronic Contracts: Distance Contracts and/or Information Society Services?

Despite the absence of a single EC definition of an 'electronic contract',
Article 2(1) DSD provides a useful starting point in defining a 'distance
contract' as

> any contract concerning the goods or services concluded between a supplier and
> a consumer under an organised distance sales or service provision scheme run by
> a supplier who, for the purpose of the contract, makes exclusive use of one or
> more means of distance communication, up to and including the moment at
> which the contract is concluded.[26]

Although a list of the means of distance communication, inserted in the
Annex, does not contain the Internet, and only e-mail, the definition has
always been considered to be wide enough to accommodate many B2C
e-contracts. The pDCR provides a revised definition of distance contracts
in Article 2(6) as 'any sales or service contract where the trader, for the
conclusion of the contract, makes exclusive use of one or more means of
distance communication'. Means of distance communication are defined in
Article 2(7) pDCR as 'any means which, without the simultaneous physical
presence of the trader and the consumer, may be used for the conclusion of
a contract between those parties'. In addition, Recital 11 pDCR removes
any potentially remaining ambiguity:'the new definition of distance
contract should cover all cases where sales and service contracts are
concluded using exclusively one or more means of distance communication
(such as mail order, Internet, telephone or fax)'.

   The fact that the new definition of a distance sale removes the
requirement for an 'organised scheme' should improve legal certainty and
create a level playing field for all traders.[27] As Howells and Schultze
indicate, 'many traders may casually slip into a distance sale contract with

---

[26] Reg 3(1).
[27] According to Rec 11.

the attendant obligations'.[28] However, note that some transactions are excluded from the scope of the Directive, and in other cases the Directive may not confer on consumers the full right to withdraw or the same level of information.[29]

The ECD refers to information society services (and providers thereof, or ISSPs). Article 2(a) and Recital 17 refer to the existing definition in Community law[30] as 'any service normally provided for remuneration, at a distance, by means of electronic equipment for the processing (including digital compression) and storage of data, and at the individual request of a recipient of a service'.[31] However, note that different aspects of the same transaction may not necessarily all fall within the scope of the ECD. As Smith explains,

> [T]he conclusion of an online contract for the sale of a book may be within the scope of the Regulations, but the fulfilment of the contract by delivery of a physical book would not be. If the book were to be downloaded in electronic form from the supplier's website, however, the whole transaction would fall within the scope of the Directive.[32]

In order to determine the scope of each instrument we also must define consumers. Unfortunately this is not a straightforward process either: the notions of 'consumer' and 'business' are blurred in an online environment; and parties do not meet in person and can in some instances transact anonymously or pseudonymously.

(ii) Notions of 'Consumer' and 'Business' in an Online Environment

We have already noted that there is no unified definition of consumers available in the EU and the same is true in English law. However, one can reliably understand a consumer to be a natural person acting for purposes which are outside his or her business.[33] The pDCR, Article 2, similarly

---

[28] G Howells and R Schulze, 'Overview of the Proposed Consumer Rights Directive', in G Howells and R Schulze (eds), *Modernising and Harmonising Consumer Contract Law* (Munich, Sellier, 2009) 6.

[29] See Art 3 DSD. In particular, information requirements, right of withdrawal and performance obligations (under Arts 4–7(1)) do not apply to contracts for the supply of foodstuffs, beverages or other goods intended for everyday consumption supplied to the home of the consumer, to his residence or his workplace by regular roundsmen, and to contracts for the provision of accommodation, transport, catering or leisure services, where the supplier undertakes, when the contract is concluded, to provide these services on a specific period. This leaves out car rental online because this comes under the transport exception (as confirmed by the ECJ in Case C-336/03, *easyCar (UK) Ltd v Office of Fair Trading* [2005] ECR I-1947) and the purchase of flight tickets for example.

[30] In Art 1(2) Directive 98/34/EC as amended by Directive 98/48/EC

[31] Further on this definition and its scope, see Edwards, above ch 1, 62.

[32] GJH Smith (ed), *Internet Law and Regulation*, 4th edn (London, Sweet & Maxwell 2007) 792, point 10-047

[33] See Art 2(e) ECD and Art 2(2) DSD. For the UK, see s 3, Consumer Protection (Distance Selling) Regulations 2000. A similar definition is found in Reg 2 of the Electronic Commerce (EC Directive) Regulations 2002.

suggests defining a consumer uniformly as 'any natural person who, in contracts covered by this Directive, is acting for purposes which are outside his trade, business, craft or profession'.[34] However, online activity has blurred the distinction between businesses and amateurs. Starting up an online web-based business no longer requires major capital investment or sophisticated infrastructure. Many 'Web 2.0' businesses in fact have few assets other than their website and their clientele. Individuals who do not conceive of themselves as commercial entrants may also find themselves unexpectedly making money in the online world. Many eBay users, for example, end up using eBay as a source of second income, selling regularly on the site. It is also the case for the new virtual world entrepreneurs who are players in the game and earning a second income at the same time. The boundaries between business and pleasure have become entangled.

'Hybrid consumers'[35] are an emerging category of e-commerce actors. They are individuals who, often unknowingly or unwillingly, display the characteristics of a business. Whilst this category of actor is not new, the use of the Internet has clearly exacerbated the tendency to earn on the side and mix play with work.

In the UK, there is no fixed definition of what 'acting in the course of business' actually covers[36] and definitions vary with the legislation applicable. When legislation applies criminal sanctions, the definition of a business is typically narrow.[37] By contrast, in the Sale of Goods Act 1979, the definition of a business is conceived widely in order to afford consumers better protection. As a result, in *Stevenson v Rogers*[38] a fisherman selling his only boat in order to replace it was considered 'in the course of business'.[39] Yet, of particular interest to eBay sellers and would-be Second Life tycoons, it is still uncertain whether the Sale of Goods Act 1979

---

[34] Art 2 pDCR states: '(1) "consumer" means any natural person who, in contracts covered by this Directive, is acting for purposes which are outside his trade, business, craft or profession; (2) "trader" means any natural or legal person who, in contracts covered by this Directive, is acting for purposes relating to his trade, business, craft or profession and anyone acting in the name of or on behalf of a trader.'

[35] They are called 'hybrid sellers' in M Morgan-Taylor and C Willet, 'The Quality Obligation and Online Market Places' (2005) 21 *Journal of Contract Law* 157.

[36] DW Oughton and JP Lowry, *Textbook on Consumer Law*, 2nd edn (London, Blackstone Press, 2000) 4.

[37] This is so, for example, with the Business Advertisement (Disclosure) Order 1977, which makes it an offence for a party in the course of business to publish, or cause to be published, an advertisement offering goods for sale to consumers, unless it is made clear that it is a business sale. The same occurs in the Trade Description Act 1968. For example, in *Davies v Sumner* [1984] 1 WLR 405, the sale of a car used by a doctor for personal as well as business needs was considered not to have the necessary regularity to allow a criminal sanction to be imposed. Also, in *Blakemore v Bellamy* [1983] RTR 303, a postal worker who often repaired and restored cars was not considered to be acting in the course of business as the work was carried out as a hobby.

[38] [1999] 2 WLR 1064

[39] In this case, the Court of Appeal decided that for the application of the Sale of Goods Act, there was no requirement for regularity of dealings and that is was sufficient that the sale was not made by a private individual.

catches the 'amateur entrepreneur'.[40] There is a fine line between a consumer *stricto sensu* who simply uses the Internet to offer for sale a few unwanted items, the individual who decides to empty the contents of lofts and garages, and the individual who actively buys goods with a view to reselling them. In the latter two cases, the activity is likely to enter the business sphere. eBay 'power sellers' are another key category of 'hybrid sellers'.[41]

Distinguishing between consumers and businesses is crucial because the law typically applies a far greater standard of protection to consumers than to businesses in transactions. Businesses are assumed to contract *inter se* 'at arm's length'—ie with equality of bargaining power—while this is not so in B2C interactions. Interestingly, when consumers contract with consumers (C2C) neither, it seems, is assumed to need special protection. Consumers buying from businesses benefit from protective national legislation such as the DSD, whilst if the parties are both classified as consumers, this does not apply.[42] A set of practical criteria enabling one to determine with more certainty when a consumer becomes a business would be most welcome, especially as any new definition of consumer is likely to be interpreted differently across Europe.[43]

(iii) Anonymity, Pseudonymity and Remote Contracting in an Online Environment

Another layer of difficulties associated with e-contracts is that parties contract at a distance, and in many cases anonymously or pseudonymously. Anonymity in contracting is again nothing new, but raises multiple problems when sales are concluded electronically. For example, some parties lack full contractual capacity, eg minor children, with exact rules varying across the EU, and issues also arise concerning age limits on sales of alcohol, etc, as well. Anonymity shrouds clear knowledge as to whether a contract is B2C, which in turn affects consumer awareness of their rights.

[40] GG Howells and S Weatherill, *Consumer Protection Law*, 2nd edn (Aldershot, Ashgate, 2005) 167.

[41] Interestingly, such difficulties, not exclusive to English law, persuaded the French legislator to include in a 'Bill on economic modernisation', considered in Parliament in the summer of 2008, the creation of a new legal classification destined to encompass power sellers on eBay and similar 'self-entrepreneurs'. The legislation was not final as of May 2009. For more on the French position, see ZDNet.fr, 'Alexander von Schirmeister, eBay France: Nous souhaitons un statut d'auto-entrepreneur pour permettre le développement de l'activité de vendeur en ligne', available on line, http://www.zdnet.fr/actualites (accessed 01 May 2008).

[42] This remains the case under the pDCR, Art 7, in its current wording.

[43] This is despite the pDCR being a maximum harmonisation Directive. For example, in France, investors can be considered consumers under certain circumstances and in the UK, under the Communications Act 2003, consumers include small businesses of up to 10 employees. For more on the concept of targeted full harmonisation and a critique of this approach, see H-W Micklitz, 'The Targeted Full Harmonisation Approach: Looking Behind the Curtain', in Howells and Shultze (eds), above n 28, 47.

The Article 7 pDCR provides that if businesses disclose that they are merely acting for consumers as agents, then the contract will not be regarded as a B2C but rather as a C2C contract, and thus falling outside the scope of the Directive. But this offers no assistance to the eBay 'power seller' problem of a business arguably posing as a consumer.[44] One practical solution, already adopted by eBay France, may be to rely on parties identifying themselves as consumer or trader via a logo. Such schemes are so far, however, voluntary, and some traders may not see compliance as worthwhile.

B. Recognition of the Validity of Electronic Contracts and Electronic Signatures

Article 9(1) of the ECD states:

> Member States shall ensure that their legal system allows contracts to be concluded by electronic means. Member States shall in particular ensure that the legal requirements applicable to the contractual process neither creates obstacles for the use of electronic contracts not result in such contract being deprived of legal effectiveness and validity on account of their having been made by electronic means.

Consequently, contracts that in the past had sometimes to be concluded in writing, eg for reasons of certainty and probativity, can now generally be entered into electronically, though some exceptions still exist in national laws. In the UK, Article 9 was not implemented as the general validity of e-contracts was already considered established.[45] On the question of 'writing', Schedule 1 of the Interpretation Act 1978 states that 'writing includes typing, printing, lithography, photography and other modes of representing or reproducing words in a visible form, and expression referring to writing are construed accordingly'. Bainbridge comments that 'this would appear to include computer storage. Words stored in a computer may be reproduced in screen or printed on paper. In any case, it is unlikely that a judge would take a restrictive view of this.'[46]

The issue of finding a viable alternative to manuscript signatures has been more complicated. In pre-electronic days, signatures were used not only to authenticate the integrity and finality of transactions, but to provide evidence of such. Digital signatures were designed to replicate these

---

[44] However, note that in the UK, for example, the Business Advertisement (Disclosure) Order 1977 SI 1977/1918 makes it an offence for a party in the course of business to publish, or cause to be published, an advertisement offering goods for sale to consumers, unless it is made clear that it is a business sale. The ECD also requires that commercial communications be identified as such (Art 6).

[45] See Electronic Communications Act 2000.

[46] D Bainbridge, *Introduction to Information Technology Law*, 6th edn (Harlow, Pearson Longman, 2008) 359.

functions, and even exceed them,[47] but have in fact proved superfluous to needs in many e-contracts. Public key encryption (PKI), as effectively favoured by the ESigDir despite its nominal 'technological neutrality',[48] has proven to be too costly and complicated for users in most low-value B2C or C2C transactions. In practice, uptake on PKI, even in B2B commerce, has been low. As a result, we provide a relatively brief account of the law in this area and refer readers to more specialised works.[49]

The ESigD defines two types of signatures: the 'electronic signature', data in electronic form that is attached to, or logically associated with, other electronic data and which serves as a method of authentication;[50] and the 'advanced electronic signature', which serves as an identification as well as authentication tool.[51]

In the UK, the Electronic Communications Act 2000 (ECA2000)[52] took a simpler approach and does not make such a drastic distinction.[53] Section 7 provides that in any legal proceedings, both an electronic signature and the certification of such signature by any person shall be admissible in evidence, with regards to the authenticity and integrity of a communication or data. However, the Act does provide for the certification of some electronic signatures under section 7(3), which are in effect the equivalent of the 'advanced signatures' identified by the Directive.[54] The ECA 2000 is 'technology-neutral', prescribing no particular technology to generate the e-signature. As a result, digital signatures can range from 'a simple typed-in

---

[47] They not only replace the handwritten signature, but also encrypt the contents of the document.

[48] See C Reed, 'Taking Sides on Technology Neutrality' (2007) 4(3) SCRIPTed 263, http://www.law.ed.ac.uk/ahrc/script-ed/vol4-3/reed.asp.

[49] For detailed discussion of the nature and regulation of encryption and digital signatures, see M Hogg, 'Secrecy and Signatures—Turning the Legal Spotlight on Encryption and Electronic Signatures', in L Edwards and C Waelde (eds), *Law and the Internet: A Framework for Electronic Commerce* (Oxford, Hart Publishing 2000) 37–54; L Brazell *Electronic Signatures Law and Regulation* (London, Sweet & Maxwell, 2004); IJ Lloyd, *Information Technology Law*, 5th edn (Oxford, Oxford University Press, 2008) 487–507.

[50] Art 2(1) ESigD.

[51] Art 2(2) defines 'advanced electronic signature' as an electronic signature which meets the following requirements: (i) it is uniquely linked to the signatory; (ii) it is capable of identifying the signatory; (iii) it is created using means that the signatory can maintain under his sole control; (iv) it is linked to the data to which it relates in such a manner that any subsequent change to the data is detectable.

[52] The Electronic Communications Act 2000, together with the Electronic Signatures Regulations 2002 (SI 2002, no 318), implement the ESigD in the UK. The Act provides rules on the legal recognition of e-signatures (including generation, verification, communication and storage of e-signatures) whilst the Regulations address the supervision of Certification Service Providers and issues of data protection.

[53] Note that under Art 5(1) of the EC Directive, advanced electronic signatures are also guaranteed legal effectiveness and admissibility. However, Art 5(1) also adds that (ordinary) electronic signatures should not be denied legal effect because they do not have the same features as advanced ones. This is apparently so in the UK implementation.

[54] The certification (or 'trusted third party') industry is tightly regulated under the Electronic Signatures Regulations 2002, especially with respect to with the supervision and the liability of certification service providers (the principal player being Verisign).

name or scanned-in signature to more complex biometric techniques, such as fingerprint scanning or signatures created by cryptographic means'.[55] Although advanced or certified signatures are not required in UK law for any purpose, Hogg[56] suggests that a certified e-signature will in practice be more useful than an ordinary one, as UK law merely provides that e-signatures are admissible in evidence, leaving questions such as provenance, authenticity or date to be determined by extraneous evidence.

In practice however, and contrary to the expectations of regulators, parties to e-contracts have leaned towards less advanced forms of electronic signatures, such as simply affixing one's name in the text of an e-mail, or on an electronic document, or using a scanned version of a written signature (see *Goodman v J Eban Ltd*[57] and *J Pereira Fernandes SA v Mehta*[58]). If the parties in consumer transactions want to protect themselves against fraud, there are easier ways to do so than PKI, such as passwords and personal identification numbers (PINs).

C. Deficiencies in the Regulatory Approach to Consumer E-contracts

In the past, Directives such as the ECD and the DSD were adopted as minimum harmonisation instruments, allowing Member States when implenting the rules to provide a higher degree of protection than the minimum prescribed by the legislation. Such an approach might be beneficial for some at the national level, but created problems for cross-border trade by failing to guarantee identical rules across Europe.[59] Because the ECD broadly follows a 'country of origin' principle[60] an information society service provider is governed by the law of the Member State in which it is established. Discrepancies in implementation create distortions in the Single Market because providers established in a country where requirements are higher than other Member States face strong competition from suppliers established elsewhere. Market newcomers will prefer to establish themselves in a Member State where the implementation is most advantageous to them. For consumer contracts, however, an e-business must meet the laws of every Member State in which consumers can purchase its products.[61]

---

[55] M O'Connor and E Brownsdon, 'Electronic Signatures' (2002) 152 *New Law Journal* 348.
[56] Hogg, above n 49.
[57] [1954] 1 QB 550.
[58] [2006] EWHC 813 (Ch). See further K Rogers, 'Signing Your e-Life Away' (2006) 156 *New Law Journal* 883.
[59] R Brownsword, 'Regulating Transactions: Good Faith and Fair Dealing', in Howells and Schulze (eds), above n 28, 87–113.
[60] Rec 22 ECD states: 'Information society services should in principle be subject to the law of the Member State in which the service provider is established.'
[61] See discussion in ch 3 below, 127

The DSD is based on the idea that it is 'essential to the smooth operation of the internal market for consumers to be able to have dealings with a business outside their country, even if it has a subsidiary in the consumer country of residence'.[62] But here again, inconsistencies in implementation have led to market distortions, and lack of harmony in consumer protection law has been identified as an obstacle to the furthering of the internal market. Fragmentation also impacts legal certainty and consumer confidence, two other key regulatory aims of the ECD[63] and the DSD.[64] As a report on cross-border e-commerce in the EU from February 2009[65] reveals,

> while e-commerce is taking off at national level, it is still relatively uncommon for consumers to use the Internet to purchase goods and services in another Member State. The gap between domestic and cross-border e-commerce is widening as a result of cross-border barriers to online trade.[66]

The report confirms that these 'obstacles have created a fragmented e-commerce internal market'.[67]

In a bid to alleviate the undesirable effects of minimum harmonisation, recent consumer protection Directives[68] have used maximum harmonisation, or full harmonisation (as it is now called), whereby Member States *cannot* apply rules providing greater consumer protection than the ones in force at EC level. This guarantees, at least in theory, a fully harmonised playing field and facilitates cross-border trade. Accordingly the pDCR adopts a policy of maximum harmonisation, in an attempt to eliminate the disparities that exist between Member States.[69] However full harmonisation has been criticised as still ineffective,[70] in particular because not all e-contracts will be fully caught by the pDCR.[71] In addition, the fragmen-

---

[62] Rec 3 DSD.

[63] Rec 7 ECD.

[64] Rec 11 DSD.

[65] Commission Staff Working Document, Report on cross-border e-commerce in the EU, February 2009, SEC (2009) 283 final.

[66] Ibid, Executive Summary, 2. Some of the identified barriers to trade relate to: (i) language, demographics, individual preferences, technical specifications or standards, internet penetration or the efficiency of the postal or payment system; (ii) the inability of consumers to access commercial offers in another member states because of mechanisms that prevent them placing orders; (iii) the lack of information on cross-border offers because it is difficult to make cross-border comparisons and because cross-border advertising is relatively uncommon; (iv) the regulatory obstacles faced by traders and the perceived difficulty to obtain effective redress when something goes wrong.

[67] Ibid, 3.

[68] See eg the Unfair Commercial Practice 2005/29/EC and the Consumer Credit Directive 2008/48/EC.

[69] See further Recs 6 and 7 of the pDCR

[70] See Howells and Schulze, 'Overview', above n 28, 6. See also Micklitz, above n 43, 47. Notably the authors feel that the legal certainty advocated in Recs 6 and 7 is illusory.

[71] At today's date, the proposal still excludes software from a right to withdraw and does not provide any further remedies if software is defective. Service contracts are also mostly excluded from the scope of the pDCR.

tation between ECD and consumer-specific instruments will persist. One cannot help but wonder if the energy expanded in moving towards a new legislative approach would not have been better channelled towards drafting a consolidated instrument for e-commerce, whether operating on full or minimum harmonisation lines. It is also important to note that if the substantive rules are not got right, the style of harmonisation will not help.

II. SUBSTANTIVE CONSUMER E-CONTRACT RULES: FIT FOR PURPOSE?

The problems raised by the formation and execution of e-contracts and the lack of clarity of the rules applicable in this area have been discussed at length over the last decade or more[72] and our coverage of some issues will thus be relatively brief. Key issues include the formation of consumer e-contracts; incorporation of terms and questions relating to unfair terms; and information and transparency requirements, as well as other rights under the DSD.

A. Formation of E-contracts

The rules on contract formation are not to be found in full in either the DSD or the ECD but in the domestic contract law of each Member State. The ECD excludes from its remit 'contracts concluded exclusively by exchange of electronic mail or by equivalent individual communications',[73] but covers contracts made via websites in Articles 10 and 11. The DSD implicitly governs all contracts made by means of distance communications, which may include e-mail contracts, but covers only B2C interactions, few of which would be formed by individually negotiated e-mails. Due to the divergences between common law and civil law systems, the European legislature felt unable to go so far as to harmonise the actual rules of formation for e-contracts across Europe in the ECD. Instead they chose to focus on the ordering process, and two common problem areas for B2C e-commerce: pricing errors by the merchant, and input errors by the purchaser. In essence, the ECD merely prescribes a good practice guide for how websites should set up their ordering process so as to minimise errors, and the consequences of errors, on both sides, but does not provide any answers to determining when a contract may be concluded.

---

[72] See eg C Gringras, *The Laws of the Internet* (London, Butterworths, 2003); Smith, above n 32, ch 10; Reed and Sutter, above n 7; R Brownsword and G Howells, 'When Surfers Start to Shop: Internet Commerce and Contract Law' (1999) 19 *Legal Studies* 287-315; J Savirimuthu, 'Online Contract Formation: Taking Technological Infrastructure Seriously' (2005) 2 *University of Ottawa Law and Technology Journal* 105, available online, http://www.uoltj.ca/articles/vol2.1/2005.2.1.uoltj.Savirimuthu.105-143.pdf (accessed 15 May 2008).
[73] Arts 10 (4) and 11(3) ECD.

As a result, the rules of formation of contracts online are still those of the national contract law, with some additions by the ECD. Under English law, for a contract to be valid, there must be an offer, matched by acceptance, consideration and an intention to create binding legal relations.[74] The contract is formed when offer and acceptance meet, ie *consensus in idem.*

(i) Offers and Invitations to Treat in E-contracts

An offer is defined in English law as 'a statement of willingness to contract on specified terms made with the intention that, if accepted, it shall become a binding contract'.[75] An invitation to treat, by contrast, is a preliminary communication, an opening to negotiations. Under traditional English contract law, a display of goods in the window[76] or in the shop by the shopkeeper is deemed only an invitation to treat, not an offer. In the leading case of *Pharmaceutical Society of Great Britain v Boots Cash Chemists (Southern) Ltd*[77] the Court of Appeal concluded *obiter* that the display of goods in a self-service shop was an invitation to treat not an offer. As Woodroffe and Lowe put it:

> [I]f the supplier were the offeror, then as soon as the consumer accepted the offer . . . a contract would be made. This could pose difficult if not insuperable problems for the supplier. A seller of goods would usually have limited stocks and be unable to meet an unexpected demand. Conversely, if it is the consumer who makes the offer when placing an order, the supplier will be in a position to choose whether to accept or reject it.[78]

Within the e-commerce context, a website selling goods or services can easily be equated to a shop window display or the shelves of a self-service shop, although this has not been tested in a UK court.[79] Some commentators cite the *Argos* case as confirming this interpretation, although the case settled out of court. In 1999, Argos advertised on its website television sets for sale at the price of £2.99 instead of £299. Many orders were placed but Argos refused to deliver the televisions, claiming that the advert on the website was not a legal offer but a simple invitation to treat; hence no

---

[74] For more on consideration and intention to create legal relations in the e-commerce context, see E Todd, *Gringas: The Laws of the Internet*, 3rd edn (Haywards Heath, Tottel Publishing, 2008) 47.

[75] R Duxbury, *Contract Law* (London, Sweet & Maxwell, 2008) 11.

[76] See *Fisher v Bell* [1961] 1 QB 394.

[77] [1952] 2 QB 795.

[78] R Lowe and GF Woodroffe, *Consumer Law and Practice*, 7th edn (London, Sweet & Maxwell, 2007) 83, point 6.15

[79] See eg ibid; AD Murray, 'Entering into Contracts Electronically: The Real WWW', in Edwards and Waelde, above n 49, 21. Also see amongst many others, J Adams and R Brownsword, *Understanding Contract Law*, 4th edn (London, Sweet & Maxwell, 2004) 59.

contract was formed until (or rather, unless) they accepted the customer's offer at the lower price.[80]

In continental Europe, by contrast, most legal regimes consider a website or a display of goods in a shop as an offer when it is made to consumers. This is potentially a difficulty for web traders since they have to respect the law of the country where a consumer is established under the ECD and the DSD. There is also in the UK potential for an advert to be construed as an offer,[81] although this would be very unusual. In the interest of legal certainty and avoidance of dispute, a clear definition in terms and conditions that a display of goods is an invitation to treat and not an offer may therefore be advisable as best practice, but respect for such a term by a court cannot be guaranteed as it may conceivably be seen as unfair to the consumer.[82] In practice, in non-e-mail contracts, the ECD rules discussed below go a long way to prescribing how to set up an online ordering process to avoid uncertainty.

(ii) Communication of Acceptance

For the contract to be formed, an acceptance needs to meet the offer. Acceptance determines the moment and the place[83] of formation of the contract. The principal importance of determining when the contract is concluded is that after the contract has been concluded one party cannot (without the consent of the other) alter the contractual terms or refuse to perform without incurring penalties for breach (unless the consumer has a post-contractual right to withdraw granted by the DSD). Thus many contractual disputes in practice boil down to disputes over when acceptance was communicated to the offeror, and a binding contract concluded.

(iii) E-contracts Made by E-mail

In English common law, the general rule, as in most other European jurisdictions, is that acceptance is only effective when communicated to the offeror. However, there is an important exception to this in relation to contracts concluded via the mail, known as the 'postal rule'. The postal rule is widely adopted in common law countries but rare in civilian legal

---

[80] See also A Guadamuz, 'Dell Involved in Massive Pricing Error', *TechnoLlama*, 10 July 2008, http://technollama.blogspot.com/2008/07/dell-involved-in-massive-pricing-error.html.

[81] As Wegenek comments (in R Wegenek (ed.), *E-Commerce, A Guide to the Law of Electronic Business*, 3rd edn (London, Butterworths Lexis Nexis, 2002) 13), 'it may not . . . always be appropriate to consider a website as an invitation to treat. For example, if there is a link to a database which indicates the number of products available, it may be correct to view this as an offer.' See *Carlill v Carbolic Smokeball Co* [1893] 1 QB 256.

[82] See further below, p 111.

[83] Issues relating to the place of formation of the contract lead to conflicts of law and jurisdiction, which are dealt with at length in ch 3 below, 124ff.

systems.[84] There has been much debate as to whether contracts formed by exchange of e-mails resemble postal contracts sufficiently that the postal rule should be applied. We have already mentioned that the ECD introduced rules designed to harmonise the legal understanding across Europe of when an e-contract is formed. However, these EC rules do not apply to 'contracts concluded exclusively by exchange of electronic mail'.[85] Would a contract partly concluded via the use of e-mail and partly via a website be subject to the ECD? We believe so, as this is the only logical explanation we can find for the use of the word 'exclusively'.[86]Also, as we will see, the ECD requires orders to be acknowledged, which technically requires the use of e-mails in many instances. In any case, when the contract is concluded via e-mail only, the general domestic rules on formation of contract, including potentially the postal rule, apply undisturbed by Articles 9–11 of the ECD.

The 'postal rule' under English law mandates that an acceptance communicated through the post by letter or telegram takes effect when it is handed over to the post office.[87] This is so in the strictest version of the postal rule even if the acceptance in fact never actually arrives.[88] By contrast, if the acceptance is sent by a method of instantaneous communication, such as telephone or telex, the contract is made at the time when the acceptance is received (the 'receipt rule').[89] The immediacy of instantaneous communications means the acceptor will notice if the communication is interrupted or breaks down, and can then take steps to resend it and thus secure conclusion of the contract.[90] By contrast, in the

---

[84] Although Reed points out that Spain uses it in relation to commercial though not consumer contracts. See Reed and Angel, above n 7, 202.

[85] Arts 10(4) and 11(3) ECD. In the UK, this exception was implemented in Regs 9(4) and 11(3) of the Electronic Commerce (EC Directive) Regulations 2002.

[86] Also Rec 39 ECD states that the exceptions to the provisions concerning contract concluded exclusively by e-mail or equivalent provided by this Directive, in relation to information to be provided and the placing not enable as a result, the by-passing of those provisions by providers of information society services. This seems to suggest, although it is not totally clear, that the ECD should apply if the exclusive use of e-mail is only in order to having to avoid the provisions in Arts 10 and 11 ECD.

[87] *Adams v Lindsell* (1818) 1 B&Ald 681. In *Cowan v O'Connor* (1888) 20 QBD 640, 642 Hawkins J held that if the acceptor replied to the offeror's telegram by sending a telegram, the acceptor's reply was considered to be given at the telegraph office from which the telegram was sent, ie the postal rule applied to telegrams.

[88] However, note that in English law this rule was refined and can only apply if it was reasonable to expect acceptance via this medium. See *Byrne v Van Tienhoven* (1880) 5 CPD 344.

[89] *Entores LD v Miles Far East Corporation* [1955] 2 QB 327 (CA) 334 confirmed by the House of Lords in *Brinkibon Ltd v Stahag Stahl und Stahlwarenhandelsgesellschaft mbH* [1983] 2 AC 34 (HL) 42. Interestingly, in a more recent case, *Apple Corps Ltd v Apple Computer Inc* [2004] EWHC 768 (Ch) para 37, Mann J suggested that the rule in *Entores* and *Brinkibon* should be reconsidered. Regarding instantaneous communications, he said that 'The law may have to move on and to recognise that there is nothing inherently wrong or heretical in allowing the notion of a contract made in two (or more) jurisdictions at the same time.'

[90] See Denning LJ pointing out in *Entores LD v Miles Far East Corporation* [1955] 2 QB 327 (CA) 334: 'In all instances I have taken so far, the man who sends the message of acceptance knows that it has not been received or has reason to know it. So he must repeat it.'

postal situation there is a clear delay between acceptance being posted and the offeror reading it. Traditionally, because the acceptor has done all he or she can to secure the contract, as the acceptance is now in the hands of a third party (the post office) the law takes the position that it is better to reward their expectations, and puts risk of non-arrival on the offeror, who is nonetheless bound.

There is no direct authority on the question whether communication by e-mail is governed by the instantaneous (receipt) rule or the postal rule. Based on analogy, it becomes obvious that there are arguments either side. On the one hand, e-mail resembles non-instantaneous, postal communication.[91] Hence, Murray[92] suggested that the postal rule should apply to e-mail acceptances, as they are 'neither direct, nor instantaneous and the acceptor sending his or her email does not know immediately whether or not the communication was successful'.[93]

On the other hand, an argument can also be made that e-mail should be treated as analogous to instantaneous communications[94] because no third *human* party is involved—this distinguishes e-mail from telegrams or normal post. Also, since e-mail is usually quick and only takes a few minutes or seconds to arrive, it is not unreasonable for the parties to actively acknowledge the receipt of emails.[95] Thus, if acknowledgement is requested by the acceptor but he or she does not receive a receipt e-mail back confirming acceptance has been received, he or she can make reason-

---

[91] This is because, unlike the telex or the telephone, e-mail is not direct between the parties, since messages are broken up into packets and travel through a number of computers connected to the networks, before they are reassembled at the recipient's end. Secondly, e-mails are not always instantaneous, nor are they reliable. The transport protocols underlying e-mails only provide a best effort service—instantaneous transmission is not guaranteed and the underlying protocols were not designed to confirm delivery for legal purposes. There is no sure means for the sender to detect whether or not the e-mail has reached the mailbox of the recipient (apart from the sender contacting the recipient to ask). Even where the acceptor has set his or her e-mail software to provide a delivery receipt, this in turn is not instantaneous, nor does it reveal whether or not the contents of or attachments to the message arrived in uncorrupted form or have actually been read.

[92] Murray, above n 79, 17–35, 24–25.

[93] Murray in fact withdraws this interpretation in his article in the 2005 collection, L. Edwards (ed), *The New Legal Framework for E-Commerce in Europe* (Oxford, Hart Publishing, 2005), 83, no 63. However, this was on the apparently mistaken assumption that the rules of Art 11(1) ECD would be applied to e-mail contracts, when, as noted above, Reg 11(3) of the UK ECD Regulationss makes it clear this is not to be the case.

[94] R Stone, *The Modern Law of Contract*, 5th edn (London, Cavendish, 2002) 52–54; also M Selick 'E-Contract Issues and Opportunities for the Commercial Lawyer' (2003) 16 *Banking and Finance Law Review* 1–45, 26–27.

[95] One solution would be for the parties to agree that, as a matter of standard practice, an e-mail is deemed to be received when the sender receives the recipient's acknowledgement of receipt, as in the 1996 UNCITRAL Model Law on Electronic Commerce, Art 14(3): under this provision, if a data message has been made conditional on receipt, the data message is treated as though it has never been sent until the acknowledgement is received (however, Art 14 is not concerned with contract formation—see Art 14(7)).

ably enquiries or resend while the contract remains unconcluded—all without causing much delay.

Treitel[96] suggests that electronic communications such as e-mail, website trading or fax occupy an intermediate position. According to Treitel, whether the acceptance has to reach the offeror depends in each case on whether the acceptor sending the message containing the acceptance had the means of knowing at once whether the communication was or was not successful. Treitel's intermediate position is unhelpful, however, in the majority of cases where the communication is successful and a contract is concluded and the only question is not *if* but *when* a contract was concluded.[97]

(iv) E-contracts Made Over the Web

Typically B2C contracts will be formed over the web, with very few contracts being individually negotiated. Those contracts are often referred to as standard form or adhesion contracts. Article 10(1) ECD[98] provides that in e-contracts made by 'electronic means', which excludes those formed by individual negotiation,[99] the ISSP must provide, prior to an order being placed, in a clear, comprehensible and unambiguous manner, information relating to:

(a) The different technical steps to follow to conclude the contract;
(b) Whether or not the concluded contract will be filed by the service provider and whether it will be accessible;
(c) The technical means for identifying and correcting input errors prior to the placing of the order;
(d) And the languages offered for the conclusion of the contract.

Article 10(3) ECD also requires that terms and conditions be made available to the consumer in a way that allows them to be stored or reproduced.[100]

Article 10 ECD is to be read in conjunction with Article 11 ECD which deals more precisely with the placing of an order and the procedure to correct errors. This article was controversial during its passing, and heavily criticised at the time of adoption for not providing any real certainty in the formation of e-contracts.[101] Effectively, as already noted, it leaves domestic

---

[96] G Treitel, *The Law of Contract*, 11th edn (London, Sweet & Maxwell, 2003) 26.

[97] In cases where the postal rule is applicable, Reed is of the opinion that the time of acceptance should be the time the electronic message was received by the network. See Reed and Angel, above n 7, 202.

[98] Implemented by Regulation 9 of the Electronic Commerce (EC Directive) Regulations 2002.

[99] See UK ECD Reg 9(4).

[100] ME Bundnitz, 'Consumers Surfing for Sales in Cyberspace: What Constitutes Acceptance and What Legal Terms and Conditions Bind the Consumer?' (2000) 16 *Georgia State University Law Review* 773.

[101] See, eg Ramberg, above n 7.

rules on formation in place, but adds some consumer protection requirements designed to clarify the ordering process and guarantee correction of
errors.

(v) Input Errors

According to Article 11(2) ECD, 'effective and accessible technical means'
must be provided to allow the consumer to identify and correct input
errors prior to placing the order.[102] Generally, websites implement this by
providing a summary page after the original response to the website by the
consumer, where the details provided are shown to the consumer and the
consumer is asked to confirm this is correct before proceeding. This raises
the question whether the confirmation summary by the business constitutes
a fresh offer, or whether it is the response by the consumer. Given the
degree of specificity of the summary (in English law at least) and the fact
the business has had time to check their stock levels and that the price is
the correct one on their side, the intuitive answer would seem to be in
English law that the business now makes an offer.[103] This certainly would
avoid most of the problems of mistake and formation which, as we have
seen, dog the common law as applied to web-based e-contracts, and is well
accepted in commercial practice. Note that if a consumer has failed to
notice a mistake even after the summary stage, rights to cancel will still be
available under the DSD, although not of course where the goods or
services are excluded, eg data or MP3s.

(vi) Placing the Order

Article 11(1) ECD first provides that the ISSP must 'acknowledge receipt of
the order to the consumer without undue delay and by electronic
means'.[104] Note again that the reference is to an 'order' not an offer. This
terminology is also adopted in the UK Regulations. The intention was that
in each Member State, national legislatures were able to choose when
implementing the legislation whether they defined 'order' as equating to
'offer' or merely as an invitation to treat. Thus Regulation 12 of the UK
ECReg 2002 unhelpfully states under the heading 'meaning of offer':
'Except in relation to regulation 9(1)(c) and regulation 11(1)(b), where
"order" shall be the contractual offer, "order" may be but need not be the
contractual offer for the purpose of regulation 9 and 11.' As a result, one

---

[102] Reg 11(1)(b) in the UK Regulations.
[103] In the UK, if the service provider does *not* provide means of allowing a person to identify
and correct input errors, then the consumer is entitled to rescind the contract (Reg 15, EC Reg
2002). However, the court has a discretion on request to refuse this remedy. Arguably the
remedy is of little use given its lack of knowledge by consumers.
[104] Reg 11(1)(a).

can assume that in contracts formed via websites, the website display itself can, as per ordinary UK common law, be interpreted as 'invitation to treat' in most circumstances. Thus, as Woodroffe and Lowe suggest, it is likely that the e-mail acknowledgement sent by the business as per Art 11(1) will in English law form a binding acceptance.[105] The acknowledgement may, it should be noted, take the form simply of the provision of the service requested.[106]

Given this, the next question concerns when the acknowledgement (required 'without undue delay') is received. The second part of Article 11(1) ECD confirms that an order, or acknowledgement of receipt of an order, is deemed to be received 'when the parties to whom they are addressed are able to access them'.[107] Neither the ECD nor the ECReg 2002, however, define the notion of 'access'. The formulation 'able to access' seems to suggest that the recipient need not have actually accessed the message, but merely that the message is potentially accessible, eg sitting in the recipient's e-mail inbox or on the supplier's server. If an e-mail acknowledging the order is sent and the customer does not access his e-mail immediately, eg because it is received outside work hours, the moment of formation of the contract can still, it is asserted, be presumed to be the time the e-mail was received into the recipient's personal mailbox. It would not seem reasonable for the purchaser to be able to delay the conclusion of a binding contract indefinitely by merely refusing to read his or her e-mail. On the other hand, what if delivery of the e-mail is delayed involuntarily, eg because the e-mail goes into a spam filter operated by an employer? Smith suggests that it is possible a contract is never formed in such circumstances, but wonders if a court would find this reasonable.[108]

Regrettably, despite funding research programmes aimed at harmonising consumer contract law across the EU,[109] the Commission has so far declined to amend the general principles of contract law to create a uniform regime on formation of e-contracts. The pDCR, which might have been a venue for such harmonisation, was published in advance of the Draft Common Frame of Reference, where it would have been natural to wait for the final results of that major study, which does inter alia reconsider contract rules in the context of e-commerce. Instead, therefore, the pDCR as introduced maintains the rules of the ECD[110] and reform of the

---

[105] Woodroffe and Lowe, above n 78, 85, point 6.20.

[106] Art 11(1).

[107] This is in essence a version of the traditional receipt rule discussed above, as opposed to the postal rule discussed in the contexct of contracts made by e-mail.

[108] See Smith et al, above n 32, para 10-088.

[109] See Study Group on a European Civil Code/Research Group on EC Private Law (Acquis Group) (eds), *Principles, Definitions and Model Rules of European Private Law, Draft Common Frame of Reference (DCFR)* (Munich, Sellier, 2009).

[110] See Rec 25 which states the rules of the pDCR are without prejudice to Arts 9 and 1, and Art 3 pDCR.

ECD itself seems currently to be indefinitely on hold. It thus seems the uncertainties of Article 11 are likely to persist for some time.

B. Incorporation of Terms and Unfair Terms in E-contracts

The Unfair Terms in Consumer Contracts Directive (UTCCD),[111] implemented in the UK by the Unfair Terms in Consumer Contracts Regulations 1999 (UTCCR)[112] provides protection from unfair terms that have not been individually negotiated[113] in contracts concluded between a business and a consumer. Any terms found to be unfair will not be binding on the consumer. The control of unfair terms in most common law countries began with the doctrine of incorporation of terms, where judges in the absence of statute found onerous terms not to be incorporated into contracts and thus unenforceable against weaker parties. Generally in this doctrine a single unfair term can be excluded and the contract still stand. Incorporation of contract terms in the online environment again raises particular problems, a matter again not harmonised in the EU or globally and thus dealt with again solely by national contract law.

(i) Online Incorporation of Terms: Click-wrap, Browse-wrap, Web-wrap

In the UK, for terms to have any legal effect, they must be incorporated into the contract. This can occur in two ways. First, incorporation can occur by signature indicating acceptance of the terms and conditions by the signatories. While e-signatures, as we have seen, exist, this is still uncommon in e-contracts. The importance of signature is that the UK courts have held that all terms of the contract signed are incorporated, even if the signatory never read them or had them specifically pointed out.[114] In the absence of a signature, incorporation requires showing a court that the terms were brought to the attention of the buyer. Three methods (other than signature) are commonly used online to incorporate terms into contracts made on or via websites: 'click-wrap', 'browse-wrap'[115] and 'web-wrap'.[116] Smith defines these methods as follows:

---

111 Council Directive 93/13/EEC of 5 April 1993 on Unfair Terms in Consumer Contracts OJ L 95/29, 21.04.1993.

112 SI 1999/2083.

113 Under Reg 5(4), it is for the seller or supplier who claims that a term was individually negotiated to show that it was. In B2C contracts, there is therefore a presumption that terms are not negotiated but rather imposed by the supplier.

114 See *L'Estrange v F Graucob Ltd* [1934] 2 KB 394.

115 See also S Hedley, *The Law of Electronic Commerce and the Internet in the UK and Ireland* (London, Cavendish, 2006) 247.

116 The terminology employing the 'wrap' expression originates with software licenses, at a time when software was still mainly distributed on permanent media such as floppy disks or later CD-ROMs, rather than over the Internet. The permanent media (eg CD-ROMs) were wrapped

'[C]lick-wrap' means that positive assent to the displayed terms (eg by an 'I agree' button) is required. 'Browse-wrap' means that the terms are accessible via a hypertext link. 'Web-wrap' denotes a notice attempting to make entry into and further use of the website conditional on posted terms and conditions.[117]

Despite an absence of UK case-law, the validity of click-wrap methods of acceptance is well accepted as equivalent to incorporation of terms by signature. The US case of *Moore v Microsoft Corporation*[118] found that the use of an 'I agree' button could and did create legal obligations.

However, 'browse-wrap' and 'web-wrap' are more controversial. The idea that conditions can be imposed on someone simply because they have browsed a website and even acquired goods or services, but made no positive indication of intent to be bound by site conditions merely available on the website, remains doubtful, at least in the UK and Europe. Some guidance may be drawn from non-electronic cases, involving standard form contracts which were not signed—these often involve tickets issued in return for payment, with the difficulty arising as to whether the ticket is a mere receipt or a contractual document incorporating terms by reference. In *Thornton v Shoe Lane Parking*,[119] the ticket issued by an automated machine at the entry to a car park stated that customers should refer to the terms and conditions displayed on the premises. The Court of Appeal held that these terms were not incorporated by reference because the car park owner had not done enough to bring the terms in question to the attention of the customer. Terms on the wall within the car park were furthermore not incorporated because they were only visible after the contract had been made, ie when the ticket was taken by the driver. More recently, in *Interfoto Picture Library Ltd v Stiletto Visual Programmes Ltd*,[120] the Court of Appeal held that a particularly onerous or unusual term which would not generally be known to the other party would require the party relying on it to show that it had been brought fairly to the other party's attention.

In the US some courts have discussed this issue. In *Specht v Netscape Communications Corporation*,[121] the Court of Appeal (2nd Circuit) considered the validity of an arbitration clause contained in a software license for software downloaded from the Internet. Multiple users downloaded a piece of software by merely clicking a 'download' button on the webpage. Before the start of the download, users were not otherwise required to explicitly assent to any terms and conditions. Terms were, however,

in clear plastic packaging and according to the vendors, opening the packaging was deemed to indicate acceptance of the terms of the license by conduct; hence the use of the idiom 'shrink-wrap' licenses.

[117] Smith, above n 32, 821.
[118] NY Sup Ct App Div 2nd Dept, 15 April 2002.
[119] [1971] 2 QB 163.
[120] [1988] 2 WLR 615.
[121] Docket No 01-7860, US Court of Appeal, 2nd Cir, 1 October 2002.

available to see if the user scrolled down to the next screen and clicked on a link, which purported to require the user to review the terms and conditions of the software license agreement before downloading. Judge Sotomayor held the terms not incorporated and the browse-wrap agreement not enforceable, because the users

> could not have learned of the existence of those terms unless, prior to executing the download, they had scrolled down the web page to a screen located below the download button. . . . A reasonably prudent Internet user in circumstances such as these would not have known or learned of the existence of the license terms before responding to an invitation to download the free software, and the defendant therefore did not provide reasonable notice of the license terms.[122]

By contrast, however, in *Ticketmaster Corp v Tickets.com Inc*,[123] the court held that a binding contract was formed where a prominent notice on the homepage explained that further use of the website was subject to the terms and conditions of use. In the UK, there is little guidance and it appears an explicit registration process is better for legal certainty of the business, even if slightly more cumbersome for users. In the meantime, however, consumer litigation as to incorporation of terms has become uncommon in the EU, and may well have been replaced by the alternative strategy of complaining that a term is unfair and should therefore not be enforced.

(ii) Unfair Terms

As already noted, almost all B2C e-contracts are not the result of negotiation. The consumer is typically presented with a standard form contract, on a 'take it or leave it' basis, and small print may hide a multiplicity of sins. Accordingly, regulations such as the UTCCD assert that 'acquirers of goods and services should be protected against the abuse of power by the seller or supplier, in particular against one-sided standard contracts and the unfair exclusion of essential rights in contracts'.

The UTCCR implement the UTCCD in the UK and under Regulation 5, a term is 'regarded as unfair if, contrary to the requirements of good faith, it causes a significant imbalance in the parties' rights and obligations arising under the contract, to the detriment of the consumer'.

First, the term needs to cause a significant imbalance between the parties, to the detriment of the consumer. Schedule 2 contains an indicative and non-exhaustive list of the terms, which may be regarded as unfair.[124] This includes terms protecting the trader from claims a consumer would

---

[122] Ibid, 20.
[123] CD Cal, 7 March 2003.
[124] Reg 5(5).

ordinarily expect to be able to make, such as ouster clauses.[125] Courts must still, however, assess a particular term on a case-by-case basis to decide whether or not it creates a significant imbalance. Under Regulation 6, the

> unfairness of a contractual term is assessed taking into account the nature of the goods or services for which the contract was concluded and by referring, at the time of the conclusion of the contract, to all the circumstances attending the conclusion of the contract and to all the other terms of the contract or of another contract on which it is dependant.

In an e-commerce environment the transparency of the process to the consumer is thus also important. Terms must be expressed in plain and intelligible language or the supplier risk the term be interpreted against him under Regulation 7.[126] Many websites now display 'privacy policies'—terms and conditions relating to what personal data can be collected from users and how it can be used—but in a manner that is clear, brief and comprehensible at least compared to the usual legalese.[127] Such plain language campaigns may yet impact on judicial views in the UK, as well as being clearly important to rulings by the Information Commissioner.

Second, the term needs to be contrary to the requirement of good faith. Commentators agree that the concept of good faith, whilst familiar to continental lawyers, is a relatively new concept for English lawyers.[128] Good faith involves fair dealing and the absence of 'sharp practice' according to Lord Bingham in the case of *Interfoto Picure Library Ltd v Stiletto Visual Programmes Ltd*.[129] Lord Bingham further refined the definition of 'good faith' in the case of *Director of Fair Trading v First National Bank Plc*[130] and noted that 'good faith in this context is not an artificial or technical concept; nor . . . is it a concept wholly unfamiliar to British lawyers. It looks to good standards of commercial morality and practice.'[131] The requirement of good faith is one of fair and open dealing. This dictates that the professional must behave in a way that enables the consumer to make a well-informed choice, having knowledge of the terms of the contract and what they imply. Any behaviour by which a business tries to camouflage terms in small print or lose it in a jungle of hyperlinks

---

125 Howell and Weatherill, above n 40, 281.

126 For more on those obligations and how they apply in the UK, see OFT, 'IT Consumer Contracts Made at a Distance, Guidance on Compliance with the Distance Selling and Unfair Terms in Consumer Contracts Regulations', December 2005, OFT 672.

127 See ICO consultation and draft Code of Practice on Privacy Notices, available on ICO website as at 29 May 2009, http://www.ico.gov.uk.

128 Woodroffe and Lowe, above n 78, 166; Howell and Weatherill, above n 40, 285.

129 [1988] 2 WLR 615, 620.

130 [2002] 1 AC 481 (HL). Note that this case was decided against the backdrop of the 1994 Regulations and not the 1999 Regulations, but this makes little difference and the case is still good law.

131 *The Director General of Fair Trading v First National Bank* [2002] 1 AC 481 (HL) para 17.

may be interpreted as contrary to the principle of good faith in the light of the above case-law.

The pDCR departs radically from the present Directive in that the indicative list of unfair terms is replaced by two new lists: a blacklist of terms that are unfair in all circumstances, and a greylist of terms presumed (as in the current Schedule) to be unfair.[132] The blacklist may be particularly useful for consumers fighting against compulsory arbitration and jurisdiction clauses which exclude the courts, as well as unfair choice of law, all common in online B2C contracts and on the blacklist. A large number of Member States already use such a device. The pDCR also strengthens the powers of consumer associations to fight on behalf of consumers in the courts. Currently, in the UK, it is primarily up to consumers themselves to litigate, despite the OFT being mandated to seek rulings under the Enterprise Act 2002.[133] In future the pDCR may require that representative action be opened up to any persons and organisations having a legitimate interest under national law. Such provision is already in place in France and has proved an effective guardian of the public interest, eg leading in 2007 to the removal of a number of clauses from AOL's Internet access contracts.[134]

C. Information and Transparency Requirements

Information and transparency requirements are imposed under the ECD, as we have already seen, in Articles 5 and 10, and under the DSD in Articles 4 and 5, respectively. As Winn and Haubold note, 'more concern could have been given to the information duties themselves of which the Electronic Commerce Directive and the Distance Selling Directive make an almost inflationary use. The lists of information duties in both Directives are long and not very well harmonised.'[135] One point to be noted is that the Directives have different targets. The ECD refers to all transactions involving information society service providers, whereas the more demanding list of requirements in the DSD is there specifically to protect consumers.

(i) Article 5 ECD

Article 5 ECD requires the provision of information concerning the identity and geographical address of the provider, contact details, any professional identification and/or authorisation (such as trade register number, super-

[132] J Stuyck, 'Unfair terms', in Howells and Schulze (eds), above n 28, 144.
[133] Part 8.
[134] See Cour de Cassation, 1ère civ, 8 novembre 2007, société AOL c/ associations UFC-Que choisir, AFA
[135] Winn and Haubold, above n 21, 577.

visory authority, professional body, VAT registration as appropriate). The European Court of Justice (ECJ) in the case of *Bundesverband v Deutsche Internet Versicherung AG*[136] considered Article 5(1)(c) ECD which requires that consumers receive in addition to the name and geographical address of the provider, the 'details of the service provider, including his electronic mail address, which allow him to be contacted rapidly and communicated with in a direct and effective manner'. In this case, Deutsche Internet Versicherung AG (DIV), an automobile insurance company, dealt exclusively on the Internet, and like many such enterprises did not provide a telephone number for consumers to use. Instead, an online enquiry form was provided, enabling customers to ask questions about the products and services. After detailed analysis, the ECJ concluded that

> [A]rticle 5(1)(c) must be interpreted as meaning that a service provider is required to supply recipients of the service, before the conclusion of a contract with them, in addition to its electronic email address, other information which allows the service provider to be contacted rapidly and communicated with in a direct and effective manner.

However, this information did not necessarily have to be a telephone number, and could be met by the electronic enquiry template the business in question provided, so long as the requirements of rapidity and effectiveness were met. If a customer who had made contact by Internet originally, subsequently found himself without electronic access, then it also had to be possible to request access to another, non-electronic, means of communication.

This decision raises a number of problems. First, how quickly must a question sent by electronic form be answered? In the German case, the norm was 30–60 minutes. Should only normal office hours 'count' or can a business take longer to answer queries out of hours? It was also left unclear if acknowledging the receipt of an enquiry and then replying within a reasonable period would be acceptable. Second, the ECJ's requirement of a non-electronic direct and effective means of communication risks placing a heavy financial burden on web-only businesses. Overall, the decision risks putting businesses that operate purely online at a disadvantage, but from a purely consumer protection perspective it should be welcomed.[137]

---

[136] Bundesverband der Vebraucherzentralen und Verbraucherverbände—Verbraucherzentrale *Bundesverband v Deutsche Internet Versicherung* AG ECJ Case C-298-/07, 16 October 2008.

[137] For a more precise account of this decision and its implication, see C Riefa, 'Bundesverband der Vebraucherzentralen und Verbraucherverbände—Verbraucherzentrale *Bundesverband v Deutsche Internet Versicherung* AG ECJ Case C-298-/07, 16 October 2008' (2008) 8(4) *E-Commerce Law Reports* 6–7; also see J Hörnle, 'Contact! The ECJ Sets e-Commerce Obligations' (2008–09) 19(5) *Society for Computers and Law*.

(ii) Information Requirements under Articles 4 and 5 DSD

Article 4 DSD is implemented in the UK in Regulation 7 of the Consumer Protection (Distance Selling) Regulations 2000. This Regulation requires that prior to the conclusion of the contract, the identity of the provider as well as its physical address be communicated to the consumer. The reason for this is that anonymity provides in many instances a shelter for fraudsters to use e-contracts to defraud users, creating distrust.[138] Regrettably, many sites still do not provide all of the most basic information essential to consumers. Indeed, an OFT web sweep revealed that 14 per cent of sites still do not provide a physical address, whilst in their previous online shopping survey, the OFT found that one-fifth of surveyed sites even failed to provide an e-mail address, contrary to Regulation 6 of the Electronic Commerce (EC Directive) Regulation 2002 (Article 5 ECD).[139]

Regulation 7 of the DSReg 2000 also requires the business to disclose the price of the goods or service, including all taxes and delivery costs where appropriate, but also information about the arrangements for payment, delivery or performance, the length of time the offer remains valid, duration of contract, and the right to withdraw from the contract.[140]

Here again compliance is an issue. For example, the OFT survey revealed that 40 per cent of sites were not fully transparent about their pricing,[141] adding extra charges at the checkout stage, when the consumer is already committed to the purchase and unlikely to back out of the purchase despite being unhappy about the additional hidden charges. This trend was confirmed by the European Commission's survey into airline sites, which revealed that one of the main problems related to 'insufficient or unclear information about price, where the price is split into a series of diverse charges, and only becomes clear at the end of the booking process'.[142] As a result of this, Article 23(1) of Regulation 1008/2008 on common rules for the operation air services in the Community[143] forces air

---

[138] See earlier discussion at p 96 of the difficulty of identifying a B2C transaction in the pseudonymous environment of eBay and other online auction sites.

[139] OFT, Web Sweep Analysis, March 2008, OFT982.

[140] For a more detailed exposé of the rules concerning pre-contractual information in distance sales, see A Nordhausen, 'Distance Marketing in the European Union', in L Edwards (ed), *The New Legal Framework for e-Commerce in Europe* (Oxford, Oxford University Press, 2005) 239–76.

[141] OFT, above n 139.

[142] Out-law.com, above n 18

[143] OJ (2008) L293/3. This article states: 'Air fares and air rates available to the general public shall include the applicable conditions when offered or published in any form, including on the Internet, for air services from an airport located in the territory of a Member State to which the Treaty applies. The final price to be paid shall at all times be indicated and shall include the applicable air fare or air rate as well as all applicable taxes, and charges, surcharges and fees which are unavoidable and foreseeable at the time of publication. In addition to the indication of the final price, at least the following shall be specified: (a) air fare or air rate; (b) taxes; (c) airport charges; and (d) other charges, surcharges or fees, such as those related to security or fuel; where the items listed under (b), (c) and (d) have been added to the air fare or air rate. Optional

services operators to disclose air fares and rates in a more transparent manner. (This was not included in the DSD as it excludes air travel and package travel.) Note, however, that an equivalent requirement in Article 5(2) ECD does exist, requiring that prices be indicated clearly and unambiguously and, in particular, inclusive of tax and delivery costs.

(iii) Impact of the pDCR on Information Requirements

If the pDCR proposal survives in its current wording, already existing information obligations are mainly retained but Article 5 ECD will be applied to all types of consumer contracts caught by the proposal, ie distance contracts as well as 'doorstep' contracts. This may create awkward clashes, since under Article 10(1) ECD, at present, the information needs to be provided 'prior to the order being placed', whereas under the pDCR the information only needs to be given before the actual conclusion of the contract. As Nordausen Scholes notes, this may still only further complicate the already messy regulation of e-contracts. Problems may also arise from the ECD being a minimum harmonisation directive while the pDCR will be a full (maximum) harmonisation directive. Since even now a large proportion of cross-border consumer contracts are e-contracts, with further growth predicted, incoherence between distance and e-contract regimes should be avoided.[144]

Nordhausen Scholes also notes that 'a chronological view shows that the information obligations in the consumer protection directives have become more and more detailed and more and more demanding as time has gone on'.[145] But is this really helping consumers?[146] Many websites deliver an overdose of contractual terms and information, overwhelming consumers rather than empowering them.[147] Winn and Haubold[148] also comment that the information overflow may well result in the contrary effect that con-

---

price supplements shall be communicated in a clear, transparent and unambiguous way at the start of any booking process and their acceptance by the customer shall be on an "opt-in" basis.'

[144] A Nordausen Scholes, 'Information requirements', in Howells and Schulze (eds), above n 28, 222–23.

[145] Ibid, 213.

[146] See Pew Internet & American Life project, 'Online Shopping: Internet Users Like the Convenience but Worry about the Security of their Financial Information', 13 February 2008, available online at www.pewinternet.org (accessed 11 March 2008), which indicates that 32 per cent of shoppers have been confused by information they have found online during their shopping or research and that 30 per cent have felt overwhelmed by the amount of information they have found online during shopping or research.

[147] See V Gautrais, 'La formation des contrats en ligne', in D Poulin et al (eds), *Guide juridique du commerçant électronique* (Montréal, Thémis, 2003) 143–64. One remarkable example is that of eBay, the online auction site, where so many policies, terms and guide documents exists that even the most versed lawyers end up literally lost.

[148] Winn and Haubold, above n 21.

sumers do not read any of the information provided.[149] Whilst technology has allowed the communication of more information to the consumer, it has to be asked if it really enables consumers to make better informed choices or if a smaller selection of truly vital data would be better.[150]

D. Right to Withdraw and Other Issues

Article 6 DSD provides consumers with a right to cancel contracts concluded at a distance within seven days, with some exceptions. The pDCR intends to set the cooling-off period at a flat 14 days to increase harmonisation across the Single Market, thus doubling the statutory limit in the UK. The key problem here for the e-commerce market is that the right to cancel does not currently apply to digital goods such as software, computer games, music, e-books or data. Such products cannot be returned once downloaded, clearly for fear that such items would merely be copied and then returned.[151] Nonetheless the market itself seems to have developed consumer-friendly norms, eg offering partly functional free trial periods for software and some games, but this does not apply to all types of digital goods. Problems may also occur with 'hybrid goods', eg a mobile broadband pay-as-you-go modem, which comes for sale only if bundled with some megabytes of data. If purchased at a distance, the right to cancel and return the modem within seven days in the UK is clear, but no such right exists in respect of the bundled data and, in practice, obtaining a refund may be difficult. Regrettably the pDCR does not bring any changes, although some were mooted at an early stage, and software still remains unreturnable.

Online auctions are also a problem. The DSD excludes 'auctions' from its scope but does not define the term. Such lack of precision has led some Member States to classify eBay and similar sites as an 'auction' and others not. Such differences in interpretation have impacted widely on the protection that consumers buying cross-border may obtain. For example, a consumer buying on eBay in France will currently be protected by the Directive with a right to withdraw, whilst a consumer in Estonia will also be protected but unable to withdraw. For a consumer in the UK there is much controversy as to whether or not she would be protected at all.[152]

---

[149] See also CP Gillette, 'Pre-approved Contracts for Internet Commerce' (2005–06) 42 *Houston Law Review* 975.

[150] Note that in 'mobile contracts' where a very limited space of 140 characters is available, the pDCR is prepared to reduce the information that needs to be provided to the bare essentials.

[151] Art 6(3) DSD. In the UK, see Reg 13(d): 'Unless the parties have agreed otherwise, the consumer will not have the right to cancel the contract . . . in respect of contracts—(d) for the supply of audio or video recordings or computer software if they are unsealed by the consumer.'

[152] For more on this question, see C Riefa, 'To Be or Not To Be an Auctioneer? Some Thoughts

The pDCR, in its current wording, strikes out the right to withdraw from online auctions altogether. This has been described as a dangerous and unjustified erosion of consumer rights, which seems unlikely to foster confidence in cross-border e-commerce.[153]

Another problem is the fact that the right to cancel is unknown to many consumers[154] and is not, in any case, well applied by businesses. In the UK, the OFT Web Sweep[155] found that 15 per cent of sites were not complying with DSReg 2000 Regulations 7(1)(a)(vi) which requires that the retailer informs the consumer of the right to cancel. In addition, the survey found that 31 per cent of surveyed sites did not refund the full cost of goods cancelled.[156] Admittedly, UK Regulation 14(5) allows a charge to be applied to the return of goods, but it cannot exceed the direct costs of recovering any goods supplied. The rules as to withdrawal are maintained in the pDCR and one can only hope that e-businesses will become more compliant.

III. CONCLUSION

As we have seen, the regulatory approach to consumer e-contracts is confused. Many different pieces of legislation are involved with with different definitions of key concepts such as 'consumer'. Because the ECD adopted a minimum harmonisation approach, national implementations have been diverse, creating disparities in the internal market. However, despite many scope issues, the provisions on validity of e-contracts have been largely successful in creating a framework in which e-commerce could develop.

Nevertheless the substantive rules applicable to consumer e-contracts are not fully satisfactory. We regret in particular that the ECD does not go further to provide a blueprint for the formation of e-contracts across the EU. The patchwork of Directives has not, in our view, worked sufficiently well to foster strong consumer confidence in electronic commerce, nor are they well enforced nationally. Clearly the Commission agrees with this view and the change of tactics to full targeted harmonisation indicates an awareness of the need to encourage consumer trust in cross-border transactions.

We are now entering a phase where e-commerce has attained a certain maturity. It is time to prepare a regulatory environment fit for purpose in

on the Legal Nature of Online "eBay" Auctions and the Protection of Consumers' (2008) 31 *Journal of Consumer Policy* 167–94; C Riefa 'A Dangerous Erosion of Consumer rights: The Absence of a Right to Withdraw from Online Auctions', in Howells and Schulze (eds), above n 28, 175–87.

153 Ibid.
154 'Internet Shopping: An OFT Market Study', Annex H, OFT, June 2007. This survey shows that 56 per cent of Internet shoppers surveyed online did not know about their right to cancel.
155 OFT, above n 139, 20–28.
156 Ibid.

the twenty-first century. The pDCR could provide a useful staging post for this. Dismayingly though, it ignores issues pertaining to software down-loaded from the Internet, excludes online auctions from the right to withdraw and ignores new forms of e-contracts concluded in virtual environments. As a result, we doubt the pDCR can in its current version achieve the anticipated results. We can only hope that the negotiations that are now to take place on this instrument can lead to a more workable framework for the future.

3

The Jurisdictional Challenge of the Internet

JULIA HÖRNLE

THE INTERNET IS, in its essence, a global network of connections. As discussed throughout this volume, it has lead to a massive increase in international contacts and contracts, for consumers and businesses alike, and hence multiplied the opportunities for cross-border disputes and conflicts. Once cross-border litigation was only of relevance to multi-national businesses; now ordinary consumers routinely find themselves embroiled everyday in transnational online disputes—when an eBay sale by a Welsh housewife to a purchaser in the US goes wrong, or a purchase from Amazon by an English consumer fails to arrive, or a Scottish laptop is infected with viruses after the download of a free game offered by a Finnish promoter. But are the rules of cross-border litigation, and the courts themselves, up to scratch to facilitate the resolution of such disputes?

The function of this chapter is to show that cross-border litigation and enforcement is so expensive and time consuming that access to redress by conventional court-based means is effectively barred for all but the largest claims (and the wealthiest litigants). For small claims, the costs and delay of cross-border litigation are frequently entirely disproportionate to the remedy potentially obtainable.

There are essentially three reasons for the high costs and delay:

- the complexity of jurisdictional rules, which complicate the finding of the appropriate available forum;
- cross-border enforcement (where necessary); and
- other cross-border aspects (such as the application of foreign law, and the need for translation).

This chapter will discuss these issues in turn, with the main emphasis on the complexity of jurisdictional rules. As this chapter will demonstrate in detail, the application of conventional jurisdictional rules to Internet disputes is enormously complex, unpredictable and uncertain, often because jurisdictional rules are based on territorial connecting factors—such as the place of performance of a contract, or the place where a tort occurs—that are highly ambiguous in Internet-related cases.

Furthermore, even if a judgment is obtained, getting damages out of a foreign defendant will usually require cross-border enforcement. This is likely to involve extra procedures, with associated costs and delay. Differences between national approaches also mean that successful claimants may still be unable to have foreign judgments enforced against defendants' assets, introducing an element of unpredictability. For example, in the US, strong constitutional protection of freedom of speech may mean that UK judgments for damages in defamation cases might not always be enforced. Finally, other cross-border aspects, such as discovering and proving what foreign law says if it is the applicable law, translation, the need to hire several legal advisors or advocates, and travelling, add further expense and delay. In practice, indeed, in many cross-border disputes the real struggle is over jurisdiction, and issues of substance are far less often litigated, with the loser on jurisdiction often then agreeing to settle.

This chapter concludes that international litigation is thus unsuitable for solving disputes in many small-value Internet disputes, and that better solutions are required if consumers are to have effective access to redress in the digital age.[1]

I. JURISDICTIONAL RULES AND THE INTERNET: PROBLEMS

Many authors have suggested that traditional jurisdictional rules are not suitable for internet cross-border disputes. For example, Burnstein points out that:

> Where activities occur—or, more precisely, where we deem them to have occurred—answers the traditional questions of jurisdiction and choice of law under conventional private international law analysis. But where activities occur might not be the right inquiry for private international law in Internet law disputes. I propose that we adapt private international law to the realities of the Internet.[2]

Perritt adds that:

> Traditional dispute resolution machinery depends on localization to determine jurisdiction. Impediments to localization [on the Internet] create uncertainty and controversy over assertions of jurisdiction. That uncertainty has two results. It may frustrate communities that resent being unable to reach through their legal

---

[1] See eg online dispute-resolution procedures, such as those offered by the Disputer (www. disputer.com).

[2] M Burnstein, 'A Global Network in a Compartmentalised Legal Environment', in K Boele-Woelki and C Kessedjian (eds), *Internet: Which Court Decides? Which Law Applies?* (The Hague, Kluwer, 1998) 23–34, 27.

machinery to protect local victims against conduct occurring in a far-off country. It also subjects anyone using the Internet to jurisdiction by any of nearly 200 countries in the world and, in many cases, to their subordinate political units.[3]

FA Mann recognised this problem as far back as 1964. He wrote that modern communications technology and cross-border media (referring to telephone, teleprinter, television and international advertising) meant that it was increasingly difficult to localise facts, events or relationships. He pointed out that the distribution of content across a multitude of countries might mean that territorial connecting factors were too readily satisfied, and would generate dissatisfaction with the rigidity of present rules.[4] These deficiencies (and dissatisfaction) have grown with the use of the Internet for global transactions and interactions.

II. THE RULES OF JURISDICTION: COMMON LAW AND BRUSSELS REGULATION RULES

Rules on jurisdiction (determining a court's competence) are not international law, but part of the domestic laws of civil procedure in each national legal system.[5] Hence, they differ from jurisdiction to jurisdiction.[6] Rules of jurisdiction, choice of law and enforcement taken together are sometimes known as conflicts of laws, or international private law.

In the EU (and the European Free Trade Area), there has been substantial harmonisation of rules on jurisdiction in civil and commercial matters in the Brussels Regulation (formerly, Convention).[7] This is on the basis of the competency contained in Article 65 of the EC Treaty on judicial co-operation in civil matters having cross-border implications. There has also been similar harmonisation in relation to the rules on choice of law in contracts ('Rome I')[8] and torts ('Rome II').[9]

In England and Wales, domestic rules, codified in the Civil Procedure Rules (CPR)[10] still govern jurisdictional disputes between English domiciliaries and non-EU domiciliaries, as well as purely domestic disputes. By contrast, however, disputes between English domiciliaries and EU domiciliaries must be determined by the harmonised Brussels Regulation

---

[3] H Perritt, 'Dispute Resolution in Cyberspace: Demand for New Forms of ADR' (2000) 15 *Ohio State Journal on Dispute Resolution* 675–703, 675–76.

[4] FA Mann, 'The Doctrine of Jurisdiction in International Law' (1964-I) 111 *Recueil des Cours* 9–158, 36–37.

[5] Mann, ibid, 9, 19; P North and J Fawcett, *Cheshire and North's Private International Law*, 13th edn (London, Butterworths, 1999) 13–14.

[6] Ibid, 9ff.

[7] Council Regulation EC/44/2001 on Jurisdiction and the Recognition and Enforcement of Judgments in Civil and Commercial Matters of 22 December 2000, [2001] OJ L12, 1–23; replacing the Brussels Convention on Jurisdiction and the Enforcement of Judgments in Civil and Commercial Matters of 27 September 1968 and the Lugano Convention on Jurisdiction and the Enforcement of Judgments in Civil and Commercial Matters of 16 September 1988.

rules. These were implemented into England and Wales by the Civil Jurisdiction and Judgments Act 1982 (CJJA).

In Scotland, the process of implementation of Brussels went even further and even wholly domestic actions, and actions between Scottish domiciliaries and non-EU domiciliaries, are governed by Brussels rules,[11] as well, of course, as actions between Scots and EU domiciliaries (including domiciliaries of other UK legal systems).

The following sections look at English law, and the harmonised EU rules, in relation to disputes about contracts and torts. The aim is to illustrate the twin problems of localising Internet interactions and determining and limiting the reach of a particular activity on the Internet. There is a greater focus on torts than on contracts, as in contracts the issue of jurisdiction is more frequently resolved by an express jurisdiction clause in the contract (a 'choice-of-forum' clause). Such clauses are usually accepted by the courts[12] subject to important special rules[13] in relation to some consumer contracts.

Because of lack of space, we will focus on jurisdiction, and only briefly look at applicable law. In particular, we will look at the consumer protection provisions of the Rome I Regulation, since they are significant in the promotion of trust in business-to-consumer (B2C) e-commerce, and their recent reform has been highly contested. We will also look very briefly at the new EC Regulation on applicable law in non-contractual obligations ('Rome II').[14]

III. CONTRACT DISPUTES

In the absence of an express choice-of-forum clause in the contract, whether jurisdiction falls under EU law (the 'Brussels Regulation') or English law (the 'common law' or CPR rules), an English court must have a ground for assuming jurisdiction. We examine some of the grounds commonly pleaded below.

A. Contract Made within the Jurisdiction

One of the common law grounds for serving a non-EU defendant with a

---

[8] Regulation (EC) No 593/2008 of 17 June 2008, OJ L177/6, 4 July 2008, replacing the Rome Convention on the Law Applicable to Contractual Obligations of 26 January 1998, OJ C027/34.

[9] Regulation (EC) No 864/2007 on the Law Applicable to Non-contractual Obligations ('Rome II') of 11 July 2007, OJ L199/40, 31 July 2007.

[10] CPR Part 6, para 3.1

[11] Civil Jurisdiction and Judgements Act 1982, Sched 8.

[12] Art 23 of the Jurisdiction Regulation EC/44/2001 and CPR 6.20(5)(d).

[13] Arts 8–14 (insurance), 15–17 (consumers) and 18–21 (employment contracts).

[14] Above, n 9.

claim from outside the jurisdiction is that the contract was made within the jurisdiction.[15] Sometimes it may be disputed where and when the contract was concluded. If a contract is made via letter by parties situated in different countries, then in English law, the so-called postal rule applies, and the contract is usually deemed formed when and at the place where the letter of acceptance is posted.[16] However, if the contract has been concluded via electronic communication, it is not always as clear where the contract was made. This matter is dealt with in detail in chapter 2.

B. Place of Performance of Contractual Obligation, or Place of Breach of Contract

Further grounds for assuming jurisdiction of English domestic rules are the place where the contractual obligation should have been performed, or the place where the breach of contract has occurred. It is often difficult to define where these occur in Internet cases.

Under the CPR, service out of the jurisdiction is also permissible where the claim is in respect of a breach of contract committed within England and Wales.[17] Real problems about localising the place of a contractual dispute also frequently occur under Brussels Regulation rules.

Brussels Regulation: Contract Rules

Under the Brussels Regulation, in principle, disputes are to be heard in the courts of the domicile of the defendant.[18] However, this basic rule is amended by special rules in numerous cases, including in disputes arising out of contracts, which allow for additional grounds of jurisdiction. The special rules for all contractual cases are found primarily in Article 5; however, further special and crucial rules relating to consumer contracts only are found in Articles 15–17.

Under Article 5(1)(a) of the Brussels Regulation,[19] under the special jurisdiction rules for contract, a court may accept jurisdiction if the place of performance of the contract giving rise to the dispute was in the forum. Article 5(1)(b) clarifies that for the sale of goods, this is the place where the goods have been, or should have been, delivered; and for services, that it is place where the services have been, or should have been, provided.

---

[15] CPR 6.20(5)(a).
[16] L Collins, *Dicey, Morris & Collins The Conflict of Laws*, 14th edn (London, Sweet & Maxwell, 2006) 377.
[17] CPR 6.20(6).
[18] Art 2(1)
[19] Above, n 6.

However it is often difficult to determine the exact place of performance for the obligation under an e-commerce contract.

As an illustration, imagine a contract where a company buys software by way of download. Imagine that the provider of the software is a company incorporated and domiciled in France, the recipient a person domiciled in Luxembourg, who uses an Internet service provider (ISP) domiciled in Belgium. The server hosting the software for downloading is located in Ireland. There are (at least) four arguable possibilities for the place of performance of the contract.

- *The location of the server which hosts the material being downloaded.* In such a situation, it could be argued that since the contractual obligation is to make available the software, this has been performed in Ireland. However, this could be completely arbitrary, and with no obvious connection to either party, and might be moved from time to time. It is thus not an ideal legal connecting factor.
- *The provider's domicile.* Since it is from this location that the provider creates and uploads the software onto the server to make it accessible, arguably this may be regarded as the place of performance of the contract (France) under Article 5(1) of the Brussels Regulation.
- *The location of the recipient's ISP.* Since the recipient's browser sends the request for the software and the software is initially received on a server of the recipient's access provider, it could be argued that this is the place of performance (Belgium).
- *The location of the recipient's desktop computer,* since this is the location to which he actually downloads the software (Luxembourg).

In the physical world, principles have long been worked out which determine, for example, when and where performance of a contract is deemed to have occurred. The problem is that equivalent principles have not been worked out in the metaphysical Internet world.

This is particularly problematic when we turn to the world of e-commerce, and in particular B2C e-commerce, where consumers make contracts online (see also the detailed discussion in chapter 2). Businesses can generally be assumed to have the resources to take legal advice on matters such as jurisdiction, but similar assumptions cannot be made for consumers. If consumers are not sure how they may resolve disputes arising out of an online contract, or in which court, then the result may be a failure of trust and confidence, which may impact on their willingness to engage in e-commerce. To prevent this, a great deal of debate has surrounded the rules in this area in recent years, both in Europe and globally.

IV. CONSUMER CONTRACTS: EC JURISDICTION AND CONSUMER PROTECTION LAWS

One of the defining features of the European approach to private international law is that there are special rules for (some) consumer contracts.[20] The policy behind special consumer jurisdiction (and applicable law) rules is that the consumer is perceived as the weaker party to the contract.[21]

To counterbalance the consumer's prima facie weaker position, the harmonised EU rules on applicable law (formerly to be found in the Rome Convention, and now, in the 'Rome I' Regulation) and jurisdiction (Brussels Regulation) provide in two ways for consumer protection.

A. Jurisdiction: Asymmetrical Rules

If the Brussels Regulation applies, a consumer is allowed to sue a foreign supplier in the local courts of the consumer's domicile. In fact, the consumer has a choice: she can sue in the state of her own domicile *or* in the domicile of the supplier (to make enforcement easier, for example).[22] But conversely, the supplier can *only* sue a defendant consumer in the consumer's local court.[23] Hence the jurisdiction rules are asymmetrical in favour of the consumer. However, even if the consumer decides to sue 'at home' she will still have to enforce the judgment abroad.

B. Applicable Law: Applicability of Mandatory Consumer Protection Laws of the Consumer's Residence

Many contracts, including standard form consumer contracts, provide for an express clause stating the applicable law in the event of a dispute. Under Article 3(1) of Rome I, such clauses are usually respected by the courts. If Rome I applies, however, the supplier cannot contract out of mandatory provisions of consumer protection law which are part of the substantive law of the consumer's residence (eg in the UK legal systems, the Consumer Credit Act).[24]

---

[20] Based on the EC Treaty (Treaty establishing the European Union (the 'Treaty of Rome') consolidated version incorporating the Maastricht and Amsterdam Treaties) Arts 3(t) and 95(3).

[21] C-96/00 *Gabriel v Schlank and Schick GmbH* [2002] ECR I-6367 para 39; Collins, *Dicey, Morris & Collins*, above n 16, 440, 1635.

[22] Brussels Regulation, Art 16(1).

[23] Ibid, Art16(2).

[24] Art 6(2) Rome I Regulation, see also Art 6(2) of Directive 93/13/EEC of 5 April 1993 on Unfair Terms in Consumer Contracts: 'Member States shall take the necessary measures to ensure that the consumer does not lose the protection granted by this Directive by virtue of the choice of law of a non-Member country as the law applicable to the contract if the latter has a close connection with the territory of the Member States.'

Mandatory rules are defined as those rules of a legal system that the parties cannot deviate from by agreement.[25] A provision of the chosen law is inapplicable *only* to the extent that it would deprive the consumer of the protection by the mandatory rules in his country of residence. In other words, in this situation, the applicable law is split: mandatory rules of the consumer's residence apply as a minimum *and* the law stipulated in the choice of law applies concurrently. The consumer's mandatory law only prevails if the consumer receives less protection under the chosen law.[26]

Thus in a consumer contract dispute, it may be necessary first to work out what the applicable law is, and secondly to decide how far it derogates from the mandatory consumer protection rules of the consumer's residence. This 'split' of the applicable law is cumbersome, and makes litigation even more uncertain and thus more expensive.

C. What Is a Consumer Contract in Brussels Regulation and Rome I?

The crucial question that must be asked is under what circumstances these rules protecting consumers will apply.

The Brussels Regulation

The special consumer contract jurisdiction rules in the Brussels Regulation apply (inter alia[27]) if 'a person *directs* commercial or professional activities to the Member State of the consumer's domicile (or to several states including that Member State)'.[28]

This is sometimes known as a 'targeting' test.[29] As some authors have pointed out, it may be sufficient for their application that consumers of a particular Member State are able to acquire goods and services through a website. This approach would mean that the consumer protection rules apply to all interactive, general audience websites.[30]

[25] Art 6(2)

[26] Collins, *Dicey, Morris & Collins*, above n 16, 1640: 'the correct interpretation . . . will enable the consumer to rely on the mandatory rules of the law of his habitual residence, if they are more favourable to him that the chosen law, or on the chosen law, if it is more favourable to him than the mandatory rules'.

[27] They also apply to a contract for the sale of goods on instalment credit terms or any other form of credit made to finance the sale of goods, Art 15(1)(a)–(b) of the Jurisdiction Regulation 44/2001/EC, above n 7.

[28] Art 15(1)(c) of the Brussels Regulation (italics added).

[29] See eg L Edwards, 'The Scotsman, the Greek, the Mauritian Company and the Internet: Where on Earth Do Things Happen in Cyberspace?' (2004) 8 *Edinburgh Law Review* 99–111, available at http://papers.ssrn.com/sol3/papers.cfm?abstract_id=1157344.

[30] L Gillies, 'European Union: Modified Rules of Jurisdiction for Electronic Consumer Contracts' (2000) 17 *Computer Law & Security Report* 395–98, 397; see also Rec 24 of the Rome I Regulation; C Clarkson and J Hill, *The Conflict of* Laws, 3rd edn (Oxford, Oxford University Press, 2006) 85; also mentioned in Collins, *Dicey, Morris & Collins*, above n 16, 442 as a possible interpretation.

However, it is more likely that the courts, in assessing whether a business directs its activities to a particular Member State, would make an overall assessment of the website in question.[31] It may take into account the nature and character of the website (eg the products sold), the language and currency used on the website,[32] marketing activities of the business external to the website (or other Internet application), such as advertisements in national print or televised media in the consumer's Member State, banner advertisements or pop-up advertising on other websites, which are clearly targeted at a particular Member State, and finally whether the website contains a genuine disclaimer.[33]

As can be seen from these criteria, targeting is a question of degree, and it is unclear how much targeting is required for the special consumer protection provisions to apply. In particular the question arises whether there is a presumption that the business directs its activities to all (Member) States, if a business does *not* specify on its website to which Member States it sells, and if the target states for its activities cannot be ascertained from the context (eg by language or currency).

Hence, businesses contracting on the Internet fear with some reason that they may be hauled into court in an unsuspected jurisdiction, or even multiple such jurisdictions, and this concern is not wholly unjustified considering the general nature of the directing/targeting test and the dearth of jurisprudence clarifying the test.

The issue has provoked considerable debate. The suggestion that e-businesses are liable to be sued in every Member State has evoked great criticism from the business community on the basis that it would drive many small and medium-sized enterprises (SMEs) out of business if they had to contend litigation in every Member State.[34] The result may be overt targeting only of a few jurisdictions, and effective partition of the Single Market, to the detriment of competition and consumer choice.

On the other side of the argument, it could be pointed out that the burden or risk of litigation in foreign EU Member States is a natural consequence of the benefits of access to (and profits from) an EU-wide consumer market.[35]

---

[31] The issue is controversial, but see the discussion in Collins, *Dicey, Morris & Collins*, above n 16, 1642–43 arguing that it is possible that the courts would adopt a targeting approach.

[32] However, Rec 24 to the Rome I Regulation (applicable law) expressly states that language and currency are not determinative (interpretation of the European Commission).

[33] See also FSA's regulatory approach as to when a person is directing financial services to the UK, similar criteria can be found in the FSA Handbook, Release 022, August 2003, ch 3, COB para 3.3.6.

[34] M Pullen 'EU's Dangerous Threat to E-commerce' [September 1999] *Legal Week*; M Jordan, 'Suffocating E-commerce at Birth' [December 1999/January 2000] *European Counsel* 15–17; M Powell and P Turner-Kerr, 'Putting the E in Brussels and Rome' (2000) 16 *Computer Law & Security Report* 23–27, 26.

[35] BEUC position paper, BEUC 183/99 'Consumer Rights in Electronic Commerce— Jurisdiction and Applicable Law on Cross-border Consumer Contracts', 8 October 1999;

One solution to this conflict is increased use of alternative dispute resolution (ADR) or online dispute resolution (ODR). Interestingly, the European Parliament, when consulted on the draft Brussels Regulation, suggested tying the consumer jurisdiction provisions to ADR. The European Parliament suggested that service providers should be allowed to contract out of the asymmetric rules on consumer jurisdiction if the supplier committed itself to co-operating in a specified ADR procedure.[36] Hence EU policymakers actively acknowledge the use of ADR as one solution to the difficulty of cross-border litigation. However, it should also be pointed out that there is no complete coverage of binding ADR services at this point in time. The US experience furthermore has been that mandatory ADR may be set up in a way that is contrary to the best interests of the consumer and very pro-business.[37]

Another solution to this conflict is to find a way to reassure businesses that the risk of being sued anywhere and everywhere without warning is low, without diminishing the protection given to consumers. This could be achieved if businesses were required always to ask their customers where they were based before concluding contracts with them, and the courts denied consumer protection if a consumer lied about his location. Businesses could use simple technology such as a drop-down menu and block consumers from jurisdictions they did not wish to target. This would prevent them from contracting with consumers in jurisdictions where they considered the laws as being too unfavourable.

This approach was originally proposed when Rome I was being debated, in Article 5(2), which at one point provided that the consumer's local law would govern a dispute if the supplier directed its activities to the consumer's Member State, unless the supplier did not know where the consumer was resident, and this ignorance was not due to the supplier's negligence. However, this provision did not survive to the final version.

Rome I

Article 6(1) of the Rome I Regulation[38] provides a similar formula to that found in the Brussels Regulation. If a business (termed 'professional' in the

---

S Dutson, 'E-commerce – European Union' (2000) 16 *Computer Law & Security Report* 105–07, 107; G Russell, 'E-commerce Law and Jurisdiction' [December 1999] *Butterworths Journal of International Banking and Financial Law* 459–61, 459.

[36] Report of the European Parliament on the Proposal for the Council Regulation on Jurisdiction, A5-0253/2000 Final, Rapporteur Diana Wallis, Art 17a, 21.

[37] See discussion of the role of ADR in EU B2C e-commerce in L Edwards and C Wilson, 'Redress and ADR in EU Crossborder E-commerce Transactions' (2007) 21 *International Review of Law, Computers and Technology* 315.

[38] The Rome Convention on Applicable Law which preceded the Rome I Regulation adopted a different test for defining a consumer contract, which involved considerable uncertainty also, and was even less well tailored to the online environment.

Regulation) directs its activities to the consumer's Member State,[39] the mandatory laws in the state of the consumer's habitual residence apply, even if there is a choice-of-law clause stipulating a different applicable law. Hence such a contract would be governed by two laws, the law of choice and the mandatory provisions of the consumer's law.[40] If there is no choice of law, the law of the consumer's residence will apply *if* the condition of directing in Article 6(1) is fulfilled. The Regulation lists certain exceptions (such as services not provided at the consumer's place of habitual residence, in Article 6(4)(a)), none of which are of particular relevance to e-commerce.[41] The Rome I Regulation, like the Brussels Regulation, thus brings a worrying degree of uncertainty to cross-border service providers.

In addition to the consumer protection provisions discussed above, private international law is also affected by the control of unfair contract terms, which make the situation even more confusing.

D. Choice-of-forum/Choice-of-law Clauses, and the Unfair Terms in Consumer Contracts Directive

As we noted briefly above, it is common (and indeed good business practice) in contracts, especially standard form consumer contracts, for an express jurisdiction clause, often alongside an applicable law clause, to be inserted in the event of a dispute. Such choice-of-forum clauses are generally respected by the courts in business-to-business contracts, but in consumer contracts, the issue arises of whether they are *fair*. The Unfair Terms in Consumer Contracts Directive[42] provides that certain terms deemed unfair are not binding on consumers. This rule, implemented in the UK by the Unfair Terms in Consumer Contracts Regulations 1999,[43] raises the question of whether an express choice of jurisdiction clause can be unfair and thus not binding on consumers. Secondly it suggests that if a choice-of-jurisdiction clause is deemed not binding, then the consumer can sue a supplier in the consumer's jurisdiction and/or challenge the jurisdiction of the supplier's local court on this basis. The issue of unfair terms, and when they are declared non-binding by the courts, is dealt with in more detail in chapter 2.

The starting point for evaluating the unfairness of a term is Article 3(1) of the Directive, which establishes three requirements[44] before a term is

[39] Rome I, Art 6(1)(b).
[40] Ibid, Art 6(2).
[41] Ibid, Art 6(4).
[42] Council Directive 93/13/EEC of 5 April 1993 on Unfair Terms in Consumer Contracts OJ L95/29, 21 April 1993.
[43] SI 1999/2083.
[44] See also *Director General of Fair Trading v First National Bank* [2000] QB 672 (CA) 686. This case has been further appealed to the House of Lords, but not on the general interpretation of the unfairness test.

deemed unfair. First, the term must not have been individually negotiated with the consumer. The burden of proof is on the business to show that a term is not a standard term and has been individually negotiated.[45] Secondly, it must be contrary to good faith. Thirdly, the term must cause a significant imbalance in the parties' rights and obligations to the detriment of the consumer.

The Annex to the Directive provides a non-exhaustive and merely indicative list of examples of clauses that cause such an imbalance and are contrary to good faith. However Article 4 of the Directive also makes clear that all the circumstances must be taken into account, including the nature of the goods and services, on a case-by-case basis. Thus a term not listed can be adjudged to be unfair, whereas a term listed may be considered to be fair in the circumstances.[46]

The most relevant of the examples of unfair clauses listed in the Annex is that contained in (q), which includes clauses 'excluding or hindering the consumer's right to take legal action or exercise any other legal remedy'. While this example does not expressly mention jurisdiction clauses, arguably a requirement for the consumer to litigate in a foreign or far-away court hinders her right to take legal action.[47]

There is also judicial support for this interpretation of the Directive. In *Océano Grupo Editorial SA v Murciano Quintero*[48] a publishing company selling encyclopedias on instalment credit terms included in its standard contract terms with consumers, who were located in different regions of Spain, a clause providing for jurisdiction in the courts at its place of business in Barcelona. Some consumers defaulted on the instalment terms and the company brought recovery proceedings in its local court. In that case, the European Court of Justice (ECJ) in a preliminary ruling decided that an exclusive jurisdiction clause in a consumer contract falls within the example listed under (q) in the Annex.[49] The ECJ argued that, since the value of the claim is likely to be small, meaning that the legal costs are disproportionate, consumers may be unable to enter an appearance. Furthermore, depending on the facts, the clause may cause a significant imbalance between the parties, contrary to the requirement of good faith if, as here, the supplier can bring and defend proceedings conveniently at its place of business, whereas the consumer has to do so at a distance.[50]

---

[45] Art 3(2) of Directive 93/13/EEC.

[46] GH Treitel, *The Law of Contract*, 11th edn (London, Sweet & Maxwell, 2003) 274; D Oughton and J Lowry, *Consumer Law*, 2nd edn (London, Blackstone, 2000) 400; R Stone *The Modern Law of Contract*, 5th edn (London, Cavendish, 2002) 252.

[47] Para 17.4 Unfair Contract Terms Guidance, published by the Office of Fair Trading in February 2001 and available on their website http://www.oft.gov.uk/Business/Legal+Powers/Unfair+Terms+in+Consumer+Contracts/unfair+guidance.htm.

[48] Joined Cases C-240-244/98 [2000] ECR I-4941.

[49] See para 22; Advocate General Saggio pointed out that even if it did not fall within the Annex, Member States can add new categories, A17.

[50] See paras 23–24; Advocate General Saggio, A18.

Similarly in an English case, *Standard Bank London Limited v Aposto-lakis*,[51] the validity of a non-exclusive jurisdiction clause was at issue, allowing the bank to sue its Greek clients at the bank's place of business in England or any other jurisdiction where the clients had assets, whereas the consumer-clients were limited to suing before the English court. The court found that the special rules on consumer jurisdiction in the Brussels Convention[52] applied and that therefore Mr and Mrs Apostolakis could only be sued in Greece and were themselves entitled to bring an action in the courts of their domicile, Greece.[53] However, the court *obiter* remarked that it would also consider the clause to be unfair under the Directive.[54] The clause caused a substantial imbalance in that the consumers would be put to substantial inconvenience and cost to sue in England, whereas the bank could sue at its place of business or at the place where a judgment would have to be enforced.[55]

V. TORT DISPUTES

Since the Internet can be accessed from anywhere in the world, the harm caused by an information tort committed on the Internet may, in some cases at least, fall anywhere and everywhere.[56] This can again cause both ordinary users and businesses serious problems in terms of fixing and predicting what courts may accept jurisdiction if a tort is committed.

A. The Fear of Being Sued Everywhere or in an Unexpected Location

A tort committed on the Internet may affect only one person and place—eg if negligent medical advice is provided via the Internet causing personal injury to one person domiciled in a particular jurisdiction—but it may also, and more commonly, affect numerous individuals, or have effects in numerous jurisdictions. The classic example is defamation: one post on a website might cause harm to a person's reputation in multiple countries if the victim has an international reputation (eg Madonna, Obama, Beckham). Similar problems arise with trademark infringement on a website of a

---

[51] [2001] Lloyd's Rep Bank 240 (QB); by contrast in *Westminster Building Company Ltd v Beckingham* [2004] All ER (D) 343 (Feb) (Technology and Construction Court) the court upheld an adjudication clause (not a jurisdiction clause) on the basis that it was not unfair in the circumstances, inter alia because the consumer had been professionally represented.

[52] Above, n 7.

[53] [2001] Lloyd's Rep Bank 240 (QB) para 42.

[54] Para 51.

[55] Para 49.

[56] H Kronke, 'Applicable Law in Torts and Contracts in Cyberspace', in Boele-Woelki and Kessedjian (eds), above n 2, 65–87, 65.

mark registered in several jurisdictions, or where a computer virus is negligently spread through a website, imparting that malicious code to anyone who happens to access the website and damaging computer equipment located in many different jurisdictions.

Even where the harm resulting from the defendant's tortious activities de facto only occurs in one jurisdiction, the global reach of the Internet can be troublesome for the unsuspecting defendant, who may be surprised at being hauled into a distant foreign court.

Arguably, this additional burden on the defendant is fair if it was foreseeable for the defendant that she would be hauled before the courts of that particular jurisdiction. But this may not be so on the Internet. For example, if a French architect operates a website that is directed at local, French customers and this website negligently carries a virus, which causes damage to the computer equipment of a Canadian user, should that Canadian user be able to sue in his local courts? This question arises not only because of the ubiquitous nature of the Internet, but also because of the fact that most businesses—even those serving only local markets—now have websites which can be accessed from anywhere in the world.

Thus the main fear of users interacting on the Internet is that they can be sued in a potentially distant jurisdiction (or multiple such jurisdictions).[57] From the claimant's point of view, the concern is whether he can sue at the place where he has suffered damage, rather than having to go to foreign court with different laws and language, and whether any remedy can be enforced at home.

As the rules on tort jurisdiction discussed in the next section demonstrate, these fears are amply justified.

B. Connecting Factors: Place of the Commission of the Tort and the Place of Damage

Looking at the connecting or localisation factors under the rules of private international law for tort, there are two logical possibilities. One connecting factor is the place where the harmful act was carried out, ie the place where the tort was committed. The other connecting factor is the place where the damage occurred.[58]

In a tort dispute between a UK domiciliary and a defendant or plaintiff domiciled elsewhere in the EU, the Brussels Regulation applies.[59] If, on the

---

[57] See the Law Commission's consultation in respect of online defamation—the main concern expressed was the potential risk of being sued on a global basis. Law Commission, 'Defamation and the Internet', Scoping Study No 2 December 2002, para 4.21.

[58] See L Edwards, 'Defamation and the Internet', in L Edwards and C Waelde (eds), *Law and the Internet*, 2nd edn (Oxford, Hart Publishing, 2000).

other hand, the defendant is not domiciled in an EU or European Economic Area (EEA) state, the English courts apply the common law rules, as stated in the CPR. Both under the Brussels rules and under the English common law rules, the claimant can sue (at his choice) in either place.[59]

In Brussels case-law, the leading case is *Bière d'Alsace v Mines de Potasse*,[61] where the ECJ had to rule on the meaning of the phrase 'place where the harmful event occurred', now used in Article 5(3) of the Brussels Regulation. The ECJ held that the phrase 'place where the harmful event occurred' could refer to either the jurisdiction where the event giving rise to the damage occurred or to the jurisdiction where the damage itself occurred.[62] This approach was followed in the case of *Shevill v Press Alliance*,[63] which related to an information tort, defamation. Although no Brussels case has yet directly dealt with an Internet tort, it seems the rules from *Bière* and *Shevill* would be followed.

Under the English domestic rules, the relevant connecting factors are similar: that either the damage was sustained within the jurisdiction[64] or that the tortious act was committed within the jurisdiction.[65] We now examine these two forks more closely.

(i) The Place Where the Tort Was Committed

As has been pointed out above, in the section about contracts, it can be difficult to pin down an activity, such as the commission of a tort, on the Internet. If a tort is committed through the provision of information, is this the place where the information is generated or accumulated, the place of uploading of the information, or the place of downloading, as this is the place where the information is accessed and read? Other possibilities include the place where the information provider is physically located or legally established, and the place where the server hosting the information is located.

As the High Court of Australia appositely pointed out in *Dow Jones v Gutnick*:

> [L]ocating the place of a tort is not always easy. Attempts to apply a single rule of location (such as a rule that intentional torts are committed where the tortfeasor acts, or that torts are committed in the place where the last event necessary to make the actor liable has taken place) have proved unsatisfactory if only because

---

59 Brussels Regulation, Art 4(2).
60 Collins, *Dicey, Morris & Collins*, above n 16, 388.
61 C-21/76 *Handelskwekerij G J Bier BV v Mines de Potasse d'Alsace* [1976] ECR 1735.
62 Ibid, para 19.
63 *Shevill v Presse Alliance SA* [1995] ECR I-415.
64 CPR 6.20(8)(a).
65 CPR 6.20(8)(b).

the rules pay insufficient regard to the different kinds of tortious claims that may be made.[66]

The answer to the question of where a tort is committed depends also on the type of tort in question.[67] For example, if the tort is defined as using a trademark in the course of trade,[68] or making a misrepresentation or misstatement,[69] the place of the commission of the tort may be different than if the tort is defined as publication.[70] In other words, not all torts committed by information disseminated through the Internet can be located by reference to the same action (such as uploading or downloading information) or by reference to the location of the same connecting factor (such as the server hosting the information, the establishment of the person producing the information, etc). Furthermore, different national courts may assert jurisdiction (or not) over identical torts via different connecting factors.

This is well illustrated by the example of defamation. Under EU law, the place where the tort of defamation was carried out is the place of publication, which was held to be the place of the publisher's establishment in *Shevill*.[71] This can be contrasted with the Australian/English approach which finds that, for defamation, publication takes place where the information is read. A series of recent cases in the English and Australian courts have established that a text, which is accessible on the Internet, is published at the place where it is downloaded.[72]

[66] *Dow Jones & Company Inc v Gutnick* [2002] HCA 56 (High Court of Australia) para 43 (first judgment).

[67] Furthermore, sometimes a tort may consist of several acts, raising the problem of defining the relevant act. A good example for this is the case of *Ashton v Rusal* [2006] EWHC 2545 (Comm) paras 62–64. In that case a Russian company 'hacked' into the computing system of a company in London and the court said that the tortious acts were committed in London on the basis that this was the place where the confidential information was stolen, where the 'safe had been cracked'. One might also argue, however, that the misuse of the information in Russia was the place where the tort was carried out. This case is an example where the Court found that the relevant acts were committed within the jurisdiction, even though the actor was outside the jurisdiction when acting.

[68] S 10 Trade Mark Act 1994; here the defendant must trade in the forum, see also *Euromarket Designs Inc v Peters and Crate & Barrel Ltd* [2001] FSR 20 (ChD) .

[69] Such as negligent misstatement, where the tort is deemed to be committed at the place of origin of the communication, see the *Domicrest Ltd v Swiss Bank Corp* [1999] QB 548 (QB). However, in other cases, the torts of negligent and fraudulent misrepresentation were found to be committed at the place of reception, see Collins *Dicey, Morris & Collins*, above n 16, 387.

[70] *Dow Jones & Company Inc v Gutnick* [2002] HCA 56 (High Court of Australia) para 98; *Harrods Ltd v Dow Jones & Company Inc* [2003] EWHC 1162 (QB) para 36; *Don King v Lewis Lennox* [2004] EWHC 168 (QB) paras 9–10, confirmed by the Court of Appeal in *Lewis Lennox v Don King* [2004] EWCA Civ 1329 (CA) para 2 and *Richardson v Schwarzenegger* [2004] EWHC 2422 (QB) para 19

[71] Above n 63, paras 24–25.

[72] *Dow Jones & Company Inc v Gutnick* [2002] HCA 56 (High Court of Australia) para 98; *Harrods Ltd v Dow Jones & Company Inc* [2003] EWHC 1162 (QB) para 36; *Don King v Lewis Lennox* [2004] EWHC 168 (QB) paras 9–10, confirmed by the Court of Appeal in *Lewis Lennox v Don King* [2004] EWCA Civ 1329 (CA) para 2 and *Richardson v Schwarzenegger* [2004] EWHC 2422 (QB) para 19.

However, it should be pointed out that an English court has recently held that there is no presumption that an article merely made available on the Internet has been published in this jurisdiction. The mere fact that the article could have been accessed in England is not sufficient for the claimant to establish jurisdiction here.[73]

(ii) The Place Where the Damage Occurred

The second connecting factor is the place where the damage itself occurred. The early case of *Mecklermedia v DC Congress*[74] illustrates how broadly jurisdiction may be asserted on the ground of damage in the forum alone. In *Mecklermedia*, a trademark infringement case, the damage to the plaintiff's reputation in the UK was mainly caused by the defendants' active marketing operations (such as leaflets and other offline marketing) in the forum (England) and only partly by the mere dissemination of information via their website, which was operated from Germany. The case illustrates how two commercial organisations, previously operating peaceably in a similar field with the same name, but in *separate* territories and *different* jurisdictions, were brought into conflict when their activities moved to the Internet by virtue of the fact that a website is in its nature accessible in all jurisdictions. In such a scenario, accepting jurisdiction based on damage to reputation within the forum, caused by users in the forum accessing the defendant's website, is, to say the least, problematic, especially if the defendant had not targeted its conduct to the forum state.[75]

In two later cases, however, the courts of both England[76] and Scotland[77] have seemed to retrench from this high watermark of 'forum shopping' acceptance. They have indicated that for, respectively, trademark infringement and passing off, the mere *possibility* of access to a 'foreign' Internet website by users in the proposed forum is not sufficient for a court in the forum to accept jurisdiction, thus weakening the precedent set by *Mecklermedia*.

It is noteworthy, and perhaps unfortunate, that neither the English nor

---

[73] *Al Amoudi v Brisard* [2006] EWHC 1062 (QB) The Court made clear that there must be a platform of facts from which it can be inferred that publication in England was likely, para 37. See also the discussion in ch 1 above, 57.

[74] *Mecklermedia Corporation v DC Congress GmbH* [1998] Ch 40 (Ch D).

[75] Although, according to the court's findings, Mecklermedia was in fact drumming up business within the UK (see 42) which may have influenced the finding against the defendants.

[76] *Euromarket Designs Inc v Peters and Crate & Barrel Ltd* [2001] FSR 20 (ChD) para 21–25; contrast this decision with the decision of the US District Court for the Northern District of Illinois, which found jurisdiction in Illinois to hear the claim on the basis of minimum contacts established by the website: *Euromarket Designs Inc v Crate & Barrel Ltd and Peters* 96 F Supp 2d 824, see above, 135.

[77] *Bonnier Media Ltd v Greg Lloyd Smith and Kestrel Trading Corporation* [2002] SCLR 977 Court of Session, Outer House, paras 19–20 (see discussion in Edwards, above n 29).

EU approach to tort jurisdiction requires an 'intention' or even objective foreseeability on the part of the defendant that damage would, or might, occur in a particular location or jurisdiction. This would limit the possible number of places where a business might be sued in tort.

By contrast, both the US courts[78] and the 'targeting' approach of the Brussels Regulation consumer contract provisions (see above p 128) attempt to limit the potential risk for businesses of having to litigate in any and every forum, just because they operate a website accessible to the world. In particular, the US courts operate a 'single publication rule,'[79] which says, very briefly, that an action relating to a publication tort can only be brought once, in the most appropriate forum. This rule is designed to promote freedom of the press and to prevent publishers being bankrupted by multiple simultaneous suits in multiple US states. Despite efforts to plead its case, the common law courts outside the US have so far staunchly resisted its introduction.[80]

One practical restriction on the full scope of jurisdiction opened up by the idea that jurisdiction can be found in any forum where damage has occurred can be found in the Brussels Regulation rules as interpreted in *Shevill*. The ECJ held in *Shevill*[81] that if the damage had been spread over several Member States, the claimant could sue in each and every juris-diction in which he or she had suffered harm, *but only for the damage suffered in that particular jurisdiction.*[82] If the claimant wishes to sue for the whole loss in one go, he or she has to bring an action in the courts of the place where the defendant carried out the tort[83] or where the defendant is domiciled or established.[84] This fits in with the general policy of the Brussels Regulation, which is that it is fairest for the defendant to be able to state their case in their own familiar courts, rather than being hauled into unexpected lands.[85]

The rules for multi-state defamation actions are similar under the English common law rules. Here also the claimant can sue for defamation in each and every jurisdiction where the statement has been downloaded.[86]

[78] See below, 143ff.
[79] See below, 148ff.
[80] See inter alia *Dow Jones & Company Inc v Gutnick* [2002] HCA 56 (High Court of Australia); *Berezovsky v Michaels* [2000] 2 All ER 986 (HL) (England and Wales); *Loutchansky v Times Newspapers Limited* [2001] EMLR 898; [2001] EWCA Civ 1805.
[81] Above, n 63.
[82] Paras 29–33.
[83] Under Art 5(3) of Reg EC/44/2001, which for defamation is the place of the publisher's establishment, see the discussion above.
[84] Under Art 2(1) of Reg EC/44/2001.
[85] Collins, *Dicey, Morris & Collins*, above n 16, 418.
[86] *Dow Jones & Company Inc v Gutnick* [2002] HCA 56 (High Court of Australia) para 98; *Harrods Ltd v Dow Jones & Company Inc* [2003] EWHC 1162 (QB) para 36; *Don King v Lewis Lennox* [2004] EWHC 168 (QB) paras 9-10, confirmed by the Court of Appeal in *Lewis Lennox v Don King* [2004] EWCA Civ 1329 (CA) para 2; and *Richardson v Schwarzenegger* [2004] EWHC 2422 (QB) para 19.

As under the Brussels rules, the claimant can only, however, recover the damage suffered in that forum.[87] In summary therefore, in both England and elsewhere in the EU, a defendant can sue in each and every jurisdiction, where the immediate[88] damage has occurred, in an action for tort.

C. Limitation of Jurisdiction under Forum non Conveniens Under the Common Law

One crucial distinction between the Brussels Regulation rules and the English common law rules needs to be highlighted. Under the common law rules, courts may exercise their discretion to examine whether England is not the *forum conveniens* (appropriate forum).[89] Under this test, the courts take into consideration other fora connected with the action, and decide if England is not the appropriate place for the case to be decided.[90] Essentially under the *forum non conveniens* doctrine,[91] the courts will assess[92] the connection of the claimant with the forum, eg in a defamation action, her reputation in the place of the forum,[93] the location of the evidence and witnesses,[94] and whether the claimant would be barred from obtaining redress elsewhere if the court struck out the proceedings.[95] If publication in England is *de minimis* compared to the main place of publication, then the courts may also refuse to hear the case, although this has not always been the case.[96] Notably, there is no requirement at all that England is the most appropriate forum, merely *an* appropriate forum. In general, the English courts have been reluctant to cede jurisdiction to a claim of *forum non conveniens* merely because the case has an Internet element and foreign defendants or plaintiffs (or both), something that in the defamation field has lead to the English legal system being described as a 'libel magnet'.[97]

In *Chadha v Dow Jones*, both claimant and defendant were resident in the US and the libel was published in a US magazine. The total distribution

---

[87] Ibid.

[88] The ECJ held in two cases that the claimant can only recover the direct damage, not any consequential harm: *Dumez France v Hessische Landesbank* [1990] ECR I 49; *Marinari v Lloyds Bank plc* [1995] ECR I 2719.

[89] See discussion in *The Spiliada* [1987] AC 460 (HL); *Berezovsky v Michaels* [2000] 2 All ER 986 (HL) (England and Wales); *Lennox Lewis v Don King* [2004] EWCA Civ 1329 (CA).

[90] *Lewis Lennox v Don King* [2004] EWCA Civ 1329 (CA), paras 25–26, referring to *Diamond v Sutton* (1866) LR 1 Ex 130 and *Schapira v Ahronson* [1999] EMLR 735 (CA).

[91] Collins, *Dicey, Morris & Collins*, n 16, 476.

[92] All of these have been mentioned in *Richardson v Schwarzenegger* [2004] EWHC 2422 (QB) para 24.

[93] *Don King v Lewis Lennox* [2004] EWHC 168 (QB) para 17; *Berezovsky v Michaels* [2000] 2 All ER 986 (HL) (England and Wales) 651–52.

[94] Lord Goff in *The Spiliada*, above n 89, 479.

[95] Ibid, 475–76.

[96] See *Berezovsky v Michaels* [2000] 2 All ER 986 (HL) (England and Wales), and cases discussed in main text following.

[97] See Edwards, above n 58.

figures were 294,346, of which 283,520 were sold in the US. Only 1,257 were sold in the England. The court at first instance declined jurisdiction and the Court of Appeal[98] confirmed this.

Furthermore in the Court of Appeal decision in *Dow Jones v Jameel*[99] the allegedly defamatory material inferring that the claimant had supported Al Quaeda in 1988, contained in the online version of the *Wall Street Journal*, was only accessed by five subscribers in England (including the claimant's lawyer). Jurisdiction had not been challenged in this case, so that the issue of *forum non conveniens* did not arise. Nevertheless the court struck out the proceedings as an abuse of process, finding that 'the cost of the exercise will have been out of all proportion to what has been achieved. The game will not merely not have been worth the candle, it will not have been worth the wick'.[100]

Chadha and *Dow Jones* show that the courts in England are empowered to strike out 'forum-shopping' actions on grounds of *forum non conveniens*, or abuse of process.[101] However, this is only likely to happen in extreme cases. As several defamation cases have shown, the English courts are slow to find that England is *forum non conveniens*: for example, in *Harrods Ltd v Dow Jones*[102] the court accepted jurisdiction, even though 'the evidence discloses a very small number of "hits" on the article as published on the web'. Similarly, the English courts accepted jurisdiction in *Lewis Lennox*, even though all parties were all resident in the US.[103] In *Schwarzenegger*, the English court assumed jurisdiction in a libel action brought by an English television presenter against the Californian Governor (and others), relating to statements made in the US during his election campaign, reported in an article by the *Los Angeles Times*, but accessible everywhere on the Internet.[104]

Forum non conveniens is not an eligible plea where the Brussels Regulation applies (although it is an eligible plea in actions between English and Scottish domiciliaries).[105] Thus if the court grants jurisdiction on the basis of the wide jurisdictional principles enunciated in *Bière d'Alsace* and *Shevill*, it will have no discretion to stay proceedings on the grounds that another forum is more appropriate.[106]

---

[98] [1999] EMLR 724 (CA).

[99] [2005] EWCA Civ 75, para 69.

[100] Ibid.

[101] See also Collins, *Dicey, Morris & Collins*, n 16, 468.

[102] *Harrods Ltd v Dow Jones & Company Inc* [2003] EWHC 1162 (QB) para 4.

[103] *Lennox Lewis v Don King* [2004] EWCA Civ 1329 (CA).

[104] *Richardson v Schwarzenegger* [2004] EWHC 2422 (QB) para 24.

[105] Collins, *Dicey, Morris & Collins*, above n 16, 472; Clarkson and Hill, above n 30, 59–60.

[106] *Group Josi Reinsurance Company SA v Universal General Insurance Company* [2000] ECR I-5925; for the Lugano Convention, see *Aiglon Limited v Gau Shan & Company Limited* [1993] 1 Lloyds Rep 164, 175; but the English Court of Appeal has held that it can still decide that England is not the appropriate forum if the conflict is between English jurisdiction and a non-EU state (such as between an English defendant and a US claimant): see *In re Harrods (Buenos Aires)*

D. Conclusions

This discussion of tort jurisdiction has shown that the rules on jurisdiction in Brussels and under the common law are complex and, for Internet cases, unpredictable. Connecting factors such as damage within the jurisdiction, and harm to reputation, may be unreasonably wide, and open the gates of courts, as has already occurred in the case of defamation in the English courts. For defendants, the risks are high that they may be sued in more than one jurisdiction, or in an unexpected jurisdiction, and this can be particularly unfortunate in the context of the media and freedom of the press, with the threat of multiple lawsuits (whether carried through or not) operating potentially to stifle freedom of speech.

VI. TORT AND APPLICABLE LAW: ROME II[107]

We move on to briefly examine how questions of choice of law are answered in cross-border Internet torts. While European harmonisation of applicable law was for a long time limited to the law applying to contracts (Rome I), this has now changed with the adoption of Regulation 864/2007. This Regulation harmonises the rules on applicable law for non-contractual liability in the EU for the first time. It applies to all non-contractual obligations in a conflict-of-law situation, including torts and unfair enrichment.

However, many of the cases relating to the Internet before the English courts have arisen from defamation, and hence it is significant that Article 1(2)(g) excludes defamation, privacy and personality rights from the scope of the Regulation. The Regulation also does not apply to Denmark.[108] Member States must apply the provisions of the Regulation from 11 January 2009.[109]

The Regulation applies universally: in other words the law applicable can be any law and need not be the law of a Member State.[110] The general, presumptive rule for torts is that the law of the country where the damage occurs will be applicable, ignoring the law of the country where the tort was committed and ignoring any indirect consequences of the tort.[111] So,

---

Limited [1992] Ch 74 (CA); *ACE Insurance SA-NV v Zurich Insurance Co and Zurich American Insurance Co* [2001] 1 Lloyd's Rep 618 (CA). However, the ECJ has now explicitly ruled that if the defendant is domiciled in a EU Member State (including the UK) and the Brussels Regulation applies, the English courts have no discretion to apply *forum non conveniens*, even where the conflict is with a non-EU jurisdiction (here Jamaica): C-281/02 *Owusu v Jackson (t/a Villa Holidays Bal Inn Villas)*, judgment of 1 March 2005 [2005] ILPr 25 (ECJ).

[107] EC Regulation 864/2007 of 11 July 2007 on the law applicable to non-contractual obligations.

[108] Art 1(4)

[109] In England, Rome II has been implemented by the the Law Applicable to Non-Contractual Obligations (England and Wales and Northern Ireland) Regulations 2008 SI 2008/2986

[110] Art 3.

[111] Art 4(1).

for example, a claim in tort for damages for harm resulting from negligent investment advice which had been supplied over the Internet would be judged according to the law of the place where the direct damage was sustained, eg where the assets relating to that investment are located.

This rule applies unless both the claimant and the defendant tortfeasor have their habitual residence in the same country.[112] Furthermore, if all the circumstances of the tort indicate that there is a closer relationship with a country other than the place where the harm was suffered and other than the country of habitual residence of the parties, then that country's law will apply.[113]

There are special rules on product liability which raise interesting issues in an Internet context. The law applicable in a product liability case is the law of the place where the claimant is habitually resident, the law where the product was acquired or the law where the damage was sustained provided that the product was marketed in that country.[114] However, if the defendant could not reasonably foresee that the product (or a product of the same type) would be marketed in any of these countries, then the law of the defendant's domicile applies.[115] This raises the question of how 'marketing' is defined in an e-commerce context. This issue is similar to the question of what amounts to directing one's activity to a particular country, discussed above in relation to the definition of consumer contracts in Brussels, and in Rome I. Again, these rules are only presumptive, and if there is a manifestly closer connection with the laws of another country (such as a closely related contract), then the laws of that other country apply.[116]

Furthermore, the Regulation contains specific rules on acts of unfair competition. These rules essentially apply the law of the country whose consumers or competitors are harmed and where the market is affected.[117] If the act of unfair competition is carried out on the Internet (eg a website using misleading advertising), or if the illegal restriction of competition affects e-commerce, in some cases it may be difficult to assess which geographical markets are affected and where consumers or competitors are actually harmed. This territorial connection factor may be particularly difficult to apply on the Internet.

The general rule on the infringement of intellectual property (IP) rights is that the law for the country in which protection is sought applies.[118] Since IP rights are rights attached to a particular territory, this rule makes sense. However, this means that if a claimant alleges, for example, copyright infringement based on content available on a website, he may have to

112 Art 4(2).
113 Art 4(3).
114 Art 5(1).
115 Ibid.
116 Art 5(2).
117 Art 6.
118 Art 8(1).

bring different claims for each territory and a different national law will apply to each claim.

The parties may agree the applicable law before the event giving rise to the obligation, if they are acting in a commercial, non-consumer capacity and provided the choice-of-law clause has been freely negotiated (ie is not a standard term).[119]

Article 27 of the Regulation provides that the application of Community law provisions shall not be prejudiced if these provisions lay down specific conflict-of-law rules for non contractual matters (as *lex specialis*). This raises the question of whether the country-of-origin rule contained in Article 3 of the E-commerce Directive[120] is such a specific conflict-of-law rule. This issue is controversial. Article 3(2) of the E-commerce Directive essentially provides that Member States must not restrict the freedom to provide information society services from another Member State. It is doubtful whether a court which applies the tort law of the place where the damage was sustained under Article 4(1) (say in a cross-border negligence case involving a website) would restrict the freedom to provide information society services. The same issue would arise where an act of unfair competition (such as certain types of misleading advertising) was addressed to a particular market and the law of that country applied.[121]

VII. THE US APPROACH TO JURISDICTION

A. The Due Process Tests

A state or federal court in the US is constrained in exercising jurisdiction over an out-of-state defendant by the due process clause contained in the Fifth[122] and Fourteenth[123] Amendments of the US Constitution. These provide, in their essential parts, that no person shall be deprived of life, liberty or property without due process of law. The due process clauses have been interpreted to impose a requirement that an out-of-state defendant must have *minimum contacts with the forum* before he or she

---

[119] Art 14(1).
[120] Directive 2000/31/EC, OJ L178/1 of 17 July 2000
[121] For further discussion, see G Smith, 'Directing and Targeting—The Answer to the Internet's Jurisdiction Problems?' (2004) 5 *Computer Law Review International* 145–51; M Hellner, 'The Country of Origin Principle in the E-Commerce Directive—A Conflict with Conflict of Laws?' (2004) 2 *European Review of Private Law* 193–213; J Hörnle 'Country of Origin Regulation in Cross-border Media—One Step Beyond the Freedom to Provide Services' (2005) 54 *International Comparative Law Quarterly* 89–126 .
[122] Applying to the federal government.
[123] Applying to states.

can be sued there, and that the exercise of jurisdiction must be in accordance with traditional notions of fair play and substantial justice.[124]

These principles have subsequently been much interpreted by the various courts. In addition, some states in the US have passed long-arm statutes establishing a list of grounds for the exercise of jurisdiction over out-of-state defendants. However in many states the long-arm statute is simply coextensive with, ie as wide as, the due process principle.

The first test of 'minimum contacts' is satisfied if the defendant purposefully avails itself of the privilege of conducting business in the forum state, or if it is foreseeable that he or she would be hauled into court there as a consequence of harmful activities intentionally directed at the forum state.[125] In tort cases, the courts have established minimum contacts on the basis of the 'effects doctrine'. This is not in fact (as the epithet may be taken to imply) jurisdiction based on mere effects, but also requires intent and knowledge on the part of the defendant. The defendant must have committed an intentional tort expressly aimed at the forum state, the harm caused thereby was suffered in the forum state, and the defendant knew that this would be the case.[126] For example, in *Panavision v Toeppen*, Mr Toeppen registered the plaintiff's trademarks as domain names and offered to sell them to the plaintiff. The court found that the defendant had directed its actions to the plaintiff's main place of business, and knew that the brunt of the harm would be suffered there.[127]

For the second part of the constitutional due process test, ie the test of traditional notions of fair play and substantial justice, the courts take into account the appropriateness of the forum (in terms of location of the evidence and the witnesses) and the interests of the respective competing jurisdictions in adjudicating the dispute. In Internet cases more emphasis seems to be placed on the first test, so this discussion is mainly focused on 'minimum contacts'.

Two key distinctions from the Brussels Regulation approach should be noted. First, the minimum contacts test has an intentional element, which is sometimes expressed as purposeful availment, or knowledge that the defendants' actions would take effect in the forum.[128] This intentional element substantially limits the opportunity for forum shopping. By contrast, as we have seen in Brussels tort cases, the courts of any country where the claimant suffered direct harm are usually entitled to adjudicate on the dispute, even if the defendant does not conduct business there, or did not direct its activities to that state.

---

124 In the seminal decision of *International Shoe Company v Washington State* 326 US 310, 316; 66 SCt 154 (1945).
125 *Calder v Jones* 465 US 783 (1984) 788–90.
126 Ibid; *Panavision v Toeppen* 141 F 3d 1316, 1321 (1998)
127 *Panavision v Toeppen*, ibid.
128 S Nauss Exon, 'A New Shoe is Needed to Walk through Cyberspace Jurisdiction' (2000) 11 *Albany Law Journal of Science and Technology* 1–55, 5.

For example, in *World-Wide Volkswagen v Woodson*, the US Supreme Court held that the claimants who had been injured in a car accident in Oklahoma could not sue the retailer of the car there, as the retailer carried on 'no activity whatsoever in Oklahoma'.[129] The court said that although in theory it was foreseeable to the defendants that the claimants might take the car to Oklahoma, this theoretical foreseeability was not sufficient.[130]

By contrast, in *Asahi v California*,[131] a narrow majority of five out of nine judges of the US Supreme Court held that a manufacturer who regularly distributes a product through various distribution chains, knowing that a certain quantity of its product is likely to end up with consumers of a particular state, has the requisite minimum contacts with that state to be sued there in a personal injury action. It is difficult to reconcile *World-Wide Volkswagen* with *Asahi*, as arguably it was also foreseeable in the former case that some of the cars sold in New York might be driven to Oklahoma, albeit that in *World-Wide Volkswagen* the defendant was the retailer of the product, who sold directly to the consumer and not a large-scale manufacturer distributing a mass-market product down a chain of sales (stream of commerce).

In the famous *Grokster* peer-to-peer (P2P) filesharing case, the US Federal District Court in California held that it had jurisdiction to decide a copyright infringement suit against Sharman Networks Ltd, the owners of Grokster/KaZaa, even though they were headquartered in Australia and incorporated in the Pacific Island of Vanuatu.[132] The court said that there was evidence that the Kazaa software had been downloaded 143 million times globally and 20 million times in the US. Although there was no direct evidence as to how many times the software had been downloaded in *California*, the court extrapolated a likely figure of 2 million from the total number of downloads. This was sufficient for a finding of the required minimum contacts with California.[133] This is a similar approach as in the stream of commerce cases such as *Asahi*.

Thus even in some (reasonably exceptional) US cases, the purposeful availment or foreseeability requirement has been interpreted fairly widely. The approach is on the whole more flexible than under Brussels rules, which may make it fairer on some defendants, but less predictable and certain for claimants thinking about future risks.

---

[129] *World-wide Volkswagen Corporation v Woodson* 444 US 286, 287, 100 SCt 559 .

[130] Ibid.

[131] Albeit that a majority held that it would constitute a violation of due process for California to exercise jurisdiction in the circumstances (the claim was between a Japanese and a Taiwanese company). *Asahi Metal Industry Co v Superior Court of California* 480 US 102, 107 SCt 1026.

[132] *Metro-Goldwyn-Mayer Studios Inc et al v Grokster et al* 243 F Supp 2d 1073 (CD California 2003).

[133] Ibid, 1087.

B. Principles Developed in US Internet Cases

Despite this flexibility, the US approach still involves analysis of the Internet transaction or activity through the lens of territoriality, with questions arising such as 'Did the defendant do business in the forum?' or 'Was it foreseeable that the defendant's actions might cause harm to the claimant in the forum?' Again, because of the difficulty of pinpointing the locus of Internet activities, and because of the ubiquity of access to the Internet, these questions are difficult to answer, and the case-law has produced contradictory outcomes on similar facts. The question of jurisdiction is therefore highly opaque and uncertain, or as Exon has put it:

> The district court decisions appear to be highly individualistic and fact dependent. The result appears to be dragging jurisprudence deeper into a quagmire of uncertainty in how to confer personal jurisdiction in cyberspace.[134]

Contrast, for example, the *Euromarket* case with *Millenium*.

In *Euromarket v Crate and Barrel*, the plaintiff alleged trademark infringement against the defendant, an Irish retail business with one shop in Dublin, who used the same name as the plaintiff, 'Crate & Barrel', as a domain name, on its packaging and on its website.[135] The US District Court found that the defendant had the required minimum contacts in Illinois, taking into account the defendant's non-Internet-related contacts, such as her participation in trade fairs and one sale to a person with an Illinois billing address, even though the goods ordered were delivered to an address in Ireland, and even though this sale was 'provoked' by the plaintiffs' law firm.[136]

In *Millenium Enterprises v Millennium Music*,[137] one music retail store, based in Oregon, sued another, based in South Carolina, for trademark infringement and unfair competition. The South Carolina music shop made a small number of CD sales through its website, one of which had been made to Oregon (again arranged by the plaintiff's law firm) and it had some non-Internet-related contacts in Oregon.[138] Nevertheless the court found that there were insufficient contacts with Oregon and dismissed the suit for lack of jurisdiction.[139]

As in the English and Brussels rules, mere access to a website as such is not sufficient to subject a party domiciled in one state to jurisdiction in another.[140] However in *Compuserve v Patterson*, the Sixth Circuit Court of Appeals found that *electronic* contacts can constitute the required

---

134 Above n 128, 26.
135 *Euromarket Designs Inc v Crate & Barrel Ltd et al* 96 F Supp 2d 824 (ND Illinois 2000).
136 Ibid, 829, 835.
137 *Millenium Enterprises Inc v Millenium Music* 33 F Supp 2d 907 (D Oregon 1999).
138 Ibid, 909.
139 Ibid, 920–24.
140 *Cybersell Inc v Cybersell Inc* 130 F 3d 414 (9th Cir 1997) 419–20.

minimum contacts with the forum jurisdiction.[141] Mr Patterson used Compuserve's services to distribute shareware software and he alleged trademark infringement and unfair competition by Compuserve. Since he had electronically registered as a shareware provider with Compuserve, based in Ohio,[142] and repeatedly uploaded software onto their system, the Court of Appeals for the Sixth Circuit found that the courts in Ohio had jurisdiction to hear Compuserve's action for declaratory relief that it had not infringed Mr Patterson's rights.[143]

A frequently cited case in Internet jurisdiction decisions is the 1997 US District Court case of *Zippo*[144] which established the influential, so-called sliding scale test, whereby jurisdiction depends on the degree of interactivity of a website. Under this test, jurisdiction is contingent on the nature and quality of commercial activity that an entity conducts over the Internet. Websites that only make information available are categorised as passive, and access to such a passive website is not a sufficient ground for the exercise of jurisdiction. By contrast, an active website, conducting business with residents in the forum state over the Internet, would be sufficient for a finding of jurisdiction. The middle ground is occupied by interactive websites, which allow a user in the forum state to exchange information with a host computer. For these middle ground websites, the exercise of jurisdiction is only proper if there is a high degree of interactivity and if the nature of the information exchange is commercial.[145]

It is important to keep in mind that the *Zippo* sliding-scale test is only a frequently cited test established by a US District Court. It cannot overrule or replace the minimum contacts test.[146] In fact it could be argued that the distinction between passive and active websites as a determinative factor is now technologically obsolete, as very few websites are merely passive showcases of information.[147] Recent decisions have placed more emphasis on targeting,[148] ie on whether the defendant has purposefully directed its activities to the forum. Judge Barbara B Crabb in *Hy Cite* severely criticised the *Zippo* test:

> First, it is not clear why a website's level of interactivity should be determinative on the issue of personal jurisdiction. . . . Even a 'passive' website may support a finding of jurisdiction if the defendant used its website intentionally to harm the plaintiff in the forum state. . . . Similarly, an 'interactive' or commercial website

---

[141] *Compuserve Inc v Richard S Patterson* 89 F 3d 1257 (6th Cir 1996).

[142] The click-wrap agreement made clear that CompuServe was based in Ohio and that the contract was deemed to be made there: ibid 1260–61.

[143] Ibid, 1264–65, 1269.

[144] *Zippo Mfg Co v Zippo Dot Com Inc* 952 F Supp 1119 (WD Pa 1997).

[145] Ibid, 1124.

[146] *Hy Cite Corporation v BadBusinessBureau.com* [2004] WL 42641 (WD Wis) 5.

[147] M Geist 'Is There a There There? Toward Greater Certainty For Internet Jurisdiction' (2001) 16 *Berkeley Technology Law Journal* 1345–1407, 1404; Exon, above n 128, 24, 35.

[148] *Hy Cite*, above n 146.

may not be sufficient to support jurisdiction if not aimed at the residents in the forum state.[149]

Likewise, in the *Step Two* case, the Third Circuit Court of Appeals emphasised that mere interactivity is not sufficient, but that the defendant must have intentionally directed its conduct at the forum state:

> The *Zippo* court similarly underscored the intentional nature of the defendant's conduct vis-à-vis the forum state. . . . Since *Zippo* several district court decisions from this Circuit have made explicit the requirement that the defendant *intentionally* interact with the forum state via the web site in order to show purposeful availment.[150]

However, other courts still rely on degrees of interactivity as set out in *Zippo*.[151] For example, in *Mar-Eco* the court found that a vehicle dealer in Pennsylvania could sue a vehicle dealer in Maryland in their local court on the basis of contacts to the forum established by an interactive website.[152]

C. Jurisdiction in Defamation Cases

In the US, the single-publication rule, well established in many US states, means that an action in respect of the same defamation can only be brought once and if the court accepts jurisdiction, and will consider the total loss to reputation alleged by the claimant.[153] This can be contrasted with the Brussels approach discussed above. At first sight the Brussels approach adopted by the ECJ in *Shevill* seems more generous to plaintiffs at least, as the claimant can bring several actions in respect of the same facts against the same defendant. However, it is costly and burdensome for a claimant to bring several actions in different jurisdictions; and may be disastrous for the defendant with attached issues of freedom of speech.

On the other hand, under *Shevill*, the claimant can recover damages for the whole loss only in the courts at the publisher's establishment. In this respect, the US approach, based on minimum contacts and targeting, is more generous as the claimant is not limited to suing at the publisher's establishment, but can bring an action for the *whole* loss in any place where

---

149 Above n 146, at 5.
150 *Toys R US Inc v Step Two SA* 318 F 3d 446 (3rd Circuit 2003) 452.
151 Eg *Mar-Eco v T&R and Sons Towing and Recovery* 837 A 2d 512 (Pa Super 2003) 517–18.
152 In that case the court even found that it had general jurisdiction over the defendant, ibid.
153 US Restatement of Torts 2d (1977) s 577A.

> (2) A single communication heard the same time by two or more third persons is a single publication.
> (3) Any one edition of a book or newspaper, or any one radio or television broadcast, exhibition of a motion picture or similar aggregate communication is a single publication.
> (4) As to any single publication
>   (a) only one action for damages can be maintained.

the due process criteria are satisfied.[154] Hence the claimant can recover the whole loss in one of several fora, not just at the place where the publisher is established.[155]

Nevertheless in a conflict between US and English jurisdictions, most claimants prefer the English courts. However, this seems not to be motivated by any advantage in jurisdictional rules, but due to a more claimant-friendly *substantive* defamation law, as in the US many defamation actions are defeated by the 'public figure' doctrine, which makes it harder for a famous person to bring an action against a media defendant.[156] English libel claims were also, at least in the past, known for the high levels of damages awarded.

D. Consumers

Another major conceptual difference between the approach to jurisdiction in the EU and the US is that there is no overarching policy against mandatory choice of forum, or 'jurisdiction' clauses, in consumer contracts in the US.[157] The general principle in the US is that a forum selection clause is enforced unless it is fundamentally unfair.[158] However, the mere existence of a jurisdiction clause is not decisive to the issue of jurisdiction. If the defendant can show that the jurisdiction clause was obtained through fraud, undue influence or overweening bargaining power, or if it is against a state's strong public policy, exceptionally, the clause does not supply the basis for jurisdiction.[159] The issue is important in relation to e-commerce as

[154] See in particular *Keeton v Hustler Magazine Inc* 465 US 770 (1984). Initially the single publication rule came to be associated with statements that the single publication took place where the newspaper or magazine was published: *Fried, Mendelson & Co v Edmund Halstead Ltd* (1922) 196 NYS 285, 287. This was then taken to mean that the applicable law should be that of the place of publication: *Zuck v Interstate Publishing Corp* 317 F 2d 727,734 (2nd Cir 1963) and Restatement of the Conflicts of Laws 2d (1971) s 150. However, a plaintiff can sue in other jurisdictions than that of the place of publication.

[155] This allows a claimant the chance to forum shop, and sue in the place with the longest limitation period.

[156] *New York Times v Sullivan* 376 US 254 (1964) and *Gertz v Robert Welch Inc* 418 US 323 (1974) establish that no public figure may recover damages for libel without a showing of actual malice—this rule of substantive defamation law causes conflict in international cases. This is especially the case where the claimants argue that the law of England or that of Australia should apply, both of which are more generous to the claimant. However this conflict cannot be solved at the level of jurisdictional rules.

[157] Geist, above n 147, 1386.

[158] *The Bremen v Zapata Off-Shore Co* 407 US 1, 12–13; 92 SCt 1907 (1972): 'a freely negotiated private international agreement, unaffected by fraud, undue influence, or overween-ing bargaining power, such as that involved here, should be given full effect'. The US Supreme Court in that case also said that 'in the light of the present-day commercial realities and expanding international trade we conclude that the forum clause should control absent a strong showing that it should be set aside' (15).

[159] Ibid and *Carnival Cruise Lines Inc v Shute* 499 US 585, 595 (1991); *Burger King Corp v Rudzewicz* 471 US 462, 486 (1985)

many major consumer giants in the field (eg eBay) include such in the standard form contracts consumers sign up to online.

In *Carnival Cruise Lines Inc v Shute*[160] the terms and conditions of a cruise line contained an express and exclusive choice of forum (Florida). One of the passengers was injured in a fall onboard a ship and sued in the Western District of Washington; that suit was dismissed for lack of jurisdiction. The US Supreme Court held that jurisdiction clauses are upheld if they passed the judicial scrutiny of fundamental fairness. The court said that it is not unreasonable for a cruise line to limit jurisdiction to one forum, as passengers come from different jurisdictions and the cruise line may otherwise risk being sued in multiple jurisdictions, ultimately constituting a cost factor, which would be passed on to consumers.[161] Hence an express choice of jurisdiction could be in the interest of consumers, as a form of prudent risk management leading to lower prices. Furthermore, the court held that there was no evidence that the purpose of the jurisdiction clause was to make litigation inconvenient for the plaintiffs.[162] The court gave short shrift to the argument that the claimants were physically and financially unable to sue in Florida and emphasised that a heavy burden of proof is required to set aside a forum selection clause on the grounds of inconvenience.[163]

The starting point of any analysis of a jurisdiction clause is that it must have been brought to the attention of the consumer before it can be incorporated into the contract.[164] In *Specht v Netscape Communications Corpn*[165] the courts made a distinction between 'browse-wrap contracts', in which the consumer is merely given warning of terms and conditions (eg through a link on the homepage of a website), and 'click-wrap contracts', where the consumer is forced to scroll through the terms and conditions and click 'I agree' or something equivalent before the contract is concluded. The court found that the terms (in this case, an arbitration clause) were not incorporated in a browse-wrap contract, as the consumer might have easily missed the link to the terms and conditions.[166] Hence a jurisdiction clause in a 'click-wrap' contract is more likely to be enforceable than one contained in a 'browse-wrap' contract.[167]

---

[160] *Carnival Cruise Lines Inc v Shute* 499 US 585, 595, 499 US 972, 111 SCt 1614 (1991).

[161] Ibid, 593–94.

[162] Ibid, 594–95.

[163] Ibid.

[164] *Spataro v Kloster Cruise Ltd* 894 F2d 44, 45–46 (2nd Cir 1990). See discussion in ch 2, 109.

[165] 306 F3d 17, 48 UCC Rep Serv 2d 761 (2nd Cir 2002).

[166] At 30–33, 35.

[167] See also *Caspi v. Microsoft Network, LLC,* 323 NJ Super 118, 732 A2d 528, 530, 532–33. (NJ Super Ct App Div 1999): this case upheld a forum-selection clause, as the subscribers to online software were required to review the terms and conditions by scrolling through them and to click 'I Agree' or 'I Don't Agree'; in *Bruce G Forrest v Verizon Communications Inc* 805 A2d 1007, 1010 (DC Court of Appeals 2002) the court also upheld a click-wrap contract forum selection clause.

More divisive is the application of the principles in *Carnival Cruise Lines* to the question of whether a jurisdiction clause contained in a standard consumer contract concluded over the Internet is valid. In particular the use of a standard jurisdiction clause in AOL's terms of service has created a spate of litigation about this issue in several states.[168]

On the one hand, consumers contracting on the Internet are also likely to come from multiple jurisdictions, so a supplier would arguably be justified in reducing the risk of being sued in multiple states. Under this approach, jurisdiction clauses may be regarded as a legitimate form of risk management, particular in mass consumer transactions on the Internet. Therefore some courts have followed the *Carnival Cruise Lines*[169] line of argument.[170]

On the other hand, a jurisdiction clause in a consumer form contract may also deprive a consumer of protective laws in his local state, in particular of the right to bring a class action and/or make litigation inefficient if the value of the claim is small compared to the cost and inconvenience of bringing a suit in another state. Hence, some courts have found that a consumer jurisdiction clause in an Internet transaction falls into the public policy exception and was unreasonable.[171]

E. Conclusion

The US approach to jurisdiction is based on general principles that are flexible, but also therefore uncertain and unpredictable in their application. This potentially leads to forum-shopping as claimants are tempted to argue that the defendant has minimum contacts, even where the links to the forum are tenuous. This tendency is slightly, but not completely, counterbalanced by a trend to base jurisdiction on targeting (so-called 'effects doctrine') rather than the interactivity of websites (or other Internet applications). Such forum-shopping makes cross-border litigation expensive and this is ultimately to the detriment of both claimant and defendant. The situation is even more unsatisfactory for consumer and other small claims disputes. Different state courts interpret the exceptions to the general enforceability of jurisdiction clauses in different ways. As a consequence,

[168] Below, n 171.

[169] Above, n 160.

[170] Eg in *Bruce G Forrest v Verizon Communications Inc* the District of Columbia Court of Appeals upheld a forum-selection clause stipulating Virginia as the forum, despite the fact that Virginia is one of two states that does not allow for class action procedures: above n 167, 1011–13; similar reasoning can be found in *AOL Inc v Booker* 781 So 2d 423, 424–25 (Fla Dist Ct App 2001) and in *Koch v AOL* 139 FSupp 2d 690, 694–95 (D Md 2000).

[171] *AOL v Superior Court (Mendoza)* 90 Cal App 4th 1, 18; 108 Cal Rptr 2d 699 (Cal App 1 Dist 2001); *Strujan v AOL* 819 NYS2d 213 (NY City Civ Ct 2006), unpublished; *AOL v Pasieka* 870 So2d 170, 171–72 (Fla Dist Ct App 2004); *Dix v ICT Group Inc* 125 Wash App 929, 937; 106 P3d 841 (Wash App Div 3 2005).

business are concerned about being sued in a different state, and consumers likewise cannot be sure whether or not a jurisdiction clause will be enforced. The need for alternative mechanisms becomes, again, as with Brussels, apparent.

VIII. CROSS-BORDER ENFORCEMENT

Even if a claimant succeeds in finding a court of competent jurisdiction and that court rules in his or her favour, if the judgment debtor does not comply with its terms, the claimant needs to enforce the judgment. If the judgment debtor does not have any assets in the jurisdiction where judgment was given, the claimant has to enforce in a foreign jurisdiction. The courts in this foreign jurisdiction are under no obligation under international law to recognise and enforce that judgment,[172] unless there is a bilateral or multilateral enforcement treaty. The most notable example is the Brussels Regulation which does establish a 'hard law' system of mutual recognition and enforcement of civil and commercial judgments within the EU and EEA.[173] Outside of such supranational agreements, however, states tend to recognise and enforce judgments,[174] on grounds such as international comity, unless there is a public policy or other ground which leads them to refuse to enforce. In some circumstances, this refusal to enforce can take a more active form. For example, an English court that does not agree with the conclusions of a foreign court about the validity of an exclusive jurisdiction clause pointing to the English courts[175] can grant an anti-suit injunction (an order issued to a person in England demanding that such a person withdraw legal proceedings in a court outside England) in an effort to halt the foreign proceedings.

For enforcement of a foreign law judgment in England under the common law rules, essentially four conditions have to be fulfilled: (i) the original court must have been competent;[176] (ii) the judgment must be final

---

172 P Schlosser 'Jurisdiction and International Judicial and Administrative Co-operation' (2000) 284 *Recueil des Cours* 9–430, 237.

173 See Brussels Regulation, discussed above, Arts 33–52. Under the Regulation, the EEA states mutually recognise and enforce civil and commercial judgments of another EEA state (Arts 33 and 38), subject to only very narrow public policy grounds (Arts 34 and 36) and a simplified enforcement procedure (Art 38). Under the Brussels rules, the courts must not examine whether the original, foreign court was the competent court (Art 35(3)). Similarly, the individual states of the US are required to enforce judgements of other US states by operation of the 'Full Faith and Credit' clause of the US Constitution. See US Constitution Art 4, s 1.

174 The liability of the debtor of the foreign judgment is regarded as a legal obligation in and of itself, without any requirement of reciprocity by the foreign state—see Schlosser, ibid, 39.

175 See *Donohue v ARMCO Inc and others* [2001] ILPr 48 (CA), overturned by the House of Lords on different grounds, see [2001] UKHL 64.

176 This is only given if the judgment debtor has either submitted to the foreign court or is present there—it seems that a mere contact over the internet may is not sufficient, Clarkson and Hill, above n 30, pp 138–39.

and conclusive; (iii) the judgment must be for a fixed sum of money; and (iv) the judgment debtor must not be able to raise a defence (such as breach against natural justice, fraud, public policy or irreconcilable judgments).[177] However, even if an obligation to recognise and enforce a judgment is accepted, there is still usually an exequator (obtaining a declaration of enforceability/registration) procedure required. The procedure involves appointing a local representative[178] and incurs translation costs,[179] which make it expensive for small claims. This will be further discussed in the next section.

IX. CROSS-BORDER ASPECTS

As Schlosser has remarked with respect to the cost of international litigation:

> For the little fellow, instituting proceedings abroad is in practice unaffordable. Normally he does not know how to find a lawyer in a foreign country. Thus he must contact a lawyer in his own country, who in turn, must engage and instruct his foreign colleague. Hence double fees are due. The fees of the lawyer consulted at home are seldom recoverable from the debtor. . . . The costs for the translation of a judgment accompanied by extensive reasons may be enormous. The costs are seldom refundable.[180]

Foreign proceedings are rendered more expensive by travel costs (of the parties, lawyers and, as the case may be, witnesses) and translation costs. If foreign law applies, experts (legal advisors and advocates or experts) on the foreign law must be instructed. Furthermore, foreign nationals suing in a foreign court frequently have to overcome discriminatory obstacles inbuilt in civil procedure. For example, in many states, foreigners instituting proceedings have to pay a deposit as security for the defendant's costs, and foreigners are discriminated against in respect to legal aid.[181]

As a consequence, for foreign litigants, the costs of international litigation are not infrequently prohibitive. In many claims the legal costs are out of proportion to the value of the claim. It is impossible to give a precise figure of these costs here—this will depend on the costs of litigation in a particular jurisdiction, on the distance between the parties, whether lawyers bill by the hour or on a fixed-fee basis (eg as a percentage of the value of the claim), whether costs are awarded to the winning party, on the availability of legal aid, whether there are translation costs, etc. By way of example, in a straightforward enforcement action, the registration and

---

[177] Ibid, 134ff.
[178] See eg Brussels Regulation, Art 40(2).
[179] Ibid, Art 55(2).
[180] Schlosser, above n 172, 215.
[181] Ibid, 216.

enforcement of a German judgment in an English court under the simplified rules in the Brussels Regulation may well cost £1,000 in translation and lawyers' costs alone.

A good example of how frustrating cross-border litigation may be can be found in the *Euromarket* case, which involved an application for summary judgment, ie a preliminary hearing, brought by a US company against an Irish trader.[182] The judge pointed out when dismissing the application for summary judgment that

> In substance neither party trades in this country. Yet well over £100,000 in costs have been expended here. No one but a lawyer could call this rational. I expressed the firm view that the parties should attempt to reach settlement.[183]

This cost factor poses serious problems for redress mechanisms in international e-commerce, especially in small claims. The cost of litigation, let alone cross-border litigation, has led to strong calls in government,[184] academic,[185] professional and judicial[186] circles for an increased use of ADR mechanisms to settle small claims arising from e-commerce.

Not just in the context of e-commerce, but more generally, there is a noticeable tendency to overcome the cost factor of (even merely domestic) litigation by encouraging the use of ADR. Courts in England have now accepted the importance of ADR in complementing litigation. Since the introduction of the CPR, courts are under an obligation to encourage ADR,[187] if appropriate, and are also empowered to impose cost penalties on parties who unreasonably refuse to participate in ADR.[188] Furthermore, the courts have recognised the validity and enforceability of ADR clauses in commercial contracts.[189]

X. A EUROPEAN SMALL CLAIMS PROCEDURE

Essentially, a small claims procedure is a simplified court procedure, allowing individuals to resolve a dispute before a court with a procedure

---

182 Above, nn 76 and 135. Note that in this case the claimant brought proceedings against the defendant in *two* courts, in England and Illinois, see above.

183 Ibid, para 8.

184 Art 17 of the E-commerce Directive 2000/31/EC published in OJ L178/1 of 17 July 2000 encourages the Member States to establish out-of-court dispute-resolution mechanisms.

185 A Patel, 'Consumer Protection and Redress—The Wider Context' (2000) 3 *Electronic Business Law* 9–10; L Gillies 'A Review of the New Jurisdiction Rules for Electronic Consumer Contracts within the European Union' [2001] *Journal of Information Law & Technology*;

186 *Cowl v Plymouth City Council* [2002] 1 WLR 803 (CA)

187 CPR Part 1.4(2)(e).

188 CPR Part 44.5; *Dunnett v Railtrack* [2002] 2 All ER 850 (CA); *Royal Bank of Canada v Secretary of State for Defence* [2003] EWHC 1841 (ChD) unreported, paras 11–13; but cf *Hurst v Leeming* [2003] 1 Lloyd's Rep 379 (ChD), where the refusal to mediate was justified on the basis that there was no real prospect of success (see p 381).

189 *Cable & Wireless Plc v IBM* [2002] 2 All ER 1041 (Comm), upholding the validity of an ADR clause.

entailing lower cost and more informality. Twenty OECD countries have such a simplified procedure.[190] These states limit the availability of the small claims procedure to claims below a certain monetary threshold, varying between €300 and €30,000.[191]

This raises the question whether small claims procedures can help *specifically* with *cross-border* disputes. The EU has recently introduced a harmonised, pan-European Small Claims Procedure,[192] which applies to cases in which the value of the total claim (excluding interest, expenses and outlays) does not exceed €2,000.[193] It came into force in the UK on 1 January 2009.[194]

As has been discussed above, the obstacles to cross-border litigation in the form of disproportionate complexity, costs and delay stem from three factors: the complexity and uncertainty surrounding the application of jurisdictional rules; the formality of the court procedure itself; and the formal requirements to achieve recognition and enforcement in a foreign jurisdiction. Does the new EU Small Claims Procedure help with any (or all) of these?

A. Jurisdictional Rules

Under the European Small Claims Procedure[195] the normal Brussels Regulation rules of jurisdiction apply to the Procedure. Thus there is no simplification of jurisdictional problems as such.[196]

B. Formality

Reduction in formality is the main point of the new EC procedure, with its aim to provide an alternative to already existing national small claims procedures.[197] For example, the Regulation provides that the procedure should normally be conducted in writing,[198] prescribes tight deadlines,[199]

---

[190] See OECD Report 'Consumer Dispute Resolution and Redress in the Global Marketplace' (2006) 24.

[191] Ibid, 26

[192] Reg (EC) No. 861/2007 establishing a European Small Claims Procedure, dated 11 July 2007, OJ L199/01, 31 July 2007

[193] Art 2(1).

[194] The Regulation has direct effect. However the Civil Procedure (Amendment Rules) 2008 (SI2008/2178), insert a new Part 78 into the Civil Procedure Rules 1998 to ensure consistency and enforceability in England and Wales.

[195] Reg 861/2007 of 11 July 2007.

[196] Ibid, Art 19.

[197] Ibid, Recital 7(l).

[198] Ibid, Art 5(1).

[199] See eg Arts 5(2), (3), 7(1).

and leaves the presentation and admissibility of evidence to the judge's discretion,[200] hence adopting an inquisitorial approach. The Regulation expressly envisages the use of videoconferencing and other online technology for the collection and presentation of evidence (such as witness statements) and for hearings.[201] Thus the Procedure simplifies the 'normal' civil litigation procedure, this being particularly relevant for those Member States who at present do not have a simplified small claims procedure and whose litigation costs are high.

C. Enforcement

Finally, as to enforcement, the Commission's original Proposal was fairly brief, simply stating that the party seeking enforcement of a foreign judgment merely has to provide the judgment and a certificate by the court having issued the judgment to be enforced.[202] The Report of the European Parliament[203] proposed considerable amendments to the enforcement provisions, stipulating that enforcement should be governed by the law in the Member State of enforcement, and that a European Small Claims judgment should be enforced under the same conditions as a domestic judgment.[204] This is essentially the position adopted in the Regulation.[205]

D. Summary

The main contribution of the European Small Claims Procedure is to provide a harmonised small claims procedure with a high degree of informality. Litigation and enforcement in a foreign jurisdiction, even under the small claims procedure, still entails additional cross-border costs.[206] Furthermore, its main limitation is that it only applies to very small value disputes, not exceeding €2,000[207] and that it would obviously only be applicable within the EU/EEA.

---

200 Ibid, Art 9.
201 Ibid, Arts 8 and 9(1).
202 Ibid, Art 18(4).
203 Text adopted by Parliament on 14 December 2006—Strasbourg, Reference A6-0387/2006.
204 Ibid, Art 21(1) .
205 Art 21—translations still required but no legal representative in the Member State of enforcement
206 OECD Report, above n 190, 28.
207 This is much lower than the current small claims limit in the English courts, which is £5,000 for most claims and £1,000 for personal injury or housing disrepair, see CPR Rule 26.6(1).

XI. CONCLUSION

The purpose of this chapter was to show that there is a 'jurisdictional challenge' for cross-border Internet disputes.

For such disputes, litigation may involve multiple sets of private international law rules, even despite some degree of regional harmonisation within the EU in Brussels and Rome I and II. The application of domestic private international law rules to Internet disputes is uncertain and unpredictable. Activities on the Internet are difficult to locate, since location is irrelevant for Internet functionality. Hence the application of the rules may have surprising or ubiquitous effects and this uncertainty enables parties to engage in 'forum shopping'. Preliminary proceedings to determine jurisdiction may be necessary, and these of themselves may add significantly to the final legal bill and lead to further delay.

Even once a judgment has been obtained, courts at the place where a defendant has assets may refuse to enforce a judgment. In contrast to litigation, arbitration awards are more easily enforced, as a consequence of the New York Convention.[208] On a regional level in the EU there is less of a problem, as recognition and enforcement of civil and commercial judgments is guaranteed under Brussels. However, enforcement in England entails a separate procedure to declare a judgment enforceable, and this also creates additional costs and delays.

Cross-border litigation imposes higher costs and delay for the parties than ordinary litigation, because of the need to instruct a foreign lawyer (frequently in addition to a local lawyer), the travel costs of the parties and witnesses, translation costs and because enforcement is more expensive. For claimants the costs of international litigation are frequently prohibitive, as in small claims the legal costs are often out of proportion to the value of the claim.

These factors mean that claimants in e-commerce, especially consumers, find legal redress practically unattainable and that access to justice is effectively barred in small claim cross-border internet disputes.[209] For defendants, the 'jurisdictional challenge' in Internet disputes means that they may be sued in a distant foreign court or even multiple foreign courts and that such a dispute may be impossible to defend, again because of cost reasons, so that a default judgment becomes inevitable. This means that at the international level access to justice through the courts is curtailed. Alternatives such as (online) arbitration or (online) mediation must be promoted and used.

Yet promotion of such alternatives is also an uphill struggle. A recent

---

[208] 330 UNTS 3 (NYC) adopted New York 10 June 1958, entered into force on 7 June 1959.
[209] See also the OECD's conclusions in relation to consumers in OECD Report, above n 190, 44.

Eurobarometer survey[210] showed that 41 per cent of people who launched a formal complaint concerning cross-border purchases were not satisfied with the way their complaint was handled. Rather than going to the courts or elsewhere for settlement, most dissatisfied consumers took no further action, and only 6 per cent brought the matter to an arbitration/mediation/conciliation body. Future work on developing a workable means of redress for disgruntled consumers in e-commerce, as well as for SMEs, remains a priority both for the UK and the EU[211] if the potential of the online Single Market is to be realised.

---

[210] See *Consumer Protection in the Internal Market—Special Eurobarometer* 252/ Wave 65.1, TNS Opinion and Social (European Commission, September 2006).
[211] See further Edwards and Wilson, above n 37 and J Hörnle, *Cross Border Internet Dispute Resolution* (Cambridge, Cambridge University Press, 2008).

4

EC Regulation of Audio-visual Content on the Internet

ELIZABETH NEWMAN

THIS CHAPTER LOOKS at how the new Audio-Visual Media Services Directive (AVMS Directive) has introduced a level of regulation to the Internet that was formerly reserved for traditional television broadcasting. The AVMS Directive is an amended version of the 1989 Television Without Frontiers Directive (TVWF Directive),[1] which was made by an amending directive[2] (Amending Directive) on 19 December 2007, and which must be implemented in Member States by 19 December 2009.

The core purpose of both the TVWF Directive and the AVMS Directive is to create a common market—in television broadcasting, in the case of the TVWF Directive, and audio-visual media services more widely, in the case of the AVMS Directive. The TVWF Directive established the so-called 'country-of-origin' principle by which television broadcasts only have to comply with the laws of the Member State from which they emanate, as opposed to the laws of any Member States into which they broadcast. This enables service providers to transmit into a number of EU countries without having to worry about compliance with local laws, so long as they comply with the laws of the country in which they are established.

The TVWF Directive and the AVMS Directive also seek to achieve a number of public policy aims such as:

- protecting children from unsuitable material;
- promoting European works to make sure that broadcasters do not simply buy in programmes from countries such as the US and Australia;
- restricting the quantity and controlling the quality of advertising and sponsorship;

---

[1] Council Directive 89/552/EEC on the coordination of certain provisions laid down by law, regulation or administrative action in Member States concerning the pursuit of television broadcasting activities (OJ L298, 17.10.1989), amended by: Directive 97/36/EC of the European Parliament and of the Council (OJ L202/60 30.7.1997).

[2] Directive 2007/65/EC amending Council Directive 89/552/EEC (OJ L332/27, 18.12.2007).

- prohibiting tobacco and alcohol advertising to children;
- prohibiting expressions of hatred;
- granting the remedy of 'right of reply', which allows people and other legal entities, such as companies, to require that any publication of inaccurate facts about them in the media, or any other publication of information which affects their legal rights, should be publicly corrected.

The 1989 Directive was made following an explosion in television and radio broadcasting across Western Europe during the 1980s as a result of a number of technological developments, including the introduction of satellite television. Because broadcast signals do not stop at national borders, and because the laws regarding this sector differed between Member States, the EU introduced the TVWF Directive to establish some minimum standards across all Member States. Amendments to the TVWF Directive in 1997 brought the Directive up to date with developments such as the introduction of teleshopping.

The new extension to the scope of the Directive has been driven by further changes in the technological delivery of audio-visual services since the 1997 amendment. In the last few years there has been a rapid expansion of fixed broadband, digital television and third generation (3G) mobile networks. Digital television was introduced via satellite and cable during the mid-1990s and by terrestrial television in 1998, and the increased channel capacity of satellite and digital cable systems led to an increase in the number of multichannel homes. During 2010–14 the analogue signals in the EU will be switched off in favour of digital. The spread of broadband, with its greater data capacity, has led to the introduction of Internet protocol television (IPTV) and Internet television, television services that are received via technologies used for computer networks. These can be distributed via the Internet or on discrete service provider networks. 3G technologies enable network operators to offer users a wider range of more advanced services, allowing users to receive broadcasting and data-casting over mobile networks. Urban cable and telephone networks will be gradually improved over the next few years, in particular by extending fibre-optic cable from local exchanges to the street cabinet or the home—replacing the old copper-wire network (which only has a limited capacity to deliver broadband through upgrades using technology such as digital subscriber line (DSL)), which will increase the broadband capacity of networks. There has also been an increase in 'time shifting', ie the use of video recorders, DVD players and personal video recorders (PVRs), which allow consumers to choose when to view scheduled broadcasts by streaming them for immediate viewing or downloading programmes to a set-top box.

These developments have resulted in what is commonly referred to as 'convergence', ie the merging of individual communications industries, such as broadcasting and telecommunications, into a single market. In practical terms, this means that consumers can make use of a number of services on a single platform or device—what was once just a mobile phone, can now be used for surfing the web, checking e-mail, watching television and listening to music, as well as making telephone calls. Equally, consumers have a choice about which platform or device on which to obtain a particular service—television programmes can be watched as scheduled broadcasts, downloaded to an iPod or watched over the Internet.

This most recent extension of the TVWF Directive aims to regulate this newly converged world, and the Directive has been renamed the Audio-Visual Media Services Directive to acknowledge that the audio-visual content it regulates is no longer available soley on television.[3]

Convergence has also had an impact on revenues that were formerly focused on a small group of broadcasters and which have now become spread more thinly among multiple platforms. Internet TV can be free, subscription- or fee-based, or supported by advertisements. Service providers are increasingly able to offer a number of bundled services as 'triple' or 'quadruple' play, which could include fixed and mobile telephone services, a television subscription and broadband access. Private subscription television is taking over from the licence fee traditionally paid for public television services. Increased competition from alternative audio-visual media services threatens to reduce conventional television viewing time, which has brought about a decline in television broadcast advertising revenue. Advertising on television has also become less attractive to businesses because of digital techniques that can be used by viewers to skip advertisements, and its decline was further hastened by the onset of worldwide recession towards the end of 2008.

I. EUROPEAN COMMISSION'S PROPOSAL TO AMEND THE TVWF DIRECTIVE

The TVWF Directive applied to television broadcasts made over wires and over the air (including by satellite) and did not apply to services provided on individual demand,[4] so did not apply to transmissions over the Internet.

The European Commission proposed amending the TVWF Directive in December 2005[5] to address the changing pattern of consumption of audio-visual media services in the EU. The Commission gave three main reasons for its proposed changes:

[3] Art 1(1) Amending Directive.
[4] Art 1(a) TVWF Directive.
[5] See European Commission Communication on the future of European regulatory audio-visual policy, 15 December 2005, and the Commission's Proposal for a Directive amending Council Directive 89/552/EEC, 15 December 2005.

- Convergence meant that viewers could watch the same or similar programmes on a range of media—on scheduled television, on-demand television or over the Internet. Audio-visual material was regulated under the TVWF Directive when it appeared on scheduled television, but not when it was broadcast as an on-demand television programme, or when it was streamed over the Internet. This meant that television broadcasters who were regulated by the TVWF Directive could find themselves in competition with other media service providers who were not regulated under the Directive. The Commission suggested that a regulatory 'level playing field' should be established between all such audio-visual media service providers, and that the scope of the Directive should be extended to all 'television-like' audio-visual media services, regardless of the means by which they are transmitted.
- The spread of advertising revenue among a wider range of services meant that traditional commercial broadcasters were struggling to stay afloat. The Commission therefore proposed amending some of the rules for television broadcasting, in particular by relaxing the restrictions in the TVWF Directive on 'spot' advertising and by expressly permitting product placement in some types of programme.
- The Commission also argued that the services not regulated by the TVWF Directive did not benefit from the regulatory certainty experienced by the regulated broadcasting services, and that the potential for compliance with a large number of local laws could restrict their development.

In relation to this last point: there is of course harmonisation of the regulation of other aspects of on-demand services, which are regulated as 'information services' under the Electronic Communications Framework Directive,[6] the E-Commerce Directive,[7] the Unfair Commercial Practices Directive[8] and the Misleading Advertising Directive,[9] and on-demand services are further regulated across the EU by a raft of self- and co-regulatory schemes that address public-policy objectives such as the protection of minors. (In the UK, self-regulation is provided through organisations such as the Internet Watch Foundation and the Association for Television on-Demand (ATVOD).) The UK, in particular, was very sceptical of the need to extend the TVWF Directive to the Internet, in the light of self- and co-regulatory systems that were working well. As an additional reason for its proposal to extend regulation under the TVWF Directive to on-demand services, the Commission cited the fact that although the E-Commerce Directive contains a country-of-origin principle,

6 2002/21/EC.
7 2000/31/EC.
8 2005/29/EC.
9 2006/114/EC.

Member States can derogate from this for public policy reasons. This reasoning has been criticised by business as being a theoretical rather than a real problem, because in fact most Member States do not derogate from the country-of-origin principle under the E-Commerce Directive.[10]

II. THE SCOPE OF THE AVMS DIRECTIVE

While the TVWF Directive regulated services transmitted in certain specific ways—over wires or over the air (including by satellite)—the AVMS Directive regulates all 'audio-visual media services' regardless of how they are transmitted. The aim of the AVMS Directive is to regulate everything that is 'television-like'. Recital 17 of the Amending Directive states:

> It is characteristic of on-demand audio-visual media services that they are 'television-like', ie that they compete for the same audience as television broadcasts, and the nature and the means of access to the service would lead the user reasonably to expect regulatory protection within the scope of this Directive.

The Directive has attempted to define the parameters of what is meant by 'television-like' (without trying to define this term itself).

Under the AVMS Directive, an 'audio-visual media service' is a service under the editorial responsibility of a media service provider, the principal purpose of which is the provision of programmes to inform, entertain or educate the general public by electronic communications networks. Audio-visual media services are regulated under two categories: 'television broadcasts' (also called 'linear' services[11]) and 'on-demand services' (or 'non-linear' services[12]).[13]

A 'programme' is defined as a set of moving images, with or without sound, constituting an individual item in a schedule or catalogue, whose form and content is comparable to that of television broadcasting, such as feature films, sports events, situation comedies, documentaries, children's programmes and original drama.[14] Recital 17 of the Amending Directive urges that, to ensure that regulation is aimed at services that are 'television-like', the notion of 'programme' should be interpreted in a dynamic way, taking into account developments in television broadcasting.

A 'media service provider' is a person with editorial responsibility for the choice of content and who determines the manner in which it is

---

[10] The European Commission's First Report on the application of Directive 2000/31/EC, in November 2003, reported (in para 37) that, contrary to the expectation of some Member States that they would have frequent need to use this derogation, this has not been the case. At this time, the Commission had received only five formal notifications, all from the same Member State and all relating to essentially the same issue.
[11] AVMS Directive, Art 1(e).
[12] Ibid, Art 1(g).
[13] Ibid, Art 1(a).
[14] Ibid, Art 1(b).

organised.[15] 'Editorial responsibility' is the exercise of effective control both over the selection of programmes and over their organisation in a schedule or catalogue. Editorial responsibility does not necessarily imply any legal liability for the content or the services provided.[16]

The definition of 'audio-visual media service' includes 'audio-visual commercial communications' (ACCs),[17] which are images used with or without sound to promote goods, services or images, and 'accompany or are included in a programme' for some sort of payment or benefit.[18] The term ACC includes television spot advertising, sponsorship, teleshopping and product placement. Public service announcements and charity appeals broadcast free of charge are not included in the definition.[19]

Audio-visual media services, other than ACCs, are either television broadcasts (linear services) or on-demand services (non-linear services). A television broadcast, or linear service, is provided for simultaneous viewing of programmes by the public on the basis of a programme schedule.[20] In this case, the viewer has no choice when to watch the programme. This definition covers, among other services, analogue and digital television, live webcasting and near video-on-demand. An on-demand, or non-linear, service allows viewers to choose what to watch and when by selecting from a catalogue of programmes compiled by a media service provider.[21] (Near video-on-demand is a service that broadcasts multiple copies of a particular programme at short intervals (eg every 20 minutes) to allow viewers to tune in at the most convenient time for them. In 2005, the European Court of Justice found that a near video-on-demand service was a scheduled service as opposed to an on-demand service, and therefore fell under the regulation of the TVWF Directive.[22])

During the EC legislative process, there was much discussion over the precise wording of these definitions. The end result is a set of rather woolly definitions. This was partly intentional, because a problem that emerged during the course of the negotiations was that the pace of technological change threatened to render the new Directive out of date even before it is implemented at the end of 2009. The drafting of the Directive therefore had to be loose enough to accommodate technological change, at least in the short term. There has been particular concern over whether concepts such as 'linear services' or 'television broadcasting' and 'non-linear' or 'on-demand' will continue to be meaningful.

The Commission wanted the AVMS Directive to be technology-neutral

---

15 Ibid, Art 1(d).
16 Ibid, Art 1(c).
17 Ibid, Art 1(a).
18 Ibid, Art 1(h).
19 Amending Directive, Rec 26.
20 Art 1(e) AVMS Directive.
21 Ibid, Art 1(g).
22 *Mediakabel BV v Commissariaat voor de Media*, Case C-89/04, 2 June 2005.

to ensure that similar services did not go on being regulated differently simply because one happened to be provided by conventional broadcast and the other by some other medium that falls outside the TVWF Directive. However, the AVMS Directive does not appear to have achieved this because by introducing a distinction between linear and non-linear services, it has set up a new distinction between different technologies. A PVR allows a viewer to record and store a copy of a scheduled programme on the set-top box in his own home and to watch it whenever he wants. This is a linear service because the programme was transmitted to the viewer according to the broadcaster's schedule. However, if a television company stores copies of programmes on its own servers and then provides them on demand to the viewer, this service would be regulated as a non-linear service. This is despite that fact that, from the viewer's point of view, the two services are more or less identical.

In March 2009, the UK government published a statement on how it proposes to proceed with the implementation of aspects of the AVMS Directive (March 2009 statement).[23] The government will give Ofcom powers to regulate UK on-demand services, and these powers will enable Ofcom to designate and delegate power to an industry-led co-regulatory body that will regulate programme content for these services. The definition of on-demand services in the AVMS Directive will be transposed into UK legislation. The co-regulator will have powers to issue guidance on the interpretation of the definition. Access providers will not be responsible for content if they do not provide content themselves, but the government expects that access providers will ensure that services to which they provide access meet the minimum standards required for UK video-on-demand services.

Ofcom will also be given powers to regulate advertising in on-demand programmes, under a co-regulatory arrangement, and the government expects that Ofcom will designate the Advertising Standards Authority (ASA) as its co-regulator in this area. The definition of advertising in the AVMS Directive will also be transposed into UK legislation, and the ASA will be able to issue guidance on the interpretation of the definition and on what advertising falls within its scope.

A. Exclusions

The following express exclusions from regulation under the AVMS Directive were introduced following publication of the Commission's initial proposals, which prompted concern over the potential extent of the proposals.

---

[23] Written Ministerial Statement on the implementation of the Audio-visual Media Services Directive, Department for Culture, Media and Sport, 11 March 2009.

(i) User-generated Videos and Private Websites

When the Commission's proposals were first published, there was concern that the amended Directive would regulate user-generated videos, such as those published on the popular MySpace and YouTube websites. This was not the Commission's intention. Recital 16 of the Amending Directive aims to dismiss this idea by explaining that a regulated audio-visual media service is a mass-media service, ie one intended for a significant proportion of the general public. Also, the intention of the Directive is that an audio-visual media 'service' is a service as defined by the EC Treaty—ie an economic activity normally provided for remuneration. The definition of audio-visual media services therefore does not cover activities that are primarily non-economic and not in competition with television broadcasting, such as private websites and services generated by private users for sharing and exchange between communities of interest. However, one can see how the framing of this exclusion is already coming under pressure. Word of mouth can popularise videos on YouTube—at what point does such a video have mass appeal? Also, YouTube announced in January 2007 that it wanted to share advertising revenue with contributors who upload popular content, and some other smaller-scale operations have similar revenue-sharing schemes in place. It is possible that the content posted by such members could fall under the Directive as the motive for posting material becomes commercial.

Another problem with the way this Directive has been framed is that it has persisted with a distinction between professional and amateur content, with professional content being subject to regulation and amateur content being excluded. However, this is based on an increasingly false dichotomy between professional content being transmitted by one to many and amateur content being transmitted one to one. With the expansion of platforms, audiences have fragmented, and the connection of professional content with content of mass appeal is no longer so straightforward. For example, plenty of videos distributed on YouTube by private individuals have the potential for mass appeal.

There is a similar problem when considering the position of service providers operating user-generated content websites. A service provider who allows users to post unlimited and unrestricted content is unlikely to be taking 'editorial responsibility' for the compilation of programmes within a catalogue and so the AVMS Directive is unlikely to apply. However, if the service provider decides (or is legally obliged) to remove copyright-infringing material, or to direct viewers to particular content, the service provider may be said to be exercising 'responsibility for the compilation' under the Directive.

Private correspondence, such as e-mail, to the extent that it has an audio-visual element, is excluded because it has no mass-media element.[24]

(ii) Electronic Versions of Newspapers and Magazines

The Directive does not regulate electronic versions of newspapers and magazines; these are expressly excluded under Recital 21 of the Amending Directive. However, it is not clear why newspapers and magazines should be excluded by virtue of a special recital, and could not rely instead on the argument that their content does not constitute programmes (eg because the audio-visual material is incidental and not the 'principle purpose' of the service). If a newspaper's website contains audio-visual news items and is exempt under Recital 21, this discriminates against a website containing identical footage but which is not associated with a printed paper. If the content is not a programme, then the recital is redundant. If the footage is excluded because it is incidental, there must be a point at which audio-visual material becomes more than incidental as a newspaper website develops into a service relying more and more heavily on audio-visual material. In that case the recital is confusing.

In the UK, a practical solution has been found to this uncertainty, at least for the time being. Since February 2007, online versions of newspapers have been regulated under the Press Complaints Commission (PCC) Code of Practice. Ofcom has indicated that it will regulate websites under the AVMS Directive only where the PCC does not consider that they fall under the PCC Code. Presumably, Ofcom considers that any service which benefits from the exemption in the AVMS Directive is regulated by the PCC, and that any service which the PCC does not regulate does not benefit from the exemption, and therefore falls (prima facie) under the AVMS Directive.

However, this still leaves a situation in which similar web-based news services provided by newspapers on the one hand and broadcasters on the other will be regulated in very different ways.

(iii) Games of Chance and Online Games

There was concern after publication of the Commission's proposals that the highly profitable European gaming industry, which includes games of chance and betting, would be caught by the Directive, and would move out of the EU to avoid the new regulation. The initial proposals would also have meant that a game played online would have been regulated, but the same game played offline would not. However, Recital 18 was added to clarify that games of chance and online games would not normally be

---

[24] Amending Directive, Rec 18.

caught because their principal purpose is not the distribution of pro-grammes—audio-visual content is incidental to their principal purpose. In theory, video games that contain non-interactive 'cutaway' video sequences could fall under the Directive, but in the UK, Ofcom has indicated that it would not consider that such sequences bring these games under the Directive.

(iv) Mere Transmission

Editorial responsibility means the exercise of 'effective control' over programmes and their organisation. Member States may specify what this means, but Recital 19 of the Amending Directive says that the definition of media service provider should exclude persons who merely transmit programmes for which the editorial responsibility lies with third parties. The AVMS Directive also does not affect the liability exemptions in the E-Commerce Directive, which release service providers from liability for information where they are acting as a 'mere conduit', 'caching' infor-mation or 'hosting'.[25] Although services that merely transmit or bundle audio-visual media services should not find themselves caught by the AVMS Directive, national interpretations of the Directive could mean that in some cases they are.

B. Two-tier Regime

Under the AVMS Directive a greater regulatory burden is placed on tele-vision broadcasts (linear services) and a lighter regulatory regime on on-demand services. The Commission proposed regulating the on-demand sector more lightly on the grounds that this was made up of newer indus-tries, often comprising small and medium-sized companies, which it did not want to drive out of Europe with the burden and expense of heavy regulation. The heavier burden of regulation was intended to fall on those television broadcasters who are used to being regulated under the TVWF Directive. However, some newer services, such as webcasting services, will be classed as linear services, and the heavier burden of regulation will also fall on them.

The AVMS Directive sets out a basic set of rules which apply to all audio-visual media services (with some variation in application for the different mediums of television broadcasting and on-demand services), and a further set of rules which apply only to television broadcasts.

---

25 Ibid, Rec 23.

III. RULES APPLYING TO ALL AUDIO-VISUAL MEDIA SERVICES

A. Country-of-origin Principle

The country-of-origin principle was established under the TVWF Directive, and ensures that all television broadcasts are required to comply only with the laws of the Member State from which they emanate (to avoid being subject to a multiplicity of laws if the broadcast is made into more than one country). This principle is extended under the AVMS Directive so that all audio-visual media services transmitted by a media service provider under the jurisdiction of a particular Member State have only to comply with the laws applicable to audio-visual media services in that Member State.[26] This simplifies things for new media service providers, who, in relation to the EU, only need to ensure that they comply with regulation in the country in which they are established. (They do, of course, need to continue to bear in mind that this does not release them from the need to be compliant with local regulations in non-EU countries—given that the Internet is accessible world-wide.) Article 2(6) also clarifies that the Directive does not apply to AVMS services intended exclusively for reception in a country outside the EU.

The TVWF Directive also set out rules that established the jurisdiction for broadcasters established outside the EU but broadcasting into the EU. Under these rules, broadcasters fell under the jurisdiction of the Member State providing the satellite capacity to broadcast into the EU, or, if the satellite capacity being used was outside the EU, the jurisdiction of the Member State from which the channel was being uplinked to the satellite. The AVMS Directive reverses this rule, so that the Member State with jurisdiction is the one providing the uplink, and only if the uplink is being provided outside the EU does jurisdiction fall to the Member State providing the satellite capacity (if any). This means that some Member States, like France, who regulated a number of non-EU broadcasters that used French satellite capacity, lose jurisdiction to other Member States, such as the UK and Germany, who have no satellite capacity, but host a number of uplinks used by non-EU broadcasters.

In the UK, the government confirmed in its March 2009 statement that non-EU satellite television channels that are uplinked from within the UK and that are not already within the jurisdiction of another Member State will have to get a broadcasting licence from Ofcom. Ofcom will be able to get providers of uplink services to stop uplinking a channel if Ofcom tells them that the channel is unlicensed. However, uplink providers will not

[26] AVMS Directive, Art 2.

have to check whether a channel is licensed before uplinking, and will not have to monitor broadcast compliance.

B. Freedom of Reception

The TVWF Directive required Member States to ensure freedom of reception for television broadcasts, and this is extended to all audio-visual media services under the AVMS Directive.[27] Obviously, there will be no need to restrict freedom of transmission in relation to material that simply complies with the provisions of the AVMS Directive. However, Article 3(1) of the AVMS Directive allows Member States to impose more detailed or stricter rules in relation to audio-visual media services, so long as such rules comply with EC law. Member States may restrict freedom of reception to back up stricter laws in certain circumstances. For television broadcasts, Member States may restrict freedom of reception when a service might harm children or incite hatred based on race, sex, religion or nationality, but only in collaboration with the Member State in which the media service provider is established and the Commission.[28] However, this exception to freedom of reception is likely to be of limited effect because the objecting Member State is in the hands of the transmitting Member State, which is only required to write to the offending broadcaster setting out the offended Member State's objections to the broadcast, but does not have to take further action. Member States may restrict freedom of reception for on-demand services on the grounds of public policy, particularly in relation to criminal offences, public health, public security and consumer protection, and Member States can restrict access to on-demand services in urgent cases without fulfilling all the normal conditions, subject to the provisions in Articles 3(4), (5) and (6) of the E-Commerce Directive.[29]

C. Qualitative Advertising Rules

All ACCs must comply with the following qualitative rules:[30]

- ACCs must be readily recognisable as such, ie they must not be misleading or surreptitious. The term 'surreptitious' was used in the TVWF Directive, which banned all forms of surreptitious advertising including product placement. Product placement is allowed under the AVMS Directive.
- ACCs must not use subliminal techniques.

[27] Ibid, Art 2a(1).
[28] Ibid, Art 2a(2).
[29] Amending Directive, Rec 35.
[30] AVMS Directive, Art 3e.

- ACCs must not prejudice respect for human dignity; include or promote discrimination on grounds of race, sex, ethnic origin, nationality, religion or belief, disability, age or sexual orientation; encourage behaviour prejudicial to health or safety; or encourage behaviour grossly prejudicial to the protection of the environment.
- ACCs for cigarettes and other tobacco products are prohibited.
- ACCs for alcoholic drinks must not be aimed at minors or encourage immoderate consumption.
- ACCs for prescription medicines are prohibited.
- ACCs must not cause moral or physical detriment to minors. They must not directly exhort minors to buy or hire products or services by exploiting their inexperience or credulity; directly encourage them to persuade their parents to purchase goods or services; exploit the trust minors place in parents, teachers or other persons; or unreasonably show minors in dangerous situations.

The Directive also requires Member States and the Commission to encourage the development of codes of conduct on the advertisement of 'junk food' during children's programmes.[31] In the UK, the Broadcast Committee of Advertising Practice (BCAP) Television Advertising Code now contains a number of provisions relating the advertisement of junk food or 'HFSS' (foods high in fat, salt and sugar), which restrict product advertising, although not the promotion of associated brands.

D. Sponsorship

The rules relating to the sponsorship of television programmes are extended to all audio-visual media services:[32]

- Sponsorship must not influence content and scheduling in a way that affects the responsibility and editorial independence of the media service provider.
- Sponsored programmes must not directly encourage the purchase or rental of goods or services.
- Sponsored programmes must identify themselves as such.
- Those whose principal activity is the manufacture and or sale of cigarettes and other tobacco products cannot sponsor programmes.
- Medicine manufacturers and sellers can use their name or image to sponsor programmes but not prescription-only product names.
- News and current affairs programmes cannot be sponsored. Member States can choose whether to prohibit the showing of a sponsorship logo during children's programmes, documentaries and religious programmes.

[31] Ibid, Art 3e(2).
[32] Ibid, Art 3f.

E. Product Placement

Product placement is any form of ACC consisting of the inclusion of or reference to a product, service or trademark so that it is featured within a programme in return for payment.[33] The UK took the view that the TVWF Directive contained an implicit prohibition of product placement because of the requirement for advertising to be identified as such and to be separate from other parts of the programme service,[34] and product placement was accordingly prohibited under the Ofcom Broadcasting Code, except in limited circumstances.[35] Other Member States, such as Spain, permitted product placement under the TVWF Directive. The situation was slightly different in relation to 'prop placement'—the use of products or services that have been supplied for less than value. The TVWF Directive was silent on prop placement, but prop placement is permitted in the UK under the Broadcasting Code, where its use is editorially justified.

Under the AVMS Directive, Member States may permit product placement in certain circumstances, and subject to certain controls. The Directive is worded so as to prohibit product placement,[36] but derogation is allowed for cinematographic works, films and series made for audio-visual media services, light entertainment and sports programmes, except in the case of children's programmes.[37] Derogation is also permitted where goods or services are provided free of charge (prop placement).[38]

Consumer groups were understandably unhappy about the introduction of product placement and, in an attempt to allay their fears, product placement can only be introduced subject to the following strict conditions aimed at protecting viewers:

- Product placement must not influence content and scheduling of programmes in such a way as to affect the responsibility and editorial independence of the media service provider.
- Programmes must not directly encourage the purchase or rental of goods or services.
- Programmes must not give undue prominence to the product in question.
- Viewers must be clearly informed of the existence of product placement by a signal at the beginning and end of a programme, and after every advertising break.[39] This rule may in fact work in favour of the adver-

---

[33] Ibid, Art 1(m).
[34] TVWF Directive, Art 10(1).
[35] Broadcasting Code, s 10.5.
[36] AVMS Directive, Art 3g(1).
[37] Ibid, Art 3g(2).
[38] Ibid.
[39] Ibid, Art 3g(2)(d).

tisers, rather than the viewers (as intended), as it is likely to allow additional promotion of products or brands for no additional fee at every advertising break, and may make product placement much more attractive and pervasive than was intended. The requirement to signal the presence of product placement does not apply to programmes that have not been produced or commissioned by the media service provider itself or an affiliated company, presumably to make sure that the new rules do not conflict with the existing practice of buying in and transmitting programmes containing product placement from outside the EU.

- Programmes must not include product placement of tobacco products, cigarettes or prescription medicines.[40]

As already mentioned, ACCs, including product placement, must not be surreptitious. The TVWF Directive required television advertising and programmes to be kept separate from one another, something that is no longer really possible with the introduction of product placement. It seems that by retaining the prohibition on surreptitious advertising, and introducing the requirement to clearly inform viewers of the presence of product placement in a programme, the AVMS Directive seeks to preserve the spirit of the separation principle even in the presence of product placement.

In the UK, an Ofcom consultation in December 2005[41] showed that, in general, broadcasters would like to see a controlled introduction of product placement, and that they did not think it would damage editorial integrity. Unsurprisingly, consumer groups opposed its introduction. Product placement would allow broadcasters to make some additional revenue from advertising, although the consultation revealed that this was unlikely to be substantial.

In its March 2009 statement, the UK government announced that it would not allow any more product placement in the UK than is currently allowed, although said it would review this decision in 2011–12. The government said that it had not found conclusive evidence that the economic benefit of introducing product placement was sufficient to outweigh the detrimental impact it would have on the quality of British television and viewers' trust in it. In the UK, recent abuses of premium-rate telephone services in broadcasting means that broadcasters need to rebuild audience trust, which the government considers is unlikely to be helped by the introduction of product placement.

---

[40] Ibid, Art 3g(3).
[41] Product Placement—a consultation on issues relating to product placement, 19 December 2005, available at htp://www.ofcom.org.uk/consult/condocs/product_placement/.

F. European Content Quotas

The requirements in the TVWF Directive for television broadcasters to devote a certain amount of time to European works and a certain amount of time, or 10 per cent of their budget, to European works created by independent producers, remain unchanged in the AVMS Directive,[42] but do not apply to television broadcasts intended for regional, rather than national, audiences.[43]

Because of their format, on-demand services cannot be required to comply with quotas in the same way. Nevertheless, Article 3i(1) of the AVMS Directive requires providers of on-demand services to promote the production of, and access to, European works, and gives some examples:

- Financial contributions to the production and rights acquisition of European works.
- A requirement for a 'minimum share or prominence of European works in programme catalogues'. It is hard to see how this would work, since service providers could list in their catalogues large amounts of European content, whether or not anyone wanted to watched it, or alternatively, could make certain popular foreign content unavailable for a time at the end of each measuring period to make sure that quotas were met.

Recital 48 of the Amending Directive also suggests that this can be achieved through the 'attractive presentation of European works in electronic programme guides'. Again, it is hard to see how such a subjective requirement could be enforced.

G. Identification

Member States must require audio-visual media service providers to identify themselves with their name, address, contact details and, where applicable, their regulatory or supervisory institution.[44]

H. Protection of Minors

For linear broadcasts, Member States must continue to ensure that programmes broadcast under their jurisdiction do not contain anything which

[42] AVMS Directive, Arts 4 and 5.
[43] Ibid, Art 9.
[44] Ibid, Art 3a.

might seriously impair the physical, mental or moral development of minors, particularly pornography or gratuitous violence.[45]

For on-demand services, Member States must make sure that services which might seriously impair the physical, mental or moral development of minors are only made available in such a way as to ensure that minors will not normally hear or see such services.[46]

I. Incitement of Hatred and Offence Against Human Dignity

Audio-visual media services must not incite hatred based on race, sex, religion or nationality.[47]

J. Rights for Cinematographic Works

Media service providers must not transmit cinematographic works outside periods agreed with rights-holders.[48]

K. Accessibility for the Disabled

Member States must encourage media service providers to make their services accessible to people with a visual or hearing disability.[49]

IV. ADDITIONAL RULES FOR TELEVISION BROADCASTS

This section sets out briefly the rules that apply only to linear transmissions, some of which already exist under the TVWF Directive, but which could affect some newer scheduled services.

A. Quantitative Advertising Rules[50]

In most types of programme, the quantity of advertisement allowed during television broadcasts has been increased under the new Directive. In particular, the rule in the TVWF Directive that there must be a gap of at least 20 minutes between advertising and teleshopping breaks within any one programme has been removed.

---

[45] Ibid, Art 22(1).
[46] Ibid, Art 3h.
[47] Ibid, Art 3b.
[48] Ibid, Art 3d.
[49] Ibid, Art 3c.
[50] Ibid, Art 18.

Some types of programme, including series, serials, documentaries, current affairs and religious programmes, will be able to contain advertising breaks at any frequency (subject to a 20 per cent per hour limit and the requirements not to jeopardise the programme's integrity, to take account of natural breaks and not to prejudice the rights of the rights-holder).[51] In these programmes, broadcasters can add additional advertising slots without necessarily increasing the length of any one slot.

The main aim of the relaxation in advertising rules is to give television broadcasters new opportunities to earn revenue from advertising. While this could mean more advertising at the expense of the quality of the viewing experience, in theory increased advertising should be controlled by the market, in that the increased viewer choice brought about by multi-channel television and competition from the Internet means that broadcasters will have to limit their advertising quotas in order to maintain a sufficiently good viewing experience to retain viewers.

In the UK, Ofcom has introduced a new Code on the Scheduling of Television Advertising, which relaxed the rules on the frequency of advertising breaks.[52] Ofcom has said it will not decrease advertising minutage and there will be no increase in the number of advertising breaks allowed on public service broadcasting (PSB) channels for programmes of 60 minutes or less, but longer programmes will be able to include as many breaks as non-PSB channels. PSB channels will be able to schedule teleshopping for up to six hours, between 12 am and 6 am, and limits on non-PSB channels will be removed.

B. Exclusive Rights and Short Extracts

The TVWF Directive allowed a Member State to prevent broadcasters having exclusive rights to certain events regarded by the Member State as being of major importance for society, and this right is preserved in the AVMS Directive.[53] Member States are required to notify the Commission with a list of all such events.[54]

The AVMS Directive introduces a new right for a broadcaster to use coverage of events to which another broadcaster has exclusive rights, for the purpose of making short reports for news broadcasts.[55] The right applies to 'events of high interest to the public'.

---

[51] Ibid, Art 11(1).

[52] Review of television advertising and teleshopping regulation, statement published 24 July 2008, available at http://www.ofcom.org.uk/consult/condocs/rada/.

[53] AVMS Directive, Art 3j(1).

[54] Ibid, Art 3j(1) and (2).

[55] Ibid, Art 3k(1).

C. Right of Reply

The right of reply gives people and other legal entities, such as companies, the right to require that any inaccurate facts published about them in the media, or any other publication of information that affects their legal rights, should be publicly corrected. The AVMS Directive preserves the right of reply in relation to television broadcasts but does not extend the right to non-linear transmissions.[56] However, guidelines for the implementation of a right of reply in relation to online media were included in the December 2006 Recommendation of the European Parliament and the Council on the protection of minors and human dignity and on the right of reply.[57]

V. IMPLEMENTATION IN THE UK

In the UK, the rules in the TVWF Directive were enforced by Ofcom through its 2005 Broadcasting Code, which applies, in the main, to radio and television content in services licensed by Ofcom, services funded by the licence fee provided by the BBC and to Sianel Pedwar Cymru. The Code does not apply to the Internet.

In general, the UK opposed the introduction of the AVMS Directive, although it did welcome the redefinition of broadcasting so as to regulate the content of all forms of 'broadcasting' transmission the same way, the liberalisation of the restrictions on advertising, and the retention of the country-of-origin principle. The UK would have preferred a reduction in regulation rather than an increase. The UK has encouraged innovative new media services by operating a 'light-touch' regulatory environment for these industries and by encouraging self-regulation, with the result that the UK has been the home to a large proportion of the EU's new media services. The UK was concerned that an increase in regulation could lead to the collapse of some small companies that could not afford to comply with an additional regulatory burden, prevent other companies setting up, and encourage the relocation of other businesses outside the EU. However, the UK was almost alone in its opposition of the new Directive and, as a result, has had to live with the provisions it does not like. For the UK, media literacy in combination with self-regulation is the answer. Media literacy means the education of citizens to enable them to take control of the content they and their children watch—the UK fought successfully to include in the AVMS Directive a provision intended to encourage media literacy throughout the EU together with a provision that would allow the Directive to be implemented through self- or co-regulatory regimes.

---

[56] Ibid, Art 23.
[57] 2006/952/EC, 20 December 2006 (OJ L378 of 27.12.2006).

Member States are required to encourage self- and or co-regulatory regimes in the areas covered by the Directive, with such regimes having to be broadly acceptable to the main stakeholders in the Member States in which the regimes apply, and provide for effective enforcement.[58] This provision acknowledges the role that industry can play in regulation, both in terms of the expertise it can offer and the importance of getting the regulated players onside if regulation is to be effective. It also recognises that many of the emerging audio-visual media service industries have already adopted successful self-regulatory arrangements.

The UK government has already proposed co-regulatory schemes for the regulation of on-demand content and advertising, as mentioned earlier in this chapter in the section on the scope of the AVMS Directive.

Ofcom has indicated that its intention is only to regulate audio-visual material on the Internet that really does look and feel like traditional broadcast television, as opposed to material that is incidental to, for example, a game or a website selling holidays. This approach follows the spirit of Recital 17 of the Amending Directive, which explains that regulation is only aimed at 'television-like' material.

VI. FINAL THOUGHTS

There is lingering controversy over whether the Commission was right to implement new regulation in relation to new audio-visual media services, or whether it should have taken the opportunity to deregulate. The TVWF Directive was introduced at a time when limited electromagnetic spectrum availability meant that only a limited number of television channels could operate, and the resulting lack of competition meant that there was a higher chance of abuse by the channels if they were allowed to operate without regulation. This is not the case now because spectrum is more widely available, for a number of reasons. Technological developments mean that it is possible to improve spectrum capacity. Digital broadcasting uses less spectrum than analogue broadcasting. There is also a move across the EU towards allocating spectrum through market methods, such as auctions, rather than allocating particular frequency bands for defined uses, on the basis that this approach drives more efficient use of the spectrum by those who have bought it. Entirely new technologies, such as IPTV mean that 'television broadcasts' no longer rely on spectrum in the same way. Since the main reason for introducing the TVWF Directive has disappeared, it is odd to find it extended rather than repealed, and the UK would have preferred to allow increased competition to replace regulation in providing the necessary checks and controls.

[58] AVMS Directive, Art 3(7).

A House of Lords report[59] appealed for the Commission's revised proposals to be subject to an impact assessment, but none was carried out. However, even after the implementation of the AVMS Directive, it is likely to remain relatively easy to avoid regulation under the AVMS Directive by locating Internet services (in particular) outside the European Economic Area. Alternatively, the imprecise nature of the definitions in the AVMS Directive may make it possible to design a service that does not fall within the terms of the Directive. But while some service providers may want to avoid the regulatory burden of the AVMS Directive, others may see compliance with its terms as a guarantee of quality of service.

[59] House of Lords European Union Committee, 3rd Report of Session 2006–07, 'Television without Frontiers? Report with Evidence', 31 January 2007.

Part III
Intellectual Property

5

'Appropriate for the Digital Age'?
Copyright and the Internet:
1. Scope of Copyright

HECTOR L MacQUEEN[1]

I. INTRODUCTION

A. The Significance of the Internet

THE LABOUR PARTY entered and won the 2005 British general election with this manifesto commitment:

> Copyright in a digital age: We will modernise copyright and other forms of protection of intellectual property rights so that they are appropriate for the digital age.[2]

Perhaps chief amongst the issues which prompted this unusual political commitment to modernisation of substantive law was the phenomenon of widespread unlicensed sharing of sound recordings of music via the Internet. Computer software and games were also shared in this way, and increasingly films and video too.[3] The music and other entertainment or so-called 'creative' industries, viewed as key economic players by government, claimed that this unlicensed activity was having a significant impact upon the 'legitimate' market for their products. These arguments were illustrated in particular by undoubtedly falling sales of music CDs and also with lurid industry-produced statistics about losses caused by 'copyright theft'.[4]

---

[1] I am grateful to the many colleagues and PhD students with whom I have discussed the issues raised in this paper, but am alone responsible for errors of fact, law and opinion contained within it. All website references were last checked on 5 June 2009.

[2] *Britain Forward Not Back: The Labour Party Manifesto 2005*, 95.

[3] See C Waelde and H MacQueen, 'From Entertainment to Education: The Scope of Copyright' [2004] *Intellectual Property Quarterly* (IPQ) 259.

[4] See eg International Federation of Phonogram Industries Digital Music Report 2009, accessible at http://www.ifpi.org/content/section_resources/dmr2009.html.

The years since 2005 have seen at least much public thinking aloud about how to fulfil Labour's undertaking, even if it seems increasingly unlikely that the electoral timetable will allow any major legislative action in consequence until 2010 at earliest.[5] By no stretch of imagination could the Gowers Review of Intellectual Property published by the Treasury in December 2006 be regarded as the systematic assessment of copyright in the digital age foreshadowed in the 2005 manifesto.[6] Such was not even the Review's primary focus. Instead what it produced was a piecemeal collection of proposals within an overall drive to achieve 'balance', 'coherence' and 'flexibility' within the 'intellectual property system' in the UK.[7] The question of what copyright law might best fit a world where information, entertainment and ideas were increasingly disseminated on the Internet was quietly left on the shelf amidst a flurry of excitement about proposals for rules on format shifting, transformative works and parody—important stuff, not unrelated to the digital age as we shall see, but scarcely going to the core of copyright. Realisation that it was not enough led to a further burst of government activity in 2008–09: a BERR consultation on legislative options in relation to illicit filesharing begun in July 2008 and closed in January 2009;[8] a UK Intellectual Property Office (UKIPO) consultation on developing a copyright agenda for the twenty-first century, published in December 2008;[9] discussion of copyright issues in the Digital Britain Interim Report published in January 2009,[10] followed by another UKIPO discussion paper on the creation of a Digital Rights Agency;[11] and a paper on strategic priorities for copyright produced by the new Strategic Advisory Board on Intellectual Property in March 2009.[12]

The question of copyright law in the digital environment thus remains a pressing one. Despite the steady growth of licensed filesharing sites, numerous court decisions around the world finding unlicensed providers and their individual users liable for infringement of copyright,[13] and more

5 The next UK General Election must be held by May 2010.

6 Available at http://www.hm-treasury.gov.uk/gowers.

7 It is very debatable whether the UK has an intellectual property 'system'. For an argument that there is a 'core concept' of intellectual property, see M Spence, *Intellectual Property* (Oxford, Oxford University Press, 2007), 12–35.

8 Accessible with government response of 29 January 2009 at http://www.berr.gov.uk/consultations/page47141.html (BERR is the Department for Business, Enterprise & Regulatory Reform).

9 UKIPO, © *the Future: Developing a Copyright Agenda for the 21st Century* (December 2008, available at http://www.ipo.gov.uk/c-policy-consultation.pdf).

10 *Digital Britain Interim Report* (January 2009), s 3.2, available at http://www.culture.gov.uk/images/publications/digital_britain_interimreportjan09.pdf. Publication of the Final Report was imminent at the time this article was completed.

11 *Copyright in a Digital World: What Role for a Digital Rights Agency* (March 2009, available at http://www.ipo.gov.uk/digitalbritain.pdf). See further below, p 190.

12 *Strategic Priorities for Copyright* (March 2009, available at http://www.sabip.org.uk/copyright-100309.pdf).

13 See eg *MGM Studios Inc v Grokster Ltd* 545 US 913 (2005); *Universal Music Australia Pty Ltd v Sharman License Holdings Ltd* [2005] FCA 1242; *Stichting Bescherming Rechten*

energetic prevention measures by Internet service providers (ISPs) encouraged by governments,[14] unlicensed activity continues virtually unabated
and may indeed be growing amongst the young. Discussion of the subject
with students alone suggests this, and it is confirmed by the findings of such
inquiries as the Digital Music Survey published by Entertainment Media
Research and the law firm Wiggin. While the 2008 edition found that the
number of illegal music downloaders had declined to 39 per cent of those
surveyed compared with the 'all-time high' of 43 per cent in 2007, this was
offset by a slight rise in such activity amongst teenagers, to 58 per cent in
that group of those surveyed.[15]

But this is not just a matter of how young people like to get their music
and films, or indeed of 'illegal' activity. Digital broadcasting is firmly established, including making available already broadcast programmes through
facilities such as the BBC iPlayer.[16] Newspapers appear in online editions
and include there podcasts of audio and video material, while broadcasters
also provide online textual versions of their news and information services.
Both groups of providers vigorously encourage interactivity with users of
their services.[17] Distance education of all kinds is increasingly carried out
online; indeed, educational institutions make increasing use of digital technology in teaching on-campus students. Course materials go online along
with recordings of lectures and use of interactive facilities, as well as
tutorial sites for communication between teachers and taught. Libraries,
public archives, galleries and museums put digitised versions of their
resources up on websites for users,[18] while universities increasingly place
staff research outputs in publicly accessible online repositories.[19] Book

---

Entertainment Industrie Nederland (BREIN) v Techno Design Internet Programming BV [2006]
ECDR 21; and the Swedish *Pirate Bay* case, decided on 17 April 2009 (see BBC News Online,
http://news.bbc.co.uk/1/hi/technology/8003799.stm). For an unofficial English translation of
the *Pirate Bay* decision, see http://www.ifpi.org/content/library/Pirate-Bay-verdict-English-trans
lation.pdf.

14 See further below, p 189.

15 Digital Music Survey 2008, available in summary at http://www.wiggin.co.uk/upldfiles/
Press%20Release%20-%202008%20Digital%20Music%20Survey.pdf. The survey reports that
51 per cent of all downloading in the UK is 'legal', making a sharp contrast with the claim in the
IFPI Digital Music Report 2009 (the basis for which is not explained) that 95 per cent of music
downloads are unauthorised and produce no revenue for rights-holders (see http://www.ifpi.org/
content/library/DMR2009.pdf, at 3, 5, 22 and 29).

16 See http://www.bbc.co.uk/iplayer/.

17 See eg http://www.scotsman.com/; compare BBC News Online (http://news.bbc.co.uk/).

18 See eg British Library (http://www.bl.uk/); National Library of Scotland (http://www.nls.uk/);
The National Archives (http://www.nationalarchives.gov.uk/); National Archives of Scotland
(http://www.nas.gov.uk/; see also Scottish Archive Network at http://www.scan.org.uk/); the
British Museum (http://www.britishmuseum.org/); National Museums of Scotland (http://www.
nms.ac.uk/); the Victoria and Albert Museum (http://www.vam.ac.uk/); National Galleries of
Scotland (http://www.nationalgalleries.org/). Note also Scottish Cultural Resources Access
Network (SCRAN) at http://www.scran.ac.uk/.

19 See eg Southampton University ECS EPrints Repository (http://eprints.ecs.soton.ac.uk/);
Edinburgh University Research Archive (http://www.era.lib.ed.ac.uk/).

publishers experiment ever more confidently with online first publication of text, supported by the development of more and more user-friendly electronic readers.[20] Google, Microsoft, Project Gutenberg and the European Digital Library project seek in different ways to make already published content available in online digital form.[21] Even governments and legislatures, whether transnational, national or local, have realised the value of the Internet as a place to give out information and interact with the people in the provision of services and the collection of data.[22] The Scottish government's online 'National Conversation' blog about independence provides a good, if flawed, example of what is now possible.[23]

All this underlines the pervasive nature of the Internet. It is now the principal means of disseminating content that not so long ago would have been available, if at all, only in analogue form and/or in particular physical locations. Social behaviour of all kinds and age-groups has changed visibly and significantly as a result, in the world of work as much as play. The Internet has become the first port of call for anyone in search of information, ideas or simply contact with like-minded people. Unparalleled opportunities also exist—through social network sites, blogs, wikis and other interactive facilities, sometimes collectively dubbed 'Web 2.0'[24]—for individuals to make public information about themselves, exchange opinions and share knowledge on every question under the sun. Huge businesses such as Google have grown up with astonishing rapidity, first to help people navigate their way around the rich and varied content now available, and then to aggregate and increase that content (not only Google Books, for example, but also Google News, Scholar, Earth, Maps, Images, Video and Street View).

Much of this activity, notably but not only filesharing, occurs in full awareness of at least a risk of copyright infringement. For some this is a cause of serious concern, whether as a good or bad thing. For others, it is

[20] See eg *The Times* 13 February 2008, Business section, 'Rival Publishers Discover Novel Battleground in Cyberspace', with editorial comment by Antonia Senior ('Publishers are Braced for the Slow Death of the Book').

[21] See http://www.googlebooksettlement.com/ (Google Books Settlement) (for discussion see ch 7); http://books.google.com/googlebooks/library.html (Google Books Library Project); http://www.bl.uk/news/2008/pressrelease20080528.html (British Library alliance with Microsoft to digitise nineteenth-century and out-of-copyright literature); http://www.gutenberg.org/wiki/Main_Page (Project Gutenberg http://www.theeuropeanlibrary.org/portal/organisation/cooperation/archive/edlproject/ (European Digital Library). Note also the Open Content Alliance (http://www.opencontentalliance.org/).

[22] See eg the websites of the UK government (http://www.direct.gov.uk/en/index.htm); the UK Prime Minister (http://www.number-10.gov.uk/output/Page1.asp); Scottish government, (http://www.scotland.gov.uk/Home); Westminster Parliament (http://www.parliament.uk/); Scottish Parliament (http://www.scottish.parliament.uk/home.htm); and Edinburgh City Council (http://www.edinburgh.gov.uk/internet).

[23] See http://www.scotland.gov.uk/Topics/a-national-conversation.

[24] See the article on this in Wikipedia (itself an example of the phenomenon) at http://en.wikipedia.org/wiki/Web_2.

simply an impediment to be ignored or confronted head on. Undoubtedly there is widespread uncertainty about what exactly the law allows. Such uncertainty is likely to be damaging: some may assert non-existent or at best doubtful rights, while others avoid socially beneficial activity out of unjustified concern about possible wrongdoing. One does not have to subscribe to the view that copyright should be a central part of the primary school curriculum to see the case for increasing accurate and objectively formulated public awareness of copyright. That process would be greatly helped if at least the general principles of copyright law could be simply and lucidly stated.[25] Even better if these principles were recognisably in tune with the realities of a digital society, and general perceptions within that society of right and wrong.

B. Making Copyright Fit for Purpose in the Digital Environment

This and the following chapter therefore explore some of the issues involved in making copyright fit for purpose in the digital environment, and attempt to go beyond the rather bland generalisations to be found in the consultations and comments made in UK government consultations and reports since 2006. The thrust of both chapters is, however, similar to those documents: copyright should support realisation of the Internet's potential for all legitimate stakeholders in a mixed but essentially market economy, ie private individuals, commercial and voluntary organisations, and public bodies. The chapters also accept that one important justification of copyright is to provide a means of rewarding creativity, and that this does indeed encourage socially beneficial and useful production. But for reasons more fully argued elsewhere,[26] these chapters are also based on the view that the law is informed by other values, such as the protection of individual personality rights, the support and use of the public domain, and the promotion and dissemination of culture (giving that word its widest possible sense). Legal recognition of these values is not inimical either to creativity or the conversion of that creativity into economic benefit for creators and their publishers.

The chapters do not, however, engage with arguments about justifications for copyright itself, or about whether we should start analysis on the basis that the law reflects some sort of basic property right in what an individual creates or is rather a special exclusive privilege carved out of a

---

[25] See further D Vaver, 'Reforming IP Law: An Obvious and Not-so-obvious Agenda' [2009] *IPQ* 143; B Fitzgerald, 'Copyright 2010: The Future of Copyright' [2008] *European Intellectual Property Review (EIPR)* 34.

[26] See HL MacQueen, 'Copyright Law Reform: Some Achievable Goals?', in F Macmillan (ed), *New Directions in Copyright Law IV* (Cheltenham, Edward Elgar, 2007); HL MacQueen, CE Waelde and GT Laurie, *Contemporary Intellectual Property: Law and Policy* (Oxford, Oxford University Press, 2007) ch 7.12–7.13.

general freedom to do what we will with creative material produced and publicly disseminated by others.[27] We must start where we are, and within the UK this means broadly within the international framework of copyright law, created by the Berne Convention, the Rome Convention so far as relevant, the Agreement on Trade-Related Aspects of Intellectual Property Rights 1994 (TRIPS Agreement), the World Intellectual Property Organization (WIPO) Treaties of 1996, and this country's continuing membership of the EU. It is possible to argue for change within these structures, of course, but only within the EU is there much realistic prospect of such arguments taking effect: the rest is pretty much a given for the foreseeable future.

The approach also takes as read that copyright applies as much to works in the digital environment as in the analogue one. There may of course be difficulties about earth-bound cross-border issues—*which* copyright law applies will often be a devilishly difficult matter to decide—but these are perhaps a little less significant for a writer based in the (not quite) harmonious EU. Thanks in particular to the WIPO Treaties, many of the issues discussed here are in fact global ones; but this chapter's point of departure is the law in the UK with due recognition of its EU setting. Perhaps the major peculiarity resulting from this is the need to take account of the EU's rules about databases. These give all databases, the making of which involved substantial investment, a special or *sui generis* form of protection, while also conferring copyright on those that, by reason of the selection and arrangement of their contents, constitute the author's own intellectual creation.[28] These rules are not replicated in other parts of the world, notably the US. Detailed treatment of this topic should be sought in the under-noted works, however, and here reference will be made to database rights only so far as incidental to use on the Internet.[29]

---

[27] See for arguments of this kind eg J Litman, *Digital Copyright* (New York, Prometheus Books, 2001), ch 12; R Deazley, *Rethinking Copyright: History, Theory, Language* (Cheltenham, Edward Elgar, 2006); M van Schijndel and J Smiers, 'Imagining a World without Copyright: The Market and Temporary Protection, a Better Alternative for Artists and the Public Domain', in H Porsdam (ed), *Copyright and Other Fairy Tales: Hans Christian Andersen and the Commodification of Creativity* (Cheltenham, Edward Elgar, 2006), 147–64; L Zemer, *The Idea of Authorship in Copyright Law* (Aldershot, Ashgate, 2007); J Boyle, *The Public Domain: Enclosing the Commons of the Mind* (Yale, Yale University Press, 2008).

[28] Copyright, Designs and Patents Act 1988 (CDPA) s 3A; Copyright and Rights in Database Regulations 1997 (SI 1997/3032), implementing Parliament and Council Directive 96/9/EC on the legal protection of databases.

[29] E Derclaye, *The Legal Protection of Databases* (Cheltenham, Edward Elgar, 2008); T Aplin, *Copyright Law in the Digital Society: the Challenges of Multimedia* (Oxford and Portland, OR, Hart Publishing, 2005); MJ Davison, *The Legal Protection of Databases* (Cambridge, Cambridge University Press, 2003); I Stamatoudi, *Copyright and Multimedia Products: a Comparative Analysis* (Cambridge, Cambridge University Press, 2002).

C. Some Other Issues not Covered

Space considerations also preclude detailed discussion of a number of other issues about copyright in the digital environment. Before we turn to the main substance of this chapter (copyright infringement), three topics may, however, be briefly noted as current at the time of writing: the responsibility of ISPs to aid in the prevention of copyright infringement, the duration of copyright, and 'orphan' works.

With regard to ISPs, the UK government has decided to legislate only to require that they (i) notify infringers using their facilities of the illegality of their conduct; and (ii) collect anonymised information about persistent infringers and provide personal details to rights-holders upon a court order to that effect.[30] This means that the government has chosen not to impose a regime necessitating the removal (or slowing) of such persistent infringers' access to the service; unlike, for example, the proposals in France.[31] The government may have considered its options narrowed by the Electronic Commerce Directive (which says that no obligation should be imposed on ISPs to screen or monitor third-party content[32]). Further difficulties were caused by the *Promusicae v Telefónica* case in 2008, where the European Court of Justice (ECJ) applied the Communications Directive 2002 to refuse to order ISPs to disclose personal details of illegal downloaders to rights-holders on privacy grounds (although noting that there might be exceptions to this to prevent crime, unauthorised use of electronic communication systems and the destruction of others' rights and freedoms, including intellectual property rights).[33] The possibility remains, however, that ISPs could be found liable under existing UK law for authorisation of copyright infringement by others whom they can control.[34] The proposed

[30] See the government's January 2009 response to the BERR consultation on legislative options to address illicit peer-to-peer (P2P) file-sharing, accessible at http://www.berr.gov.uk/files/file49907.pdf and referred to in Action 13 of the *Digital Britain Interim Report* (January 2009, accessible at http://www.culture.gov.uk/images/publications/digital_britain_interimreport jan09.pdf). See also a government-brokered Memorandum of Understanding on unlawful file-sharing of music and film published on 24 July 2008 and accessible at http://nds.coi.gov.uk/environment/fullDetail.asp?ReleaseID=375009&NewsAreaID=2&NavigatedFrom Department=True. The UKIPO website reports that in an initial three-month trial under the Memorandum, each of the six ISPs involved issued 1,000 notifications per week to infringers identified by rights-holders (http://www.ipo.gov.uk/c-policy-p2p.htm). See generally ch 1.
[31] For the 'three strikes and you're out' French law (the *loi Hadopi*), passed by the French National Assembly and Senate on 12 and 13 May 2009 respectively, see http://en.wikipedia.org/wiki/HADOPI_law#cite_note-4. 'Hadopi' is an acronym for Haute Autorité pour la Diffusion des Œuvres et la Protection des Droits sur Internet. The law is now subject to constitutional review and possible challenge for inconsistency with EU legislation.
[32] E-Commerce Directive, Art 14; see further below, p 197 n 70.
[33] Case C-275/06 *Productores de Música de España v Telefónica de España SAU* [2008] ECR I-271; Directive 2002/58/EC of the European Parliament and of the Council of 12 July 2002 concerning the processing of personal data and the protection of privacy in the electronic communications sector. See generally ch 14.
[34] See further CDPA s 16(2), and MacQueen, Waelde and Laurie, above n 26, paras 4.63–4.70.

Digital Rights Agency, to be funded and run by rights-holders and ISPs under the government's watchful eye, may well be a further mechanism by which ISPs will be subjected to pressure to go beyond their legislative obligations and take further 'voluntary' actions to bring filesharers to heel.[35]

The *duration of copyright* has become significant for the Internet in various indirect ways. Most prominent is the term of sound-recording copyright—50 years from the end of the year of publication[36]—because the sound-recording industry is lobbying hard for a near-doubling of the period, to 95 years. The European Commission was persuaded to issue a proposal for a Directive to this effect in July 2008, but the measure has failed to gain the whole-hearted support of the Member States or (so far) of the European Parliament, which has recommended extension to 70 years only.[37] The importance of this for the digital environment is that many of the most popular sound recordings made in the 1950s—and soon in the 1960s—are falling into the copyright-free public domain and so becoming available for unlicensed Internet transmission. A much longer copyright term would thus have a significant effect upon exactly how the Internet's role as an enduring repository for this material might develop over the next decade.

Another but rather different issue arising from the length of copyright term is that of the *'orphan work'* whose author cannot be identified, whether as a result of anonymity, pseudonymity or simple obscurity. This makes it impossible to know when the work's copyright term, determined in the case of literary, artistic, dramatic and musical works by calculating 70 years from the end of the year the author died, comes to an end. The partial frustration of projects to digitise library holdings, at least if this is to be carried out with the express consent of all rights-holders, is one possible result of the law's insistence that no use can be made of anonymous and pseudonymous works without an elaborate and potentially costly prior process of 'reasonable inquiry' about the author's true identity.[38] Further, there is no provision at all for the problem of the merely obscure author. The potential significance of the whole issue is highlighted by the British Library's calculation that some 40 per cent of its copyright holdings are orphan works.[39] Some solution to this difficulty is clearly needed to facil-

---

35 See UKIPO, *Copyright in the Digital World: What Role for a Digital Rights Agency* (March 2009, available at http://www.ipo.gov.uk/digitalbritain.pdf). The Agency may also be a rights clearance house and a dispute resolution forum. At the time this chapter was completed it seemed doubtful whether the Agency would in fact be brought into existence.

36 CDPA s 13A.

37 For the Commission proposal, see http://ec.europa.eu/internal_market/copyright/docs/term/proposal_en.pdf. For the European Parliament's recommendation, made on 23 April 2009, see BBC News Online, http://news.bbc.co.uk/1/hi/entertainment/8014734.stm. See further Opinion, 'Creativity Stifled? A Joint Academic Statement on the Proposed Copyright Term Extension for Sound Recordings' [2008] *EIPR* 341.

38 CDPA ss 9(4), (5), 12(3)–(6), 104.

39 The British Library Manifesto, Intellectual Property: A Balance (September 2006) (accessible at http://www.bl.uk/news/pdf/ipmanifesto.pdf).

itate the goal of digitising our cultural heritage to be accessible to all.[40] Google's aggressive approach, to digitise all books and put them online unless a copyright owner makes itself known and objects, appears to have had some success in the US where (subject to the approval of a court due to be decided in September 2009) it has formed the basis for a general settlement with groups representing rights-holders.[41]

II. SCOPE OF COPYRIGHT: INFRINGEMENT IN THE DIGITAL ENVIRONMENT

A. Introduction: The Right to Copy

There is a simple point inherent in the very name of copyright. It starts with the idea of a right to copy works of the kind protected by the law: literary, dramatic, musical and artistic works, films, sound recordings and broadcasts, to use the categories of the Copyright, Designs and Patents Act 1988. The right is exclusively vested in somebody in relation to every work, so that only with that rights-holder's permission may anyone else lawfully copy any such work. The right to copy here, in other words, is one about excluding copying without authority; such copying is a wrong.

In the digital world, however, copying of protected works occurs constantly and necessarily: every time a software program is loaded into a computer RAM, or a surfer opens up a webpage, to take two simple examples occurring several million times a day around the world. There is, in other words, a *need* to copy before any and every *use* of digital material, whether long or short, commercial or non-commercial, intentional or accidental, serious or casual. Where there is such a basic technological requirement, the question ought surely to arise whether the correct starting point for legal analysis of copying is from the standpoint of a wrong being committed. Might the right to copy in this context be one more appropri-

[40] See US Register of Copyrights, Report on Orphan Works (2006) (accessible at http://www. copyright.gov/orphan/); Gowers Review, ch 4.91–4.99, recommendation 13; Publishers Association Position Paper on Orphan Works (October 2007), accessible at http://www. publishers.org.uk/en/home/copyright/issues_and_papers/; Commission Green Paper, *Copyright in the Knowledge Economy* (Brussels, COM(2008) 466/3). Note also the Commission recommendation (2006/585/EC, L 236/28), encouraging Member States to create mechanisms to facilitate the use of orphan works, as well as the Final Report and Memorandum of Understanding produced by a High Level Expert Group on Digital Libraries on Digital Preservation, Orphan Works and Out-of-Print Works (see http://ec.europa.eu/information_society/activities/digital_libraries/experts/ hleg/meetings/index_en.htm); and the Joint Copyright Guidelines produced in the UK in April 2008 by the British Academy and the Publishers Association (http://www.britac.ac.uk/reports/ copyright-guidelines/index.html), s 8.

[41] See http://www.googlebooksettlement.com/ (Google Books Settlement). It is by no means clear at the time of writing whether the court will approve the settlement. See also ch 7.

ately vested in the population at large rather than being subject to any single person's authority and control?

B. Transient Copying

Such, of course, has not been the approach of law-makers to the matter over the three decades or so since copyright in the digital world began to press itself upon them as a matter worthy of attention. They were rather moved to make clear that the concept of copying extended to the 'temporary' or 'transient' reproduction typically occurring with digital works, where generally the copy's life ended when the use of the work stopped with either the software or the computer being switched off by the user.[42]

In Europe, the process began with the Software Directive 1991 and continued with the Database Directive 1996.[43] But in a somewhat absurd manner each Directive also provided rather circular and question-begging exceptions to the effect that persons with rights to use software or access a database (and so make temporary reproductions thereof) could do so without infringing copyright as a result.[44] The absurdity reached its height in the Copyright in the Information Society (InfoSoc) Directive 2001.[45] As one Article brought temporary reproduction within the scope of copyright infringement unless licensed,[46] another carefully set out an exception allowing unauthorised temporary reproduction.[47] Apart from software and databases, which are left with their own rules, there is no infringement where temporary reproduction is an 'integral and essential part of a technological process' with its 'sole purpose' being either a 'transmission of the work in a network between third parties by an intermediary' or a 'lawful use of the work', and the resultant copy has 'no independent economic significance'. A decision of the ECJ on the interpretation of these words is awaited in *Infopaq International A/S v Danske Dagblades Forening*.[48] The opinion of Advocate General Trstenjak was issued on 12 February 2009: she declared, amongst many other points, that the essential circumstance

---

[42] In the UK note CDPA s 17(6), an early statutory statement that transient copying is infringement.

[43] Council Directive 91/250/EEC on the legal protection of computer programs (henceforth Software Directive 1991), Art 4(a); European Parliament and Council Directive 96/9/EC on the legal protection of databases (henceforth Database Directive 1996), Art 5(a).

[44] Software Directive 1991, Art 5(1); Database Directive 1996, Art 6(1).

[45] European Parliament and Council Directive 2001/29/EC on the harmonisation of certain aspects of copyright and related rights in the information society (henceforth InfoSoc Directive 2001).

[46] Ibid, Art 2.

[47] Ibid, Art 5(1).

[48] Case C-5/08 *Infopaq International A/S v Danske Dagblades Forening*, judgment forthcoming. See also ch 7.

for a 'transient' reproduction was that it should last only for a very short time.

The elaborate structure of the rule is designed to ensure that neither the technical operations of the Internet (the transmission of data in small packets from computer to computer across networks), nor the ordinary activities of users of websites, constitute a massive and continual series of copyright infringements. That extraordinary result could have been equally well or still better avoided by tackling the issue on the alternative, and surely more sensible, basis that temporary reproduction would only exceptionally (if ever) be infringement—perhaps, for example, when such a reproduction *did* have an independent economic significance. Indeed, 'independent economic significance' might be a better starting point for defining when *any* copying becomes relevant for copyright purposes, eg the making of a copy which deprives the rights-holder of a sale that would otherwise be made in the marketplace for its work. Certainly it looks a more readily intelligible criterion than the vague metaphysics involved in determining whether or not a copy is 'temporary' or 'transient'. It can also be related to the Berne Convention's idea that a rights-holder's 'normal exploitation' of its copyright should not be prejudiced by any exception to that right.[49]

C. Public Communication Right: Making Available

Copyright has never been limited to the right to copy, and the need to go further has very often been driven by the means, sometimes but not always technological, through which works reach their audience. Thus print involved the making of copies by the printer/publisher, but generally this was with the consent of the rights-holder, the author of the work concerned. What really mattered, because it generated revenue, was the transfer by sale of printed copies to the public. This, at least so far as concerned the first dealing with the copies, was accordingly brought within the scope of the copyright-owner's exclusive rights; to be joined more recently by rental and lending transactions involving published copies of the work.[50] To broadcast works likewise became an exclusive right within the scope of copyright, although even more clearly a method of exploiting works not involving the creation of copies.[51] This built on established rights to control public performances, previously the main way in which dramatic and musical works in particular reached their audiences, which

---

[49] See further below, pp 203–204; also IVIR Study on the Implementation and Effect in Member States' Laws of Directive 2001/29/EC on the Harmonisation of Certain Aspects of Copyright and Related Rights in the Information Society (February 2007, henceforth IVIR InfoSoc Study), 22–24, 30–39.

[50] In the UK see now CDPA ss 18 and 18A.

[51] Broadcasting is now subsumed in the public communication right: see further below, p 194.

again did not result in the circulation of physical copies of the script or score concerned.[52]

There is thus nothing surprising or contrary to copyright principles in the introduction of a new right designed to accommodate transmission on the Internet and bring it within the sphere of exclusive rights. This is the public communication right, which first saw the light of day in the WIPO Copyright Treaty of 1996,[53] was picked up for the EU in the InfoSoc Directive,[54] and was implemented in the UK from 31 October 2003 by the Copyright Regulations 2003.[55] Public communication is about the electronic transmission of works to their audiences. The UK implementation first brings broadcasting (including cablecasting) under the new head. However, it also extends to making a work available to the public by electronic transmission in such a way that members of the public may access it from a place and at a time individually chosen by them.[56] This describes Internet transmission, and makes clear that only the rights-holder or its licensee may so transmit a work.[57] Anyone else making copyright material generally available on the Internet—eg sound recordings or videos via peer-to-peer (P2P) networks such as Napster or social networking websites such as YouTube—is an infringer. Public communication right has thus been the basis on which music-recording companies have since 31 October 2003 begun successfully to sue individual members of P2P networks as distinct from the creators and suppliers of the software enabling such networking to take place.[58] The right also clearly applies to the 'streaming' of material across the Internet as well as to enabling others to download or make copies of works.[59]

---

[52] CDPA s 19.

[53] WIPO Copyright Treaty 1996, Art 8. See further J Ginsburg, 'The (New?) Right of Making Available to the Public', in D Vaver and L Bently (eds), *Intellectual Property in the New Millennium* (Cambridge, Cambridge University Press, 2004), arguing that the international right does not reach all forms of Internet transmission.

[54] InfoSoc Directive, Art 3.

[55] Copyright and Related Rights Regulations 2003 (SI 2003/2498), reg 6, now CDPA s 20.

[56] CDPA s 20(2)(b).

[57] The distinction between broadcasting and making available at a time and place chosen by the user may not always be very sharp. For example, on my digital television I can record programmes for later viewing or, more significantly, 'pause' an ongoing transmission while I take a telephone call or make a cup of tea, then 'resume' it at the point where I had left off once I am ready to do so. See, for more technical discussion, IVIR InfoSoc Study, 27–28.

[58] For a UK case decided against individual file-sharers as copyright infringers, see BBC News Online, 27 January 2006, http://news.bbc.co.uk/1/hi/entertainment/4653662.stm. On 19 August 2008 the BBC reported a case from the Patents County Court in which a computer games producer had been awarded £6,000 damages plus £10,000 costs against a woman who unauthorisedly uploaded one of its games for use by file-sharers on the Internet (http://news.bbc.co.uk/1/hi/technology/7568642.stm). I have not traced any judgment in these cases in either the law reports or legal databases.

[59] See *Union des Associations Européennes de Football v Briscomb* [2006] EWHC 1268 (Ch); OLG Hamburg, Urteil vom 7.7.2005, 5 U 176/04, ZUM 2005/10, 749–751 (*Streaming offer* case); IVIR InfoSoc Study, 26–27.

What else does this new right cover? In the *Rafael Hoteles* case the ECJ said that it

> must be interpreted broadly. Such an interpretation is moreover essential to achieve the principal objective of that Directive, which, as can be seen from its ninth and tenth recitals, is to establish a high level of protection of, inter alios, authors, allowing them to obtain an appropriate reward for the use of their works.[60]

The ECJ went on to hold that transmissions by a hotel proprietor of copyright material on television to different persons in their individual hotel bedrooms required copyright licences as public communication. The case is thus mainly concerned with broadcasting, but other comments in the judgment have a bearing on liability for Internet transmission.

So whether communication to an individual sitting in a hotel bedroom was 'public' was argued, but the Court observed that the letter and the spirit of the Directive (and of the preceding 1996 WIPO Treaty) meant that the public or private nature of the place where the communication took place was immaterial. The 'making available' element of the public communication right reinforced this interpretation: the essence of that element was the recipient's ability to choose the place and time of the communication, and this would be rendered meaningless if her choice of a private place made a difference. So it matters not to the communicator's liability whether recipients are in their studies, Internet cafés or airport lounges, or indeed accessing the communication on mobile devices.[61] Even more clearly, it would seem, it does not matter that the communicator is working from a private space in making the work available to the public.

That the communication might be made only to a limited number of the public—eg subscribers to a website or members of a network who gained access through user names and passwords—probably does not matter either. As with the public performance right, it is the nature of the audience that counts—are they members of the public?—not whether anyone without restriction may choose to receive the communication.[62] The ECJ seems to confirm this interpretation by identifying hotel customers as 'a public' distinct from other 'publics', when holding that the copyright author's licence to the television broadcasters to communicate its work to the public covers only 'direct' users of the broadcasts. These are 'owners of

---

[60] Case C-306/05 *Sociedad General de Autores y Editores de España (SGAE) v Rafael Hoteles SA* [2006] ECR 11519, para 36.

[61] An argument that the conclusion that there could be public communication in a private place infringed Art 8 ECHR (privacy) was rejected by the court, on the basis that it was the hotel making its room available to the public which was being made liable rather than the customer in the private room (para 53).

[62] L Bently and B Sherman, *Intellectual Property Law*, 3rd edn (Oxford, Oxford University Press, 2008) 151–52; MacQueen Waelde and Laurie, above n 26, para 4.53–4.54; WR Cornish and D Llewelyn, *Intellectual Property*, 6th edn (London, Thomson: Sweet & Maxwell, 2007) para 12.32.

reception equipment who, either personally or within their own private or family circles, receive the programme'. This does not extend to occupants of hotel bedrooms receiving the work by way of a further transmission process inside the hotel.[63] They are a new and different public for the work, and a further licence is needed before the material can be communicated to them. A 'public' is constituted by 'a fairly large number of persons', and in determining the relevant numbers it is relevant to consider 'the fact that, usually, hotel customers quickly succeed each other',[64] ie it is not a matter of 'freezing' the audience at any particular moment in time.

Moreover, whether or not customers switch on the televisions is unimportant; or, putting the point more generally, whether or not members of the public actually access the communication. The language of the Directive—'may access'—makes clear that creation of the possibility of reception of the communication is sufficient. In the Internet context, this must raise the question whether inserting hypertext links to other sites without permission of the latter's owner is potentially an infringement of that person's public communication right.[65] The ECJ notes that the seemingly very wide potential liability is somewhat restricted by a statement in the InfoSoc Directive recitals: 'the mere provision of physical facilities for enabling or making a communication does not in itself amount to communication within the meaning of this Directive'.[66] Thus, according to the ECJ, merely installing television sets in the bedrooms would not be enough for liability, whereas transmitting signals to be picked up by those televisions would complete the infringement. Hyperlinks seem to provide an intermediate case: neither a physical facility nor a transmission, but undoubtedly something which enables communication to the public. The answer to this may be that in many cases the public enabled to receive the communication by the hyperlink is anyway part of the public at which the linked site is already aimed, rather than a new public in the sense discussed in the previous paragraph. But the matter may be finely balanced in many cases, especially those of deep-linking, which evades home pages and other original controls on access.[67]

Litigation in the Netherlands, Belgium and Ireland has raised the question of whether an ISP can be liable as a person 'making available' infringing material even although that material is placed upon its servers by

---

[63] *Rafael Hoteles*, paras 41, 42 (citing WIPO Guide to the Berne Convention).

[64] *Rafael Hoteles*, para 38.

[65] See eg *Shetland Times v Wills* [1997] FSR 604; Bently and Sherman, above n 62, para 6.6.2. Note also the Belgian case of *Google v Copiepresse* [2007] ECDR 5 where the court held that the public communication right of newspapers were infringed by Google's display of links on its search website enabling users to access stories on the newspapers' websites which had been captured and stored in the defendants' server caches.

[66] InfoSoc Directive, recital 27; *Rafael Hoteles*, paras 45–47.

[67] See further Aplin, above n 29, 147–51. Aplin also argues that 'in-line linking', where a hyperlink is triggered, not by a user, but by an embedded instruction to the user's browser, is a public communication of the material to which the link is made (ibid, 155–56).

others.[68] An argument might again be advanced about whether merely providing facilities for communication amounts to 'making available', and about whether the facilities offered by an ISP amount to the 'physical' kind explicitly excluded from liability in the InfoSoc Directive and discussed in the *Rafael Hoteles* case. The ISP is able to plead a liability exemption under the Electronic Commerce Directive 2000, benefiting intermediaries playing a wholly passive role as mere conduits between suppliers and users of infringing material. This exemption appears, however, to be mainly for the

> automatic, intermediate and transient storage of the information transmitted where
> (a) this takes place for the sole purpose of carrying out the transmission in the communication network, and
> (b) the information is not stored for any period longer than is reasonably necessary for the transmission.[69]

So this may not reach the situation where the ISP is the carrier for a file-sharing service on which the storage is longer term rather than merely the link between the respective computers of the uploader and the downloader.

There is, however, also an exemption under the Directive for 'hosting', or storage, of information at another's request, albeit this makes no direct reference to transmission activities. The exemption shields the ISP from liability so long as it does not know of illegal activity in relation to the material stored and is unaware of facts and circumstances from which illegal activity would be apparent.[70] Hence, an ISP that sought to attract unlicensed filesharers' business, or advertised its potential use for filesharing without warning against unlicensed activity, would not be able to shelter here from liability under the public communication right. Further, once notified of infringing content, the ISP must act expeditiously to remove or disable access upon learning or becoming aware of the activity.[71] But the Directive expressly provides that no obligation should be imposed on ISPs actively to screen or monitor third-party content; the onus is on rights-holders to establish that the facilities are being used for infringing storage and communication.[72]

---

[68] See *Stichting Bescherming Rechten Entertainment Industrie Nederland (BREIN) v Techno Design Internet Programming BV* [2006] ECDR 21 (Court of Appeal of Amsterdam); *SABAM v SA Tiscali (Scarlet)*, [2007] ECDR 19, District Court of Brussels. Note also *EMI v Eircom*, High Court of Ireland 2008/1601 P, settled in January 2009 on the basis that the ISP defendant would henceforth operate a 'three strikes and you're out' policy against file-sharers using its facilities. On such policies see further above, p 189, nn 30–33.

[69] European Parliament and Council Directive 2000/71/EC on certain legal aspects of Information Society services, especially electronic commerce in the Internal Market (E-Commerce Directive), Art 12; implemented in the UK by the Electronic Commerce (EC Directive) Regulations 2002 (SI 2002 no 2013), reg 17. The exemption 'includes' the situation quoted in the text, and it is not clear how much wider it might go.

[70] E-Commerce Directive, Art 14; Electronic Commerce Regulations, reg 19. See also chs 1 and 7.

[71] E-Commerce Directive, Art 14; Electronic Commerce Regulations 2002, reg 19(a)(ii).

[72] Unsurprisingly there are no equivalent words in the Electronic Commerce Regulations

Some other points mentioned in the *Rafael Hoteles* case may be more briefly treated to conclude this section on public communication rights. Just as it did not matter there whether or not customers switched on the televisions, whether or not they received the same communications by way of the transmission, or whether they were received simultaneously or at different times, was also unimportant. But the ECJ did not decide whether the unlicensed communicator had to make a profit or receive some other benefit from the activity to be liable for it, but held that the hotel clearly did do so in the case before it, since it affected both the hotel's standing and the price of its rooms.[73] The view of the Commission, that profit or other benefit is not a precondition of liability, is borne out by the absence of any reference to such a requirement in the Directive, and may also be supported, at least in the UK, by the fact that no such requirement exists in relation to public performance right either.[74]

D. Copying in the Digital Environment: Downloading

It has been forcefully argued that there is an overlap between public communication and reproduction (especially temporary reproduction) rights, and that this causes significant difficulties in practice for rights clearance since it leads to a need for multiple licences and payments in respect of what are in essence 'unitary acts of usage'.[75] A possible example of such double liability can be seen in the Belgian case of *Copiepresse v Google*,[76] where the court held that both rights were infringed by Google's storage in server caches of copies of webpages (reproduction right) and the display of links on its search website making these copies accessible to users (public communication right). But if there is overlap, it is by no means total. Public communication rights in relation to the Internet are about 'making available': that is to say, putting it crudely, it is about the communicator's conduct, not the recipient's, about uploading rather than downloading. Copying is therefore still a potentially relevant form of infringement in

2002. Note, however, BBC News Online, 30 January 2006, http://news.bbc.co.uk/1/hi/technology/4663388.stm, for an order of the High Court of England and Wales requiring 10 ISPs to hand over information about 150 file-sharers detected using their networks.

[73] *Rafael Hoteles*, para 44. Advocate General Sharpston had likewise felt it not necessary to decide this particular point (paras 56–57 of her Opinion).

[74] Bently and Sherman, above n 62, ch 6.5; MacQueen, Waelde and Laurie, above n 26, ch 4.52-4.58; Cornish and Llewelyn, above n 62, ch 12.32.

[75] IVIR InfoSoc Study, 22–25.

[76] *Copiepresse v Google* [2007] ECDR 5, Brussels Court of First Instance (TGI), 13 February 2007; noted by IVIR InfoSoc Study, 55–56; B van Abroeck and M Cock, 'Belgian Newspapers v Google: 2–0' (2007) 2 *Journal of Intellectual Property Law & Practice* 463; S Klein, 'Search Engines and Copyright' (2008) 39 *International Review of Intellectual Property and Competition Law* 451; M Turner and D Callaghan, 'You Can Look but Don't Touch!' [2008] *EIPR* 34. See also ch 7.

relation to unlicensed downloading activity, whether that be by way of saving material to disk or another website, or printing it.

There is a further crucial point about copying as infringement in the digital environment. A fundamental flowing from the existence of copyright, closely related to the protection of privacy, is that it enables authors and creators to decide *not* to publish or disseminate their works.[77] Traditionally, many such privately created works were first made and fixed in such analogue forms as paper and canvas, and no doubt many still are; but today they are equally, if not more, likely to be 'born digital', created and stored on disks and computers. Perhaps the commonest example of digital creation is by photographers using digital cameras, camcorders and mobile phones to capture their images, which may then continue to be held in the machine or be downloaded elsewhere but still in digital rather than printed form. The Internet increasingly provides convenient storage space for all this material, which can otherwise overwhelm or at least awkwardly clutter the limited capacity of even the most memory-rich piece of hardware. Moreover it adds the benefit of relative permanence against the turnover of machinery in households and the ever-present risk of loss of or damage to disks. It is certainly not the case that such storage use of the Internet should necessarily be seen as equivalent to publication of the material stored, or as giving other users some implicit licence to access or use it.

On many storage sites, of course, the position can be readily made clear. When I store my photographs on the Flickr website, for example, I have to choose whether to make them private or public.[78] If I opt for privacy, I can nonetheless open up the images to family or friends whom I invite; while if I choose to go public, I have a further choice to make between complete openness or some form of Creative Commons licence seeking to regulate the reuse of my material by others.[79] I have made use of all the options mentioned so that the position on my collection is generally clear to anyone who comes across it. But the question remains what should the default position be in storage sites in the absence of such structures: available to all or not? Whatever the answer, the protection of individual privacy in supporting decisions not to publish material must be a factor additional to the 'independent economic significance' earlier supported as an element in defining what kinds of copying should constitute infringement of copyright in the digital environment.[80]

---

[77] See for a recent example *HRH The Prince of Wales v Associated Newspapers (No 3)* [2008] Ch 57 (CA) (although note that there was some limited dissemination of the work in this case amongst the Prince's private circle).

[78] See http://www.flickr.com/.

[79] On Creative Commons licences, see further below, pp 221–2.

[80] See above, p 193.

E. Extraction and Reutilisation of Database Contents

Finally in this section, reference should be made to the exclusive rights in the *sui generis* database right, which concern an extraction of substantial parts from the database and reutilisation of the material thus extracted.[81] The interest of their formulation and application lies in their having been designed specifically with digital content in mind. In essence the rights parallel the reproduction and public communication rights in copyright. Unauthorised extraction is the permanent or temporary transfer of database contents to another medium (eg a printout), although this need not involve removal of the content from the database.[82] The ECJ has rather opaquely said that this does not make mere unlicensed consultation of the database an infringement.[83] Extraction is to be given a wide meaning: the concept is not limited to physical taking, and also includes taking that is preceded by the taker's critical evaluation of the material.[84] Reutilisation is making database content available to the public by any means, thus including online transmission and distribution or rental/lending of the database.[85] Extraction and reutilisation may be carried out directly or indirectly (ie from a copy of the original database). The substantiality of the part of the database extracted or reutilised may be measured quantitatively or qualitatively; the fact that a relatively insubstantial quantity of a database's content nevertheless has significant intrinsic value does not make the material qualitatively substantial. Repeated and systematic extraction or reutilisation of insubstantial parts of database contents may amount to the extraction or reutilisation of a substantial part if the actions either (i) conflict with normal exploitation of the database, or (ii) unreasonably prejudice the legitimate interests of its maker.[86] This is in line with the recommendation made earlier in this

[81] Database Directive 1996 art 8(1), implemented in the UK by Copyright and Rights in Databases Regulations 1997 (SI 1997/3032), Reg 16.

[82] Database Directive 1996 Art 7(2)(a), implemented by Databases Regulations 1997, Reg 12(1).

[83] Case C-203/02 *British Horseracing Board v William Hill Organization Ltd* [2004] ECR I-10415, para 54 (cf Database Directive 1996 recital 44 and Databases Regulations 1997, Reg 12(2), (4)). The *Horseracing* case contains extensive discussion of the extraction and reutilisation rights, and has been drawn upon elsewhere in this paragraph to elaborate the statutory wording being paraphrased here. See also Case C-545/07 *Apis-Hristovich EOOD v Lakorda AD*, 5 March 2009.

[84] Case C-304/07 *Directmedia Publishing GmbH v Albert-Ludwigs-Universität Freiburg*, 9 October 2008.

[85] Database Directive 1996 Art 7(2)(b), implemented by Copyright and Rights in Databases Regulations 1997, Reg 12(1).

[86] Database Directive 1996 Art 7(5), implemented in part by Copyright and Rights in Databases Regulations 1997, reg 16(2) (normal exploitation conflict and unreasonable prejudice requirements omitted).

chapter, explicitly bringing into the realm of infringement concepts which actually have their origin in the international regime for copyright exceptions, or defences to claims of copyright infringement.[87]

III. CONCLUSIONS

The conclusions of this chapter may now be briefly stated before directing the reader on to the further discussion and overall conclusions given in the next. The law of copyright infringement has been adapted to the digital environment through the introduction of the public communication right. While this new right is intelligible in principle, its precise scope and its interaction with other forms of copyright infringement remain problematic in several important respects. The basic right protected by copyright, that of preventing others from making copies, remains important in the digital context with regard to unauthorised downloading; but this has been distorted by the addition of the notion of a 'transient' copy as infringement. Apart from the uncertainty about what exactly is covered by the idea of transience, difficulties are created for the basic operation of the Internet. As a result an exception has had to be created, when a more helpful approach might have been to work with the idea, based on the Berne Convention and the Database Directive, that only activities which prejudice the rights-holder's economic position or are in conflict with normal exploitation should be treated as infringements. Such an approach would have been much more consistent with a policy aimed at the realisation of the Internet's potential for all rather than the protection of commercial interests alone.

POSTSCRIPTS

1. The Digital Britain Final Report was published on 15 June 2009 (accessible at http://digitalbritainforum.org.uk/report/). The Government proposes initially to give OFCOM power to impose two duties on ISPs to help reduce illegal file sharing: (1) to notify persons using their servers illegally; (2) for repeat infringers, a court-based process of identity release and civil action. If these measures do not work reasonably soon, ISPs will be empowered to use intermediate technical measures such as bandwidth reduction or protocol blocking. (See above, pp 189–90.)

2   The ECJ issued its *Infopaq* decision on 16 July 2009. The court held

---

[87] See further Derclaye, above n 29, 100–19, 276–78 (arguing that the rights of extraction and reutilisation are 'broadly adequate').

that the reproductions of electronic news articles involved in the preparation of an electronic 'cuttings' service by an agency were not 'transient' copies within the meaning of Article 5 of the Infosoc Directive. (See above, pp 192–3.)

6

'Appropriate for the Digital Age'? Copyright and the Internet: 2. Exceptions and Licensing

HECTOR L MacQUEEN[1]

THIS CHAPTER CONTINUES the discussion begun in its predecessor, and considers issues about copyright exceptions and licensing in the digital environment.

I. COPYRIGHT EXCEPTIONS IN THE DIGITAL ENVIRONMENT

A. International Background

Since its generalisation in the Copyright Act 1911, UK copyright law has provided for exceptions or limitations upon the exclusive rights of copyright owners, for the benefit of users of their works. In the Copyright, Designs and Patents Act 1988 (CDPA) they are described as 'permitted acts', and the relevant sections are nearly 60 in number.[2] The international copyright framework allows for such exceptions to copyright, but does not spell out in any detail what their content should be. There are some specific provisions;[3] but most important is Article 9(2) of the Berne Convention which offers the following general guidance about exceptions, often described as the 'three-step test'.[4] The Convention's Member States may:

---

[1] I am grateful to the many colleagues and PhD students with whom I have discussed the issues raised in this paper, but am alone responsible for errors of fact, law and opinion contained within it. All website references were last checked on 5 June 2009.

[2] CDPA Part I Chapter III (ss 28–76, also including ss 31A–F, 40A, 44A and 50A–D).

[3] Berne Convention, Arts 2bis (political and legal speeches, lectures, addresses), 10 (quotations, illustration for teaching), 10bis (news reporting), 13 (musical works once recording authorised).

[4] See further M Senftleben, *Copyright, Limitations and the Three-step Test: An Analysis of the Three-step Test in International and EC Copyright Law* (The Hague, London and New York, Kluwer, 2004).

permit the reproduction of [literary and artistic] works in certain special cases, provided that such reproduction does not conflict with a normal exploitation of the work and does not unreasonably prejudice the legitimate interests of the author.

The 'three steps' are, then, that (i) exceptions are allowed only in 'certain special cases'; (ii) there must be no conflict with normal exploitation, and (iii) there must be no prejudice to the author's legitimate interests. These open-ended tests, introduced to the Convention only in 1967, both reflect and perpetuate distinct national approaches to copyright exceptions, but have become central to international development of the law, being explicitly referred to as guiding criteria in the Agreement on Trade-Related Aspects of Intellectual Property Rights 1994 (TRIPS Agreement),[5] the World Intellectual Property Organization (WIPO) Copyright Treaty 1996,[6] and the Copyright in the Information Society (InfoSoc) Directive.[7] Significantly, however, where the Berne Convention speaks of the three-step test as 'permitting' exceptions, the later instruments talk rather of 'confining' or restricting their availability; a point to which we return below.[8]

B. Purposes of Copyright Exceptions

The purposes of copyright exceptions are various.[9] They may be seen as reflecting some public interest of wider significance than the private benefit of the copyright owner, the realisation of which should not be dependent on the latter's consent. Examples of such wider interests include education, news reporting, efficient public services or the protection of the disabled. Again, there may be a perception that rights must come to an end somewhere: for example, that they should not extend into the regulation of wholly private or non-commercial activity, or protect the rights-holder's interests outside the economic or market sphere. So long as the user is not competing with the rights-holder's product, or depriving it of an initial sale or other return from the work, there is no need for copyright protection. A still more functional justification argues that exceptions cover common and socially beneficial uses of copyright works where formal permission requirements would impose excessively burdensome transaction costs on all

---

[5] TRIPS, Art 13.

[6] WIPO Copyright Treaty, Art 10.

[7] European Parliament and Council Directive 2001/29/EC on the harmonisation of certain aspects of copyright and related rights in the information society (the InfoSoc Directive), Art 5(5).

[8] See further C Geiger, J Griffiths and R M Hilty, 'Towards a Balanced Interpretation of the "Three-step Test" in Copyright Law' [2008] *European Intellectual Property Review* (*EIPR*) 489.

[9] See generally R Burrell and A Coleman, *Copyright Exceptions: The Digital Impact* (Cambridge, Cambridge University Press, 2005).

concerned such that the uses might not happen at all without the liberation provided by the exceptions.

C. The Digital Challenge

Rights-holders have always had difficulty with exceptions, however, and there is a long history including problems with audio and video recorders and photocopiers as instruments by which users private, professional or commercial might seek to take the benefit of the law's provisions in their favour. The arrival of the Internet, and the possibility that a copy made within an exception might itself be instantly and perfectly copied and trans-mitted across networks to third parties, whether or not these were also beneficiaries of an exception, reinforced this natural hostility. The differ-ence this time was that law-makers responded to these concerns in a much more repressive way than had ever been the case with earlier devices for easy and accessible copying.[10]

International instruments began, as already noted, to talk about the three-step test as a way of restricting the scope of exceptions. The InfoSoc Directive recitals state:

> [T]he provision of . . . exceptions [to copyright] . . . should . . . duly reflect the increased economic impact that such exceptions . . . may have in the context of the new electronic environment. Therefore the scope of certain exceptions may have to be even more limited when it comes to certain new uses of copyright works.[11]

Article 5 of the Directive sets out what is at first sight a long list of copy-right exceptions to be available in the EU Member States, including the one for temporary reproduction already discussed.[12] But closer inspection reveals that this is the only one of the long list which Member States must adopt, and that all the others mentioned are optional. This is because Article 5 was one of the major battlegrounds in the formation of the Directive, thanks not only to the general issues about exceptions already described, but also because of significant differences of approach within the pre-existing national laws. The compromise that enabled the Article to go forward was that most existing exceptions remained permissible, thus allowing Member States to leave their laws as little changed as possible. But the concession was also at the expense of Member States' freedom (had

---

[10] Eg the arrival of the videocassette recorder in the 1980s prompted the introduction of an exception for 'time-shifting' (CDPA s 70). The result, despite the horror-struck protestations and legal actions of the film and television industries, was not their utter destruction. See C Anderson, *The Long Tail: How Endless Choice is Creating Unlimited Demand* (London, Random House, 2006) 199–200.

[11] InfoSoc Directive, Rec 44.

[12] See above, p 192.

they wished to exercise it) to develop new exceptions: the optional list is also an exclusive list.[13] In this freezing of the current laws is the first specific indication of a more restrictive approach to exceptions, coupled with the further possibility that Member States might opt to drop exceptions hitherto granted within their systems. Certainly the notion that *new* exceptions specially tailored for the digital world might be developed at either national or European levels appeared to be cut off.

D. Exceptions under the InfoSoc Directive

The exceptions actually listed in the InfoSoc Directive do not, for the most part, seem particularly tailored to the digital environment—unsurprisingly, given the background just described. Of course, many of the classical exceptions used in the analogue world were and are perfectly capable of application in the digital one, eg teaching and research for non-commercial purposes, quotation for the purposes of criticism or review, use of works of architecture or sculpture located in public places, incidental inclusion of one work in another, and use for the purpose of caricature, parody or pastiche. The exception for news reporting was pleaded, albeit unsuccessfully, by Google in defence of their news service and its aggregation on Google servers of material from other news websites in a case in Belgium.[14] The exception for private copying, obviously of great potential significance in the digital world, remains, subject to the condition that rights-holders receive fair compensation (ie through the levy system); but there is an important addition here, to the effect that the compensation must take account of the application or non-application of 'technological measures' to the work.[15] This will be returned to later; here it suffices to note that this exception, of great importance in France for instance, was not implemented in the quite different tradition of the UK. This, incidentally, well illustrates the absence of European harmonisation following the InfoSoc Directive.[16]

A study by the Amsterdam Institute for Information Law suggests that 'only a very small number of limitations included in the [InfoSoc] Directive seem to be the result of a specific attempt to adapt the system . . . to the digital environment'.[17] Apart from the adjustment to the private copying

---

[13] InfoSoc Directive, Rec 32.

[14] *Google v Copiepresse* [2007] ECDR 5. See generally ch 7.

[15] InfoSoc Directive, Art 5(2)(b). See also Recs 35 and 39 on fair compensation and technological protection measures.

[16] Note, however, that the European Commission is consulting on the levy systems: see http://ec.europa.eu/internal_market/copyright/levy_reform/index_en.htm#member_states.

[17] IVIR Study on the Implementation and Effect in Member States' Laws of Directive 2001/29/EC on the Harmonisation of Certain Aspects of Copyright and Related Rights in the Information Society (February 2007) (the IVIR InfoSoc Study) 43–44.

exception just mentioned, the Institute lists only the exceptions for publicly accessible libraries, educational establishments, museums and archives.[18] This confines their ability to make reproductions to the supply of copies for no direct or indirect economic or commercial advantage (eg to a reader wishing to make a copy for private study or non-commercial research, or to themselves for purposes of preservation). The exception is explicitly not extended to public communication of material in their collections save by way of dedicated terminals on the establishments' premises enabling individual members of the public to access it for purposes of research or private study.[19] Recital 40 of the Directive underlines the restrictive approach: the exceptions 'should not cover uses made in the context of online delivery of protected works. . . . Specific contracts or licences should be promoted which, without creating imbalances, favour such establishments and the disseminative purposes they serve.'[20]

E. Exceptions as 'User Rights'?

The emerging, apparently restrictive, online-unfriendly and possibly abolitionist approach to exceptions on the international stage naturally produced an opposite response, characterising them as 'user rights', as significant within copyright as the rights of owners. The concept of 'user rights' even won judicial support (or at least use) in the Canadian Supreme Court.[21] It is based around ideas of the public domain where there is a general freedom to do with others' creative work that which is not prohibited, and an argument that copyright carves out of that public domain a limited set of rights for authors and their publishers for functional reasons.[22] The copyright exceptions in some sense merely articulate specific instances of the public domain and the general freedom to make use of what is found there.[23] Human rights come into play as well, notably freedom of expression, privacy and rights to education.[24] This freedom, which is a recurrent

---

[18] InfoSoc Directive, Art 5(2)(c), (3)(n).

[19] Note too that this exception does not apply where the works concerned are subject to purchase or licensing terms.

[20] For a German decision (*Subito*) on the extent to which a not-for-profit document delivery service which included online activity came within the library exception of German law (Landgericht München, 15 December 2005, Az.: 7 O 11479/04), see discussion in IVIR InfoSoc Study, 47.

[21] *Law Society of Upper Canada v CCH Canadian Ltd* [2004] 1 SCR 339.

[22] See eg C Waelde and H MacQueen (eds), *Intellectual Property: The Many Faces of the Public Domain* (Cheltenham, Edward Elgar, 2007); W Davies and K Withers, *Public Innovation: Intellectual Property in a Digital Age* (London, Institute of Public Policy Research, 2006).

[23] J Cahir, 'The Public Domain: Right or Liberty?', in Waelde and MacQueen (eds), above n 23, 35–52, cogently criticises the use of rights language in relation to the freedom of the public domain.

[24] See the European Convention on Human Rights, Arts 8, 10 and First Protocol, Art 2; also P Torremans (ed), *Copyright and Human Rights: Freedom of Expression, Intellectual Property,*

word in such approaches, is further reflected in the inability of the rights-holder to seek remuneration for use within copyright exceptions, and it is argued that another concomitant is, or should be, a prohibition on attempts to contract out of or around the exceptions.[25]

In the UK it is difficult to accept such arguments as a matter of current law without considerable qualification, no matter how sympathetic one may be to the underlying general approach. They are hard to reconcile with the Berne Convention and CDPA language of 'permitted acts', especially when the latter also starts with the proposition that 'copyright is a property right'.[26] The public domain may then simply be that which is left over by copyright protection or other relevant intellectual property rights. The CDPA's many permitted acts are generally spelled out with such specificity and detail as to make it very doubtful that they are only particular instances of some more general freedom for users. A detailed recent analysis concludes that it is 'generally possible to contract out of the permitted acts'.[27] In a number of instances (education providing one especially prominent example[28]), particular exceptions cease to be available where a collective licensing scheme is in place. Where the private copying exception exists in other Member States of the European Union, it does so, in compliance with the InfoSoc Directive,[29] alongside a system of levies on the equipment that lets such copying take place, ensuring that rights-holders gain remuneration for the use made of their works, albeit indirectly. The French Cour de Cassation has, however, rejected the idea of a right to private copying arising from the exception to that effect in French law. The Court held that overriding the exception by technological protection measures is within the normal exploitation of a digital work.[30]

On the other hand, one can point in the UK to the existence (if it has survived the implementation of the InfoSoc Directive) of a general 'public interest' limitation on the exercise of copyright at common law, albeit this

Privacy (London, Kluwer, 2004); J Griffiths and U Suthersanen (eds), *Copyright and Free Expression* (Oxford, Oxford University Press, 2005); C Geiger, 'Author's Right, Copyright and the Public's Right to Information: A Complex Relationship (Rethinking Copyright in the Light of Fundamental Rights)', in F Macmillan (ed), *New Directions in Copyright Law* V (Cheltenham, Edward Elgar, 2007) 24–44.

25 See LMCR Guibault, *Copyright Limitations and Contracts: an Analysis of the Contractual Overridability of Limitations on Copyright* (The Hague, Kluwer, 2002).

26 CDPA s 1(1).

27 Burrell and Coleman, above n 9, 69.

28 CDPA ss 35(2), 36(3). See also s 31D on disability exceptions.

29 See above, p 206.

30 *Studio Canal v Perquin et Union fédérale des consommateurs Que choisir*, 28 February 2006, case no 549, Bull 2006 1 no 126, 115 (the *Mulholland Drive* case). See also *Studio Canal v Perquin et Union fédérale des consommateurs Que choisir*, Paris Court of Appeal, 4 April 2007, Gaz Pal 18/07/2007 no 199, 23; and note the similar Belgian decision, *Test Achats v EMI Recorded Music Belgium*, Brussels Court of Appeal, 9 September 2005, case 2004/AR/1649.

has been handled very gingerly by the courts in modern times.[31] In *Ashdown v Telegraph Newspapers*[32] the Court of Appeal also recognised that human rights may sometimes at least temper the full enforcement of copyrights, implicitly qualifying the view of the first instance judge in the case that '[t]here is no room for . . . further defences outside the code which establishes the particular species of intellectual property in question'.[33] The US has its very open-ended 'fair use' doctrine, the determination of which 'includes' (ie is not limited to) such matters as whether the use is of a commercial nature or for non-profit educational purposes, the amount and substantiality of the portion used in relation to the whole work, and the effect of the use upon the market or the value of the work.[34] This certainly provides the courts with some flexibility of response to change in the way copyright works are disseminated and used, whether arising from new technologies, social behaviour or institutional structures.

F. Further Reform

The revision of the copyright exception regime is very much on the current agenda in the UK. Part of the remit of the Gowers Review of Intellectual Property in 2006 was to determine, in the context of intellectual property rights fit for the digital environment, 'whether provisions for 'fair use' by citizens are reasonable'. For some this looked ominous, in the light of the apparently developing agenda for the restriction, or even elimination, of exceptions; but in the event the Gowers Review summarised its position as follows:

> Balanced and flexible rights should enable consumers to use material in ways that do not damage the interests of right holders and will help ensure that citizens have trust in the system. They will enable cultural institutions to preserve our heritage, and help research institutes to further knowledge by using ideas protected by others.[35]

The Report went on to propose the development of exceptions for education (to ease the provision of digital material for students on the distance learning programmes facilitated by the Internet[36]) and for libraries

---

[31] See HL MacQueen, CE Waelde and GT Laurie, *Contemporary Intellectual Property: Law and Policy* (Oxford, Oxford University Press, 2007) ch 5.47, for a summary of the leading modern cases.

[32] *Ashdown v Telegraph Newspapers* [2002] Ch 149 (CA).

[33] Ibid, para 20 (Sir Andrew Morritt VC).

[34] US Copyright Act 1976, s 107.

[35] Gowers Review of Intellectual Property (December 2006) 4 (Executive Summary) (available at http://www.hm-treasury.gov.uk/gowers).

[36] Ibid, paras 4.13–4.19. Note the previous recommendation to similar effect made in 1997 by the National Committee of Inquiry into Higher Education (Chairman Sir Ron Dearing), *Higher Education in the Learning Society*, para 13.34 and recommendation 43.

(to enable them to make archival copies of all works in their collection for preservation purposes, and to shift such copies from one format to another to ensure that the archive was not made obsolete by technological change).[37] Turning to the activities of individuals, Gowers recommended that a limited private copying exception should be created to allow 'format shifting' by consumers, ie moving content from one lawfully acquired carrier (say a CD) to another (say an MP3 player) for greater ease and personal convenience of use.[38] All this, argued Gowers, would be within the scope of the exceptions allowed under the InfoSoc Directive.

Indeed, the Report continued, the UK could take advantage of the optionality of the Directive list to add an exception found there because of its place in the laws of several other Member States, namely one for parody, caricature or pastiche.[39] The possibilities for work of this nature were increased by the malleability of digital content, and since it could engender both cultural and economic benefit, it should not be hampered by the need to seek rights-holders' permissions. Similar thoughts led Gowers to suggest one further exception clearly outside the scope of the InfoSoc Directive, for creative, transformative or derivative works, such as those produced by digital 'sampling' of others' music recordings. Transformative work of this kind, it was suggested, was at least sometimes recognised as fair use in the US, and the UK should urge change upon the EU, always, of course, within the three-step test of the Berne Convention.[40]

Most of these issues (but significantly, perhaps, not the matter of transformative works) were taken up in a UK Intellectual Property Office consultation published in January 2008.[41] But this may well be given further context by activity in the European Commission, which in November 2007 produced a relatively brief review of the InfoSoc Directive for the Council, the European Parliament and the Economic and Social Committee, in the course of which exceptions are discussed.[42] The main concern of the document is to identify which of the exceptions have been taken up by the Member States, how they have been implemented, and how they have operated in the courts and in practice, rather than to reconsider the whole approach of the Directive. The exceptions specifically

---

[37] Gowers Review, above n 35, paras 4.78–4.84.
[38] Ibid, paras 4.72–4.76.
[39] Ibid, paras 4.89–4.90.
[40] Ibid, paras 4.85–4.88.
[41] UKIPO, *Taking Forward the Gowers Review of Intellectual Property: Proposed Changes to Copyright Exceptions* (January 2008) (the UKIPO Consultation). It is a matter of some concern that in mid-June 2009 this consultation had yet to produce any report, or indeed the second round of consultation promised on the UKIPO website (http://www.ipo.gov.uk/c-policy-copyexceptions.htm).
[42] Commission Staff Working Document, Report to the Council, the European Parliament and the Economic and Social Committee on the application of Directive 2001/29/EC on the harmonisation of certain aspects of copyright and related rights in the information society (November 2007).

discussed, however, are those for private copying, reporting current events, quotation for criticism or review, parody, and the benefit of libraries. In July 2008 the Commission published a Green Paper entitled 'Copyright in the Knowledge Economy',[43] which discussed copyright exceptions within the context of the best dissemination of knowledge in the online environment for the purposes of research, science and education, emphasising in particular exceptions for libraries, archives, and teaching and research purposes.

G. Library and Similar Exceptions

Taking first here exceptions for the benefit of libraries, the Commission's 2007 paper draws attention to developments in related areas of European policy:

> [T]he Commission Recommendation of 24 August 2006 on the digitisation and online accessibility of cultural material and digital preservation recommends that Member States adopt legislation allowing multiple copying and migration of digital cultural material by public institutions for preservation purposes.[44] . . . As scanning and indexing are arguably outside the scope of the library exception, a copyright subgroup has tackled this issue as part of the Commission's 'Digital Libraries' project.[45] [Footnote references as in the original text.][46]

The aim of these activities is the highly attractive one of providing European citizens with access to the continent's cultural heritage via the Internet, and deploying digital technology to allow individual searching for and use of material. Much of that will be in the copyright-free public domain; but that which is not will require some form of copyright exception or limitation to become part of the resource. The InfoSoc Directive does not enable this in its present form.

Such matters therefore also lie beyond the scope of the current UK consultation on copyright exceptions. Extension of the very limited current scope of the UK version of the libraries and archives is suggested, so that it will cover all kinds of work, not just literary, dramatic and musical works; enable format shifting for preservation purposes; and cover museums and

---

[43] Brussels, COM(2008) 466/3.

[44] Commission Recommendation 2006/585/EC of 24 August 2006 on the digitisation and online accessibility of cultural material and digital preservation, para 9.

[45] Communication 'i2010:Digital Libraries', Brussels 30.9.05 COM(2005) 465 final, followed by a recommendation on the digitisation and online accessibility of cultural material and digital preservation, OJ 236 of 31.8.06, 28.

[46] Commission Staff Working Document, Report to the Council, the European Parliament and the Economic and Social Committee on the application of Directive 2001/29/EC on the harmonisation of certain aspects of copyright and related rights in the information society, 5.

galleries as well.[47] With regard to digitally preserved archive copies, the consultation notes a British Library submission to Gowers:

> Best practice for digital data storage is to hold a number of copies on mirror servers to ensure that works are not lost if one digital copy is lost or corrupted. . . . The issue becomes more acute where works are of high cultural importance and where only one copy ever existed, eg manuscripts of literary and political figures.[48]

The argument that the exception should therefore enable the making of more than one preservation copy is countered by fears that the revenue of rights-holder could be adversely affected if the copy was also used for other purposes such as inter-library loan or online delivery. Context for such fears is provided by library collaboration in such projects as Google Books, which aims to make copyright material freely available online in public libraries and not-for-profit educational institutions. All of these activities are, as already noted, anyway outside the scope of what the InfoSoc Directive specifically allows the library exceptions to do with digital material; but has the balance been rightly located in the present law? Are the full possibilities of the digital environment in overcoming the limitations of the physical being realised?

Take a simple example. If a unique copy of a work in a publicly accessible library or archive, say the private letter or manuscript of a public figure who died within the last 70 years, is withdrawn from public handling because of its fragile state, and is instead digitised, is that digital copy to be available only to would-be readers physically on the premises of the library or archive? There is clearly benefit for those members of the public who, for a variety of perfectly understandable reasons, are not able to visit the library or archive in person, while there seems to be no loss of revenue to the rights-holder (the public figure's estate) in making the work also available online, or in transmitting a digital copy of it attached to an e-mail to a remote reader, or in posting a print-out of the digital copy to that reader. The case for an approach like this in the context of museums and galleries, where typically the work will exist in a unique copy, seems even stronger.

H. Exceptions for Individuals

Moving on from the concerns of institutions, the mission of which includes holding collections of copyright material and making them available to the public, the UK consultation also raises some acute questions about the reform of exceptions conceived primarily for the benefit of individual

---

[47] UKIPO Consultation, 28–30.
[48] Ibid, para 179.

users. A particular example is the exceptions for private study and non-commercial research. The main reform proposed here is to extend the exception from literary, dramatic, musical and artistic works to all categories of copyright work, including sound recordings and films.[49] In general terms, this seems an obviously sensible development of the law within the scope of the InfoSoc Directive, and one that has been pressed for particularly by academic bodies to take account of the interests of scholarship and teaching in expanding fields such as cultural and media studies.[50] But at the moment the benefit of the exception is available to anyone, and not just to those carrying out study or research in academic institutions. The consultation paper therefore raises the possibility that the individual who downloads a sound recording or a film from some un-licensed source and makes it available online may be able to defend a claim of copyright infringement on the basis that the activity was to enable that person's private study or non-commercial research, even although such study could otherwise only have been carried out by purchasing, renting or borrowing the sound recording from an authorised source generating revenue for the rights-holder.[51]

Various unattractive solutions to this difficulty are canvassed in the consultation paper: confining the benefit of the expanded exception to those working in academic institutions or studying on courses or programmes leading to formal qualifications, or limiting the amount of the work that can be copied under the exception. While it would be helpful to make clear that research in academic institutions is non-commercial (a point of some uncer-tainty in the present law), it is far from clear why those genuinely pursuing research or study out of private or personal interest rather than in the course of their employment or education should not also have the benefit of the exception. There may also be difficulty in defining the academic institutions in which research of the right kind is carried out.[52] There will certainly be enormous difficulty in defining appropriate limitations upon the amount of a work that can be taken under the exception. Musicologists, for example, will have serious problems in studying or researching the history of popular music recordings unless tracks can be examined as a whole. Moreover, copying will often be necessary since much of the source material is no longer made available by rights-holders. It would also follow that such activity does not deprive the rights-holder of a sale.[53]

---

[49] Ibid, paras 116–41.

[50] See eg British Academy Review, *Copyright and Research in the Humanities and Social Sciences* (September 2006).

[51] Gowers Review, above n 35, paras 146–60.

[52] There may be less difficulty in defining institutions in connection with whose courses and programmes students may carry out private study, since there is already a fairly comprehensive definition of 'educational establishment' in CDPA s 174 and Copyright (Educational Establish-ments) Order 2005 (SI 2005/223).

[53] I owe this example to Professor Nick Cook FBA, Director of the AHRC Research Centre for the History and Analysis of Recorded Music, Royal Holloway, University of London.

214 Hector L MacQueen

In the end, the best approach to the problem of the unlicensed filesharer pleading the exception for private study or non-commercial research would seem to lie in the dictionary definitions of study and research and the overarching concept of fair dealing. The definitions are, respectively, the application of the mind to the acquisition of knowledge and a process either of search or investigation undertaken to discover facts and reach new conclusions by the critical study of a subject or by a course of scientific inquiry, or a systematic investigation into and study of materials and sources, to establish facts or collate information.[54] No doubt some, and perhaps even many, filesharers could show that their activities fell within these definitions; but the burden would be upon them to prove that such was the case. Filesharing is a two-way activity: what one downloads is also available to others, and the private study exemption does not apply to making materials available for third-party private study.[55] Further, research would probably require some end-product in view, such as publication of results. Finally, the filesharer's activity would in the UK also have to be 'fair dealing', at which point we may return to the three-step test, and consider how far the activity conflicts with normal exploitation and unreasonably prejudices the legitimate interests of the rights-holder. A more than trivial library of unlicensed copies of works otherwise available on the authorised marketplace seems unlikely to be regarded as fair dealing, no matter how much private study its owner engages in there.

An issue that the UK consultation cannot address, because the rule in question is laid down in the InfoSoc Directive,[56] is the limitation of the research exception to non-commercial research. For the UK this was a narrowing down of the previous law. As already noted, this causes difficulties of application in the academic world,[57] and may cause tricky questions in other sectors, eg when government commissions social research from a private consultancy firm. There is a similar exception to the *sui generis* database right of extraction (but not reutilisation).[58] A European Commission staff working paper published in 2004 questioned whether differences between copyright exceptions and the more limited exceptions for the *sui generis* right may mean problems for owners and

---

[54] For these definitions, see the *Oxford English Dictionary*; note also the Australian and New Zealand cases of *De Garis v Neville Jeffress Pidler* (1990) 18 IPR 292 (Fed Ct Aus); *Television New Zealand v Newsmonitor Services* [1994] 2 NZLR 91 (High Ct NZ); and *Copyright Licensing v University of Auckland* (2002) 53 IPR 618 (NZ).

[55] See *University of London Press Ltd v University Tutorial Press Ltd* [1916] 2 Ch 601; *Sillitoe v McGraw-Hill Book Co (UK) Ltd* [1983] FSR 545.

[56] InfoSoc Directive, Art 5(3).

[57] It is discussed at length in the British Academy Review (above n 50).

[58] European Parliament and Council Directive 96/9/EC on the legal protection of databases, Art 9(b), implemented by Databases Regulations 1997, Reg 20(1)(b); E Derclaye, *The Legal Protection of Databases* (Cheltenham, Edward Elgar, 2008) 131–33 (critical of the exceptions as too narrow).

users of databases.[59] An example may be the provision that making a database available for on-the-spot reference use in a library or similar public institution constitutes reutilisation for which a licence is needed, although *lending* the database through such an establishment otherwise than for direct or indirect economic or commercial advantage is freely allowed.[60] As well as being odd in itself, this seems inconsistent with the InfoSoc Directive exception for dedicated terminals in libraries discussed above.[61] How it fits with the European Court's comment, also cited above,[62] that mere consultation of a database is neither extraction nor reutilisation, is likewise unclear. But again these are questions that the UK exercise cannot address.

I. A New Approach?

Much of the foregoing is concerned only with the detail and specific application of particular exceptions, confined as it is by the unsatisfactory constraints imposed by the peculiar history and structure of the InfoSoc Directive. The Amsterdam Institute study for the European Commission on the InfoSoc Directive is the only recent document to take a principled overarching approach to the reform of the law on exceptions, its objectives being balanced and harmonised rules across the European Union that will create the legal certainty cross-border online businesses want to have.[63] The study recommends what it calls a two-tiered approach, with a set of mandatory exceptions based on human rights and Internal Market considerations, plus the adoption of an 'open norm' which gives Member States the freedom to provide for further exceptions. Mandatory exceptions based on human rights (mostly freedom of expression) would include criticism and review, news reporting, parody, use for educational purposes, and provision for the disabled; while Internal Market considerations include private copying, research and private study, and exceptions for libraries, archives and museums. The open norm is not spelled out in any detail beyond the limitations of the three-step test and the absence of significant effect upon the single European market.[64] The flexibility such an open norm might give in meeting future social and technological needs is appealing, but if it is to gain its place in European copyright law it may need fleshed out in greater detail, perhaps deploying the US 'fair use' clause

[59] Commission Staff Working Paper on the review of the EC legal framework in the field of copyright and related rights, SEC (2004) 995, para 2.1.3.2. See also the Report of the Royal Society (London), *Keeping Science Open* (London, 2003) ch 5.
[60] Databases Regulations 1997, Reg 12(2), (4).
[61] At p 207.
[62] At p 200.
[63] IVIR InfoSoc Study, ch 2.
[64] Ibid, 65–67.

as a source of relevant further factors to be considered.[65] Whether or not the 'open norm' would have a 'subsidiary' or gap-filling role in relation to the particular exceptions, or be something stronger and more overarching in function, would also have to be decided.

II. TECHNICAL PROTECTION MEASURES AND RIGHTS MANAGEMENT INFORMATION SYSTEMS

One further issue that has already been touched upon occasionally in this chapter, but which the UK consultation cannot address because the rules are laid down firmly (if obscurely) in the InfoSoc Directive, is that of the legal protection for technical protection measures (TPMs) and electronic rights management information systems (RMIs) for digital works.

Just as digital technology made copying necessary, easy and perfect, so it also enabled the development of defence mechanisms to prevent, or at least make more difficult, such copying where it was taking place without the copyright-owner's licence or consent. Simple examples include encryption so that the work becomes available only if the device on which it is accessed contains a 'key' making decryption possible (so, for example, sound recordings downloaded from the iTunes store can only be played on an iPod machine);[66] the use of activation codes of the kind familiar to any purchaser of Microsoft Office software; or the Flickr website system already described[67] by which an uploader of photographs may prevent third-party access to them. In a commercial context, these digital walls or fences became the point at which rights-holder and would-be user can make bargains about the terms and conditions of use. In reality, for the user this is generally a matter of 'take it or leave it', not negotiation.

A further technique by which transmission and reuse can also be regulated digitally is the incorporation within works of electronic rights management information systems—electronic tags or 'fingerprints' which enable works to be identified and traced electronically wherever they may be in use, lawfully or, more importantly, otherwise. The identification usually includes the names of the software and the copyright-owner, and lists the respective rights of the rights-holder and the lawful user. The information in the system often comes up on the computer screen when the work is installed or run. These systems are of particular importance in identifying the source of a work that has been transmitted across the Internet and in

---

[65] The approach in the new Israeli copyright law, promulgated in 2007: see OF Afori, 'An Open Standard "Fair Use" Doctrine: A Welcome Israeli Initiative' [2008] *EIPR* 85.

[66] Another example familiar from case-law is the lock systems used in conjunction with the global but regionally divided distribution of the Playstation computer games console: *Sony Computer Entertainment v Owen* [2002] EMLR 34; *Sony v Ball* [2005] FSR 9; *Kabushiki Kaisha Sony Computer Entertainment v Stevens* [2005] HCA 58.

[67] Above, p 199.

their most extreme form may involve the transmission of data about users back to the copyright-holder whenever the work is accessed or played.[68]

Since the whole aim of these digital rights management (DRM) systems is to prevent unlicensed access to, use and transmission of digital works, and set up opportunities to contract and charge for these activities, an obvious issue is what to do about attempts to circumvent them by those unwilling to pay the rights-holder's price. Maintaining the effectiveness of some form of DRM was clearly vital to the realisation of the commercial potential of digital technology and the Internet. What the InfoSoc Directive therefore did, following and developing a precedent set by the Software Directive,[69] was to confer legal protection upon both TPMs and RMIs, making it equivalent to copyright infringement to circumvent an effective technological measure or to remove or alter without authority rights management information associated with a copy of a work or appearing in connection with a public communication of it. To be liable, the infringer had to know or have reasonable grounds for knowing what he was doing; the innocent who accidentally or unknowingly interferes with a work's DRM systems will escape responsibility. The liabilities extend to those who manufacture or deal commercially in devices designed to circumvent TPMs, or who knowingly distribute, import or communicate to the public works the RMIs of which have been altered or removed.[70]

A crucial difference between the TPM and the RMI protections, however, is that only for the latter are the circumvention wrongs tied to actual copyright infringement. The alteration or removal of RMI, or the dealing in an RMI-stripped/altered digital work, must be done with knowledge or reason to believe that the action in question induces, enables, facilitates or conceals an infringement of copyright.[71] Nothing similar limits the protection of TPMs; and from this it seems to follow that circumvention of a measure that is not aimed at copyright infringement but at the exercise of a copyright exception, such as private study or non-commercial research, will still be caught as infringement of the TPM right. Indeed, TPMs could go even further and prevent access to a work which had either fallen out of copyright at the end of its term, or had never had copyright at all in the first place.

The realisation that TPM protection could effectively go beyond copyright led to heavy criticism from the time of its conception. The InfoSoc Directive attempted a compromise solution in its notorious Article 6(4), said by one distinguished commentator to have been 'so twisted by

---

[68] In November 2005 BMG withdrew a 'copy control' mechanism which was said to be capable of use of this kind, after threats of litigation founded on rights of privacy in various countries: see BBC News Online, http://news.bbc.co.uk/1/hi/technology/4430608.stm.

[69] Art 7(1)(c). Note also CDPA s 296 as originally enacted.

[70] InfoSoc Directive, Arts 6 and 7, implemented in the UK as CDPA ss 296ZA–296ZG.

[71] CDPA s 296ZG (1), (2), implementing InfoSoc Directive, Art 7(1).

conflicting demands as to resemble Laocoön wrestling with the serpents'.[72] In essence Member States must set up mechanisms for lawful users of works prevented from exercising copyright exceptions by TPMs to complain and have a remedy—in the UK, the Secretary of State has the power to issue directions to the copyright owner or an exclusive licensee if it is that person who is exercising the relevant copyright.[73] However, none of this applies to 'copyright works made available to the public on agreed contractual terms in such a way that members of the public may access them from a place and at a time individually chosen by them'.[74] The legislation also says nothing about work out of or never in copyright and issued digitally supported by TPMs.

No complaints have been made to the UK Secretary of State under these provisions since their implementation on 31 October 2003. Perhaps the most cogent critique has come from by the British Library, arguing that the possible obsolescence of any given DRM system as technology evolves may in due course make it impossible to access older digital works for any purpose, never mind fair dealing under the library exceptions already discussed.[75] But this scenario has yet to materialise. Uncertainty shrouds the explanation for the lack of formal complaint: do the legislation's contortions effectively ensure that complaints are unlikely to be worthwhile, are frustrated users simply unaware of the possibility of complaint, or are exceptions in fact operating despite TPMs?[76] It is certainly true that some major content providers have become more relaxed or liberal about the use of TPMs in recent times. From January 2008 EMI, Warners, Virendi Universal and Sony BMG, the four largest sound recording companies, are all making material available without copy controls, albeit at higher prices than the same material with DRMs attached.[77] Apple announced in January 2009 that it would follow a similar policy with its iTunes sales.[78] Some TPMs allow copying for limited periods of time or on

72 WR Cornish and D Llewelyn, *Intellectual Property*, 6th edn (London, Thomson: Sweet & Maxwell, 2007) ch 20.79. The UK implementation (CDPA s 296ZE) is no less contorted. For images of Laocoön and the serpents, and more information about his tragedy, see http://en.wikipedia.org/wiki/ Laoco%C3%B6n.

73 Cf the altogether more powerful French Autorité de Régulation des Mesures Techniques (ARMT), discussed in N Jondet, 'La France v Apple: Who's the Dadvsi in DRMs?' (2006) 3(4) *SCRIPT-ed* 473 accessible at http://www.law.ed.ac.uk/ahrc/script-ed/vol3-4/jondet.asp. The ARMT has now been renamed Haute Autorité pour la Diffusion des Œuvres et la Protection des Droits sur Internet (HADOPI): see further p 189 n 31 above.

74 CDPA s 296ZE(9), implementing InfoSoc Directive, Art 6(4), fourth para.

75 The British Library Manifesto, Intellectual Property: A Balance (September 2006) (accessible at http://www.bl.uk/news/pdf/ipmanifesto.pdf).

76 A study which casts light on what is happening is P Akester, 'Technological Accommodation of Conflicts between Freedom of Expression and DRM: The First Empirical Study' (Centre for Intellectual Property and Information Law, University of Cambridge, 2009), accessible at http://www.law.cam.ac.uk/faculty-resources/summary/technological-accommodation-of-conflicts-between-freedom-of-expression-and-drm-the-first-empirical-assessment/6286.

77 See BBC News Online, http://news.bbc.co.uk/1/hi/technology/7175338.stm.

78 See BBC News Online, http://news.bbc.co.uk/1/hi/technology/7813527.stm.

a limited number of occasions, thus enabling the private user to make back-ups or shift formats to allow the content to be played on MP3 players, personal computers or in-car sound systems.[79]

How, then, should the law be made fit for the digital age?[80] A powerful argument clearly exists for linking the rules against circumvention of TPMs to copyright infringement in the same way as the rules against alteration or removal of RMIs.[81] The effect of this would be the legitimation of circumvention for purposes other than infringing the copyright in the protected work. On the other hand, merely legitimating circumvention would not benefit the technologically unsophisticated user, who would be left dependent on the development of businesses making and supplying easy-to-use circumvention devices.

It would not be easy to go further and legislate for a requirement that DRMs recognise generally when a user is exercising the benefit of a copyright exception. For example, a system that depended on self-certification by the user would probably be too open to abuse. But attention has been drawn to the solution of one content platform which offers a dedicated service for universities and libraries, with DRMs that enable activities normal within such institutions, such as lending of copies.[82] Again, websites that give disabled people special access facilities might also enable them to get the benefit of the exceptions in their favour. Such models might be encouraged or supported by requiring producers to make positive efforts to allow use of the exceptions.

A further option could be a rule that DRMs must be made to expire with the copyright in the supported work. Here the difficulties look to be more legal than technological: for authored works issued digitally with DRMs when the author is still alive, it cannot be foretold when the copyright will come to an end. An altogether different approach would make DRMs the *only* protection available for digital works, since from the point of view of the rights-holder it has all, and more than, the benefits of copyright. The difficulty with this is that the sole incentive for the rights-holder to make the work available in the copyright-free world is profit, and the same profits can be made selling a few copies at a high price or many at a low: so the incentive may fail to achieve the widespread

---

[79] Some examples are given in an article on BBC News Online, 11 December 2007 (http://news.bbc.co.uk/1/hi/technology/7136527.stm).

[80] Some recent recommendations by various bodies within the UK are summarised in MacQueen, Waelde and Laurie, above n 31, para 7.61.

[81] Such an argument is set out in detail in IVIR InfoSoc Study, 95–101.

[82] IVIR InfoSoc Study, 108. The content platform in question is not identified in the study. It later recommends (ibid, 133) that the limitations which the Study elsewhere proposes should be mandatory (see above, p 215) should by law be accommodated by TPMs. See also Commission Staff Working Document (2007) s 3.4 for an agreement in Germany between the national library, on the one hand, and the Federation of Phonographic Industries and the Booksellers and Publishers Association, on the other, allowing the former to circumvent TPMs on CDs, CD-ROMs and e-books.

dissemination and use of works. All that would protect the user and general public interests recognised in current copyright law is individual and collective bargaining power. That might be supplemented with relevant consumer protection rules, but these might end up looking quite a lot like copyright, which would rather undermine the point of abolishing it in the first place. In any event, none of the current stakeholders seem interested in getting rid of copyright, so the discussion is probably best focused on the regulation of DRMs within that framework.

III. LICENSING

A. Relationship between Exceptions and Contractual Provisions

Inherent within this discussion of DRMs is the wider question of the relationship between copyright and contract law, in particular whether copyright exceptions may be overridden by agreement between the parties. Since licensing rather than sale, rental or lending is the characteristic transaction in the digital environment, the matter is critically significant for present purposes. The recent conclusion that the general answer to the question is yes has already been quoted;[83] but Burrell and Coleman, the authors of the study in question, also make the point that several exceptions to the general position exist, many of them in the digital context.[84] Hence, any term or condition of an agreement purporting to prohibit the permitted act of temporary reproduction of a database necessary for the purpose of access to and normal use of the database contents by a person with a right to use the database is void.[85] A number of other acts in relation to computer programs which are permitted to a lawful user thereof cannot be overridden by contract—ie making a back-up copy of the program,[86] decompilation with the aim of creating a new program,[87] and observing, studying or testing the functioning of a program to determine its underlying principles.[88] Burrell and Coleman argue that a piecemeal approach is to be preferred to any blanket principle for or against contractual overriding of copyright exceptions, and that one should distinguish between different types of fair use in this regard.[89]

Taking such an approach, some exceptions seem unlikely to be meaningfully overridden by contract—or DRMs, for that matter. Criticism and

[83] See above, p 208.
[84] Burrell and Coleman, above n 9, 69.
[85] CDPA ss 50D(2) and 296B.
[86] CDPA s 50A.
[87] CDPA s 50B.
[88] CDPA s 50C.
[89] Burrell and Coleman, above n 9, 70.

review, parody and news reporting provide reasonably clear examples, at least where the works in question can generally be accessed, digitally or otherwise.[90] On the other hand, the library community has argued vociferously for several years that the licence agreements which enable readers to be provided with access to commercially provided databases and other digital material frequently override the exceptions for the benefit of libraries, inadequate though these already are. The British Library has claimed that in a random sample of 30 of its licences, 28 were found to be 'more restrictive than rights that currently exist within copyright law'.[91] If there is a problem here—and obviously much more empirical evidence would be required to show that there is—then it may provide a case for further regulatory intervention.

B. Open Access Licensing

Not all licensing is restrictive by comparison with copyright, and some of what is available in the digital context might almost be said to eliminate copyright altogether as an owner's right. Schemes abound, with names ranging from 'Copyleft' and 'General Public Licence' to 'Open Source' and 'Creative Commons', their shared feature being that the copyright owner declares in advance the uses of the work generally allowed to any member of the public without further specific consent or any licence fee. These general permissions may cover the whole range of restricted acts, or make a selection from within them. The Creative Commons scheme, for example, allows the rights-holder to declare that anyone may make use of a work, choosing whether or not to insist on attribution of source and exact reproduction only, or to allow commercial use, or to insist on the licensee likewise granting licences with regard to resultant works on the same terms and conditions ('share-alike').[92] Such licences are seen by their promoters as embracing rather than fearing the possibilities of digital technology; but they do face some formidable legal difficulties. One of the most complex is the basic question of enforceability, on either side of the transaction, or against third parties; another (assuming initial enforceability) is whether, and if so, how and to what extent such a licence may be revoked.[93] The

[90] Ibid, 70–75.

[91] The British Library Manifesto, Intellectual Property: A Balance (September 2006) (accessible at http://www.bl.uk/news/pdf/ipmanifesto.pdf).

[92] See the Creative Commons website, http://creativecommons.org/; MacQueen, Waelde and Laurie, above n 31, ch 21.29.

[93] See P Johnson, '"Dedicating" Copyright to the Public Domain' (2008) 71 *Modern Law Review* (*MLR*) 587. For a Dutch decision upholding the enforceability of a Creative Commons licence, see *Curry v Audax Publishing BV* [2006] ECDR 22. See also a Spanish case *SGAE v Fernandez*, 17 February 2006, and in the US, *Jacobsen v Katzer* 535 F 3d 1373 (Fed Cir 2008), likewise upholding the enforceability of an open-source licence. A claim that licensing copyright material for no return constituted the anti-trust (competition) law offence of predatory pricing

practical importance of such questions is that many grant open access licences in idealistic enthusiasm and without real understanding of their legal rights, and then find that others less innocent are making hay with the grass that they sowed.

Creative Commons licences in which authors have the right to claim attribution and to allow or prevent derivative works as they see fit recognise the significance in the digital world of the moral rights of attribution and integrity. The author's name must continue to be connected with the work, and the work must not be treated in a way that damages its integrity and the author's honour and reputation.[94] Moral rights recognise a role of individuals in creative production and their right to maintain their personal expressions in the forms they chose to give it. Moreover, rights of integrity contribute to the preservation of cultural heritage for later generations.[95] These rights seem all the more important in the 'mash-up' world of the Internet. Fears that such rights put the author in the position of censor and lead to the stultification of derivative or transformative uses of others' work seem exaggerated and indeed unlikely, especially if the liability requirement of damage to the original author's honour and reputation is kept in mind. There are in any event questions about the extent to which moral rights can be transferred to others than the author, waived or set aside altogether (a subject on which there is, however, considerable diversity internationally).[96]

C. Public Sector Information Reuse

A significant development with some of the characteristics of open access concerns the licensing of copyright public sector information (PSI) for reuse by persons other than the public body which first generated the material. Following a Directive in 2003 implemented in the UK in 2005,[97] most public bodies are now under an obligation to license reuse of their material to those requesting it.[98] Terms and conditions may be imposed,[99]

was rejected in a decision of the US Court of Appeals Seventh Circuit: *Wallace v IBM, Red Hat and Novell* 467 F 3d 1104 (2006).

[94] CDPA ss 77–89.

[95] See eg MT Sundara Rajan, 'Moral Rights in Information Technology: A New Kind of "Personal Right"?' (2004) 12 *International Journal of Law and Information Technology (IJLIT)* 32. Cf P Masiyakurima, 'The Trouble with Moral Rights' (2005) 68 *MLR* 411.

[96] For comparative information, see E Adeney, *The Moral Rights of Authors and Performers: An International and Comparative Analysis* (Oxford, Oxford University Press, 2006) chs 2I, 7.43, 8K, 9L, 12G, 14J, 16G, 18G.

[97] Parliament and Council Directive 2003/98/EC on the re-use of public sector information, implemented in the UK by the Re-use of Public Sector Information Regulations 2005 (SI 2005/1515).

[98] Some public bodies are excluded, eg archives, libraries, museums, galleries public sector broadcasters, educational and research establishments (PSI Regulations 2005, Reg 5(3)).

[99] PSI Regulations 2005, Reg 12.

but there is an Information Fair Trader Scheme for the accreditation of authorities in this regard (which can be carried out online in its basic version).[100] The principles of the scheme involve a commitment to *openness*, defined as meaning that generally all information created by the organisation will be licensed for any use, by any customer; *transparency*, meaning that terms, conditions and pricing policies should be clearly, simply and accessibly explained; and *fairness*, meaning that all applicants and licensees should be treated alike for the same types of reuse, and that the organisation should not use its market power to compete unfairly. Standard charges are to be used as far as reasonably practicable, and charges should not exceed the sum of the cost of collection, production, reproduction and dissemination of documents plus a reasonable return on investment.[101] Where appropriate and possible, electronic processes are to be used throughout the process of licensing, from initial request to delivery of the material.[102] The Office of Public Sector Information has promulgated 'click-use licences' which can be used online for Crown and Parliamentary copyright material, and encourages other public authorities to develop similar facilities.[103] Nearly 18,000 click-use licences were granted between April 2001, when the scheme started, and May 2009.[104]

Space precludes any more detailed treatment of the PSI reuse rules here;[105] but they provide an interesting illustration of possibilities for automated online contracting subject to regulation of the contracts for fairness in accordance with broad equitable principles. Whether the private sector needs to generate self-regulating mechanisms of this kind to encourage greater consumer confidence in the fairness of their prices and other terms and conditions must be a moot point. It is certainly unlikely that government would or could seek to intervene in detail in the various markets involved, even if that was otherwise desirable.

[100] See further the Office of Public Sector Information website at http://www.opsi.gov.uk/ifts/index.htm.

[101] PSI Regulations 2005, Reg 15.

[102] PSI Regulations, Regs 10, 11(2).

[103] See further the Office of Public Sector Information website at http://www.opsi.gov.uk/click-use/index.htm.

[104] This and other relevant statistics, regularly updated, on the Office of Public Sector Information website at http://www.opsi.gov.uk/about/website-statistics/licensing-statistics.htm.

[105] Or debate on whether public sector information ought to be protected by copyright and other intellectual property rights at all, or should be freely available to all, as happens in the US. See eg S Saxby, 'Crown Copyright Regulation in the UK—Is the Debate Still Alive?' (2005) 13(3) *IJLIT* 299; P Weiss, 'Borders in Cyberspace: Conflicting Public Sector Information Policies and their Economic Impacts', in *Open Access and the Public Domain in Digital Data and Information for Science: Proceedings of an International Symposium* (Washington DC, National Academies Press, 2004), accessible at http://www.primet.org/documents/weiss%20-%20borders%20in%20cyberspace.htm.

IV. CONCLUSIONS

The question pursued in this and the preceding chapter is how copyright may support realisation of the Internet's potential for all legitimate stake-holders. It seems clear that the commercial possibilities require copyright protection coupled with some form or other of digital rights management. But it is equally clear that the individual consumers for whom the commercial products are ultimately intended will not accept a merely passive role in this marketplace. Filesharing sites are one outcome of the great rebellion against the sound-recording industry, the roots of which lie in high pricing of CDs from the 1980s on, and which finally boiled over with Napster and its unlicensed successors around the world. More recently, the resistance to DRM systems preventing all use beyond mere access to the material seems to have persuaded the sound-recording industry to move to the provision of more liberal systems or to drop tech-nological protection altogether, using price variations between protected and unprotected products as the way to maintain and perhaps start to regrow revenue. There are lessons here for rights-holders and law-makers. The protection of copyright and DRM cannot, and should not, entail complete control for the rights-holder over use and dissemination of the copyright work. That this is increasingly recognised and accepted is reflected in the objective of rights-holders in debates about copyright being articulated more and more as 'monetisation' of the content; that is to say, ensuring as far as possible that the use which cannot be prevented none-theless produces some sort of revenue stream. The old analogy between the Internet and a 'pay-and-play' jukebox seems to come ever closer to reality, except that the contents of the Internet appear to be limitless.

The limitations for copyright, whether expressed through the definition of restricted or permitted acts—by way of infringement or exception—must therefore free individuals to take advantage of the possibilities opened up by digital technology. This can be simple stuff: making a second CD to keep and play in the car, or an MP3 file to store and play on a mobile phone, or downloading an image to be a screen-saver on a laptop. For many, perhaps most, this will be as far as it goes. For others, more creative possibilities exist, using the technology to develop new works; and so long as these are sufficiently new—or 'original', in copyright's time-honoured phrase—then they too should be free from the claims of others' copyrights.

The worlds of education, research and news reporting, together with the preservation and conservation of cultural heritage, all of which have the objective of making content as widely accessible as possible, seem also to demand a more flexible and responsive copyright regime. Individual excep-tions allowing research and study, for example, will be of small value if the places where research and study take place (on or offline) cannot make the material available in the ways that people want to use them. In many instances, the changes needing to be made are relatively minor ones, bringing the law up to date with the technology, and enabling the technology to be used so that the traditional functions of educational, library and similar institutions can be performed better. The risk to commercial interests in such changes seems small.

Perhaps the hardest question to answer is the one about the relationship between copyright and contract and the DRM systems that uphold the latter. To what extent should copyright act as a brake or limitation upon contractual freedom? In an ideal world, where producer and would-be user bargained freely, equally and in good faith about the terms and conditions of use, there would be no need for copyright. But copyright came into existence at least partly because the world was not ideal, and it was relatively rare for producer and user to be able to negotiate face to face. To some extent, the interactive power of digital technology has reduced the problem: it is more possible for producer and user to negotiate directly with one another than ever before. But still the hard truth is that digital technology makes most possible automated, not negotiated contracting; the one choice the user has most of the time is whether or not to contract on the producer's terms. For a long time now contract law has generally accepted that it must seek to regulate such transactions to protect the weaker party from abuse. Nor are we talking only about individual users here, but also about institutions whose raison d'être is the collection, preservation and dissemination of copyright material for the benefit of users, and who must enter contracts with producers to fulfil these missions. For now, copyright law is the bastion from which the user interest can best defend itself against overreaching contracts.

Ironically, copyright may also turn into a redoubt for rights-holders when dealing with the intermediaries who seek to be something more than just the conduits by which works reach their audiences. The Google Book Settlement in the US, under which Google will digitise and put online the entire contents of a number of US academic libraries, exemplifies above all the power which that organisation now wields. Rights-holders are more or less compelled to decide whether to opt in or out of what Google wants to do with their works, with no room for negotiation about the terms for opting in.[106] But copyright does at least mean that those who opt in will receive royalties (if any are earned, of course), while also empowering those who wish to stay out to do so. In this context, copyright may yet be a shield with which monopolisation of access to the world's culture and information can be resisted rather than achieved.

---

[106] For the Google Books Settlement, see http://www.googlebooksettlement.com/. See also HL MacQueen, 'Editorial: The Google Book Settlement' (2009) 40 *International Review of Intellectual Property and Competition Law* 247.

7

Search Engines and Copyright: Shaping Information Markets

CHARLOTTE WAELDE[1]

I. INTRODUCTION

SEARCH ENGINES ARE powerful tools. While Internet service providers (ISPs) may be the gatekeepers to the Internet,[2] search engines make accessible the content of the Internet.[3] It is said that 80 per cent of Internet users who are searching for a specific site will start their search using a search engine.[4] A meaningful use of the Internet without search engines is therefore virtually impossible.[5] There is, however, the potential for harm. By controlling the accessibility of Internet content, search engines inevitably create winners and losers through the inclusion or exclusion of that content. It is vital, therefore, that a regulatory environment not only lays out a regime in which the innovative work of the search engine can flourish, but does so whilst also recognising the harms that can be inflicted on the interests of other stakeholders.

Much of the legal environment within which search engines work was devised before the Internet was conceived, but it has increasingly been revised and updated with the digital in mind. But technological development invariably outstrips legal regulation, often leaving the law struggling to cope. Even where revised, the law might have surprising and sometimes

---

[1] My grateful thanks go to Tobias Bednarz, research associate, SCRIPT, and to Arne Kolb, one-time research associate SCRIPT and now lead cellist for Broken Records, for research work done in connection with this chapter.

[2] See ch 1.

[3] Search Engines have also been described as the gatekeepers of public communication. See W Schulz, T Held and A Laudien, 'Search Engines as Gatekeepers of Public Communication: Analysis of the German Framework Applicable to Internet Search Engines Including Media Law and Anti Trust Law' (2005) 6(10) *German Law Journal* 1419.

[4] L Otterwell and D Bray, 'Search for Answers—Search Engine Functionality and Infringement Concerns' [2005] *Copyright World* 154.

[5] German Federal Court of Justice, I ZR 259/00, 17 July 2003, 'Paperboy'.

228   *Charlotte Waelde*

unforeseen effects when applied to a particular set of facts: most notably where innovative technologies and the law collide.[6]

The purpose of this chapter is to examine one aspect of the regulatory framework—the law of copyright—as it applies to search engines.[7] Aggregating, indexing and making information from third parties accessible is the raison d'être of a search engine. During this process, third-party content is reproduced, adapted and further made available—activities that are usually within the exclusive domain of the content owner. As will be discussed below, the law of copyright has had significant impact on the search engine 'business' and on business models deployed by the search engine. Taken to its extremes, copyright law also has the potential (at least within certain jurisdictions) of bringing search engine activity to a halt. Disputes have arisen between search engines and the content owners (such as the entertainment company, the publisher, the author) in which the law has been applied at times hesitantly, at others bullishly, to the business followed, and the technology deployed, by the search engine. The skirmishes represent, in essence, a quest for control over content: the desire of the content owner to retain control over how that content is used, and, where possible, to extract revenues for its use; pitted against the business model deployed by the search engine. It might be argued that the public interest benefits delivered by search engines in making information accessible should render their activities beyond the reach of copyright law. But it should not be forgotten that search engines, most particularly the larger ones, are powerful, valuable businesses and as such vigorously pursue returns for their shareholders[8] however much the satisfaction of a public interest might also result from their activities. A change in the technology or business model might compromise, rather than satisfy, that same public interest.

Taking these factors into account, this chapter narrates and comments upon the intersection between the law of copyright and search engine activities, questioning developments in light of the public interest benefits embedded within the law. The analysis will look to the law in the UK as it is derived from European initiatives, comment on developments in other Member States and make comparisons with the position in the US. Throughout the chapter it should be borne in mind that a key factor is the relationships and interplay as between the content owner (often referred to elsewhere as the rights-holder), the search engine, the user and the public interest(s)—the latter of which may, or may not, align itself with any one of the other interests in this framework.

---

[6] Eg *Navitaire Inc v Easyjet Airline Co & Anor* [2004] EWHC 1725 (Ch).
[7] For a discussion on search engines and trade mark law, see ch 8.
[8] Although few search engines exist for charitable ends it is notable that Google has recently announced a philanthropic initiative. See http://www.google.org.

A. Search Engines: History

From small beginnings in 1990 when the first tool for searching the Internet, Archie, was developed, the search engine 'market' is now thriving. Wikipedia[9] notes an impressive number of search engines (over 2,000 in May 2009), placing them into such categories as 'general' which includes Google, Live Search (formerly MSN) and Yahoo! (the latter which had been in negotiations with Microsoft over a sale—negotiations that later broke down); 'metasearch' engines which include Excite and Webcrawler; blog search engines; and news search engines, to name but a few.

B. Search Engines: Statistics

While, as indicated, there are many active search engines, the name that will crop up most often in this chapter is 'Google'. Figure 7.1 shows which search engines were used most often by searchers in the UK in the four weeks ending 22 March 2008.[10] As the statistics show, Google has by far

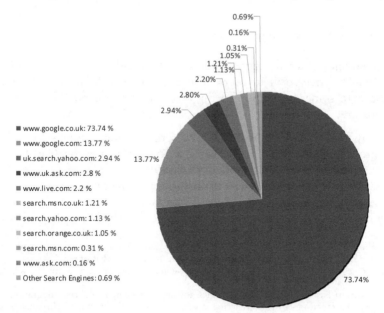

Figure 7.1 Most popular search engines in the UK for the four weeks ending 22 March 2008

    9 http://en.wikipedia.org/wiki/List_of_search_engines.
    10 The figures were compiled by Hitwise and are available at http://weblogs.hitwise.com/robin-goad/2008/04/how_popular_is_googles_pages_from__the_uk_search_option.html.
Hitwise makes available most interesting statistics on search engines and search engine activity.

the largest share of the market, and a market capitalisation at the start of 2009 in excess of US$175 billion.[11] Google has earned this lead by being one of the most innovative search engines and the pioneer in many of the informational market sectors it currently occupies. This innovation, coupled with the value of the company, has made Google the target of many and varied law suits.[12]

C. Search Engines and Copyright

Whilst copyright is relevant for protecting elements of the search engines' own functionality such as the software (see chapter 10), this chapter will focus on the application of copyright law to three areas. Firstly, to the caching process generally which is integral to search engine functionality and also to the caching of thumbnail images; secondly, to an example of search engine activity, that of news aggregation; and thirdly, to an example of a business model developed by Google—the Google Book Search.

D. The Way a Search Engine Works

Search engines generally aggregate information and make that available in a more constructive form to users. There is no legal definition of a search engine with some descriptions being broader than others.[13] The key components are:

- a crawler—a program which searches the web and copies (or spiders) content and stores it on a server also known as a cache (e.g. Google's server also known as the Google cache);
- a searchable index (database) of words appearing on the pages;
- a search engine programme/search interface which the user queries and which then looks up the index, the results of which are returned to the

---

[11] See eg http://www.finance.yahoo.com. In May 2009 there were several news stories pointing out that Google's market capitalisation was in excess of that of GE.

[12] For a website which has collated information on many of the cases, see http://www.linksand law.com/. See also ch 8.

[13] At its most basic, a search engine copies and indexes content. A broad definition might encompass the function of the search engine which is to search documents for keywords and return a list of the documents in which the keywords are found (see http://smartbiz connection. com/advertising_glossary_index.htm). A narrower definition might focus on the use of bots (spiders, robots, crawlers) to search the Web taking the information to create a searchable index of the Internet (see http://www.numatek.com/glossary/glossary-s.html). Here the engine has several components: search engine software, spider software, an index (database), and a relevancy algorithm (rules for ranking) (see http://www.virtechseo.com/seoglossary.htm) and generates results based on a user's search criteria. See also http://www.themarketingbureau. co.nz/Search_Engine_Glossary.htm.

user[14] along with a link to the webpages the user may (or may not) be looking for.[15]

Google also operates a feature whereby, when search results are returned by the search engine, there will often be a second link saying 'cached'. This is a snapshot of the webpage as it stood when the Google robot (Googlebot) visited the page. The page contains a disclaimer explaining that it is only a cached copy and that the page may not be current: 'Google's cache is the snapshot that we took of the page as we crawled the Web. The page may have changed since that time.'[16] A link to the current page is included in the disclaimer. Google has provided these cached links with its search results since 1998.[17] A website owner can prevent a cached link appearing in a number of different ways.[18] Instructions to web crawlers can be inserted into the metatags of a page in such a way that either the page will not be picked up by the search engine at all[19] or it will prevent a link being made to the cached version.[20] Websites can also be removed from the index;[21] and will be removed if a request is made so to do.[22]

To a copyright lawyer, the copying and making available of copied material involved in these processes[23] raise a number of legal questions.[24]

---

[14] B Allgrove and P Ganley, 'Search Engines, Data Aggregators and UK Copyright Law: A Proposal' [2007] *European Intellectual Property Review (EIPR)* 227.

[15] As was pointed out in *Field v Google Inc* (US District Court District of Nevada, No CV-S-04-0413-RCJ-LRL, 12 January 2006), 'Internet search engines like Google's allow Internet users to sift through the massive amount of information available on the Internet to find specific information that is of particular interest to them. . . . There are billions of Web pages accessible on the Internet. It would be impossible for Google to locate and index or catalog them manually. . . . Accordingly, Google, like other search engines, uses an automated program (called the "Googlebot") to continuously crawl across the Internet, to locate and analyze available Web pages, and to catalog those Web pages into Google's searchable Web index' (para 7).

[16] See eg http://64.233.183.104/search?q=cache:rS2qjpSb95sJ:www.law.ed.ac.uk/+edinburgh +law+school&hl=en&ct=clnk&cd=2&gl=uk—a cached version of the Edinburgh Law School site on 14 March 2008.

[17] *Field v Google Inc*, above n 15, para 12.

[18] See S Ott, 'Der Google Cache—Eine milliardenfache Urheberrechtsverletzung?' [2007] *Medien Internet und Recht* 195.

[19] An instruction to disregard completely the webpage can also be contained in the robots.txt file. This is the file in the top-level directory of a website which is analysed first by web crawlers. See http://en.wikipedia.org/wiki/Robots_Exclusion_Standard.

[20] The latter can be achieved by the simple command in HTML code (META NAME= "ROBOTS" CONTENT="NOARCHIVE").

[21] See http://www.google.com/support/webmasters/bin/answer.py?answer=61062. Again, the result will be that the webpage will not appear as a search result at all.

[22] Ott, above n 18, 195.

[23] Otterwell and Bray, above n 5, 22. Allgrove and Gangley, above n 14, 227, speak of two copies: (1) temporary copy made when robot trawls the Internet in order to analyse and index the content; (2) cached copy: 'copy of the HTML of the indexed page stored in a temporary repository called cache'.

[24] Linking is a key feature of search engine functionality. It is often argued that it infringes copyright law, particularly where the linked to sites contain material which infringes copyright—eg P2P sites facilitating access to unauthorised music files. See eg the agreement attained between Eircom and the music industry http://tjmcintyre.com/2009/01/three-strikes-for-ireland-eircom-music.html. See also chs 1 and 5.

II. COPYRIGHT AND CACHING

A. UK (European) Law

When a page is cached, the whole or part of it is copied. Copyright will reside in the whole or elements of the page, such as the text and any images. The Copyright Designs and Patents Act 1988 (CDPA) section 17(1) provides that 'copying . . . means reproducing the work in any material form. This includes storing the work in any medium by electronic means'.[25] Moreover, section 17(6) CDPA provides that 'copying . . . includes the making of copies which are transient or are incidental to some other use of the work'.[26] Therefore, even if the copying is temporary, it is likely that copyright will be infringed if there is no authorisation.

The provision of links to cached versions of webpages in the manner described above might also amount to a communication to the public of a protected work and thus an infringement of copyright?[27] Section 20 CDPA (Infosoc Directive Article 3) provides for liability where a protected work is made available by electronic means 'in such a way that members of the public may access it from a place and at a time individually chosen by them'.[28] A question arises as to whether the cached copy is 'made available to the public' within the meaning of this section. The European Court of Justice (ECJ) considered the meaning of this provision (as found in the Infosoc Directive[29]) in *SGAE v Rafael Hotels*.[30] The ECJ held that limited subsets of the public, including sets of unconnected users of the same service, could amount to 'the public'.[31] One might argue that the link to the cached page is only provided to the single user who initiates a search, and does thus not fall under this provision. However, it may be problematic to maintain that view in the light of the ECJ's ruling in *SGAE*.[32] It would also appear to be irrelevant as to whether the user actually clicks on the cached link, as it is sufficient that 'members of the public *may* access

[25] CDPA s 17(1).

[26] CDPA s 17(6).

[27] CDPA s 20.

[28] CDPA s 20(2)(b).

[29] European Parliament and Council Directive 2001/29/EC on the harmonisation of certain aspects of copyright and related rights in the information society (the InfoSoc Directive), Art 3. See also ch 5.

[30] Case C-306/05 *Sociedad General de Autores y Editores de España (SGAE) v Rafael Hoteles SA* [2007] ECDR 2 (SGAE).

[31] Ibid, para 51. Allgrove and Ganley see this as establishing a rule that spatial discontinuity does not foreclose a communication to the public. See Allgrove and Ganley, above n 14, 232, citing the opinion of Advocate General Sharpston and the judgement of the ECJ

[32] Ott, above n 18, 195, para 3, analysing the parallel provision in the German copyright code. Both provisions are based on the same EC Directive and should therefore be interpreted uniformly.

it'.[33] Thus it would seem that making a cache available in this way would amount to a communication to the public under the CDPA and thus an infringement if done without authorisation.

(i) Exceptions and Defences

There are a number of possible exceptions available in domestic law which are derived from the Infosoc Directive.[34] For instance, section 28A CDPA (Infosoc Directive Article 5(1)) provides:

> Copyright . . . is not infringed by the making of a temporary copy which is transient or incidental provided three conditions are fulfilled:
>   (1) it is an integral and essential part of a technological process;
>   (2) the sole purpose of which is to enable a) a transmission of the work in a network between third parties by an intermediary or b) a lawful use of the work;
>   (3) and the copy has no independent economic significance.

While it could be argued that caching is an integral and essential part of a technological process, what it does not do is to enable a transmission of the work between third parties. Rather, one of the purposes of the copying is to index the page. It is an interesting question as to whether caching enables a lawful use of the work. One might be tempted to argue that the lawful use is that of the user finding the link to the page, it being lawful for the user to call up the webpage. However, it would appear that this is not the 'work' for the purposes of this exception. The work is rather the one that has been cached and is used to produce the index. Moreover, it is difficult to argue that the cached copy has no independent economic significance. Search engine functionality depends upon the cache and it thus lies at the heart of the search engine business model. It would seem that this exception is not relevant to the caching process.

Some guidance may be forthcoming soon from the ECJ on a number of these issues. The Højesteret in Denmark referred questions to that court in relation to the operation of a media monitoring analysis business, Infopaq.[35] In particular, the ECJ was asked what is meant by temporary and transient acts, and whether the context in which they take place is relevant. For example, whether a reproduction can be regarded as transient where the reproduction is processed by the creation of a text file on the basis of an image file; and whether the stage of the technological process at which temporary acts of reproduction take place is relevant to whether they constitute an integral and essential part of a technological process. The

---

[33] Allgrove and Ganley, above n 14, 232.

[34] European Parliament and Council Directive 2001/29/EC on the harmonisation of certain aspects of copyright and related rights in the information society and implementing regulations. Copyright and Related Rights Regulations SI 2003/2498.

[35] Case C-5/08 *Infopaq International*. The ECJ has now handed down judgment. For a brief postscript, see p 266.

way in which a media monitoring analysis business like Infopaq works shares many features with the more general search engine business, most notably in the context of temporary and transient acts. Therefore, the answers are likely to be relevant to the issues raised above, albeit that the extent to which the ruling will be applicable to general search engine business will depend on the extent of the convergence between the respective technologies and the contexts in which they are used in their own markets' spaces. At the time of writing, Advocate General Verica Trstenjak had handed down her opinion (20 February 2009) but it was not available in English. Judging by the analysis produced by a number of commentators,[36] 'reproduction' has been given a very wide interpretation, which, if followed by the ECJ, would seem apt to capture search engine activities including caching.

Another question may be as to whether the cached webpages are really temporary.[37] Google stores the webpages in its cache at present for approximately 14–20 days.[38] Although this has been regarded as temporary in US law,[39] the same result may not be arrived at under the CDPA. It has been described as a 'moot point' whether proxy server caching by universities, libraries and others to avoid congestion could fall under the temporary reproduction section.[40] But there are other difficulties. Providing access to cached webpages is unlikely to be considered a technological necessity. It is rather an end in itself, offering the user who searches the Internet an additional service.[41]

Going beyond the CDPA and Infosoc Directive, a defence might be available for a search engine making cached copies under the 'mere conduit' provisions in the E-Commerce Directive.[42]

Article 12 of the E-Commerce Directive provides that the service provider will not be liable where it:

> (a) did not initiate the transmission;
> (b) did not select the receiver of the transmission; and
> (c) did not select or modify the information contained in the transmission.
>
> (2) The acts of transmission and of provision of access include the automatic, intermediate and transient storage of the information transmitted where:
> (a) this takes place for the sole purpose of carrying out the transmission in the

---

[36] See in particular http://www.ipkat.com.

[37] Above p 232.

[38] *Field v Google Inc*, above n 15, para 46.

[39] Ibid.

[40] H MacQueen, C Waelde and G Laurie, *Contemporary Intellectual Property: Law and Policy* (Cambridge, Cambridge University Press 2007) para 5.17

[41] Ott, above n 18, 195.

[42] Directive 2000/31/EC of the European Parliament and of the Council of 8 June 2000 on certain legal aspects of information society services, in particular electronic commerce, in the Internal Market (the E-commerce Directive), Art 12 implemented in the Electronic Commerce (EC Directive) Regulations 2002 SI 2002 No 2013 (E-Commerce Regulations) Reg 17. See also ch 1.

communication network, and

(b) the information is not stored for any period longer than is reasonably necessary for the transmission.

However, this also seems difficult to apply to caching by search engines. Transient copying is not a transmission; the information is not provided by a recipient of the service; and the content is selected and modified by search engines.[43]

It might be argued that the 'caching' defence in the E-Commerce Directive (Article 13) could provide a limitation on liability but here, as with Article 12, difficulties arise.

Article 13 E-commerce Directive

Where an information society service is provided which consists of the transmission in a communication network of information provided by a recipient of the service, the service provider (if he otherwise would) shall not be liable for damages or for any other pecuniary remedy or for any criminal sanction as a result of that transmission where—

(a) the information is the subject of automatic, intermediate and temporary storage where that storage is for the sole purpose of making more efficient onward transmission of the information to other recipients of the service upon their request, and

(b) the service provider—

(i)   does not modify the information;

(ii) complies with conditions on access to the information;

(iii) complies with any rules regarding the updating of the information, specified in a manner widely recognised and used by industry;

(iv) does not interfere with the lawful use of technology, widely recognised and used by industry, to obtain data on the use of the information; and

(v) acts expeditiously to remove or to disable access to the information he has stored upon obtaining actual knowledge of the fact that the information at the initial source of the transmission has been removed from the network, or access to it has been disabled, or that a court or an administrative authority has ordered such removal or disablement.

Although this provides a defence for caching, most commentators are of the view that it does not apply to search engines. For example, the defence applies; 'where an information society service is provided which consists of the transmission in a communication network of information provided by a recipient of the service'. Providing access to the cached webpages is not a transmission; neither has it been provided by a recipient of the service.

B. The Position in Europe

Unlike Austria, Portugal and Spain, the UK has not expressly extended the

---

[43] Allgrove and Ganley, above n 14, 233.

mere conduit, caching, and hosting defences in the E-Commerce Directive
to cover search engine functionality.[44] The recent Gowers Review asserted
that the defences in the E-Commerce Directive applied also to search
engines[45] but did not provide reasons. Moreover, in 2005 the UK government held consultations on the question of whether the regulations should
be extended[46] to search engine activities, but declined the opportunity to
do so on the basis that there was insufficient evidence of a necessity.[47] It
would thus seem that under UK law the daily activities of search engines do
indeed infringe the law of copyright.

III. US LAW

A quick glance across the Atlantic shows how greatly the legal environment
differs there. In 2006 in F*ield v Google Inc* the use of Google's cache was
challenged.[48] Field, a poet, found a number of his works in Google's cache
and argued that Google infringed his rights to reproduce, distribute and
publicly display[49] his works each time that a user clicked on the cached
link. The court disagreed and found that there was no direct infringement
of copyright. In the US, courts had previously established that direct
infringement by ISPs requires a volitional act: automated copying by
machines is not sufficient.[50] This reasoning was applied to the search
engine in Field: 'the automated, non-volitional conduct by Google in
response to a user's request does not constitute direct infringement under
the Copyright Act'.[51] Despite this finding of non-infringement, the court
went on to discuss the defences that Google had put forwards. Field was
aware of, but had chosen not to implement any of the strategies available to
prevent caching.[52] This was interpreted as Field having granted an implied
licence.[53]

[44] B Allgrove, 'The Search Engine's Dilemma—Implied Licence to Crawl and Cache?' [2007] *Journal of Intellectual Property Law & Practice* 437, 438.
[45] Gowers Review of Intellectual Property (HM Treasury London, 2006), http://www.hm-treasury.gov.uk/media/6/E/pbr06_gowers_report_755.pdf, 69, para 4.69.
[46] See The Department for Trade and Industry, DTI Consultation Document on the Electronic Commerce Directive: The Liability of Hyperlinkers, Location Tool Services and Content Aggre-gators (London, DTI, 2005). See also G Arthur, 'Considering an Extension' [2005] *Copyright World* 154.
[47] Allgrove, above n 44, 438.
[48] *Field v Google Inc*, above n 15. See also case comment by S Saxby, 'News and Comments on Recent Developments from around the World' (2006) 22 *Computer Law & Security Report* 183, 189–90 and 'Case Comment' [2006] *Computer and Telecommunications Law Review* N88.
[49] US Copyright Act Title 17 s 106.
[50] *Religious Tech Ctr* 907 F Supp at 1369–70; *CoStar Group* 373 F 3d at 555; *Sega Enters Ltd v Maphia* 948 F Supp 923, 931–32 (ND Cal 1996).
[51] *Field v Google Inc*, above n 15, para 19. For discussion see MD Lawless, 'Against Search Engine Volition', available at SSRN: http://ssrn.com/abstract=984563
[52] Above nn 23 and 24.
[53] Field was also estopped from asserting the copyright claim on the basis, inter alia, that he

On the question of fair use, the court went through the four factors to be found in the US Copyright Act (17 USC s 107).

1. the purpose and character of the use, including whether it is of a commercial nature or is for non-profit educational purposes;
2. the nature of the work protected by copyright;
3. the amount and substantiality of the portion used in relation to the work as a whole; and
4. the effect of the use upon the potential market for or value of the protected work.

Courts traditionally have given the most weight to the first and fourth factors. As the list of factors is non-exhaustive, courts have also sometimes considered:

5. whether the alleged copyright infringer acted in good faith.

On the first factor, and in finding that the use of Field's work was transformative, the court found that several points weighed heavily in Google's favour. Not only did it meet a different user need by enabling a user to locate and access information that was otherwise inaccessible, but in addition, it allowed a user to detect changes that might have been made to a particular webpage. It was made clear that Google did not intend for the cached page to be substituted for the original. The court also considered that Google's status as a commercial enterprise did not negate fair use, as Google did not display advertising to the user or offer any other form of commercial transaction. The second factor weighed slightly in Field's favour. While his (Field's) work was considered creative, this was balanced against the fact that by publishing the work on the Internet and by including a 'robot.txt', he had sought to make his work widely available for free. On the third factor, it was acknowledged that Google had copied the whole of the work, but the court considered that this operation was no more than necessary for the caching function. On the fourth factor, the court found no evidence of a market for Field's work or of a market for licensing search engines to cache pages. This factor therefore weighed heavily in Google's favour. Finally, the court considered that Google had acted in good faith by providing means to prevent caching and, in the instant case, by removing the cached web page as soon as it knew of Field's discontent. A balance of all the factors 'demonstrates that if Google copies or distributes Field's copyrighted works by allowing access to them through cached links, Google's conduct is fair use of those works as a matter of law'.[54]

knew of Google's allegedly infringing conduct well before any supposed infringement of his work took place but remained silent. *Field v Google Inc*, above n 15, paras 23 and 24.

[54] Ibid, para 43.

The court went on to consider whether Google was also entitled to the caching copyright safe harbor for online service providers in the US Digital Millennium Copyright Act (DMCA).[55]

Section 512(B) DMCA provides in its relevant part:

(b) System caching.—
(1) Limitation on liability.—
A service provider shall not be liable for monetary relief, or, except as provided in subsection (j), for injunctive or other equitable relief, for infringement of copyright by reason of the intermediate and temporary storage of material on a system or network controlled or operated by or for the service provider in a case in which—

(A) the material is made available online by a person other than the service provider;

(B) the material is transmitted from the person described in subparagraph (A) through the system or network to a person other than the person described in subparagraph (A) at the direction of that other person; and

(C) the storage is carried out through an automatic technical process for the purpose of making the material available to users of the system or network who, after the material is transmitted as described in subparagraph (B), request access to the material from the person described in subparagraph (A), if the conditions set forth in paragraph (2) are met.

The court found that Google's cache for approximately 14–20 days is temporary; that the requirements of section 512(b)(1)(B) were met because Field transmitted the webpages to Google's crawler at Google's request and that Google is a person other than Field; and that section 512(b)(1)(C) was satisfied because Google's storage is carried out by an automated technical process. The safe harbour requirements were thus satisfied.[56]

A. Transatlantic Divergence

So what trends do we see so far? Application of the law in the UK, and the law applied in limited case law in the US, show clear differences. In the UK caching would appear to be an infringement of copyright per se; in the US it is not. In the UK there appear to be no exceptions or defences available to an action of infringement. If the activity did infringe in the US, then it would appear that the defence of fair use would be available, as would limitations on liability in the safe harbour provisions under the DMCA. Given that much of UK copyright law now derives from European initiatives (in particular the temporary reproduction provisions as well as the

---

[55] See generally ch 1

[56] The ruling was largely followed in the Pennsylvanian case of *Parker v Google Inc* (US District Court Eastern District of Pennsylvania, No 04-CV-3918, 10 March 2006); see also E Mills, 'Google Wins a Court Battle' zdnet.com (16 March 2006), http://news.zdnet.com/2100-9595-6050667.html.

caching defences), it may be that the same outcome would be attained in other EU countries as in the UK.[57] However, the availability of a safe harbour provision might differ given, as noted above, a number of other countries have provided for limitation of liability on search engine activities.

The key point for this chapter is therefore that in the UK it is the content owner who has control over content vis-à-vis this aspect of search engine activities. In other words, it would appear that a content owner could stop a search engine from caching its content. So why have there been no cases on caching in the UK? A challenge by a content owner would have a profound impact on the accessibility of that content for the user. A search engine would no longer be able to make the cache from which the index is derived. A user would no longer be able to find the content. It would seem that because the search engine fulfils an essential function for the content owner, there is a symbiotic relationship between the content owner and the search engine. Through this it can be argued that the public interest in accessibility of information is satisfied.[58] But it would appear that the public interest is only satisfied because of this truce between the search engine and the content owner. In other words, the satisfaction of the public interest is not fulfilled through the application of the law, but is a by-product of a private (if unspoken) bargain. The question then arises as to what happens if that landscape changes? If either the content owner or the search engines wanted to alter their strategy, what then of the public interest? By contrast in the US it would appear from *Field* that it is the search engine which has the upper hand in relation to control over content, as the court ruled that caching per se was not an infringement of copyright. But this too would seem problematic. What if there is a change in the significance of caching which may be used for other purposes, or in the business model pursued by either side? Perhaps it would be preferable to bring these search engine activities within the copyright framework now, and to use the flexibilities in the law to excuse socially beneficial behaviour, than to leave them outside the regulatory framework altogether.

Finally for now, it is important to note how search engines are developing their own form of safe harbour. Works will be cached, but that caching can be prevented through the use of technology. Content owners are thus able to 'opt out' of the system. Copyright therefore seems to become less of a set of exclusive rights in the hands of the owner, and more of a right to be opted into when desired.[59]

---

[57] Although there is always room for national divergence in interpretation especially before the matter may have been adjudicated by the ECJ—and sometimes afterwards as well. See also the discussion in ch 8.

[58] Which raises questions beyond the scope of this chapter as to the obligations a search engine may or may not have to content owners in making content available, and how that is done.

[59] It is also interesting to speculate on the extent to which in choosing the opt-out provision might enable the owner of content to 'censor' its availability—an issue that has long been of

IV. CACHING AND THUMBNAIL IMAGES

So far the discussion has centred on works protected by copyright in general—with no distinction between categories (literary, artistic, musical and dramatic). However, specific types of searches, notably image searches, have raised their own problems. One example is Google's Image Search, which displays low-resolution thumbnail images in response to text-based queries which are stored in the search engine cache. Clicking on the thumbnail will display the thumbnail image and the third-party website that hosts the full-size version. As a result of this process, content stored on third-party websites can be viewed through Google's website.[60]

A. UK and Thumbnail Images

As with caching generally, it would appear that this process of caching thumbnail images infringes UK copyright law. Among the copyright concerns would be: the copy of the image which is cached when the crawler trawled the page containing the original image; the creation of a low-resolution small version; and the provision of a thumbnail picture in the results of a search query. These steps all suggest infringement of section 17 CDPA when displaying the thumbnail picture, and of section 20(2)(b) CDPA[61] (Infosoc Directive Article 3) when making that available to the public. As the thumbnail is not an integral and essential part of a technological process, but an additional service for search engine users in itself, the exception in section 28A CDPA (Infosoc Directive Article 5(1))would not apply. Nor would the defences in the E-commerce Directive be likely to be available for the reasons given above.[62]

B. Germany and Thumbnail Images

Going beyond the UK shores, there have been a couple of interesting cases in Germany dealing with thumbnail images, one heard by the District Court of Hamburg,[63] and the other by the District Court of Erfurt.[64] The

concern in the law of copyright, see eg *Church of Scientology v Spaink* Dutch Court 4 September 2003.

60 This description is taken from DC Glazer and S Herman, 'Thumbnail Hazards, Continued' [2007] *Copyright World* 172. The question of framing brings its own copyright questions that will not be further elaborated on here, see Otterwell and Bray, above n 4, 22.

61 These infringing acts are the ones identified by German courts. The parallel German provisions are authoritative where litigated in Germany. See LG Erfurt, 3 O 1108/05, 15.03.2007, para 22.

62 Above pp 234 and 235.

63 Case No 308 O 449/03.

64 Case No 3 O 1108/05.

District Court of Hamburg held that thumbnail images displayed alongside news stories without permission infringed copyright. The court was aware of, and discussed, the US case of *Kelly v Arriba*[65] (see below[66]), but noting the differences in the legal systems (Germany has no broad fair use defence) found itself unable to consider the benefits of a visual search engine to the public as articulated in that case. The District Court of Erfurt, on the other hand, did stress the public benefits of the inclusion of thumbnails and pointed out that such use could be excluded if the copyright owner so desired using a robots.txt file.

While both of the German cases were heard in District Courts, the findings suggest that the legal landscape may differ both within and among European states.

C. France and Thumbnail Images

The Tribunal de Grande Instance in Paris heard a case concerning thumbnail images in May 2008.[67] A photographers' collecting society sued Google Inc for infringement of copyright over a number of images which belonged to its members, including Henri Cartier-Bresson and Depardon, and were available through Google Image. In an interesting, and what might be described as surprising judgment, the Tribunal ruled that the law applicable to Google's infringing activities was that of the US.[68] The Tribunal applied a translation of section 107 of the US Copyright Act, ultimately finding that Google's actions amounted to fair use. On the first factor the Tribunal found that Google treated all content on the Internet in the same way and that it did not generate revenue directly from the provision of images. Hence 'La première condition est donc totalement remplie.' On the second factor the Tribunal said simply: 'La deuxième condition (la nature des oeuvres protégées) en l'espèce des images n'a pas été débattue par les parties.'[69] On the third condition the Tribunal noted that the process of caching (and thus reproduction) was automatic, the purpose of this process was to speed up access to the Internet, and that Google did not stockpile the images. 'La troisième condition de l'exception de "fair use" est également remplie.' Finally, and on the fourth factor, the

---

[65] *Kelly v Arriba Soft Corp* (280 F 3d 934 (CA9 2002) withdrawn, refiled at 336 F 3d 811(CA9 2003)).

[66] p 242.

[67] TGI Paris, 20 mai 2008, SAIF c/ *Google France et Google Inc.*

[68] Google pointed to Art 5.2 of the Berne Convention in support of its argument that the law of the place where the infringing act took place was the law to be applied

[69] On the question of moral rights which might have been infringed by the change in size and nature of the images, the Tribunal said : 'En tout état de cause, la dénaturation de l'image ressort du droit moral des artistes et non de leur droit patrimonial qui est le seul apporté à la SAIF.' It is thus interesting to speculate whether this outcome might have been different had the artists brought individual cases and directly alledged infringement of moral rights.

Tribunal was unconvinced that the activities of Google interfered with the potential market of the artists. On the contrary, the benefit to the artists of having their works obtainable on the Internet was stressed, so satisfying the fourth fair use factor.

D. US and Thumbnail Images

While the application of the US fair use doctrine by a French court might seem surprising,[70] it is unsurprising that this provision has already been applied in the US in two cases, *Kelly v Arriba Soft Corp* and *Perfect 10 v Google*, in which the flexibility of its application has produced some interesting results.

In 2003 in *Kelly* the Court of Appeals for the Ninth Circuit decided that, while the reproduction of copyright-protected images to create thumbnails, and the use of those thumbnails by an image search engine, infringed the copyright in the original images, the activity was excused under fair use.[71] In considering the fair use factors,[72] the court found that on the first, the use by Arriba, which was 'to help index and improve access to images on the internet and their related web sites',[73] benefited the public by 'enhancing information-gathering techniques on the internet'.[74] Being of lower resolution than the originals, their use served a different purpose and was therefore transformative. On the second, while the creative nature of the works mitigated against fair use, the fact that the images had already appeared on the Internet weighed only slightly in Kelly's favour. On the third, once again it was acknowledged that the works were reproduced in their entirety, but this was necessary 'to allow users to recognize the image and decide whether to pursue more information about the image or the originating web site'.[75] Finally, on the fourth factor, the court found that the low-resolution thumbnails were not substitutes for the originals, nor was Kelly's market harmed because the search engine did not licence them to other parties—findings in favour of the search engine. Overall, the court found that the use of the images as thumbnails was a fair use.

A slightly different result was attained in 2007 when the Court of Appeals revisited similar issues in *Perfect 10 v Google*.[76] A central feature

---

[70] For an article arguing against such 'spillover' effects, see P Geller 'Conflicts of Laws in Copyright Cases: Infringement and Ownership Issues' (2004) 51 *Journal of the Copyright Society of the USA* 315, available at SSRN: http://ssrn.com/abstract=602901

[71] *Kelly v Arriba Soft Corp*, above n 65.

[72] Above p 237.

[73] *Kelly v. Arriba Soft Corp*, above n 65, 9071.

[74] Ibid, 9073

[75] Ibid, 9075.

[76] *Perfect 10 Inc v Amazon.com Inc* 487 F 3d 701 (9th Cir (US) 2007). Perfect 10 sued Google as well as Amazon for its A9 search. As Google provided the image search functionality for Amazon, the cases were joined for the appeal sub nom *Perfect 10 v Amazon.com*; for a case

of this case was that the complaint concerned unauthorised images. Perfect 10 offered photographs of nude models for subscribed customers and licensed reduced-sized versions of these images for download to mobile phones.[77] On the Internet, unauthorised copies of Perfect 10's pictures appeared on third-party webpages. These pages were crawled and cached by Google. Thumbnails of the pictures were created and subsequently displayed as part of the results in Google's image search. Perfect 10 alleged Google was liable for direct infringement of copyright in the original pictures by displaying the thumbnails, and by linking to the full-sized unauthorised pictures using the framing technique. It was also alleged that Google was contributorily and vicariously liable through framing the original pictures. The District Court for the Central District of California held that Perfect 10 was unlikely to prevail on its claim of direct, contributory or vicarious infringement arising out of Google's linking to the full-size pictures using the framing technique. However, the court found Perfect 10 likely to prevail on its claim that the use of thumbnails directly infringed copyright.[78]

In the Court of Appeals, the finding of the District Court was reversed on the claim of direct infringement. It agreed with the District Court's 'server test': a computer owner who stores an image as electronic information and serves that electronic information directly to the user is displaying the electronic information. Applying this, using the thumbnails prima facie infringed the copyright owner's exclusive display right.[79] However, the defence of fair use was available. Google's use of thumbnails was highly transformative as the thumbnails were not only used as images, but in addition incorporated in a new work—an 'electronic reference tool';[80] while the pictures were creative, they had already been published; while Google copied the image as a whole, this was necessary to achieve the transformative use; and finally, the Court of Appeals found that the District Court had rightly held that Google's use of thumbnails did not hurt Perfect 10's market for full-size images, there being no evidence as to whether the download of the thumbnails on to mobile phones had actually occurred.[81]

comment, see Glazer and Herman, above n 60 and 'Case Comment' [2007] *Computer and Telecommunications Law Review* N176.

[77] *Perfect 10 Inc v Google* 416 F Supp 2d 828 (CD Cal 2006).

[78] For an analysis of this ruling, see DC Glazer and K Camacho 'Thumbnail Hazards' [2006] *Copyright World* 160, 10.

[79] Interestingly the court did not refer to the necessary volitional element that was a feature of *Field v Google Inc*, above n 15, and *Parker v Google Inc*, above n 52.

[80] *Perfect 10 v Amazon.com*, above n 76, 15471 'the nature of Google's search engine, particularly in light of its public benefit, outweighs Google's superseding and commercial uses of the thumbnails in this case'.

[81] In the view of the District Court Google's use of the thumbnails encroached on that of Perfect 10 in that it could serve the same purposes as Perfect 10's activities to license its pictures for download to mobile phones. Above n 77, 29. Yet, the Court of Appeals paid less attention to

> Weighing [the] significant transformative use against the unproven use of Google's thumbnails for cell phone downloads, and considering the other fair use factors, all in light of the purpose of copyright, we conclude that Google's use of Perfect 10's thumbnails is a fair use.[82]

On the question of contributory infringement through linking to sites containing unauthorised copies, while the court found that the third-party websites containing the full-sized copies of the images directly infringed copyright by reproducing, displaying and distributing unauthorised copies, Google substantially assisted these third-party websites in distributing those infringing copies. Recalling *A&M Records Inc v Napster Inc*,[83] the court noted that the operator of a computer system could only be considered to be liable for contributory infringement if it has actual knowledge that specific infringing material is available using its system, and can take simple measures to prevent further damage to works protected by copyright yet continues to provide access. As these were factual questions, they were remanded to be answered by the District Court.[84]

E. Transatlantic and European Divergence

So once again we see differences in the application of the laws of the US and UK (and other European jurisdictions) in their responses to the copying that takes place when images are cached. In the UK, in general it would appear to be an infringement of copyright though there have been no cases challenging the practice. In Germany, the picture is not so clear, with courts finding both for and against liability, while in France, the activity has been excused through the application of US law on fair use. In the US, while caching in general appears not to be an infringement of copyright, caching of thumbnail images is, though this is excused under fair use. In addition, caching of unauthorised images and making those available may amount to contributory infringement, although that liability might be limited if mechanisms are deployed to prevent public access.

There has been some disquiet as a result of this latter finding, and although it remains to be seen what findings of fact the District Court comes up with, it does leave some uncertainty for search engines. If it is found that there is a method by which access could be denied to works which infringe copyright, search engines would need to deploy that technology to comply with an order. As is well known, Napster, the subject of a

---

this point, as 'the district court did not find that any down loads for mobile phone use had taken place', *Perfect 10 v Amazon.com*, above n 76, 15471.

[82] *Perfect 10 v Amazon.com*, above n 76, 15474.

[83] 239 F 3d 1004 (9th Cir 2001).

[84] Finally, the court found Perfect 10 unlikely to prevail in its claim for vicarious liability as Google had no ability, right or duty to control the conduct of the third-party sites.

similar order, closed soon thereafter.[85] However, and as will be argued below, it may be that the court was striving for a balance between the content owner and the search engine. If the search engine is to profit from the content of others, some obligations may be imposed that would be of benefit to those content owners, although these may not emanate directly from copyright law.

Those who worry about such obligations being placed on search engines argue that they (search engines) play such a vital role in accessibility of content that they should be left to ply their trade without additional obligations being imposed. However, and as has been argued above, search engines 'profit' from the content provided by others and do so because they are in business. Also as suggested above, while it might be considered that the act of caching per se should not amount to an infringement of copyright since that is how the search engine works, technology moves fast. What might seem to be an 'innocent' act, of benefit to the public at present, may develop into a different feature of the search engine business model as time moves on. By placing this outside the scope of copyright law, this facet of the information market is unregulated, at least by copyright. An aspect of this can be seen in *Kelly*. Yes, the activity infringed, but that finding enabled the court to examine the activity under the principles of fair use. In a few years' time, and faced with different facts, the fair use balance may tip in the other direction. An extension of this balancing act can be seen in *Perfect 10*. While there was direct infringement in this case, it was excused under fair use. It was for a finding of fact as to whether Google was contributorily liable, and if such a finding was upheld, whether (and perhaps bearing in mind the difficulties caused to Napster) a 'simple' mechanism might be found to enable Google to prevent access to infringing works. Here we see the court regulating activity by copyright using the array of provisions available to it, and in so doing, trying to find a balance between the interests of the content owner and the activities of the search engine.

So, in balancing these interests, are the goals of copyright also fulfilled? The balance in *Perfect 10* appears, broadly, that if a search engine is to use content belonging to others, then an obligation may be imposed whereby the search engine must help to inhibit access to unauthorised material. This is certainly in the interests of the content owner. The direct benefit to the public interest is less obvious. By stretching a little it could be argued that, on matters of provenance, it is indeed in line with the public interest goals that the user knows the origin of the material and that it is non-infringing—an obligation not unlike the requirement of attribution and

---

[85] *A & M Records, Inc v Napster, Inc* 114 F Supp 2d 896 (ND Cal 2000), aff'd in part, rev'd in part, 239 F 3d 1004 (9th Cir 2001). Cf *IO Group Inc v Veoh Networks Inc* USD NDC Case C06-03926.

integrity. But if these, and other arguments of that ilk, are accepted, the goals become malleable. Whilst is not necessarily a bad thing in the digital era, where technological innovation inevitably poses new challenges, any such shifts should take place in full knowledge of the consequences for the other elements of, and interests, in the framework. Whether this is best pursued on a case-by-case basis, as is currently what appears to be happening, must be a moot point.

V. NEWS AGGREGATION

A field into which search engines have extended their activities, and which has caused some controversy, is that of news aggregation. A web content aggregator is an individual or organisation which gathers web content and/or applications from different online sources for reuse or resale.[86] News aggregator services are web content aggregators in the news sector which collect news information from a variety of channels. As the news sector is characterised by a large number of different channels and agencies producing and distributing news information in different forms, languages and formats, it is often difficult for users to keep track of news items on a chosen topic. In this situation, news aggregators can provide useful services which save the user a great deal of time.[87] There are two categories of news aggregators: those that simply gather news information from various sources and put them on their websites; and those that gather, process and distribute content to suit their users' needs. Google News[88] is an example of the former;[89] *Infopaq International*[90] of the latter.

One way to find news content of interest on Google News is to search using a certain keyword. Google News then returns a list of results from different sources. Each entry contains the headline, the first few sentences of a news story and sometimes a low-scale image.[91] The headline and the picture constitute a link to the full article on the original content provider's website.[92] The consistency of this business model with copyright law has

[86] S Chowdhury and M Landoni 'News Aggregator Services: User Expectations and Experience' [2006] 30 *Online Information Review* 100, 101.
[87] Ibid.
[88] http://news.google.com. Although you can get 'personalised' news sent directly to your inbox from Google news.
[89] Chowdhury and Landoni, above n 86, 102.
[90] Above n 35.
[91] The news story and thumbnail do not necessarily come from the same source. It seems that the top news stories which Google displays on its Google News home page without the need for a search offer pictures even if these come from a different source.
[92] A more thorough description is given by Chowdhury and Landoni, above n 86, 103: '[Google News] provides news stories gathered from various news sources throughout the world and presents them in eight different categories, arranged by the most relevant news first. It provides three types of feeds: (1) section feeds, where the user can get a feed for any Google News section; (2) in search results feeds, where the user can also get a feed for any search done

been questioned in different jurisdictions as content owners and news aggregators seek to exert control over the content and of the market space. Within this, it seems generally acknowledged that news aggregators significantly increase traffic to the news websites.

> Hitwise tracks 800,000 sites divided into 170 industry categories. One of those categories is our News & Media—Print category which covers Newspaper and Magazine websites (3,180 sites total). For the week ending 11/18/06 (based on our US sample), Google was the #1 site sending traffic to the category at 13.66%, Search Engines as a whole were responsible for 22.44% of traffic for that same week.[93]

A. Europe

In the different European jurisdictions there has been limited case-law considering the consistency of news aggregation with copyright law.[94] *Handelsblatt v Paperboy*[95] in Germany in 2003 concerned Paperboy, a search service for current news offering news clippings, headlines and in some cases short phrases indicating the content of the publication.[96] The Federal Court of Justice found that Handelsblatt could not require Paperboy to stop offering news clippings on copyright grounds: 'This is so because it has been neither argued, nor is it obvious that, through the manner in which Paperboy displays publications, parts of works capable of copyright protection could be used individually.'[97] Including short excerpts

on Google News; and (3) in the customized news feeds, where the user can create a feed of a customized news page. Google Alerts is a specific service that sends automatic e-mails to users when there are new items on a chosen topic. Users can personalize the news front page by creating sections of their own topics. Amongst others, users can choose for either country-specific or source-specific searching criteria; or users can search for news articles published in any specific news source, any specific location.'

[93] D Sullivan, 27 November 2006, http://blog.searchenginewatch.com/blog/061127-123545.

[94] One of the earliest in Denmark was *Danske Dagblades Forening (DDF) v Newsbooster* [2003] European Copyright and Design Reports 5. A Danish court found that an online news service's practice in selecting, compiling and deep linking to online news articles infringed the publishers' database rights under Danish law. The case dealt with the legality of deep linking rather than the question whether a link containing material protected by copyright infringed and said nothing about the consistency of the Newsbooster's business model with copyright law. See also A Wernblad, 'Denmark: Electronic Commerce—Intellectual Property' [2002] *Computer and Telecommunications Law Review* N147.

[95] *Verlagsgruppe Handelsblatt GmbH v Paperboy* [2005] European Copyright and Design Reports 7.

[96] The court gives an example: '[K.Express]: Express Online—News Thursday, 25 February 1999, 02.39am News Lower House of the German Federal Parliament: huge row ["es krachte gewaltig"] Chancellor versus CSU-Leader exp Bonn—the oral battle was hard, the choice of words pithy. Government and Opposition granted each other on the second . . . Investors Predecessor-Government Distortion Union FDP-fight 759 words, 5,550 bytes.'

[97] Above n 95.

from the text of the original news report was not an infringement of copyright in this case.[98]

However, a different conclusion, albeit based on different facts, was reached in Belgium in *Copiepresse v Google Inc.*[99] In this case the President of the Civil Court of First Instance in Brussels—on appeal from Google—confirmed that Google's practice of providing news clippings infringed the publishers' copyright in the original news reports.[100] Two aspects of the service came under scrutiny. The first was the caching of the report and providing access to the article; the second was the question of infringement by the display of excerpts from news articles on Google News. On the first, it was noted that the whole of the news reports in question could be retrieved via the cached link on http://google.be. The court held that the caching and storing of the news reports constituted copying, and allowing users to access these stored news reports constituted communication to the public. The conduct was not saved by Infosoc Directive Article 5(1) (the equivalent of section 28A CDPA (temporary copy)) in Belgian law[101] as, even if it was accepted that the reproduction by caching is an integral part of the technical indexation process, it is not the sole purpose as it is also used to grant access to the cached sites.[102] On the second aspect of the service, the court found that while, in general, headlines and some lines of the original news report are not original for the purposes of copyright law and are therefore not protected, some of the snippets and headlines were sufficiently 'marked by the personality, the stamp of the author' and

[98] The unofficial translation provided by the European Copyright and Design Report does not do justice to the original wording, which in the end is clearer: '[Es ist nicht ersichtlich] daß durch die Art und Weise, wie Paperboy Veröffentlichungen nachweist, selbständig urheberrechtlich schutzfähige Werkteile genutzt werden könnten.' The court also found that deep linking does not conflict with copyright or with the publishers' database rights

[99] *Copiepresse SCRL v Google Inc* [2007] European Copyright and Design Reports 5. For general comments see B Van Asbroeck and M Cock, 'Belgian Newspapers v Google News' [2007] *Journal of Intellectual Property & Practice* 463; M Turner and D Callaghan, 'You Can Look But Don't Touch! The Impact of the Google v Copiepresse Decision on the Future of the Internet' [2008] *EIPR* 34–38.

[100] The court also found that Google infringed the publishers' moral rights—a point that will not be further explored in this chapter. An analysis of the reasoning is provided by B Van Asbroeck and M Cock, 'Belgian Newspapers v Google News: 2–0' [2007] *Journal of Intellectual Property Law & Practice* 463. Note also that Copiepresse took the European Commission to court in Belgium over its news aggregation services. The case was dismissed on technical grounds although Copiepresse said that it would seek to reapply to the court. See http://www.out-law.com/page-9227.

[101] They should be substantially the same, as they are both based on Art 5(1) of the Infosoc Directive.

[102] Google had tried to convince the court that it only provided the installations and it was the Internet user who created the copy when clicking on the cached link. This followed on from the logic behind the District Court's reasoning in *Field v Google Inc*. The claim in *Copiepresse* was more broadly worded and encompassed caching and the grant of access—a factor emphasised by the court. Indeed, it has been suggested that in the US, a claim worded similarly might have more success than the one in *Field v Google*. The Belgian court also pointed out that Google did not merely link to the articles but that the reports were stored in Google's memory—akin to the server test established in *Kelly v Arriba Soft Corp* and confirmed in *Perfect 10 v Amazon.com Inc.*

therefore enjoyed protection. It concluded therefore that both acts gave rise to a prima facie case of copyright infringement.

Google argued a number of defences. The first was that its news service qualified as a press review for the purposes of Article 21, section 1 of the Belgian Copyright Law which allows, without prior authorisation of the copyright holder, quotations which have the 'purpose of criticism, polemic, education, review or for scientific works';[103] the second that Article 22, sections 1(1) and 2 which allow for the reproduction, for the purpose of information, of brief excerpts of works on the occasion of news reporting[104] provided a defence; and the third that its freedom of expression enshrined in Article 10 of the European Convention on Human Rights would be curtailed if it was to be enjoined from providing news clippings. The court rejected all three arguments. The quotation exception could only be invoked in the case of a quotation used to illustrate or defend an opinion; the exception for reporting news was only applicable where the works are accessory to the news reporting and not the very object of it; and freedom of expression was already taken into account in the legislation through the exceptions to copyright.[105]

By holding Google liable for copyright infringement and finding that no defence was available to the search engine, *Copiepresse v Google Inc* is thus the first decision which holds that news aggregation is incompatible with copyright law. Some have said that it is a lawsuit 'that seriously threaten[s] web search itself'.[106] But how likely is it that other courts will follow the Belgian approach?

B. UK

If the case were to come before a court in the UK many of the points tackled in the Belgian order would fall to be decided in the UK according to substantially similar provisions, as most of these aspects have been harmonised on EU level. But would this also entail achieving the same result? One question would be whether the snippets displayed on Google News actually amount to a substantial part of the original work.[107] If they

---

[103] Van Asbroeck and Cock, above n 99.

[104] Ibid.

[105] Google's argument that press publishers who do not use existing technical means to prevent indexation implicitly consented to such indexation was put aside by the simple statement that the prior consent is one of the fundamental copyright principles. P Laurent, 'Brussels High Court Confirms Google News' Ban—Copiepresse SCRL v Google Inc— Prohibitory Injunction/Stop Order of the President of the High Court of Brussels' (2007) 23 *Computer Law & Security Report* 290, 292.

[106] D Sullivan, 'Google's Belgium Fight: Show Me the Money, Not the Opt-Out, Say Publishers', SearchEngineWatch.com (20 September 2006), http://blog.searchenginewatch.com/blog/060920-152314.

[107] To infringe, the reproduction must be substantial whether measured quantitatively or qualitatively.

do not, then the communication to the public would not infringe copyright. That would leave open caching which, as argued above, does infringe UK law. The question would then arise as to whether that infringing act might be excused given the lawfulness of the final presentation of the material to the public—akin to the argument that it can be fair dealing to copy the whole of a work in order to deal fairly with a part (see below). On fair dealing, it would seem that the relatively limited parameters of the criticism or review fair dealing defence[108] would not be available to Google as it has been argued that review requires some dealing with the original work 'other than condensing that work into a summary'.[109] However, it is notable that the wording of the Infosoc Directive,[110] which, in part, strove to harmonise limitations and exceptions throughout Member States, speaks of 'quotations for purposes *such as* criticism or review',[111] suggesting that the exceptions should not be limited to these categories. Another possibility could be the defence of fair dealing for the purposes of reporting current events.[112] While, as outlined above, the defence did not work in Belgium, UK courts have consistently stated that the defence is of wide scope and should be interpreted liberally[113] albeit that the events need to be current.[114] Furthermore, it may be argued that in certain circumstances it will still be fair dealing to copy the whole of a work in order to deal fairly with part[115] thus introducing the possibility that the caching would be excused under this head where presentation of the snippets amounts to fair dealing. Certainly there are difficulties, not least of which is that Google will be displaying material not all of which could be regarded under the law as current. But the analysis suggests that a different conclusion could be achieved in these circumstances, giving control through the law of copyright, while at the same time excusing behaviour that contributes to the circulation of news—a goal that is itself recognised in the Berne Convention.[116]

(i) InfoPaq

One other point to note, and by virtue of which the law may be clarified in due course, is the reference that has been made to the ECJ in *Infopaq*.[117] As

108 CDPA s 30(1)
109 Above n 37, para 5.29.
110 Above n 34.
111 Infosoc Directive Art 5(3)(d).
112 CDPA s 30(2).
113 *Pro Sieben Media v Carlton UK Television* [1999] FSR 610 (CA)
114 *Ashdown v Telegraph Group Ltd* [2002] Ch 149 CA; *HRH the Prince of Wales v Associated Newspapers Ltd* (No 3) 2006 EWHC 522; [2006] EWCA Civ 1776.
115 Above n 40, para 5.26 using the example of the need to call up the whole of a webpage where part only is to be used.
116 Berne Convention Art 2(8). 'The protection of this Convention shall not apply to news of the day or to miscellaneous facts having the character of mere items of press information.'
117 Case C-5/08. See n 35. See also the postscript on p 266.

described above,[118] the questions asked in this reference concern the operation of a news aggregation service offering bespoke services to its clients.
A number of the questions concerning transient copyright were noted. In
addition to these, questions have been asked about whether the storing and
subsequent printing out of a text extract from an article in a daily
newspaper, consisting of a search word and the five proceeding and five
subsequent words, could be regarded as acts of reproduction; whether a
'lawful use' (see Article 5(1) of the Infosoc Directive) can include the
scanning by a commercial business of entire newspaper articles, subsequent
processing of the reproduction, and the storing and possible printing out of
part of the reproduction, consisting of one or more text extracts of 11
words, for use in the business's summary writing, even where the rights-
holder has not given consent to those acts; and whether that activity can be
regarded as constituting 'certain special cases which do not conflict with a
normal exploitation' of the newspaper articles and 'not unreasonably
[prejudicing] the legitimate interests of the rights-holder.[119]

As can be seen, these questions are key to the lawfulness or otherwise,
within copyright law, of the news aggregation activities of search engines.
Clarification by the ECJ of these points should lead to (greater) convergence in case-law in Member States and thus a move towards a more level
playing field for content providers and news aggregators in the Community. What remains to be seen is the extent to which the ECJ might, or
might not, explicitly or implicitly, take into consideration the wider
copyright goals when considering the questions. As has been argued, news
aggregators provide extremely useful services for the public, enabling them
to keep track of many and varied news sources and reports. But whether
that can, or indeed should, be recognised as falling directly within the
public interest concerns of the law must be debatable.

---

[118] Above pp 233 and 234.

[119] The full text of the relevant questions is as follows: 'Can the storing and subsequent
printing out of a text extract from an article in a daily newspaper, consisting of a search word and
the five proceeding and five subsequent words, be regarded as acts of reproduction which are
protected (see Art 2 of the Infosoc Directive)? 9. Does "lawful use" (see Art 5(1) of the Infosoc
Directive) include any form which does not require the copyright holder's consent? 10. Does
"lawful use" (see Art 5(1) of the Infosoc Directive) include the scanning by a commercial business
of entire newspaper articles, subsequent processing of the reproduction, and the storing and
possible printing out of part of the reproduction, consisting of one or more text extracts of 11
words, for use in the business's summary writing, even where the rightholder has not given
consent to those acts? 11. What criteria should be used to access whether temporary acts of
reproduction have "independent economic significance" (see Art 5(1) of the Infosoc Directive) if
the other conditions laid down in the provision are satisfied? 13. Can the scanning by a
commercial business of entire newspaper articles, subsequent processing of the reproduction,
and the storing and possible printing our of part of the reproduction, consisting of one or more
text extracts of 11 words, without the rightholder's consent be regarded as constituting "certain
special cases which do not conflict with a normal exploitation" of the newspaper articles and
"not unreasonably [prejudicing] the legitimate interests of the rightholder" (see Art 5(5))?'

C. US

There have been several disputes in the US involving news aggregation and copyright, none of which have yet been fully aired in court. In March 2005 the Agence France Presse (AFP), the world's oldest news agency, filed a $17.5 million law suit in the US District Court for the District of Columbia against Google News.[120] AFP alleged that the posting of AFPs headlines, photographs and news summaries without permission infringed copyright.[121] El-Shibib reports that US District Judge Gladys Kessler was reluctant to dismiss AFPs copyright claims and instead granted both parties more time to demonstrate or discount alleged copyright infringements.[122] However, the District Court ultimately did not need to decide on the matter as AFP and Google reached a licensing agreement on 6 April 2007 which enabled Google News to index AFP content. Although the specific terms of the agreement have not been disclosed, it is widely believed that Google made a financial commitment.[123] Associated Press (AP) then filed a law suit against news aggregator Moreover Technologies Inc.[124] As to copyright infringement, AP claimed[125] that 'Moreover infringes its copyright through reproduction and display of identical copies of the articles including the headlines, and images'; and that Moreover also caches this material, enabling its users to gain access to unlawful copies. Should the portion of the work be considered to be infringing (under UK law there would be some doubt as to whether a headline would receive protection and there may also be a question about substantiality) the US court may consider it to be covered by fair use, guided by the analyses in *Kelly v Arriba Soft Corp*[126] and *Perfect 10 v Amazon.com Inc.*[127] However, it did not seem mere coincidence that AP drafted its claims in a very similar way to the claims brought by Copiepresse in Belgium. No doubt emboldened by Copiepresse's success, AP may have felt its chances had risen after that case. Sadly the US court did not get the opportunity to judge the issue as the case

---

120 *Agence France Presse v Google Inc* (filed 15 March 2005).
121 T El-Shibib, 'USA: Copyright—Settlement of Dispute Concerning Licence Agreement' (2007) *Entertainment Law Review* N110. Official documents, including the complaint related to *Agence France Presse v Google Inc*, can be found at http://dockets.justia.com/docket/court-dcdce/case_no-1:2005cv00546/case_id-113951/.
122 Ibid.
123 E Goldman, 'AFP v Google Settles', Technology & Marketing Blog (7 April 2007), http://blog.ericgoldman.org/archives/2007/04/afp_v_google_se.htm .
124 *Associated Press v Moreover Technologies Inc*, 07 CIV 8699 (SDNY complaint filed 9 October 2007)
125 A link to the complaint filed is provided by E Goldman, 'AFP v Google News Redux—AP v Moreover', Technology & Marketing Blog (11 October 2007), http://blog.ericgoldman.org/archives/2007/10/afp_v_google_ne_1.htm.
126 Above n 65.
127 Above n 76.

settled in August 2008. The terms of the settlement have not been disclosed.[128]

D. Licensing Agreements and Technological Solutions[129]

No doubt spurred on by this litigious activity, two trends can be discerned in the marketplace. The first is for licensing agreements between news aggregators and publishers; the second is the development of technology to permit, on certain terms, access to news stories.

(i) Licensing Agreements

The first deal between a news aggregator and a news publisher which received significant attention was in August 2006 and involved AP and Google. Google agreed to pay AP for use of its news stories and pictures. The next deal came in 2007 when AFP and Google settled their law suit. As the District Court judge is reported to have been reluctant to dismiss AFPs claims, many believed that this deal also involved payment. Even before August 2006 there were numerous licensing schemes in place between contract aggregators and content providers, although these may not have necessarily involved payment. Examples are the agreements between Google and the *New York Times*, *Le Monde* and *The Times*, where, for example, Google may have enhanced access to the publisher's archive which was otherwise only accessible with user registration. The former online editorial director of *The Times* and the *Sunday Times*, Peter Bale, is reported to have said that Times Online had 'benefited tremendously' from traffic coming from Google News.[130]

The issue of payment is an important one. If payment is made in respect of these licensing deals in the US, fair use may no longer be available as a defence. This is because a market will have developed for selling news reports thus negating the fourth fair use factor. Perhaps because of this, Google (after the first statements announcing the AP deal) added that it had not paid AP to use its content but that new innovative services would be launched in the near future. Doubts have been expressed as to whether any of these innovative services will be forthcoming.[131]

---

[128] http://investing.businessweek.com/research/stocks/private/snapshot.asp?privcapId=31715.

[129] Licensing and technology are of course the recurrent 'solution' to many of the difficulties encountered including for example that of ISPs and piracy (see ch 1); Google Library Program (see below and ch 5).

[130] M Sweney, 'Publishers Warned Over Google News Deal', MediaGuardian, 3 October 2007, http://www.guardian.co.uk/media/2007/oct/03/digitalmedia.pressandpublishing/print.

[131] JC Perez, 'Google's Associated Press Licensing Deal Short on Results', Infoworld, 2 August 2007, http://www.infoworld.com/article/07/08/02/Google-AP-deal-yields-nothing_1.html.

(ii) Technology

But it is not just litigation and licensing deals that shape the market. A proposed technological solution, Automated Content Access Protocol (ACAP), has been designed to enable content owners to place permissions on their site which can then be read by crawlers. As stated on the website: 'ACAP is destined to become the universal permissions protocol on the Internet, an open, non-proprietary standard through which content owners can communicate permissions for access and use to online intermediaries.'[132] While it is said that the alliance is one between search engines and content owners, including news aggregators, it appears that none of the major search engines have engaged with the initiative.[133] Neither is it entirely clear as to what permissions will be given to search engines. Might there be permission, for example, to link, or to cache? What, then, if these activities are lawful within the jurisdiction in which permission is given? Might a practice develop in which permissions replace copyright, a practice clearly having close parallels in other discussions in which contract is used to contour copyright?[134] If this does develop, control will lie firmly in the hands of the content owners, in turn raising questions over the place of the public interest.[135]

E. Future Trends

As was highlighted at the start of this section, it seems generally accepted that news aggregator services provided by search engines significantly increase traffic to news websites. Why, then, do the providers of the news content want to 'bite the hand that feeds them'? The answer will come back to one of the fundamental points identified above: control. Even if no payment is made to the news aggregators, once the principle of licensing is established it is much easier for the news sites to control their content. While the news aggregators may continue to argue either that no licence is actually necessary because there is no copyright infringement and/or that the activities fall under fair dealing or fair use, that a deal has been agreed would seem to put them in a much weaker position vis-à-vis the content providers. The question then arises, when revisiting copyright principles, of whether that actually matters. Deal or no deal, the news aggregators make

---

132 For information, see http://the-acap.org/.
133 For a sceptical note, see R Paul, 'A Skeptical Look at the Automated Content Access Protocol', 13 January 2008 http://arstechnica.com/articles/paedia/skeptical-look-at-acap.ars/1.
134 See chs 5 and 6.
135 For comment on the initiative, see SEC(2007) 1710, Commission Staff Working Document accompanying the Communication from the Commission to the European Parliament, The Council, the European Economic and Social Committee and the Committee of the Regions on Creative Content Online in the Single Market (COM(2007) 836 final) para 3.2.8.

it possible for a user to find news content from a wide variety of sources for the benefit of the consuming public, thus satisfying this element of the public interest. As has also been argued above, assuming that the activity is regulated by copyright, it enables flexibility in decision making (where that flexibility exists in national laws) to excuse certain behaviours which are in the public interest. Difficulties may arise where regulation takes hold through the technology. Here, it is the content providers that enable or deny access to the works, on terms that may or may not reflect the public interest benefits inherent in the law of copyright. This in turn brings into sharp relief all the arguments that have been raised in recent years over the use of technical protection measures when making content available, which can deny to user the benefits of such relaxations as fair dealing[136] as well as fundamental questions over regulation of the Internet through code.[137]

The analysis so far suggests that while copyright law generally applies to the activities of search engines, at times the application has the potential to stifle publicly beneficial activities (such as search engine caching in the UK); while at other times, search engines may be required to act on behalf of content owners, for reasons outside of the goals embedded in the law (such as removal or making inaccessible of infringing material). Furthermore, there are signs that at times, while the joint interests of the search engine and the content owner might be met through (unarticulated) agreement so both may ply their trade, there is little or nothing in this that would take into account the public interest, which becomes merely a by-product of the pursuit of commercial interests.

VI. GOOGLE BOOK SEARCH

We turn now to a different project in which Google is engaged: Google Book Search (formerly Google Print).[138] In this project, Google states that its goal is to 'digitize the world's books in order to make them easier for people to find and buy'.[139] It differs from the other aggregation projects described above in that it does not gather information that is already available on the Internet, but rather books are manually scanned[140] and then made available through one of two programs:

- *Google Books Partner Program (formerly Print Publisher Programme):* Google scans and saves the complete book. Users can see a few pages or

---

[136] See chs 5 and 6 and the discussion on the various business models, including the newspaper industry, under threat in the Internet era in ch 11.

[137] See eg L Lessig, *Code and other laws of Cyberspace* (New York, Basic Books, 1999).

[138] See also ch 6.

[139] See http://books.google.com/.

[140] For an insight into what can happen when the scanning takes place too fast, see http://www.techcrunch.com/2007/12/06/google-books-adds-hand-scans.

the whole of the book depending on the permission given by the publisher.

- *Google Books Library Project (formerly Print Library Project):* Google scans and saves complete book. Where the book is protected by copyright the users only see a few lines of text ('snippets') and not more than three instances per search plus a link to a site where the book can be purchased, or a library where it can be borrowed. Where the term of copyright has expired, then the complete book is available for download.

A. The Program, the Project and Copyright

The Google Books Partner Program raises no copyright issues as it is based on agreement between the publisher and Google. The Google Books Library Project does, however, have implications for copyright as Google scans books and makes available the snippets without permission from the publisher who is often the owner of the copyright after taking an assignation (or exclusive licence) from the author. Google gives publishers the opportunity to opt-out of having their portfolios of books scanned either before the scanning takes place, or after the book has been scanned and made available. Before the scan is made, the publisher can give notice to Google that the work should not be included in the database. If the scan has already been made and is in the database, Google will remove this on request by the publisher. This strategy, Google argues, is legitimised by the notice and take-down provisions enacted in many domestic laws.[141] The publishers and authors, perhaps unsurprisingly, object to this business model. As with the other initiatives described above, the key issue is one of control over content.

(i) Case-law Challenges

In 2005, the Author's Guild launched an action against Google in the US.[142] This was a class action on behalf authors alleging 'massive' copyright infringement of their rights through the reproduction of their works without consent. In October 2005, in an action co-ordinated and funded by the Association of American Publishers, a request for injunctive relief was filed against Google alleging infringement of the exclusive rights of the publishers by way of the reproduction and distribution of their books.[143] As will be discussed below, a negotiated settlement between these parties was made public in November 2008.

---

[141] In Europe, the E-commerce Directive, above n 42. In the US, the Digital Millennium Copyright Act 1998.

[142] No 05 CV 8136 (SDNY, filed 20 September 2005).

[143] *McGraw-Hill Companies, Inc v Google*, No 05 CV 8881 (SDNY, filed 19 October 2005).

In Germany, a petition by WBG (a German publisher) for a preliminary injunction against Google (Regional Court Hamburg) was withdrawn in June 2006 after the court indicated that the petition was unlikely to succeed.[144] It was said that the presentation of snippets from the books was unlikely to infringe German copyright law, and that it was unlikely that German copyright would apply to scanning/copying of the books as that activity took place in the US.

In France, also in June 2006, the publishing group La Martinière sued Google France and Google Inc for infringement of their intellectual property rights. La Martinière was joined in the law suit in October 2006 by Syndicat national de l'Edition (SNE), an association representing 400 publishers.[145] This action is still pending.

(ii) The Arguments

Google argues that it is not liable for infringement of copyright. Pointing to the choices that the publisher has for opting out of the programme, Google is of the view that this negates any infringement liability. Further, and in the US at least (which is where the scanning takes place), if infringement were found, Google argues that it has a defence as the scanning of the work amounts to fair use as does the presentation of snippets.[146] Unsurprisingly others, and in particular publishers and authors, do not agree with these views. They complain that Google's argument turns the exclusive rights granted to copyright owners on their head by saying that there is a right to reproduce a work unless the content owner opts out.[147] Copyright has always been about exclusivity for the owner, not the user. On the matter of fair use and copying of the entire work, some deny that the copying of the whole of a work could ever be regarded as fair even where it enabled a use which is fair (in this case, the presentation of the snippets[148]). Also on the question of fair use, where the use impacts on the commercial interests of the rights-holder, US case-law suggests that it is unlikely to be regarded as fair.[149] In both US actions the applicants have stressed the commercial nature of the project—Google aims to increase its advertising revenue from the programme.[150]

[144] *WBG (German publisher) v Google*. For information, see http://www.linksandlaw.com/google-print-timeline-3-book-search.htm.
[145] See the BBC News website at http://news.bbc.co.uk/1/hi/entertainment/5052912.stm.
[146] See eg the Official Google Blog. Google Print and the Authors Guild, 20 September 2005, http://googleblog.blogspot.com/2005/09/google-print-and-authors-guild.html.
[147] Note the Belgian court in *Copiepresse SCRL v Google Inc* [2007] European Copyright and Design Reports 5 did not accept the arguments.
[148] Above n 143.
[149] Eg *Field v Google Inc*, above n 15.
[150] On this, Google says that 'We don't place ads on a specific book result unless the copyright holder has given us permission to display portions of the book and wants to show ads.' The revenue is shared between Google and the publisher. http://books.google.com/googlebooks/facts.html.

B. Shaping Business Strategies within Jurisdictional Divergences

Although the issues remain unsettled, these arguments are the basis on which Google has shaped its business strategy for scanning and making books available though this programme, and within which Google seeks shelter. The differences in the laws of various jurisdictions must mean that Google feels more comfortable in some countries than others with regard to the processes involved, from scanning books to presentation of the results. The US fair use doctrine,[151] with its inherent flexibilities, does not have a counterpart in the majority of European countries (or elsewhere). In carrying out its scanning activities in particular, Google and those developing similar projects are likely to gravitate to the US where they may be shielded by the law. On the availability of content, because the law has uncertain parameters, fewer books will be searchable than might otherwise be the case. Many libraries joining the project, whether in the US or elsewhere, only agree to the scanning of material in the public domain. Beyond that, Google tends to concentrate on older books and those out of print.[152]

All this also has an impact upon cultural diversity. Because Google relies on broad fair use in the US for scanning the books and carries out that activity within the US, it is more likely that these will be in English than in other languages, to the impoverishment of non-English language speakers. Perhaps sensitive to this last point, Europe has, since 2005, been working on its own Digital Libraries Initiative. The plan is to make

> Europe's diverse cultural and scientific heritage (books, films, maps, photographs, music, etc.) easier and more interesting to use online for work, leisure and/or study. It builds on Europe's rich heritage combining multicultural and multilingual environments with technological advances and new business models.[153]

While there are some notable collections already available within Europe, it would appear that the ambitious project is still grappling with copyright issues.[154]

The availability of content can vary from the perspective of the user even within Member States of the EU where many laws should be at least

---

[151] US Copyright Act Title 17 s 107, above p 237.

[152] According to Google, those books should be favoured because they are more worth making searchable/visible, but one may suspect that Google wants to await the outcomes of the litigation before it spends money on the scanning of copyrighted books because Google might be required to delete/not use the copies made.

[153] http://ec.europa.eu/information_society/activities/digital_libraries/what_is_dli/index_en.htm.

[154] See eg Commission Recommendation of 18 May 2005 on collective cross-border management of copyright and related rights for legitimate online music services (2005/737/EC); and COM(2007) 836 final Communication from the Commission to the European Parliament, the Council, the European Economic and Social Committee and the Committee on Creative Content Online in the Single Market (SEC(2007) 1710).

approximated even if not harmonised. This can be seen in the aftermath of the ruling issued against Google in the Belgian case of *Copiepresse v Google Inc*[155] discussed above. When Google lost, one part of the order granted against the search engine required it to remove content in which copyright belonged to the French and German publishers from its Belgian website or pay a fine of €1 million daily. As a result, Google almost immediately removed access to over 10 sites within the .be domain, although the same content remained available from other Google sites such as Google.com.[156] That content would still have been accessible to users within Belgium, but perhaps not all users would have thought to search on different sites. One can imagine that an adverse decision for Google in the cases brought by La Martinière and SNE[157] may result in the non-availability of the content in the form served by Google within the .fr domain—but not elsewhere.

C. The Google Book Program and the Public Interest

While in the uncertain environment control over content may lie in the hands of the publishers, the result, it would seem, would do little to make these works available to the consuming public.

This leads to consideration of the place of one of the public policy goals of copyright in relation to the Google Book Program. Although the Book Program does not itself result in the creation of new works, a question arises as to whether it increases accessibility of existing works. One way to show that Google Book Search does help to attain this goal might be to compare the numbers of times a work is accessed by a user on Google Book Search with the number of uses of a work in hard-copy format (such as through book sales or library loans). However, obtaining evidence from Google that might support or undermine the claim is no easy task. Information on such matters as numbers of users, what they search for, whether a 'find' through the book search is likely to result in the downstream sale of a book, are said to be 'things that Google doesn't talk about'.[158] A Google search has, however, revealed that Heather Hopkins of Hitwise, a company that analyses web behaviour, said that 'Last week [August 2006] 15.93% of downstream visits from Google Book Search UK went to websites in the Hitwise Shopping and Classifieds—Books category.'[159] This suggests, although not nearly as clearly as one might like, that Google Book Search might enhance downstream sales—users may be obtaining access to works they might not otherwise have known about or have been able to find.

---

[155] Above n 99.
[156] http://blog.searchenginewatch.com/blog/060920-152314.
[157] Above n 145.
[158] E-mail communication by Google, February 2008.
[159] http://twopointouch.com/2006/08/31/googles-book-statistics/.

While perhaps not overly robust, this is at least an argument, moulded and adapted for the digital era, for why, despite the challenges posed for the law of copyright as it has existed and been justified at least in the UK since 1709,[160] the Book Search might be supported from within the existing law.

D. Google Book Settlement

But time has not stood still. As indicated above, several challenges have been mounted against Google Book Search. In 2008 it appeared that Google and the Authors Guild had managed to settle their differences in an agreement that has come to be known as the Google Book Settlement (the Settlement).[161] The Settlement is subject to ratification by the New York District Court in a fairness hearing which was due to have taken place on 11 June 2009. However, for reasons that will be explained below, this has been postponed until 7 October 2009.[162]

The Settlement proposes the establishment of a Book Rights Registry (the Registry). The purpose of the Registry, which is essentially a collecting society, is to maintain a database of rights-holders, collect their contact details and information regarding requests with respect to uses of books, and then to co-ordinate payments to rights-holders. Google will pay US$34.5 million for the set up costs of the Registry which will thereafter be funded through 63 per cent of the income stream received by Google through its commercial operation of the Books database. The Registry will be managed by equal numbers of authors and publisher representatives. No other stakeholder class (eg libraries, readers, academic users) will be represented or have a vote.

Google will obtain its revenue stream through selling access to the database of books which will mainly be those protected by copyright but out of print. Access licences will be available to educational institutions, libraries (free viewing will be giving via one terminal) and consumers. Revenue will also be earned through advertising. Books in the public domain will continue to be made available free of charge. Books which are protected by copyright and in print will not be available in the database unless the rights-holder opts to have them included. Rights-holders can

---

160 Statute of Anne 1710, the first Copyright Act.

161 Full information available at http://www.googlebooksettlement.com.

162 If it is ratified, then the publishers in *The McGraw-Hill Companies, Inc et al v Google Inc* will dismiss their separate suit against Google. Given that the case has been raised as a class action, in deciding whether or not to approve the settlement a court's typical concern is whether the settlement is 'fair, reasonable, and adequate' to class members, FED R CIV PROC 23(e)(2) quoted by J Grimelmann, 'The Google Book Search Settlement: Ends, Means, and the Future of Books' [April 2009] *The American Constitution Society for Law and Policy* 15. It must also be consistent with the public interest. *Bailey v Great Lakes Canning, Inc*, 908 F 2d 38, 42 (6th Cir 1990).

exclude their books from some or all of these uses and can also remove their books altogether from the database (if already digitised) so long as the request is made on or before 5 April 2011. Thereafter a book can be prevented from being made available but cannot be 'de-digitised.' Nor can Google be stopped from digitising it. With respect to books that have already been digitised without permission, Google will make available US$45 million, and pay between US$60 and US$5 for each work.

(i) The Views So Far

It has taken a while for comment on the Settlement to emerge, no doubt because the terms are complex. What should come as no surprise to anyone is the self-interest of the parties evident in the terms of the Settlement. There are, however, differences of opinion as to how that self-interest should be interpreted. Supporters of Google agree with the search engine that the aim to free the printed word shines through. Those who are more circumspect point to the position of monopoly that will be occupied by Google if the Settlement is agreed and argue that Google's only aim is to dominate this market.[163]

One key aspect of the Settlement concerns so-called orphan works. An orphan work is generally understood as a work still believed to be protected by copyright but for which the owner cannot be found despite carrying out reasonable searches. With the ubiquity of digitisation combined with the malleability and ease of repurposing protected works, so the difficulties posed in trying to find copyright owners have been amplified. This has led, in recent years, to a number of proposals being brought forwards which would give those digitising and making available orphan works some immunity in the event that they used the work but then the rights-holder emerged and claimed infringement. One of the most developed was the Orphan Works Act[164] in the US. This measure was proposed after a lengthy study of the issue by the US copyright office and would have limited the amount of damages a rights-holder could claim from someone making an orphan work available provided a reasonable search had been carried out in trying to find that rights-holder.[165] The process stalled in the autumn of 2008 as political attention focused on the economic crisis. Other jurisdictions are also working on the problem. In Europe there have been extensive discussions and meetings to examine possible solutions to this issue. One of the most recent culminated in a report on orphan works

---

[163] For a synopsis of the arguments on both sides, see J Grimmelmann 'How to Fix the Google Book Search Settlement' (2009) 12(10) *Journal of Internet Law* 1.

[164] HR5889 and related Bill S 2913.

[165] The full report and other information on orphan works is available at http://www.copyright.gov/orphan/

promulgated by the i2010: Digital Libraries High Level Expert Group.[166] However, as in the US, progress is lamentably slow as focus remains on weighty economic matters.

In essence, the Settlement is a type of orphan works agreement forged by private parties in the face of public regulatory failure. Because this is a class action it has been brought on behalf of all authors who have an interest in a US copyright.[167] In addition the publishers have agreed to drop their action in the event that the Settlement is ratified at the Fairness Hearing. The Settlement thus immunises Google from being sued for past and future reproduction and making available of orphan works and works that turn out not to be orphaned. However, that immunity would apply only to Google and not to any other party that might want to follow this business model—such as Amazon. If other organisations want also to digitise books which they consider to be orphan, while they could do so, they would run the risk of being sued and have no guarantee that they would be able to negotiate a 'safe harbour' similar to that granted to Google.

Another key and related issue is that of payment. As indicated, Google will make available US$45 million for digitisation that has already occurred, and then give 63 per cent of future revenues to the Registry for distribution amongst copyright owners. Many of the books already digitised are likely to be orphan works.[168] After five years the revenues will be distributed amongst the rights-holders who have registered with the Registry and to defray the costs of the Registry. There is thus a conflict of interest as between those who have signed up to the Registry and 'owners' of orphan works.

Others have raised serious questions as to whether those who initiated the Authors Guild action could possibly be said to represent authors as a class. It was a question Google raised in the initial court papers but dropped as settlement was reached. In the Settlement, the Authors Guild claim to represent everyone who has a US copyright interest in a book.[169] All authors are then bound by the deal unless they opt out. But in order to obtain a deal that bound all of the members of the class, Google only had to negotiate with 10 individuals. Would-be competitors then face an insurmountable hurdle in that they would have to deal individually with

---

[166] i2010: Digital Libraries High Level Expert Group—Copyright Subgroup, Final Report on Digital Preservation, Orphan Works, and Out-of-Print Works (4 June 2008).

[167] Because of the Berne Convention and national treatment, so the nationals of all signatory states to the Berne Convention will have US copyright in their published works. Berne Convention Art 3. In May 2009 there were 164 Contracting Parties to the Berne Convention.

[168] Google has spent $7 million on a campaign to alert authors to the settlement—so many may come forwards. See Grimmelmann, above n 163, 14 who quotes that a notice has even gone to *Nauru Bulletin* (circulation 700). But there will be many other authors who may not.

[169] Grimmelmann, above n 163, 3. Indeed, eventually the Authors Guild will represent all of those who sign up to the Registry—but all authors will be included unless they opt out.

aggrieved authors and, ultimately, be faced with potentially expensive law suits in order to compete in the market and drive down the price of the books and of access.[170]

The reality is that there were significant pressures on both sides to settle this action. For Google, had they been sued and lost, potential payments for each and every digitisation of a book that had been carried out without permission might have amounted to in excess of US$100,000. For the Authors Guild there was the unthinkable outcome that a court may have found Google's behaviour to be fair use. And for both there was the prospect of years, and years, and years, of litigation as the case progressed its way through appeal after appeal. Such uncertainty is expensive not only in financial terms, but also in terms of the energy and focus that could be much better expended elsewhere—in innovating, in growing the business and in concentrating on the creation of new works. So private parties have come to a negotiated settlement where regulation failed, 'While the public authorities slept, Google [and the Author's Guild] took the initiative.'[171]

Or that is how it seems. At the time of writing opposition to the Settlement was starting to build. Not only has the date for indicating claims to Google been moved back by four months and the Fairness Hearing moved to October, but in addition there are reports that the Department of Justice in the US has been talking to Google about the antitrust concerns it has with regard to the position of monopoly in which the Settlement would place Google.[172] It remains to be seen whether the Fairness Hearing takes place and, if it does, whether the Settlement is ratified. Thus the jury is still out: has Google sought to free or to monopolise the printed word? Is it acting in the public interest in pursuing the Book Program? Or purely pursuing its own business interests? Or is the truth somewhere between the two?

VII. CONCLUSION

Diverse but interrelated strands have informed the discussion in this chapter. At the outset it was suggested that, contrary to the opinion held by many, search engine activity and behaviour should be regulated by the law of copyright. Many search engines are businesses and where these are owned by shareholders, their prime goal is to increase profits and return dividends to those owners. Search engines work by using content belonging

---

[170] P Samuelson, 'Legally Speaking: The Dead Souls of the Google Booksearch Settlement', *O'Reilly Radar*, 17 April 2009. http://radar.oreilly.com/2009/04/legally-speaking-the-dead-soul.html.

[171] R Darnton, 'Google & the Future of Books' (2009) 56(2) *New York Review of Books* 12 February 2009. Quoted here in a different context.

[172] See eg the *Wall Street Journal* http://online.wsj.com/article/SB124095639971465549.html#mod=rss_whats_news_technology.

to third parties in a multitude of different ways. As has been identified above, many of those activities are capable of meeting one or more of the public interest goals which underpin the law of copyright, albeit that the shape of the public interest being satisfied may have to be rethought. To argue that search engine activities should lie outside the law of copyright is to place them outside this framework. Paradoxically, it is often on public interest grounds that this argument is made: because the activities of search engines fulfil a public interest (such as in the accessibility of information), so they should be unregulated by copyright law as otherwise their more innovative manoeuvres might be stifled. But, and has been shown, where there are flexibilities in the law and these are used creatively, the framework can be applied to encompass these public interest goals. Placing search engines outside the framework would be dangerous. A large swathe of their activities would be unregulated. Aspects that are innovative and in the public interest today might change and be merely in the interests of the search engine (or the content owner) tomorrow. It is more difficult, then, to draw them back into this framework when, as is inevitable, there are changes in behaviour, in the business model or in the technology that may have significant copyright implications. So if one is to accept that the functions performed by the search engine do have value within the context of the goals to be achieved by the copyright framework, how then to recognise that, whilst at the same time ensuring the interests of the content owners are respected?

One way might be to rethink the copyright framework in light of the new and different ways in which public interest goals might be conceived of and met. Two examples from the activities described above spring to mind. One is the provision of the technology to prevent caching of webpages and/or from those caches being made available to the searcher. The other is the 'opt-out' option in Google Book Search. While at present these 'turn copyright on its head' the results do have public interest benefits. Should, then, the framework of the law be rethought in order to encourage these socially beneficial outcomes? But such a strategy is likely to be impracticable. Many changes have been made to the law of copyright over the last decade. Each seems to become more contentious than the last,[173] and none has proposed such a radical rethink. But the law already does have its own flexibilities. As has been seen above, in some jurisdictions there are defences to actions of infringement. One of the most flexible is the fair use doctrine in the US, which explicitly permits the public interests within the law to be balanced against the interests of the copyright owner. The downside of using this type of defence is that its application on a case-by-case basis might be argued to cause too much uncertainty. In

---

[173] The proposal by the EC to increase the term for sound recordings is likely to arouse strong passions. See eg M Kretschmer, Letter to the Editor, 'Copyright Extension Will Benefit Few', *Financial Times* 18 February 2008.

addition, a small change in facts might favour one party over another. A different, or complementary, strategy might be found in the application of the safe harbour provisions of the E-Commerce Directive and the DMCA. While it has been argued that these are inapplicable, certainly within the UK for search engine activity, within other Member States and within the US the situation might differ. Developing new safe harbour provisions specifically for search engines built around the public interest goals, either already existing within copyright law or reshaped to meet the digital challenges, might give sufficient incentive to search engines to act in a socially responsible manner.[174] Indeed, many of the strategies adopted by search engines, notably those on opt out, could be seen as self-development of safe harbour provisions within the shadow of the existing law. Much better that proper public consideration is given to the parameters of these provisions lest they develop—possibly with the connivance of the content holders—into provisions that might further the interests of the search engine and content owners whilst sidelining the public interest.

Finally, there is the question of regulation by technology. A glimpse of its potential is given above in the discussion of the ACAP. The reported absence of search engines from the discussions suggests that the sector does not perceive this initiative to be in their interests. Clearly, acknowledging that such a solution might provide something of an answer to the friction between the search engines and content owners would be for the search engines to acknowledge that the content owners have the right to control the content and the way in which the search engines engage with that content. While content owners must necessarily act to an extent in the public interest (content must be made available to the user: that is its purpose) their interests and those of the public are not wholly contemporaneous. Through technology it might be possible to hide strategies being played out that would be to the detriment of the public (such as limiting the contours of fair dealing, cartel behaviour, censorship). Better, surely, that the regulation be transparent and designed to promote copyright's public interest goals than hidden, lurking behind automated access protocols.

Content will not stop being produced; content owners will not stop making available content; search engines will not stop innovating; users will not stop wanting access to content. The question is whether the regulatory environment is optimal for the future development of a balanced and orderly information marketplace in which innovation can thrive, interests of content owners be respected, and the public interest furthered.

---

[174] See eg in G Dinwoodie and M Janis, 'Confusion Over Use: Contextualism in Trademark Law' (2007) 92 *Iowa Law Review* 1597, 1665 discussing a paper by Van Houweling where it is suggested that safe harbours in the copyright regime be designed 'more generously but to extract collateral concessions from beneficiaries that further the policies of the relevant legal regime'. See also M Lemley, 'Rationalizing Internet Safe Harbors' (10 April 2007), Stanford Public Law Working Paper No 979836, available at SSRN: http://ssrn.com/abstract=979836

POSTSCRIPT

The ECJ issued its judgement in *Infopaq International A/S v Danske Dagblades Forening* (Case C-5/08) on 16 July 2009.

The ECJ indicated that, when considering the work in which copyright resides, it was appropriate to look at parts of works as well as the whole work. The various parts of a work are protected by copyright to the extent that they embody the author's own intellectual creation (para 39). While single words would not qualify for copyright protection, whole sentences and parts of sentences could (paras 46, 47). So, the response to the question as to whether the reproduction of 11 words would infringe would depend on whether it represented the authors' intellectual creation. That was for the national court to determine (para 48). Further, and given the data capture process employed by Infopaq was cumulative in that several key words might be specified as search terms, this was likely to result in the reproduction of lengthy extracts which were 'liable to reflect the originality of the work in question' such as to reflect the originality of the author (para 50).

On the matter of transient copyright and whether the copying of the cuttings were transient, the ECJ, stressing that the provisions derogated from the general principle and so needed to be restrictively construed (paras 56–58), said that they were not transient within the meaning of Article 5 of the Infosoc Directive.

Overall, the ECJ emphasised what it perceived to be the focus of the Infosoc Directive (recitals 9–11) which is to provide a high degree of protection to the author and to enable them to receive an appropriate reward for reproduction of those works (para 40).

Although the application is for national courts, it would seem that a media monitoring business such as Infopaq would need permission within Member States of the EU to ply its trade, and that caching processes and news aggregations businesses carried out by search engines will infringe copyright within those same Member States unless permission is granted. (See above pp 233–4, 250–1.)

8

Search Engines, Keyword Advertising and Trade Marks: Fair Innovation or Free Riding?

TOBIAS BEDNARZ and CHARLOTTE WAELDE[1]

I. INTRODUCTION

THE OVERARCHING QUESTION for this chapter on search engines, keyword advertising and trade marks is: in selling keywords which correspond to registered trade marks belonging to third parties, does a search engine innovate fairly, or does it free ride on the rights of the trade mark owners? To address this from a legal perspective and establish whether the practice is contrary to trade mark law, a key question, and the one on which this chapter will focus, is whether selling trade marks as keywords amounts to an infringing use of the trade marks. The developing case-law in Europe (European Court of Justice (ECJ), UK, Germany, France) and the US will be analysed and compared. Related sub-themes concerning the wider impact of the practice emerge: to what extent might high-tech companies pursuing innovative business strategies be helped or hindered in their efforts by the uncertain application of laws developed prior to the advent of the Internet? Should business expect to have to develop different business strategies for different jurisdictions based on the uncertain and mixed outcome of litigation? Or in this era of globalised trade might it be reasonable to want some coherence in regulatory frameworks? To what extent are the underlying policy goals of trade mark law met or subverted by the practice of keyword advertising? Might keyword advertising lead to regulatory competition in which authorities mould the

[1] Links to documents retrievable online have last been checked in June 2009. Unless otherwise indicated, foreign case-law and literature has been translated by the authors. This chapter has its origins in a seminar Charlotte Waelde attended in Haifa in 2006. Our thanks for research assistance go to Arne Kolb, one-time SCRIPT research associate and now lead cellist with Broken Records and author of ch 10.

law in order to promote what they may perceive to be innovative practices, or prohibit what they perceive to be unfair practices?

In discussing these issues the search engine that will be most often mentioned is Google. In common with chapter 7 on search engines and copyright, while Google is most certainly not the only search engine to whom the law is applicable, it is the one that has been the subject of the majority of the reported litigation because of its innovative behaviour, its market lead and the perception that it has deep pockets.

A. Background

Search engine providers offer their services free of charge to Internet users. For income, the search engine business model relies on revenues from advertising, the biggest part of which is generated through keyword advertising. The example of Google illustrates how critical keyword advertising is to their financial success: in 2008, 97 per cent of Google's revenue came from advertising (US$ 21.1 billion)—66 per cent of this from Google's own websites (keyword advertising activities); 31 per cent from network sites; and 3 per cent from other licensing and revenue.[2]

Every time a search engine is used to find something on the Internet, it not only returns results pertinent to the search terms entered by the user, but it also displays small advertisements, also called sponsored links, most commonly above or beside the actual search results. The display of these advertisements is by no means random. Rather, each advertisement is associated with certain keywords and is triggered every time the search term(s) match one of the keywords. It is the advertisers who specify the keywords. The advertisers can also indicate where those advertisements should be placed on the search page, whether at the top or along the right-hand side (see Figure 8.1). Revenue comes from the advertisers who pay to the search engine a specified amount each time an internet user clicks on a sponsored advertisement (click-through). The ranking of the advertisements on the page depends on a combination of factors. For Google it includes other advertisers' bids; the quality score of advertisements in any particular search calculated by the click-through rate; the relevance of the advertisers' text and keywords; and account history. The minimum bid for a keyword takes into account the quality of the landing page (where the user gets to when she clicks on the advertisement) including the relevancy and originality of the content.[3]

---

[2] Unaudited   accounts   available   at   http://investor.google.com/releases/2008Q4_google_earnings.html.

[3] See the instructions at http://www.google.co.uk/intl/en/ads/. See also the description by J Grimmelmann, 'Rescuecom Oral Argument Report' (laboratorium.net, 4 April 2008), http://laboratorium.net/archive/2008/04/04/rescuecom_oral_argument_report.

Figure 8.1

An example of a search for 'law school' in August 2009 gave the results shown in Figure 8.1.

Key to the legal disputes is that search engines permit advertisers to 'buy' keywords that are the same as or similar to trade marks registered by third parties. So when a user searches for 'coca cola', advertisements for 'Pepsi Cola' might appear if Pepsi Cola has bid on the 'coca cola' trade mark. This, it is argued by the trade mark owners, causes consumer confusion, dilution of the trade mark, unfair competition (passing off) and leads to misleading advertising. Search engines, on the other hand argue, that their business model does not make use of the trade mark, and even if it did, it does not lead to consumer confusion or to the dilution of well-known trade marks. Further, if there is a problem for trade mark law, it is the advertisers who are responsible as it is they who choose the keyword, not the search engine.

In considering whether this is fair innovation or free riding, the focus of the comment in this chapter is on the key question as to whether in the keyword advertising programme 'use' is made of the trade mark for the purposes of trade mark infringement. The examination will be as to the liability of the search engine—as opposed to the advertiser who chooses a certain trade mark as a keyword. A successful litigation strategy directed against the search engine is, in practical terms, the most favourable strategy for the trade mark owner as she will have only the number of search engines in the marketplace as potential defendants. The search engine is, in other words, a potential 'choke point', the behaviour of which is likely to be more easily shaped in response to litigation than that of theoretically limitless advertisers using trade marks in an advertising strategy. Typically, the trade mark is only used to trigger the advert but remains invisible to the search engine user. It is on these most problematic cases that this chapter will focus.[4]

B. Infringing Use of a Trade Mark

The concept of trade mark use permeates trade mark law. From the ability to acquire distinctiveness—and therefore trade mark rights—by using a sign,[5] through the need to show genuine use of a trade mark so that it is not expunged from the register,[6] so the requirement of use shapes and moulds trade mark law. It is also of paramount importance in the context of infringement. Both the UK Trade Marks Act 1994 (TMA) section 10 and the EU Trade Marks Directive[7] (TMD) Article 5(1) provide that if a trade mark is not used, there can be no infringement. While this is uncontested, there is an ongoing debate as to the nature of that use: is any use sufficient? Or is there an implied requirement that the use of a trade mark must be of a certain kind or quality to entail infringement? Many believe this is the case and argue that for there to be infringement, not only must a sign identical or similar to a registered trade mark be used, but that it must also be used as a trade mark, ie in a trade mark specific way. But what, then, constitutes such a use as a trade mark? These are the recurring questions in all of the jurisdictions focused on here, and while the debate is differently nuanced and is considered of variable importance in each legal system, academic interest in the question of use has blossomed in general,[8] in

---

[4] If the trade mark is reproduced in the text of the advert, this mention may well amount to an (additional) infringement on its own. Such use, however, is far less problematic to judge than the use of the keyword as a trigger only.

[5] Trade Marks Act 1994 (TMA) s 3(1); First Council Directive 89/104/EEC of 21 December 1988 to approximate the laws of the Member States relating to trade marks (TMD) Art 3(3); Council Regulation (EC) No 40/94 of 20 December 1993 on the Community trade mark (CTMR), Art 7(3). See generally H MacQueen, C Waelde and G Laurie, *Contemporary Intellectual Property: Law and Policy* (Oxford, Oxford University Press, 2007) paras 14.59ff.

[6] TMA s 46, TMD Art 10 and CTMR Art 15; generally MacQueen, Waelde and Laurie, above n 5, paras 14.93ff.

[7] Note that the TMD and the CTMR have now been replaced by codified versions. See Directive 2008/95/EC of the European Parliament and of the Council of 22 October 2008 to approximate the laws of the Member States relating to trade marks (codified version) and Council Regulation (EC) No 207/2009 of 26 February 2009 on the Community trade mark (codified version).

[8] Some of these are as follows: M Daly 'An Analysis of the American and European Approaches to Trade Mark Infringement and Unfair Competition by Search Engines' (2006) 28 *European Intellectual Property Review* (*EIPR*) 413–17; M Hüsch, 'Keyword Advertising – Rechtmäßigkeit

relation to the Internet and, of relevance to this chapter, with respect to keyword advertising.[9]

Seemingly paradoxical at first glance, the test of use as a trade mark is applied to limit the scope of trade mark protection. That it would be undesirable to have boundless trade mark rights has been emphasised in the UK by the late Laddie J in *Wagamama v City Centre Restaurants*.[10] Analysing whether the trade mark owner's monopoly should apply in cases where consumers might be confused but not as to the origin of the goods and services offered by the trade mark owner and the alleged infringer, he said:

> If the broader scope were to be adopted, the Directive and our Act would be creating a new type of monopoly not related to the proprietor's trade but in the trade mark itself. Such a monopoly could be likened to a quasi-copyright in the mark.[11]

Applying the 'use as a trade mark' criterion is one way to prevent such a broad monopoly. This concept provides a threshold test in relation to infringement: if a trade mark is not 'used as a trade mark' by an unauthorised third party, then there can be no infringement and the examination goes no further. Only once use as a trade mark has been dealt with do the questions of confusion and dilution for the purposes of infringement fall to be considered.

The role played by consumer confusion within the trade mark system remains central: the touchstone of liability has always been tied to consumer confusion. As trade marks operate in the consumer society, so their purpose is to ensure that the consumer is not confused by inappropriate

suchwortabhängiger Werbebanner in der aktuellen Rechtsprechung' (2006) 9 *Multimedia und Recht* 357–61; D McGhee 'Looking Beyond "Use" in Predicting Advertiser Liability for Using Competitors' Marks in Online Advertisement' (2008) 20(4) *Intellectual Property & Technology Law Journal* 9–12; J Moskin, 'Virtual Trademark Use: The Parallel World of Keyword Ads' (2008) 11(8) *Journal of Internet Law* 12–15; E Ullmann, 'Wer sucht, der findet—Kennzeichenverletzung im Internet' (2007) 109 *Gewerblicher Rechtsschutz und Urheberrecht* 633–39; G Westkamp, 'Hyperlinks, Circumvention Technology and Contributory Infringement—A Precarious Tale from German Jurisprudence' (2006) 1 *Journal of Intellectual Property Law & Practice* 309–13.

9 S Blakeney, 'Adverse to AdWords? An Overview of the Recent Cases Relating to Google AdWords' (2007) 13 *Computer and Telecommunications Law Review* 83–87; S Blakeney, 'Keyword Advertising: Will the ECJ Provide an Answer?' (2008) 14 *Computer and Technology Law Review* 209–12; Z Efroni, 'Keywording in Search Engines as Trademark Infringement—Issues Arising from Matim Li v. Crazy Line' (2007) 38 *International Review of Industrial Property and Copyright Law* 204–23. C Manara and F Glaize, 'AdWords: la Cour de cassation en touche un mot à la CJCE' (Juriscom.net, 24 May 2008), http://www.juriscom.net/actu/visu.php?ID=1069; N Shemtov, 'Searching for the Right Balance: Google, Keywords Advertising and Trade Mark Law' (2008) 30 *EIPR* 470–74; E Tardieu-Guigues, 'Google/AdWords, une partie de gagnée ?' (2007) (30) *Revue Lamy Droit de l'Immatériel* no 996; E Tardieu-Guigues, 'L'autorisation de la marque d'un tiers dans des mots clés sur un moteur de recherche ne porte pas atteinte au droit de marque (sous certaines conditions)' (2008) (34) *Revue Lamy Droit de l'Immatériel* no 1128.

10 [1995] FSR 713.
11 Ibid, 730–31.

uses by third parties—the consumer interests being safeguarded by traders taking issue with each other when they think their rights are being encroached upon. At one end of the spectrum, in cases of double identity when a sign identical to a registered mark is used in connection with identical goods and services, it is not necessary to show consumer confusion—it is assumed.[12] For some uses falling within this category—such as comparative advertising[13] or where there is a prior use[14]—defences have been developed to excuse acceptable behaviour. Moving along the spectrum, where the unauthorised sign is the same as the registered mark and used in connection with the similar goods or services, or where it is similar to the registered mark and used in connection with identical or similar goods or services, then confusion must be shown.[15] Further along still are well-known marks where no consumer confusion is necessary to find liability; rather the focus is on the harm to the well-known mark.[16]

The importance of the concept of consumer confusion remains unchanged even if one accepts that only a use as a trade mark can infringe. It should, however, be noted that the test of whether a certain use is a use as a trade mark entails an enquiry as to the perception of the relevant public.[17] The perception of the relevant public is also critical in assessing whether there is a likelihood of confusion. It could therefore be argued that the 'use as a trade mark' test imports notions of consumer confusion. This is particularly important where an identical mark has been used for identical goods and services. As noted above, neither the legislative provisions, nor the case-law, require a likelihood of confusion to be shown in these circumstances. Although resort to the perception of the relevant public is therefore not foreseen by the letter of the law, accepting the use as a trade mark test entails precisely this enquiry.

The contours of what constitutes an infringing trade mark use have been shaped to a large extent by the ECJ.

(i) The European Court of Justice and Infringing Use

Although the ECJ has not yet had an opportunity to rule upon the question of infringing trade mark use in connection with search engines and keyword advertising,[18] general questions run through the ECJ's case-law,

---

[12] Eg CTMR Art 8(1)(a); TMD Art 5(1)(a).

[13] Eg EC Directive 97/55/EEC on Misleading and Comparative Advertising; Directive 2006/114/EC of the European Parliament and of the Council of 12 December 2006 concerning misleading and comparative advertising (codified version); TMA s 10(6).

[14] Eg CTMR Arts 106 and 107; TMD Art 4(5).

[15] CTMR Art 8(1)(b); TMD Art 5(1)(b).

[16] CTMR Art 8(5); TMD Art 5(2).

[17] See below pp 272–7.

[18] It has, however, received in this regard six references for a preliminary ruling until now; see below pp 292–7. Note that it was announced in June 2009 that the opinion of the Advocate

although to date the rulings have done little to bring clarity to this area. National courts have interpreted these judgements in domestic litigation in line with their own understanding of the role of trade marks within national borders, the legal framework itself being largely harmonised by European measures.

An early example which encapsulates many of these issues concerned the football club Arsenal and a seller of football memorabilia, Mr Reed. Arsenal owned a number of registered trade marks comprising pictures and words including 'Arsenal' and 'Arsenal Gunners'.[19] Mr Reed sold merchandise (scarves, shirts and other items) outside the club grounds on which the names and logos were placed. So the issue was one of double identity where a sign was used that was identical to a registered trade mark in relation to goods and services that were identical to those for which the mark was registered. Mr Reed had a prominent statement on his stall informing his customers that the goods were not official merchandise of the club. Mr Reed argued in the UK High Court, and the late Laddie J agreed, that Mr Reed's use of the marks would not be perceived by his customers as indicating trade origin, but as a 'badge of support, loyalty or affiliation'. Thus the signs were not being 'used as trade marks'.[20] Acceptance of this argument would have meant that merchandising would have been outside the scope of trade mark law. However, it was felt that sufficient uncertainty surrounded the issue to ask the ECJ to adjudicate on the general question of whether a registered mark would be infringed if it was being used in such a way that did not signify trade origin.[21] The ECJ did not directly answer that question. Instead the Court said that

> the essential function of a trade mark is to guarantee the identity of origin of the marked goods or services to the consumer or end user by enabling him, without any possibility of confusion, to distinguish the goods or services from others which have another origin.[22]

General in these cases would be delayed. See http://www.worldtrademarkreview.com/daily/Detail.aspx?g=77a2869e-f958-4d93-b368-b3986550b225.

[19] For representations of the logos, see MacQueen, Waelde and Laurie, above n 5, para 15.9.

[20] *Arsenal Football Club Plc v Reed* (No 1) [2001] 2 CMLR 23 [58].

[21] The questions were: (i) where a trade mark is validly registered and (a) a third party uses in the course of trade a sign identical with that trade mark in relation to goods which are identical with those for whom the trade mark is registered; and (b) the third party has no defence to infringement by virtue of Art 6(1) of the Council Directive of December 21, 1988 to approximate the laws of the Member States relating to trade marks (89/104); does the third party have a defence to infringement on the ground that the use complained of does not indicate trade origin (i.e. a connection in the course of trade between the goods and the trade mark proprietor)? (ii) If so, is the fact that the use in question would be perceived as a badge of support, loyalty or affiliation to the trade mark proprietor a sufficient connection?

[22] Case C-206/01 *Arsenal Football Club Plc v Reed* [2002] ECR I-10273 [48]. Six months before *Arsenal* the ECJ had already acknowledged that not every use is use for the purposes of TMD Art 5 and that use for purely descriptive purposes did not fall under this provision; see Case C-2/00 *Hölterhoff v Freiesleben* [2002] ECR I-4187.

It went on to point out that

> the exclusive right under Article 5(1)(a) of the Directive was conferred in order to enable the trade mark proprietor to protect his specific interests as proprietor, that is, to ensure that the trade mark can fulfil its functions

and that

> [t]he exercise of that right must therefore be reserved to cases in which a third party's use of the sign affects or is liable to affect the functions of the trade mark, in particular its essential function of guaranteeing to consumers the origin of the goods.[23]

Applying this reasoning to the facts of the case, the ECJ held that this essential function was affected as Reed's use of the Arsenal names and logos created the impression of a commercial link between the merchandise and the Arsenal football club. A defence was not available in the context of a mark being used as a badge of allegiance or loyalty, as it was possible that consumers who came across the goods after they have been taken away from Mr Reed's stall displaying the relevant disclaimer would perceive the goods as originating from the trade mark owner, ie Arsenal.[24]

On return to the High Court, Laddie J found that the ECJ had disagreed with the findings of fact he had made at the trial and so was not bound by its conclusion.[25] Accordingly, there was no trade mark infringement by Matthew Reed.[26] Ultimately on appeal to the Court of Appeal,[27] that court applied as the appropriate standard whether the use of the sign was likely to affect or jeopardise the guarantee of origin—echoing the words of the ECJ. In the instant case the use of the Arsenal marks was such as to create an impression of a trade link between Arsenal and the goods. Whether or not the signs were (also) perceived as badges of affiliation was irrelevant to the function of the mark as a guarantee of origin.[28]

Subsequent ECJ decisions on trade mark use have followed the *Arsenal* trend and all reiterated that the use of a third party mark is infringing if it affects 'the functions of the trade mark, in particular its essential function of guaranteeing to consumers the origin of the goods or services'.[29] So while there is always an infringement if the origin function is compromised,

---

[23] Case C-206/01 *Arsenal v Reed*, above n 22, [51].

[24] Ibid, [56]–[57].

[25] *Arsenal Football Club Plc v Reed* (No 2) [2002] EWHC 2695 (Ch) [27].

[26] Ibid, [29].

[27] *Arsenal Football Club Plc v Reed* (No 2) [2003] EWCA Civ 696, [2003] 3 All ER 865.

[28] But see the Scottish case *Dyer v Gallacher* [2006] GWD 7-136 where Gallacher was acquitted of criminally infringing the registered trade marks of Glasgow Rangers FC by selling hats and scarves bearing the word "Rangers" or an "RFC" monogram without any licence from the club to enable him to do so.

[29] Case C-245/02 *Anheuser-Busch Inc v Budejovický Budvar, národní podnik* ECR I-10989 [59]; Case C-48/05 *Adam Opel AG v Autec AG* [2007] ECR I-1017, [2007] ETMR 33 [21]; Case C-17/06 *Céline SARL v Céline SA* [2007] ECR I-7041 [16]; Case C-533/06 *O2 Holdings Ltd v Hutchison 3G UK Ltd* [2008] ECR I-4231, [2008] 3 CMLR 14 [57].

this particular formula allowed the ECJ to remain silent as to whether it would also see it as an infringement if only other functions of a mark are compromised.

The extent to which this test entails an enquiry which is normally only required when assessing likelihood on confusion is illustrated by *Adam Opel v Autec*,[30] which also concerned a case of double identity between signs and goods. The figurative mark 'Opel' registered by Adam Opel, not only for its cars but also in connection with replica toy cars, was used by Autec on their replica remote-controlled toy cars. When it was asked whether this was 'use as a trade mark',[31] the ECJ emphasised that although the signs and the goods were identical, the use would only be prohibited if it was liable to affect the functions of the trade mark, in particular its original function. It concluded that if the relevant public did not perceive the Opel logo on the toys as an indication that the toys were produced by Opel or a company economically linked with Opel, the referring court would have to judge that the essential function was not affected.[32]

More recently in *L'Oréal v Bellure*[33] the ECJ returned once again to the issue of the essential function of a trade mark. In his opinion, Advocate-General Mengozzi had identified a 'gradual development . . . of the concept of protection under Article 5(1)(a) of trade mark functions other than as a guarantee of origin' in the existing case-law, concluding that 'the protection which the trade mark enjoys as a result of the exclusive right conferred in Article 5 . . . goes beyond the need to protect the trade mark's function of origin'. Taking up this point, the ECJ stated that:

These functions [under Article 5(1)(a)] include not only the essential function of the trade mark, which is to guarantee to consumers the origin of the goods or services, but also its other functions, in particular that of guaranteeing the quality of the goods or services in question and those of communication, investment or advertising.[34]

How this is to be interpreted is far from clear. Does it mean that, for instance, the advertising function is to be protected only when the origin

---

[30] Case C-48/05 *Adam Opel v Autec*, above n 29.

[31] The referring German Regional Court, Nürnberg-Fürth, hesitated to find trade mark infringement as the relevant public did not perceive the Opel logo on the toy cars as an indication that the toy was manufactured by Opel but rather saw it as a sign of a truthful, reduced-scale reproduction of the actual car.

[32] Case C-48/05 *Adam Opel v Autec*, above n 29, [21]–[24]. As the affixation could not be prohibited unless it was likely to affect the functions of the trade mark, the onus was on the trade mark owner to show that it does have that effect. On remand, the referring court made the assessments indicated by the ECJ and ruled that the original function was not affected. Consequently, it held that there was no infringing use; LG Nürnberg-Fürth (4 HK O 4480/04–11.05.2007). This was affirmed by the appeal court; OLG Nürnberg (3 U 1240/07–29.04.2008). However, Opel has appealed to the Federal Court of Justice which has not handed down judgment as yet.

[33] Case C-487/07 *L'Oréal v Bellure NV*.

[34] Ibid, [58].

function is implicated? Or might it mean that protection for, inter alia, the advertising function is in addition to the origin function and will come into play not only when the origin function is affected but also when it is not?[35] These questions are likely to be critical when assessing whether the function of a trade mark, and most notably the advertising function, has been affected in the process of keyword advertising.

The 'confusion' evident in the meaning and interpretation of this concept of infringing use and its relation to the functions of a trade mark in ECJ case-law is far from satisfactory. While the English courts have historically distinguished between infringing and non-infringing uses in cases of identity between marks and goods or services using the criterion of 'use as a trade mark' (see below), the 'test' used has been to determine the impact of the use on the customer. When Laddie J considered in *Arsenal v Reed* whether there was use as a trade mark, he looked at 'whether or not a particular sign has been used in a trade mark sense, what counts is the likely impact of the use on the customer, that is to say, what would the customer's perception be'.[36] While this may be seen as a mechanism to limit the trade mark owner's monopoly (if the consumer is not confused at this stage, there can be no question of infringement), it presents great difficulties from a harmonisation perspective as it requires a reading of Article 5(1)(a) that is not directly supported by the text. That this can lead to divergences in interpretation and application as between EU Member States can be seen in the national cases on keyword advertising discussed below.

In one case the ECJ has been clear on what does not amount to infringing use. At the same time the case offers some explanation as to why it might be desirable to distinguish between legitimate and illegitimate uses of another person's trade mark. At the oral hearing in *Hölterhoff v Freiesleben*[37] the European Commission had argued that there are situations in which it would be inequitable to allow the trade mark owner to prohibit all use of the trade mark yet where the TMD does not contain any provision to preclude him from doing so. The Commission referred to a case in which a question mark has been registered as a trade mark in respect of magazines. It reasoned that the owner of the mark should not be

---

[35] Very recently, two references for a preliminary ruling by the Austrian Highest Court of Justice and the German Federal Court of Justice have specifically pointed to whether these functions should also be protected under TMD Art 5(1)(a). See below pp 293 and 295. A Griffiths, 'The Trade Mark Monopoly: An Analysis of the Core Zone of Absolute Protection under Art 5(1)(a)' [2007] *Intellectual Property Quarterly* 312–49, who states that to protect the advertising function under TMD Art 5(1)(a) could limit consumers' freedom of choice and restrict rather than enhance competition. In his view 'any extension of the exclusive property rights of trade-mark owners to protect the wider economic functions of their trade marks therefore requires a careful balancing act'. Given that these functions are already protected under Art 5(2) 'it is therefore not necessary or appropriate for the core zone to have to perform this task', ibid, 322–23.

[36] *Arsenal Football Club Plc v Reed (No 1)* [2001] 2 CMLR 23 [58].

[37] Above n 22.

allowed to prevent the use of question marks, even for purely grammatical purposes, on the covers of other magazines. However, no relevant limitation in Article 6(1) or elsewhere could stop the trade mark owner.[38] The Commission therefore concluded, and Advocate General Jacobs followed, that not every use can give rise to an infringement. While the ECJ did not refer to this example in its judgment, it held that a purely descriptive use of a trade mark not to indicate the origin of goods but simply to denote certain characteristics of those goods would not be infringing use. It remains to be seen whether this case can easily be reconciled with the recent ruling in *L'Oréal*.

It is, of course, for the national court to apply the rulings of the ECJ to the facts before them, both in giving judgment in the case referred to the ECJ and in respect of other similar cases brought before them. The discussion on *Arsenal* has shown that the fear that the opaque nature of the case-law could give rise to inconsistencies in national interpretation is borne out even within a single jurisdiction, and, as will be seen from the cases below, there are significant divergences as between jurisdictions.

II. SEARCH ENGINES, KEYWORD ADVERTISING, TRADE MARKS AND NATIONAL CASES ON INFRINGING USE

A. UK

There have, to date, only been two cases in the UK courts concerning a challenge to search engine trade mark practices. In the first, *Wilson v Yahoo!*,[39] Mr Wilson represented himself and so the arguments were not perhaps explored in quite as much depth as might have been the position had he been legally represented (as Yahoo! was). That said, the case not only gave some insight into current thinking in the English High Court, but in addition, and as will be explained below,[40] seems to have prompted Google to change its business practice in the UK.

This case concerned the Community Trade Mark (CTM) 'Mr Spicy' which Mr Wilson had registered in classes 29, 30 and 42 of the CTM register. Mr Wilson brought an action against Yahoo! arguing that when 'Mr Spicy' was typed into Yahoo!'s search bar the first return to come up was for Sainsbury's and 'Delicious meal ideas for all occasions www.sainsbury's.co.uk, food news, inspiration and recipes from Sainsbury's on-line', and second for Pricegrabber where the entry began with the

---

[38] Opinion of Advocate General Jacobs in Case C-2/00 *Hölterhoff v Freiesleben* [29] and [37].
[39] *Wilson v Yahoo! UK Ltd* [2008] EWHC 361 (Ch), [2008] ETMR 33.
[40] See below pp 304ff.

Figure 8.2

Figure 8.3

word 'spicy' followed by 'www.pricegrabber.co.uk, compare prices on a variety of products at Pricegrabber' (as at 14 December 2006).

A search for 'spicy' in March 2009 revealed the results in Figure 8.2, while a search for 'mr spicy' revealed the results in Figure 8.3.

The High Court was asked about, and dealt with, the question of use. According to the Court:

> [t]he trade mark in this case is not used by anyone other than the browser [internet user] who enters the phrase 'Mr Spicy' as a search query in the defendants' search engine. In particular, the trade mark is not used by [Yahoo!]. The

response of the defendants to the use of the trade mark by the browser is not use of the trade mark by the defendants. That is enough to decide the case in the defendants' favour.[41]

The High Court went on to apply the ECJ's ruling in *Arsenal*, saying:

[i]n my judgment, this case, very comfortably and clearly, comes within paragraph 54 of the decision in that case; that is, Mr Wilson is not able to prohibit the use of the words 'Mr Spicy' even when they are being applied to goods identical to those for which the mark is registered if that use cannot affect his own interest as proprietor of the mark having regard to its functions. That is satisfied here.[42]

Thus there was no infringement. In assessing the importance of *Wilson v Yahoo!* for the legality of keyword advertising in the UK, it is essential to bear in mind the peculiarities of the case. The advertisers had only booked 'spicy' as a keyword, ie a purely descriptive term.[43] Yahoo!'s service, however, functioned so as to display the advertisement every time an Internet user searched for the term 'spicy' or any other phrase containing it. This is why Morgan J came to the conclusion that only the Internet user searching for 'Mr Spicy' used this term and therefore Mr Wilson's trade mark, but not the advertiser or the search engine provider.[44] *Wilson v Yahoo!* is therefore a rather special and not typical case of keyword advertising. Although it clarified some aspects of the law of keyword advertising, it cannot be assumed that UK courts would in consequence reject the notion of use as a trade mark if the search engine had sold a distinctive third-party trade mark as a keyword.[45]

This seems to be confirmed by the decision in the second case, *Interflora v Marks and Spencer*.[46] Although in this case the trade mark owner, Interflora, sued the advertiser, Marks and Spencer, Interflora not only

---

[41] *Wilson v Yahoo! UK Ltd*, above n 39, [64].

[42] Ibid, [65].

[43] Ibid, [31] and [68].

[44] In this regard the UK case-law is in line with a recent decision of the German Federal Court of Justice. In its *pcb* decision (22.01.2009–I ZR 139/07) it was concerned with the same technique, this time employed by Google and called 'broad match'. It held that the advertiser who had booked a descriptive term did not use as a trade mark a sign registered for a competitor mark containing also this descriptive term. It thereby rejected the opposite position, according to which the advertiser would have been liable unless he included the third-party mark as a so-called 'negative keyword'. Such 'negative keywords' prevent adverts from being displayed even if they normally would have pursuant to the 'broad match' option. Even if one accepted the latter view, the German provision transposing TMD Art 6(1)(b) would apply in the instant case, which limits the exclusive right of the trade mark owner in cases where the mark is used as an indication of the characteristics of goods and services.

[45] This at least teaches experience from Germany where the Federal Court of Justice—on the same day as the *pcb* decision (above n 44)—decided to stay proceedings in the *bananabay* case (22.01.2009–I ZR 125/07) and refer to the ECJ whether chosing a sign identical with a third party's trade mark as a keyword consitutes 'use' for the purposes of Art 5(1)(a) TMD; see below pp 295ff.

[46] *Interflora Inc v Marks and Spencer plc* [2009] EWHC 1095 (Ch).

claimed that Marks and Spencer had committed an infringing act, but in addition that Google had committed acts for which Marks and Spencer were jointly liable. Interestingly, *Wilson v Yahoo!* does not appear to be referred to by any of the parties. Arnold J noted that the implications of keyword advertising were currently subject of very different treatment in Member States of the EU and summarised the existing six national references to the ECJ for a preliminary ruling.[47] Ultimately, he held that there was a 'real possibility that the rulings by the ECJ on the existing references will not clearly resolve all the issues of law which arise in the present case', and, without giving any view of what the possible answer to any of the questions might be, ordered a reference to be made although at the time of writing the questions had not been finalised. It is increasingly apparent that clear guidance from the ECJ is sorely needed to smooth the inconsistencies and uncertainties in the law.

B. Germany

By contrast with the UK, there have been a number of cases in Germany. In the majority, the trade mark owner has sued the advertiser rather than the search engine,[48] but in two, the defendant has been the search engine. In neither of these was the search engine found liable.[49]

At first glance, the relatively small number of cases against search engine providers might come as a surprise. It can, however, be explained on three counts. First, there is in Germany a general view that search engine providers' involvement in keyword advertising does not amount to a trade mark infringement in and of its own.[50] In Germany, search engine providers are regarded as merely providing the environment in which advertisers choose their keywords. It is therefore the advertiser who is considered as the potential perpetrator of an alleged trade mark infringement, but not the search engine provider.[51]

The second explanation is more complicated and draws on particularities of the German legal system and the implications of the cases against advertisers for the liability of a search engine. German law recognises an additional category of liability, the *Störerhaftung*. Not only can the person (and/or accessory) who commits a trade mark infringement be found liable, but so can the person who causes a disturbance to the trade mark owner's rights. The broad principle behind this is that liability can be found if the defendant contributed to the infringement of the trade mark and, in so

---

[47] See below pp 292–7.
[48] See below nn 56, 57 and 104.
[49] LG München I (02.12.2003–33 O 21461/03); OLG Hamburg (04.05.2006–3 U 180/04).
[50] M Schaefer, 'Kennzeichenrechtliche Haftung von Suchmaschinen für AdWords—Rechtsprechungsüberblick und kritische Analyse' (2005) 8 *Multimedia und Recht* 807, 808.
[51] See eg ibid, 808.

doing, causes a disturbance to the right conferred by law on another. To find liability it must be shown that the defendant was legally able to prevent the infringement but failed to investigate whether an infringement would arise, although he could have reasonably have been expected to do so. Intent or negligence does not need to be shown.[52] In the two existing cases against search engine providers it was argued that they were liable for disturbance. It is, however, important to emphasise the interdependence of the liability for trade mark infringement on the side of the advertiser, and the disturbance liability for contributing to this infringement on the side of the search engine provider. The acts of the search engine provider are only actionable if they result in an infringement of the trade mark.[53] In other words, the search engine provider can only be found liable if the acts of the advertiser also are considered an infringement. It is therefore important as to how the German courts judge the advertisers' activities. As will be shown, they are divided as to whether choosing a third party's trade mark as a keyword should be considered use as a trade mark. Consequently, only those courts that see the advertiser's action as an infringing use would even consider whether a search engine is liable for disturbance.

Third, an action against search engine providers seems not to be attractive for trade mark owners. Once liability for disturbance is established, it is remedied by an injunction prohibiting the contributing act. In contrast with liability for trade mark infringement, however, it cannot result in the award of any damages.[54]

When assessing liability in disturbance, the most contentious question raised in the German courts is that of trade mark use. Does an advertiser, in choosing as a keyword a sign registered for a competitor, use that sign as a trade mark? If this question is answered in the negative, there is no scope for the search engine's liability for disturbance. The first step is to consider the function of a mark by reference to the now-familiar test: a sign is used as a trade mark if the use at least also serves to distinguish the goods and services of one company from those of others.[55] Whether this is the case is assessed by reference to the relevant public's perception—for present purposes from the point of view of an ordinary, well-informed, rational and attentive search engine user. While these criteria are universally acknowledged by the German courts, Higher Regional Courts disagree as

[52] In the words of the Higher Regional Court of Braunschweig when discussing keyword advertising: 'Als Störer kann . . . auch auf Unterlassung in Anspruch genommen werden, wer, ohne Täter oder Teilnehmer zu sein, in irgendeiner Weise willentlich und adäquat kausal zur Verletzung eines geschützten Gutes beiträgt, sofern er die rechtliche Möglichkeit zur Verhinderung dieser Handlung hatte und eine ihm zumutbare Prüfungspflicht verletzt hat' (OLG Braunschweig (11.12.2006–2 W 177/06) [27]).
[53] Schaefer, above n 50, 809.
[54] BGH (09.07.1958–V ZR 202/57).
[55] This is the standard test the Federal Court of Justice applies in light of the relevant ECJ decisions; see BGH *Russisches Schaumgebäck* (03.02.2005–I ZR 45/03) [18]; BGH *MetroBus* (5.2.2009–I ZR 167/06) [60].

to whether the average search engine user perceives the use of the trade mark as a keyword as a means to indicate origin. On the one hand, the Higher Regional Courts of Braunschweig, Dresden, Stuttgart and München have held that the choice of a trade mark as a keyword is use as a trade mark,[56] stressing that although the trade mark is not necessarily visible for the search engine user, its use triggers the display of both the search result and the advertisement and thus lures users to the infringer's website. Advertisers therefore use the trade mark by reference to its function of distinguishing goods and services of the owner from those of other companies when they create the impression that the advertisement leads to the trade mark owner's website. On the other hand, the Higher Regional Courts of Köln and Frankfurt have held that the average Internet user does not perceive the use of a trade mark as a keyword as an indication of origin.[57] Two explanations are given. First, it is assumed that the average user is unaware of the fact that the advertisements are chosen according to the search term and so do not perceive the advertisements as an indicator of origin linked to the trade mark. Second, even assuming that the relevant public was aware of the fact that the advertisements are context sensitive, these courts emphasise that search results and advertisements are clearly separated in terms of their position and colouring. Thus, search engine users will not be led into thinking that only advertisements for those products are displayed which are manufactured by the owner of the trade mark that had been entered as a search term. Recently, the debate reached the Federal Court of Justice with the *bananabay* decision where the question has been referred to the ECJ for a preliminary ruling.[58] Until the ECJ gives guidance on this point, it is unclear whether the practice of choosing trade marks as keywords amounts to trade mark infringement on the part of the advertiser.

This uncertainty has an important impact on search engine providers. As liability for disturbance presupposes trade mark infringement on the part of the advertiser, search engines would appear to be safe from liability before those courts that do not consider choosing a trade mark as a keyword is use as a trade mark. In two cases, however, German courts have dealt in greater detail with disturbance liability of search engine providers—before ultimately rejecting it.

---

[56] OLG Braunschweig (11.12.2006–2 W 177/06); OLG Dresden (09.01.2007–14 U 1958/06); OLG Braunschweig (12.07.2007–2 U 24/07); OLG Stuttgart (09.08.2007–2 U 23/07); OLG München (06.12.2007–29 U 4013/07).

[57] OLG Köln (31.08.2007–6 U 48/07); OLG Frankfurt (26.02.2008–6 W 17/08). This point of view is also shared by the majority of scholarly contributions on the matter: see eg Ullmann, above n 8, 638; Hüsch, above n 8, 358–59; Schaefer, above n 50), 810; and A Kur, 'Confusion over Use?—Die Benutzung „als Marke" im Lichte der EuGH-Rechtsprechung' (2008) 57 *Gewerblicher Rechtsschutz und Urheberrecht Internationaler Teil* 1–12, 10.

[58] BGH *bananabay* (22.01.2009–I ZR 125/07); see also below pp 295ff.

In 2003 before the Lower Regional Court of München I[59] the claimant, a software producer, took action against Google after having successfully obtained an injunction against the advertiser. The court first determined that the advertiser's choice of a sign identical to the distinctive part of the claimant's trade name as a keyword was use as a trade mark and therefore infringing. Turning to Google, the court considered the legal grounds of disturbance. It considered that Google itself did not use the relevant keyword but only offered the data-handling process which made it possible for users to link the self-chosen keyword to an advertisement displayed on Google's platform. The Munich court pointed out that the disturbance was not obvious as the mark was not well known. It found that it would be unreasonable to impose a duty to investigate further on Google in the circumstances, as this would require efforts on the part of Google which would be disproportionate given, firstly, the sheer number of keywords and their constant changeability, and, secondly, the consequent burden of such investigation which would, in essence, force Google to conduct comprehensive assessments as to the legal rights as between competitors and the respective advertisements. The court concluded that the situation would be different if Google had actual knowledge of an infringement and was in a position in which it was technically possible and reasonable to stop it. On this latter point, as Google had applied its take-down system when it was notified by the claimant, liability could not arise.

In the second case in 2006 before the Higher Regional Court of Hamburg the claimant sued Google Germany on grounds of disturbance and argued that it contributed to an infringement by providing help to advertisers when they chose their keywords and by displaying the advert. A further contribution was alleged in that the claimant's trade mark had not been blocked from use as a keyword. On the first two claims the court found that it was Google Ireland which concluded the contract with the advertiser and not Google Germany, and that it was Google Inc in the US which provided the website www.google.de. Google Germany was no more than an agent for the sale of the AdWord programme and for these claims not the right defendant.[60] As far as the third claim was concerned, it was shown that Google Germany was involved in the complaint procedure set up by Google Inc to respond to trade mark objections. While the court doubted that it was Google Germany which had the authority to block keywords, it felt it could leave this question open because even if there had been a contribution on the part of Google Germany, this could only entail liability if Google Germany had also been under a duty to investigate whether an infringement would take place. The court found that such a duty could only arise once Google Germany was informed of the alleged

[59] LG München I (02.12.2003–33 O 21461/03).
[60] OLG Hamburg (04.05.2006–3 U 180/04) [152]–[168].

infringement.[61] As the advertisement was no longer displayed after Google Germany had been properly notified, there was no liability. Finally, the court pointed out that an abstract knowledge on the part of Google Germany that trade marks could be infringed through keyword buying did not create an earlier duty to investigate given that it was only a selling agent.[62]

In Germany, therefore, the prior condition for finding that search engines are liable for trade mark infringement in running their keyword advertising activities appears to be that there is a trade mark infringement on the part of the advertiser. Such an infringement, in turn, presupposes use as a trade mark and as such that the function of the mark as an indicator of origin is compromised. Beyond that it would appear from the two existing cases that liability for disturbance would only arise where it could be shown that the search engine has knowledge of the infringement, and failed to take action to mitigate the allegedly infringing use. By stipulating that any duty on the part of the search engine must be reasonable, German courts retain a large margin of flexibility which, from the perspective of the search engine, could be perceived as uncertainty in the application of the law.

C. France

France, by comparison with other jurisdictions, has experienced a plethora of cases concerning keyword advertising strategies. Where claims have been directed against the advertiser, French courts have, with little detailed analyses, found the advertiser liable for trade mark infringement:

> [B]y selecting the mark . . . in order to display a commercial link to their own company the defendants have committed an act of trade mark infringement.[63]

Commentators, too, have had little difficulty in accepting that the advertiser should be liable: '[T]he advertiser's liability does not present any difficulty'.[64] The one exception to this trend was the first instance decision

---

61 Ibid, [169].

62 Ibid [171].

63 TGI Nanterre, 14 déc 2004, *CNRRH, PT c/ Google France, Tiger, BT Innaconsulting*. Similar conclusions were drawn in TGI Paris, 24 juin 2005, *Sté La Agence des Medias Numériques (AMEN) c/ Sté Espace 2001 et Sté Google France*; TGI paris, 19 oct 2005, *Sté Free c/ Sté Lyonnaise Communication Noos*; TGI Paris, 8 déc 2005, *SA Kertel c/ SA Google France, Sté Google Inc et Sté Cartephone*; TGI Paris, 27 avr 2006, *Auto IES c/ Google France, Car Import, Direct-infos Com, Ebay France, Pierre B*; TGI Paris, 31 oct 2006, *Iliad c/ Google France, Helios*; TGI Paris, 22 févr 2008, *Sté Ideo Technologies c/ Sté Jdeo Solutions*, TGI Lyon, 13 mars 2008, *Rentabiliweb Europe SARL, Mr J D c/ Mr N B, Mr H P, Clic-event.com SARL, Sté Le Net créatif, Google France SARL*; TGI Paris, 14 mars 2008, *Sté Citadines c/ Sté Google France, Sté Google Inc, Sté Faraway24.com et Fredy W.*

64 F Glaize and A Nappey, 'Les liens publicitaires sur internet', in C Gavalda and P Sirnelle (eds), *Lamy droit des médias et de la communication* (Rueil-Malmaison, Lamy, 2007) étude 473 (loose-leaf collection, version November 2007) no 473-16.

Atyra v Google.[65] In rejecting a claim for trade mark infringement, the Tribunal noted that the claimant's mark was not used to indicate the defendant's products and that the actual advertisements did not contain the trade mark and clearly identified the defendant. It held that such use did not amount to trade mark infringement.[66]

More interestingly for present purposes is that most cases in France have been directed against the search engine. The trade mark owner has been successful in the overwhelming majority of these (if not under trade mark law, then liability has been found under tort law[67]) and in many cases a finding of liability has led to the search engine being required to pay considerable compensation,[68] in some cases in excess of €300,000.[69]

Two aspects in the search engine's behaviour have given rise to claims for trade mark infringement:

- the provision of the so-called keyword generator; and
- the display of advertisements triggered by trade mark keywords in response to a search.

---

[65] TGI Strasbourg, 20 juill 2007, *Sté Atyra c/ Sté Google France et autre.*

[66] The finding has been met with considerable scepticism amongst French scholars who consider this ruling to be 'unusual' due to its 'original way of approaching the facts' (P Tréfigny, 'Les liens commerciaux: et si c'était la solution ? Quoique . . .' (2007) (11) *Propriété industrielle*, comm 87), revealing an 'extremely restrictive vision of trade mark law' (E Tardieu-Guigues, 'Google/AdWords, une partie de gagnée ?' (2007) (30) *Revue Lamy Droit de l'Immatériel* no 996). It has not been possible to challenge the predominant view in French courts as can be seen from a subsequent judgment of the First Instance Court of Paris where the court held that the defendant's actions had 'the aim to direct an internet user searching for [the claimant's trade mark] to the internet site exploited by [the claimant] through an advertising hyperlink . . . [The defendant] therefore attaches to the . . . signs the role to identify [and] individualise the products promoted on that site and therefore uses [them] as a trade mark'; TGI Paris, *Ideo Technologies v Jdeo Solutions*, above n 63.

[67] TGI Paris *Kertel v Google*, above n 63; TGI Paris, 9 mars 2006, *Promovacances, Karavel c/ Google France*; TGI Paris, 7 janv 2009, *Voyageurs du Monde et Terres d'Aventure v Google et autres.*

[68] In *Hôtels Méridiens v Google* Google was ordered by the appeal court to pay €80,000 in damages (the court even lowered the amount (€150,000) that the first instance judges had fixed); CA Versailles, 24 mai 2007, *Sté Google France c/ Sté des Hôtels Méridien.* Google's competitor Overture was ordered to pay €140,000 in damages in *Accor v Overture* (again the appeal court lowered the amount (€200,000) fixed in the first instance); CA Versailles, 2 nov 2006, *Stés Overture c/ Sté Accor.* Most recently, the First Instance Court of Paris has required Google to pay €200,000 and €150,000 to the two claimants respectively in *Voyageurs du Monde v Google*, above n 67. Note, however, that the figures cited here and in the following note were aggregate sums; this is because in many cases the liability of the search engine was based not only on trade mark law, but also unfair competition, general tort law or misleading advertisement. It should be recalled that damages would not be available as a remedy in Germany; see above p 281.

[69] In *Louis Vuitton Malletier v Google* the appeal court ordered the Google companies to pay €300,000 (the first instant court had awarded €200,000); CA Paris, 28 juin 2006, *Sté Google France c/Sté Louis Vuitton Malletier.* Note, however, that this case differs from the typical keyword advertising case in that the trade mark was reproduced in the text of the advert itself. In *GIFAM v Google* the total amount of damages payable even exceeded €300,000; CA Paris, 1 févr 2008, *Groupement interprofessionnel des fabricants d'appareils d'équipement ménager (Gifam) et autres c/ Sté Google France, Google Inc. et Google Ireland Ltd.*

The keyword generator is a statistical tool that is provided by Google to potential advertisers to use during the process of creating an advertisement. It reveals the number of times any particular word has been searched for and lists other expressions deemed contextually similar (eg synonyms or expressions that contain the keyword). Among these may well be registered trade marks. It is the display of these trade marks that has sometimes been seen by French courts as an infringement.

In finding the search engine liable, emphasis has been placed by the French courts on four different criteria which, while not present in all cases, are germane to many:[70]

- the use of the trade mark is characterised by the display of the trade mark within the list of keywords created by the keyword generator;
- Google therefore plays an active role as it suggests trade marks as possible keywords through its keyword generator;
- this use is commercial in nature as it creates revenue for Google; and
- this use happens in a context which corresponds to the goods and services for which the trade mark is registered, as Google tries to offer keywords as relevant as possible.

There have been a good number of first instance courts in which the search engine has been held liable for trade mark infringement.[71] On appeal trade mark owners have been even more successful with, it would appear, all cases decided in their favour. This notwithstanding, there are contentious issues surrounding the liability of search engine providers for trade mark infringement.

One problematic point has proved to be the *règle de spécialité*, ie the requirement that the use of a third-party trade mark must be for goods or services identical or similar to those for which the mark is registered for there to be infringement. It seems doubtful that search engines do that: their services will rarely be identical or similar to the goods and services of the trade mark owner. Many French courts have overcome this obstacle indirectly: while the search engine does not sell the goods and services for which the mark may be registered (eg flights and holidays) it sells the trade mark as a keyword to a third party to do just that. The argument was explained in some detail by the First Instance Court of Nanterre in *CNRRH v Google*, where, as well as the liability of the advertiser,[72] the liability of the search engine was considered:

70 See also F Glaize, 'Liens publicitaires: suggérer, est-ce contrefaire?' (2008) (36) *Revue Lamy Droit de l'Immatériel* no 1220.

71 TGI Nanterre *CNRRH v Google*, above n 63; TGI Paris *AMEN v Espace 2001*, above n 63; TGI Paris *Free v Noos*, above n 63; TGI Paris *Kertel v Google*, above n 63; TGI Paris *Auto IES v Google*, above n 63; TGI Lyon *Rentabiliweb v Google*, above n 63; TGI Nanterre, 13 oct. 2003, *Sté Viaticum et Sté Luteciel c/ Sté Google France*; TGI Nanterre, 2 mars 2006, *Sté des Hôtels Méridien c/ Sté Google France*, affirmed by CA Versailles *Google v Hôtels Méridien*, above n 68.

72 See above n 63.

Google is not a competitor of CNRRH. It does not have an activity in the same sector. However, it reproduced the trade mark Eurochallenges in its keyword list in order to offer it to its advertising customers which notably exercised the same activity as the services specified by the trade mark. [Google] therefore does use the trade mark Eurochallenges as a trade mark. Thus, even if its activity is not identical or similar to that protected by the trade mark Eurochallenges, it is undeniable that its activity consists of offering and selling advertising space consisting of sponsored ads of clients who in their turn have an activity identical or similar to the trade mark. In fact, if the trade mark that is offered as a keyword was not in any way related to the customer who wishes to have a sponsored link, the latter would not choose it as a keyword triggering the display of the link.[73]

Some first instance courts have rejected this approach. So, in *Kertel v Google* the First Instance Court Paris stated that

as far as the Google companies are concerned, to propose a keyword to an advertiser does not constitute a trade mark infringement. . . . In fact, if Google uses the mark 'Kertel' to reference and present the advertiser's sponsored links . . . this use of the sign is not accompanied by any offer of products and services specified in the registration of the opposing mark but is part of an activity of a provider of advertising services.[74]

The courts which follow this line of argument interpret the *règle de spécialité* more restrictively. While they require that the products and services of the alleged infringer and the trade mark owner be similar or identical, the majority of courts adopt the indirect approach described above and consider that if the search engine uses the trade mark to trigger advertisements, it is using the trade marks for identical or similar products if the advertisers' products are identical or similar.[75]

Some French courts have voiced even more fundamental reservations as to the search engine's liability for trade mark infringement. They reject the

---

[73] TGI Nanterre *CNRRH v Google*, above n 63, affirmed by the CA Versailles, 23 mars 2006, *Sté Google France c/ Sté CNRRH et al*. A similar reasoning was also given in TGI Nanterre *Viaticum v Google*, above n 71; TGI Nanterre *Hôtels Méridien v Google*, above n 71; TGI Nanterre, 17 janv 2005, Sté *Accor c/ Sté Overture et Sté Overture Services Inc*, TGI Paris *AMEN v Espace 2001*, above n 63; CA Aix en Provence, 6 déc 2007, *Sté TWD Industries c/ Sté Google France et Sté Google Inc*, TGI Lyon *Rentabiliweb v Google*, above n 63. Achieving the same end result with a slightly different reasoning CA Paris *Gifam v Google* (above n 69).

[74] TGI Paris *Kertel v Google*, above n 63. See also similarly TGI Paris, *Promovacances v Google*, above n 67; TGI Paris *Auto IES v Google*, above n 63; TGI Paris *Iliad v Google*, above n 63; TGI Paris, 13 févr 2007, *Laurent C c/ Sté Google France*. Note, however, that the search engine in these cases and in the cases cited in n 76 has still been held liable for its keyword advertising under the provisions against unfair competition or misleading advertising or under general tort law.

[75] In Germany this requirement does not play an important role. It is of indirect importance for the search engine's *Störerhaftung* only insofar as the advertiser's trade mark infringement, which the search engine's liability builds on, requires that the goods or services offered by the trade mark owner and the advertiser be identical or similar. If this is not the case, there can be no infringement on the part of the advertiser and consequently no liability for disturbance on the part of the search engine. Beyond that liability for disturbance only requires that the search engine somehow contributed to the infringement.

view of the majority of French courts which see the search engine as an active infringer. Rather, they see the advertiser as playing the active part while the search engine's actions alone do not amount to a trade mark infringement. In *GIFAM v Google* the First Instance Court of Paris held in relation to the keyword generator that 'Google . . . cannot be blamed for acts of trade mark infringement' as the 'illegal acts arise only once the advertiser has chosen one of these signs as a keyword without having the authorisation of the owner.'

Turning to the display of the advert, the court pointed out that

> only the advertiser, when choosing the keywords, or the internet user, when using it for a search, link the sign (the keyword) to the good or service offered (by the advertiser) or searched for (by the internet user).[76]

So while there are debates as to whether the search engine uses the thir-party trade mark at all, and, if so, whether this use is for goods or services identical or similar to the trade mark owner's, there is very little explicit discussion about whether this use is a use as a trade mark. Given the line of ECJ cases and the extensive discussion in Germany, it is surprising that the question of the affect of the search engine's activities on the functions of the trade mark appears only sporadically in French case-law.[77] The only example where the doctrine was discussed on the side of the search engine[78] was *Atrya v Google*. The First Instance Court of Strasbourg pointed out that the claimant's mark was not used to indicate the defen-dant's products and that the actual advertisements did not contain the trade mark and clearly identified the defendant. It concluded that

> the simple use of the protected mark in the keywords invisible for internet users does not generate any likelihood of confusion in the mind of the latter, who can-not err about the origin of the commercialised products, and subsequently does not constitute a trade mark infringement.[79]

---

[76] TGI Paris, 12 juill 2006, *Groupement interprofessionnel des fabricants d'appareils d'équipe-ment ménager (Gifam) et autres c/ Sté Google France*. It applied the reasoning again when granting an interim injunction in *Citadine v Google*, TGI Paris, réf, 11 oct 2006, *SA Citadines c/ Sté Google Inc et SARL Google France*. See also (in the context of unfair competition) T com Paris, 31 oct 2007, *Trednet c/ Bodxl, Google France*. Note, however, that the TPI was overruled by the CA Paris in *Gifam v Google*, above n 69 and that at the trial stage in *Citadine v Google* it did find trade mark infringement, above n 63. This notwithstanding and a final decision in *Gifam v Google* from the Cour de cassation pending (see Cass comm, 27 janv 2009, *Sté Google France c/ Gifam et autres*), the TPI Paris reaffirmed its assessment in January 2009 in *Voyageurs du Monde v Google*, above n 67.

[77] Legal commentary in France has not addressed the issue widely either. One commentator has simply said that the French Intellectual Property Act does not require use as a trade mark for there to be infringement. See N Martin, 'Des conditions de la contrefaçon à celles de la faute en passant par la qualification d'hébergeur, le TGI de Strasbourg relance le débat sur les liens commerciaux' (2007) (31) *Revue Lamy Droit de l'Immatériel*, no 1026. For views which seem to accept there is a use doctrine, see E Tardieu-Guigues, 'L'autorisation de la marque d'un tiers', above n 9.

[78] As well as on the side of the advertiser, as the court applies the same reasoning to both actors; see TPI Strasbourg *Atrya v Google*, above n 65.

[79] *Atrya v Google*, above n 65.

Most French courts finding in favour of the trade mark owner, however, assume at least implicitly that the search engine's activities affect the functions of the trade mark. One example is from the Court of Appeal of Versailles where, in *Overture v Accor*, some of the advertisers were entitled to use the mark as they commercialised the products offered under the mark, while others, who did not commercialise the products, were not. The court held that 'the use as a keyword to offer authentic services does not affect the essential function of the mark as its purpose is precisely to permit the internet user to identify the origin of the services'. But the search engine's activities were found infringing where 'the sponsored link does not effectively give access to authentic services but serves as an eye catcher to offer competing services'.[80]

An explicit rejection of the use as a trade mark requirement was exhibited by the Appeal Court of Aix-en-Provence in *TWD Industries v Google* when it stated that the use that the French provision prohibiting trade mark infringement targets 'concerns all acts by which an economic operator reproduces a mark while it is not necessarily required that the use of the infringing mark be carried out "as a trade mark"'. It concluded that the search engine has 'directly infracted the trade mark owner's exclusive rights, which have not the exclusive purpose to guarantee the origin of a product'.[81] It is a moot point whether this view is compatible with the judgments of the ECJ. In May 2008, the Cour de Cassation recognised that there is disagreement in French courts as to the use as a trade mark requirement, and referred the question to the ECJ.[82]

Legal commentators in France are divided on the question of whether the search engine commits a trade mark infringement. Some defend the liability of search engines under trade mark law. For example, it has been noted that the whole business idea of Google AdWords is contextual advertising, ie to link advertisements to the semantic context of the advertiser. In so doing it designates the advertisers' products and services and not its own, and that the *règle de spécialité* must be applied accordingly.[83] Others disagree and reject trade mark liability on the part of the search engine. Tardieu-Guigues[84] argues that not only is the trade mark not used by the search engine to designate products and services but only to determine where to display an advertisement, but in addition the search engine does

---

[80] CA Versailles *Overture v Accor*, above n 68.
[81] CA Aix en Provence *TWD Industries v Google*, above n 73.
[82] See below pp 292ff.
[83] See eg Glaize, above n 70; Martin, above n 77.
[84] E Tardieu-Guigues, 'Liens commerciaux, contrefaçon ou non? A la recherche d'une solution convaincante . . .' (2008) (36) *Revue Lamy Droit de l'Immatériel* no 1194. She also points out that prohibiting the search engine from using trade marks as keywords would lead to undesirable consequences in particular by extending the rights of the trade mark owner as a result of the operation of Google's broad matching technique where the use of a keyword would be barred even for sectors beyond those for which the trade mark is registered.

not know whether the advertiser legitimately chooses a trade mark. She compares keyword advertising to the offline environment, arguing that for print media, it is accepted that an advertiser may place an advertisement in the context of one of his competitors. In that case, it is common ground in French law that whether or not there is trade mark infringement depends on the content of the advertisement itself.

D. Differences between the Member States

As can be seen from the discussion above, the UK, Germany and France exhibit three very different approaches to keyword advertising. The court jurisprudence is the least developed in the UK where there has been only one opportunity to consider liability of the search engine with questions in the second case having been referred to the ECJ. The first case was one in which the concept of infringing use seems to have been embraced: the deployment of trade marks by search engines in keyword advertising is not use as a trade mark for these purposes. In Germany the majority of the cases have been against advertisers rather than the search engine with mixed results. While the courts follow the ECJ jurisprudence on 'use', the outcomes are inconsistent. Where the search engine has been the subject of suit, use has played an indirect, but important, part. So far, no search engine has been held liable for trade mark infringement. Where courts have analysed the search engine's activities under trade mark law, they have done so on the legal grounds of disturbance, an action that cannot result in monetary compensation for the trade mark owner. In France the approach differs again. There have been many cases, the vast majority of which have been directed (also) against the search engine. In most, the search engine has been found liable. However, the notion of use as a trade mark, at least as it seems to be understood in other jurisdictions (and by the ECJ), has not featured to any significant extent in the reasoning, with the *règle de spécialité* being an important factor coupled with the view that it is the search engine that has an active role in reproducing the trade mark.

The differences are influenced by the approach that each jurisdiction takes to the functions of a trade mark, and the understanding of where the parameters of the monopoly conferred by the mark should lie. Whilst it is accepted across jurisdictions that a trade mark has its raison d'être in the consumer society, allowing the owner to send certain signals to the consumer about the goods and services associated with the mark, how broadly that monopoly should be construed has been, and is, a matter for debate.[85]

---

[85] MacQueen, Waelde and Laurie, above n 5, paras 13.4–13.19.

The British courts are largely consistent in their attempts to keep the power of the trade mark within fairly tight boundaries; the approach taken in the High Court in *Arsenal*[86] is one example of that strategy. Traditionally, UK trade mark law has recognised that there can be non-infringing use of a trade mark. Under the Trade Marks Act 1938 (ie before European harmonisation), there was a general view that trade mark use could either be use as a trade mark,[87] which would be infringing, or descriptive use, which would not.[88] To differentiate the two, courts looked at the 'likely impact of the use on the customer, that is to say, what would the customer's perception be'.[89] The insight that not every use of a trade mark is use as a trade mark is therefore not new to UK trade mark law.

As with the UK, German law has a tradition of restricting the trade mark owner's monopoly by requiring a *markenmäßigen Gebrauch*, ie use in a trade mark sense. Such use was assumed where a not insubstantial part of the relevant public perceived the sign as a badge of origin of the goods bearing it, or as an advertising campaign of the trade mark owner. A sign was not seen as being used as a trade mark if that use was descriptive, decorative or oral.[90] While the old German law is not exactly the same as the recent judgments of the ECJ, in both cases the emphasis is on the main function of a trade mark—as an indicator of origin.

France, on the other hand, presents a completely different picture. It seems that French trade mark law has never had use as a trade mark requirement. On the contrary, French courts and French law have traditionally offered significant protection to trade mark owners.[91] Tardieu-Guigues notes that

> the French judge has always protected the trade mark owner's rights in an extensive manner, under the influence of article L. 544 of the French Civil Code, which provides that the property right is 'the right to enjoy and dispose of things in the most absolute way . . .'. And even if community and French jurisprudence have questioned this absolutism, one has to note . . . the tendency in courts to grant the trade mark owner an enlarged protection. In fact, not so long ago, the Cour de cassation affirmed that a 'trade mark infringement results from the

---

[86] *Arsenal v Reed* (No 1), above n 20, and *Arsenal v Reed* (No 2), above n 25.

[87] See TMA s 4 and also s 64, which defines trade mark restrictively as 'a mark . . . in relation to goods for the purpose of indicating, or so as to indicate, a connection in the course of trade between the goods and some person having the right . . . to use the mark'.

[88] H Norman, 'Time to Blow the Whistle on Trade Mark Use?' [2004] *Intellectual Property Quarterly* 1; R Sumroy and C Badger, 'Infinging "Use in the Course of Trade": Trade Mark Use and the Essential Function of a Trade Mark', in J Phillips and I Simon (eds), *Trade Mark Use* (Oxford, Oxford University Press, 2005) para 10.33.

[89] Laddie J when analysing the law under the 1938 Act in *Arsenal v Reed* (No 1), above n 20, [56].

[90] See R Ingerl and C Rohnke, *Markengesetz*, 2nd edn (Beck, Munich, 2003) § 14, para 92, referring extensively to case-law.

[91] In *Hölterhoff v Freiesleben*, above n 22, for example, the French government submitted that TMD Art 5(1)(a) conferred absolute protection against unauthorised use of the trade mark; see Advocate General Jacob's opinion [25].

reproduction of the characteristic elements of a sign protected as a trade mark whatever the use that is made of it'[8], or still 'the trademark owner can oppose the commercial employment of its mark for purposes other than those serving the commercialisation of his products'[9], or still 'what is reproachable is the use of a reproduced trade mark for economic and social activities[10].[92]

[8]   Cass Com, 23 nov 1993, Propr Intell 1994, no 51, p 64.

[9]   CA Paris, 19 nov 1994, Juris-Data, no 000015.

[10]   CA Paris, 26 oct 1994, PIBD 1995, 579, III, 8.

It is these approaches to the contemporary role of the trade mark which shape thinking in domestic courts in relation to the use as a trade mark which, in turn, has a significant impact in a finding of liability or of non-liability of the search engine in relation to keyword advertising.

E. References to the European Court of Justice

To date (June 2009), the ECJ has received six requests for a preliminary ruling. Generally speaking, the referring courts seek clarification as to how European trade mark law should treat keyword advertising. More specifi-cally, all of them ask whether keyword advertising amounts to infringing use. Drawing on the discussion above, this section examines the questions that have been referred to the ECJ and considers the issues that may be examined by the court. In so doing it highlights suggestions that some referring courts have made as to how the questions might be answered.

On 20 May 2008 both the French Supreme Court and the Austrian Highest Court of Justice decided to stay proceedings on keyword adver-tising cases before them and to lodge references for a preliminary ruling to the ECJ.

In France, three keyword advertising cases reached the Cour de cass-ation at the same time and were referred for preliminary rulings: *Google v Viaticum*, *Google v CNRRH* and *Google v Louis Vuitton Malletier*.[93] In its questions in *Google v Viaticum*[94] the court first asked whether the use of a third-party trade mark by the search engine is an infringing use for the purposes of TMD Article 5(1)(a) and (b) and CTMR Article 9(1)(a) and (b). In doing so it referred to those actions on the part of the search engine that French courts have identified as potentially infringing: the suggestion of which trade marks to chose in the keyword generator and the display of

[92]   E Tardieu-Guigues, 'Une interprétation extensive des articles L 713-2 et L 713-3 du Code de la propriété intellectuelle dans le cadre de la vie des affaires' (2006) (19) *Revue Lamy Droit de l'Immatériel* no 559.

[93]   Cass comm, 20 mai 2008, *Sté Google France c/ Sté Viaticum et Sté Luteciel*; Cass comm, 20 mai 2008, *Sté Google c/ Sté CNRRH et autres*; Cass comm, 20 mai 2008, *Sté Google France et Sté Google Inc c/ Sté Louis Vuitton Malletier.*

[94]   Cass comm *Google v Viaticum*, above n 93; Case C-237/08 *Google France v Viaticum and Luteciel*, reference for a preliminary ruling [2008] OJ C209/27.

the advertisements.[95] The Supreme Court emphasised that the advertisements linked to 'sites offering goods identical or similar to those covered by the trade mark registration' and thus alluded to the debate surrounding the *règle de spécialité*. By its second question the court wanted to know whether the search engine, when offering keyword advertising, qualified as an information society service and could therefore benefit from the exception in E-Commerce Directive Article 14. In this case its liability would be limited.[96] The second case, *Google v CNRRH*, not only concerned the search engine's but also the advertiser's liability. In addition to repeating the questions as to the search engine's liability and the application of E-Commerce Directive Article 14, the court also asked the ECJ whether the advertiser's activities amounted to an infringing use for the purposes of TMD Article 5(1)(a) and (b) and CTMR Article 9(1)(a) and (b).[97] Finally, *Google v Louis Vuitton Malletier* again concerned the search engine's liability. Yet the case was atypical insofar as the trade mark at issue—Louis Vuitton—had a reputation and the allegedly infringing advertisements led to sites where counterfeited Louis Vuitton handbags were offered. The Supreme Court therefore repeated its question as to the E-Commerce Directive Article 14 and amended its question as to the search engine's liability in that it clarified that the advertisements were 'advertising links to sites offering infringing goods'. Given the reputation of the Louis Vuitton mark, the court, in a third question, also asked whether the search engine's actions infringed TMD Article 5(2).[98]

In Austria, the Oberster Gerichtshof analysed the trade mark implica-

---

[95] In the official translation, Google, in its keyword advertising activities, is described as a 'paid referencing service who makes available to advertisers keywords reproducing or imitating registered trade marks and arranges by the referencing agreement to create and favourably display, on the basis of those keywords, advertising links to sites offering goods identical or similar to those covered by the trade mark registration'; see the reference in Case C-237/08 *Google v Viaticum*, above n 94.

[96] Directive 2000/31/EC of the European Parliament and of the Council of 8 June 2000 on certain legal aspects of information society services, in particular electronic commerce, in the Internal Market, Art 14 provides for an exception to an information society service merely hosting third party information. In Germany, this question has not arisen as this exception only applies where information society services are subject to compensation claims. However, as far the liability for disturbance is concerned compensation is not availably as a remedy; see above p 281. See generally ch 1.

[97] The advertiser's potentially infringing actions were described as 'the reservation . . . of a keyword triggering . . . the display of a link proposing connection to a site operated by that operator in order to offer for sale goods or services, and which reproduces or imitates a trade mark registered by a third party in order to designate identical or similar goods'; see Case C-238/08 *Google France v CNRRH et al*, reference for a preliminary ruling, [2008] OJ C209/27.

[98] See Case C-236/08 *Google France and Google Inc v Louis Vuitton Malletier*, reference for a preliminary ruling [2008] OJ C209/26. Several issues could be addressed by the ECJ in this regard. Is infringing use for the purposes of TMD Art 5(1) the same as for Art 5(2)? And if the search engine's actions were deemed infringing use for the purposes of Art 5(2), does this use take unfair advantage of or is it detrimental to the distinctive character or the repute of the mark?

tions of keyword advertising in *BergSpechte v trekking.at*, a case in which the trade mark owner sued an advertiser who offered competing services.[99] The court first asked whether using the trade mark as a keyword amounted to an infringing use for the purposes of TMD Article 5(1). It then concentrated on cases of double identity (ie those envisaged in TMD Article 5(1)(a)) and asked whether the trade mark owner's exclusive right is infringed 'regardless of whether the accessed advertisement appears in the list of hits or in a separate advertising block and whether it is marked as a "sponsored link"'.[100] Finally, the court turned to cases where an identical sign is used for similar goods and services or a sign similar to the trade mark is used for identical or similar goods and services (ie those envisaged in TMD Article 5(1)(b)) and asked 'is the fact that the advertisement is marked as a "sponsored link" and/or appears not in the list of hits but in a separate advertising block sufficient to exclude any likelihood of confusion?'[101]

In its reasoning the court clarified why it chose to distinguish the two situations. In its view it was possible that ordinary, well-informed, rational and attentive Internet users would associate in their minds the trade mark with the advertisement. In these circumstances, the court believed that the use of a trade mark as a keyword is, in principle, capable of affecting the origin function of the trade mark. This would mean that in double-identity cases, using a trade mark as a keyword would be infringing even where the layout and the positioning of the advertisement make it clear that it does not emanate from the trade mark owner. Those facts would only be relevant in all other cases where they would be decisive in determining whether there is a likelihood of confusion. But the court also explained that—should the ECJ judge that the origin guaranteeing function is not affected—it would be necessary to analyse the trade mark's communications and advertising function. It would then be necessary to consider whether a use can be prohibited under TMD Article 5(1) which compromises these functions only and not the origin function of the trade mark.

The Hoge Raad der Nederlanden also faced questions of keyword advertising in *Portakabin v Primakabin*, a dispute between a trade mark owner and an advertiser.[102] In keeping with the other references, the court started by asking whether the advertiser, who uses a trade mark as a keyword, uses it within the meaning of TMD Article 5(1)(a) and whether it makes a difference if the advertisement is displayed in the search results or

---

99 OGH (20.05.2008–17 Ob 3/08b); the decision can be found at http://www.ris.bka.gv.at/Jus/.

100 Case C-278/08 *Die BergSpechte Outdoor Reisen und Alpinschule Edi Koblmüller GmbH v Günter Guni and trekking.at Reisen GmbH*, reference for a preliminary ruling, [2008] OJ C223/30.

101 Ibid.

102 Hoge Raad der Nederlanden (12.12.2008–C 07/056 HR); available at http://zoeken.rechtspraak.nl/.

103 Case C-558/08 *Portakabin Limited and Portakabin BV v Primakabin BV*, reference for a preliminary ruling, [2009] OJ C55/10.

in an advertising section identified as such.[103] The court then focused on the criterion that any use must be for goods and services similar or identical to those for which the trade mark is registered. The judges asked whether it made a difference in this regard if the advertiser offered similar or identical goods or services (i) in the advertisement itself and (ii) on the site to which Internet users are directed when clicking on the sponsored link. The next two questions arise from the particular facts of the instant case in which the trade mark owner produced modular portable buildings and the advertiser resold these products new or second-hand. If the use of a trade mark, as a keyword, is to be characterised as use as a trade mark, the court wished to know whether this falls under one of the exceptions to the exclusive right as (i) an indication of characteristics of the goods and services (TMD Article 6(1)(b)) or (ii) as a necessary indication of the intended purpose of a product (TMD Article 6(1)(c)). Moreover, it asked whether the trade mark owner's right was exhausted (TMD Article 7) where the goods offered by the advertiser had been marketed in the European Community under his trade mark or with his permission. The last two questions are of more general interest. The Hoge Raad asked whether any of the foregoing questions must be answered differently if the advertiser chooses keywords which produce the trade mark deliberately with minor spelling mistakes, but the trade mark is reproduced correctly on the advertiser's website. Finally, the court addressed the relationship between TMD Article (5)(1) and Article 5(5) when it referred the question to the ECJ as to whether—assuming the advertiser's actions do not constitute a use under TMD Article 5(1)—Member States are entitled to grant protection under TMD Article 5(5) if the use of the sign without due cause takes unfair advantage of, or is detrimental to, the distinctive character or the repute of the trade mark, or whether in so doing, national courts must consider 'Community-law parameters associated with the answers to the foregoing questions.'

The last court to lodge a reference for a preliminary ruling with the ECJ was the German Bundesgerichtshof. The *bananabay* case was a conflict between producers and traders in erotic toys and—again—a dispute between a trade mark owner and an advertiser.[104] The Federal Court of Justice referred to the ECJ the question of whether there is use for the purposes of TMD Article 5(1)(a) if an advertiser provides a keyword that is identical to a third-party trade mark. In doing so the court emphasised the fact that the promotional link

---

[104] BGH *bananabay* (22.01.2009–I ZR 125/07); available at http://www.bundesgerichtshof. de/index.php?entscheidungen/entscheidungen. On the same day the Federal Court of Justice decided two other keyword advertising cases where it did not see the necessity for a reference to the ECJ. In its *Beta Layout* decision (22.01.2009–I ZR 30/07) it held that there is no likelihood of confusion if a company name is used as a keyword to trigger competitors' advertisements which are clearly marked as such. In the *pcb* decision (22.01.2009–I ZR 139/07) it was held that merely booking the descriptive part of a third party trade mark did not amount to trade mark infringement; see above n 44.

appears in an advertising block set apart from the list of search results . . . is marked as a sponsored link and the advertisement itself does not comprise the sign nor contain any reference to the trade mark proprietor or to the products it is offering for sale.[105]

In its reasoning the court described the analysis that it thought needed to be conducted when assessing the legality of keyword advertising under trade mark law. It shared the view of the Austrian Oberster Gerichtshof insofar as the German court also believed that it would be essential to determine whether, for a use to be use as a trade mark for the purposes of TMD Article 5(1)(a), it is sufficient if this use only affects the communication and advertising function of the trade mark without compromising its origin function. If so, the sign would have been used as a trade mark in the instant case 'because the identical keyword causes the display of the competitor's advert on the internet page resulting from the search and therefore a dilution of the advertising appeal emanating from the claimant's sign'.[106] If, however, the origin function of a trade mark also needs to be affected, is this also the case with keyword advertising? According to the court, this should be answered in the affirmative if one accepts that this function is already compromised where the advertiser uses the foreign trade mark to promote his own goods and services.[107] On the other hand, it would need to be answered in the negative if one required the origin function to be affected such that the use created the impression that there was an economic link between the goods and services and the trade mark owner.[108] In that case, the advertisement being clearly marked as such would militate against such an impression. Unlike its Austrian counterpart, the German court thus seems hesitant to ignore the fact that the advertisement was clearly marked as such when deciding whether there is use as a trade mark.

Most recently, in the British case *Interflora v Marks and Spencer* Arnold J indicated that he will refer questions on keyword advertising to the ECJ although these had not been drafted at the time of writing.[109]

---

105 See for the official English translation case C-91/09 *Eis.de GmbH v BBY Vertriebs-gesellschaft mbH*, reference for a preliminary ruling, not yet published in the Official Journal but available at http://curia.europa.eu/jurisp/cgi-bin/form.pl?lang=en.

106 BGH *bananabay*, above n 104.

107 Ibid. In this regard the Federal Court of Justice refers to *O2 v Hutchison* where, when explaining why the use of a competitor's trade mark in comparative advertising was use as a trade mark, the ECJ stressed that this use was 'aimed . . . at promoting the goods and services of that advertiser'; see EJC *O2 v Hutchison*, above n 29. In the following sentence, however, the ECJ also referred to the fact that the 'advertiser seeks to distinguish his goods and services by comparing their characteristics with those of competing goods and services'. Note that this is not the case with keyword advertising.

108 Ibid.

109 *Interflora v Marks and Spencer*, above n 46, [93]. BGH *bananabay*, above n 104.

The current state of the law surrounding search engines, keyword advertising and trade marks in Europe is thus in turmoil. As can be seen from these cases that have been referred to the ECJ, there is some common ground from the referring courts as to the points on which clarity is needed. Whether the judgments will bring that much needed clarity is a moot point, and one that has already been alluded to and which will be taken up again later in this chapter.

F. US

(i) The Use Doctrine

It is not only European legal systems that have struggled to find the right balance when assessing keyword advertising under trade mark law. Difficulties can also be observed in the US where proponents and opponents of the so-called 'use doctrine' have conducted a lengthy and spirited debate.[110] The questions are similar to those raised in Europe identifying the need that, for there to be trade mark infringement, a sign identical or similar to the plaintiff's trade mark must have been used by the defendant as a mark, ie to indicate the source or sponsorship of the defendant's products.[111] In US litigation, however, the use as a trade mark criterion becomes a threshold test for courts in the early stages of proceedings which needs to be adequately alleged by the claimant before a case can proceed to the trial stage. The most vocal dialogue amongst academics from the US has taken place between Graeme Dinwoodie and Mark Janis on the one hand, neither of whom supports the trade mark use doctrine, and Stacey Dogan and Mark Lemley on the other, both of whom consider that it has a useful

---

[110] An overview of the relevant issues is provided eg by M Barrett, 'Internet Trademark Suits and the Demise of Trademark Use' (2006) 39 *University of California Davis Law Review* 371–457; G Dinwoodie and M Janis, 'Confusion Over Use: Contextualism in Trademark Law', University of Iowa Legal Studies Research Paper Number 07-24, September 2007, http://ssrn.com/abstract=927996; G Dinwoodie and M Janis, 'Lessons from the Trademark Use Debate', University of Iowa Legal Studies Research Paper Number 07-23, September 2007, http://ssrn.com/abstract=1001130; S Dogan and M Lemley, 'Trademark and Consumer Search Costs on the Internet' (2004) 41 *Houston Law Review* 777; S Dogan and M Lemley, 'Grounding Trademark Law through Trademark Use', Stanford Public Law and Legal Theory Working Paper Series, Research Paper No 961470, September 2007, http://ssrn.com/abstract=961470; JS Fabian 'Rescuecom Corp v Google, Inc: A Misuse of the Federal Trademark Doctrine of Commercial Use' (2008) 3 *Journal of Business & Technology Law* 147–60; E Goldman, 'Trademark Use in Commerce Revisited', Technology & Marketing Blog, 14 April 2008, http://www.ericgoldman.org/archives/2008/04/trademark_use_i.htm; MP McKenna, 'Trademark Use and the Problem of Source in Trademark Law', 18 January 2008, http://ssrn.com/abstract=1088479; ZJ Zweihorn, 'Searching for Confusion: The Initial Interest Confusion Doctrine and its Misapplication to Search Engine Sponsored Links' (2006) 91 *Cornell Law Review* 1344–81.
[111] Dogan and Lemley, 'Grounding Trade Mark Law', above n 110, 1682.

role to play.[112] Dinwoodie and Janis argue that the doctrine has no historical basis in the law; its adoption would prevent trade mark law from regulating new information markets; it would lead to inefficiency in the marketplace as (short-term) consumer confusion would be unregulated; and its adoption would ignore many of the subtle advantages that can be gained in shaping consumer behaviour through sensitive application of trade mark law in the consumer marketplace.[113] Dogan and Lemley, on the other hand, argue that the use doctrine is indeed part of the historical development of trade mark law. Their thesis is that that the law needs to leave certain aspects of trade mark use unregulated lest traders fear to use trade marks for legitimate purposes within trade such as for comparative advertising campaigns, reselling goods and, often beyond the marketplace, for free speech purposes. They consider it an important concept because of its potential to limit the power of trade marks.

Although the use doctrine shares many characteristics with the parallel debate in Europe, there are a number of significant differences. Unlike the UK and Germany, where traditionally there has been a distinction between infringing and non-infringing use,[114] US trade mark law seems not to have recognised use as a trade mark as a separate element in the trade mark owner's prima facie case. Rather it has been the notion of likelihood of confusion alone that has formed the core of trade mark liability. In this regard it is important to note that, under US trade mark law, likelihood of confusion must always be shown in order to succeed with an infringement claim[115]—even in cases of double identity.[116] As 'non-trademark use is highly unlikely to cause actionable confusion',[117] arguably, those cases where there is no use as a trade mark could also be filtered out by courts when assessing consumer confusion. This suggests that the use doctrine in the US does not fulfil the same functions as its European counterpart. In Europe, the most important consequence of requiring use as a trade mark is that courts retain flexibility in cases of double identity. Without use as a trade mark, any use would automatically lead to an infringement as likelihood of confusion need not be demonstrated. But if the use doctrine

---

112 See, notably, the discussion that took place through the papers Dogan and Lemley, 'Trademark and Consumer Search Costs on the Internet', above n 110; Dinwoodie and Janis 'Confusion Over Use', above n 110; Dogan and M Lemley, 'Grounding Trademark Law', above n 110; Dinwoodie and Janis, 'Lessons', above n 110.

113 Dinwoodie and Janis, 'Confusion Over Use', above n 110.

114 See above p 290.

115 See Lanham Act s 32(1), 15 USC s 1114(1), for registered and s 43(a)(1), 15 USC s 1125(a)(1), for unregistered trade marks; this notwithstanding it can be observed that '[c]ases where a defendant uses an identical mark on competitive goods hardly ever find their way into the appellate reports. Such cases are "open and shut" and do not involve protracted litigation to determine liability for trademark infringement' (JT McCarthy, *McCarthy on Trademarks and Unfair Competition*, 4th edn (St Paul, West Group, 1996, updated 2009) § 23:20).

116 Recall that in those cases TMD Art 5(1)(a) does not require a likelihood of confusion; see above p 272.

117 McCarthy, above n 115, § 23:11.50.

does not introduce additional flexibility, what exactly is its purpose? Two answers can be suggested. On the one hand, the use doctrine would allow cases where there is no use as a trade mark to be struck out at a pre-trial stage. Proponents of the use doctrine argue that, although these claims could also be neutralised at trial stage when assessing likelihood of confusion, this would be a very fact-specific task which would be unnecessarily costly and uncertain.[118] On the other hand, especially in the context of keyword advertising, the recent trend has been to bring claims against intermediaries, such as search engines, based on direct infringement.[119] Those who advocate the use doctrine reject this development for blurring the direct/ indirect infringement dichotomy and see in the use doctrine the theoretical basis for 'curtailing [this] utterly new form of trademark claim against parties that do not promote their own products or services under the protected mark'.[120]

(ii) The Use Doctrine in US Courts

In a large number of cases in the US, trade mark infringement through keyword advertising has been claimed—and several of these cases have been brought against search engines challenging their keyword strategies. In most instances, it has been alleged that the search engine is directly liable for trade mark infringement although contributory and vicarious liability has also been a feature of some cases (eg *GEICO v Google*[121]). The prior question in some (but not all) of the cases, and one on which lower courts (notably the Second and other Circuits) and academic commentators are divided, is the question of whether keyword advertising constitutes trade mark use.

(a) Second Circuit

In *Rescuecom v Google*[122] the US District Court for the Northern District of New York relied on the reasoning in the earlier case of *1-800 Contacts Inc v WhenU.com Inc*[123] which dealt with liability for the use of trade marks for pop-up advertisements. WhenU offered a downloadable software called SaveNow which generated pop-up advertisements when users landed on websites relevant to SaveNow categorical search terms. In order for an advert to appear the advertiser had to bid for a certain category beforehand.[124] 1-800 sued WhenU for causing their competitors' ads to pop-up

---

[118] Dogan and Lemley, 'Grounding Trademark Law', above n 110, 1695.
[119] See for the parallel situation in France the list provided above n 62.
[120] Dogan and Lemley, above n 118, 1693 and 1673.
[121] *Government Employees Insurance Co v Google Inc*, 330 F Supp 2d 700 (ED Va 2004) 704.
[122] *Rescuecom Corp v Google Inc*, 456 F Supp 2d 393 (NDNY 2006).
[123] *1-800 Contacts Inc v WhenU.com Inc*, 414 F 3d 400 (2d Cir 2005).
[124] This means that, unlike search engines engaged in keyword advertising, WhenU did not allow advertisers to bid on trade marks but only on categories of keywords. The court

when the 1-800 website was accessed. 1-800's trade mark, however, did not appear in the advert itself. While the District Court granted the request for a preliminary injunction, the Court of Appeals for the Second Circuit dismissed the claim. It first emphasised that use of a trade mark was a threshold requirement.[125] This was then held not be met in the instant case as a 'company's internal utilization of a trademark in a way that does not communicate it to the public is analogous to a individual's private thoughts about a trademark'.[126] Further, placing contextual advertising in pop-up ads was akin to paid product placement in 'real world' stores, itself not an actionable trade mark infringement.

Relying on this reasoning, the *Rescuecom* court held that Google's alleged sale of trade marks as keywords did not satisfy the threshold requirements of trademark use:

> Even if plaintiff proved, as it alleges, that defendant is capitalizing on the good will of plaintiff's trademark by marketing it to plaintiff's competitors as a keyword in order to generate defendant's own advertising revenues, that plaintiff's competitors believed defendant is authorized to sell its trademark, or that Internet users viewing the competitors' sponsored links are confused as to whether the sponsored links belong to or emanate from plaintiff, none of these facts, alone or together, establish trademark use.[127]

Neither could Rescuecom rely on its claim that Google had altered the search results because there was

> no allegation that plaintiff's trademark is displayed in any of the sponsored links, or that defendant's activities prevent a link to plaintiff's website from appearing on the search results page.[128]

There was no trademark use because there was 'no allegation that defendant places plaintiff's trademark on any goods, containers, displays, or advertisements, or that its internal use is visible to the public'.[129] Google's motion to dismiss the claim was therefore granted.

As District Courts in the Second Circuit have also repeatedly rejected claims against advertisers for lack of trade mark use[130] there was a clear

---

explains that '[i]nstead, the SaveNow directory terms trigger categorical associations (eg www.1800Contacts.com might trigger the category of "eye care"), at which point, the software will randomly select one of the pop-up ads contained in the eye-care category to send to the C-user's desktop' (ibid, 412).

125 It explained: 'Not only are "use," "in commerce," and "likelihood of confusion" three distinct elements of a trademark infringement claim, but "use" must be decided as a threshold matter because, while any number of activities may be "in commerce" or create a likelihood of confusion, no such activity is actionable under the Lanham Act absent the "use" of a trademark' (ibid, 412).

126 Ibid, 409.

127 *Rescuecom v Google*, above n 122, 401.

128 Ibid, 402.

129 Ibid, 403.

130 *Merck & Co v Mediplan Health Consulting Inc*, 431 F Supp 2d 425 (SDNY 2006); *Site*

trend within the Second Circuit not to regard keyword advertising as trade mark infringing. This, however, changed in April 2009 when the US Court of Appeals for the Second Circuit vacated the first ruling in *Rescuecom v Google* and remanded the case for further proceedings.[131] While the Court of Appeals did not challenge the threshold nature of trade mark use, it found that Rescuecom had adequately alleged trade mark use by the search engine. The Court of Appeals reasoned that the District Court had erred in thinking that it was bound by *1-800 Contacts v WhenU*. In the Court of Appeals' view, that case was significantly different from the facts in *Rescuecom v Google* in two respects. First, WhenU 'did not use, reproduce, or display the plaintiff's mark *at all*' but used the website address to trigger pop-up adverts. Second, under WhenU's programme advertisers could not request or purchase keywords to trigger their advertisements. By contrast, Google displayed, offered and sold Rescuecom's trade mark and encouraged its purchase through the Keyword Suggestion Tool. Google's objection that the inclusion of a trade mark in an internal computer directory could not constitute use was rejected as Google's recommendation and sale of the trade mark were not internal uses. Moreover, *1-800 Contacts v WhenU* did not imply that an internal use precludes a finding of trade mark use.[132] Finally, Google's comparison of its policy with legitimate offline product placements in stores was immaterial as such practice is not infringing because there is no trade mark use but because it does not create a likelihood of confusion.[133]

After this ruling, it is doubtful whether there is still any scope for a trade mark use defence for search engines in the Second Circuit.[134] It also remains to be seen whether courts in the Second Circuit will continue to dismiss cases against advertisers on this ground, as so far, they also have relied heavily on *1-800 Contacts v WhenU*.

(b) Other Circuits

As indicated above, other circuits in the US have placed less emphasis on the use doctrine, and/or proceeded directly to the question of whether there is confusion. In a preliminary ruling in *GEICO v Google* the court held that the defendants' keyword triggered advertising could constitute

---

Pro-1 Inc v Better Metal LLC, 506 F Supp 2d 123 (EDNY 2007); *Fragrancenet.com Inc v Fragrancex.com Inc*, 493 F Supp 2d 545 (EDNY 2007) and *S&L Vitamins Inc v Australian Gold Inc*, 521 F Supp 2d 188 (EDNY 2007).

[131] *Rescuecom Corp v Google Inc*, 562 F 3d 123 (2d Cir 2009).

[132] Ibid, 129.

[133] Ibid, 130.

[134] For an initial assessment by Professors G Dinwoodie and M Barnett, see E Goldman, 'Graeme Dinwoodie on Rescuecom v Google', Technology & Marketing Blog, 15 April 2009, http://blog.ericgoldman.org/archives/2009/04/graeme_dinwoodi.htm; and E Goldman, 'Margreth Barrett on Rescuecom v Google', Technology & Marketing Blog, 9 April 2009, http://blog.ericgoldman.org/archives/2009/04/margreth_barret.htm.

trademark use. The US District Court for the Eastern District of Virginia explained:

> Contrary to defendants' argument, the complaint is addressed to more than the defendants' use of the trademarks in their internal computer coding. The complaint clearly alleges that defendants use plaintiff's trademarks to sell advertising, and then link that advertising to results of searches.[135]

In August 2005 Judge Leonie M Brinkema issued a written opinion which did not deal with the question of trade mark use but did hold that GEICO had only established likelihood of confusion with regard to advertisements that featured GEICO's trade marks in the content of the advertisements. After this written opinion, GEICO and Google settled the case.[136]

In *800-JR Cigar v GoTo.com*[137] the US District Court for the District of New Jersey held that that there was trade mark use by the search engine through: accepting bids from JR Cigar's competitors that paid for prominence in search results; ranking its paid advertisers before any 'natural' listings in a search results list, thus injecting itself into the marketplace and acting as a conduit to steer potential customers from JR Cigar to JR Cigar's competitors; and its 'search term suggestion tool', which identified JR Cigar's marks as effective search terms and marketed them to JR Cigar's competitors. The parties settled after this decision was issued.[138]

In *Google v American Blind & Wallpaper Factory*[139] the search engine moved for summary judgment to declare that, as a matter of law, its sale of trademarked keywords in its AdWords program did not constitute use in commerce under the Lanham Act. The court analysed the existing relevant case-law within the Ninth Circuit, which had focused on likelihood of confusion rather than trade mark use and concluded that these cases suggests 'that the Ninth Circuit would assume use in commerce here'.[140] It therefore held that the sale of trade marks as keywords was use as a trade mark. The case was finally scheduled to go on jury trial in November 2007. However, in early September 2007 Google and American Blinds reached a settlement in which they agreed to dismiss the litigation, with prejudice; neither party accepted liability or admitted to wrongdoing and each paid its own costs.[141] This agreement was reached about two weeks after American

---

135 *GEICO v Google*, above n 121, 403.

136 SH Klein 'Geico and Google Settle Trade Mark/Keyword Advertising Lawsuit' (2006) 1 *Journal of Intellectual Property Law & Practice* 167, 169.

137 *800-JR Cigar Inc v GoTo.com Inc*, 437 F Supp 2d 273 (DNJ 2006).

138 EH Cohen and H Huffnagle IV, 'Inconsistent Rulings Continue to Plague Keyword Advertising' (2008) 41(1) *Maryland Bar Journal* 22, 26.

139 *Google Inc v American Blind & Wallpaper Factory Inc*, 2007 WL 1159950 (ND Cal 2007).

140 Ibid, 5.

141 L Rosencrance, 'American Blinds Drops Suit Against Google', *Computerworld*, 4 September 2007, http://www.computerworld.com/action/article.do?command=viewArticleBasic&articleId=9034322.

Airlines filed the same claims against Google on 16 August 2007.[142] In July 2008, however, this case was also settled by the parties. The exact terms of the settlement are unknown.[143]

Somewhat surprisingly after its settlement with Google, the latest developments regarding the search engine liability for keyword advertising was again initiated by American Airlines. This time the airline sued Yahoo! Inc, alleging that the search engine's trade mark policy

> constitutes . . . use in commerce [of American Airlines' trade marks] . . . with full knowledge that consumers are likely to be confused and lured away from the websites that they intended to visit, and with the goal of financially benefiting Yahoo! to the detriment of American Airlines[144]

So, until recently the US courts were split on the question whether keyword advertising is 'trade mark use'. Where this question was affirmed, it was done even though the sponsored links were identified as paid advertisements and did not contain the claimant's trade marks.[145] The sharp contrast between the interpretation of trade mark use by the Second and other Circuits is reminiscent of the ongoing divergences as between and within Member States of the EU. In light of the appeal ruling in *Rescuecom v Google*, however, these differences will diminish. Be all this as it may, an overview of the existing proceedings against Google indicates that the search engine is wary of letting cases progress to the trial stage. Where Google's motion to dismiss a case has been unsuccessful, the search engine and claimant have always come to a settlement. This is why there has as yet been no court ruling on whether the sale of trade marks as keywords by search engines constitutes a trade mark infringement. It remains to be seen whether *American Airlines v Yahoo!* will bring about more clarity in this regard.

III. BEYOND USE

The analysis above has concentrated on infringing use and explained how some courts bring this criterion into play as a threshold question. If there is

---

[142] *American Airlines Inc v Google Inc*, 4:07-CV-487-A (ND Tex). All documents related to this case can be found at http://news.justia.com/cases/featured/texas/txndce/4:2007cv00487/169927/#20080718.

[143] E Goldman, 'American Airlines and Google Settle Keyword Advertising Lawsuit', Technology & Marketing Blog, 19 July 2008, http://blog.ericgoldman.org/archives/2008/07/american_airlin_1.htm.

[144] Para 78 of the complaint in *American Airlines Inc v Yahoo! Inc*, 4:08-CV-626-A (ND Tex); see http://dockets.justia.com/docket/court-txndce/case_no-4:2008cv00626/case_id-181052/. More information on the case is provided by E Goldman, 'Yahoo Countersues American Airlines for Declaratory Judgment', Technology & Marketing Blog, 1 December 2008, http://blog.ericgoldman.org/archives/2008/12/yahoo_countersu_1.htm and E Goldman, 'Fifth Circuit Denies Yahoo's Jurisdictional Appeal in American Airlines Case', Technology & Marketing Blog, 12 March 2009, http://blog.ericgoldman.org/archives/2009/03/fifth_circuit_d.htm.

[145] Cohen and Huffnagle, 'Inconsistent Rulings', above n 138, 26.

no use, so the investigation need proceed no further. But if there is trade mark use, it is just the start of the analysis. Thereafter the issues of identity of mark and goods, and similarity of mark and goods and confusion, emerge. The important question then is: would the consumer be confused into thinking the trade mark owner was the origin of the goods advertised in the sponsored links? This is a difficult question to answer in the absence of empirical research. In relation to well-known marks, questions of dilution arise: the activity of the search engine, without due cause, must take advantage of, or free ride on the reputation of the well-known mark to found liability.[146] As the preliminary question is still to be definitively settled by a higher court, let alone these subsequent questions, it is likely to be some time before the law surrounding the practice of the sale of trade marks as keywords by search engines is settled.

A. Wider Implications

Three sub-themes were identified in the introduction to this chapter:

- To what extent should high-tech companies pursuing innovative business strategies be helped or hindered in their efforts by the uncertain application of laws developed prior to the advent of the Internet, and should they have to develop different business strategies for different jurisdictions based on the uncertain and mixed outcome of litigation?
- To what extent are the underlying policy goals of trade mark law met or subverted by the practice of keyword advertising?
- Might the practice lead to regulatory competition in which authorities mould the law in order to promote what they may perceive to be innovative practices, or prohibit what they perceive to be unfair practices?

(i) Change in Business Models

The court cases have had a profound impact on the way Google (and other search engines) conducts business. This becomes evident through an examination of the terms and conditions governing the AdWord strategy. As from 5 May 2008 Google changed its business practice in the UK and Ireland. Before that date Google's policy did not permit advertisers to bid for keywords that corresponded to registered trade marks. So, Sainsbury's could not bid for Tesco; Celtic Sheepskin could not bid for Ugg. If competitors' trade marks were used, Google had a procedure by which the use could be

---

[146] At least for those jurisdictions subject to the CTMR and the TMD and which have incorporated the relevant provisions into domestic law.

stopped.[147] From 5 May 2008 that policy changed. It now states the following:

> When we receive a complaint from a trademark owner, we only investigate the use of the trademark in ad text. If the advertiser is using the trademark in ad text, we will require the advertiser to remove the trademark and prevent them from using it in ad text in the future. Please note that we will not disable keywords in response to a trademark complaint. In addition, please note that any such investigation will only affect ads served on or by Google.[148]

While some commentators found the change unexpected, it would seem that Google was simply bringing its UK strategy into line with that in the US and other countries after *Wilson v Yahoo!*,[149] countries where, although the law is not settled, Google may feel confident of 'winning' in court.

Business analysts have argued that the shift radically alters the contours of keyword advertising for all of the players. It has been suggested that the change will send the cost of bidding on AdWords 'skyrocketing',[150] thus increasing revenue for Google and increasing the costs for trade mark owners and advertisers. Hitwise, a firm of Internet analysts, suggested that the majority of searches are now 'navigational'. In other words, searchers use trade marks to find what they are looking—in other words they search for, for example, 'Coca Cola' and 'Myspace', rather than non-navigational terms such as 'fizzy drinks' or 'social networking sites'.[151] Hitwise also noted that in the three-month period prior to Google's change in policy in the UK, '91.8% of brand searches ended up on the brand owners' websites in the UK, compared to just 84.2% in the US'.[152] During that period the policy operated in the US was the one now operating in the UK. These figures can be interpreted in two ways. On the one hand, it could be argued that by allowing competitors to bid on trade marks, consumers are faced with more choice as to websites to visit, and they take up that opportunity. On the other hand, it could be suggested that sponsored links are confusing and that consumers are diverted to competitors' sites although they expect the trade mark owner's.

---

[147] 'When we receive a complaint from a trademark owner, our review is limited to ensuring that the advertisements at issue are not using a term corresponding to the trademarked term in the ad text or as a keyword trigger. If they are, we will require the advertiser to remove the trademarked term from the ad text or keyword list and will prevent the advertiser from using the trademarked term in the future. Please note that any such investigation will only affect ads served on or by Google.' http://www.google.com/tm_complaint_AdWords.html before May 2008.

[148] This is the same policy as that in the US and Canada.

[149] Above n 39.

[150] Netimperative, 'Google Sparks Controversy with Trademark Policy Change' (7 April 2008) http://www.netimperative.com/news/2008/april/7/google-sparks-controversy-with-trademark-policy.

[151] Robin Goad Analyst Weblog, 'Google Delivers over a Third of All UK Traffic—Trademark Changes Will Have a Significant Impact', http://weblogs.hitwise.com/robin-goad/2008/04/google_delivers_over_third_uk_internet_traffic_trademark_changes_big_impact.html.

[152] This 'gap' of about 7 per cent was borne out by other statistical analyses carried out by Hitwise; ibid.

Meanwhile Google has further liberalised its trade mark policy. As of 4 June 2009 it allows advertisers to buy trade marks as keywords in another 190 countries and regions.[153] Trade mark complaints about the mere use of the trade mark as a trigger will no longer be investigated by Google; only complaints alleging the use of a trade mark in the text of an advertisement will be followed. Thus, Google now applies in these areas the same trade mark policy as in the US, the UK, Ireland and Canada. Importantly, for the rest of the EU Member States the policy remains unchanged for now.[154]

In response to the various defeats in France it was reported that Google modified the text in which it presents its keyword generator. More specifically, it now provides links to trade mark databases as well as the *Registre du commerce et des sociétés*, the French trade register where every individual and legal entity acting as a merchant must be registered. Google's hope seemed to be that if it offered an easy way for its customers to check whether or not the keywords they are about to chose are registered trade marks, liability would arise only if they did not bother to check for third-party rights. But even after this, the French courts continued to hold Google liable for trade mark infringement.

The impact that the ECJ judgements have on the search engine business model could be profound. If the ECJ rules that keyword advertising is use per se, that would call into question the basis on which the business model is constructed. It would fundamentally alter the relationship between the search engine and the trade mark owner and, depending on the stance taken by the trade mark owner, may seriously question the economic viability of search engines. It is little wonder that the judgments are keenly awaited.

B. Compatibility with the Rationales for Trade Mark Law

A related question to that of changing business models concerns the compatibility of the behaviour with the rationales for trade mark law. As has been stressed many times, trade marks exist in the consumer environment to ensure that consumers can be informed of, and do not become confused by, the origin of goods and services sold under the mark. Given that a consumer has no *locus standi* to sue, this rationale can be subsumed by the trade mark owners' interests, albeit that the two are supposed to

---

153 Google, 'Updates to AdWords Trademark Policy', https://adwords.google.com/support/bin/answer.py?answer=143903.

154 A second change, taking effect on 15 June 2009, relates to Google's policy in the US where the use of trade marks in the texts of adverts is now permitted if these 'appear to be submitted by resellers; informational sites; the makers or resellers of components or parts for the goods and services related to the trademark term; or compatible components or parts for the goods and services related to the trademark term', Google, 'Updates to US Trademark Policy', https://adwords.google.com/support/bin/answer.py?answer=145407.

dovetail. Although the question of confusion within the meaning of trade mark law arising through keyword advertising has not been investigated in any detail in this chapter, there is, as suggested above, both case-law and commentary which is sceptical that a consumer could be confused as a result of the practice. Certainly on the statistical analysis, and as indicated above, more consumers go to sites other than those belonging to the brand owner where competitors are able to bid on trade marks. But is that because the consumer is confused? Or is it rather that consumer choice has been expanded? A good deal more empirical research would be needed before this could be answered with any confidence. In the absence of such research it is at least as arguable that the activities of Google benefit the consumer, as it is to say the consumer is confused.[155]

It is also the case that the rationales underpinning trade mark law are, or should be, if not exactly the same, at least grounded in the same underlying philosophy no matter the jurisdiction. However, and as has been seen in the survey of cases, the outcomes in national courts vary dramatically even within those regions working within the same regulatory framework.[156] It is perhaps in this respect that the observer might have sympathy for the search engine seeking to ply its trade within and across borders, and having to juggle strategies in response to national preferences.

C. Regulatory Competition (Tinkering)

There appear to have been few direct regulatory initiatives in response to the keyword advertising litigation. Regulators, at least for now, seem to prefer to see the existing law applied to regulate the disputes that arise between the parties. The one exception may be the State of Utah. In March 2007 it enacted the Trademark Protection Act, SB 236, which attempted to create a new class of state-registered trademarks known as 'electronic registration marks' which could be infringed if used as a keyword or if a keyword-triggered advertisement was likely to cause confusion with the mark. The proposals were the subject of significant criticism, and although passed into law, the measure was repealed in 2008.[157] Seemingly undeterred, the legislature made another attempt in March 2009 to pass legislation dealing with keyword advertising. This was also unsuccessful.[158]

---

155 Note also that Google has announced that it will soon begin to sell targeted advertisements, at least in the US. That, of course, brings in a set of different trade mark issues. See JE Vascellaro, 'Google to Tie Ads to Surfers' Habits', *Wall Street Journal* 12 March 2009, http://online.wsj.com/article/SB123675503793992831.html.

156 In this chapter, the UK, Germany and France.

157 E Goldman, 'Utah Amends Trademark Protection Act (But Only After Some Drama)', Technology & Marketing Law Blog, 7 March 2008, http://blog.ericgoldman.org/archives/2008/03/utah_amends_tra.htm.

158 E Goldman, 'Utah HB 450 Dies in Utah Senate Without a Vote', Technology & Marketing Law Blog, 13 March 2009, http://blog.ericgoldman.org/archives/2009/03/utah_hb_450_die.htm.

It seems that there are few plans by regulators to develop targeted legislation which would, in any event, be bound to be controversial. Legislate too far in favour of the business model of the search engine, and the powerful trade mark lobby would undoubtedly respond with vigour. Legislate too far in favour of the trade mark owner, and the innovative practices of the search engine (and others of that ilk) may be extinguished. The strategy, at least at present, seems to be to leave the stakeholders to find their own way through—and assume that the consumer interest is satisfied as a by-product of their litigation strategies.

D. Fair Innovation or Free Riding?

The central question asked at the outset was whether keyword advertising was a fair innovation within the information marketplace, or whether it was one of free riding by the search engine on the rights and interests of trade mark owners. As will have been seen from the discussion, if the application of trade mark law is the standard by which that question should be answered, then the outcome is far from clear, either as a matter of the application of the law, or in relation to the policy base on which the law rests. For some jurisdictions where liability is found as a matter of routine (eg France), the search engine is a free-rider. For others where the current state of case-law suggests that the search engine would not be found liable (eg the UK), the search engine is a fair innovator. The prior, and more interesting question, is as to whether the practice *should* be regarded as fair innovation, or whether that section of the marketplace should be subject to the control of the trade mark owner. It would seem, as suggested, that empirical research is sorely needed to inform this discussion.

IV. CONCLUSION

Even after the ECJ and appeals courts in the US have issued their judgments, even if the search engine business model is not in tatters, the law on search engines, keyword advertising and trade marks is likely to remain chaotic. In Europe, while the question of use might become clearer, the questions of confusion and dilution will still need to be worked out. In addition, even if the law provides room for search engines to engage in the practice, some trade mark owner friendly Member States such as France may well continue to condemn the practice using other legal avenues, such as unfair competition and general tort law—areas in which there is no harmonisation.[159] This hiatus is no doubt in large part due to the confused nature of the rationales on which the law is based, which are themselves a

---

[159] See also TMD Rec 6.

product of the confusion in the underlying policy goals, confusion which in turn is played out in domestic court interpretations of what role trade mark law should play within the consumer society.

Within this search engines are obliged to adapt their business strategies to national interpretations of the law while their activities cross borders. As it becomes increasingly possible to erect virtual borders along national lines, so search engines may think again as to where they wish to do business. The ultimate question, for the search engine, may become one of when it becomes too expensive to do business within a particular territory. Would a search engine withdraw their services from a jurisdiction? And if so, does that place the trade mark owner in a stronger, winning position? And what about the consumer in whose name trade mark law exists, and putatively in whose interests the search engines and trade marks owners do battle in court?

Despite the pressing questions over the current state and role of the law in regulating the proper boundaries between the search engine and trade mark holder in relation to the keyword advertising strategy, it is perhaps too early (and indeed undesirable at this stage) for regulators to step in to regulate their relationship, particularly as the regulators themselves are unclear as to the underlying rationales for the law and the policy being pursued. Better that the innovators and trade mark owners should take time to come to an accommodation in this new digital marketplace, with the regulator keeping a watching brief, but ready to enter the fray should either overstep the mark to the detriment of the consumer.

9

Domain Names and Trade Marks: An Uncomfortable Interrelationship

CAROLINE WILSON

I. GENERAL INTRODUCTION

Recent figures on domain name registrations indicate that over 174 million domain names have been registered globally.[1] There are also more categories of top level domains (TLDs) available[2] and more ways of abusing the domain name registration process[3] than ever before. Domain name terminology and domain name acronyms continue to evolve. All this means that it is simply no longer possible, even if it were desirable, in a chapter of this length to critically review domain name and trade mark disputes: there are too many disputes[4] and too many fora[5] for the same. Instead, the purpose of this chapter is to provide a critical background to—and insight into—the interrelationship, at times uncomfortable, between domain name regulation and trade mark law from a (primarily) UK perspective.

The first parts of this chapter comprise an introduction to domain names, including the basics of domain name terminology, and background on the regulation of .uk domain names. Thereafter, the definition of 'trade mark' and relevant provisions of the UK Trade Marks Act 1994 and practice will be briefly discussed, and finally the role of trade mark law in a domain names context will be critically summarised.

Three disclaimers or limitations relating to this chapter should be noted. The first relates to the range of primary and secondary sources cited (as will be seen, there is heavy reliance on online sources at the expense of

---

[1] Nominet, 'Domain Name Industry Report' (2008) 5. Report available at http://www.nic.uk/digitalAssets/32856_Domain_name_industry_report2008.pdf.

[2] See below.

[3] Eg so-called domain name tasting: the practice of registering a domain name and using the period before registration fees are due in order to test the marketability of said domain name. See below.

[4] See below.

reliance on more traditional secondary literature[6]). Put simply, the fast-moving nature of domain name developments means that the secondary literature in this area can be out of date by the time it is published. That factor, combined with space limitations, justifies placing emphasis and analysis on (currently[7]) relevant primary sources and policy documents rather than synthesising the full corpus of academic and practitioner literature. Second, this chapter concerns domain names and trade marks. A whole range of interesting, non-trade mark domain name issues[8] are therefore beyond its scope. Finally, the domain name/trade mark nexus has always represented a challenge for trade mark law in an information technology (IT) context—and had been the principal one for many years. Now, however, it is one among many issues in this area as the trade mark/IT legal policy debate moves on.[9] That is not to imply that domain name disputes and domain name policy are not interesting or important from a trade mark perspective (or vice versa), but merely reflects the increased policy certainty relating to the trade marks/domain name relationship; a certainty[10] born of the evolution of trade mark jurisprudence on domain names and the growing maturity of domain name regulation, and in particular the development of the alternative dispute resolution (ADR) systems developed for resolving domain name disputes.

B. What Is a Domain Name?

As not all readers will be familiar with the terminology and institutions of domain names, this section provides a basic introduction to domain names, domain name institutions and a critical overview of relevant domain name terminology. How domain names can be abused and a brief discussion of aspects of domain name ADR follow. Reflecting the local jurisdictional focus in this chapter, this section concludes with a brief introduction to the regulation of .uk domain names.

---

[5] See below.

[6] A wide range of such literature is, however, available. There are too many journal articles to mention here, but key texts include T Bettinger, T Willoughby and S Able, *Domain Law and Practice: An International Handbook* (Oxford, Oxford University Press, 2005) and D Lindsay, *International Domain Name Law* (Oxford, Hart Publishing, 2007). Information concerning a wider range of TLDs can be found via J Olsen, S Maniatis and N Wood, *Domain Names: Global Practice and Procedure* (London, Sweet & Maxwell, looseleaf publication).

[7] The domain name law and policy in this chapter is correct as at 6 March 2009.

[8] These are too numerous to note here, but range from issues such as use of trade marks as metatags; whether a domain name should be considered as being a property right; to more recent issues of DNS governance and geopolitical representation (on this issue, see eg ICANN, 'Draft Plan for Improving Institutional Confidence' (26 February 2009), available at http://www.icann.org/en/jpa/iic/draft-iic-implementation-26feb09-en.pdf.)

[9] To, for example, trade mark issues relating to Internet advertising. See ch 7.

[10] But is this a certainty based on an assumption of a false equivalence between trade marks and domain names? See below.

C. Introduction to Domain Names

The primary technological function of the Domain Name System (DNS) is to map Internet Protocol (IP) addresses (ie unique numbers that identify each and every computer linked to the Internet) to the equivalent domain name—a process termed name resolution. A domain name is simply a human-friendly address (www.soton.ac.uk[11] is, for example, easier to remember than 152.78.128.78[12]) but technically it is the IP number behind each domain name that holds the location of a website.

The DNS itself constitutes a database, known as the root zone, created by the Internet Assigned Numbers Authority (IANA[13]), spread over 13 root servers[14] which constitute the entry point to the DNS. Somewhat akin to the international postal and telephone systems, the DNS is hierarchical and this is reflected in the structure of domain names: there are commonly three, sometimes more, levels in this hierarchy, reading from right to left with the domain name registrant's chosen name being located in the lowest hierarchical level of the domain name. In the example shown in Figure 9.1 there are three hierarchical levels.

Figure 9.1 Example of a domain name

Traditionally, domain names are considered to fall into one of two categories based on their TLD: generic top level domains (gTLDs[15]) and country code top level domains (ccTLDs;[16] see Table 9.1). More recently, this traditional TLD terminology has been extended to reflect the introduction of new gTLDs[17] (see below for a critique).

---

[11] The domain name for the University of Southampton website.

[12] The equivalent IP number. This is an example of what is known as an IPv4 IP address. See below.

[13] See below.

[14] Further information regarding these root servers can be found at http://root-servers.org.

[15] These are generic (traditionally thought to mean non-geographical) TLDs, ie TLDs assigned on the basis of RFC 1591: they comprise semantic terms consisting of three (eg .com) or more (eg .museum) letters.

[16] These are geographical TLDs, ie the TLD assigned to a nation or dependent territory on the basis of ISO 3166: they consist of two letters that correspond to the relevant geographical entity, eg .uk for the UK and .us for the US.

[17] Details of the gTLD expansion programme can be found at http://www.icann.org/topics/new-gtld-program.htm.

Table 9.1 The current accepted classification of active gTLDs[a]

gTLD[b]	gTLD categorisation	Availability of gTLD	Responsibility for gTLD registration regulation/policy[c]
.aero	sTLD	Restricted to the global aviation community	Société Internationale de Télécommunications Aeronautiques SC (SITA) (http://www.information.aero/gateway/index_html)
.asia	sTLD	Restricted to the Pan-Asia and Asia Pacific region	DotAsia Organisation (http://www.registry.asia/)
.biz	uTLD[d]	Businesses	NeuLevel (http://www.neulevel.biz/)
.cat	sTLD	Catalan linguistic and cultural community	Fundació puntCat (http://www.domini.cat/en_index.html)
.com	uTLD[e]	Unrestricted	Verisign Global Registry Services (http://www.verisign.com/information-services/index.html)
.coop	sTLD	Co-operative organisations	Dot Cooperation LLC (http://www.nic.coop/)
.edu	sTLD	Certain US post-secondary institutions	Educause (http://net.educause.edu/edudomain/)
.gov	sTLD	US government	General Services Administration (http://www.dotgov.gov/)
.info	uTLD	Unrestricted	Afilias Limited (http://www.nic.info/gateway/index_html and http://www.info.info/)
.int	sTLD	International organisations	IANA .int Domain Registry (http://www.iana.org/domains/int/)
.jobs	sTLD	Human resource management community	Employ Media LLC (http://www.goto.jobs/)

.mil	sTLD	US military	DoD Network Information Center
.mobi	sTLD	Consumers and providers of mobile products and services	mTLD Top Level Domain Ltd (dotMobi) (http://mtld.mobi/)
.museum	sTLD	Museums and related persons	Museum Domain Management Association (MuseDoma) (http://musedoma.museum/)
.name	uTLD	Individuals	Global Name Registry Ltd (See http://www.name/)
.net	uTLD	Unrestricted	Verisign Global Registry Services (http://www.verisign.com/information-services/index.html)
.org	uTLD	Unrestricted	Public Interest Registry (PIR) (http://www.pir.org/)
.pro	uTLD	Licensed professionals	Registry Services Corporation (RegistryPro) (http://www.registrypro.pro/)
.tel	sTLD	Contact data for businesses and individuals	Telnic Ltd (http://www.nic.tel/)
.travel	sTLD	Entities whose primary area of activity is in the travel industry	Tralliance Corporation (http://www.travel.travel/)

aInformation collated from the ICANN and assorted gTLD registrar or sponsor websites (please see below for the respective URLs).

bFormally, arpa is also a gTLD, but this TLD is reserved exclusively for the purposes of Internet infrastructure, and so is not included as an active gTLD here.

cPlease note that the organisations listed here are not necessarily the Registry for the relevant gTLD, as the Registry function is sometimes delegated to another organisation.

dAlthough ICANN describe this as a sTLD it should be noted that in the IANA root zone database this is classified as 'generic'.

eAlthough ICANN describe this as an uTLD it should be noted that in the IANA root zone database this is classified as 'generic'.

At present there are 257 active TLDs, of which 247 are usually classified as ccTLDs (which are rather too numerous to list in this chapter[18]) and 20, as listed in Table 9.1, are usually classified as gTLDs.[19] As noted above and discussed below, this usual classification requires further refinement.

The number of sub-domains available varies according to the TLD. Within some TLDs, such as .com and .it, the domain name registrant registers within the second level domain (SLD) (eg microsoft.com and coca-cola.it), whilst within others the domain name registrant registers within the third level domain (eg .uk) or lower (eg .museum). Where a domain registrant can register in the SLD, the chosen name will be unique within that TLD, whereas with registrations in the third level domain or lower, the chosen name can be registered under different sub-domains available within the same TLD. The implications of this for trade mark proprietors are discussed below.

D. Institutions

The most high-profile institution is almost certainly the Internet Corporation for Assigned Names and Numbers (ICANN[20]), a non-profit-making organisation responsible for the general management of the domain name system, with a particular role as to the management of gTLDs. ccTLDs are traditionally more directly the province of IANA,[21] which is itself operated by ICANN. ICANN itself has a number of important constituent elements,[22] but it should be noted that questions have been raised as to the representativeness and legitimacy of ICANN.[23]

Each TLD has a domain name registry, the body responsible for the assignation of domain names, domain name register management and the management of the TLD primary name servers. However, domain name registration typically occurs via intermediary organisations called domain

18 Instead, please see http://www.iana.org/domains/root/db/.

19 Since 1999 ICANN has been actively engaged in the introduction of new gTLDs, with the original seven gTLDs being added to in 2000 and 2003–04. A third, and more extensive, stage of gTLDs expansion is expected in 2009 (at the time of writing, information on this most recent gTLD expansion was expected to be made available at http://www.icann.org/en/topics/new-gtld-program.htm.), and ICANN has offered competition and linguistic reasons for expanding the number of gTLDs (see ICANN Generic Names Supporting Organisation, Board Report, 'Introduction of new Generic Top-Level Domains' (11 September 2007) 12–14, available at http://gnso.icann.org/issues/new-gtlds/council-report-to-board-pdp-new-gtlds-11sep07.pdf.).

20 http://www.icann.org/. ICANN can be regarded as the key international organisation for gTLD policy formulation.

21 http://www.iana.org/. IANA also performs important technical functions regarding number resources and protocol assignment. See http://www.iana.org/about/.

22 The structure of ICANN is summarised at http://www.icann.org/structure/.

23 Eg, see Centre for Democracy & Technology, 'ICANN and Internet Governance: Getting Back to Basics' (July 2004), available at http://www.cdt.org/dns/icann/20040713_cdt.pdf.

name registrars,[24] which act on behalf of domain name applicants and registrants vis-à-vis the registry.

D. Selected Domain Name Terminology

The literature discussing domain names, and the DNS itself, is riddled with jargon and acronyms. The main terms relating to TLDs and domain name dispute resolution are described in this section,[25] but, as argued below, the current taxonomy of domain names is confusing and sometimes inaccurate.

The traditional terminology used to describe TLDs (ie gTLDs and ccTLDs) is not adequate. The introduction of gTLDs *has* led to some new TLD terminology, principally the subcategorisation of gTLDs into sTLDs (sponsored gTLDs) and uTLDs (unsponsored gTLDs). sTLDs are defined by ICANN as:

> '[gTLDs operating] under policies established by the global Internet community directly through the ICANN process' and uTLDs as: '[specialised gTLDs that have] a sponsor representing a specific community that is served by the TLD. The sponsor thus carries out delegated policy-formulation responsibilities over many matters concerning the TLD.[26]

As Table 9.1 indicates, there is not complete agreement as to whether *all* gTLDs are to be categorised as being either sTLDs or uTLDs.

Although not every TLD is available to a prospective domain name registrant to register in (as noted below, many ccTLDs have strict nationality requirements and, as described in Table 9.1, some gTLDs are restricted), once a domain name has been successfully registered, what does the registrant actually have? Although there is still some uncertainty as to the legal status of a domain name,[27] it will usually be specified in the Registry and registrar contracts that the registrant is a domain name *holder* for the duration of the registration contract, with the registrant having a right *in personam* rather than a right *in rem*.[28] Further, domain names are sold on a 'first come, first served' basis in most cases.[29]

---

[24] Just for gTLDs that fall under the aegis of ICANN, there are more than 900 domain name registrars, with the numbers of registrars accredited for gTLDs increasing all the time. See http://www.icann.org/registrars/accredited-list.html for the current list of ICANN-accredited registrars.

[25] Further, a full list of commonly used domain name acronyms can be found at http://gnso.icann.org/acronyms.html.

[26] See http://www.icann.org/registries/.

[27] See eg S. Burshstein, 'Is a Domain Name Property?' (2005) 1 *Journal of Intellectual Property Law & Practice (JIPLP)* 59–63.

[28] Eg see the .uk material below.

[29] Eg see the .uk material below. However, there are exceptions: for example, when new gTLDs have been launched, ccTLDs redelegated or new ccTLDs launched there has commonly been a pre-registration period before open first-to-file registration in which potential registrants could, variously, 'reserve' (usually termed 'sunrise periods'. Eg the Intellectual Property Claim

The traditional gTLD/ccTLD classification, even where supplemented with the (helpful but not always consistently applied) sTLD/uTLD distinction (as set out in Table 9.1) provides an inadequate domain name taxonomy for current gTLDs[30] in three key respects. Firstly, .asia, .cat, .edu, .gov and .mil, due to their regional or restrictive national registration policies, do not easily fall within the accepted perception of a gTLD.[31] This author believes it preferable that a different term (which could also accommodate .arpa), *atypical TLDs* (aTLDs) be used to describe these TLDs.

Second, current TLD taxonomy does not reflect the fact that ccTLD use has also evolved. A range of ccTLDs, including .cc,[32] .fm,[33] .me[34] and .tv[35] are now actively marketed for non-national semantic, rather than geographical, use. This more commercial use of ccTLDs parallels the development of sTLDs and, it is proposed, merits terminological recognition to enable traditional 'national' ccTLDs and the more commercial and generic use of certain ccTLDs to be easily distinguished.

Third, this author has previously argued[36] that the introduction of the .eu TLD meant that there was a new type of TLD—*the regional (rTLD)*. The subsequent introduction of the .asia and .cat TLDs adds further weight to the argument that such TLDs are a discrete category of TLD.

In summary, the increasing sophistication of the domain names industry merits a more nuanced categorisation of TLDs that more accurately reflects the contemporary roles played by the various TLDs. The suggested taxonomy is set out in Figure 9.2.

Service during the launch of the .biz TLD was intended to allow trade mark proprietors to register their marks as domain names) and/or compete (via auction, as in the .asia launch, or lottery, as in the .biz launch) for their chosen domain name.

30 Which could be exacerbated upon the introduction of further new gTLDs. See n 19 above. This eventuality appears likely as, at the time of writing, ICANN's Generic Names Supporting Organization (GNSO) was engaged in developing a policy to guide the introduction of new gTLDs (the most recent information concerning this policy-development process can be found at http://www.icann.org/topics/new-gtld-program.htm).

31 See n 16 above.

32 For the Cocos (Keeling) Islands: the .cc TLD is actively promoted as a TLD for 'commercial company' and other such terms (see http://www.enic.cc/).

33 For the Federated States of Micronesia: the .fm TLD is actively promoted as a TLD for radio stations and providers of digital audio content (see http://www.dot.fm/).

34 In late 2007, ICANN agreed to the delegation of .me for Montenegro (see http://www.iana.org/reports/2007/me-report-11sep2007.html). .me is expected to go live during 2008, and will be targeted at individuals (see http://www.nic.me/).

35 For Tuvalu, which is actively promoted to television companies and to providers of web-based multimedia content. (see http://www.tv).

36 See C Wilson, 'Internationalised Domain Names: Problems and Opportunities' [2004] *Computer & Telecommunications Law Review* 174–181.

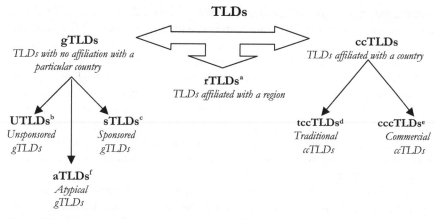

Figure 9.2 A new functional categorisation of TLDs

[a]This proposed TLD type would comprise .asia, .cat and .eu. Grouping these TLDs together into a discrete type of TLD makes more sense that the current view that .asia and .cat are gTLDs and .eu a ccTLD.

[b]This subcategory of gTLDs would be the same as the standard view of what constitutes an uTLD, comprising .biz, .com, .info, .name, .net, .org and .pro.

[c]This subcategory of gTLDs would be smaller than the standard view of what constitutes a sTLD, comprising .aero, .coop, .int, .jobs, .mobi, .museum, .tel and .travel.

[d]The majority of ccTLDs are what I have termed traditional ccTLDs (tccTLDs); domain name registration within a tccTLD is intended to infer a connection or association with the relevant country (tccTLD registries typically have strict rules relating to residency so as to ensure that domain name applicants have such a connection).

[e]As noted above, a small number of ccTLDs, eg .tv, have or are developing away from the traditional ccTLD model (a trend also noted in Bettinger (ed) *Domain Name Law and Practice. An International Handbook* (Oxford, Oxford University Press, 2005) 19); I have termed such ccTLDs commercial ccTLDs (or cccTLDs). Such TLDs are being used and promoted for non-national and supra-national purposes—one that is more akin to a sTLD. Where an assigned ccTLD has the linguistic potential to be used for descriptive purposes, ie the two letters that make up the ccTLD could be an acronym for a generic community or activity, moving to the cccTLD model is a possibility for that ccTLD. (ccTLD redelegation would, however, normally be required for this to take place).

[f]This is a proposed new subcategory of gTLDs consisting of .arpa, .edu, .gov and .mil. Alternatively, it could be placed outside gTLDs and ccTLDs as a discrete type of TLD, rather than as a gTLD subcategory (ie alongside gTLDs, ccTLDs and the proposed rTLD types).

II. ABUSE OF DOMAIN NAMES

Domain names can be abused in a variety of ways. Before establishing how this may occur, it is important to be clear as to what the function of a domain name is generally accepted to be, and what it should be.

The *technological* function a domain name has been set out above, but what is the *practical* function of a domain name? Subject to the relevant Registry and registrar terms and conditions, as well as being the 'address' of a website, a domain name may feature in an e-mail address and, in the future, may relate to a telephone number.[37] Thus a domain name functions as an *identifier*—as means of accurately navigating websites,[38] for example. The *legal* function of a domain name is defined in the contractual relationship between registrant and registry. Although this varies from TLD to TLD, in general the legal function might be said to flow from the non-abusive registration and use of the domain name, with the domain name itself comprising a contractual right limited in time. The issue of the legal status of domain names is briefly considered below. One can thus conceptualise domain name function as being one that, while not subject to territorial limitations,[39] is subject to legal limitations[40] which include temporal restrictions.[41]

The classic and still prevalent form of domain name abuse is known as cybersquatting[42] which includes a number of variants including typo-squatting.[43] Increasingly, commentators are arguing that that the *focus* of cybersquatting has evolved from a resale model into an advertising-based model.[44] There is much merit in this argument. This author takes the view that this evolution has emerged from an original resale focus via a range of tactics including domain name extortion and profiteering,[45] and brand tarnishing[46]—activities that domain name ADR (see below) appear to have

[37] Via Telephone Number Mapping (ENUM). ENUM is an international public database linking telephone numbers to Internet names and other Internet-related destinations and identities: it is intended to increase the ease-of-use of Voice-over-Internet Protocol (VoIP) technology, allowing the VoIP experience to more resemble that of traditional telephony. ENUM UK services were launched on 7 October 2008 (see http://www.nominet.org.uk/enum/launch/).

[38] Although many users navigate websites use a search engine rather than manually entering a URL, the reliability of search engines in finding useful content is also determined by the reliability of the DNS (as argued in C Wilson, 'The Domain Name WHO-IS Debate: The Privacy Concerns of Domain Name Registrants and Spam Recipients', AHRC Privacy Workshop, Edinburgh (September 2005)).

[39] Domain names are global.

[40] As defined by the ambit of the contractual relationship between registrant and registry (and, also, the registrar).

[41] Domain name registrations typically are for a two-year period, although some registrars offer longer registration periods.

[42] The scope of cybersquatting does vary slightly according to the legal context, but it can be generally characterised as the abusive registration of domain names which are regarded as being bad faith registrations vis-à-vis certain pre-existing third party rights. Eg under the US Anticyber-squatting Consumer Protection Act of 1999 so-called 'cyberpiracy' is extended to trademarks, business names and the names of famous persons (15 USC s 1125(d)), whereas under the auspices of the Uniform Dispute Resolution Process (UDRP) cybersquatting only relates to trade marks (UDRP, para 4(a), available at http://www.icann.org/udrp/udrp-policy-24oct99.htm).

[43] This involves the abusive registration by a third party of a misspelled version of an existing domain name (or registered or unregistered trade mark).

[44] See CT Varas, 'Sealing the Cracks: A Proposal to Update the Anti-cybersquatting Regime to Combat Advertising-based Cybersquatting' [2008] *JIPLP* 246–61, 248.

[45] Domain name extortion (as in *BT (and others) v One in A Million* [1998] EWCA Civ 1272) is rarely seen nowadays, following the advent of the UDRP and other forms of domain name dispute resolution. Profiteering (a term used here to refer to the acquisition and reselling of domain names for more modest profits), however, does continue.

[46] This could range from the classic tactic of the posting of pornographic, or other highly offensive content, by the cybersquatter on the 'squatted' site (which is generally is clear-cut

been successful in addressing. Whether current forms of domain name ADR, and domain name regulation in general, are successfully combating advertising-based cybersquatting has, however, been doubted.[47]

Collectively, the various forms of cybersquatting can be seen as being harmful inasmuch as they frustrate the identification of, and legal functions associated with, domain names. There are a number of other forms of domain name abuse, with so-called domain name tasting[48] being one such recent concern.

A. Domain Name ADR

The domain name community can be regarded as a pioneer[49] in online forms of ADR (also known as online dispute resolution (ODR)). Although there are a wide variety of domain name ADR systems,[50] the most important is almost certainly the uniform dispute resolution process (UDRP).

The UDRP is an online arbitration-influenced administrative process

cybersquatting) to the registration of protest and so-called '-sucks' sites (which, depending on the facts, may or may not constitute cybersquatting, and certainly raises concerns relating to freedom of expression). Interestingly, the nexus of such tarnishing activities appears to have moved in recent months from standard websites to accounts in social networking sites such as Facebook and Twitter, where there have been examples of fake and protest corporate accounts set up (sometimes referred to as 'brand-jacking'). There is also a longer-established practice of setting up a fake social networking account purporting to be that of a famous individual. To date, where brand-jacking and fake individual social networking accounts are identified, these accounts can be removed under the terms of service: consideration of whether such an informal and ad hoc process (at least compared to domain name dispute ADR) should be formalised in the future is an issue that is beyond the scope of this chapter.

[47] See n 44 above.

[48] This is an abuse of the domain name registration process, rather than of domain names per se (although there is an intersection with cybersquatting as domain name tasting is a tactic used for cost-effective advertising-based cybersquatting). Domain name tasting works as follows: traditionally, domain name registration processes do not require registration fees to be paid concurrently with the submission of the domain name application; there is a short 'grace period' for payment of fees—usually five days—in which applicants can use a domain name without incurring cost. This allows a 'try before you buy' mentality to develop, with the registrant being able to decide if the domain is worth keeping. As noted above, domain name tasting may facilitate advertising-based cybersquatting, but irrespective of whether the actual domain name registration is abusive, a common business model here is establishing 'link farm' websites whereby the domain name applicant places pay-per-click advertisements on the website. Towards the end of the grace period, the registrant can make an assessment whether sufficient traffic has been generated so that advertising revenue is likely to exceed the domain name registration costs, and if they do the registration fee is paid to secure the domain (if not, no fee is paid and the domain name registration process automatically comes to an end). ICANN is aware of this issue (see http://public.icann.org/issues/domain-name-tasting) and the related practice of domain kiting (where the domain name registration is repeatedly deleted during the grace period and re-registered, thus securing ongoing de facto free use of the domain).

[49] L Edwards and C Wilson, 'Redress and Alternative Dispute Resolution in EU Cross-border E-commerce Transactions' (2007), European Parliament Briefing Note IP/A/IMCO/NT/2006-31. Available at http://www.europarl.europa.eu/comparl/imco/studies/0701_crossborder_ecom_en.pdf

[50] Eg see the Nominet DRS for .uk domain names outlined below.

available for the most serious types of trade mark-related domain name disputes—those involving so-called cybersquatting. The legal basis of the UDRP lies in the contract between the Registrar[51] and the domain name registrant. The registrant submits to the UDRP as part of the registration process. The UDRP provides for the cancellation, transfer or change of domain name registrations where:[52]

- the registrant's domain name is identical or confusingly similar to the complainant's trade mark;
- the registrant has no rights or legitimate interests in the domain name;
- the domain name has been registered and is being used in bad faith.

A neutral and independent panellist or panellists[53] (who cannot be contacted directly by either party to the dispute) will then decide whether or not the domain name(s) at issue should be transferred. The parties to the dispute are required to provide written submissions, upon which the UDRP panel will base its decision.[54] The whole process is essentially conducted online; there are no in-person hearings except in extraordinary cases.[55] Under the UDRP, either party retains the option to take the dispute to a court of competent jurisdiction for independent resolution, although in practice this is rarely done.[56]

There is a choice of dispute resolution providers[57] who, increasingly, offer multilingual services.[58] The number of UDRP disputes is significant: for example in 2008 the most popular UDRP provider alone heard 2,329 complaints.[59] Accredited registrars are contractually bound to take the necessary steps to enforce a UDRP decision, such as transferring the name that is the subject of the dispute.

While it is not possible to engage in an in-depth analysis of UDRP decisions in this chapter, there are interesting trends evident in recent literature. Edwards and Wilson[60] noted that while empirical research on the

---

[51] Registrars are accredited by ICANN, the body also ultimately responsible for gTLD registers, the UDRP and the approval of both accredited registrars and UDRP providers.

[52] UDRP para 4a. See http://www.icann.org/udrp/udrp-policy-24oct99.htm. These three factors are cumulative.

[53] UDRP para 7.

[54] UDRP para 15. There is no provision in the UDRP for panel members to undertake their own investigation.

[55] UDRP para 13.

[56] In the first five years of the UDRP, approximately 70 losing registrants went on to file a court case; most of these being filed in the US (see T Bettinger, Willoughby and Able, above n 6, 984).

[57] See http://www.icann.org/dndr/udrp/approved-providers.htm.

[58] See Wilson, above n 36, 179.

[59] WIPO statistics, 2008 (see http://www.wipo.int/amc/en/domains/). The most recent statistics available for the other dispute-resolution providers show that in 2007 the National Arbitration Forum (NAF, see http://www.arb-forum.com/) recorded 1,805 and the Asian Domain Name Dispute Resolution Center (ADNDRC, see http://www.adndrc.org/adndrc/index.html) recorded 34 filings in the same period. At the time of writing, the newly launched ADR.eu had recorded just one case in 2009 (see http://www.adr.eu/).

[60] Edwards and Wilson, above n 49.

UDRP seems to show a superficial appearance of bias in UDRP decision outcomes towards large company complainants, the system cannot be said to be biased as the preponderance of successful large company complainants can largely be explained by the high number of default decisions (ie where the complainant is unopposed by the registrant). What can be concluded is that trade marks play a central role in the UDRP[61] and many other domain name ADR systems, although whether the UDRP and other such domain name ADR systems currently offer an adequate remedy against modern forms of cybersquatting is debatable.

B. .uk Domain Names

.uk is the ccTLD for the UK and the .uk registry is Nominet.[62] Registrants register names in the third-level domain within .uk, under one of the appropriate SLDs, each SLD being subject to specific SLD Rules (see Table 9.2).[63]

The registration process is online and automatic[64] and only domain name applications that are identical to an existing .uk domain name are rejected.[65] A .uk registrant is therefore part of a 'contractual triangle' with Nominet and their chosen registrar. The status of a .uk domain name is clear. Nominet's terms and conditions state:

> A domain name is not an item of property and has no 'owner'. It is an entry on our register database reflected by our nameservers which we provide as part of this contract.[66]

---

[61] There have been proposals to expand the ambit of the UDRP beyond trade marks (eg to include proprietary pharmaceutical names and other names). The principle source of such proposals can be found in the WIPO Report, 'The Recognition of Rights and Use of Names in the Internet Domain Name System' (available at http://www.wipo.int/export/sites/www/amc/en/docs/report-final2.pdf), but all such proposals have thus far come to naught.

[62] http://www.nominet.org.uk/.

[63] See http://www.nominet.org.uk/registrants/aboutdomainnames/rules/.

[64] A .uk domain name, like most TLDs, is subject to an online application process, usually via a registrar than directly to the Registry. The actual cost and time taken to register a .uk domain name will differ according to which registrar (a list of available registrars can be found at http://www.nominet.org.uk/registrars/becomeregistrar/taglist/)—and, sometimes, which SLD—is used, but a .co.uk domain might cost around £20 for a two-year registration and registration can take seconds (although it may take 24–48 hours for the Nominet Registry database to be updated to reflect this). Registrations generally operate on a first-come, first-served basis, with no pre-registration examination, but it is clear (see http://www.nominet.org.uk/registrants/about domainnames/legal/terms/) that subsequent to registration, third parties may be able to establish a right to the registered domain name.

[65] Although the same domain name under .uk cannot be registered by another company, it could be registered under different a different SLD (eg soton.ac.uk would not prevent the registration of soton.me.uk) or TLD (eg soton.ac.uk would not prevent the registration of soton.com). Also, confusingly similar variations (using the same example as before, 'suton' and 'sotton' or even 'soton' in a non-English language, would be examples of confusingly similar registrations) are registrable within the same TLD.

[66] Nominet, 'Terms and Conditions of Domain Name Registration', clause 10, available at http://www.nominet.org.uk/registrants/aboutdomainnames/legal/terms/. Unlike in the US (see

Table 9.2 .uk SLDs

Sub-domains[a]	Intended users of sub-domains
SLDs operated by Nominet	
.co.uk	Commercial entities and purposes
.ltd.uk	Private limited companies
.me.uk	Personal names
.net.uk	ISPs' infrastructure
.org.uk	Not-for-profit entities
.plc.uk	Public limited companies
SLDs operated by Nominet, but for restricted use	
.nic.uk	Network use only
.sch.uk	Schools
SLDs administered by third-party registrars as trustees	
.ac.uk	Higher and further education and research institution
.gov.uk	National, regional, and local government bodies and agencies
.mod.uk and .mil.uk	Military and related purposes
.nhs.uk	National Health Service
.police.uk	Police forces

Source: information collated from the Nominet website.

[a]As can be seen, these SLDs are semantic, rather than geographic, in character. Geographic SLDs under the .uk TLD (such as .sco.uk for Scotland and .cym.uk (Cymru) for Wales) do not currently exist.

.uk domain names are, therefore, contractual rights. The registrant has responsibility to maintain the accuracy of the contact details[67] having asserted the right to use personal details relevant to the domain name registration. The registrant also undertakes that the registration does not infringe third-party intellectual property rights, including trade marks, and confirms that the registrant has the right to register the domain name.[68]

C. .uk Dispute Resolution

A cause of action might be found in trade mark law or passing off (see below) where there is a domain name dispute, but there has been relatively little court-based domain name litigation in the UK (or elsewhere) when

eg *Kremen v Cohen* 325 F 3d 1035 USPQ 2d 1502 (9th Cir Cal 2003)), there is no real UK authority supporting the view that domain names constitute property rights.

[67] Nominet, 'Terms and Conditions', above n 66, clauses 4 and 7.2.
[68] Ibid, clauses 4 and 7.4, 7.5.

compared with the reliance on forms of ADR to resolve domain name disputes. Such ADR systems have an advantage over litigation in terms of speed and cost.

Nominet has an ADR policy for .uk domain names which binds the parties by virtue of contract law. In particular, Nominet's terms and conditions state (where DRS stands for Dispute Resolution Service):

> You agree to be bound by:
> The DRS policy and DRS procedure, and;
> if there is a dispute, the version of the DRS policy and DRS procedure (available on our website) which applies at the time that proceedings under the dispute resolution service start, until the dispute is over.[69]

The Nominet DRS policy itself has been characterised as a variant[70] on the UDRP. It is a broader ADR system as it applies where the third party has 'rights'[71] rather than just being a registered trade mark proprietor. A complainant is required to prove, on a balance of probabilities, that two elements are present: that the complainant has rights in respect of a name or mark which is identical or similar to the domain name and that the domain name in the hands of the Respondent (ie the domain name registrant) is an abusive registration.[72] A non-exhaustive list of factors which complainants may use to support a claim of abusive registration,[73] and which respondents can use to evidence that a registration is not abusive,[74] can be found in the DRS policy.

Should the parties be unable to resolve the matter between themselves, and where information mediation is not successful, the DRS provides for a

---

[69] Ibid, clause 14. The current DRS Policy is available at http://www.nominet.org.uk/disputes/drs/policy/ and the DRS Procedure at http://www.nominet.org.uk/disputes/drs/procedure/.

[70] See K Brimstead, 'Domain Name Disputes. .uk Domain Name Disputes—Still a Cybersquatter's Charter?' [2002] *Computer Law & Security Report* 201–04. This article considers what is known as Version 1 of the Nominet DRS (which applied from September 2001 to October 2004); however, this journal article still has some relevance, namely to the current version of the DRS (version 2). In the view of this author, one of the most helpful aspects of the Nominet DRS (and certainly an improvement in the UDRP) is that there is an element of quality control via a body that reviews DRS decisions: the Experts Review Group (ERG, see http://www.nominet.org.uk/disputes/drs/experts/expertsgroup/). The ERG was introduced on 1 October 2006. Although it cannot change any DRS decision, the ERG is a useful mediating influence on the development of DRS policy and practice. A further asset of the DRS process is that it allows time for the parties to the dispute to resolve matters between themselves before an Expert is appointed (cf the UDRP, above).

[71] Nominet DRS Policy, 2(a)(i), available at http://www.nominet.org.uk/disputes/drs/policy/?contentId=3069.

[72] Ibid, 2(a)(i) and (ii).

[73] Ibid, 3. In summary, these are: cybersquatting, blocking registrations and unfair disruption of the claimant's business (various modes of achieving this are listed). There is also a rebuttable presumption that a registration is abusive if the claimant shows that the respondent made an abusive registration in three or more Dispute Resolution Service cases in the two years before the complaint in issue was filed (this is known as the 'three strikes rule').

[74] Ibid, 4. In summary, genuine use of the domain name, legitimate connection with a mark, and legitimate non-commercial or fair use of the domain name.

Nominet Expert to be appointed,[75] triggering payment of a fee.[76] Where a complainant prevails, the domain name registration in question may be cancelled, suspended, transferred or otherwise amended.[77] A DRS decision may be appealed[78] and does not replace litigation: any DRS current or future proceedings will be suspended (pending the outcome of such litigation) where legal proceedings relating to the domain name in question are issued in a court of competent jurisdiction.[79] DRS proceedings are usually managed online (or by post, fax, etc), although there is provision for in-person hearings.[80] It can be regarded as a relatively quick and cheap way of resolving domain name disputes.

It is noteworthy that permission was refused in the one known application for judicial review of the Nominet DRS.[81]

III. WHAT IS A TRADE MARK?

This section provides a very brief overview of the provisions of the UK Trade Marks Act 1994 (TMA), relevant to domain names.

A. Introduction

As is generally recognised, a trade mark is a sign whose legal function is to indicate the origin or source of goods or services;[82] the trade mark may be registered,[83] resulting in a limited property right.[84] For the purposes of this chapter, the key limitations of the property right can be conceptualised as

---

[75] Nominet experts have legal and/or technical background. An expert will be appointed to a DRS case on a strict 'cab-rank' basis (see http://www.nominet.org.uk/disputes/drs/experts/), ie the parties to the dispute have no choice as to who is appointed.

[76] Nominet DRS Policy, 21.

[77] As part of the terms and conditions the registrant agrees to be bound by the DRS—see above.

[78] Nominet DRS Policy, 18.

[79] Ibid, 20.

[80] Ibid, 14.

[81] *Application for Judicial Review on the Application of CyberBritain Group Limited v Nominet UK Limited* (CO/8360/2005) of 4 August 2005. However, as the refusal was based on undue delay, this gives little insight.

[82] The practical function of this is that consumer choice is enabled—as argued by S Maniatis, 'Trade Mark Use on the Internet', in J Phillips and I Simon (eds), *Trade Mark Use* (Oxford, Oxford University Press, 2005) 254. On the same page, he argues that whilst trade marks are *distinguishing signs*, the alphanumeric nature of domain names mean that they are *disguising signs*; with respect, this author disagrees with that analysis. It is submitted that domain names—like trade marks—are, in fact, distinguishing signs: this must be axiomatic given the role of the domain name as an identifier: the fact that a domain name is, in effect, a proxy for an IP number is *not* functionally significant in the view of this author.

[83] Discussion of unregistered trade marks, in the UK protected by the law of passing off, will only be briefly noted in this chapter.

[84] See TMA ss 2(1) and 22.

being *geographic* (trade marks are territorial rights) and *functional* (trade marks are registered according to the categories[85] of goods and services to which they will be used).[86] As will be seen below, a wide variety of signs can be registered as trade marks.

(i) The Trade Marks Act 1994

In the UK, trade mark law is governed by the TMA[87] as amended. Following the submission of a trade mark application (and the appropriate fees) a six-month period is likely to elapse before the UK Intellectual Property Office (UKIPO) issues a registration certificate for a successful application. Trade mark applications which are not straightforward take more time.[88] Applications are examined[89] for the absolute grounds of refusal[90] (and, if required, hearings and appeals may take place), then published and a period set aside for opposition by third parties (and, if required, an opposition process takes place, where relative grounds for refusal can be raised)[91] before a mark is registered. A UK trade mark registration covers England, Scotland, Wales, Northern Ireland and the Isle of Man, and (at additional cost), can be extended to also cover Jersey and Guernsey.[92] UK trade marks are registered for period of 10 years, renewable for further 10-year periods.[93]

Under the TMA there is a presumption that a mark ought to be registered unless there is a specific objection to it.[94] The grounds for refusing a

---

[85] Trade marks are registered within categories and sub-categories of goods and services. The so-called Nice classification (established by the Nice Agreement Concerning the International Classification of Goods and Services for the Purposes of the Registration of Marks of 15 June 1957, as revised at Stockholm on 14 July 1967, and at Geneva on 13 May 1977, and amended on 28 September 1979) is the principal classification system for trade marks.

[86] There are, of course also *legal* limitations (only certain marks can be registered as trade marks—see TMA ss 3–5) and *temporal* limitations (trade mark registrations last for a discrete period of time, TMA s 42(1), albeit they can be renewed—TMA s 42(2)).

[87] This was enacted in order to implement EU legislation in relation to trade marks.

[88] See the UKIPO timeline, available at http://www.ipo.gov.uk/tm/t-applying/t-costtime.htm. On the same webpage it is noted that the cost of registering a UK trade mark is £200 for one class, with £50 for each additional class applied for. Although trade mark applicants can apply (online or by post) directly themselves, most would utilise the services of a trade mark attorney to manage the trade mark prosecution process (ie the process of applying for a UK trade mark), thus incurring additional cost. This is a much slower process than a .uk domain name registration, and although the trade mark registration costs are approximately twice as expensive as a single .uk domain name registration for a similar period (see n 94 above), the actual registration costs would be expected to be higher than this where a trade mark agent is used and where there are multi-class applications.

[89] TMA s 37.

[90] In contrast, domain names have traditionally been registered on a first-come, first-served basis.

[91] TMA s 38.

[92] TMA s 108.

[93] TMA s 42.

[94] See TMA ss 3–5.

registration are divided into two categories: absolute[95] and relative.[96] The relative grounds[97] are based on third-party rights, whereas the absolute grounds[98] are concerned with objections based on the mark itself rather than a conflict with another mark. Priority is, within the complexities of the relative grounds for refusal,[99] first-to-file, subject to Convention priority rights.[100]

Different forms of signs are potentially registerable as UK trade marks.[101] Based on UKIPO guidelines[102] and practice such signs can be categorised as follows:

- conventional trade marks (eg pictorial marks such as words and devices (logos, pictures/drawings) and combinations of words and devices);
- non-conventional trade marks (eg slogans,[103] three-dimensional marks,[104] colour marks[105] and sensory marks[106]).

[95] TMA ss 3–4.

[96] TMA ss 5–6.

[97] However, trade mark applicants must now be actively opposed under the relative grounds for refusal by the proprietor of the earlier trade mark following recent changes to UKIPO practice (see http://www.ipo.gov.uk/tm/t-decisionmaking/t-law/t-law-notice/t-law-notice-relative grounds.htm). As a result, although much opposition to domain name registration is post-registration rather than being a feature of the domain name registration process, the de facto position for objecting to registration based on third-party rights for trade marks is now closer to that for domain names.

[98] The UKIPO does examine for the absolute grounds.

[99] Not only can UK trade mark proprietors oppose applications for an identical mark for identical classes of goods or services (TMA s 5(1)), but in some circumstances they can also oppose applications for similar marks and applications for similar or dissimilar goods and services (see TMA ss 5(2) and 5(3)). Further, in limited circumstances, the relative grounds for refusal permit parties with no registered trade mark to use other rights oppose a UK trade mark application (TMA s 5(4)). Also, proprietors of so-called well-known trade marks may be able to restrain, by injunction, use in the UK of an identical or similar trade mark (registered for identical or similar goods and services): see TMA s 56. The scope for objection to trade mark registration is, therefore, clearly wider than that for domain names within the domain name dispute resolution process.

[100] TMA s 35. As the UK is a signatory of the Paris Convention (The Paris Convention of 20 March 1883, as revised at Brussels on 14 December 1900, at Washington on 2 June 1911, at The Hague on 6 November 1925, at London on 2 June 1934, at Lisbon on 31 October 1958, and at Stockholm on 14 July 1967, and as amended on 28 September 1979), Convention priority may be claimed, ie a trade mark applicant may 'back date' an application for a UK trade mark to that of an earlier trade mark application made in another Paris Convention country. The contrast, here, with the domain name registration system is marked.

[101] TMA s 1(1). See also http://www.ipo.gov.uk/tm/t-applying/t-should/t-should-different.htm.

[102] See the *UKIPO Manual of Trade Mark Practice*, ch 3: 'Examination and Practice', 40, available at http://www.ipo.gov.uk/tmmanual-chap3-exam.pdf).

[103] *Erpo Möbelwerk v OHIM (The Principle of Comfort)* (Case C-64/02 P 2004) makes it clear that applications for slogans may be refused due to their descriptive content or for failing to appropriately indicate the origin of the goods or services in question.

[104] Shape marks must be appropriately represented in the trade mark application (*Koninklijke Philips Electronics BV v Remington Consumer Products Ltd* (Case C-299/99)) and certain shapes, which I would categorise as inherent (TMA s 3(2)(a)), functional (TMA s 3(2)(b)) and valuable (TMA s 3(2)(c)) shapes, are not registrable.

[105] A specific shade may be a sign under the TMA, provided that the applicant describes the colour using a code from an internationally recognised colour identification system, such as

Not only can the *form* of a trade mark vary from, for example, word marks to sound marks, but four different types of trade mark are recognised under the TMA: what might be called ordinary trade marks,[107] certification marks,[108] collective marks[109] and well-known trade marks.[110] This functional variation is not seen in domain names. All four types of trade mark can be infringed where a third party uses[111] an identical mark for identical goods or services[112] or similar marks for similar or dissimilar goods and services.[113] There is also a form of contributory infringement.[114] There are a number of defences to trade mark infringement,[115] and there are also criminal offences relating to trade marks in UK law.[116] A wide range of remedies[117] and sanctions[118] for trade mark infringement are available.

B. Trade Mark Law in a Domain Names Context

Following the earlier discussion of domain names and of UK trade mark law, in this section, the relationship between domain names and trade mark

Pantone. (*Libertel Groep BV v Benelux-Merkenbureau* (Case C-104/01)). Combinations of colours are subject to additional requirements (*Heidelberger* (Case C-49/02)).

[106] I would define sensory marks as including auditory (ie sound) marks, gustatory (ie taste) marks and olfactory (scent) marks. In fact, following *Sieckman* (Case C-273/00) gustatory and olfactory signs are unlikely to be registrable. Auditory signs are potentially registrable where a statement that they are sound marks is made and appropriate description, eg by musical notation, is employed in the trade mark application (*Shield Mark BV v Kist* (Case C-283/01)).

[107] See TMA s 1(2).

[108] Which are explicitly recognised in the TMA, being defined in s 50(1) as marks used in relation to goods and services certified by the trade mark proprietor in respect of origin, material, mode of manufacture or performance of service, quality, accuracy or other characteristics. Certification marks differ from standard trade marks in that they are not used by the trade mark proprietor, but rather by authorised third parties in respect of goods or services meeting the standards of the certification in question (see the *UKIPO Manual of Trade Mark Practice*, ch 4: 'Certification and Collective Trade Marks', 2, available at http://www.ipo.gov.uk/tmmanual-chap4-certcoll.pdf).

[109] Which are explicitly recognised in the TMA, being defined in s 49(1) as marks distinguishing the goods and services of an association, the association being the trade mark proprietor here. These marks thus perform a guarantee of origin function.

[110] TMA s 56. Well-known trade mark proprietors may obtain injunctions to prevent the use in the UK of marks identical or similar to (and in relation to identical or similar goods) the well-known trade mark.

[111] Trade mark 'use' is considered in TMA ss 10(4) and 103(2).

[112] TMA s 10(1).

[113] TMA s 10(2), (3).

[114] TMA s 10(5). There is no real equivalent to this in domain name regulation.

[115] TMA s 10(6): comparative advertising; s 11(1): limitations on the effect of a trade mark; s 11(2)(a): use of own name or address; s 11(2)(b): use of certain indications; s 11(2)(c) use necessary for intended purpose; s 11(3); the locality defence; s 12 and 12(2): exhaustion.

[116] TMA ss 92(1), 92(2), 92(3), 94 and 95.

[117] Principally damages, account of profits, injunctions, erasure, etc, of the offending sign from the trade marks registry, delivery up, and destruction or forfeiture of infringing goods (see, variously, TMA ss 14–16, 18, 19 and 56–58).

[118] TMA s 92.

law will be critically considered. The analysis will begin by considering the broad similarities and differences between domain names and trade marks. It will move to consider trade marks in the context of domain name litigation and conclude with a reflection on the domain name/trade mark nexus.

(i) Domain Names and Trade Marks Compared

There are three fundamental differences between domain names and trade marks. First, the latter is clearly a property right, whilst the former is not treated as such (see above). Second, identical trade marks may be registered and owned in the same jurisdiction by a number of parties provided that they are registered, and used, in respect of different classes or goods and services, whereas identical domain names cannot be registered. Third, trade marks are subject to territorial limitations, whereas domain names are global.

In addition, word marks that are registered trade marks may also be registered as domain names and domain names may be registered as trade marks, but domain names can only employ a limited use of characters,[119] whereas any character in any font can be used in a word mark. Further, trade marks can take a wide variety of additional forms, including pictures, symbols and sounds, although the way in which the different forms of sign are treated can differ. Clearly, therefore, a trade mark is both potentially more diverse in form and afforded a greater degree of protection in law than is a domain name.

While both domain names and trade marks require registration, the procedure for achieving that registration differs markedly. As illustrated above, the UK trade mark registration process is lengthier, more detailed and expensive than that of a .uk domain name, with pre-grant examination and opposition of the mark by trade mark examiners. Domain names, by contrast, are automatically registered on a first-come, first-served basis provided they are not identical to an earlier domain name. Further, third party opposition to trade marks is an inherent part of the trade mark regis-

---

[119] Ie a combination of letters and numbers. Domain names are also generally limited in length, eg to a total of 32 characters (for IPv4 address), with the actual limit depending on the TLD in question and, sometimes, the registrar used. Traditionally, only a subset of US-ASCII characters (the ASCII LDH (the American Standard Code for Information Interchange, Letters, Digits and Hyphen) code points, meaning the letters a–z and A–Z, the digits 0–9 and hyphens (-); although the symbol @ cannot be used in domain names, it can be used in e-mail addresses) could be used for domain names, but the increasing availability of internationalised domain names (IDNs)—domain names using non-English letters or characters—at the SLD and below, means that within some TLDs non-English letters, characters and script may be used in domain names. At the time of writing, 11 IDNs at the TLD were being evaluated and tested, including Arabic, Han Chinese, Cyrillic and Hebrew, but these are not yet live (see http://www.iana.org/reports/2007/testetal-report-01aug2007.html). For more information on IDNs, see Wilson, above n 36, and http://www.icann.org/topics/idn/.

tration process,[120] whereas for most TLDs (as in .uk), opposition to a domain name registration can only take place after the domain name has been registered, the usual procedure here being to utilise the available domain name ADR processes.[121] Nevertheless, there is some evidence that the trade mark registration process increasingly resembles the domain name application process, principally due to the fact that in the UK trade marks are no longer examined on relative grounds. There is also some evidence that trade mark registration procedures are influencing those for domain names: in common with most trade mark systems UK trade mark law affords some flexibility in trade mark renewal, a system that is being copied by the introduction of domain name redemption grace periods (RGPs) in some TLDs.[122]

In terms of disputes, domain name registrants are almost always subject to mandatory online ADR systems, but both parties to a domain name dispute could also engage in litigation. By contrast, the trade mark system contains no mandatory ADR (although parties to a trade mark dispute may voluntarily seek a form of ADR). It would be invidious to attempt to 'compare' domain name ADR and trade mark infringement—the two mechanisms clearly have very different characteristics.[123] How a UK domain name dispute involving trade mark issues would be approached is the topic of the next section.

(ii) Domain Name Litigation and the Role of Trade Marks

Consideration of case-law dealing with the intersection between trade marks and domain names gives some interesting insight into the domain name/trade mark relationship.

---

120 An example of pre-grant opposition.

121 Almost all TLDs offer a form of online ADR, adherence with the ADR in question usually being a condition of domain name registration. All the main gTLDs are subject to a form of online ADR, mainly to the UDRP, although there are also additional gTLD online ADR systems, eg the Política de Resolució de Conflictes sobre Requisits d'Admissibilitat del .cat for .cat domain names (see http://www.icann.org/udrp/). Most ccTLDs have a national online ADR policy (see eg the Nominet DRS, discussed below), but not all (eg .tr for Turkey) currently do. See below.

122 Eg, although renewal of UK domain names should take place before the expiry of the registration, it is possible for renewal to take place up to six months after expiry, subject to the payment of an additional fee— TMA s 43(3). See http://www.icann.org/ regarding the ICANN RGP where a similar system allows renewal 30 days after expiry.

123 As noted above. For example, domain name ADR is generally cheaper, quicker and easier than litigation (although some systems, like the UDRP, require trade mark registrations) and, where successful, results in the domain name being redelegated (or remaining with) the rightful party. However, no damages are available and there are no defences as such within most domain name online ADR systems, arguably with implications for freedom of expression. In contrast, UK domain name litigation is expensive and time-consuming, but the conception of infringement (and available remedies and sanctions) is more flexible and there are a (limited) range of defences (but no defence of parody, for example). A key aspect is that domain name online ADR is about establishing who is the sole and rightful holder of a domain name, whereas in domain name litigation identical or similar trade marks may be allowed to coexist.

In the UK the key such authority remains *BT (and others) v One in A Million*.[124] This was a classic instance of cybersquatting in which One in a Million registered (but did not much use) a range of domain names containing UK trade marks (including bt.org) and offered to sell these domain names to the trade mark proprietors for thousands of pounds. Facing claims of trade mark infringement and passing off, One in a Million's actions were found by the Court of Appeal to constitute passing off via the domain name registration constituting an instrument of fraud. It was accepted that such activities could also constitute trade mark infringement.[125]

It is clear from this that a domain name registration can infringe UK trade mark law where it incorporates a UK trade mark. It is also clear that the law of passing off may provide a remedy (although the likelihood of success in any passing-off action is difficult to predict). Trade mark law can thus be seen as enhancing and reinforcing domain name regulation. Also, as we have seen earlier, domain names may also be registered as trade marks.

However, is the close relationship between domain names and trade marks helpful? The marked differences in the nature of domain names and trade marks (as well as the differences that remain in registration procedure) mean that in some key respects it is often unhelpful for domain names to be treated as being somehow equivalent to trade marks. Some of these issues have already been mentioned above. The key such respect is that domain names are *not* property rights and they are *not* equivalent to trade marks, although the main element of a domain name might also be registered as a trade mark. For example, there is only one globally available (and not restricted as to the goods and services referred to therein) wilson.com, and within the DNS the registrant of this domain name has no particular rights to the name 'wilson' within other active TLDs. In contrast, in each trade mark jurisdiction there may be a range of trade mark proprietors of the mark WILSON, each for different goods or services—in other words, there is likely to be a significant number of (national) WILSON trade mark proprietors all wishing to have high-profile domain name registrations. In the trade mark system, with its territorial nature and classification system, multiple proprietors of the same mark can coexist. This is not the case in the DNS, where competing registrants have to settle for alternative names, or domain names under a different TLD. The proliferation of new gTLDs and the introduction of IDNs further complicates the situation for domain name registrants, and ICANN will need to have carefully considered the trade mark problems of launching yet more gTLDs, as previously used mechanisms for resolving demand for the same

---

[124] [1998] EWCA Civ 1272.
[125] TMA s 10(3).

domain name under a new TLD[126] have not, in the view of this author, been adequate.

In conclusion, trade marks are important to the domain name registrant and in domain names practice,[127] but treating them as being equivalents—in either substance,[128] procedure[129] or policy[130]—amounts to a false equivalence. Trade marks and domain names can rightly be regarded as being *interrelated*, but are not equivalents.

IV. SUMMARY: THE DOMAIN NAME/TRADE MARK NEXUS

In this chapter, the background (with some critical analysis) to domain names and UK trade mark law has been provided and the relationship between domain names and trade marks considered. Although, in the past, trade mark law might have been seen as the principal influence on the regulation of domain names, there are now some instances where domain name practices have in fact influenced the trade mark regime. So, from a policy perspective, the domain name/trade mark relationship is increasingly a two-way one. However, as argued above, we should shy away from treating domain names as being equivalents of trade marks.

---

[126] Where a new TLD is launched or IDN availability is announced, most registries have allowed trade mark proprietors to pre-register; however, where more than one trade mark proprietor pre-registers, then which party secures the domain name registration is, often quite literally, a lottery.

[127] As many domain name practitioners have a trade mark background, this was probably inevitable.

[128] Eg regarding a domain name registration as being a property right.

[129] Although some trade mark influence on domain name procedure, eg the introduction of the RGP, can be helpful, too much influence would vastly increase the time, cost and burden of domain name registration.

[130] Eg, although the emphasis in the UDRP placed on trade marks is helpful, to an extent, in managing the interrelationship between domain names and trade marks, other trade-mark-influenced domain name policies seem less helpful. Principally here there is the example of gTLD expansion: if gTLD expansion is one means of giving trade mark proprietors more 'choice' of TLDs, then this is unhelpful. This is because (i) the extent of gTLD expansion that would be necessary to give enough 'choice' to trade mark proprietors to allow the extent of mark coexistence (due to the classification system) found in the trade mark system is unimaginable; and (ii) unlike trade marks, domain names do not have to be 'used' so one brand proprietor could easily register in all the (expanded) gTLDs. Extensive gTLD expansion could, thus, degenerate into a revenue-raising exercise.

10

Protection of Computer Software

ARNE KOLB

I. INTRODUCTION

COMPUTER SOFTWARE IS an innovative and thriving industrial sector and one of great economic importance. Software is widely used in business and in private. It is often hidden in many products—from cars and mobile phones, to stereos and cameras. There are a number of stakeholders with different and often conflicting interests engaged in this field. For example, software *developers* are caught between wanting strong legal protection for their own software and needing the ability to use and to build on the work and ideas of others without having to worry about being sued for copyright or patent infringement. *Competitors* tend to have an interest in developing software with a very similar 'look and feel' to existing software—or at least software that is interoperable—in order to entice customers to use their products. *Customers* are interested in innovative, affordable and interoperable software that does not take too long to learn to use. Interoperability is of great importance as a new device or piece of software may be unattractive if it does not work with other devices, programs or existing files used by the customer, even if it is flawless in itself. The developer of the original software thus has an interest in preventing the creation of software with a similar 'look and feel', while competitors want to do exactly that.

The most important legal regimes relevant for software protection are copyright, patents and design law as well as the law of breach of confidence and contract.[1] This chapter will focus on UK copyright and patent law, but with a European and international perspective. During the analysis many of the themes introduced above will become apparent in the case-law and comment. For instance, in *Microsoft Corp v Commission of the European Communities*[2] interoperability was of great importance, while in *Navitaire*

---

[1] See generally DI Bainbridge, *Software Copyright Law*, 3rd edn (London, Butterworths, 1997) 11–16.
[2] T-201/04 [2007] 5 CMLR 11.

Inc v *Easyjet Airline Co Inc*[3] a major issue was the look and feel of software.

II. SOFTWARE AND INTELLECTUAL PROPERTY

The fundamental rationale for the intellectual property regime—to provide enough incentive for innovation by offering sufficient reward in form of intellectual property rights without stifling innovation by too strong monopoly rights—seems simple. However, in practice it is anything but as it encompasses complex constellations of interests and mechanisms for balancing them.[4] For example, the position in terms of access to affordable legal advice of a small entrepreneur-led information technology company differs significantly from that of a multinational company with a large in-house intellectual property department; the legal obligations on the market leader in a dominant position for a particular software application differ markedly from the obligations on its competitors; the business strategies and exploitation opportunities with accompanying enforcement mechanisms will be different for companies relying on the proprietary software model as compared to companies embracing free and open source software.

The emergence of software, a relatively new phenomenon, challenged the existing and long-estabished intellectual property regime and in so doing raised complex questions. Does the intellectual property regime provide protection for software? Is software a literary work under copyright law? Is it a patentable invention under patent law? Is the standard of protection under the existing regimes adequate, or would it be better to give protection under a *sui generis* system?[5] Which parts of software can or should be protected—source code, screen displays, program structure? Are legitimate stakeholder interests protected sufficiently? Are there enough safeguards against the abuse of the intellectual property system? Is the law clear enough, or is legislation needed to eliminate legal uncertainty? Will older case-law be applied to this new technology, or will cases be distinguished? Is there a need for international regulation and harmonisation?

Over time, different answers have been given to these questions, with the result that the legal protection given to software in different jurisdictions has varied quite significantly. This has also been driven by changes in the computer industry. Early computers were massive mainframe machines, built and used by few. Hardware manufactures developed bespoke soft-

---

[3] [2006] RPC 3.

[4] For a general discussion of the justification of intellectual property rights, see EC Hettinger, 'Justifying Intellectual Property' (1989) 18 *Philosophy and Public Affairs* 31–52.

[5] For a current take on this question, see L Diver, 'Would the Current Ambiguities within the Legal Protection of Software be Solved by the Creation of a Sui Generis Property Right for Computer Programs?' (2008) 3 *Journal of Intellectual Property Law & Practice* 125–38.

ware, little of which was interoperable. The law governing trade secrets and contracts provided sufficient legal protection.[6] Unauthorised copying was not common because of the tailored nature of the software. Even until the 1970s, hardware was thought to be the most important aspect of the business, with software merely an add-on. A common view was that software should not be protected by copyright or patents in the hope that this might stimulate trade in computer hardware.[7]

This view changed as the computer industry evolved and computers became more common. In the 1970s, software piracy became an increasing problem.[8] At this stage, it was far from clear to what extent software *was* protected through copyright or patents, or to what extent it *should* be protected by those regimes. Although many of the basic questions have now been answered by legislation and in case-law, the debate still continues as to how software might or should best be protected. In respect of patents, this reached a climax when the EU Parliament rejected the proposal for the Directive on the Patentability of Computer-Implemented Inventions[9] on 6 June 2006.

Important milestones along the path of legal protection included the WIPO Model Provisions on the Protection of Computer Programs,[10] published in 1978, based mainly on copyright law. These model provisions had a strong influence on thinking about the most appropriate form of protection, and in the 1980s and 1990s the copyright system was generally regarded as most appropriate. The US adopted the copyright approach in 1980,[11] and the EU followed with the Council Directive of 14 May 1991 on the legal protection of computer programs[12] (the Software Directive). Finally, the Agreement on Trade-Related Aspects of Intellectual Property Rights 1994 (TRIPS Agreement)[13] and the World Intellectual Property Organization (WIPO) Copyright Treaty 1996[14] required that computer programs, whether in source or object code, be protected by copyright as literary works within the meaning of Article 2 of the Berne Convention.

However, copyright only protects one aspect of software, namely the expression of an idea and not the idea itself. Attempts to extend copyright

[6] BL Smith and SO Mann, 'Innovation and Intellectual Property Protection in the Software Industry: An Emerging Role for Patents?' (2004) 71 *University of Chicago Law Review* 243–47.
[7] E Gratton, 'Should Patent Protection be Considered for Computer Software-related Innovations?' (2003) 7 *Computer Law Review and Technology Journal* 223.
[8] Smith and Mann, above n 6.
[9] Proposal for a Directive of the European Parliament and the Council on the Patentability of Computer-Implemented Inventions, COM(2002) 92.
[10] World Intellectual Property Organization, 'Model Provisions on the Protection of Computer Software' (1978) WIPO Publication No 814.
[11] Computer Software Copyright Act, 12 December 1980, Pub L No 96-517, 94 Stat 3015, 3028 (1980).
[12] 91/250/EEC.
[13] Agreement on Trade-Related Aspects of Intellectual Property Rights, Art 10(1).
[14] WIPO Copyright Treaty, Art 4.

to cover the principles or ideas behind a literal expression led to the development of complicated legal tests in the US, such as the structure–sequence–organisation test[15] and the abstraction–filtration–comparison test,[16] which were partly also applied by European courts.[17] Advances in reverse engineering and the need for interoperability made protection by way of trade secrets complex and no longer apt for software.

To allow for stronger protection of software ideas and principles, US courts increasingly extended patent protection. This started with the ruling in *Diamond v Diehr*,[18] which departed from former more restrictive rulings such as *Gottschalk v Benson*,[19] and Europe followed this tendency.[20] In *Gottschalk v Benson*, an application was filed for a method for converting binary-coded decimal numerals into pure binary numerals using a general-purpose computer. The US Supreme Court held that the process was not patentable because the claim was directed to an algorithm alone. This decision was widely taken to confirm that software by itself was not patentable. In *Diamond v Diehr*, a claim was made for the execution of a process for moulding raw, uncured synthetic rubber utilising a computer programme that calculated when to open the press by implementing a mathematical algorithm. While the patent examiner had initially rejected this application, citing *Gottschalk v Benson*, the US Supreme Court held that the invention was patentable.

The current position in Europe in general, and in the UK in particular, is that the less important question is whether software attracts copyright protection (in most cases it undoubtedly does because of the low threshold for protection). The more important question is as to what amounts to infringement. For patents, by contrast, the problem lies more in the question as to whether a patent can be granted in the first place or whether the software invention is excluded subject matter and thus cannot be patented.

III. COPYRIGHT PROTECTION

In the UK, it was unclear for a long time whether and to what extent computer programs were protected by copyright. Although the Copyright Act 1956 made no mention of computer programs, many writers considered them protected as literary works. This opinion was confirmed

15 *Whelan Associates Inc v Jaslow Dental Laboratory Inc* [1987] 797 F 2d 1222.
16 *Computer Associates International Inc v Altai Inc* [1992] 982 F 2d 693.
17 T Cook, 'EC Draft Patent Directive: "I Wouldn't Start From Here if I Were You"—Intellectual Property Protection for Computer Software in Europe and the Proposed New Directive on Computer-implemented Inventions' (2002) 18 *Computer Law & Security Report* 197.
18 [1981] 67 L Ed 2d 155.
19 [1972] 409 US 63.
20 For an overview, see DJM Attridge, 'Challenging Claims! Patenting Computer Programs in Europe and the USA' (2001) 1 *Intellectual Property Quarterly* 22.

in a couple of interim hearings.[21] However, the question was never answered in full trial. The 1977 report of the Whiteford Committee pointed to the uncertainty and shortcomings of copyright law in relation to computer programs. The Copyright Amendment Act 1985 brought the long-awaited clarification that computer programs were protected by copyright law as literary works. Now, and despite ongoing debates on whether copyright is the correct or adequate regime for protection of computer programs,[22] it is beyond dispute that computer programs are protected as literary works.[23]

However, the Copyright Designs and Patents Act 1988 (CDPA) does not attempt to define computer programs. Given the speed of development in this area, a definition could quickly become dated. In general, a computer program is a set of instructions to a computer. Both the source code (the human-readable form of instructions that comprise a program, usually written by a programmer) and the object code (machine-executable instructions, usually generated from source code by a computer running a compiler software) attract copyright protection.[24]

A. The Basic Position

The application of copyright protection to computer software is straightforward: copyright is a property right subsisting, inter alia, in original literary works[25] if certain requirements are met. A computer program is a literary work for these purposes.[26] The person who creates the work is the author of the work[27] and as a default the first owner of any copyright in it,[28] unless the work was made by an employee in the course of his employment, in which case the employer is the default first owner of copyright.[29] Protection is automatic and begins with the creation of the work. There is no need for registration. Copyright in a literary work expires 70 years after the end of the calendar year in which the author died.[30]

The copyright owner has a comprehensive set of exclusive rights over the work. For example, he has the exclusive right to copy the work, to issue copies of the work to the public, or to make adaptations of the work.[31] His

---

[21] *Sega Enterprises Ltd v Richards* [1983] FSR 73; *Gates v Swift* [1982] RPC 339.

[22] One for many: SE Gordon, 'The Very Idea! Why Copyright Is an Inappropriate Way to Protect Computer Programs' (1998) 20 *European Intellectual Property Law Review* 10.

[23] CDPA s 3(1)(b).

[24] S Lai, *The Copyright Protection of Computer Software in the United Kingdom* (Oxford, Hart Publishing, 2000) 2.

[25] CDPA s 1(1)(a).

[26] CDPA s 3(1)(b).

[27] CDPA s 9(1).

[28] CDPA s 11(1).

[29] CDPA s 11(2).

[30] CDPA s 12(2).

[31] CDPA s 16(1).

copyright is infringed if anybody does—either directly or indirectly—any of the acts restricted by copyright in relation to the work as a whole or any substantial part of it, unless the copyright owner authorises him to do so.[32] To balance these exclusive rights with the legitimate interests of others and the public interest, the CDPA permits certain acts (so called 'permitted acts') in relation to copyright works regardless of any authorisation of the copyright owner.[33] These copyright exceptions only allow specific acts (eg copying, performing or temporary reproduction) to be undertaken in relation to certain protected works (eg literary, dramatic, musical and artistic works). As a computer program is a literary work, all of the exceptions/defences available for literary works also apply to computer programs unless otherwise stated. Those exceptions include, for example, fair dealing with a work for the purpose of non-commercial research,[34] private study,[35] and review or criticism.[36] Next to these, the CDPA provides specific exceptions for *lawful* users of computer programs. According to the Act, a lawful user is a user who has a right to use the program, whether under a license or otherwise, eg under one of the general exceptions mentioned above.[37] A lawful user may take advantage of the exceptions in CDPA s 50, which include the right to:

- make a backup copy of the program which is necessary for a lawful use;[38]
- convert it into a version expressed in a higher-level language, ie to decompile it, for the sole purpose of obtaining the information necessary to create an independent program which can be operated with the decompiled or with another program;[39]
- observe, study or test the functioning of the program to determine its ideas and principles while loading, displaying, running, transmitting or storing the program which he is entitled to do;[40]
- copy or adapt it if this is necessary for his lawful use and in particular if this is necessary for the purpose of correcting errors in it.[41]

The acts permitted by these sections cannot be prohibited or restricted by any contractual clause; such clauses are void.[42] It is also important to note that the exceptions listed in the CDPA are exhaustive, with the exception of

---

[32] CDPA s 16(2) and (3).
[33] CDPA, part I, ch III.
[34] CDPA s 29(1).
[35] CDPA s 29(1).
[36] CDPA s 30(1).
[37] CDPA s 50A(2).
[38] CDPA s 50A(1).
[39] CDPA s 50B.
[40] CDPA s 50BA.
[41] CDPA s 50C.
[42] CDPA s 296A.

a narrow public interest defence, which is disputed in scope and existence.[43]

Of these exceptions, decompilation is of utmost importance. This originates from the Software Directive, in which the importance of software interoperability was recognised:

> [T]he function of a computer program is to communicate and work together with other components of a computer system and with users and, for this purpose, a logical and, where appropriate, physical interconnection and interaction is required to permit all elements of software and hardware to work with other software and hardware and with users in all the ways in which they are intended to function.[44]

For example, if someone wanted to develop a new word processing program, details would be needed of the operating system on which it should run as well as information on file formats of competing word processors so that the new software could permit the user to open and write files in the relevant format. In the absence of this information the new program would be unlikely to be able to interoperate with existing programs and would thus have a slim, if not non-existent, chance of succeeding on the market. To enable developers to obtain this interface information, the CDPA permits the decompilation of software but does not permit the copying of the interface itself.

To be an infringement the copyright owner would thus need to show the following:

- copyright subsists in the software (a low threshold);
- the act complained is of a restricted act (eg copying);
- the act relates to a substantial part of the work;
- the copyright owner did not authorise or consent to the act;
- the act does not fall within the permitted acts;
- the act is not in the public interest.

B. Substantial Part of the Work

In many software copyright cases, the question of whether a *substantial* part of the work had been copied can be problematic. Substantiality is a question of quality and quantity.[45] Even if a relatively small part of a program is taken, this can constitute infringement when this part is an important part of the program. It has been suggested that every part of a

---

[43] For copyright and the public interest, see A Sims, 'The Public Interest Defence in Copyright Law: Myth or Reality?' (2006) 28 *European Intellectual Property Review* (*EIPR*) 335; A Sims, 'The Denial of Copyright Protection on Public Policy Grounds' (2008) 30 *EIPR* 189.

[44] Council Directive of 14 May 1991 on the legal protection of computer programs, 91/250/EEC, Rec 10.

[45] DI Bainbridge, *Intellectual Property*, 5th edn (Harlow, Longman, 2002) 194.

computer program without which the program would not run properly is to be considered a substantial part. This would mean that even very insignificant and trivial lines of code would be substantial parts[46] and thus infringed if copied. This has been rightly rejected in *Cantor Fitzgerald International v Tradition (UK) Ltd.*[47] In keeping with the function of copyright law to protect the author's skill and labour, the correct question to ask is whether the part taken represents a substantial part of the author's skill and labour.[48]

C. Copying and Indirect Copying: The Look and Feel of Computer Programs

Another problematic area is the question of what amounts to *copying* of a computer program for the purposes of the law of copyright. There are several ways a program can be copied. The most obvious is literal copying, where the program code itself (or parts of it) are copied. This happens, for example, when a program saved on a disk is copied to another disk. However, copyright law also recognises non-literal copying in relation to computer programs. Non-literal copying refers to an act where elements of a program are taken, eg its structure, functions or sequence of operations (its 'look and feel'), but without literally copying parts of the code. This form of copying raises many legal questions.

John Richardson Computers Ltd v Flanders[49] was the first leading case in the UK to address the 'look and feel' of computer programs. The defendant had worked for the claimant on a program designed for stock control and label printing in a pharmacy. When the defendant left his employment and joined a new firm he wrote a new version of the program which competed with that of his former employer. While the new version added some new features, it had a very similar user interface and followed the same scheme as the first. There was no literal copying because the original version of the program had been written for a BBC computer, while the new version was written for an IBM computer in a different programming language. Referring to the abstraction–filtration–comparison test adopted in the US case of *Computer Associates International Inc v Altai Inc,*[50] Ferris J held that parts of the defendant's version infringed the claimant's copyright in the BBC version because non-literal elements of the program had been copied.

---

[46] See the Australian case *Autodesk v Dyason* [1992] RPC 95.
[47] [2000] RPC 95.
[48] *Cantor Fitzgerald International v Tradition (UK) Ltd* [2000] RPC 95.
[49] [1992] FSR 497.
[50] [1992] 982 F 2d. 693.

In *Ibcos Computers Ltd v Barclays Mercantile Highland Finance Ltd*,[51] Jacob J rejected Ferris J's approach, and in particular the application of the abstraction–filtration–comparison test. In this case, the second defendant, a computer programmer called Mr Poole, had worked on the claimant's accounts payroll package for agricultural dealers. After leaving Ibcos he developed a competing accounts package for the first defendant. It was held that literal copying had taken place. Both program suites contained many common mistakes in the 'comment' lines (these are program lines that are not executed, but merely make it easier for programmers to understand the code) and the same redundant code had been used. In the absence of any plausible explanation for this by Mr Poole, this was deemed enough to prove literal copying.

In addition to establishing a precedent for the burden of proof, *Ibcos* confirmed that non-literal copying can infringe copyright. Although rejecting the application of the abstraction–filtration–comparison test referred to in *John Richardson Computers Ltd v Flanders*, Jacob J agreed that 'most literary copyright works involve both literal matter (the exact words of a novel or computer program) and varying levels of abstraction (plot, more or less detailed of a novel, general structure of a computer program)', and that 'it [is] right to have regard . . . not only to . . . "literal similarities" but also to . . . "program structure" and "design features".' *Ibcos* recognised that software developers often invest substantial skill, labour and judgement in the design of the program structure and its design features, and that these efforts are worth protecting through copyright. This basic position on non-literal copying was also confirmed by *Cantor Fitzgerald International v Tradition (UK) Ltd*,[52] which made an analogy between the structure and architecture of a computer program and the plot of a play.

By contrast with these three cases, which took an expansive approach to the extent of copyright protection and the copying of non-literal elements, *Navitaire Inc v Easyjet Airline Co Inc*,[53] a more recent case, has narrowed the extent of protection, an approach that has been confirmed in *Nova Productions Ltd v Mazooma Games Ltd*.[54] In *Navitaire*,[55] the claimant (N) sought damages for the infringement of their airline booking system Open-Res, which was licensed to the defendant (E) until E introduced its own replacement software eRes that was developed by the second defendant (B). It was not disputed that E wanted a system that was in practice indistin-

[51] [1994] FSR 297.
[52] [2000] RPC 95.
[53] [2006] RPC 3.
[54] [2006] EWHC 24.
[55] For a discussion of this case, see S Stokes, 'The Development of UK Software Copyright Law: From John Richardson Computers to Navitaire' (2005) 11 *Computer and Telecommunications Law Review* 129–33.

guishable from the OpenRes system. Also, it was not disputed that the defendants did not have access to the source code of OpenRes.

N claimed that the copyright in OpenRes had been infringed by, among other things, 'non textual copying'—similar to copying the plot of a book, the defendants had copied the 'business logic'. However, it was held that there was no copying and that the analogy with a plot is a poor one because two completely different computer programs can produce an identical result at any level of abstraction. A program like OpenRes 'does not have a plot, merely a series of pre-defined operations intended to achieve the desired result in response to the requests of the customer'.[56]

To illustrate his argument, the late Pumfrey J, who presided over the case, gave the example of a chef who invents a new pudding which is thereafter always made using his written recipe. Pumfrey J found that a competitor who successfully emulated the pudding (without having access to the original recipe) and recorded his recipe did not infringe copyright in the earlier recipe, even if the end result, the 'plot and purpose' of both puddings, is the same.[57]

> Navitaire's computer program invites input in a manner excluded from copyright protection, outputs its results in a form excluded from copyright protection and creates a record of a reservation in the name of a particular passenger on a particular flight. What is left when the interface aspects of the case are disregarded is the business function of carrying out the transaction and creating the record, because none of the code was read or copied by the defendants. It is right that those responsible for devising OpenRes envisaged this as the end result for their program: but that is not relevant skill and labour. In my judgment, this claim for non-textual copying should fail.
>
> I do not come to this conclusion with any regret. If it is the policy of the Software Directive to exclude both computer languages and the underlying ideas of the interfaces from protection, then it should not be possible to circumvent these exclusions by seeking to identify some overall function or functions that it is the sole purpose of the interface to invoke and relying on those instead. As a matter of policy also, it seems to me that to permit the 'business logic' of a program to attract protection through the literary copyright afforded to the program itself is an unjustifiable extension of copyright protection into a field where I am far from satisfied that it is appropriate.[58]

It followed that the claimant lost most of the claims with the exception of some of the screen layouts, which were held to qualify as artistic works under the CDPA and infringed the defendant's software.

Is this legal development regarding the 'look and feel' of software to be welcomed from a policy point of view? Is it fair that after *Navitaire* it is easier to develop a computer program that is, from the users' point of view,

---

[56] [2006] RPC 3, paras 125–27.
[57] Ibid, para 127.
[58] Ibid, paras 129–30.

very similar to an existing program of a competitor? It is safe to say that in most cases it will be easier and cheaper to develop a program if its 'final look and feel', its functionality and user interface are known from the start—even if the program code itself is written from scratch. The creator of the original software might feel that the competitor is freeloading on the skill, labour and effort that went into developing the 'look and feel' in the first place.

The developer should perhaps look to other ways to claim advantage. While for custom software the developer can ensure that efforts are rewarded by building costs into the price, this is more problematic in relation to standard software for the mass market. Development costs can only be recouped through selling the software on the open market where customers may be faced with cheaper, but lawful (within the meaning of *Navitaire*) copies. Nevertheless, the first-mover advantage—the advantage gained by the initial occupant of a market segment—might be enough to allow for the recouping of the initial investment.

From the customer and consumer point of view, this legal development has to be welcomed. Having the ability to transfer techniques and skills used with one software program to another is likely to save a great deal in time and resources. This may mean that a consumer is more likely to switch products, perhaps in turn increasing the incentive for new program development to satisfy increased demand.

The decision of the European Court of First Instance (CFI) in *Microsoft Corp v Commission of the European Communities*[59] also raised issues of interoperability and consumer protection, this time from the perspective of competition law. The case illustrates how the exercise of intellectual property rights can be restricted by other areas of the law.[60] The case had two threads: one concerned the bundling of the Windows operating system with the Windows Media Player, the other Microsoft's refusal to supply competitors with interoperability information and to license the use of that information to enable competitors to develop own products for the workgroup server operating systems market. It is that latter thread that is of interest to this discussion. In 1998, Sun Microsystems asked Microsoft to provide the information necessary to allow its own workgroup server operating system to operate seamlessly with Microsoft's Windows personal computer operating system and other Windows-based software. Microsoft refused to disclose that information by reference to its intellectual property rights. The European Commission started an investigation into the behaviour by Microsoft. In its decision of March 2004,[61] the European

[59] T-201/04 [2007] 5 CMLR 11.
[60] For a comment on the case from an intellectual property view, see I Eagles, 'Microsoft's Refusal to Disclose Software Interoperability Information and the Court of First Instance' (2008) 30 *EIPR* 205.
[61] COMP/C-3/37.792.

Commission ordered Microsoft to make the interoperability information available, allow its use on reasonable and non-discriminatory terms, offer a version of the Windows Client PC Operating System which did not incorporate Windows Media Player, and imposed a fine of €497,196,304. Microsoft appealed to the CFI. The CFI upheld the Commission's decision in most parts and confirmed that Microsoft had misused its market power and breached Article 82 EC. While confirming that, in principle, even dominant firms are free in their decision not to license their intellectual property, when a market player occupies a dominant position a refusal to do so can constitute an abuse of a dominant position under 'exceptional circumstances',[62] which had been established in this particular case. Microsoft was therefore obliged to disclose and license the interoperability information, notwithstanding the subsistence of intellectual property rights.[63]

While some might consider that this extra regulatory tier on the exercise of copyright is unjustifiable, it should be remembered that the application of this aspect of competition law to curb the exercise of copyright can only come into play when the player is in a dominant position. In addition, and as the point has been made above, preventing user lock-in to a single system or software and promoting the freedom to choose among different interoperable systems fosters innovation, reinforcing the justification for intellectual property.

IV. SOFTWARE PATENTS

As mentioned at the start of this chapter, copyright protection is often not considered sufficient for the protection of computer programs because of the uncertainty and narrowness of its application and the protection it affords in infringement cases. Patents, by contrast, give much stronger rights and, judging by the numbers of software patents that exist, notably in the US, developers clearly consider them to grant worthwhile protection. However, while there are few major hurdles to obtaining a software patent in the US, that is not the case in Europe where the legal framework under the European Patent Convention (EPC) excludes computer programs *as such* from patentability. The differences in approach between the systems has fuelled a heated debate about the proper extent of protection for computer software under the patent system, highlighting the alleged injustices that result from having such different regimes in a globalised marketplace.

---

[62] The test of exceptionality refered to in this decision had been laid down in previous decisions, most refined in *Radio Telefis Eireann (RTE) and Independent Television Publications Ltd (ITP) v Commission of the European Communities* 'Magill' (C 241 & 242/91 P) [1995] ECR I-743; [1995] 4 CMLR 718 and *IMS Health GmbH & Co OHG v NDC Health GmbH & Co KG* (C-418/01) [2004] ECR I-5039; [2004] 4 CMLR 28.

[63] For further analysis of the role and extent of exceptional circumstances, see ch 13.

The arguments for and against patenting software are polarised. Patent law is economic law and should be primarily assessed by its economic merits.[64] There are many different costs associated with patents. As a patent grants a monopoly right, so competition will be diminished for the period of the patent, free market mechanisms changed and unwanted network effects could be amplified.[65] Other costs include the costs of patenting, compliance costs of ensuring non-infringement, costs of uncertainty and litigation costs.[66] To be justified, these negative effects or costs have to be outweighed by the overall positive effects of patents. Two benefits are generally put forward: patents provide an important incentive for innovation; and the requirement of public disclosure enables further innovation by competitors (information function). In short, patents facilitate innovation. Proponents of software patents generally argue that this is as true for software patents as for patents for other inventions and that therefore there is no reason to treat software differently, ie to exclude it from patentability.

Opponents of software patents generally argue that the special nature of software and the economic conditions of the software industry tip the balance towards the adverse effects of monopoly rights and away from the incentives for innovation—which might or might not be found in other areas of equal or greater innovative activity. While the nuances of the argument are complex, it is notable that software innovation proceeded at immense speed for years without any software patents, and the amazing success story of free and open source software[67] hint at the fact that innovation in the area of software is not necessarily linked to proprietary models, suggesting that software is indeed different to other areas of innovation.

As the policy framework underlying software patents is vague, it is perhaps unsurprising that the law designed to express the policy is open to diverging interpretations. That factor, combined with a European patent system that is in need of reform, has resulted in an uncertain legal landscape in Europe for developers, competitors and users alike.

A. The Computer Program Exclusion

In general, a patent may be granted for inventions that are new, involve an inventive step and are capable of industrial application.[68] However, in the UK, as in the rest of Europe, certain subject matter is excluded from

---

[64] R Bakels and PB Hugenholtz, 'The Patentability of Computer Programs. Discussion of European-level Legislation in the Field of Patents for Software' (2002) *JURI* 107–36.

[65] Ibid, 21.

[66] *Aerotel* v *Telco, Macrossan's Application* [2006] EWCA Civ 1371, para 20.

[67] See ch 11.

[68] Patents Act 1977 s 1(1).

patentability including programs for computers *as such*. The relevant provision in the UK Patents Act 1977 states:

> (2) It is hereby declared that the following (among other things) are not inven-
> tions for the purposes of this Act, that is to say, anything which consists of—
>
> . . .
>
> (c) a scheme, rule or method for performing a mental act, playing a game or
> doing business, or a *program for a computer*;
>
> . . .
>
> but the foregoing provision shall prevent anything from being treated as an
> invention for the purposes of this Act only to the extent that a patent or applica-
> tion for a patent relates to that thing *as such*.[69]

It is these two small words 'as such' that have caused problems and inconsistencies in interpretation. Determining what makes the difference between
a patentable invention and a computer program *as such* has become subject
of heated legal debate over the last decades. Since the provisions of the UK
Patents Act 1977 implement a parallel provision in the European Patent
Convention 2000 (EPC), namely Article 52, this debate spans all members
of the EPC, and has been subject of numerous decisions by the European
Patent Office (EPO) and national courts.

Unfortunately, the rationale behind the computer program exemption is
far from clear. There is no evident underlying purpose behind the
exemption provisions in section 1 of the Patents Act 1977, which include
not only a program for a computer but also a scheme, rule or method for
performing a mental act, playing a game or doing business.[70] It would seem
that the categories form a disparate group without a common, overarching
concept.[71] Unfortunately the EPC *travaux préparatoires*—the official record
of the negotiations to the EPC treaty—do not give any further guidance
as to interpretation. As two recent studies of those documents have
revealed,[72] the wording of the exemptions are more a result of various
compromises made throughout the negotiation processes than principled
development. As a result, the framers left many questions to be answered
by the Boards of the EPO.

---

[69] Patents Act 1977 s 1(2) (emphasis added). Note that the wording of the Patents Act differs
from the parallel provision in Art 52(2) and 52(3) EPC. However, this is generally not taken as
having a different meaning (see *Aerotel v Telco, Macrossan's Application* [2006] EWCA Civ
1371, para 6).

[70] Patents Act 1977 s 1(2)(c). S 1(2)(a) a discovery, scientific theory or mathematical methods;
(b) a literary, dramatic musical or artistic work or any other aesthetic creation whatsoever; (d)
the presentation of information.

[71] *Aerotel Ltd v Telco Holdings* [2006] EWCA Civ 1371, see para 9.

[72] J Pila, 'Article 52(2) of the Convention on the Grant of European Patents: What Did the
Framers Intend? A Study of the Travaux Preparatoires' (2005) 36 *International Review of
Intellectual Property and Competition Law* 755; J Pila, 'Dispute over the Meaning of 'Invention'
in Article 52(2) EPC—The Patentability of Computer-implemented Inventions in Europe'
(2005) 36 *International Review of Intellectual Property and Competition Law* 173.

Given the European dimension of the question, the next section will describe briefly the European patent system before turning to discuss the leading decisions of the Boards of the EPO and the courts of the UK, and analysing their interplay.

B. The European Patent System

Patents within Europe are mainly governed by national law. Despite efforts dating back to the 1970s, the Member States of the EU have not managed to agree on a Community Patent System that would allow the grant of one single patent valid throughout the EU and subject to uniform interpretation by a European court.

However, national patent law has been harmonised to a certain level through the EPC[73] which was signed in 1973. The EPC contains substantive provisions on patentability and exclusions, the most important of which for this discussion is Article 52 mentioned above. The EPC also established the EPO. Patent applicants can file a single application with the EPO, which will then be subject to one examination process. If successful, the applicant will obtain a bundle of patents in respect of any number of designated signatory countries. Those patents have the same effect as if granted by the domestic patent offices.

Except for a time-limited post-grant opposition procedure,[74] power over enforcement and revocation of patents is exercised by the national courts which are not bound by the decisions of the EPO (EPC 2000, Article 64).[75] This creates a situation in which a patent granted by the EPO may be found to be valid in one country, but is unenforceable in another because of divergent decisions by national courts. Further, if a patent applicant chooses not to apply for a patent via the EPO but files the application at a national patent office, that patent office will decide on the application according to national law. In the event that the applicant is not happy with the decision of the patent office, an appeal must be made to the national courts. Hence, a patent application can have different outcomes in different European countries. This has resulted in calls for reform which will be described at the end of this chapter after an examination of the leading software patent cases.

---

[73] To be sure, the EPC is not part of EU law, and its members include, apart from the Member States of the EU, Switzerland, Liechtenstein, Turkey, Monaco, Croatia, Former Yugoslav Republic of Macedonia, Norway, San Marino and Iceland.

[74] EPC 2000 Arts 99–105.

[75] I Erdos, 'A Measure to Protect Computer-implemented Inventions in Europe' (2004) 8 *Journal of Information, Law and Technology (JILT)* 1.

C. Software Patent Cases

Over the last decades, a range of approaches regarding the patentability of software has been adopted in Europe, often leading to the same or similar result, albeit based on different reasoning.

In the 1980s, the EPO adopted the position that, while programs for computers as such are excluded from patentability by EPC 2000, Article 52(2), if the claimed subject matter had a technical character it was not excluded from patentability. In one of the leading decisions of the Board of Appeals, *Vicom/Computer-related Invention*,[76] the Board explained its reasoning:

> Generally speaking, an invention which would be patentable in accordance with conventional patentability criteria should not be excluded from protection by the mere fact that for its implementation modern technical means in the form of a computer program are used. Decisive is what *technical contribution* the invention as defined in the claim when considered as a whole makes to the known art.[77]

According to this decision, and a number following on using the same reasoning, claims could be made regarding a computer system when programmed (apparatus claim) and regarding an equivalent method (method claim) provided they had the necessary *technical* character. The method claimed was, in effect, a method performed by a running and suitably programmed computer, and the apparatus claimed was, in effect, a computer programmed to carry out the method.

However, it was not until 1998 that the Board of Appeal first addressed the allowability of claims to computer programs *in themselves* (program claims). Such claims can be important for the patent applicant because in certain circumstances the method and apparatus claim will not provide sufficient protection, eg when the applicant intents to exploit his invention by selling computer programs on disks or by Internet download. Without a computer program claim, only the contributory infringement provisions can be invoked to establish liability.[78] These are based on fault and not strict liability, and no protection is given against production and sale of such programs if they are intended for use abroad. In *IBM/Computer Program Product*,[79] the Board concluded that a program is not excluded from patentability if, when run on a computer, it produces a further technical effect that goes beyond the normal physical interactions between a program and a computer. Hence, the mere *potential* of a program to produce a technical effect when run on a computer is sufficient. The Board found it

[76] [1986] T208/84.
[77] Para 16 (emphasis added).
[78] Patents Act 1977 s 60(2).
[79] [1999] TI173/97.

illogical to grant a patent for both a method and the apparatus adapted for carrying out the same method, but not for the computer program product, which comprises all the features enabling the implementation of the method and which, when loaded in a computer, is indeed able to carry out that method.[80]

Such claims are allowed whether the program is claimed for itself or on a carrier, such as a disk.

In the UK, The Court of Appeal adopted the technical contribution approach of the EPO with the rider that novel or inventive purely excluded matter does not count as 'technical contribution'. This position was developed through the rulings in *Genentech's Patent*,[81] *Merrill Lynch's Application*,[82] *Gale's Application*[83] and *Fujitsu's Application*.[84] In *Merrill Lynch*, the issue was whether an improved data-processing system for implementing an automated trading market for securities was excluded subject matter. Referring to *Vicom*, the Court found that this would be the case if the claimed invention made no technical contribution to the known art. The court added that inventive excluded matter could not count as a technical contribution. While the court recognised that if a computer program produced a new technical effect, it would normally be patentable, it held that the computer system in question did not do so. It was merely a method of doing business and hence not patentable. Similarly, and also referring to *Vicom*, the Court of Appeal in *Gale* considered that 'difficult cases can arise where the computer program, whether in hardware or software, produces a novel technical effect either on a process which is not itself a computing process . . . or on the operation of the computer itself', but held that the claimed invention—an improved way of calculating square roots programmed onto a ROM—was not of that type, and its incorporation in a device having no novelty could not alter this position. In *Fujitsu*, the patent application related to a computer programmed for modelling synthetic crystal structures and displaying the resulting image. Again, the question was whether there was a technical contribution such that the invention consisted of something more than a computer program per se. The court recognised that the boundary line between what was and what was not a technical contribution was not a clear one, and that each case had to be decided on its own facts. In the end, the court concluded that no technical contribution could be found in Fujitsu's system.

However, this concordance between the Boards of the EPO and UK courts turned into open disagreement after the EPO began to change its practice towards the more generous 'any hardware' approach (if the claim involves the use of or is to a piece of physical hardware, however mundane,

---

[80] Para 9.8.
[81] [1989] RPC 147.
[82] [1989] RPC 561.
[83] [1991] RPC 305.
[84] [1997] RPC 608.

EPC 2000, Article 52(2) does not apply) in the 'trio' of decisions, *Pensions Benefit System Partnership*,[85] *Hitachi/Auction Method*[86] and *Microsoft/Data Transfer*.[87]

In *Pensions Benefit*, claims were made for a method and apparatus for controlling a pension benefits program. On the method claim, the question was whether it represented merely a method of doing business as such, or if the method was technical, that would still make it a method of doing business, but not a method of doing business *as such*. The Board held that '[t]he feature of using technical means for a purely non-technical purpose and/or for processing purely non-technical information does not necessarily confer technical character to any such individual steps of use or to the method as a whole' and found that the claimed method, although referring to various computing means, contained only steps having purely adminis-trative, actuarial and/or financial character. It followed that the method was excluded from patentability under EPC 2000 Article 52(2)(c) in combi-nation with Article 52(3). By contrast, the Board treated the apparatus claim quite differently. Because the claimed computer system had the character of a concrete apparatus in the sense of a physical entity, it was not excluded from patentability, and hence it was an invention in terms of EPC 2000 Article 52(1) regardless of the fact that it was programmed for use in the field of business and irrespective of the question as to whether the apparatus had new features not known from prior art. The latter only mattered for the test whether the invention involved an inventive step. Here, the Board found that the improvement envisaged by the invention was essentially economic and therefore could not constitute an inventive step. Hence, in the end, the apparatus claim also failed.

The approach taken in *Pension Benefit* was further refined in *Hitachi*. This case concerned a computerised auction method. Again, a claim was made for a method and an apparatus. Following *Pensions Benefit*, the apparatus was not considered excluded subject matter because it comprised technical features such as a server, client computers and a network. With regard to the method claim, the Board expressly disagreed with the approach taken in *Pension Benefit* and argued that method and apparatus claim should be treated in the same way. Hence they came to the conclusion that 'a method involving technical means is an invention within the meaning of Art 52(1) EPC'. The Board recognised that its broad inter-pretation of the term 'invention' covers trite activities such as writing using pen and paper, but pointed out that this does not make all methods involving technical means patentable as they still have to meet all other requirements for patentability. For the assessment of the inventive step,

[85] [2000] T931/95.
[86] [2004] T258/03.
[87] [2006] T424/03

only those features which contribute to a technical character would be taken into account. Because the technical features of the auction system in question did not constitute an inventive step, the Board refused the application.

Microsoft Data Transfer is the last case in the trio and confirms the approach taken in *Hitachi*. This case concerned a method of facilitating data exchange between different programs running on a computer using an enhanced clipboard. Because the claimed method used technical means, ie was implemented on a computer, it was held to be an invention within the meaning of Article 52(1) EPC 2000. In relation to the product claims, the Board found that a program on a computer-readable medium has technical character because it relates to a technical product. However, *Microsoft Data Transfer* differs from *Hitachi* as the Board gave no express indication of whether it only considered features with technical character when assessing the inventive step.

What impact did these recent decisions of the EPO have in the UK? In the conjoined appeals in *Aerotel v Telco, Macrossan's Application*,[88] the Court of Appeal considered the different approaches taken and dismissed the EPO's 'any hardware' approach (which had previously been rejected by the Court of Appeal in *Gale*) and observed that it was bound by earlier decisions in *Merrill Lynch, Gale* and *Fujitsu*. According to *Aerotel/Macrossan*, the following approach should be taken:

- Properly construe the claim.
- Identify the actual [or alleged] contribution.
- Ask whether the contribution falls solely within excluded subject matter.
- Check whether the actual or alleged contribution is actually technical in nature.

This test is a reformulation of the 'technical effect approach' as laid down in *Merrill Lynch*, with the third step being the application of the 'as such' qualification.

Not only did the Court of Appeal find the decisions of the EPO in the trio 'mutually contradictory', but in addition it found that the EPO Board wrongly took a narrow view of what was meant by 'computer program' in Article 52 EPC 2000—the narrow view being that computer programs, as an abstract conception, are just a set of instructions. The correct and wider view, according to the Court of Appeal, was that a computer program also encompasses the instructions contained on the media such as the computer disk. The court argued that the narrow view 'render[s] the exclusion without real content', which contrasts with the intention of the framers of the EPC 'to exclude computer programs in a practical and operable form'.

However, the Court of Appeal in *Aerotel/Macrossan* clearly did not want

---

[88] [2006] EWCA Civ 1371.

to be antagonistic, and sought to find common ground with the EPO. The Court of Appeal formulated a series of questions to be asked of an Enlarged Board of Appeals:

> (1) What is the correct approach to adopt in determining whether an invention relates to subject matter that is excluded under Article 52?
>
> (2) How should those elements of a claim that relate to excluded subject matter be treated when assessing whether an invention is novel and inventive under Articles 54 and 56?
>
> (3) And specifically:
>
> (a) Is an operative computer program loaded onto a medium such as a chip or hard drive of a computer excluded by Article 52(2) unless it produces a technical effect? If so, what is meant by 'technical effect'?
>
> (b) What are the key characteristics of the method of doing business exclusion?

In 2006 the Board of Appeal of the EPO delivered a decision[89] in which it criticised the approach taken in *Aerotel/Macrossan* and seemed to suggest that the Court of Appeal failed to apply Article 52 EPC 2000 in good faith.[90] The Board emphasised that the requirements of invention, novelty, inventive step and susceptibility of industrial application are separate and independent criteria. Therefore, the examination as to the existence or otherwise of an invention within in the meaning of Article 52 should not be mixed up with other patentability requirements as was the case with the *Aerotel/Macrossan* approach. The Board considered that the approach was irreconcilable with the EPC and suggested that it was rooted in a layman's concept of invention, being a novel and often inventive contribution to the known art.

The divergence between the UK and the EPO was aggravated by a change of practice in the UK Intellectual Property Office (UKIPO). After *Aerotel/Macrossan*, the UKIPO issued a set of guidelines, stating that

> the Office takes the view that *Aerotel/Macrossan* must be treated as a definitive statement of how the law on patentable subject matter is now to be applied in the United Kingdom (UK). It should therefore rarely be necessary to refer back to previous UK or EPO case law.

The guidelines went on to discourage applications for programs in themselves: 'whilst examiners will continue to assess each case on its merits, it seems likely that few claims to programs in themselves (or programs on a carrier) will pass the third test'.[91] As a result, the UKIPO declined numerous software patent applications, resulting in a number of appeals against those decisions.

---

[89] Duns Licensing Associates/Estimating sales activity [2006] T154/04.

[90] For a discussion of the decision, see N Gardner and P England, 'European Union: Patents—Exclusion from Patentability' (2008) 30 *EIPR* 5–6.

[91] Patent Office Practice Note [2007] RPC 8.

Six of these appeals were joined in *Astron Clinica Ltd & Others v The Comptroller General of Patents, Designs and Trade Marks*.[92] In its ruling in January 2008, the England and Wales High Court tried to reconcile—at least in part—what seemed to be an outright clash between the UK and the EPO. The court argued that there was nothing in *Aerotel/Macrossan* that prohibited the patentability of computer programs as such and reached the conclusion

> that claims to computer programs are not necessarily excluded by Article 52. In a case where claims to a method performed by running a suitably programmed computer or to a computer programmed to carry out the method are allowable, then, in principle, a claim to the program itself should also be allowable. I say 'in principle' because the claim must be drawn to reflect the features of the invention which would ensure the patentability of the method which the program is intended to carry out when it is run.[93]

The court held that the hearing officer at the UKIPO erred in law when he rejected the claims in all six cases.

In *Symbian Ltd v Comptroller-General of Patents*,[94] the Court of Appeal took a similar view to the England and Wales High Court in *Astron Clinica*. This case concerned an improved method for accessing a dynamic link library on a computing device such as a mobile phone. A dynamic link library is a collection of small programs which deal with general computer functions and which can be used by other programs on the machine. The prior art of linking to those subroutines was either to link by name or link by ordinal. Both methods have disadvantages: linking by name requires more memory and time to process, while linking by ordinal is prone to errors when functions of the link library are added or modified. Symbian's contribution to the prior art was to split the link library into a section of existing functions, which would be linked by ordinals, and a section for added functions, which would be linked by name. With this method, the computer would run faster without sacrificing reliability.

The court confirmed that *Aerotel/Macrossan* did not represent a departure from the existing domestic law and that the approach in *Aerotel/Macrossan* should lead to the same results as the approach taken in previous decisions. Hence, the fundamental question ought to be whether the invention is a technical contribution to the state of the art, and the best guidance for answering this question is to be found in *Vicom*. The court held that Symbian's new method of linking was a technical contribution to the state of the art because it solved a technical problem within the computer itself—a computer programmed according to that method is a faster

---

[92] [2008] EWHC 85 (Pat). For a case discussion, see D Pearce, 'Astron Clinica: Computer Program Product Claims in UK Patents' (2008) 18 *Computers and Law* 4 February.
[93] Para 51.
[94] [2008] EWCA Civ 1066.

and more reliable computer. Hence, the court found that the invention was patentable.

So while *Symbian* may have clarified what had been blurred by *Aerotel/Macrossan* and its interpretation by the UKIPO, it could neither hide the difficulties in trying to reconcile all of the prior decisions, nor could it hide the fact that the application of the technical contribution criterion remains challenging in practice. One further noteworthy case decided by a hearing officer in the UKIPO suggests *Aerotel/Macrossan* may not have changed the law as much as some commentators have thought it has—at least as regards practice of hearing officers in the UKIPO.

A patent application by Kabushiki Kaisha Toshiba concerned a mechanism for calculating the optimum routing for cables used in large industrial plants. The hearing officer decided that the contribution fell within excluded subject matter, being a combination of a mathematical method, mental act and a program for a computer as such. In so doing she said:

> The interpretation of section 1(2) has recently been given further consideration by the Court of Appeal in *Symbian Ltd's Application* [2008] EWHC Civ 1066. Symbian arose under the computer program exclusion, but as with Aerotel, the Court gave guidance of a more general nature on section 1(2). Although the Court approached the question of excluded matter primarily on the basis of whether there was a technical contribution, it was quite clear (see paragraphs 8–15 of the decision) that the structured four-step approach to the question in Aerotel was never intended to be a new departure in domestic law; that it remained bound by its previous decisions which rested on whether the contribution was technical; and that any differences in the two approaches should affect neither the applicable principles nor the outcome in any particular case. Indeed the Court at paragraph 59 considered its conclusion in the light of the Aerotel approach. It therefore remains appropriate for me to apply the Aerotel test, but with due regard to the clarification that Symbian provides as to when a computer program makes a technical contribution.

Following the delivery of the *Aerotel/Macrossan* judgement by the Court of Appeal, there was some correspondence between Lord Justice Jacob in the Court of Appeal and Alain Pompidou, the then President of the EPO. M Pompidou wrote to Jacob LJ in February 2007, stating that at that time there was not a proper legal basis for the referral to the Enlarged Board of Appeals as suggested by Jacob LJ because there were not enough differences between the current Board of Appeal decisions relating to Article 52 EPC 2000 exclusions and those of the domestic court. This position was not shared by Alain Pompidou's successor, Alison Brimelow from the UK. In a letter in October 2008 she referred a number of questions to the Enlarged Board of Appeal,[95] questions that have been described by some commentators as being key to resolving the differences between EPO and

[95] G 3/08, Official Journal EPO 1/2009, 32.

domestic practice and for clarifying the law in this area. The questions were broadly as follows:

Question 1: Claim category

Can a computer program only be excluded as a computer program as such if it is explicitly claimed as a computer program?

Question 2: Claim as a whole

(a) Can a claim in the area of computer programs avoid exclusion under Article 52(2)(c) and (3) merely by explicitly mentioning the use of a computer or a computer-readable data storage medium?
(b) If question 2(a) is answered in the negative, is a further technical effect necessary to avoid exclusion, said effect going beyond those effects inherent in the use of a computer or data-storage medium to respectively execute or store a computer program?

Question 3: Individual features of a claim

(a) Must a claimed feature cause a technical effect on a physical entity in the real world in order to contribute to the technical character of the claim?
(b) If question 3(a) is answered in the positive, is it sufficient that the physical entity be an unspecified computer?
(c) If question 3(a) is answered in the negative, can features contribute to the technical character of the claim if the only effects to which they contribute are independent of any particular hardware that may be used?

Question 4: The activity of programming

(a) Does the activity of programming a computer necessarily involve technical considerations?
(b) If question 4(a) is answered in the positive, do all features resulting from programming thus contribute to the technical character of a claim?
(c) If question 4(a) is answered in the negative, can features resulting from programming contribute to the technical character of a claim only when they contribute to a further technical effect when the program is executed?

The Board invited observations by third parties—an exercise that closed at the end of April 2009 and the results of which are available on the EPO website. At the time of writing (May 2009) perhaps unsurprisingly no further comment from the EPO had yet been forthcoming. A number of those who submitted briefs[96] challenged the legal basis on which the exercise had been undertaken. While this is of course important, it is perhaps to be hoped that the matter will be given the attention it deserves in order to clarify this area of the law for the benefit of all stakeholders.

D. Reform of the Patent System

It has become clear that there is a significant level of legal uncertainty across Europe in the field of software patents. Not only does this result in major costs,[97] but it can also put many small and medium-sized enterprises at a disadvantage as they may be unaware of what could be patented to their benefit.[98] Most software patents granted by the EPO are granted to non-European companies, putting European companies at a competitive disadvantage.[99]

Despite this uncertainty, attempts to clarify and harmonise the rules relating to the patentability of software in Europe have proved more difficult than might have been anticipated. The imperative to make a choice as to the level of protection to be granted to software by patent law within a broad spectrum of possibilities inevitably focuses the political debate on the key question as to whether software patents are desirable in Europe or not.[100] In this discussion, references to and comparisons with the US software industry and US patent system are inevitable.

In 1999 the European Commission commissioned a study on 'The Economic Impact of Patentability of Computer Programs',[101] which addressed, inter alia, the question of whether Europe should extend the scope of software patentability. While this study tended to suggest a positive response to this question, patent advocates and adversaries clashed. Plans to expand patent protection for software were scaled back and instead the European Commission focused on the problems of legal uncertainty and diversity. A proposal for a Directive on the Patentability of Computer-Implemented Inventions[102] (CII Directive) was published in February 2002.

---

96 Eg Joseph Straus, Re: Case No G3/08, Referral of the President of the European Patent Office under Article 112 (1) (b) EPC of October 22, 2008, Statement According to Article 11 b Rules of Procedure of the Enlarged Board of Appeal.

97 A Duffus, 'The Proposal for a Directive on the Patentability of Computer-implemented Inventions' (2002) 16 *International Review of Law, Computers & Technology* 337.

98 L Egitto, 'Certifying Uncertainty: Assessing the Proposed Directive on the Patentability of Computer Implemented Inventions' (2004) 9 *JILT* 7.

99 Ibid.

100 For an overview, see A Guadamuz, 'The Software Patent Debate' (2006) 1 *Journal of Intellectual Property Law & Practice* 196–206.

101 Study Contract ETD/99/B5-3000/E/106.

102 Proposal for a Directive of the European Parliament and the Council on the Patentability of Computer-Implemented Inventions, COM(2002) 92.

Because the EPC is not part of EU law, the CII Directive would have the left the EPC unchanged, but it would have bound the courts of the EU Member States to interpret national and European patents in accordance with the Directive.[103] The Directive did not aim to make major changes to substantive law. Instead, the idea was to reinforce the 'technical contribution' criterion.[104] However, as no clear definition of 'technical' could be devised, the question was raised as to whether the Directive would have substantially decreased legal uncertainty, or whether it would have merely codified uncertainty.[105] At the end of the co-decision procedure involving the European Parliament and the European Commission, the Parliament rejected the common position in the second reading in June 2006, thus putting an end to this proposal. Subsequently the European Commission declared that it would respect this decision and would not present a new proposal covering the same area, unless the Parliament invited it to do so.

Whether this was a real victory for the software patent opponents is questionable since the rejection only confirmed the status quo as defined by the relatively liberal practice of the EPO. Nevertheless, it was a voice that could be heard across the Atlantic. US computer magazines put out headlines such as 'Europe Votes for Innovation—Action Could Change the Patent Landscape Here, Too',[106] and commented 'in the light of the European Union's ruling not to grant patents on software, it is time for the US to give serious though to revamping its patent system'.[107]

Next to the failed CII Directive, two other efforts at harmonising European patent law deserve mention: the Community Patent and the effort to establish a European patent court. Although neither of those specifically target software patents, they are nevertheless likely to solve some of the issues.

The endeavours to create a Community Patent reach back to the 1970s. Unlike the patents granted under the EPC, the Community Patent would not just be a bundle of national patents subject to enforcement by national courts, but an independent patent right effective throughout Europe and subject to a unitary European jurisdiction. This would solve the current problem that under the EPC revocation of a patent after expiry of the nine-month opposition period, and enforcement of patents, must be carried out through national courts in individual countries. This can not only be very costly and time consuming if carried out in several countries, but can also lead to different outcomes depending on the views of the national

---

103 R Bakels and PB Hugenholtz, 'The Patentability of Computer Programs. Discussion of European-level Legislation in the Field of Patents for Software' (2002) *JURI* 107–31.

104 C Koboldt, 'Much Pain for Little Gain? A Critical View of Software Patents' (2003) 8 *JILT* 1.

105 Egitto, above n 98, 4.

106 J Rapoza, 'Europe Votes for Innovation' [2005] *eweek* 40 (18th July).

107 PJ Britt, 'Patently Absurd? Report Calls for Patent System Revamp' [2006] *EContent* 11 (January/February).

courts. The latter is an especially pressing issue for software patents as the application of existing patent law is—as seen above—far from uniform in this area. However, despite ongoing efforts over decades, no agreement has yet been reached.

To circumnavigate the unresolved issues surrounding the Community Patent, the slightly less ambitious route has been to establish a European patent court—the subject of the European Patent Litigation Agreement (EPLA). The EPLA seeks to improve the enforcement of European patents, enhance legal certainty and promote the uniform application and interpretation of European patent law through the creation of a single European patent court with exclusive jurisdiction over European patents. The agreement was drafted by the Working Party on Litigation set up by the Contracting States of the European Patent Organisation in 1999. However, the political future of this proposal remains to be seen. The EPLA is very controversial among proponents and opponents of software patents. The EPO is one of the leading proponents of the treaty and believes that '[I]n a clear and direct way, *all* patent holders in Europe would benefit from the EPLA, as well as competitors seeking to challenge patents and also the general public at large.'[108] In contrast, the Foundation for a Free Information Infrastructure (FFII) sees in the EPLA a vehicle to make software patents granted by the EPO 'outside its competence' enforceable.[109] In 2007, the European Commission put forward a new proposal on a Unified Patent Litigation System (UPLS) inspired by the EPLA proposal. The latest step in this is the recommendation from the Commission to the Council to authorise the Commission to open negotiations for the adoption of such an agreement.[110] Whether and when this initiative might progress remains to be seen.

V. OUTLOOK

Given the speed of change in software development and the industry, it is clear that the applicable elements of the intellectual property regime should be kept constantly under review. Although software has now been a feature of our daily lives for several decades, as has been seen, the intersection between intellectual property law and the protection of software is far from clear, particularly in the field of patents. What is clear is that we are a long way from being at the end of developments in this field—either legal or technical. The coming years should prove to be most challenging and interesting.

---

[108] http://www.epo.org/topics/issues/eply.html.
[109] http://epla.ffii.org/analysis.
[110] Recommendation from the Commission to the Council to authorise the Commission to open negotiations for the adoption of an Agreement creating a Unified Patent Litigation System, SEC(2009) 330.

11

Free and Open-Source Software

ANDRÉS GUADAMUZ

I. INTRODUCTION

PERHAPS NO OTHER software-related topic is more written about, and more misunderstood, than that of free and open-source software (FOSS). The size of the software market is a good indication of the economic importance of software. For 2006, the total information technology (IT) market encompassed US$1.16 trillion, of which software made up US$394 billion.[1] While most of the market belongs to commercial and or proprietary software,[2] the growing importance of computer programs developed through non-traditional means is palpable. Not only has open-source software become a recognisable phenomenon outside of the techno-enthusiast circles, but some open-source programs such as Firefox have achieved a surprisingly high level of market penetration.[3] Google is the largest corporate user of FOSS in the world, and their developers are known to often state that 'Every time you use Google, you're using Linux.'[4]

Given the commercial relevance of software, the written instructions which make up a computer program, generally known as source code, have become a valuable commodity. The complexity and cost of a program can be measured in terms of its source lines of code (SLOC), which give an estimate of the amount of programming time required to create the product. A commercial operating system can have as many as 40 million SLOC, and is developed by a team of 1,800 programmers.[5] By contrast, Debian 3.0, an open-source operating system, is said to have 105 million SLOC, and has been developed by a multinational community without a

---

[1] Business Software Alliance, Research and Statistics, http://www.bsa.org/country/Research%20and%20Statistics.aspx.

[2] See below, p 366.

[3] Sixteen per cent of the total browser market as of February 2008, according to thecounter.com, see: http://www.thecounter.com/stats/2008/February/browser.php.

[4] C DiBona, 'Joining OIN', Google Blog (2007), http://googleblog.blogspot.com/2007/08/joining-oin.html.

[5] V Maraia, *The Build Master: Microsoft's Software Configuration Management Best Practices* (Indianapolis, IN, Addison-Wesley, 2005) 78.

commercial strategy.[6] Given such costly endeavour, open-source software development seems a counter-intuitive method of coding software. So why does it still exist? Why do thousands of programmers give their time to release source code to the wider community? And most importantly, how is it achieved? What are the legal implications of such a development method? This chapter will address some of these questions.

II. A BRIEF HISTORY OF FOSS

FOSS can be traced back to the creation of the Unix operating system[7] which was developed between 1969 and 1970 by a small team at AT&T Bell Labs.[8] AT&T had been the subject of an antitrust suit in 1949, which resulted, amongst other things, in the signing of a consent decree in 1956 to settle the suit in accordance with stipulations established by the Sherman Antitrust Act.[9] This consent required the company to reveal any patents it held and to license them to competitors. The practical effect of this was that AT&T could not profit from its work on Unix. It disbanded the team that had been developing the operating system and started selling it cheaply and with no guarantees, support or bug fixes of any kind.[10] As the source code was made available, this prompted users to band together and start working on fixes to known problems.[11] In 1974, AT&T was the subject of yet another antitrust suit, which resulted in it parting company with the Bell part of the enterprise, allowing it to commercialise Unix. Eventually, the company released a definitive version of the software in 1979, increased its price and ceased making the source code available to the public.[12]

During this process, and as early as 1973, the software had been rewritten to accommodate new hardware variations. Changes were constantly made by different teams within Bell Labs and the wider academic community—notably from the University of California at Berkeley. It was this unique environment of sharing between experts leading to the creation of Unix which set the tone for the future evolution of the free software and open-source movements.[13]

---

[6] JJ Amor et al, 'Measuring Woody: The Size of Debian 3.0' (2004) 5(10) *Reports on Systems and Communications* 1.

[7] An operating system, eg MS-DOS, UNIX, Linux, OSX or Windows, is a computer program that allows a computer to run; it serves as the basic interface between the user and the computer.

[8] G Moody, *Rebel Code: Linux and the Open Source Revolution* (London. Penguin, 2002) 13.

[9] Ch 647, 26 Stat 209, 15 USC s 1–7.

[10] Ibid, 14–16.

[11] J Naughton, *A Brief History of the Future* (London, Weidenfeld & Nicholson, 1999) 172–74.

[12] HE Pearson, 'Open Source: The Death of Proprietary Systems?' (2000) 16(3) *Computer Law & Security Report* 151–56.

[13] Moody, above n 8, 5–12.

The 1980s saw the culmination of the development of Unix. Many companies started selling their own versions of the operating system, and the academic community began distributing its own version called Berkeley Software Distribution (BSD).[14] In 1984, a software developer named Richard Stallman, who had been involved with MIT, formed the Free Software Foundation (FSF) to support the nascent ideas of sharing information in the shape of developing free software and to accommodate the GNU[15] project.[16] The 1980s saw the development of software under the auspices of the FSF, encouraging the sharing of code between developers who had never met each other. The FSF had been attempting to generate a new Unix system, but they were missing some key components, notably a kernel,[17] for their operating system.[18]

The movement gained mainstream recognition in 1990 with the development of a new Unix-based kernel[19] called Linux. This began as a hacker project by Finnish programmer, Linus Torvalds. He had been waiting for the developments coming from the FSF relating to their Unix-based clone system, but was impatient and wanted to run it right away. The fact that the FSF had not created a kernel prompted Torvalds to develop his own. He called it Linux and placed it on the Internet for free, asking programmers to improve it.[20] Torvalds secured feedback from other programmers by making the source code for the Linux operating system available to be examined by anybody who wished to do so. This led to the development of different versions (known as distributions) of Linux, giving this operating system an unparalleled amount of stability and security, as the community was in charge of its support.

The term 'open source' itself is relatively new; it was coined during a meeting in February 1998 in Palo Alto, California by a group of software developers with links to Linux.[21] The group met to plan a new strategy in response to the ground-breaking announcement by Netscape that it would be opening its operations and providing the source code of its popular Internet browser to the public. Netscape decided to do this prompted by fierce competition from Microsoft.[22] Netscape believed that this gesture

---

[14] MK McKusick, 'Twenty Years of Berkley Unix: From AT&T-owned to Freely Redistributable', in C Di Bona, S Ockman and M Stone (eds), *Open Sources: Voices from the Open Source Revolution* (Sebastopol, CA, O'Reilly & Associates, 1999) 31–46.

[15] GNU is a recursive acronym that means 'GNU is Not UNIX'.

[16] R Stallman, *The GNU Project* (1998), http://www.gnu.org/gnu/thegnuproject.html.

[17] The kernel is the fundamental part of an operating system. It is a piece of software responsible for providing access to the computer's hardware by other software applications.

[18] R Stallman, 'The GNU Operating System and the Free Software Movement', in Di Bona, Ockman and Stone (eds), above n 14, 53–70.

[19] See above n 17.

[20] Moody, above n 8, 31–35.

[21] Open Source Initiative, *History of the OSI* (2001): http://www.opensource.org/docs/history.html.

[22] It may even be said that Microsoft's competitive tactics against Netscape were excessive and even predatory, and they prompted the anti-trust case brought by the US Department of Justice

would give them a precious opportunity to sell the open-source software development approach to the corporate world.[23]

The need to create a term to describe this approach had become pressing. Until then, the most common way to describe output produced through the non-proprietary approach was by using the expression 'free software'. It was apparent to many software developers that this movement had a tarnished reputation in the business world as a result of association with some of the more radical ideas held by people linked to Stallman and the FSF. In short, it was thought that trying to sell a more commercial non-proprietary approach would not work if they kept referring to the work as 'free software'. A more business-friendly philosophy was needed, along with a new name. Hence 'open source' was coined, a term that was considered less ideological.[24] Many developers welcomed the move, helped in great part by the Linux community using the existing network of websites, message boards and magazines.[25] The rest, as they say, is history.

III. KEY CONCEPTS AND DEFINITIONS

A. Common Characteristics of FOSS Licences

It will be clear from the above discussion that there are two names given to open-source developments: free software and open-source software, referred to together by the acronym FOSS. Contrary to popular misconception, it is important to note that FOSS does not necessarily mean free of charge, and it is not a movement opposed to traditional intellectual property protection. In its more general form, FOSS is simply software that is subject to later modifications by the user or other developers by allowing free access to its source code.[26] In this light, non-proprietary software is considered such if it is released under a licence that allows later modifications, also known as 'forks', together with legal documents which enable others to make their own modifications and distribute them accordingly. FOSS licences also allow a wide range of freedoms for consumers that they

against Microsoft. A roadmap to the case can be found here: http://www.stern.nyu.edu/networks/ms/top.html.

[23] Open Source Initiative, above n 21.
[24] Moody, above n 8, 144–55.
[25] Open Source Initiative, above n 21.
[26] Source code is the programming statement expressed in a programming language that exists before the program is compiled into an executable application. The executable form of the software is generally known as the object code, and can only be read by the machine (see Figure 11.1).

Source code	Object code
#!/usr/bin/perl use LWP::Simple; use Math::BigInt; my $html = get my($prime) = $html =~ m{<blockquote>([^<]+)</blockquote>}; $prime =~ tr{0-9}{}cd; $prime = Math::BigInt->new($prime); my $binary = ''; while ($prime > 0) { $binary = pack('N', ($prime % 2**32)) . $binary; $prime /= 2**32; } $binary =~ s{^\0+}{}; local *FH; open(FH, '| gunzip -acq') or die 'cannot gunzip, $!'; binmode FH; print FH $binary;	

Figure 11.1 Source code and object code

would otherwise not have, such as making copies of the work, or installing and distributing the software.

It is important to stress that there are ideological differences in the choice of either open-source or free software. The FOSS acronym is a compromise between the different philosophies. This author prefers the use of the term 'non-proprietary software' as an umbrella definition that refers to the different subcategories encompassed by this movement. It also covers different types of works, from those offered in exchange for payment, to those that are offered freely to the public. This would include works that are in the public domain,[27] something not included in the definitions of open-source software or free software. Another acceptable term is 'libre software'.[28] This leads to another common acronym: free, libre and open-source software (FLOSS).

Having discussed the general definition of the non-proprietary software model, it is necessary to explain how it fits with other types of software

[27] This is software that has been placed in the public domain specifically by their authors, and is known as public domain software to distinguish it from other types. In software development, public domain does not necessarily mean free; it is simply a legal term to refer to works that are not copyrighted. See Free Software Foundation (FSF), *Categories of Free and Non-Free Software* (2008), http://www.fsf.org/licensing/essays/categories.html.

[28] Libre is a word present in various Romance languages that means free as in freedom, not free as in having no monetary cost. For more on this use, see Working Group on Libre Software, *Free Software/Open Source: Information Society Opportunities for Europe?* (2000), http://eu.conecta.it/paper.pdf.

development, particularly commercial software ownership and proprietary software. Proprietary software is usually defined as a computer program, '[the] use, redistribution or modification [of which] is prohibited, or requires you to ask for permission, or is restricted so much that you effectively can't do it freely'.[29] This is the opposite of non-proprietary software, for which there is a possibility of having access to the code and changing it. It must also be stressed that commercial software is a subset of proprietary software, but not all proprietary software is necessarily commercial.

Commercial software is a program that is created specifically to be marketed and sold.[30] There are several types of software that are offered free of charge, but cannot be changed. Examples of this would be freeware and shareware. Freeware is software that is offered to the public free of charge, but cannot be changed in any way because it is protected by copyright and closed so that the user cannot incorporate its programming into anything else they may be developing. Shareware is software distributed free on a trial basis with the understanding that if the user wants to continue using it, they must acquire a licence. Some software developers offer a shareware version of their program with a built-in expiration date (eg after 30 days, the user can no longer get access to the program). Other shareware (sometimes called liteware) is offered with certain capabilities disabled in the hope that the user will buy the complete version of the program.[31] Another type of proprietary software that should not be confused with non-proprietary software is called a demo. This is software that presents a limited edition of a program, distributed at no cost over the internet, usually before the general commercial release of the software. The objective is to promote the program by presenting some of its features in the hope that users will later buy the full version.

B. Free Software

The free software movement is centred on the concepts and philosophies of developing programs and distributing them freely. As described earlier, the term arose from Richard Stallman's own experiences as a programmer in the 1980s. For a while, the term 'free software' was synonymous with the non-proprietary philosophy of software development. As personal computers became widespread, software programmers continued to exchange pieces of code amongst themselves, providing better ways of developing software in a more efficient manner. Sharing code is an efficient way of programming, as it brings together the work and experience of pro-

[29] FSF, see above n 27.
[30] Ibid.
[31] Ibid.

grammers around the globe, reducing costs and making it easier to find errors. Other factors that have served as an important motivation for sharing code stem from the fact that programmers engaged in the movment mostly worked for non-profit organisations and academic institutions. Ownership of the intellectual property was thus less important than it might be now. Stallman described it as follows:

> Whenever people from another university or a company wanted to port and use a program, we gladly let them. If you saw someone using an unfamiliar and interesting program, you could always ask to see the source code, so that you could read it, change it, or cannibalize parts of it to make a new program.[32]

The decision to create the FSF and the GNU project came from the personal disillusionment felt by Stallman after the collapse of the early software-sharing community, and a notable increase in the development of proprietary software. Stallman explains that software began to have restrictions imposed in the shape of proprietary licences telling users they could not access the source code to modify the software, or share it with other people with a view to enhancing its functionality. If the user engaged in any tinkering with the code, then he stopped being a hobbyist and became a pirate.[33] Eventually, Stallman and other like-minded programmers created a powerful software development force under the general principles of non-proprietary software.

Stallman defines free software as having the following four characteristics:

- The freedom to run the program, for any purpose (freedom 0).
- The freedom to study how the program works, and adapt it to your needs (freedom 1). Access to the source code is a precondition for this.
- The freedom to redistribute copies so you can help your neighbor (freedom 2).
- The freedom to improve the program, and release your improvements to the public, so that the whole community benefits (freedom 3). Access to the source code is a precondition for this.[34]

As understood by the proponents of free software, programmers and other developers can charge for the software if it is their desire to do so, but the same underlying freedoms must exist whether or not it is acquired for a monetary fee. The user must still have all of the freedoms described, with access to the source code as the most basic requisite.[35]

According to the GNU project, there are several types of free software, some that conflict with the values advocated by the FSF, and some that do

---

[32] Stallman, above n 16.
[33] *Revolution OS*, directed by JTS Moore (2001).
[34] FSF, *The Free Software Definition* (2007), http://www.fsf.org/licensing/essays/free-sw.html.
[35] FSF, *Selling Free Software* (2006), http://www.fsf.org/licensing/essays/selling.html.

not. The main category is an overarching free software definition, which states that the software qualifies as free software if it 'comes with permission for anyone to use, copy, and distribute, either verbatim or with modifications, either gratis or for a fee. In particular, this means that source code must be available.'[36]

The FSF has promulgated a policy of making available software termed 'free software', stating that the software must follow the philosophy described. If the program comes with too many restrictions, it will not be granted certification. Certain restrictions are acceptable if these are not excessive.[37] One of the main restrictions is that of subsequent licensing, under which software must be maintained as 'free'.

C. Open Source

In its broadest sense, open source is the opposite of 'closed source', the traditional proprietary approach to software development in the commercial world. Closed source is software 'in which the customer gets a sealed block of bits which cannot be examined, modified, or evolved'.[38] The common thread in both free software and open-source software is that the source code remains available for examination, modification and peer review.

As mentioned, the official definition was based on the Debian Free Software Guidelines, a licensing model written by software developer Bruce Perens and which accompanies the Debian GNU/Linux system, a Linux distribution.[39] These existing documents were improved and modified by developer Eric Raymond and form what is known as the 'open-source definition' (OSD). The definition not only requires that open-source software should make available the original code, but also sets the following principles underlying all open-source software:

> *Free Redistribution:* this means the software will have no restrictions regarding further distribution as part of another package.
> *Source Code:* the source code will be made available for examination, either by including the software in the software package or by making it available at a public location.
> *Derived Works:* the licence must allow modifications and the development of derived works.
> *Integrity of The Author's Source Code:* the licence may allow restrictions about changes to the original source code only if the distributor assumes the responsibility of fixing any problem found with the software.

36 FSF, above n 27.
37 Ibid.
38 E Raymond, 'Keeping an Open Mind' [1999] *Cyberian Express* April, http://tuxedo.org/~esr/writings/openmind.html.
39 The guidelines can be found at: http://www.debian.org/social_contract.html#guidelines.

No Discrimination Against Persons or Groups: OSS can be used both for 'abortion clinics and anti-abortion activists'.[40]

No Discrimination Against Fields of Endeavour: the licence will not discriminate the usage of the software for specific fields of work.

Distribution of License: there will be no need for the development of additional licences for those who receive the software from any party other than the licensee.

Licence Must Not Be Specific to a Product: if the software is distributed within a larger software bundle, the software will still be subject to the larger product license.

The Licence Must Not Restrict Other Software: this means that there will not be any restrictions placed on other software being distributed under the same software bundle.[41]

The main characteristic of open source as underpinned by these points is the idea of peer review of a work. By allowing more people access to the code that makes up a program, that software will gain in dependability, stability and security. In the words of Raymond, 'open source puts the software customer in the driver's seat, dramatically lowers total cost of ownership, and is the only recipe that works for high reliability'.[42]

Since the original coining of the term, open source has gained substantial recognition in technical circles. But the success has come at a price. As the term gained more credibility and popularity, there was nothing to prevent a software developer releasing a software program and labelling it 'open source' as a marketing ploy. This was possible without the software actually fulfilling any of the requirements under the definition, or even where it fell into the proprietary category. The lack of an enforcement mechanism prompted several activists to create the Open Source Initiative (OSI) to analyse software licenses and measure them against the OSD, and hence to certify software as genuinely open source.[43] The OSI maintains a public list of all software that it has certified, thus enabling consumers and others to know whether the software they are using is indeed open source.[44]

D. Copyleft

The third most important concept to understand in FOSS licences is that of copyleft. Copyleft is a legal mechanism contained in a licence which maintains the general freedoms awarded to users of software licensed as FOSS,

[40] Interview with Bruce Perens. *Revolution OS*, above n 33.

[41] Open Source Initiative, *The Open Source Definition*, Version 1.9 (2006), http://opensource.org/docs/osd.

[42] Raymond, above n 38.

[43] Open Source Initiative, *Certification Mark* (2006), http://opensource.org/docs/certification_mark.html.

[44] The list is maintained at: http://opensource.org/licenses.

but by acquiring a program released as copyleft, the user agrees that the software will not be used to develop closed-source applications derived from it.[45] This is done via a clause that requires all derivatives arising from the original code to be released under the same freedoms as those under which they were received.

Copyleft was developed from a perceived need to protect the fruits of non-proprietary development. After several years of producing computer programs through sharing expertise and offering the code to the public, some programmers started taking the source code, tweaking it and selling it as commercial proprietary software. Their development costs were thus very low.[46] Copyleft licensing became the only means of stopping companies from profiting from non-proprietary products and then creating products that went against the spirit of the free software movement.

Copyleft is an elegant legal solution that imposes a restriction through a chain of software distribution. The contractual clause ensures the propagation of a licence through that same chain, aptly named 'viral contracts' by Radin, who defines them as 'contracts whose obligations purport to "run" to successor of immediate parties'.[47] These contracts spread in a viral form as the licensee must include the terms of the licence in any subsequent 'fork' distributed because that obligation is part of the contract. Subsequent licensees will have to impose the same contractual terms in further licences they promulgate in perpetuity.

Despite the fact that copyleft licences tend to promote the free software principles and the definitions drafted by the FSF and Stallman, some of the contractual restrictions in copyleft licences have prompted criticism from enterprises and commercial users. Copyleft is a strong tool to keep code open, but it may also prove overly restrictive for enterprises wishing to profit from those derivatives.

IV. FOSS LICENCES

A. Licence Ecology

This chapter has so far described the underlying philosophies and principles that determine the development strategy known as FOSS. These are implemented and enforced through legal documents. Although the definitions and principles are important, one could argue that licences are

---

[45] LE Rosen, *Open Source Licensing: Software Freedom and Intellectual Property Law* (Upper Saddle River, NJ, Prentice Hall, 2004), 105.

[46] FSF, *Copyleft: Pragmatic Idealism* (2005), http://www.fsf.org/licensing/essays/pragmatic.html.

[47] MJ Radin, 'Humans, Computers, and Binding Commitment' (2000) 75(4) *Indiana Law Journal* 38.

the one thing that separates proprietary and non-proprietary software models.

The inclusive nature of the definitions of free and open-source software mean that there is a large number of software licences that fall into one or other camp.[48] At the time of writing, the OSI listed 72 certified licences while the FSF identifies more than 100.[49]

As FOSS licences cover such a broad spectrum, classification is difficult. One could distinguish them as either FSF or OSI certified, but as has been pointed out, there is substantial overlap between the definitions and hence the licences. One way to categorise them is as either copyleft or non-copyleft. The common elements of FOSS licences are:

- *Attribution.* Copyright notices are to be kept intact, and the author(s) will be attributed in the code.
- *Access to the source code.* This is the most basic common element in all licences. The source code will be included either with the distribution, or is to be made available to the public in an open source repository.[50]
- *User rights.* Users are granted a non-exclusive right to use, copy and distribute the work.
- *Derivatives.* All open-source licences allow developers to make modifications to the source code and make those modifications available to the public. This modification may come with restrictions, such as the one present in copyleft licences.

The most basic FOSS licence is the BSD licence,[51] which is short and concise. There are several variations of the licence, evidencing its popularity within the FOSS community. The main part is the assignation of rights, which states:

Redistribution and use in source and binary forms, with or without modification, are permitted provided that the following conditions are met:
—Redistributions of source code must retain the above copyright notice, this list of conditions and the following disclaimer.
—Redistributions in binary form must reproduce the above copyright notice, this list of conditions and the following disclaimer in the documentation and/or other materials provided with the distribution.
—Neither the name of the <ORGANIZATION> nor the names of its contributors may be used to endorse or promote products derived from this software without specific prior written permission.[52]

---

[48] Research by the author has uncovered a total of 129 unique FOSS licences.
[49] Some of them are on both lists. See http://www.fsf.org/licensing/licenses/.
[50] Such as SourceForge, located at http://sourceforge.net.
[51] http://www.opensource.org/licenses/bsd-license.php.
[52] Ibid.

This is a permissive licence with regard to the range of rights granted to the user, as it allows all redistribution of the software both in binary and source code. Other short and elegant OSS licences, eg the MIT licence, take a similar approach.[53]

The most comprehensive non-copyleft, open-source licence is the Apache 2.0 licence,[54] which is more restrictive than both the BSD and MIT licences. This is an important legal document because the Apache Software Foundation produces the Apache HTTP Server software, one of the most widely used open-source programs in the world.[55] The Apache licence maintains the freedom to redistribute the software in binary or source code form, the freedom found in most FOSS licences, but adds the right to create derivative works from the original.[56] The redistribution and modification of the work are allowed provided the copy or derivative work is included with proper attribution of the originator(s) of the program, and that the copyright notices attributing ownership of the code to the original programmers are attached. This approach falls short of the viral clause included in copyleft licences and demonstrates one of the main differences between the licensing models. Another interesting feature included in the Apache licence is the assignment of copyright and grant of patent licence despite the fact that the Apache Software Foundation (drafters of the patent) have stated that that they do not own, and have not applied for, any software patents.[57]

A new development in FOSS licensing is that some developers have been using open licences not originally designed for software. One example is Creative Commons, a project started by Lawrence Lessig following the licensing ideals of FOSS, but directed towards the protection of creative works, such as literary, artistic and musical creations.[58] Although Creative Commons licences are not designed to cover software and source code, there is nothing in the way in which they are drafted that excludes them from being used to licence software.

---

[53] http://www.opensource.org/licenses/apache2.0.php.

[54] See full text at http://www.opensource.org/licenses/apache2.0.php.

[55] As of February 2008, Apache commands 51 per cent of the total web server market, while some competitors, such as Google Server, are based on Apache code. See Netcraft, *February 2008 Web Server Survey* (2008), http://news.netcraft.com/archives/2008/02/06/february_2008 _web_server_survey.html.

[56] In UK law, this would be known as 'adaptations'.

[57] Apache Software Foundation, Apache License v2.0 and GPL Compatibility, http://www. apache.org/licenses/GPL-compatibility.html.

[58] For more about Creative Commons, see N Elkin-Koren, 'What Contracts Can't Do: The Limits of Private Ordering in Facilitating a Creative Commons' (2005) 74(2) *Fordham Law Review* 375; and S Dusollier, 'The Master's Tools v the Master's House: Creative Commons v Copyright' (2007) 29(3) *Columbia Journal of Law & the Arts* 271.

B. GNU General Public Licence Version 2

The GNU General Public License (GPL) is the most important licence in the FOSS movement. At the time of writing, 68 per cent of all projects listed in the SourceForge open-source repository are released under the GPL.[59] But what makes the GPL the licence of choice for non-proprietary development?

The GPL was first drafted in 1985[60] by Richard Stallman in order to accommodate the ideas of free distribution of source code implemented by the FSF.[61] The GPL is the first copyleft licence, and as such is designed to maintain the four freedoms in the FSF definition, but it also contains the copyleft clause.[62] Version 2 of the licence, drafted by Stallman and Moglen, was released in 1991.[63]

The GPL is the legal framework that sustains most of the copyleft system.[64] It reads as a mixture of a legal contract[65] and an ideological manifesto. The preamble to the work restates clearly some of the most common beliefs of free software movement and non-proprietary approach, with several admonitions about the meaning of the word 'free'. The key point is that the source code must be made available to the users. The preamble states:

> For example, if you distribute copies of such a program, whether gratis or for a fee, you must give the recipients all the rights that you have. You must make sure that they, too, receive or can get the source code. And you must show them these terms so they know their rights.[66]

The licence specifies that this is achieved by two means: by protecting the software through copyright; and by providing the users with a licence that gives them the freedom to use and modify the software in any way they see fit if they meet the stated conditions. The main body of the licence reiterates these ideas. Section 1, for example, states:

> 1. You may copy and distribute verbatim copies of the Program's source code as you receive it, in any medium, provided that you conspicuously and appropriately publish on each copy an appropriate copyright notice and disclaimer of warranty; keep intact all the notices that refer to this License and to the absence

---

[59] Out of 73,978 listed projects, 50,013 were released with the GPL. See http://sourceforge.net/softwaremap.

[60] However, the official dating of version 1 is 1989. This is because the GPL was known originally as the EMACS General Public License.

[61] Stallman, above n 18, 59.

[62] Moody, above n 8, 26–29.

[63] Ibid.

[64] The full text of version 2 of the licence can be found at http://www.gnu.org/licenses/old-licenses/gpl-2.0.html.

[65] Some people do not believe that the GPL is a contract, a question that will be discussed in detail later.

[66] FSF, GNU General Public License v2, Preamble.

of any warranty; and give any other recipients of the Program a copy of this License along with the Program.[67]

This section also mentions that the user can make monetary charges when distributing the copy as long as the charges are for expenses in making copies of the software. This is consistent with the general free software characteristic that does not discriminate against commercial software as long as it is not proprietary commercial software.

Many of the provisions of the GPL can be found in other non-proprietary software licences. What makes the GPL different to most others is section 2(b) as this is where the restrictions against using the software to create commercial software are specified. The section reads:

> 2. You may modify your copy or copies of the Program or any portion of it, thus forming a work based on the Program, and copy and distribute such modifications or work under the terms of Section 1 above, provided that you also meet all of these conditions: . . . b) You must cause any work that you distribute or publish, that in whole or in part contains or is derived from the Program or any part thereof, to be licensed as a whole at no charge to all third parties under the terms of this License.[68]

This is the best example of the copyleft clause, as any software developed using the open-source code of the program must ensure that the GPL is transferred to further users of the derivative software. As evidenced by the widespread adoption of the GPL version 2, this is indeed a viral licence because derivatives must be released under the same licence, thus ensuring downstream use of the licence terms.[69]

Despite the fact that copyleft licences tend to promote the free software principles and the definitions drafted by the FSF and Stallman, some of the contractual restrictions in licences such as the GPL have come in for criticism from enterprises and commercial users.[70] Despite this, the GPL has stood well against most challenges, as exemplified by its longevity and the relatively small amount of litigation that it has generated.[71]

There is another version of the GPL, called the GNU Lesser General Public License (LGPL).[72] This version is almost identical to the GPL but does not contain a copyleft clause. This is because there is sometimes need for software to interact with non-FOSS code and to do so a non-copyleft

---

[67] Ibid, s 1.

[68] Ibid, s 2(b).

[69] See A Guadamuz, 'Viral Contracts or Unenforceable Documents? Contractual Validity of Copyleft Licenses' (2004) 26(8) *European Intellectual Property Review* 331.

[70] For some criticisms, see A Guadamuz, 'Legal Challenges to Open Source Licences' (2005) 2(2) *SCRIPT-ed* 301.

[71] See JS Miller, 'Allchin's Folly: Exploding Some Myths about Open Source Software' (2002) 20 *Cardozo Arts & Entertainment Law Journal* 491.

[72] http://www.gnu.org/licenses/old-licenses/lgpl-2.1.html.

version is required or else the linking libraries would have to be released under the GPL.

C. GPL Version 3

While the longevity and success of the GPL have been a testament to its legal validity,[73] the FSF felt that it was time for an updated version, giving the opportunity to fine-tune some legal issues and to respond to developments in the free software community. Prior to the release of the draft, Stallman and Moglen identified key issues they believed needed to be addressed by the licence.[74] These were as follows:

- *Internationalise the licence.* While GPL version 2 was drafted with US law in mind, it aimed to meet the international copyright principles present in the Berne Convention.[75] While most issues of enforcement have taken place outside of the US,[76] it was felt that the licence required clarity in international compliance.
- *Standard setting.* Stallman and Moglen argued that the GPL has become an international standard for the FOSS industry, so any update should take this factor into consideration.
- *Responding to changing circumstances.* The FOSS community, and in particular the principles of free software, are faced with new threats, such as patentability of software, trusted computing and digital rights management (DRM). The GPL must change to meet those threats.[77]

So, what is contained in the new licence? There have been some major changes in both style and substance. The GPL has never been known for its conciseness and clarity, so it is unfortunate that version 3 is longer and more opaque than its predecessor.[78] This is a real problem, as even before being updated, the GPL was subject to much differing legal interpretation.[79]

The drafting process was an interesting exercise in governance. The FSF must be commended for the inclusive and open process through which it undertook discussions on drafting. The first draft of the GPL version 3 was

[73] For further legal analysis of its validity, see R Gomulkiewicz, 'De-bugging Open Source Software Licensing' (2002) 64 *University of Pittsburgh Law Review* 75.

[74] E Moglen and R Stallman, 'GPL Version 3: Background to Adoption' (5 June 2005), http://www.fsf.org/news/gpl3.html.

[75] Berne Convention for the Protection of Literary and Artistic Works 1886.

[76] J Höppner, 'The GPL Prevails: An Analysis of the First-ever Court Decision on the Validity and Effectivity of the GPL' (2004) 1(4) *SCRIPT-ed* 662, at http://www.law.ed.ac.uk/ahrb/script-ed/issue4/GPL-case.asp.

[77] Stallman and Moglen, above n 74.

[78] GPL v3: http://www.fsf.org/licensing/licenses/gpl.html.

[79] R Gomulkiewicz, 'General Public License 3.0: Hacking the Free Software Movement's Constitution' (2005) 42(4) *Houston Law Review* 1015, 1034–36.

made available for public discussion in January 2006. The website on which it was made available was open for public comment, and hundreds of notes from the community were shared for all to see. Two more drafts were made available which were the subject of closed and open meetings, conferences and discussion that included stakeholders and GPL users in general. Although the participation was unprecedented in such a drafting exercise, it must be said that the end result seems to have suffered from too much compromise. The text of the GPL version 3 is nearly unreadable in places.

The document which identified the need for a redraft prompted expectations that the GPL v3 would overhaul the protection of GPL software vis-à-vis software patents and it would update the copyleft clause present in the existing section 2(b). Although these are topics covered in the final text, the real surprise came with regards to DRM and in particular technical protection measures (TPMs). The new GPL makes a statement on the future of open-source usage in the entertainment industry by including strong wording against TPMs. One of the most contentious parts is section 3 on DRM:

> No covered work shall be deemed part of an effective technological measure under any applicable law fulfilling obligations under article 11 of the WIPO copyright treaty adopted on 20 December 1996, or similar laws prohibiting or restricting circumvention of such measures.[80]

This paragraph specifically excludes all works distributed under the GPL from the anti-circumvention measures in the WIPO Copyright Treaty[81] (WCT) by stating that the licensed software shall not constitute 'an effective technological protection measure', thus making it inapplicable for protection. In other words, the distribution of derivatives with works that contain certain restrictive types of DRM is prohibited. This is an elegant legal solution to the perceived problem, as it excludes all relevant software from anti-circumvention legislation by contractual means.

Surprisingly, and contrary to what many expected, GPL version 3 seems to direct all of its power against TPMs but not software patents. This is perhaps a reflection of the fact that some of the biggest free and open-source software players in the US are acquiring patents as well.[82] Stallman and Moglen seem pragmatic regarding software patents and recognise that FOSS developers may be involved in complex patent licensing transactions. Hence their implicit recognition of the status quo.[83]

---

[80] S 3 of GPL v3.

[81] Specifically, Art 1 WCT, which states that 'Contracting Parties shall provide adequate legal protection and effective legal remedies against the circumvention of effective technological measures.'

[82] Apache, IBM and Novell have applied for thousands of software patents in the US. For more about this, see A Guadamuz, 'The Software Patent Debate' (2006) 1(3) *Journal of Intellectual Property Law & Practice* 196.

[83] See their draft rationale at http://gplv3.fsf.org/rationale.

Version 3 expands on the implicit patent licensing in GPL version 2, making it an explicit patent grant in section 11. The new patent grant reads:

> Each contributor grants you a non-exclusive, worldwide, royalty-free patent license under the contributor's essential patent claims, to make, use, sell, offer for sale, import and otherwise run, modify and propagate the contents of its contributor version.

In addition to this, GPL version 3 adds paragraphs relevant to patents that are drafted with specific issues in mind. In particular, there is a paragraph that seems to be drafted to respond to patent licence agreements between Microsoft and some FOSS developers, such as Novell.[84] Another issue-specifc section relates to so-called Tivoisation of code, which is an existing loophole present in previous versions by which modified code released under the GPL is distributed to the public but locked using hardware (such as the copyleft code contained in TiVO players).[85]

These drafting practices are, in the author's opinion, the biggest problem with the GPL. A document that is supposed to act as the constitution of the free software ideals should not be bogged down in these details.

Another big change in GPL version 3 is that it revamps the old copyleft section 2(b). As explained earlier, under the current GPL the copyleft aspects only apply to derivative works that are distributed to the public. In other words, you take a work under the GPL, change it and then distribute your own adaptation. Then you have to redistribute it under the GPL. This simple rule generally resulted in clear-cut cases in which the GPL would apply, and those where it would not. For example, imagine that a hardware developer creates a driver module that interacts with the Linux kernel (distributed under the GPL). It is not part of the kernel, but it interacts with it. Under GPL version 2, it is clear that this module is not a derivative, and therefore it does not need to be distributed under the GPL.

What happens with GPL version 3? The situation with derivatives is less straightforward. The copyleft section in the new GPL has been given a boost. Users and developers still have the right to install and use GPL software without restrictions. Developers also have the right to privately modify the software, unless they have initiated a patent suit 'against anyone for making, using or distributing their own works based on the Program'. The problem is that of modifications that are distributed. Consider section 5(c) (the old section 2.b):

---

[84] This is the Patent Cooperation Agreement—Microsoft & Novell Interoperability Collaboration, signed October 2006, see http://www.microsoft.com/interop/msnovellcollab/patent_agreement.mspx.

[85] C O'Riordan, 'Tivoisation Explained—Implementation and Harms', FSF Europe Briefing paper (December 2006).

(c) You must license the entire work, as a whole, under this License to anyone who comes into possession of a copy. This License will therefore apply, along with any applicable section 7 additional terms, to the whole of the work, and all its parts, regardless of how they are packaged. This License gives no permission to license the work in any other way, but it does not invalidate such permission if you have separately received it.[86]

This would certainly apply to anyone who includes any sort of modification of code into her work. Imagine, for example, that you include modified modules from the Linux kernel in your work so as to be compatible with the kernel. An initial reading of section 5(c) would lead one to believe that the entire program would need to be licensed under the GPL. However, there is an exception for compilations. Section 5 reads in a later paragraph:

A compilation of a covered work with other separate and independent works, which are not by their nature extensions of the covered work, and which are not combined with it such as to form a larger program, in or on a volume of a storage or distribution medium, is called an 'aggregate' if the compilation and its resulting copyright are not used to limit the access or legal rights of the compilation's users beyond what the individual works permit. Inclusion of a covered work in an aggregate does not cause this License to apply to the other parts of the aggregate.[87]

This seems like excessive protection. The wording generates legal uncertainty—something picked up by commentators of the draft.[88] The paragraph tries to rationalise specific cases in which the revamped GPL copyleft section will apply by inventing a new definition as to what a compilation is. Software distributed in the same distribution medium has to be GPL if it is a 'compilation', but not if it is an 'aggregate'. Why create the new terminology?

All of the above points make for an interesting legal mechanism, but one that seems unnecessarily complex. Those developing small and medium FOSS projects looking for a licensing scheme may very well think twice about migrating to the new version. Although the licence was issued last year, adoption has been slow. According to a survey by Evans Data, by September 2007 only 6 per cent of FOSS projects had migrated to GPL version 3. More worryingly, 43 per cent of respondents claimed that they would never implement the new licence.[89] Time will tell if this approach is maintained.

[86] S 5(b) GPL v3.
[87] S 5 GPL v3.
[88] For a series of comments, see: http://gplv3.fsf.org/comments/.
[89] E Corradetti, 'Open Source Developers Staying Away From GPLv3, New Evans Data Survey Shows', Evans Data Corporation (25 September 2007), http://www.evansdata.com/press/viewRelease.php.

V. SOME LEGAL ISSUES

A. Contract or Licence? The Problem with Consideration

The issue of the legal nature of open-source licences has generated controversy in legal circles. Some FOSS proponents, particularly those in the free software camp, are adamant that FOSS licences are not contracts, but copyright licenses. This may seem like an arcane legal distinction, but it raises important questions about enforcement, jurisdiction, applicable law and even about the validity of the licence. There may also be different legal effects in some jurisdictions depending on whether a contract is a contract for sale of goods, or a contract for sale of services.[90]

A licence documents a legal relationship through which the licensee is granted permission to perform acts that could not otherwise be done legally. When one buys commercial software, the licence allows the licensee to install a copy of the program on a computer—an act that would otherwise infringe copyright. In some jurisdictions, licences are contracts, and are classified as a specific type of contractual obligation. However, in other countries, licences are not contracts.

The question at the heart of this dichotomy between contracts and licences rests on the issue of reciprocity, known in common law jurisdictions as consideration.[91] A typical argument is presented by FOSS advocate and blogger Pamela Jones, when she asks: 'Why isn't it a contract? Because there are no further agreed-upon promises, no reciprocal obligations.' [92] The lack of reciprocity is also mentioned by Moglen:

> A contract . . . is an exchange of obligations, either of promises for promises or of promises of future performance for present performance or payment. The idea that 'licenses' to use patents or copyrights must be contracts is an artifact of twentieth-century practice, in which licensors offered an exchange of promises with users: 'We will give you a copy of our copyrighted work,' in essence, 'if you pay us and promise to enter into certain obligations concerning the work.' With respect to software, those obligations by users include promises not to decompile or reverse-engineer the software, and not to transfer the software.[93]

---

[90] For a discussion of a distinction between software as sale of goods or sale of services in software, see A Taubman in the Introduction to this edition and HL MacQueen, 'Software Transactions and Contract Law', in L Edwards and C Waelde (eds), *Law and the Internet: Regulating Cyberspace* (Oxford, Hart Publishing, 1997).

[91] Famously defined in *Currie v Misa* (1875) LR 10 Ex 153 as 'some right, interest, profit or benefit accruing to one party, or some forbearance, detriment, loss or responsibility given, suffered or undertaken by the others'.

[92] See P Jones, 'The GPL Is a License, not a Contract' [2003] *Linux Weekly News* 3 December, http://lwn.net/Articles/61292/.

[93] E Moglen, *Enforcing the GNU GPL* (2001), http://www.gnu.org/philosophy/enforcing-gpl.html.

The problem with this interpretation is that it comes from a jurisdiction-specific analysis of contract law. In most civil law and mixed legal systems, such as Scotland, contracts are present when the requirements of offer and acceptance have been met.[94] This means that unilateral acts can constitute contracts under the appropriate conditions.[95] However, in common law jurisdictions the additional requirement of consideration must be met. This is the reason why Jones and Moglen place so much emphasis on the issue of reciprocity in FOSS licences. It is argued that open-source systems are usually offered for free, which would mean that the important contractual step of consideration is missing. Therefore, FOSS licences should be classified as unilateral legal acts, and not contracts as such.

One could argue, however, that there is consideration in some FOSS licences, particularly in copyleft licences. Risking oversimplification of the rich case-law dealing with consideration and contract formation in common law, one could generalise the concept as one of reciprocity, as has been expressed earlier. If one defines consideration as such, then it would be possible to see how copyleft clauses would fulfil the requirement of consideration in jurisdictions where it is required. Copyleft clauses impose an obligation to release modifications under the same licence as the one under which it was obtained. The contract then would be formed like this: making the software available under a FOSS licence would be the offer, using the software under those conditions would be the acceptance, while consideration would be met by the obligation imposed in the copyleft clause. However, some scholars disagree that copyleft clauses meet the requirement of consideration. Giles, for example,[96] argues that copyleft is, at best, illusory consideration, and has found several cases to support his view. Of note he cites the case *British Empire Films Pty Ltd v Oxford Theatres Pty Ltd,*[97] where the courts found unilateral promises that depended entirely on the will of one of the parties as illusory consideration. As expressed by O'Brian J:

> It is common ground that the plaintiff is obliged to supply nothing, and a supposed consideration which is entirely dependent upon the will of the plaintiff whether it will ever become operative is illusory.[98]

However, this does not seem to be a useful analogy, as the promises dealt with in illusory consideration case-law are very specific, and seem not to translate well into the realm of open-source software. For example, participants in the software development community may have their options

---

[94] HL MacQueen and JM Thomson, *Contract Law in Scotland*, 2nd edn (Edinburgh, Tottel, 2007) 54–56.

[95] Ibid, 56–59.

[96] B Giles, '"Consideration" and the Open Source Agreement' (2002) 49 *NSW Society for Computers and Law*, http://www.nswscl.org.au/journal/49/Giles.html.

[97] [1943] VLR 163.

[98] Ibid, 168.

seriously curtailed if they use copyleft software, as they will be under a very real obligation to release modifications under the same licence as the one under which they received it. True, they may choose not to use the software, but is that not the case in all contracts? In other words, once they have accepted the terms and conditions of the licence by using the software and modifying it, the obligation imposed on them seems very real, and not illusory at all.[99]

The contract/licence dichotomy was discussed at length in a recent case in the United States, *Jacobsen v Katzer*,[100] which dealt precisely with this question.

The case involved Robert Jacobsen, an open-source developer partici-pating in an open-source project called the 'Java Model Railroad Interface' (JMRI), a model train software released under the Artistic License.[101] Jacobsen received a letter demanding licence fee payments from a company named Kamind Associates, owned by Matthew Katzer, which had obtained software patents over model railroad software.[102] Jacobsen decided to pre-empt legal action and sued Katzer first, alleging that the patent was invalid on the grounds of obviousness, and for failure to meet disclosure requirements. He later amended the complaint to include copyright infringement, claiming his software pre-dated Katzer's.

The US District Court for the District of Northern California ruled on a motion to dismiss by the defendants, and on a motion for preliminary injunction from the plaintiff. The District Court granted some of the motions to dismiss, denied others and denied the claim for preliminary injunction. The important part of the decision for the current discussion is the analysis of the copyright infringement claims. The District Court declared that because the software was released to the public online through an open-source licence, there was therefore permission to use the software. The Artistic License is not a copyleft licence: it allows modifi-cation and the creation of derivatives, provided that those doing so doing insert prominent notices on each file, and perform one of the following:

> (a) place your modifications in the Public Domain or otherwise make them Freely Available, such as by posting said modifications to Usenet or an equivalent medium, or placing the modifications on a major archive site such as ftp.uu.net, or by allowing the Copyright Holder to include your modifications in the Stan-dard Version of the Package.
> (b) use the modified Package only within your corporation or organization.
> (c) rename any non-standard executables so the names do not conflict with

---

[99] Credit must go to FOSS legal expert Robert Gomulkiewicz, who explained some of these ideas in an e-mail discussion in the Cyberprof mailing list. Other FOSS experts who come on the side of thinking of the licences as contracts is OSI legal counsel Larry Rosen. See Rosen, above n 45, 59–66.
[100] 2007 US Dist. LEXIS 63568; 535 F 3d 1373 (Appeal).
[101] http://www.opensource.org/licenses/artistic-license.php.
[102] US patent 7,216,836.

standard executables, which must also be provided, and provide a separate manual page for each non-standard executable that clearly documents how it differs from the Standard Version.

(d) make other distribution arrangements with the Copyright Holder.[103]

The District Court made it clear that such restrictions are not copyright restrictions but contractual obligations.

> Based on the both the allegations in the amended complaint and the explicit language of the JMRI Project's artistic license, the Court finds that Plaintiff has chosen to distribute his decoder definition files by granting the public a non-exclusive license to use, distribute and copy the files. The nonexclusive license is subject to various conditions, including the licensee's proper attribution of the source of the subject files. However, implicit in a nonexclusive license is the promise not to sue for copyright infringement. . . . Therefore, under this reasoning, Plaintiff may have a claim against Defendants for breach the nonexclusive license agreement, but perhaps not a claim sounding in copyright. . . . However, merely finding that there was a license to use does not automatically preclude a claim for copyright infringement. . . . The condition that the user insert a prominent notice of attribution does not limit the scope of the license. Rather, Defendants' alleged violation of the conditions of the license may have constituted a breach of the nonexclusive license, but does not create liability for copyright infringement where it would not otherwise exist.[104]

The District Court stated that there should be no presumption of a copyright infringement claim, and that such claim should be proven before the plaintiff can make its case. If the plaintiff cannot provide evidence that such a claim may be successful in court, then Jacobson could only rely on the contractual elements of the licence in order to seek redress—in other words the failure to place attribution notices is not enough to make a copyright claim, only a contractual one. Interestingly, the District Court understood perfectly the trade-off in open-source licences that rests at the very heart of the contract/licence dichotomy: if the user complies with the licence, there is permission to use the software, and therefore there is no copyright infringement. But if there is no claim for copyright over the work, the only claim possible is breach of contract.

Katzer appealed the District Court ruling, and it made its way to the Court of Appeals for the Federal Circuit (CAFC), which overturned the decision holding that open-source licences set out permissions to use the work, and if the licence disappears, then the user would be infringing copyright. The ruling makes for interesting reading:

> In this case, a user who downloads the JMRI copyrighted materials is authorized to make modifications and to distribute the materials provided that the user follows the restrictive terms of the Artistic License. A copyright holder can grant the

---

[103] http://www.opensource.org/licenses/artistic-license.php
[104] *Jacobsen*, 2997 WL 2358628 at 7.

right to make certain modifications, yet retain his right to prevent other modifi-cations. Indeed, such a goal is exactly the purpose of adding conditions to a license grant. The Artistic License, like many other common copyright licenses, requires that any copies that are distributed contain the copyright notices and the copying file.[105]

It is heartening that the CAFC has understood the concepts behind open-source licensing. In various passages, it clearly appreciated the basis of the movement and the underlying rights. The CAFC has delivered the high-est instance recognition to open licences—an encouraging sign for FOSS development. The appeal has also pleased many in the FOSS community. For example, the ruling closely follows the reasoning presented an *amicus curiae* arguing against the District Court ruling. In it, the OSI, the Linux Foundation and others argued that 'it would be enormously beneficial to public licensing for this Court to state clearly a rule regarding the impor-tance of interpreting public licenses in a manner consistent with their unique nature and federal copyright policy'.[106]

Despite the final decision in *Katzer*, this author still considers that it is preferable to classify FOSS licences as contracts. Why is the FSF adamant that its licences, in particular the GPL, are not contracts? There are practical reasons why some FOSS proponents insist on licences not having contractual strength. Moglen is on record as stating that the GPL primarily rests on copyright and the international protection awarded by the Berne Convention. He is uneasy with the global variability of contract law, and concerned that a judge in one jurisdiction may impose local contract law interpretations which may affect the project globally.[107] By using copyright instead of contract it is in the licensee's best interest to make sure that the licence is valid as he would otherwise be infringing copyright. Moglen says:

> So all that I do is bring an infringement action. It is the defendant's responsibility to prove license and the only credible license for the defendant to plead is my license, because code is not otherwise available except under that license.[108]

This seems a rather negative view of copyright licensing—as if all use of the licensed work should be considered a priori infringement until proven otherwise. A similar example might be if one invites a guest home, and the moment they enter the premises, trespass is claimed. The invitation can be seen as a unilateral licence allowing the guest to perform an action they

---

[105] Ibid at 13.

[106] AT Falzone and CK Ridder, Brief of Amici Curiae Creative Commons Corporation, the Linux Foundation, the Open Source Initiative, Software Freedom Law Center, Yet Another Society, the Perl Foundation, and Wikimedia Foundation, Inc. in Support of Plaintiff-Appellant and Urging Reversal (2008), http://jmri.sourceforge.net/k/docket/cafc-pi-1/ccc_brf.pdf.

[107] M Hardin, 'Interview Eben Moglen, Legal Counsel, Free Software Foundation', Auskadi Blog (2004), http://auskadi.civiblog.org/blog/_archives/2005/6/25/972325.html.

[108] Ibid.

would not otherwise have a right to do. However, as discussed above in *Jacobsen v Katzer*, there is a real possibility that the user will not have a claim in copyright and so the obligations contained in the licence could only be enforced through contract.

The above analysis is important point if one considers the practicalities in FOSS development. Code is passed between and modified by people all over the world. It is possible to imagine a situation where code has reached a developer in such a modified state that the original owner will no longer be able to claim copyright over it. English courts have considered the minimal amount of code that would be infringing by following the general qualitative test in cases of copying from another work. In both *Richardson Computers v Flanders*[109] and *Ibcos v Barclays*,[110] the courts found that if there had been any copying from a protected original work, there had to be an analysis of whether such copying had been substantial to determine infringement. Even quantitatively minimal copying might be qualitatively substantial. This is evident in the case of *Cantor v Tradition*,[111] where copying of original source code took place from former employees of a financial services company. In this case, expert witnesses found that only 2 per cent of the original source code had been copied, accounting for only 2,952 lines of code out of 77,000. The lines of code were deemed to be of importance for some modules in the resulting software, but the copying was not considered sufficient to find infringement. The copier nonetheless agreed to take financial responsibility for the infringed code and offered to pay for it. One could thus imagine a situation where enough changes have occurred to create a new work—one where the original code would no longer be subject to copyright.

B. Enforcement

Considering there are such large numbers of participants and projects, a surprising feature of FOSS is the very small number of cases that have been brought to court. There are perhaps two reasons. Firstly, FOSS projects are, for the large part, small and medium-sized endeavours, where large numbers of participants only make one-off contributions.[112] The small size of the projects, coupled with the fact that most of the developers are not motivated by profit,[113] means that litigation will not be a priority for developers. As there is a strong sense of community in the open-source

---

109 *John Richardson Computers Ltd v Flanders and Chemtec Ltd* [1993] FSR 497.
110 *Ibcos ComputersLtd v Barclays Mercantile Highland Finance* [1994] FSR 275.
111 *Cantor Fitzgerald International v Tradition (UK) Ltd* [1999] Masons CLR 157.
112 J Lerner and J Tirole, 'Economic Perspectives on Open Source', in J Feller et al (eds), *Perspectives on Free and Open Source Software* (Cambridge, MA, MIT Press, 2005) 55–57.
113 R Ghosh, 'Understanding Free Software Developers: Findings from the FLOSS Study', in Feller et al, above n 112, 34–42.

environment,[114] conflict is usually resolved internally. Second, the FSF has a very effective enforcement body for policing implementation of the GPL called GPL-violations.org.[115] It is a non-profit branch of the FSF which monitors GPL usage, informs the public about infringement, names and shames perpetrators, and, if necessary, issues cease-and-desist letters to the offenders.[116] In an industry that is famously risk-averse, and where profits can be tight, it pays to comply with low-impact enforcement measures such as cease-and desist letters. Similarly, companies that use open-source software rely heavily on the community for updates, bug fixes and for providing interoperability checks. GPL-violations.org serves as an effective mechanism for keeping the community on one's side.

Nonetheless, there has been some litigation involving open source and, particularly, the GPL. The first case involved open-source developer MySQL, the makers of a widely used database software released under the GPL. MySQL brought an action against NuSphere—a software company that it believed was using its source code to produce proprietary software—something which contravenes the terms of the GPL.[117] This suit was filed in response to a claim by NuSphere against MySQL claiming 'breach of contract, tortious interference with third party contracts and relationships and unfair competition'.[118] MySQL's counter-claim was for 'trademark infringement, breach of the interim agreement, breach of the GPL license, and unfair and deceptive trade practices'.[119] This case was settled out of court[120] in an agreement that seems to have suited MySQL as NuSphere agreed to comply with the terms and conditions of the GPL.

The GPL has been the subject of three separate injunctions in German courts. Harald Welte is an open-source developer working for the netfilter/iptables team, which is software used in the Linux kernel. Welte is also one of the main supporters of GPL-violations.org. Part of his strategy has been to file complaints in German civil courts to help with enforcement strategies. The first injunction was filed in 2004 against network equipment manufacturer Sitecom.[121] Welte claimed that Sitecom offered a wireless network router which operated with firmware containing netfilter software

---

114 C Kelty, 'Trust among the Algorithms: Ownership, Identity, and the Collaborative Stewardship of Information', in R Ghosh (ed), *Code: Collaborative Ownership and the Digital Economy* (Cambridge, MA, MIT Press, 2005) 127–31.

115 http://gpl-violations.org/.

116 S O'Mahony, 'Guarding the Commons: How Community Managed Software Projects Protect their Work' (2003) 32(7) *Research Policy* 1179.

117 K Nikulainen, 'Open Source Software: Why Is it Here and Will it Stick Around?' (2004) 1(1) *SCRIPT-ed* 149, http://www.law.ed.ac.uk/ahrc/script-ed/docs/opensource.asp.

118 This, of course, lends credence to the previous discussion about contracts. A FAQ about the case can be found at http://www.mysql.com/news-and-events/news/article_75.html.

119 Ibid.

120 http://www.mysql.com/news-and-events/press-release/release_2002_14.html.

121 Landgericht Muenchen No 21 0 6123/04. An English version of the injunction can be found at http://www.jbb.de/judgment_dc_munich_gpl.pdf.

released under the GPL. Although Sitecom did not modify the software, it did not keep the copyright notices, and it 'closed' netfilter/iptables in that it ceased to offer it under the GPL. The claimants asked the court to order that the defendant ceased

> distributing and/or copying and/or making available to the public the software 'netfilter/iptables' without at the same time . . . making reference to the licensing under the GPL and attaching the license text of the GPL as well as making available the source code of the software 'netfilter/iptables' free of any license fee.[122]

The Munich District Court agreed with the claim and issued the injunction. This case is of tremendous importance for the validity of FOSS licences. Firstly, the Munich District Court recognised that the GPL is valid contract in accordance to German law. Moreover, it upheld the contractual validity of the main clauses, including the copyleft clause.[123]

The second injunction was issued in 2005 also by the Munich District Court in a case also brought by Welte.[124] The complaint was made against Fortinet, a manufacturer of firewall software. Welte and GPL-violations.org claimed that Fortinet was using Linux in its own code without releasing the modifications under the GPL. Interestingly, Welte was able to bring an action against Fortinet when another developer assigned code—called initrid—that was being used by the defendants. The injunction mirrors that issued in Sitecom. Eventually Fortinet settled out of court and announced its compliance with the terms and conditions of the GPL stating that:

> The source for the Linux Operating System Kernel and other GPL licensed components, including Fortinet's modifications, is available upon written request at the cost of CD copying and distribution. Additionally, Fortinet and its partners are providing written copies of the GPL license terms with all Fortinet product shipments.[125]

To conclude Welte's hat-trick, in 2006 he obtained another ruling against network hardware manufacturer D-Link for similar violations, this time in Frankfurt.[126]

While these three victories for the GPL have been widely publicised in FOSS circles, the litigation that made technology news headlines was that of *SCO v IBM*.[127] In March 2003 the SCO Group—a well-known software developer of Unix-related products—filed a lawsuit against IBM alleging that the company was infringing its intellectual property over the Unix kernel. SCO claimed that back in 1985, AT&T and IBM signed a contract to produce a version of Unix called AIX. In 1995, SCO purchased all of the

122 As cited by Höppner, above n 76.
123 For a more detailed analysis of the case, see Höppner, above n 122.
124 Landgericht Muenchen No 21 0 7240/05.
125 http://www.fortinet.com/news/pr/2005/pr042505_gpl.html.
126 Landgereicht Frankfurt No 2-6 0 224/06.
127 *Caldera Sys, Inc v Int'l Bus Machs Corp* (D Utah 2003) (No 03-CV-0294).

intellectual property related to Unix from AT&T, hence the infringement claims. SCO argued that they own part of the code for AIX used in the Linux kernel code included with all Linux distributions. As a result of this action, IBM countersued SCO, claiming that the company has been infringing its (IBM's) copyright and patents, and alleging that SCO was in violation of the GPL because they used and modified the Linux kernel licensed with the GPL.[128]

The case is still ongoing[129] despite the fact that most commentators seem to believe that SCO's claims are baseless. At the heart of the problem is that SCO has been unable to prove ownership of vital components of code used in Linux. Moreover, when disclosing code, it has been shown that the elements to which they laid claim had already been released under other FOSS licences, including the BSD.[130] At the time of writing SCO had filed for bankruptcy,[131] and experts agree that FOSS users 'have little to fear from this litigation because SCO will struggle in proving IBM did not have the right to contribute its derivative and independent code to Linux'.[132]

In addition to the litigation over contracts and copyright, a recent FOSS concerned competition law. In *Wallace v IBM*,[133] the Seventh Circuit Court of Appeals found that the GPL did not contravene US antitrust law. Software developer Daniel Wallace claimed that he wanted to compete against the Linux operating system by selling derivatives or writing an operating system from scratch, but that this was not possible because Linux is offered for free. According to Mr Wallace, the GPL is part of a conspiracy because it makes software free forever, and it is impossible to compete against free products. Mr Wallace clearly missed the point of the definition of free software outlined above. Free is not free as in beer, but free as in freedom. Mr Wallace lost the case in the first instance because he could not prove that he had suffered an antitrust injury. Judge Easterbrook stated:

> Many more people use Microsoft Windows, Apple OS X, or Sun Solaris than use Linux. IBM, which includes Linux with servers, sells mainframes and supercomputers that run proprietary operating systems. The number of proprietary operating systems is growing, not shrinking, so competition in this market continues quite apart from the fact that the GPL ensures the future availability of Linux and other Unix offshoots.[134]

128 KD Goettsch, 'SCO Group v IBM: The Future of Open-Source Software' [2003] *University of Illinois Journal of Law, Technology & Policy* 581.
129 The most recent developments in this case can be followed http://www.groklaw.net.
130 G Lehey, *SCO's Evidence of Copying between Linux and UnixWare* (2004), http://www.lemis.com/grog/SCO/code-comparison.html.
131 US Bankruptcy Court for the District of Delaware, 07-11337-KG The SCO Group, Inc.
132 A LaFontaine, 'Adventures in Software Licensing: SCO v IBM and the Future of the Open Source Model' (2005) 4(2) *Journal on Telecommunications & High Technology Law* 449.
133 *Daniel Wallace v IBM, Red Hat and Novell*, 467 F 3d 1104.
134 Ibid, 6.

All of the above litigation and enforcement strategies point to the conclusion that FOSS licences are legally valid, and that the movement rests on firm legal foundations.

C. FOSS in Practice

The various technical and legal considerations explored above are important, but beyond that, what is the relevance of open-source software in everyday life? After all, the intricacies of the various licences and underlying philosophies seem to be most relevant to specialist lawyers and 'Internet geekdom'. However, the significance of FOSS to the wider public makes it an important subject of legal study.

FOSS is playing an increasingly important role in mainstream software development. Even so, it is common to read about FOSS in terms of its opposition to proprietary and commercial software from many commentators including prominent advocates of free and open-source software.[135] This rather combative approach seems to be diminishing in relevance as FOSS develops and follows a philosophy of peer production and open distribution of code.[136] The key question, then, is as to whether it forms a viable system of creating computer programs.

It is difficult to measure the adoption of FOSS in the wider community. While Linux has not managed to take a part of the operating system market away from Microsoft Windows, FOSS has proven to be an excellent system for servers, with some projects, such as Firefox, having made their way into mainstream use.[137] The FOSS community seems vibrant and active with SourceForge hosting 257,594 separate projects on its site. A survey of open-source communities amongst more than 3,000 projects found 127,006 identifiable individuals programming code.[138]

Software relies entirely on source code. One could say that computer code is the currency of the information age, as the writing of instructions takes expertise and time. Code, then, is a valuable commodity within the digital environment. Without code, computers are useless. FOSS is mostly a system for producing code in a cheap manner by harnessing the power of crowds of programmers who are willing to write and share it with the wider community through the use of open licences. If one accepts the idea

---

[135] R Stallman, 'Why Software Should Not Have Owners', in J Gay (ed), *Free Software, Free Society: Selected Essays of Richard M Stallman* (Boston, GNU Press, 2002) 47–52.

[136] For more about the concept of peer production, see Y Benkler, *The Wealth of Networks: How Social Production Transforms Markets and Freedom* (London, Yale University Press, 2006) 59–90.

[137] S Weber, *The Success of Open Source* (Cambridge, MA, Harvard University Press, 2004) 190–92.

[138] R Ghosh and VV Prakash, 'The Orbiten Free Software Survey' (2000) 5(7) *First Monday*, http://firstmonday.org/issues/issue5_7/ghosh/index.htm.

of code as a commodity, FOSS is a runaway success. The latest version of the Debian operating system has 213 million SLOC, while the Linux kernel has 5.2 million SLOC. To put things into perspective with proprietary software, Windows XP has 29 million SLOC, Windows Vista has 50 million SLOC, and Mac OSX (based largely on open-source code) has 86 million SLOC.[139]

The commercial successes enjoyed by FOSS developers are a good indicator of its viability, a phenomenon reinforced by the enthusiasm with which public administration bodies around the world have embraced open source. The EU seems to be at the forefront of FOSS adoption. In 2002, a report for the European Commission recommended that, wherever possible, public administrations in the EU should fund software projects and purchase software that fulfilled certain characteristics compatible with open licences.[140]

As a result of this and other research projects,[141] the Commission adopted the European Public Licence (EUPL),[142] the latest addition to the expanding open-source licence portfolio. While the licence is initially intended to be used as the official release method for projects funded under the IDABC framework, it is also the first open-source licence with an officially sanctioned translation in the 23 official languages of the EU, making it particularly useful for public-sector administrations within Member States.

FLOSS has been adopted in the European public sphere as it moves towards e-governance and e-democracy, allowing cost-effective, stable and secure access to information technologies. The German federal government has signed an agreement with IBM to purchase computers for use in its offices that will have Linux installed, thus greatly reducing their costs and increasing security.[143] The Spanish region of Extremadura decided to move into open-source operating systems in public institutions and had a total of 100,000 computers running Linux by the end of 2003.[144]

Another area in which FOSS has proved important is in developing countries. A simple cost comparison shows the clear advantages of this type of technology for countries that do not have the resources to purchase expensive proprietary commercial software licences. For example, German

139 Figures from H Dahdah, 'Tanenbaum Outlines his Vision for a Grandma-proof OS' [2007] *Computer World*, http://www.computerworld.com.au/index.php/id;1942598204;pp;1; and G Robles, *Debian Counting* (2004), http://libresoft.dat.escet.urjc.es/debian-counting/.
140 R Ghosh et al, 'Free/Libre and Open Source Software: Survey and Study', CORDISS Report D18, (2002), part II B, 23–26.
141 Eg R Ghosh et al, *Study on the Economic impact of open source softwareon innovation and the competitiveness of the Information and Communication Technologies (ICT) sector in the EU*, Contract ENTR/04/112, http://ec.europa.eu/enterprise/ict/policy/doc/2006-11-20-flossimpact.pdf.
142 Full text and accompanying documents can be found at http://www.osor.eu/eupl.
143 'IBM signs Linux deal with Germany', BBC News, 3 June 2002, http://news.bbc.co.uk/1/hi/business/2023127.stm.
144 AE Cha, 'Europe's Microsoft Alternative', *Washington Post* 3 November 2002, A01.

Linux distributor SuSE calculates that the cost of proprietary licences for operating system and applications generally used for constructing a Windows-based web server would cost almost €6,000; this generally includes the licences for one system.[145] In contrast, a SuSE Linux distribution that contains all of those applications and can be installed in an unlimited number of systems would only cost €90, and many Linux distributions can even be downloaded directly from the Internet without cost.

One drawback is that free or low-cost Linux distributions come with no support. Support must be purchased at extra cost. In addition, some distributions such as Red Hat Enterprise Linux are offered at considerably higher prices than the free download ones. The additional costs often represent the payment for full support—and the package usually covers unlimited licences. A study by Forrester Research of 140 large firms in North America found that, even taking into consideration some of the more expensive Linux distributions, the cost of every server machine running Linux was 60 per cent less than a comparable server running Windows.[146] Others, however, have pointed out that the migration from an environment running proprietary software and operating systems into a FLOSS operating system is considerably more expensive than expected. For example, the local government in Munich commissioned a study to calculate the cost of migration from Windows to Linux. The study found that there was no noticeable difference in cost between migrating to Linux and migrating to a later proprietary Windows version. On the contrary, the study estimated that the migration might cost as much as €3000 per client in hardware, software and training.[147] Yet others have pointed to examples of cheap migrations.[148] For developing countries, and in particular the least-developed countries, migration would not generally be a problem as there are often no operating systems to migrate from.

Along with the cost benefits, FOSS has other characteristics that makes it valuable for developing countries. As has been stressed, source code is made available in all FOSS licences, which means that programmers can make changes to how the software works. This would give those in developing countries flexibility in adapting the software to their needs—particularly to make language ports.[149] Good examples of this are the many non-English Linux distributions, often in languages that would not warrant

---

145 Figures taken from http://www.suse.com/en/private/products/suse_linux/prof/winprice.html.

146 J Giera, 'The Costs and Risks of Open Source', Forrester Research Report (2004).

147 Unilog Management, *Client Study for the State Capital Munich: Executive Summary of the LHM 2002* (2003), http://www.forget-me.net/Linux/free-software-study-munich.pdf.

148 See eg R Benner, 'Migration from Windows to Linux Saves Thousands' [2004] *IT Manager's Journal*, http://www.itmanagersjournal.com/software/04/01/09/2231250.shtml.

149 P Krakowski, 'ICT and Free Open Source Software in Developing Countries' (2006) 223 *IFIP International Federation for Information Processing* 319.

the interest of commercial developers.[150] Proprietary software, by contrast, is offered to the user as a block of sealed bits that cannot be changed. Even attempting to reverse engineer and decompile proprietary software could be considered unlawful in many jurisdictions.[151]

A further advantage for developing countries is the reliability and security of non-proprietary software when compared to proprietary software. Faulty, vulnerable or buggy software can cost considerable sums of money. For example, a survey of IT specialists by *CIO Magazine* found that companies spend 7–8 per cent of their computer-related budgets on security. Another report from 2001 calculates that faulty software costs companies in the US a staggering US$78 billion a year.[152]

However, the ultimate advantage of FLOSS for developing countries is that it offers a powerful tool to encourage the development of native technologies, enabling the move from imitation to innovation. True, there will be an initial need to copy and share source code originating from developed countries, but once this has been achieved, then indigenous innovation could take over. In the words of Wayne Marshall, a Unix programmer in Guinea: 'Open-source advocates can be sure that Africans get community; Africans get bazaar.'[153]

With these advantages, one should not be surprised that public institutions in developing nations are looking at non-proprietary software in a favourable manner. It has the potential to help these nations bridge the digital divide through enhancing their technological capability.

A good example of a country in which FOSS has been widely adopted is China, a country heavily involved in the development of indigenous tools for e-governance. The flexibility of the non-proprietary model can be seen in the development of a Chinese distribution of Linux called Red Flag Linux aimed at Chinese consumers.[154] Another version of Linux called Yangfan Linux (which means 'raise the sails') supported by the Chinese government is set to replace Windows and Unix on all computers and servers in the Chinese government.[155] A survey of Chinese software developers conducted by Evans Data Corporation found that about two-thirds of those developers are planning to write OSS-related applications in the next year, a figure that shows the extent to which this model is growing in

---

[150] Eg Ubuntu Linux is distributed with support for 100 languages (they claim 'from Afrikaans to Zulu'). Other noteworthy distributions are Dreamlinux in Brazilian Portuguese; gnuLinEx in Spanish; and Asianux in Chinese, Korean and Japanese.

[151] For more about the law of decompilation, see P Samuelson and S Scotchmer, 'The Law and Economics of Reverse Engineering' (2002) 111 *Yale Law Journal* 1575.

[152] M Levinson, 'Let's Stop Wasting $78 Billion a Year', *CIO Magazine* 15 October 2001, http://www.cio.com/archive/101501/wasting.html.

[153] W Marshall, 'Algorithms in Africa', *Linux Journal* 1 June 2001, http://www.linuxjournal.com/article.php?sid=4657.

[154] http://www.redflag-linux.com/.

[155] M Berger, 'inuxWorld Expo: Chinese Government Raises Linux Sail', *Infoworld* 13 August 2002, http://archive.infoworld.com/articles/hn/xml/02/08/13/020813hnchina.xml.

China.[156] India is another country where non-proprietary software is making strong advances. It was calculated that in January 2004, 10 per cent of all commercial computers sold in India contained Linux as their operating system.[157]

The eventual success of non-proprietary software in such populous countries as India and China could be the greatest encouragement for the use of this model in developing nations. The size of these markets alone would provide serious incentives for other countries to replicate the experiences in China and India—and if successful, it might even create a proprietary/non-proprietary divide.

VI. CONCLUSION

There can be little doubt that the software industry is still one of the powerhouses of the global economy despite the recent financial downturn. For example, in 2007 the global worldwide spending on software amounted to US$257 billion.[158] Given the economic importance of software, it is clear that any discussion about its legal protection is of the utmost interest to producers, consumers and regulators, who want a share of the growing demand for computer programs to be satisfied in their countries.

This chapter has described and analysed just a few of the many areas of relevance to FOSS development and distribution. It is common to see this topic treated in a shrill and partisan manner from both promoters and detractors of the movements. While it is clear that proprietary producers and commercial developers may see their share of the market reduced by FOSS, it would be a mistake to look at open source as a potential harm. There are many possibilities for the coexistence of the models despite the protestations of those at the fringes. As a personal anecdote, I am writing this on a Mac, a closed operating system that uses some open-source code, using both Microsoft Office and NeoOffice (an open source replacement for Microsoft Office), and have done some research on Firefox. Intransigence? The reality is that there is growing interaction between proprietary and non-proprietary systems.

The gradual acceptance of FOSS as a valid commercial strategy is shown by looking at how it has been adopted by the two largest software companies in the world, IBM and Microsoft, both of which are involved in a struggle for the profitable server market. IBM dominates the hardware

156 Evans Data Corporation. *Chinese Development Survey*, Vol 2 (2002), http://www.evans data.com/n2/surveys/chinese_toc_02_2.shtml.
157 'Linux, Microsoft Face Off in India', Reuters, 11 August 2003, http://news.com.com/2100-1016_3-5062158.html.
158 Plunkett Research, *InfoTech Industry Overview* (2008), http://preview.tinyurl.com/5e2gwg.

market[159] while Microsoft is still ahead in software sales. IBM has thrown its considerable financial weight behind open source in order to dent Microsoft's software dominance. Back in 2000, IBM announced that it would make an unprecedented investment of US$1 billion in Linux.[160] Since then, IBM has become the biggest supporter of FOSS models as a valuable and profitable business model.[161] The fact that it still remains strong in the software market should serve as an indication that the strategy has been at least partially successful. Similarly, Microsoft has been shifting its attitude towards FOSS. While the software giant was initially opposed to open-source licensing and ideals,[162] it has been slowly moving towards a policy of peaceful coexistence, even releasing its own FOSS licences.[163] This has been quite a shift from the company that at one point had discussed in leaked documents the use of fear, uncertainty and doubt tactics in order to minimise the threat of Linux and FOSS to Microsoft's market share.[164] As with many other commercial strategies, it is not clear why Microsoft shifted its approach to FOSS. It may, however, have been motivated by IBM's success in harnessing the power of the FOSS community.

[159] S Malik et al, 'IBM Servers, Worldwide, 2007', Gartner Research Report G00150814 (2007).

[160] J Wilcox, 'IBM to spend $ 1 billion on Linux in 2001', *CNET News.com* 2000, http://news. cnet.com/news/0-1003-200-4111945.html.

[161] J West, 'How Open Is Open Enough? Melding Proprietary and Open Source Platform Strategies' (2003) 32(7) *Research Policy* 1259.

[162] See Guadamuz, above n 70.

[163] Such as the OSI-approved Microsoft Public License (Ms-PL), see http://www.opensource. org/licenses/ms-pl.html.

[164] These are known as the Halloween Documents. See http://edge-op.org/iowa/www. iowaconsumercase.org/011607/6000/PX06501.pdf.

12

Scholarly Communications and New Technologies: The Role of Copyright in the Open Access Movement

CHARLOTTE WAELDE

I. INTRODUCTION

'OPEN'. A SMALL word, but when used in the same breath as 'Internet' or more broadly, 'information and communication technologies', it has expansive, sometimes overlapping, and often confusing meanings. 'Open' is used in relation to software, standards and access amongst other categories of technologies and content. The use of the term brings with it connotations of non-proprietary, of accessibility, and of sharing. In other words, it is imbued with notions and concepts that run counter to propertisation and control of technologies and content. Open source in relation to software has been considered in chapter 11. The purpose of this chapter is to consider the term in relation to the open access and scholarly communications movement. The central focus will be on the role of copyright in that movement. The pressures, often competing, underlying the historic and present shape of the movement will be described, some predictions for the future made, and ideas put forwards for the role that copyright might (or might not) play in that future.

Borrowing from the Budapest Open Access Initiative,[1] the open access movement combines:

> An old tradition (the willingness of scientists and scholars to publish the fruits of their research in scholarly journals without payment), with a new technology (the Internet), to make possible an unprecedented public good (free access to scholarly communications at the point of use).

---

[1] http://www.soros.org/openaccess/read.shtml.

395

A. Definitions and Scope

Neither of the terms 'scholarly communication' and 'open access' have legal definitions. The term 'scholarly communication' generally denotes something that is more than the output of research in the form of a published article. It is often taken to mean the academic process from the inception of an idea, through the research needed to investigate and elaborate upon that idea, to making the research available to the interested community in the form of the published output.[2] Because this entire process underpins scholarly communications, a great deal needs to change in order to bring about the transformation from the traditional methods of publishing to open access. Areas where long-standing and accepted practice need to be transformed include the research institution within which the academic carries out the research; methods of research funding by virtue of which the academic can fund the research; the libraries and archives within which the idea can be researched; the publishers who provide the editorial input; and the journal within which the output can be made available to the user of the research. Whereas the focus of this chapter is the availability of the final output and the role that copyright plays in that, it is important to recognise that this output cannot be viewed in isolation, but is dependent on this process and the support that underlies it. This gives goes some way towards explaining why the move to open access in scholarly communications is far from easy.

As will be seen below, there has been much discussion regarding the meaning of 'open access' when used in conjunction with scholarly communications. Examples include those ranging from free and unrestricted access to, and use of, published outputs (the journal article) in ways that go beyond the parameters of the law of copyright (ie where the article can be 'freely' copied without regard to the limitations placed on reproduction by fair dealing[3] or other specific legislative relaxations[4])—better referred to as open content; to more restricted meanings, focusing on the free accessibility of the scholarly outputs at the point of use—in other words, free to the reader/user. This chapter is concerned with the latter, and with respect to which leading commentators have identified two main paths by which the goal may be achieved. One is the 'green' path: the process whereby a researcher self-archives post-print scholarly outputs at the point of publication (or sometime thereafter). Here, the self-archiving is likely to take place in an institutional repository such as Edinburgh Research Archive.[5]

---

2 See American Library Association Scholarly Communication Toolkit, Scholarly Communication: Definition and Background at http://www.ala.org/ala/acrl/acrlissues/scholarlycomm/scholarlycommunicationtoolkit/librarians/librarianbackground.cfm, citing S Thorin, 'Global Changes in Scholarly Communication', presented at e-Workshops on Scholarly Communication in the Digital Era', 11-24 August 2003, Feng Chia University, Taichung, Taiwan.

3 Copyright Designs and Patents Act 1988 (CDPA) ss 29 and 30 in particular.

4 Eg CDPA ss 32–36A for the education sector.

5 This functions as a repository and archive and can be found at http://www.era.lib.ed.ac.uk/.

The other path is the 'gold' path which refers to publication in an open access, peer-reviewed journal to which there is free access for the reader/ user at the point of use.[6] Much of the comment below refers to initiatives taken along the green path.

While it is acknowledged that there are, and always will be, individual academics who are keen proponents of the open access initiative and who regularly publish their works on an open access basis (such as authors who make their scholarly works available under a Creative Commons licence[7]), this chapter is concerned rather with the institutional structures and processes that underpin scholarly publishing more generally which need to change if the open access movement is to become widespread, and the role of copyright in the work in helping or hindering the process of change. The focus in the chapter is also on the scholarly journal. The making available of academic books[8] and datasets[9] face other challenges in the move towards open access more broadly, and are ones that will not be further considered here.

This chapter considers the issues that have arisen from an international, European and domestic (UK) perspective. It should be recognised that while the open access movement is global, there are certain characteristics of the UK academic sector that make moves to open access particularly challenging. As will be discussed below, these include such factors as modes of public funding of research; the shape of the publishing business; the peer-review processes organised by publishers; and the link between academic promotion and publications, often in select academic journals.

Finally, this discussion of open access and scholarly communication is but one example of the changes being wrought by new technologies on traditional 'information businesses' with consequent impacts on organisations, communities and individuals who have to change and adapt to the new information environment. Perhaps the highest-profile example has been the music business[10] where there has been an outpouring of discussion on the changing nature of the business model underpinning this sector in

---

6 S Harnad, T Brody, F Vallieres, L Carr, S Hitchcock, Y Gingras, C Oppenheim, H Stamer-johanns and E Hilf, 'The Access/Impact Problem and the Green and Gold Roads to Open Access', (2004) 30(4) *Serials Review*, available at http://dx.doi.org/10.1016/j.serrev.2004.09.013. See eg the open access journal *SCRIPT-ed* (the 'gold' path) at http://www.law.ed.ac.uk/ahrc/script-ed.

7 See eg A Guadamuz González, 'GNU General Public License v3: A Legal Analysis' (2006) 3(2) *SCRIPT-ed* 154, http://www.law.ed.ac.uk/ahrc/script-ed/vol3-2/guadamuz.asp.

8 A few high-profile academic authors have published their books under a Creative Commons licence. See eg L Lessig, *Free Culture; The Future of Ideas; and Code Version 2:0*.

9 It is the Database Directive (Directive 96/9 of the European Parliament and of the Council of 11 March 1996 on the legal protection of databases) implemented in the Regulations (the Copyright and Related Rights Regulations 2003, SI 2003/2498) that provides the legal frame-work for datasets, rather than the law of copyright. See generally C Waelde and M McGinley, 'Public Domain; Public Interest; Public Funding: Focussing on the 'Three Ps' in Scientific Research' (2005) 2(1) *SCRIPT-ed* 71, http://www.law.ed.ac.uk/ahrc/script-ed/vol2-1/3ps.asp.

10 See chs 5 and 6.

response, most particularly, to peer-to-peer (P2P) filesharing. Another example is the newspaper business—an industry that is facing great challenges from the move to online news.[11] The discussion in this chapter should be seen in that broader context—as an example of the culture changes that are forced upon these traditional industries, and of the role that the law of copyright plays in that changing culture.[12]

II. THE EMERGENCE AND GROWTH OF THE OPEN ACCESS MOVEMENT

The academic journal publishing market is a crowded one. The first English language scholarly journal, *Philosophical Transactions* (Figure 12.1), was published in 1665 and is still available today. But it is now only one[13] amongst thousands of academic titles in the marketplace vying to make the fruits of scholarly research available to the reader.[14]

One might be forgiven for thinking that this move towards open access only began with the emergence of the Internet. This, however, is not the case. A history of 'landmark' events has been charted by Peter Suber, who is a knowledgeable proponent of the open access movement.[15] His timeline contains a wealth of information about the movement, noting that it started in 1966 when the Educational Resources Information Centre (ERIC) was launched in the US to make bibliographic information relating to journal articles available on an open access basis, information that was supplemented by links to the full text of the source document where

[11] For an exchange of views between eminent US intellectual property academics on what the industry might do in response to challenges, see http://http://www.mediainstitute.org/IntellectualProperty/VPD_021909.html. For a story by the *New York Times* on media coverage of the events in Iran in June 2009 in the wake of the elections, see http://www.nytimes.com/2009/06/29/business/media/29coverage.html.

[12] Rich and reflective academic writing exists around the notion of open access and scholarly communications, the depth of which reflects the diverse nature of the movement, and the multifold interests that underlie it. This wealth of literature reveals the diverse backgrounds of the stakeholders and commentators, including, notably, librarians and information and computer scientists. A very useful list bringing together some of the more influential writings has been complied by Charles Bailey under the heading 'Scholarly Electronic Publishing Bibliography', at http://www.digital-scholarship.org/sepb/sepb.html. Because the movement is dynamic and initiatives occur on almost a daily basis, a great deal of interesting topical comment is provided in blogs. Two particularly informative ones are 'Open Access Archivangelism' by Stephen Harand, at http://openaccess.eprints.org/, and 'Open Access News' headed by Peter Suber, at http://www.earlham.edu/~peters/fos/fosblog html, both of which give insights into the numerous themes, sub-themes and interests involved.

[13] Or rather two, having been split into part A dealing with physical sciences, and part B dealing with life sciences.

[14] Figures relating to absolute numbers of journal titles in the market are hard to come by. In an article by GG Moghaddam, 'Scholarly Electronic Journal Publishing: A Study Comparing Commercial and Nonprofit/University Publishers', available at http://eprints.rclis.org/archive/00009171/01/Scholarly_Journals_Publishing.pdf, the author notes that in 2003 the top 15 commercial publishers of e-journals produced 5,027 electronic journal titles between them.

[15] http://www.earlham.edu/~peters/fos/timeline.htm.

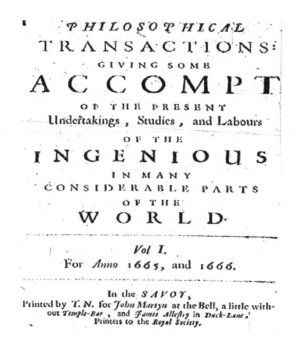

Figure 12.1

available. It shows that the movement gained momentum through the 1990s (corresponding to the growth of the Internet) where around 95 open access events are documented for that decade. In 2007 he charted over 100 entries, including such items as ERIC announcing a programme to digitise 40 million pages of microfiche documents for open access, and the Ministry of Culture in Spain making funding available for open access repositories throughout the country. Suber notes that he waits for a period before adding new events so that he can decide whether they might truly be seen as landmark. A recent inclusion was the motion that was approved by the Faculty of Arts and Sciences at Harvard University to make all scholarly outputs from the Faculty available on an open access basis.[16]

A. Academic Publishing

Traditional methods of hard-copy scholarly publishing, reliant as they have been on the traditional printed word, have resulted in the development of an interdependent set of relationships in the UK through which academic

---

[16] http://www.earlham.edu/~peters/fos/2008/02/text-of-harvard-policy.html and for comment see http://www.earlham.edu/~peters/fos/2008/02/more-on-imminent-oa-mandate-at-harvard.html.

journals have flourished by making available scholarly articles to a broad readership. The main actors are the academic publishers, the universities and the academics. Academic publishers have provided the mechanism (the journal) through which works are made available to the reader, and which have incorporated key components of quality control: from editorial organisation through to the administration of peer-review processes—means by which the quality of the academic contribution is judged by peers. The construct has been one that has proved its worth for universities. This is particularly so with the introduction of the first Research Assessment Exercise (RAE) in 1986.[17] The RAE is a mechanism by which the quality of academic outputs within the higher-education sector is judged by peers. The exercise is one that not only allows an institution to review the quality of its own research, both individually and by reference to other universities, but also, and importantly, it is the basis on which funding decisions are made. The higher the academic esteem of an institution and its constituent elements, the more public money for research is directed towards research endeavours.[18] In this way, the needs of the academic have also been met. Because academic promotion is almost entirely dependent on the quality of academic output, academics have sought to be published in the most prestigious journals of their relevant discipline in order to advance their careers. Academics have also willingly acted as key players in the peer-review process. Publishers draw their peer-review panels from those academics with strong reputations in the relevant field. In turn, being part of this process is considered an important academic tribute.

Then along came the Internet, disrupting these relationships and the business model upon which they are based. It soon became apparent that ever-wider dissemination of the fruits of publicly funded research to interested parties, both within academia and beyond, could be achieved through the medium of the Internet. This realisation came in tandem with other pressures faced by the sector. Library support services are confronted with ever-increasing demands for content and rising journal subscription costs but shrinking budgets,[19] and these are set within universities which are themselves dealing with finite budgets and many and diverse demands for resources. But there are also those who feel pressure from beyond this immediate circle. Research councils also have responsibility for allocating dedicated research funds drawn from the public purse to the sector and, under obligations to ensure that knowledge goes beyond the immediate

---

[17] For information on the RAE, see http://www.rae.ac.uk.

[18] Ibid.

[19] And rising journal subscription costs. See eg F McLellan, 'Publishers Face Backlash Over Rising Subscription Costs' (2004) 363(9402) *The Lancet* 44–45; C Bergstrom, and T Bergstrom, 'The Costs and Benefits of Library Site Licenses to Academic Journals' (2004) 101(3) *Proceedings of the National Academy of Sciences of the USA* 897–902.

academic community and transfers more broadly, a desire to see the fruits of that funded research being made as widely available as possible. But these research councils also have relationships with the publishing sector that have been nurtured over many years, and which have had mutually beneficial outcomes. Policymakers, for their part, being the source of the public funding supporting the academic sector, are keen to see the benefits of that funding nurture a competitive UK economy, of which open access to scholarly publications is considered a small, but important element. Yet those same policymakers need to balance the interests and demands of all of the stakeholders, including the publishers—whose greatest fear is the disappearance of their business model.

(i) The Place of Copyright

Copyright is only one small piece of the overall jigsaw, but it is a key part. Its relevance manifests itself in two ways: first, in the way by which copyright has been exploited in the traditional publishing model; and second, through the limits on exploitation to be found within the law of copyright. On the first point, regarding the traditional publishing model noted above, publicly funded researchers have historically assigned copyright in scholarly outputs to the publisher.[20] This has enabled publishers to exploit the work to the exclusion of all others in whatever way they thought best and most profitable. Sometimes the academic will have received a reward in the form of an upfront payment or royalties; sometimes the prestige of publication will have sufficed. Attribution has always been a key feature, bringing benefits both to the academic and the publisher: the academic through enhancing her reputation, and the publisher through enhancing sales on the back of that reputation.

The exclusivity of exploitation has been of prime importance to the publisher. While the academic may have desired her work to feature in more than one title, understandably the publisher wanted control over exploitation. If a scholarly work appeared in more than one place, sales may have been depressed. By requiring assignation of copyright the publishers' control was ensured both in the primary (journal) market as well as over subsidiary markets (translation, photocopying, etc) Open access leaves the traditional publisher vulnerable. If a scholarly work appears to be free at the point of use on the Internet, then sales of the traditional hard-copy journal may falter. If sales falter, then publishers become financially vulnerable and the services they have traditionally supplied in this area are endangered.

The second way in which copyright is relevant within the open access

---

[20] This in turn begs the question as to whether the academic has the title so to do which she will not if the employee rule in CDPA s 11 applies. See below n 55.

movement relates, as indicated, to the parameters of copyright. That copyright gives exclusive rights of reproduction,[21] dissemination[22] and communication to the public[23] to the owner of the right means that permission is required from the owner for the act of placing an article in a repository or within an open access journal, browsing and downloading of the work by the user, as well as any form of onward transmission and dissemination. While, as argued above, open access should not be confused with open content, copyright permissions are still needed if open access is to function in the way anticipated. In other words, permission is needed from the owner of the copyright in a scholarly work if that work is to be made available on an open access basis and be capable of being lawfully accessed by the user. Whereas the place of copyright is acknowledged in many of the key landmark events in the open access movement, there does not yet appear to be a uniform view as to how the tensions between open access on the one hand, and the practice of assigning exclusive rights to publishers on the other, should be resolved; nor on what permissions should appropriately be granted to maximise the impact of open access.

One further point needs to be made. Open access in scholarly communications is of relevance across the academic disciplines, from the fine arts to the pure sciences. However, much of the comment and the research in the area relates to the sciences, and not to the arts, humanities and social sciences. For instance, an inquiry by the UK Science and Technology Select Committee into academic publishing[24] limited itself to scientific, technical and medical (STM) publishing, noting that: 'The market for journals in the social sciences, arts and humanities has different characteristics.'[25] From a copyright perspective, some of these differences will lie in the layers of protected works that might be incorporated into a scholarly output. While, in the interests of good scholarship, academics in these disciplines limit themselves as much as their science colleagues to acceptable limits on borrowing, it is more likely that substantial parts of third-party works might, with permission, be incorporated into an original output—eg illustrations and pictures. This in turn makes the rights that can be granted to third parties in respect of exploitation more complex. Permissions have to be obtained for all the works that might be included in the one output, and those permissions may relate to the different categories of works, such as literary, artistic, dramatic or musical works.[26] In addition, less research in the humanities is funded via research councils as compared with the sciences where research is generally more expensive. Therefore there has

---

[21] CDPA s 17.
[22] CDPA s 18.
[23] CDPA s 20.
[24] House of Commons Science and Technology Committee Report 2004: 'Scientific Publications: Free for All?' See below n 59.
[25] Ibid, s 2, para 6.
[26] CDPA s 1(1)(a).

not been the tradition of research councils for the humanities driving the move towards open access by making it a condition of funding that scholarly outputs arising as a result of that funding be placed in open access repositories within a certain time of publication[27] or be published in open access journals. So while the general points to be made below relate to open access across the disciplines, some are specific to the sciences, and many have developed from foundations in the sciences.[28]

B. International, Regional and Domestic Settings

The open access movement is on the agenda of many diverse organisations and groupings at international, regional and domestic levels. One of the key aims was to get the principle of open access endorsed, not only by those who would need to engage with the initiative in the sense of making their works freely accessible (the academic), but also by those who could make this happen (the funders), as well as by those who would need to support it more broadly (the policymakers and regulators). In so doing careful thought has been given at times as to what copyright permissions would need to be granted in order to realise the vision. At other times the role and place of copyright seems to have been glossed over.

(i) International Declarations

In 2002 a group of interested parties came together in Budapest, funded by the George Soros Foundation through the Open Society Institute, and formulated the Budapest Initiative on Open Access. This was a call to make all scholarly publications freely available

> on the public internet, permitting any users to read, download, copy, distribute, print, search, or link to the full texts of these articles, crawl them for indexing, pass them as data to software, or use them for any other lawful purpose, without financial, legal, or technical barriers other than those inseparable from gaining access to the internet itself. The only constraint on reproduction and distribution, and the only role for copyright in this domain, should be to give authors control over the integrity of their work and the right to be properly acknowledged and cited.[29]

As can be seen, the copyright permissions which are sought under this

---

[27] Eg the Wellcome Trust, a leader in the field of open access. For further information, see http://www.wellcome.ac.uk/About-us/Policy/Spotlight-issues/Open-access/Policy/index.htm, and below n 63.

[28] For further thoughts on the differences, see M Heath M Jubb and D Robey, 'E-Publication and Open Access in the Arts and Humanities in the UK' [2008] *Ariadne* issue 54, 30 January, available at http://www.ariadne.ac.uk/issue54/heath-et-al/.

[29] http://www.soros.org/openaccess/read.shtml.

declaration go significantly further than the limits of copyright. In other
words, the user should be free to carry out many of the acts restricted by
copyright. Where the declaration seems to stop short is in the authorisation
of derivative works, at least beyond the acceptable limits of using a
substantial part of the work for the purposes of fair dealing.[30] That said,
the declaration is not entirely clear on this point as it speaks of 'the *only*
[emphasis added] role for copyright' being to ensure attribution and
integrity. These requirements of attribution[31] and of integrity[32] are, of
course, quite in keeping with the scholarly processes open access is designed
to support. Attribution of the work of others, together with respect for the
work of others, has always been integral to good scholarship.

The scope of copyright in open access was again considered in 2003,
when the Berlin Declaration on Open Access to Knowledge in the Sciences
and Humanities was formulated and opened for signature.[33] For this, open
access contributions must satisfy two conditions:

> The author(s) and right holder(s) of such contributions grant(s) to all users a free,
> irrevocable, worldwide, right of access to, and a license to copy, use, distribute,
> transmit and display the work publicly and to make and distribute derivative
> works, in any digital medium for any responsible purpose, subject to proper
> attribution of authorship (community standards, will continue to provide the
> mechanism for enforcement of proper attribution and responsible use of the pub-
> lished work, as they do now), as well as the right to make small numbers of
> printed copies for their personal use.
>
> A complete version of the work and all supplemental materials, including a
> copy of the permission as stated above, in an appropriate standard electronic for-
> mat is deposited (and thus published) in at least one online repository using
> suitable technical standards (such as the Open Archive definitions) that is sup-
> ported and maintained by an academic institution, scholarly society, government
> agency, or other well-established organization that seeks to enable open access,
> unrestricted distribution, inter operability, and long-term archiving.[34]

Here the permissions are more tightly crafted, with reference being specifically made to derivative works and to the possibility of making a small
number of copies for personal use. There also seems to be an attempt to
take attribution and integrity from their rather opaque constraints provided
for in the law, by requiring these to be respected in accordance with good
scholarship.

While the international declarations set a vision for scholarly communications and open access, at the European and domestic levels policymakers

---

[30] Above n 3.
[31] CDPA ss 77–79.
[32] CDPA ss 80–82.
[33] http://oa.mpg.de/openaccess-berlin/berlindeclaration.html.
[34] This initiative has been followed by conferences at CERN 2004, Southampton 2005, Golm
2006, Padua 2007, Dusseldorf 2008.

have struggled with developing strategies through which that vision might be realised.

(ii) Europe

In Europe there has been a plethora of policy documents and communications referring to open access. From a rather slow start, these now exhibit increasing sophistication and awareness of the many factors to be taken into account in moving towards a coherent and structured framework. In 2000 a decision was taken to create what was called 'the European Research Area'.[35] A specific concern within the EU was the realisation that Europe lags behind both the US and Japan in terms of investment in research. In order to stimulate greater investment, one of the many strategies was to increase accessibility of research outcomes, noting that to facilitate the plan, 'the relevance and consistency of the intellectual property arrangements used to implement public research programmes should also be improved'.[36] In an interim evaluation of the research area programme in 2007, it was acknowledged that the underlying intellectual property issues were broader and more complex than originally identified.[37]

Although documents which deal more directly with open access and scholarly communications have noted that copyright is important, there seems to have been an odd reluctance to tackle the issue head on. This is evident from a reading of a report on the publishing sector produced in early 2006.[38] This study, which focuses on the economic and technical evolution of the scientific publication markets in Europe, brought together much of the current state of knowledge and thinking in the area of open access and scholarly communications, particularly in relation to the organisational and technical issues which are so vital to its operation. However, the report only noted copyright in passing, arguing that research councils had a key role to play in shaping copyright contracts to ensure that research results could be made available in repositories. While it also noted that 'publishers have become more permissive over time, in particular in terms of the posting of published material on individual web pages', the report went on to suggest that 'it would be good to investigate precise legal solutions that would provide legal certainty to authors, but also potentially

[35] Communication from the Commission to the Council, the European Parliament, the Economic and Social Committee and the Committee of the Regions: Towards a European Research Area Brussels, 18.1.2000 COM(2000) 6 final.

[36] See the comments of Research Commissioner Philippe Busquin announcing the launch of the European research area in a press release, 'Science without frontiers? A European Research Area', 24 January 2000, ref RCN: 14195.

[37] See in particular Commission paper 'Inventing our Future Together, Preliminary Results, Public Consultation, Green Paper on the ERA' September 2007, Sharing Knowledge, s 4.4, available at ec.europa.eu/research/era/pdf/preliminaryresults-eraconsultation_en.pdf.

[38] 'Study on the Economic and Technical Evolution of the Scientific Publication Markets of Europe', Final Report, January 2006, ISBN 92-79-01029-8.

to other parties, in terms of dissemination of published material' and recommended that further work be carried out in this area.[39] In advance of a European conference on open access in 2007[40] a petition containing over 18,000 signatures was presented to the European Commission urging it to endorse guaranteed public access to publicly funded research results.[41] This petition was based on one of the recommendations in the publishing study which read in part:

> The following actions could be taken at the European level: (i) Establish a European policy mandating published articles arising from EC funded research to be available after a given time period in open access archives, and (ii) Explore with Member States and with European research and academic associations whether and how such policies and open repositories could be implemented.[42]

The open access conference was itself announced in a communication from the Commission, in which a number of the threads that had emerged from discussions pertaining to the European research area and the digital libraries initiatives were drawn together[43] and which laid out the challenges facing the sector, and proposed a plan of action as to how the desired results might be achieved. The Commission stated that their aim was to signal the importance of access to, and dissemination of, scientific information, and to launch a policy process.[44] On copyright, the Commission noted that the practice of assigning copyright to publishers can have a 'negative impact on access and dissemination' and that these practices should be reflected upon.[45] There is, however, precious little further guidance or strategy in the document to suggest what might be needed to be done,[46] noting only that the aim is not

[39] Ibid, Recommendation C2.
[40] Held in October 2007.
[41] http://www.ec-petition.eu/
[42] The remainder of the recommendation is as follows: Recommendation A1. Guarantee Public Access to Publicly-Funded Research Results Shortly after Publication. Research funding agencies have a central role in determining researchers' publishing practices. Following the lead of the US National Institutes of Health and other institutions, they should promote and support the archiving of publications in open repositories, after a (possibly domain-specific) time period to be discussed with publishers. This archiving could become a condition for funding. In the Green Paper, 'The European Research Area: New Perspectives Brussels', 4.4.2007, COM(2007) 161 final, the Commission stated that 'Europe should stimulate the development of a "continuum" of accessible and interlinked scientific information from raw data to publications, within and across different communities and countries.' On intellectual property it was recognised that 'A major hindrance is the inconsistent, and often inadequate, rules and approaches for managing intellectual property rights (IPR) resulting from public funding.'
[43] Communication from the Commission to the European Parliament, the Council and the European Economic and Social Committee on scientific information in the digital age: access, dissemination and preservation. Brussels, 14.2.2007 COM(2007) 56 final.
[44] Ibid, 2.
[45] Above n 43, p 5.
[46] Note that this is one of the few documents where a clear distinction is made between copyright and database right and the difference in what is protected within Europe. What the Commission has done is to earmark over €51 million for the development of open access journals and repositories as part of the infrastructure needed to support the movement.

the introduction of Community rules on copyright contract law—an area which has not been harmonised at Community level—but a reflection on the way in which authors exercise their rights in the digital environment.[47]

The development of any strategy in an organisation as broad and diverse as the EU, and governed by institutions pursuing broad and diverse agendas, carries the potential for conflict in policies. As part of the European research area, knowledge transfer has been identified as a key theme and as such the subject of a number of initiatives. In formulating policy to stimulate knowledge transfer as between educational institutions and industry,[48] the Commission acknowledged that, although open access is increasingly being endorsed by universities as an effective path for dissemination of research results, there are times when formal protection is needed for an underlying innovation if it is to be commercialised. When taking decisions on whether or not to make research outputs available under open access, the benefits that might accrue should be weighed against the future benefit that might be lost through disclosure of information: 'It is therefore important to ensure that researchers are aware of the benefits of both approaches and that decisions are made on the basis of socio-economic impact.'[49] This is far from a ringing endorsement for open access. Further it was highlighted in the report that, as the rules governing ownership of publicly funded research and development results varied throughout Europe, 'it may be appropriate to revisit in the near future the question of a single European ownership model for publicly funded research',[50] a proposal that has now been followed up in a further recommendation by the Commission on the management of intellectual property in knowledge transfer activities.[51] In this document the Commission recommends that institutions take measures to:

> Promote the broad dissemination of knowledge created with public funds, by taking steps to encourage open access to research results, while enabling, where appropriate, the related intellectual property to be protected[52]

and in implementation suggests that institutions should:

> Develop and publicise a publication/dissemination policy promoting the broad dissemination of research and development results (eg through open access publi-

---

[47] Above n 43, 5.
[48] Communication from the Commission to the Council, the European Parliament, the European Economic and Social Committee and the Committee of the Regions, Improving knowledge transfer between research institutions and industry across Europe: embracing open innovation. Brussels, 4.4.2007, COM(2007) 182 final.
[49] Ibid, s 2.2.
[50] Ibid.
[51] Commission Recommendation on the management of intellectual property in knowledge transfer activities and Code of Practice for universities and other public research organisations Brussels, 10.4.2008 C(2008)1329
[52] Ibid, Recommendation 4

cation), while accepting possible delay where the protection of intellectual property is envisaged, although this should be kept to a minimum.[53]

These statements are accompanied by the recommendation that in order to promote transnational knowledge transfer, the owner of the intellectual property arising from publicly funded research should be defined by clear rules, and that institutional ownership rather than 'professor's privilege' (the assumption that the academic will own the intellectual property) is considered the default legal regime for intellectual property ownership at public research organisations in most EU Member States. On this last point, and although the Commission falls short of a recommendation that institutions should own the intellectual property arising from publicly funded research, it certainly seems to give a strong steer in that direction. One of the difficulties with such a strategy is that it does not distinguish between the various types of intellectual property rights. It is clear from a reading of the Commission's communication and recommendation that the principal concern is with patents.[54] This explains the emphasis on protecting the products of research by way of, for example, a patent application before publication of the research results. However, the problem in failing to distinguish clearly between these and other types of intellectual property rights, in particular copyright, is that confusion may be caused for open access strategies. It is the owner of the copyright in the scholarly output who needs to give permission for it to be included in an open access journal or repository. It is the academic author who has historically given this permission to publishers and which now, in the UK at least, leads to the presumption that the author is the owner of the copyright in the scholarly work unless there is a specific agreement otherwise.[55] Taking such a broad brush approach in policy documents to intellectual property and to ownership risks causing confusion on the already tricky path to open access as to who would have the power to consent to publication of the scholarly output.[56]

So, open access is firmly on the European agenda. However, and while over the years the place and importance of the role of copyright in the open access movement seems to have become better understood by the

---

[53] Above n 51, Appendix 1, Recommendation 7.

[54] This is reminiscent of the Bayh–Dohl Act in the US which mandates institutional ownership of IP within universities and with respect to which it is unclear as to whether it has had the outcomes intended. See C Leaf, 'The Law of Unintended Consequences', *Fortune Magazine*, September 2005, available at http://money.cnn.com/magazines/fortune/fortune_archive/2005/09/19/8272884/index.htm.

[55] See in particular *Noah v Shuba* [1991] FSR 14 (an implied term against the application of the employer rule in CDPA s 16(2)); *Stephenson, Jordan and Harrison v Macdonald and Evans* (1952) 69 RPC 10 (copyright in lectures belonged to lecturer); above n 20.

[56] It is perhaps difficult to envisage that an academic institution would ever have the processes in place to give permission to each and every time an academic within the institution wished to publish a paper.

regulators at European level, these documents seem to suggest that there is something of a reluctance to tackle the copyright issues head on. It is acknowledged that intellectual property in general, and copyright in particular, need to be given quite some thought as to how they might best be used to support the open access movement. What, however, seems to be lacking at present is any coherent strategy or joined-up approach as to how this might be taken forwards.

(iii) UK

In the UK, open access has been the subject of, inter alia, a declaration by senior representatives of the higher-education sector in Scotland, a Science and Technology Select Committee report, and is on the agenda of the research councils and other organisations supportive of the movement.

In 2004, a Scottish Open Access Event took place at which a declaration was signed by the representative of a number of higher-education institutions.[57] Little was said about copyright in the declaration, apart from a call to universities and research institutions to '[r]eview intellectual property policies, to ensure that researchers have the right and duty to provide an open access version of their research.'[58] But the support at this level for the general open access vision seems to be confirmed.

Policymakers have also been active in the field. Open access was the subject of the report in 2004, 'Scientific Publications: Free for All?' by the House of Commons Science and Technology Committee, noted above.[59] The Committee broadly encouraged the government to engage with open access and adopt a number of strategies, most particularly directed towards encouraging researchers to deposit scientific research outputs in open access repositories (the 'green' path). The Committee recognised that copyright was 'crucial to the success of self-archiving'.[60] The Committee recommended that investigations should be carried out to ascertain the impact of a strategy whereby authors would retain their copyright, rather than assigning it to publishers.[61] Despite this endorsement and call for action to be taken by the government, little progress seems to have been made. Indeed, in the government's response, copyright suddenly became intertwined with concerns over plagiarism, defamatory and libellous material.[62] Whereas it was noted that there is currently much activity going

[57] http://scurl.ac.uk/WG/OATS/declaration.htm.
[58] Ibid.
[59] Above n 24. As noted above, the focus of the investigation was on publishing in the sciences and not the arts and humanities.
[60] Above n 24, para 126.
[61] Above, n 24.
[62] 'It is important that authors' work is protected from plagiarism and any move to assign control of copyright to institutions will need to take into account how an institution will monitor and address plagiarism issues. Institutions will have an additional administrative burden to

on in the open access arena, it was made clear that any change would be incremental, rather than government mandated.

Implementation of the open access vision seems to have been left in the hands of some of the funders of higher education, although it has been far from straightforward nor have the funders all chosen the same strategy. The Wellcome Trust, a medical research charity which funds research into human and animal health, was an early and active supporter.[63] The Trust says that what it seeks are 'initiatives that broaden the range of opportunities for quality research to be widely disseminated and freely accessed' and that it 'support[s] unrestricted access to the published output of research'.

In a policy statement, updated in February 2008, the Trust stated that it required

> electronic copies of any research papers that have been accepted for publication in a peer-reviewed journal, and are supported in whole or in part by Wellcome Trust funding, to be made available through PubMed Central (PMC) and UK PubMed Central (UK PMC) [two open access repositories] as soon as possible and in any event within six months of the journal publisher's official date of final publication

and that it

> encourages—and where it pays an open access fee, requires—authors and publishers to license research papers such that they may be freely copied and re-used (for example for text and data-mining purposes), provided that such uses are fully attributed.[64]

The statement deals with a number of complex copyright issues which permeate the open access movement. In the first sentence, the Trust is mandating that peer-reviewed research outputs need to be made available through its open access databases 'as soon as possible and in any event within six months of the journal publisher's official date of final publication'. The Trust is thus using its position as a funder to mandate a required outcome. This is, however, qualified to the extent that the paper must be made available immediately—or within six months of publication. This last point responds to strategies deployed by some publishers in the face of changing business models. Firstly, in response to increasing pressure, many

protect the rights of authors. There is also the issue of legal liability on institutional repositories if material is found to be libellous, fraudulent or defamatory. Mechanisms will have to be introduced to allow them to deal with these occurrences.' Government response to Recommendation 51 in Science and Technology Committee Fourteenth Report, Appendix 1.

63 The Wellcome trust has committed resources to investigating business models that could support the open access movement and commissioned and published two influential reports: *Economic Analysis of Scientific Research Publishing*, September 2003, ISBN 1 841290 47 5; and *Costs and Business Models in Scientific Research Publishing*, April 2004, ISBN 1 84129 051-3. Finding a sustainable business model remains a challenge.

64 http://www.wellcome.ac.uk/About-us/Policy/Spotlight-issues/Open-access/Policy/index.htm.

publishers no longer tend to take an assignation of copyright in the scholarly output, but rather an exclusive licence. They argue that this leaves authors with what they have been asking for—ownership of the copyright. Whilst this might be welcomed, the exclusivity of the majority of the licences, coupled with the practice of seeking a licence covering all of the exclusive rights granted by copyright for the full term, means that such a licence differs little from an outright assignation certainly as far as exploitation by either the author or any third party is concerned. Second, the requirement by the funder was in response to tactics publishers were deploying in permitting or refusing permission for the deposit of a paper in a repository, and when that could be done. Some publishers permitted deposit (self-archiving—the 'green' road) after a certain period of time, and some of those permitted deposit of a copy of the paper *before* it was refereed, and some permitted deposit of a post-publication copy *after* it had been refereed. Others still allowed deposit of the refereed final copy after a certain period. This led, in a number of instances, to different versions of substantially the same paper appearing multiple times in a variety of places. Clearly, the most authoritative is the post refereed version.[65] This is what the Trust, at best, requires to be deposited, so the pressure here is really on the publishers.[66] On the exclusive copyright parameters, the Trust encourages both publishers and contributors to ensure that the works may be 'freely used and copied' but then seemingly limits this to a fairly narrow category of uses by stating 'for example, for text and data mining purposes'. While the copies made for these purposes would need a licence,[67] it does not go so far as is called for by the international declarations.

Other UK funders also support open access, although none have gone as far as the Wellcome Trust.[68] The Research Councils UK (RCUK)[69] issued a position statement on access to publicly funded research in 2005 which was subsequently updated in 2006. While the statement urges that, where appropriate, researchers should deposit the outcomes of publicly funded research in an open access repository, this is subject to 'current copyright and licensing policies, for example embargo periods or provisions limiting the use of deposited content to non-commercial purposes, are respected by authors'. In September 2008 the RCUK was given the results of research it had commissioned earlier that year. The purpose of the research was to

---

[65] The best, from an authoritative point of view, would be the final PDF with page numbers, etc. However, there are many who would prefer not to use PDFs because of the difficulties they cause for text and data mining. In addition, the Trust would have no authority over the publishers to mandate that copy be deposited as the publisher, in the UK at least, would have copyright in the typographical arrangement of the work. CDPA ss 1(1)(c) and 8(1).

[66] SHERPA maintains a database of publishers giving information about their open access policies at _http://www.sherpa.ac.uk/index.html. A brief glance shows the diversity in approach.

[67] The process almost inevitably requires that a cache be made. For the copyright implications of caching in the UK context, see chs 5 and 7.

[68] For a listing, see http://www.sherpa.ac.uk/juliet/

[69] http://www.rcuk.ac.uk/default.htm.

'identify the effects and impacts of open access on publishing models and institutional repositories in light of national and international trends, including the impact of open access on the quality and efficiency of scholarly outputs, specifically journal articles'.[70] The research found that there was a growing trend towards open access in research institutions, albeit that there were significant differences as between disciplines; that open access enabled wider and quicker dissemination of research results; that there remained significant costs associated with open access; and that there was no inherent reason why the position of publishers (with the exception of learned publishers) should be jeopardised vis-à-vis the academic community.[71] The findings in the report have prompted the RCUK to increase their support for open access through further encouraging the deposit of articles in open access repositories, and increasing support for publication in open access journals including through pay-per-publication models.[72]

These moves by RCUK to further support open access publishing are taking place in an environment in the UK in which the traditional methods for judging academic outputs described above (the RAE) are changing. It has been recognised that the costs of organising and running the RAE are unsupportable. A new framework—the Research Excellence Framework (REF)—is being constructed.[73] This will be based on new criteria, in which there will be quantitative indicators, including bibliometric indicators. Because a criterion is likely to be citation counts for articles, many educational institutions are now taking steps to ensure that their academics deposit scholarly outputs in research archives and, depending on the ownership of the copyright in the article, into open access repositories. This method of judging research excellence through citation counts, and linking that to public funding for universities, seems to have done more than any other strategy to galvanise institutions into taking the steps needed, and put the processes into place, to facilitate open access to research outputs amongst their academics.[74]

70 Open Access to Research Outputs, Final Report to RCUK, September 2008, SQW Consulting, available at http://www.rcuk.ac.uk/cmsweb/downloads/rcuk/news/oareport.pdf.

71 Ibid, 7.

72 For full details, see http://www.rcuk.ac.uk/access/default.htm.

73 For information, see http://www.hefce.ac.uk/Research/ref/.

74 The Research Information Network has commissioned work to develop a scholarly communications toolkit. This toolkit 'will provide guidance to relevant stakeholders in relation to each principle constituting the statement of principles, and their roles in applying them. It will encourage reflection on how the agendas of different stakeholders might be aligned behind common goals and conflicts of interests resolved.' http://www.rin.ac.uk/files/Goals%20for%20 Public%20Policy%20-%20Scholarly%20Communications%20Statement%20of%20Principles. pdf. It will no doubt help research institutions when developing their policies and process for open access.

B. So Where Are We Now?

The events noted above are but drops in the ocean of the open access movement.[75] Returning to Peter Suber's timeline of key events, this illustrates how many initiatives are taking place around the globe.[76] While copyright is a building block without careful consideration of which open access cannot happen, many other hurdles need to be overcome. Quite apart from the structural processes identified above, repositories need to be built; processes developed to facilitate the deposit in, and retrieval of scholarly works from, those repositories; mechanisms put in place to enable works to be found ideally across a multitude of repositories; new ways of rewarding researchers developed that go beyond the traditional scholarly output in a peer-reviewed articles; means found to encourage academics to place their materials into repositories; ways found to ensure provenance of the works; and sustainable business models constructed—to name just a few of the challenges.

Although copyright may only play a small part in the open access landscape, it is a key part. As was mentioned above, it is copyright on which publishers rely for exclusivity of exploitation and through which they sustain their current business models—whether it be through taking exclusive licences of rights, or issuing embargo periods on placing works into repositories. In other words, in the current phase of development towards open access, copyright gives control over the work, and it is the work that is of value in the marketplace. It is also copyright that causes some to fear using scholarly works that are already available. Given the high profile that has been given to copyright in the digital sector, particularly with entertainment industries seeking to control their business models in the face of the rise of P2P networks and uncontrolled reproduction of music files, and suing individuals and institutions as a result,[77] there is a general awareness of copyright amongst the public and in the academic sector. Unfortunately, this can result in an overcautious approach by the users of works protected by copyright, with the result that perfectly lawful acts of reproduction and dissemination can be inhibited: whether that be within the parameters of the legislation such as fair dealing, or within the permissions granted in a licence.

A question might then arise as to why the impact that digital technologies has had on the scholarly communications and open access movement has not been as high profile as it has been in, say, the music sector. A

---

[75] One other important initiative emanating from the private sector, while not what might be considered open access as such in the sense being discussed in this chapter, but which will certainly have reverberations in this field is the Google Book Program and the Google Book Settlement. For full discussion, see ch 7. Google Scholar is another important private-sector initiative.

[76] Above n 15.

[77] See ch 5.

number of reasons can be suggested. Firstly, in the academic sector copyright litigation is the exception and not the norm,[78] no doubt due to the
symbiotic relationship between stakeholders that none is keen on disman-
tling, at least before it is known what will replace it. Second, and unlike the
position in the music sector, there are many and varied elements that need
to be changed and developed if open access is to work. No more than a
P2P network is needed to access and distribute music files, and many users
seemed unconcerned about the effect upon the entertainment industry's
business model despite valiant attempts by the industry to persuade them
that it is important less the flow of new works dries up for lack of
investment. By contrast, the historical benefits brought by the publishing
industry to academia are generally well known (even if the niceties of
copyright are not) and appreciated by many. A further factor might be at
play. At present it is not quite clear how to measure whether open access
actually 'works' in the sense of achieving the intended goals. It is based on
the premise that if fruits of publicly funded research are made widely
available, then logically they should be used to a greater extent than is
currently the case as the basis of further research. One of the key issues,
therefore, is how to measure whether that goal is being met. One
measurement of the use made of scholarly works in relation to traditional
hard-copy journals has been that of citation counts: in other words, how
many times has a journal, or an article in a journal, been cited by others.
This, as discussed above, is one of the measures likely to be used for the
REF. That said, it is a rather crude metric which could be open to manipulation. It is one that is more common in, and applicable to, the sciences
than the humanities. A most interesting report from the Research Information Network[79] found that while the evidence tended to suggest that
there were more citations for articles self-archived in repositories as distinct
from the same or similar articles available in a subscription journal, and
that deposit of articles in open access repositories seemed to be associated
with larger numbers and earlier citations, much of the evidence used inconsistent methods and covered different subject areas. This finding does not
quite deliver the resoundingly positive note for open access that may have
been desired and expected, and is now the subject of further research.[80]

---

[78] There are notable exceptions. One example in the UK is *Universities UK v Copyright
Licensing Agency* [2001] RPC 36. Another example currently being litigated in the US is where
Cambridge University Press, Oxford University Press and Sage Publications have filed suit
against Georgia State University for what they allege to be wilful violation of their copyright
through the making available of protected publications for teaching (rather than research)
purposes. A copy of the complaint is available at http://www.publishers.org/main/PressCenter/
documents/GSUlawsuitcomplaint.pdf.
[79] UK Scholarly Journals 2006 Baseline Report: An Evidence Based Analysis of Data Concerning Scholarly Journal Publishing, Area 4, 67ff, available at http://www.rin.ac.uk/data-scholarly-
journals.
[80] See http://www.rin.ac.uk. But others of course disagree and argue that statistics show a clear
increase in citation count both in time (open access encourages earlier citations) and in volume.

The results will be important in deepening understanding of the effects of open access publishing.

III. CONCLUSION AND PREDICTIONS

When considering the spread of the open access movement, there seems to be little doubt that it will continue to expand, both through publications in the increasing numbers of open access journals[81] and through self-archiving by researchers of scholarly outputs in repositories.[82] Technical, organisational and process solutions to many of the current obstacles will be found. Technological developments will make it possible to search across repositories, thus increasing the value of open access; standards will emerge for ordering and searching outputs; solutions will be found the current financial discussions as to who should pay for sustaining open access.[83] It seems that much of this is likely to be driven by innovation on the ground. Where direction does come 'from above', open access may be a by-product of the pursuit of other goals—such as increasing research funding. The open access landscape in a decade is likely to look quite different from that of today.

The law of copyright will not be an impediment in this; it will be a backdrop against which community standards of attribution and integrity will be respected. Repository managers and researchers will become better at stating clearly what may be done with the fruits of the research in terms of reproduction and the creation of derivative works; the margins of permissions will become less opaque, enabling greater reuse. These boundaries will be set by the working needs of the academic community and users of the research rather than by the publishers and the fuzzy edges of the law. And the publishers? Their business model will change and they will find new and other ways of working in the information environment, although it is not possible to predict precisely what that will be. One innovation might be to exploit the powerful position they now occupy in their ability

See eg C Hajjem, Y Gingras, T Brody, L Carr and S Harnad, 'Open Access to Research Increases Citation Impact' (2005) citation code 11687, available at http://eprints.ecs.soton.ac.uk/11687/. But, of course, yet others disagree. See I Craig, A Plume, M McVeigh, J Pringle and M Amin, 'Do Open Access Articles Have Greater Citation Impact? A Critical Review of the Literature' (2007) 1(3) *Journal of Informetrics* 239–48. The authors of this last article are all from publishing houses. For a bibliography of studies of the 'Effect of Open Access and Downloads ("Hits") on Citation Impact', see http://opcit.eprints.org/oacitation-biblio.html, a page maintained by the Open Citation Project based at the University of Southampton.

[81] For a directory of open access journals and to get an indication of the increasing numbers, see http://www.doaj.org/.

[82] For arguments that a scholar has a responsibility to make the results of research available on an open access basis, see J Willinsky, *The Access Principle: The Case for Open Access to Research and Scholarship* (Cambridge, MA, MIT Press, 2006), available at http://mitpress.mit.edu/catalog/item/ebook.asp?ttype=2&tid=10611.

[83] See above n 63 for the models proposed by the Wellcome Trust.

to see, track and to make use of usage statistics. As has been argued by Guédon:

> With usage statistics you move faster and stand closer to the realities of research than with citations. . . . The strategic possibilities of such knowledge are simply immense. They resemble the marketing possibilities emerging from the study of consumer habits and profiles.[84]

Guédon goes so far as to suggest that publishers may be able to use this information to influence the direction of science because it would enable the publishers to monitor and evaluate scientists. As they could monitor and evaluate scientists, so that knowledge might in turn be valuable for, and feed into, the research funding process. Whether this would ever become a reality remains to be seen. All that can be said with certainty is that, just as the open access landscape will look different in a decade, so too will the academic publishing sector.

---

[84] J-C Guédon, 'In Oldenburg's Long Shadow: Librarians, Research Scientists, Publishers, and the Control of Scientific Publishing' (2001), Proceedings Creating the Digital Future: Association of Research Libraries 138th Annual Meeting, Toronto. Note also the concerns over Phorm, http://www.phorm.com/, a mechanism to gather ISP data on Internet users so that advertisements may be better targeted. A number of the newsworthy stories have been collated by the Register at http://www.theregister.co.uk/2008/02/29/phorm_roundup/– a. See also ch 16.

13

Intellectual Property, Competition and the Internet

ABBE EL BROWN[1]

I. INTRODUCTION

THE RELATIONSHIP BETWEEN intellectual property (IP) and the Internet continues to evolve. Contemporary challenges concern metatags,[2] search engines,[3] patents over key technologies[4] and the place of IP in massively multiplayer online role-play games (MMORPGS), often called virtual worlds. A common factor is the potential for IP owners to control and influence the use and development of the Internet and the opportunities it offers. Refusing to allow technology to be used unless a large payment is made, or for a new purpose in a new field (or a new world?) might, in the most general terms, be called 'anti-competitive'. From the more legal perspective, concerns at reliance on IP rights, through collusive agreements and unilateral conduct by powerful entities, can raise competition questions. This chapter provides an introduction to and overview of the relationship between IP and competition in respect of the Internet with reference to patents[5] and copyright,[6] using examples drawing

---

[1] Some aspects of this chapter build upon consideration of copyright, human rights and the prohibition on abuse of a dominant position in C Waelde and AEL Brown 'A Practical Analysis of the Human Rights Paradox in Intellectual Property Law: Russian Roulette', in W Grosheide (ed) *The Human Rights Paradox in Intellectual Property Law* (Cheltenham, Edward Elgar, forthcoming). The author is also grateful to her students in classes in Information Technology Law, Intellectual Property Law and Information: Control and Power (Honours and LLM, on campus and by distance learning) at the University of Edinburgh in 2006/7, 2007/8 and 2008/9. All links referred to were accurate as at 7 April 2009.

[2] *Reed Executive Plc v Reed Business Information Ltd* [2004] EWCA Civ 159 [2004] ETMR 56.

[3] See chs 7 and 8.

[4] Such as the Amazon one-click patent which was re-examined in 2007, see commentary at http://igdmlgd.blogspot.com/2007/10/amazon-one-click-patent-rejected-by-us.html or the patents asserted by Microsoft in the European Commission interoperability investigation considered further below, p 436.

[5] As considered in ch 10, the patentability of software related inventions is controversial, but patenting is increasingly frequent.

[6] As considered in ch 10, copyright will exist in respect of software, although movements such as Creative Commons and open source provide a new perspective on its exercise and impact.

on hypothetical new blog technology, standards and MMORPGs. It does so from a global perspective and uses the EU as a case study.

II.THE INTERFACE BETWEEN IP AND COMPETITION

A. Overview

At the heart of the relationship between IP and competition is the question of whether or not they are in conflict. IP confers the exclusive right to control the use of the results of innovation and creativity. Thus if a patent is obtained for a key aspect of next-generation blog technology, only the patent owner or others with its consent could use this;[7] no one else could offer the same service on more attractive terms or use the technology as the starting point for commercial development of, say, 'blog 4.0.' Alternatively, a patent for technology enabling avatars to move to Everquest[8] from World of Warcraft,[9] where they might already have enjoyed wearisome success, could lead to the patent owner controlling when players (and avatars?) might be able to make that move.[10]

In contrast, competition law can be summarised as enabling and creating market conditions where participants develop new products, and compete vigorously for business, without external restrictions.[11] The ability of an IP owner to control the use of technology could therefore be inconsistent with competition. The view that IP and competition are inherently in conflict can, however, be challenged.

---

[7] See eg UK Patents Act 1977 (PA) s 60 and Trade Related Aspects of Intellectual Property Rights (TRIPS) Art 28, http://www.wto.org/english/docs_e/legal_e/27-trips_01_e.htm.

[8] http://everquest.station.sony.com/.

[9] http://www.worldofwarcraft.com.

[10] Consistent with their rights? See R Koster 'Declaring the Rights of Players' [and comment] http://www.raphkoster.com/gaming/playerrights.shtml. Note in this regard movements in MMORPGs towards open and interoperable technology and standards (considered more generally below, p 429). See sources and discussion at http://www.raphkoster.com/2007/10/10/interoperability/, SF Kane 'Passporting' of Avatars and Property between Virtual Worlds' (2007) 9(12) *E-Commerce Law and Policy* 10–11 and commentary at http://www.techcrunch.com/2008/07/08/ibm-and-second-life-announce-interoperability-project-but-bridging - virtual-worlds-is-the-wrong-answer/. The author is also delighted to acknowledge discussions on this issue at Gikii 2007 in response to her paper 'Playing to Win or the Game's the Thing: Competition and Human Rights in Virtual Worlds', http://www.law.ed.ac.uk/ahrc/gikii/docs2/brown.pdf.

[11] For more detailed analysis, see ch 20 in H MacQueen, C Waelde and G Laurie, *Contemporary Intellectual Property Law and Policy* (Oxford, Oxford University Press, 2007); P Lowe and L Peeperkorn, 'Intellectual Property: How Special is its Competition Case' and G Ghidini and E Arezzo 'On the Intersection of IPRs and Competition Law With Regard to Information Technology Markets', both in CD Ehlermann and I Atanasui (eds), *European Competition Law Annual 2005: The Interaction between Competition Law and Intellectual Property Law* (Oxford, Hart Publishing, 2007), 91–100 and 105–8, respectively; and R Whish, *Competition Law*, 6thedn (Oxford, Oxford University Press, 2008) 1–19.

IP rights have their own internal limits:[12] threshold criteria for the right to exist (including originality in respect of copyright and novelty and inventiveness in respect of patents),[13] restricted territory,[14] limited duration,[15] infringement tests (involving construction of patent claims, assessment of substantial part and evaluation of the allegedly infringing technology),[16] and exceptions and defences to infringement (such as private or experimental use or fair dealing).[17] Obtaining a patent in respect of new blog technology would not confer, therefore, the right to control all present and future activities in the web communications field, wheresoever they might occur.[18]

Further, there is some uncertainty as to the object of competition: is it to benefit consumers (by enabling lower prices or better products); to benefit competitors (by enabling smaller businesses to stay open with higher prices and to be able to use technology to provide the same products as others); to increase efficiency (on which basis, if competitors cannot manage their businesses so as to offer lower prices or attractive products they should close); or to bring about wider social benefits (eg enabling several smaller local shops to remain open might be considered preferable to having one large supermarket, or bringing about wide access to technology now might be more important than narrow reward and future innovation)?[19] There have been moves towards an holistic view of competition, within which all these factors are to be taken into account.[20] It can be argued, therefore, that increased innovation and new product development can be broadly consistent with competition and its aims.[21]

[12] See generally A Gowers, 'Gowers Review of Intellectual Property' (2006), http://www.hm-treasury.gov.uk/gowers, ch 4.

[13] Eg Copyright Designs and Patents Act 1988 (CDPA) s 1; TRIPS Arts 9 and 27; PA ss 1–4. See also ch 10.

[14] PA s 60; CDPA s 16; also TRIPS Art 1.

[15] TRIPS Arts 12 and 33; PA s 25; CDPA s 12.

[16] CDPA s 16(3), *Nova Productions Ltd v Mazooma Games Ltd* [2007] RPC 25; PA s 60(1), *Kirin-Amgen Inc v Transkaryotic Therapies Inc (No 2)* [2005] RPC 9.

[17] PA s 60(5); CDPA ss 29–30. See also chs 5–7.

[18] See in particular *Navitaire Inc v EasyJet Airline Co Ltd (No 3)* [2006] RPC 3; MacQueen, Waelde and Laurie, above n 11, 9–17; TF Cotter 'The Procompetitive Interest in Intellectual Property Law' (27 January 2006) Berkeley Center for Law and Technology *Law and Technology Scholarship (Selected by the Berkeley Center for Law & Technology)* paper 15, http://repositories.cdlib.org/cgi/viewcontent.cgi?article=1016&context=bclt.

[19] For further analysis, see S Bishop and M Walker, *The Economics of EC Competition Law: Concepts, Applications and Measurement*, 2nd edn (London, Sweet & Maxwell, 2002) esp 1–6, 11–27; RP Malloy and J Evensky (eds), *Adam Smith and the Philosophy of Law and Economics* (Dordrecht, Kluwer, 1994); and V Korah, 'The Interface Between Intellectual Property Rights and Competition in Developed Countries' (2005) 2(4) *SCRIPT-ed* 429, http://www.law.ed.ac.uk/ahrc/script-ed/vol2-4/korah.asp, s 2.

[20] See eg Speech of EC Competition Commissioner Neelie Kroes, 23 September 2005 to Fordham Corporate Law Institute, http://ec.europa.eu/comm/competition/antitrust/art82/index.html.

[21] See also eg PA Geroski, 'Intellectual Property Rights, Competition Policy and Innovation: Is There a Problem?' (2005) 2(4) *SCRIPT-ed* 422, http://www.law.ed.ac.uk/ahrc/script-ed/vol2-4/

It can also be argued that IP rights themselves encourage investment and engagement in innovation and creativity.[22] This could be so directly through development of patented blog 3.0 technology and its publication as part of the patent process. There could also be a more indirect impact, as others would be required to invent around the patent during its term (leading to blog 3.5 or 5.8?). Further, after the patent has expired, others could develop the patented technology, which may lead to, say, the more direct development of blog 4.0. Using competition law to restrict the activities of an IP owner—through, for instance, requiring technology to be licensed—could therefore be a significant deterrent to innovation now and in the future.[23]

It is not universally accepted that IP has a wholly positive impact on innovation and creativity.[24] Particular scepticism can be seen in the information and communications fields, where there is support for a more collaborative and open approach to innovation—one that is less dependent on IP.[25] The very discussion suggests, however, that IP and competition should not be assumed to conflict. Further, in the twenty-first century commentators,[26] regulators[27] and courts[28] have largely taken a more cohesive

geroski.asp and discussion in W Cornish and D Llewelyn, *Intellectual Property: Patents, Copyright, Trade Marks and Allied Rights*, 6th edn (London, Sweet & Maxwell, 2007) 46–48, 404, 797–800.

[22] See eg UK Commission on Intellectual Property Rights, 'Integrating Intellectual Property Rights and Development Policy' (2003), 'Overview', http://www.iprcommission.org/graphic/documents/final_report.htm; Gowers Review, above n 12, 1, 3, 12, 15; Korah, above n 19, s 1:1; RM Sherwood, *Intellectual Property and Economic Development* (Boulder, CO, Westview Press, 1990).

[23] For comment in this regard when competition first entered IP litigation, see A Robertson 'Compulsory Copyright Licensing under EC Law' (1992) 108(Jan) *Law Quarterly Review* 39–43; R Thompson, 'Magill: ECJ Upholds Use of Article 86 to Control Conduct of Copyright Holders on Ancillary Markets' (1995) 6(4) *Entertainment Law Review* 143–46; I Govaere, *The Use and Abuse of Intellectual Property Rights in EC Law* (London, Sweet & Maxwell, 1996) 9, 135.

[24] Gowers Review, above n 12, 19–20; U Suthersanen, G Dutfield and KB Chow (eds), *Innovation Without Patents: Harnessing the Creative Spirit in a Diverse World* (Cheltenham, Edward Elgar, 2007); Adelphi Charter on Innovation, Creation and Intellectual Property, http://sitoc.biz/adelphicharter/adelphi_charter_document.asp.htm.

[25] Gowers Review, above n 12, 3, 21; evidence from hearings of US Federal Trade Commission and Department of Justice, 'Competition and Intellectual Property Law and Policy in the Knowledge-Based Economy', http://www.ftc.gov/opp/intellect/detailsandparticipants.shtm# February% (sessions focussing on IP, innovation, competition and software). See also Access to Knowledge treaty initiative http://www.cptech.org/a2k/.

[26] See eg Geroski, above n 21; G Ghidini, *Intellectual Property and Competition Law. The Innovation Nexus* (Cheltenham, Edward Elgar, 2006); G Tansey [Comment], 'Whose Rules, Whose Needs? Balancing Public and Private Interests' 662, 665–66, 668 and J Drexl 'The Critical Role of Competition Law in Preserving Public Goods in Conflict with Intellectual Property Rights' 709, 719–20, both in KE Maskus and JH Reichman (eds), *International Public Goods and Transfer of Technology Under a Globalized Intellectual Property Regime* (Cambridge, Cambridge University Press, 2005); D Kallay *The Law and Economics of Antitrust and Intellectual Property* (Cheltenham, Edward Elgar, 2004); and the collection of contributions in SD Anderman (ed), *The Interface between Intellectual Property Rights and Competition Policy* (Cambridge, Cambridge University Press, 2007).

[27] In the EU, Commission Regulation 772/2004 on the application of Article 81(3) of the

view of the fields. With this starting point, it is not necessarily inconsistent with competition for there to be a refusal to license blog or MMORPG technology which is the subject of patent or copyright. Each case must be assessed individually: but by whom and on what basis?

B. Individual Assessments

(i) The Decision-maker

An important distinction between IP and competition arises here. IP legislation creates rights to be enforced by courts. Competition legislation sets out, in general terms, conduct that is prohibited: for example, the competition legislation of the UK prohibits abuse of a dominant position in a market if it may affect trade within the UK.[29] There is a similar provision in the EC Treaty.[30] In the UK jurisdictions, questions of abuse can be considered by a court hearing private actions in two main circumstances: continuing our examples, this could be done as the basis of a claim, if a competitor considers itself to have suffered[31] as a result of being unable to

Treaty to categories of technology transfer agreements, available at http://eur-lex.europa.eu/ LexUriServ/LexUriServ.do?uri=CELEX:32004R0772:EN:HTML ('TTBE') and Guidelines on the application of article 81 of the EC Treaty to technology transfer agreements (2004/C 101/02), available at http://europa.eu/eur-lex/pri/en/oj/dat/2004/c_101/c_10120040427en 00020042.pdf ('TT Guidelines'); in Australia, see the Intellectual Property and Competition Review Committee 'Review of Intellectual Property Legislation under the Competition Principles Agreement' (September 2000), http://www.ipaustralia.gov.au/pdfs/ipcr/finalreport. pdf, 202–15, considering Trade Practices Act 1974 (Cth) (Australia) (TPA) s 51(3). See also earlier developments in the US: US Department of Justice and Federal Trade Commission Antitrust Guidelines for the Licensing of Intellectual Property (1995), http://www.usdoj.gov/atr/ public/guidelines/0558.pdf, cf the 'Nine No Nos' of the 1970s set out by BB Wilson, Deputy Assistant Attorney General, Antitrust Division, before the Michigan State Bar Antitrust Law Section, 21 September 1972, available at http://www.cptech.org/cm/ninenonos.html.

[28] See EU cases considered below, pp 435ff. See also in the US *Illinois Tool Works, Inc v Independent Ink, Inc*, 396 F 3d 1342 (Fed Cir) 2005, rev'd, 126 SCt, 1281 (2006); H Hovenkamp, MD Janis and MA Lemley, 'Unilateral Refusals to License' (2006) 2(1) *Journal of Competition Law & Economics* 1–42 regarding refusals to supply more generally in the US; and for possible application to IP, *New York Mercantile Exchange, Inc v Intercontinental Exchange, Inc* 323 F Supp 2d 559, and EM Fox 'A Tale of Two Jurisdictions and An Orphan Case. Antitrust, Intellectual Property and Refusals to Deal' (2005) 28 *Fordham International Law Journal* 952.

[29] Competition Act 1998 (UK) s 18 (CA).

[30] Art 82 EC Treaty, which requires an affect on trade between Member States. See p 432.

[31] *Garden Cottage Foods Ltd v Milk Marketing Board* [1984] 1 AC 130, *Crehan v Inntrepreneur Pub Co* [2004] EWCA Civ 637. See also UK Office of Fair Trading Discussion Paper, 'Private Actions in Competition Law Effective Redress for Consumers and Business', http://www.oft. gov.uk/shared_oft/reports/comp_policy/oft916.pdf, cf EC White Paper on compensating consumer and business victims of breaches of the competition rules, April 2008, http://ec.europa. eu/comm/competition/antitrust/actionsdamages/index.html. For initial references in relation to the US, see *Arista Records et al v Lime Wire et al*, No 06-CV-5936 (SDNY) of December 2007, see discussion in KR Logan et al, 'Antitrust Development in the Media and Entertainment Industries', http://globalcompetitionreview.com/ara/17_mediaent.cfm.

provide blog 3.0; or as a response to an IP infringement action, say if the competitor went ahead with blog 3.0.[32] For these arguments to survive an early procedural challenge there must be a nexus[33] between the abuse (which may in exceptional cases include the raising of the action itself)[34] and the alleged infringement. However, there has not yet been a case in which such matters have been taken to a full trial with evidence and argument.

Competition questions, including those involving IP, can also be considered by regulators. Competition regulators (like IP rights) tend to be national, with the notable exception of the European Commission. Competition regulators have a mixed role: administering and enforcing legislation, while also working with industry in a more collaborative manner.[35] Regulators might start an investigation on their own initiative[36] or in response to a consumer or competitor complaint, [37] as was the case with investigations into Microsoft in the EU[38] and in the US.[39] A regulatory investigation can lead to the imposition of remedies (such as orders to supply and to offer products or services separately)[40] and to penalties.[41] These decisions can be subject to review by a court.[42]

---

[32] This argument has been developed from Art 82 having direct effect (*Van Gend en Loos* [1963] ECR 1) and should prevail over inconsistent national law; see UK European Communities Act 1972 ss 2(1) and (4), as interpreted in *R v Secretary of State for Transport ex p Factortame (No 2)* [1991] 1 AC 603, 659.

[33] *Intel Corp v VIA Technologies Inc* [2003] FSR 33 ('*Intel v VIA*'); *Sportswear Co SpA v Stonestyle Ltd* [2007] FSR 2.

[34] *ITT Promedia NV v Commission of the European Communities* (T111/96) [1998] ECR II-2937 ('*Promedia*') (CFI), 30 56, 60, 61, 73; proceedings could not reasonably be considered an attempt to assert the rights of the dominant undertaking, but to be approached restrictively so as not to frustrate access to courts. *Intel v VIA*, above n 33, took a more open approach, paras 48–51, but *Promedia* was referred with approval in *SanDisk Corp v Koninklijke Philips Electronics NV* [2007] FSR 22. Cf in the US, the Noerr–Pennington doctrine: see Federal Trade Commission (FTC) Staff Report, 'Enforcement Perspectives on the Noerr Pennington Doctrine' (2006), http://www.ftc.gov/reports/P013518enfperspectNoerr-Penningtondoctrine.pdf.

[35] See eg The UK OFT Guidelines 'Assessment of Market Power', OFT 415, http://www.oft. gov.uk/shared_oft/business_leaflets/ca98_guidelines/oft415.pdf.

[36] See Council Regulation 1/2003 Art 5 on the implementation of the rules on competition laid down in Arts 81 and 82 of the Treaty http://eur-lex.europa.eu/smartapi/cgi/sga_doc? smartapi!celexapi!prod!CELEXnumdoc&lg=EN&numdoc=32003R0001&model=guichett.

[37] See eg UK OFT details at http://www.oft.gov.uk/contactus.

[38] See EC Commission Decision relating to a proceeding under article 82 of the EC Treaty (Case COMP/C-3/37.792 Microsoft) March 2004, available at http://ec.europa.eu/competition/ antitrust/cases/decisions/37792/en.pdf, regarding bundling and interoperability information. Regarding fresh investigation in 2008, see announcement from BBC News website, http://news. bbc.co.uk/1/hi/business/7187750.stm and Commission Press Release http://europa.eu/rapid/ pressReleasesAction.do?reference=MEMO/08/19&format=HTML&aged=0&language=EN &guiLanguage=en.

[39] For sources and overview of the US antitrust investigation into operating systems and web browsers, see http://www.usdoj.gov/atr/cases/ms_index.htm.

[40] In *NDC Health v IMS Health* Case COMP D3/38.044 (OJ 2002) L59, 18 available via http://ec.europa.eu/comm/competition/antitrust/cases/decisions/38044/en.pdf, para 215, the EC Commission ordered negotiation with the involvement of an independent expert. A more interventionist and structured approach was taken in Commission Microsoft Decision, above n 38,

(ii) How?

Competition cases involve both detailed factual analysis and the application to the law of economic principles—which are themselves open to different interpretations.[43] Cases have been criticised as moving too slowly for innovative industries, such as those related to the Internet, with the field having moved on by the time of a decision.[44] As an example, the European Commission's investigation of Microsoft began in 1998 and Microsoft announced in 2007 that it would not appeal the decision of the Court of First Instance (CFI). It has also been argued that the court or regulator might not have sufficient understanding of the industry and its innovation to justify its decision and any intervention.[45]

(iii) A Global Approach?

National or regional competition regulators may be concerned about questions relating to IP and the Internet—but as always with the Internet, questions may arise in more than one country. Consider a startup blog service provider in the UK, faced with a complaint from the owner of Australian, UK and US patents in relation to a key piece of technology, which the patent owner refuses to license: might there be different outcomes in respect of any resulting competition investigations? As noted, IP rights are national rights,[46] but there is some global consistency in the

---

with a trustee appointed to have custody of the information and to monitor negotiation towards terms which were to be reasonable and non-discriminatory (Commission Microsoft Decision, above n 38, 273–80). This aspect of the order was annulled by the Court of First Instance as outwith the power of the Commission in *Microsoft Corp v Commission of the European Communities* (T-201/04) [2007] 5 CMLR 11, H43, H45, H47-8, H51, paras 50, 83; for Commission changes in approach, see Commission Press Release IP/09/349 http://europa.eu/rapid/pressReleasesAction.do?reference=IP/09/349&format=HTML&aged=0&language=EN&guiLanguage=en. Regarding the terms of the licence, see M Valimaki 'A Flexible Approach to RAND Licensing' (2008) 29(12) *European Competition Law Review* (*ECLR*) 686–91.

[41] Eg Commission Microsoft Decision, above n 38, 299, Art 3. For details of the compliance disputes which followed, see eg Commission Press Release IP/05/1695 http://europa.eu/rapid/pressReleasesAction.do?reference=IP/05/1695&format=HTML&aged=0&language=EN&guiLanguage=en and Commission SPEECH/07/647 http://europa.eu/rapid/pressReleasesAction.do?reference=SPEECH/07/647.

[42] Eg *Microsoft Corp v Commission of the European Communities* (T201/04 R 2) [2005] 4 CMLR 5 (regarding application for interim relief from compliance with Commission Microsoft Decision, above n 38); CFI Microsoft, above n 40.

[43] This is considered further below regarding network effects and innovation rates, p 434.

[44] See eg D Garrod and B Keane, 'EU v Microsoft: Competition Wins' (2008) 18(5) *C&L* 29 and comments in the Channel Register from 22 October 2007, http://www.channelregister.co.uk/2007/10/22/microsoft_europe_agreement/comments/#c_81595.

[45] See consideration in 'Different Models of Allocating Oversight Responsibilities', Report of the International Competition Network Working Group on Telecommunications Services, Appendix II, http://www.internationalcompetitionnetwork.org/media/library/conference_5th_capetown_2006/AppendixII.pdf.

[46] See generally chs 5–10 above.

extent of IP protection in the light of international treaties.[47] Australia, the UK and the US also have competition laws, in Australia under the term 'trade practices'[48] and in the US 'antitrust'.[49] Partly owing to differences in economic development,[50] however, there has been no international standardisation of competition, with attempts made early in the Doha Development Agenda round of discussions[51] to include competition in the World Trade Organization being unsuccessful.[52] Yet there has been increased voluntary co-operation and exchange of learning between national competition agencies through the International Competition Network.[53]

MMORPGS do not, despite cogent arguments for parallel internal governance of virtual worlds,[54] and their substantial markets and economies,[55] have any competition law—yet. But in any event, that and the extent to which real-world IP rights and disputes are already entrenched in respect of virtual worlds[56] suggests that real-world courts and regulators may consider themselves able to determine competition questions involving virtual worlds. When so doing they would again apply (one) terrestrial competition law.

Competition issues arising will be considered, therefore, on the basis of local competition laws.[57] There is some substantive consistency between

[47] Initially through treaties such as the Berne and Paris Conventions (http://www.wipo.int/treaties/en/) and more recently mandatory harmonisation for members of the World Trade Organization (WTO) through TRIPS. See P Drahos 'Negotiating Intellectual Property: Between Coercion and Dialogue', in P Drahos and R Mayne (eds), '*Global Intellectual Property Rights. Knowledge, Access and Development*' (Basingstoke, Palgrave Macmillan, 2002).

[48] TPA, above n 27.

[49] Sherman Act ss 1 and 2.

[50] Different levels of development did not of course prevent TRIPS, see n 47. See P Marsden, *A Competition Policy for the WTO* (London, Cameron May, 2003) for consideration of the challenges of an international competition system.

[51] See Doha Ministerial Declaration WT/MIN(01)/DEC/1, paras 23–25, http://www.wto.org/english/thewto_e/minist_e/min01_e/mindecl_e.htm#interaction; see Decision of General Council 1 August 2004 WT/L/579 http://www.wto.org/english/tratop_e/dda_e/draft_text_gc_dg_31july04_e.htm. See also Marsden, above n 50, 60ff for early overview of WTO discussions.

[52] For resources and overview, see WTO webpage, 'Interaction between Trade and Competition Policy', http://www.wto.org/english/tratop_e/comp_e/comp_e.htm.

[53] For further background, see http://www.internationalcompetitionnetwork.org/index.php/en/about-icn.

[54] Eg FG Lastowka and D Hunter, 'The Laws of the Virtual Worlds' (2004) 92 *California Law Review* 3.

[55] Eg Second Life Linden dollars can be exchanged for US dollars, http://secondlife.com/whatis/currency.php. See also E Castranova 'A First-hand Account of Market and Society on the Cyberian Frontier' (2001) 2(1) *Gruter Institute Working Papers on Law, Economics, and Evolutionary Biology*, http://www.bepress.com/cgi/viewcontent.cgi?article=1008&context=giwp.

[56] Property issues in virtual worlds: see report via http://secondlife.typepad.com/second_life_lawsuit_bragg/court_order_finding_arbitration_provision_unconsionable_rosedale_stays_in_suit_bragg_v_linden_l/; regarding the place of IP in virtual worlds, see also http://secondlife.com/corporate/tos.php, cl 3; cf W Barfield 'Intellectual Property Rights in Virtual Environments: Considering the Rights of Owners, Programmers and Virtual Avatars' (2006) 39 *Akron Law Review* 649 and A. Jankowich 'EULAw: The Complex Web of Corporate Rule-making in Virtual Worlds' [Spring 2006] *Tulane Journal of Technology & Intellectual Property* 1.

[57] See ch 3.

these laws of larger real-world economies. For example, the laws of the EU, the UK (whose competition legislation has been seen to be similar and closely related to that of the EU as a whole),[58] the US and Australia each prohibit, essentially, agreements which might have a collusive or anti-competitive effect[59] and abuse of market power.[60] This could cover exclusive licences between large companies so that only they can each use key patented aspects of blog technology and refusals to grant a licence to another company to use blog technology, either in itself or to develop the next generation product. Yet the conduct of global businesses might have different impacts in each country; and varying aspects of their conduct might be considered objectionable when set against the finer points of national competition laws (including, from the EU perspective, a focus on EU integration)[61] and different economic approaches.[62] An individual analysis, therefore, is still required in each case. In the light of this, the next section focuses on European competition law in the context of IP and the Internet.

III. THE INTERNET, IP AND EU COMPETITION LAW

A. Anticompetitive Agreements

(i) An Introduction

Article 81 EC Treaty provides:

(1) The following shall be prohibited as incompatible with the common market: all agreements between undertakings, decisions by associations of undertakings and concerted practices which may affect trade between Member States and which have as their object or effect the prevention, restriction or distortion of competition within the common market, and in particular those which:

(a) directly or indirectly fix purchase or selling prices or any other trading conditions;

(b) limit or control production, markets, technical development, or investment;

(c) share markets or sources of supply;

(d) apply dissimilar conditions to equivalent transactions with other trading

---

[58] When CA s 18 is applied, it must, pursuant to CA s 60 and Regulation 1/2003 Art 3(1) (above n 36), be done in a manner consistent with how Art 82 would be applied. The provisions are frequently applied and considered without distinction, eg *Intel v VIA* (above n 33).

[59] Sherman Act s 2; CA s 2; Art 81 EC Treaty; TPA s 45.

[60] Sherman Act s 2; CA s 18, Art 82 EC Treaty; TPA s 46.

[61] See Bishop and Walker, above n 19, and V Korah, *Intellectual Property Rights and the EC Competition Rules* (Oxford, Hart Publishing, 2006) ch 1.

[62] See eg Fox, above n 28; D Kanter, 'IP and Compulsory Licensing on Both Sides of the Atlantic—An Appropriate Antitrust Remedy or a Cutback on Innovation' (2006) 27(7) *ECLR* 351–64.

parties, thereby placing them at a competitive disadvantage;

(e) make the conclusion of contracts subject to acceptance by the other parties of supplementary obligations which, by their nature or according to commercial usage, have no connection with the subject of such contracts.

(2) Any agreements or decisions prohibited pursuant to this Article shall be automatically void.

(3) The provisions of paragraph 1 may, however, be declared inapplicable in the case of:

—any agreement or category of agreements between undertakings;

—any decision or category of decisions by associations of undertakings;

—any concerted practice or category of concerted practices,

which contributes to improving the production or distribution of goods or to promoting technical or economic progress, while allowing consumers a fair share of the resulting benefit, and which does not:

(a) impose on the undertakings concerned restrictions which are not indispensable to the attainment of these objectives;

(b) afford such undertakings the possibility of eliminating competition in respect of a substantial part of the products in question.

Staying with blog technology, consider the grant of an exclusive licence to manufacture and sell blog technology which is the subject of a UK patent, in circumstances where the patent owner was not in a position to so manufacture and sell the technology. This licence might seem consistent with the aims of dissemination of the proceeds of innovation, wider use of Internet opportunities and encouragement of further innovation by payment of some kind to the patent owner. The exclusive nature of the licence, however, could clearly 'limit or control production, markets, technical development' within Article 81(1), and might therefore be void, pursuant to Article 81(2).

An initial issue, given the transnational nature of the Internet, might be the need in Article 81 for an effect on competition 'within the common market'. This requirement is not surprising, given, as noted above, the focus of the EU on integration.[63] Yet European courts and regulators have developed a low threshold requirement in this respect[64] and this would probably be satisfied even by the UK focus of the licence proposed. This sits well with the reality of Internet-related business, as a UK blog provision business will clearly have potential impact throughout the EU (and beyond).

To come within Article 81(1), agreements must also 'have as their object or effect the prevention, restriction or distortion of competition'. The aim of the exclusive licence could be said to enable the innovative blog technology to be available to consumers, rather than to impact upon

---

[63] See above n 30.

[64] Commission Guidelines on the effect on trade concept contained in Articles 81 and 82 of the Treaty [2004] OJ C101/81, *Societe Technique Minière v Maschinenbau Ulm* [1966] ECR 235.

competition. EU courts and regulators have made it clear, however, that exclusive licences of IP can nonetheless come within Article 81(1). The wider economic benefits in respect of innovation and their impact on competition in that market must be assessed,[65] and such analysis is always complex. The relevant principles in respect of agreements dealing with patents and copyright in respect of software are now set out in the Technology Transfer Block Exemption of 2004 (TTBE).[66] If the licence is within the TTBE, then Article 81(1) does not apply.[67] There are also Guidelines on the application of Article 81 of the EC Treaty to technology transfer agreements (TT Guidelines). Notably, the TT Guidelines recognise the complex relationship between IP, competition and innovation, particularly in fast-moving and dynamic industries.[68]

(ii) The Technology Transfer Block Exemption

Licences of patents and software copyright are exempt from Article 81(1), unless the agreement or a particular provision is addressed specifically in the TTBE. The TTBE is applicable if the parties to a licence are competing (eg Typepad[69] and Blogger[70]) and their combined market share is not more than 20 per cent.[71] If they are not competing (eg (possibly) Blogger and Amazon[72] or Blogger and Twitter[73]), then the TTBE will apply if the individual market share of each party is not more than 30 per cent.[74] If these requirements are satisfied, then if a licence includes any 'hardcore' restrictions,[75] it cannot be exempt under the TTBE; if it has 'excluded' restrictions, it might still be exempt if these clauses can be severed from the rest of the agreement.[76]

What is a 'hard core' and 'excluded' restriction depends, again, on whether the parties are competitors. If the parties are competing, examples of 'hard core' clauses are those restricting the ability of the licensee to

---

[65] See *LC Nungesser KG v Commission of the European Communities* (C-258/78) [1981] ECR 45 (Art 81 was formerly Art 85 EC Treaty) and see consideration of this case in MacQueen, Waelde and Laurie, above n 11, paras 20.27–20.28.

[66] See above n 27 and below. See in particular Art 1(b).

[67] On the basis of Art 81(3)–TTBE Art 2 (above n 27). Note that the European Commission has over the years issued a series of block exemptions in different fields: see http://ec.europa.eu/comm/competition/antitrust/legislation/legislation.html. See MacQueen, Waelde and Laurie, above n 11, paras 20.30–20.33 for overview and history of block exemptions and changes to the regulatory system.

[68] See s III and paras 5–17, 25, 32–33, 132–203 (in particular 138–39) of the TT Guidelines (above n 27).

[69] http://www.typepad.com/.

[70] https://www.blogger.com/start.

[71] TTBE Arts 1(j) and 3(1).

[72] http://www.amazon.co.uk/

[73] http://twitter.com/

[74] TTBE Arts 1(j) and 3(2).

[75] See full list in TTBE Art 4.

[76] See full list in TTBE Art 5.

exploit the technology (unless this is indispensable to prevent disclosure of the licensor's confidential know-how)[77] or clauses allocating markets, although it is permitted to restrict sublicensing in particular territories.[78] If parties are not competing, then the only excluded restriction is a limit on the licensee's ability to exploit the technology or its ability to conduct research and development—unless, again, this is indispensable to prevent disclosure of the licensor's confidential know-how.[79]

How does the TTBE work in practice? It was introduced after much consultation[80] and its aim was to enable a dynamic and informed balancing of the benefit of the agreement and its impact on other competitors and consumers.[81] This was considered particularly necessary as the previous block exemption[82] was highly formulaic and agreements could be brought within it which still had a negative impact on competition. Some have argued, however, that the focus of the current TTBE on individual circumstances and assessment, notwithstanding the further guidance provided in the TT Guidelines,[83] has introduced too much uncertainty for business and innovation.[84]

These uncertainties arise because the assessment of key concepts—market definition, competitors and market share—is not straightforward. These issues are ever present in competition law and have given rise to significant case-law and regulatory statement, some of which is considered below in respect of abuse of dominance.[85] The TTBE also provides its own guidance, stating that the questions are to be assessed in respect of the relevant product and technology markets; that parties will be competing if they operate without infringing the other's IP rights; will be part of the same market if their offerings are substitutable for users by reason of price and use and for suppliers if they could realistically supply the other goods in response to a change in price of products of others;[86] and that market share is to be assessed mainly on the basis of available sales data[87] with, importantly given the evolving nature of provision and use of blogs and

---

[77] TTBE Art 4(1)(d).

[78] TTBE Art 4(1)(c)(iii).

[79] TTBE Art 5(2).

[80] See http://eur-lex.europa.eu/LexUriServ/LexUriServ.do?uri=OJ:c:2003:235:0010:0054:en:PDF.

[81] See TTBE Recs 3–8.

[82] Commission Regulation 240/96 of 31 January 1996 on the application of Article 85(3) of the Treaty to certain categories of technology transfer agreements, http://eur-lex.europa.eu/smartapi/cgi/sga_doc?smartapi!celexapi!prod!CELEXnumdoc&lg=en&numdoc=31996R0240&model=guichett.

[83] TT Guidelines, paras 34–117.

[84] P Treacy and T Heide, 'The New EC Technology Transfer Block Exemption' (2004) 25(9) *European Intellectual Property Review* (*EIPR*) 414–20.

[85] See below p 435.

[86] TTBE Art 1(j).

[87] TTBE Art 8(1) and (2).

MMORPGS,[88] the recognition that market share and market can change over the term of an agreement.[89]

(iii) A Wider Question

If an agreement cannot have the benefit of the TTBE, Article 81(3) may still mean that the agreement is not prohibited. As is considered below,[90] this may be important in the Internet context in respect of patent pools and standards. It is frequently helpful for consumers, and efficient for business, for all products in a field to use the same technologies, or at least ones that are compatible and interoperable. One means of doing this is through formal industry standards, with an example being the GSM standard administered through the European Telecommunications Standards Institute (ETSI), which deals with telecommunications technology in Europe.[91] Owners of IP which is part of a standard could, however, have a significant ability to affect competition and the operation of the market.[92]

In recognition of the risks of reliance on IP in relation to technology which is part of a standard, standards-setting bodies have required that businesses subscribing to the standard disclose IP which is 'essential'[93] to it; and that they license that IP on a fair, reasonable and non-discriminatory basis to other members of the body.[94] This has been done both by bodies

---

[88] For commentary on the TTBE more generally, see H Ullrich, 'The Interaction between Competition Law and Intellectual Property Law: An Overview' and 'Panel II: EU Policy Issues. A Critical Examination of the TT Block Exemption Regulation and TT Guidelines', S Bishop and D Gore, 'From Black and White to Enlightenment? An Economic View of the Reform of EC Competition Rules on Technology Transfer', L Kjoelbye and L Peeperkorn, 'The New Technology Transfer Block Exemption Regulation and Guidelines' and S Anderman 'Technology Transfer and the IP/Competition Interface' in Ehlermann and Atanasui (eds), above n 11, respectively, xxxii–li, 34–45, 141–160, 161–209 and 211–36.

[89] TTBE Art 4(3) and 8.

[90] See below p 430.

[91] See website http://www.etsi.org/WebSite/homepage.aspx and regarding 'interoperability' http://www.etsi.org/WebSite/Standards/Interoperability.aspx. See also W3C http://www.w3.org/. For consideration of the place of standards in relation to the internet and their potential consequence, see Commission Microsoft Decision, above n 38, 17–18, 33ff and 197.

[92] See detailed analysis in MA Lemley, 'Intellectual Property Rights and Standard-Setting Organizations' (2002) 90 *California Law Review* 1889 and KJ Koelman, 'An Exceptio Standardis: Do We Need an IP Exemption for Standards?' (2006) 37(7) *International Review of Intellectual Property and Competition Law* 823–43. See also policy discussion at the World Intellectual Property Organization in March 2009 at the Standing Committee on the Law of Patents, see Standards and Patent Secretariat Document, http://www.wipo.int/edocs/mdocs/scp/en/scp_13/scp_13_2.pdf, IP Watch discussion, http://www.ip-watch.org/weblog/2009/03/25/concerns-voiced-at-wipo-over-potential-conflicts-between-ip-and-standards/, and Summary by the Chair http://www.wipo.int/edocs/mdocs/scp/en/scp_13/scp_13_7.doc; see also the Dynamic Coalition on Open Standards at the Internet Governance Forum, eg http://igf-dcos.org/dcos-statement-on-procurement-in-support-of-interoperability-and-open-standards/.

[93] The question of essential has led to its own disputes: *Nokia Corp v Interdigital Technology Corp* [2007] EWHC 3077 (Pat) 2007 WL 4587096.

[94] See also Valimaki above n 40; P Treacy and S Lawrance, 'FRANDly Fire: Are Industry Standards Doing More Harm than Good?' (2008) 3(1) *Journal of Intellectual Property Law &*

supportive of IP and private control of standards, such as ETSI,[95] and those that are more open, such as the Storage Networking Industry Association (SNIA) which relates to data storage and information management.[96] The SNIA also requires that a member should leave the standard if there is no such licensing.[97]

Further, different parts of important technology may be the subject of various patents. In such a case, without a license of one patent it may not be possible for technology that is the subject of another patent to be used without infringing the first patent.[98] The solution to this could be a patent pool, where all relevant patent owners agree to cross-license their patents, with the end-product then available for license to others.

Both standards and patent pools can be consistent with and support innovation and consumer benefit.[99] The TTBE does not apply, however, to licensing agreements with more than two parties and specifically does not apply to patent pools;[100] and despite their potential benefits, standards agreements are likely to come within Article 81(1), given their requirement of use of particular technology[101] and the provisions as to licensing terms.[102] Such licences must be assessed on their own merits using the TT Guidelines, therefore, to establish whether they come within Article 81(3).[103]

The TT Guidelines address standards and patent pools. They set out in detail the factors to be taken into account, in each case in balancing the benefits for innovation and dissemination and the wider impact on compe-

Practice 22–29; note also discussion there of arguments that non-disclosure could limit the ability to enforce a patent; and A Gupta, 'Are Open Standards a Prerequisite to Open Source? A Perspective in Light of Technical and Legal Developments' (2009) 15(1) *Computer and Telecommunications Law Review* (*CTLR*) 3–8.

95 See 'Intellectual Property Rights in ETSI', http://www.etsi.org/WebSite/AboutETSI/IPRs InETSI/IPRsinETSI.aspx, providing link to ETSI Rules of Procedure, Annex 6, ETSI Intellectual Property Rights Policy (2008) ('ETSI IP Policy'), cl 4, 6.1. 6bis, 15(6). If this is not done, work on the standard can be suspended, there can be further consultation, and, ultimately, the standard may not proceed or, if the standard is already in place, it may no longer be recognised or it may be modified: see ETSI IP Policy cl 6.2, 6.3, 8.1.2, 8.1.3, 8.2.

96 See website http://www.snia.org/tech_activities/standards/.

97 See SNIA IP Policy v 3 (2006), http://www.snia.org/about/corporate_info/ip_policy/SNIA_ IP_Policy_v3.0_Final.pdf, esp paras 2.6, 3.3.2, 3.3.4, 3.4, 3.5.1, 3.5.2 and 5.1. See further analysis of patents and open standards in M Välimäki and V Oksanen, 'Patents on Compatibility Standards and Open Source—Do Patent Law Exceptions and Royalty-Free Requirements Make Sense?' (2005) 2(3) *SCRIPT-ed* 397, at http://www.law.ed.ac.uk/ahrc/script-ed/vol2-3/valimaki. asp.

98 Which could amount to a patent thicket—for discussion from another field, see G Ohana et al, 'Disclosure and Negotiation of Licensing Terms Prior to Adoption of Industry Standards: Preventing Another Patent ambush?' (2003) 24(12) *ECLR* 644–56.

99 See eg ETSI Guidelines for Antitrust Compliance (2008), http://www.etsi.org/WebSite/ document/Legal/ETSI_Guidelines_for_Antitrust_Compliance.pdf.

100 TTBE Rec 7.

101 Art 81(1) (b).

102 Art 81(1) (a).

103 TT Guidelines, para 3.

tition in that market.[104] In early 2009, there was as yet no formal decision from EC regulators on Article 81(3) and standards, although the European Commission had engaged with the ETSI in respect of its IP policy, which led to change in 2005.[105] US competition authorities considered similar questions in 2006 in relation to the VITA open standard and its impact on competition and innovation.[106] Revealingly, the regulator considered that it would not oppose the disclosure and licensing requirements.[107]

(iv) Summary

IP agreements relating to development and use of Internet technology can raise competition questions. In the EU, the TTBE and TT Guidelines attempt to address these in a dynamic and informed manner. This should enable further innovation to occur, and IP to be enjoyed, while delivering solutions consistent with competition, albeit at the price of some certainty.[108] Yet, as noted at the outset, a key concern in respect of competition, IP and the Internet is the potential for an IP owner to hold an industry to ransom. Even if an agreement relating to a key technology was found to come within Article 81(3)) or the TTBE, it may still involve abuse of a dominant position.[109] This is now considered.

[104] TT Guidelines, paras 167, 210ff. For academic debate and consideration, see Panel Discussion III, 'Patent Pools'; AD Melamed and D Lerch, 'Uncertain Patents, Antitrust and Patent Pools'; P Plompen, 'The New Technology Transfer Guidelines (TTG) as Applied to Patent Pools and Patent Pool Licensing, Some Observations Regarding the Concept of 'Essential Technologies'; and H Ullrich, 'Patent Pools: Approaching a Patent Law Problem via Competition Policy', all in Ehlermann and Atanasui (eds), above n 11, at, respectively, 239–53, 273–93, 295–303, 305–28.

[105] The ETSI IP Policy of 2008 (above n 95) replaced a policy put in place in 2007. For comment on competition issues with the previous rules, see P Treacy and S Lawrance, 'Patent Misuse and Patent Ambush: The Competition Authorities get to Grips with IP' (2006) 5 *European Current Law* xi–xvi. Also available at http://www.bristows.com/?pid=46&level=2&nid=861, s 2.

[106] See website http://www.vita.com/vso-stds.html.

[107] See US Department of Justice Press Release, http://www.usdoj.gov/atr/public/press_releases/2006/219379.htm. For analysis of this, see P Treacy 'Safer Standard Setting', http://www.bristows.com/?pid=46&level=2&nid=1013 (originally published in *Competition Insight Magazine*). For wider analysis of standards, see H Ullrich, 'The Interaction between Competition Law and Intellectual Property Law: An Overview', in Ehlermann and Atanasui (eds), above n 11, xvii–xxix; Ghidini and Arezzo, above n 11, 108–15.

[108] See full analysis of Art 81, IP and competition in Korah, above n 61, chs 4–6.

[109] By limiting production, markets or technical development these examples might come within paras (a) and (b) of Art 82 and see TT Guidelines para 1(2). See *Michelin v Commission* [1983] ECR 3461 ('*Michelin*'); *Tetra Pak v EC Commission* [1990] ECR II-309 ('*Tetra Pak*'); and *Compagnie Maritime Belge v EC Commission* [2000] ECR I-1365 confirming the potential relevance of Art 82.

B. Abuse of a Dominant Position

(i) Basic Principles

Article 82 EC Treaty provides:

> Any abuse by one or more undertakings of a dominant position within the common market or in a substantial part of it shall be prohibited as incompatible with the common market insofar as it may affect trade between Member States.
>
> Such abuse may, in particular, consist in:
>
> (a) directly or indirectly imposing unfair purchase or selling prices or other unfair trading conditions;
>
> (b) limiting production, markets or technical development to the prejudice of consumers;
>
> (c) applying dissimilar conditions to equivalent transactions with other trading parties, thereby placing them at a competitive disadvantage;
>
> (d) making the conclusion of contracts subject to acceptance by the other parties of supplementary obligations which, by their nature or according to commercial usage, have no connection with the subject of such contracts.

(ii) Article 82 and the Internet

Given the points made above, it is perhaps not surprising that the European Commission has been active on the basis of Article 82 in relation to IP and standards. In August 2007, it launched an investigation into Rambus. The Commission was concerned that Rambus had made excessive requests for royalties for dynamic random access memory chip (DRAM) patents forming part of a standard and had failed to disclose these patents as part of the standards-setting process.[110] The Commission has also taken a critical approach to refusals to supply and license technology which has, through market success and initial industry engagement, become a more informal standard.[111] Further, the Commission and courts have confirmed in cases involving valuable information, both real world and Internet related, that in exceptional circumstances refusal to license or supply key

---

[110] COMP /38.636. See EC Commission Press release http://europa.eu/rapid/pressReleases Action.do?reference=MEMO/07/330&format=HTML&aged=0&language=EN&guiLangu age=en, referring to a previous US FTC investigation and remedy in relation to Rambus' alleged non-disclosure of patents which were part of an industry standard. In April 2008, the District of Columbia Court of Appeals overturned the regulatory decision, *Rambus Inc, v Federal Trade Commission*, http://pacer.cadc.uscourts.gov/docs/common/opinions/200804/07-1086-1112217. pdf; see also Treacy and Lawrance, above n 105, s 2. In February 2009, the US Supreme Court declined to hear the case, see http://www.rambus.com/us/news/press_releases/2009/090223.html.

[111] See Commission Microsoft Decision, above n 38, 33ff, 119ff, 120–30, 188; and IMS Commission Decision, above n 40, paras 20 20, 26, 75–92, 123. This was also considered by the ECJ in that case, *IMS Health GmbH & Co OHG v NDC Health GmbH & Co KG (Case C-418/01)* [2004] ECR I-5039 ('*IMS*') see paras 29, 30.

technology can be abuse of a dominant position—irrespective of whether it is the subject of an IP right.[112]

EU competition law could be used, therefore, to fetter more excessive behaviour of IP owners in relation to the Internet. Like Article 81, Article 82 applies only in respect of conduct with an impact on trade between Member States. Again[113] this requirement is likely readily satisfied, given the number of Internet service providers, Internet consumers, Internet businesses and IP owners that have links to EU Member States.[114]

Yet, as with Article 81, careful analysis of Article 82 is required in each case. There is no equivalent of Article 81(3), the TTBE and the TT Guidelines. It is well established, however, that owning and exercising an IP right will not necessarily lead to a dominant position in a market and that refusing to license IP will not necessarily be an abuse.[115] It is not enough for an IP owner to seem powerful and to engage in conduct which some others do not like, in relation to technology that they might see as essential for their proposed activities. The relevant principles are considered below.

(iii) What Is the Market, Properly Defined?

The market must first be assessed and the European Commission has set out market definition guidelines.[116] The two key components are supply and demand side substitutability and geography—as was the case with the market definition guidance given in the TTBE considered above. Given that a patent confers exclusive rights, it might seem that there could be no substitutes; however, while a patented blog related technology must be novel to be patented in the first place,[117] it may be able to be used for a similar purpose as other blog-related technologies or other means of communication. Assessing this actual and potential substitutability can involve collecting evidence from consumers, potential competitors and surveys.[118] For example, do consumers see the patented technology as one of several that enables consumers to write blogs or communicate, or do they see it as the only means of communication in a particular manner (eg if it links a blog with a new form of media communication)? How readily would they

---

[112] Eg CFI Microsoft, above n 40, H16, paras 107,112, 116, 124, 269–89.

[113] See above p 426.

[114] See above pp 423, 425, 427 and eg EC Commission Information Society Portal, http://ec.europa.eu/information_society/ecowor/ebusiness/index_en.htm.

[115] *Volvo AB v Erik Veng (UK) Ltd* (238/87) [1988] ECR 6211 ('*Volvo v Veng*').

[116] Commission Notice on the definition of the relevant market for the purposes of Community competition law [1997] OJ C372/03, http://eur-lex.europa.eu/smartapi/cgi/sga_doc?smartapi!celexapi!prod!CELEXnumdoc&lg=en&numdoc=31997Y1209(01)&model=guiche ti ('Market Definition Notice').

[117] See above n 13.

[118] Consider CFI Microsoft, above n 40, paras 23–28, 480–664; for an example in respect of patents, albeit in the pharmaceutical field, see *Tetra Pak,* where the ECJ considered products, possible market shares, and territory in relation to patents—see paras 1, 3, 5.

switch product? What factors would be relevant—price or technical quality? Could another provider provide the same service? What obstacles might it face? These questions must be assessed in each case in the light of the competition question arising. There may be different results and app-roaches depending on whether the concern is in respect of past or potential conduct and in relation to the short or longer term.[119]

Regarding geography, it might seem that a UK patent could only impact upon the UK, and so that should be the market; yet where courts have considered geographical markets in patent cases, it has been accepted that these markets can be international.[120] In the context of the Internet and blog technology, a global market assessment is likely appropriate, subject to the question of language and translation technologies.

(iv) Assessment of Dominance

Within the defined market, it must then be assessed whether or not the IP owner is in a dominant position. If the market is all technology relating to Internet communications for use in the English language, then it is less likely that one UK patent owner is in a dominant position in that market. It is tempting to characterise this issue in terms of market share; and indeed, if the owner of copyright in key software has an 80 per cent market share, then it is very likely to be dominant. But the test is whether an entity can act to an appreciable extent independently of competitors and consumers in the market—eg increase price or decrease supply—without loss of customers and/or competitor activity.[121]

In terms of what this might mean, the UK Office of Fair Trading (OFT) Guidelines,[122] which build on EU guidelines and case-law, provide a helpful summary of the approach that might be adopted by the European Commission in relation to Article 82. An IP owner with a market share of 40 per cent might still be dominant in respect of the relevant period,[123] depending on how that market operates—perhaps all other participants have a very small market share.[124] The key issue is the extent of any external constraints on the behaviour of the IP owner and in particular the barriers facing others who might wish to enter the market.[125]

[119] These matters are considered in the Market Definition Notice. Regarding markets, IP and technology, see also Govaere, above n 23, 131, 136, 139–40; and M Monti, 'Article 82 and New Economy Markets', in C Graham and F Smith (eds), *Competition, Regulation and the New Economy* (Oxford, Hart Publishing, 2004) 18–31.
[120] *Intel v VIA* paras 1, 8, 12, 16, 18, 91, and CFI Microsoft, para 29. More generally, see Drexl, above n 26.
[121] *Michelin*, para 30; *F Hoffmann La Roche & Co AG v Commission of the European Communities* [1979] ECR 461 para 39.
[122] See above n 35.
[123] OFT Guidelines, 4.2.
[124] Ibid, 2.12.
[125] Ibid, 2.10, 3.1-5.

Particularly important in this regard in the Internet and communications field are network effects,[126] consumer attitudes and IP. A patent or copyright over a key technology, piece of software or information structure could be a significant barrier to another seeking to provide its own service. There could be a next-generation combination of blog technology and Internet protocol telephony which is patented and which is not interoperable with other communication forms. If this became instantly accepted and used by consumers, it would not appealing for new consumers to use anything else if they were unable to speak to the large number of existing users of the other technology. These apparent network effects may in fact be readily overcome, however, in a dynamic and innovative industry where new, better and cheaper systems are regularly developed and adopted. In such a case, owners of IP in respect of relevant underlying technology might not be considered to be dominant.[127]

(v) Abusive Conduct

IP owners should not be criticised merely because they are in a dominant position in a market—it is not holding the dominant position that is prohibited, but its abuse. Decisions in the Microsoft case have been criticised as ignoring this distinction, and as imposing an unjustified burden on the powerful;[128] yet it is well established that those holding a dominant position are subject to additional responsibilities and restrictions.[129] So where is the line?

Some guidance can be obtained from the cases introduced at the start of this section. In *Volvo v Veng* in 1988, the European Court of Justice (ECJ) stressed that although the right to prevent third-party manufacture and refusal to license remained the very subject matter of IP,[130] in exceptional circumstances[131] a refusal to license could be abuse of a dominant position. Seeking to establish the parameters of this led to a substantial line of jurisprudence. In the 1990s the well-known case of *Magill*, involving television listings protected by copyright, was the first time the ECJ found that there was abuse.[132] The ECJ also stated that there would be the necessary 'exceptional circumstances' if: there is no actual or potential substitute for the

---

126 See MA Lemley and D McGowan, 'Legal Implications of Economic Network Effects' (1998) 86 *California Law Review* 479; Kallay, above n 26, 42–3, 90–109 133–53; Ghidini, above n 26, 39, 66–67, 104–07; M Messina, 'Article 82 and the New Economy: Need for Modernisation?' (2006) 2(2) *Competition Law Review*, available via http://www.clasf.org/CompLRev/Issues/Vol2Issue2Art3Messina.pdf.
127 OFT Guidelines s 5, in particular 5.15, 5.21–22, 5.34, 5.36.
128 J Appeldoorn 'He Who Spareth the Rod Hateth His Son? Microsoft, Super-dominance and Article 82' (2005) 26(12) *ECLR* 653–58.
129 *Michelin*, para 57.
130 *Volvo v Veng*, para 4(2).
131 Ibid, para 9—with some examples provided that are not relevant here.
132 *RTE and ITP v EC Commission* [1995] ECR I-743 ('*Magill*').

work protected by IP in respect of which a licence is sought; the work would be used for the development of a new product for which there is unmet consumer demand;[133] the refusal will exclude competition in a secondary market;[134] there is no objective justification for the refusal of the licence.[135]

These criteria were considered in 1997 in *Tierce Ladbroke*,[136] which involved licences to televise horse races in different countries; in 1998 in *Oscar Bronner*,[137] which was not an IP case but concerned access to a successful local newspaper distribution network; and in 1999 in *Micro Leader*, in respect of attempts, through contract and differential pricing, to prevent parallel importing from Canada to France of French language software.[138] These cases suggested that all elements of the *Magill* test need not in fact be met. In 2004, however, the ECJ in *IMS*, a case concerning access to means of presenting pharmaceutical data which was protected by copyright, suggested that the *Magill* criteria are both exhaustive and cumulative.[139] *IMS* provided some clarification and development: the ECJ held that 'indispensable' required there to be no economically viable alternative (whether for technical, legal or economic reasons)[140] available to a business or combination of businesses of the same size as the dominant undertaking;[141] that the 'secondary market' need only be hypothetical;[142] and that without the licence there must be a total lack of competition (not just on the part of the access seeker).[143]

---

133 Ibid, para 54.

134 Ibid, para 54.

135 Ibid, para 55.

136 *Tierce Ladbroke SA v Commission of the European Communities* (T504/93) [1997] ECR II-923 [1997] 5 CMLR 309 ('*Tierce Ladbroke*'), paras 130–32.

137 *Oscar Bronner GmbH & Co KG v Mediaprint Zeitungs- und Zeitschriftenverlag GmbH & Co KG* (C7/97) [1998] ECR I-7791 [1999] 4 CMLR 112 ('*Oscar Bronner*'), paras 39–45.

138 *Micro Leader Business v Commission of the European Communities* (T198/98) [2000] All ER (EC) 361 [1999] ECR II-3989 [2000] 4 CMLR 886 ('*Micro Leader*') paras 1–4, 9, 50, 54–55.

139 *IMS* H11, para 38. For analysis of this decision, see E Derclaye 'The IMS Health Decision and the Reconciliation of Copyright and Competition Law' (2004) 29(5) *European Law Review* (*ELR*) 687–97; B Ong, 'Building Brick Barricades and Other Barriers to Entry: Abusing a Dominant Position by Refusing to License Intellectual Property Rights' (2005) 26(4) *ECLR* 215–24; and C Stothers, 'IMS Health and its Implications for Compulsory Licensing in Europe' (2004) 26(10) *EIPR* 467–72.

140 *IMS* paras 28–29; D Ridyard, 'Compulsory Access under EC Competition Law—A New Doctrine of Convenient Facilities and the Case for Price Regulation' (2004) 25(11) *ECLR* 669–73. This has been argued to be based on the essential facilities doctrine, considered in detail by the Advocate General in *Oscar Bronner* AGO, paras 28, 35–53 regarding infrastructure and essential facilities cases in the UK, EU and US. Courts have, however, steered clear of this label and to the extent it has been considered it seemed part of analysis of, or support for, the lack of objective justification or indispensability requirements, or a barrier to others entering the market such that there might be dominance. See also IMS Commission Decision, above n 40, 62–4 and CI Nagy, 'Refusal to Deal and the Doctrine of Essential Facilities in US and EC Competition Law: A Comparative Perspective and a Proposal for a Workable Analytical Framework' (2007) 32(5) *ELR* 664–85; and see also OFT Guidelines, 5.13.

141 *Oscar Bronner*, paras 41–45.

142 *IMS*, paras 42–44.

143 *IMS* para 37, consistent with *Magill*, paras 55–56.

The need for a new product to be proposed by the access seeker has been strongly criticised—notably on the basis that while it might be objectionable to prevent new product development, it can also be undesirable to prevent others competing in a market in respect of a technology, particularly when the technology protected by the IP has become a standard.[144] The very focus on the *Magill* criteria has also been criticised as inconsistent with the initial flexibility of 'exceptional circumstances' as seen in *Volvo v Veng*.[145]

Yet just before the ECJ decision in *IMS*, the European Commission took a wider and more flexible approach to refusal and abuse in its consideration of the behaviour of Microsoft.[146] In assessing whether Microsoft's refusal to supply interoperability information was abuse, the Commission focused on all the circumstances of the situation, rather than on the tests suggested from *Magill* and the other cases considered above.[147] On this approach, it did not matter that Microsoft's competitors did not propose to develop a new product; the refusal to supply indispensable interoperability information was found to be abuse on the basis of a combination of patterns of conduct, disruption of levels of supply and the risk of elimination of competition.[148] Further, the Commission was very concerned at the network effects considered to be enjoyed by Microsoft and negative impact on consumers and innovation.[149] The Commission rejected the argument that Microsoft's IP rights in the information protocols might provide objective justification for the refusal to share the information;[150] however, the Commission also expressed concern that its actions should not have an overly negative impact on encouragement of innovation. This consideration by the Commission of encouragement of innovation might suggest a new approach to ensuring a balance of encouragement, reward and supporting third-party innovation during the term of the IP right.[151] The broader, more flexible approach, and the possible new innovation balance, were challenged by Microsoft when it sought to annul the

---

[144] D Geradin, 'Limiting the Scope of Article 82 EC: What Can the EU Learn from the U.S. Supreme Court's Judgment in Trinko in the Wake of Microsoft, IMS and Deutsche Telekom' (2004) *Common Market Law Review* 41; D McCann, 'European Union: Competition Law—Abuse of Dominant Position' (2006) 17(4) *International Company and Commercial Law Review* N27–31, N30.

[145] Korah, above n 19, ss 3.2.2 and 4.1.

[146] Commission Microsoft Decision, above n 38.

[147] Ibid, 46–47.

[148] Ibid, 151–74. The Commission referred to the evolution of Microsoft's market shares, the update of its new technologies, competitors' statements, the heterogeneity of computer networks, the level of uptake of alternatives, Microsoft's behaviour and customer evidence. The Commission rejected explanations from Microsoft at 174–85.

[149] Ibid, 186–89.

[150] Ibid, 190.

[151] Ibid, 190–98. See also Korah, above n 19, s 4.3.1 and S Vezzoso, 'The Incentives Balance Test in the EU Microsoft Case: a Pro-innovation 'Economics-based' Approach?' (2006) 27(7) *ECLR* 382–90.

European Commission's decision before the CFI. Yet rather than consider these questions, the CFI judgment focuses on whether the (by then available) *IMS* test was in fact satisfied. The CFI considered that the *IMS* test was indeed met on the facts[152] and therefore did not comment on whether the more flexible approach was appropriate.[153] The CFI proceeded, however, to stretch the *IMS* test, considering that the potentially problematic 'new product' requirement should be seen more as a need for 'technical development' by others;[154] and that the question of elimination of competition should be assessed on the basis of a risk of elimination of viable competition.[155] The CFI also considered that the EC Commission's assessment of IP, innovation and objective justification did not involve the introduction of a new test.[156]

Whatever 'technical development' and 'viable competition' might mean, they are likely to be less linked to consumer demand and more linked to technical and early stage progress and support of competitors.[157] It is also interesting to note that a more flexible approach to exceptional circumstances is advocated in the European Commission's ongoing review of Article 82,[158] as is the suggested innovation balance and direct competitor access to interoperability information, even where investment has been incurred in developing that and acquiring IP.[159]

So this issue is unlikely to have been laid to rest; and for now it is unclear when refusal to license IP might be abuse of a dominant position in terms of Article 82. The *Magill* and *IMS* tests, even as now interpreted by

[152] CFI Microsoft, paras 331–33, 336. See paras 103–06, 108–10, 118–53, 207–66, 337–422 regarding interoperability and indispensability, also I Eagles and L Longdin, 'Microsoft's refusal to disclose software interoperability information and the Court of First Instance' (2008) 30(5) *EIPR* 205–08.

[153] This was consistent with the nature of the review which the CFI could undertake, see consideration CFI Microsoft, paras 84–90.

[154] Ibid, paras 621–65, esp 647.

[155] Ibid, paras 560–620.

[156] Ibid, paras 666–703, notably paras 690–91, 695, 697–98.

[157] See Garrod and Keane, above n 44; B Batchelor, 'The Fallout from Microsoft: the Court of First Instance Leaves Critical IT Industry Issues Unanswered' (2008) 14(1) *CTLR* 17–22 and detailed analysis in D Howarth and K McMahon, '"Windows has Performed an Illegal Operation": The Court of First Instance's Judgment in Microsoft v Commission' (2008) 29(2) *ECLR* 117–34 and S Anderman, 'Microsoft v Commission and the Interoperability Issue' (2008) 30(10) *EIPR* 395–99. Regarding interoperability and other regimes more generally, see MAC Dizon, 'Decompiling the Software Directive, the Microsoft CFI case and the I2010 strategy: How to Reverse Engineer an International Interoperability Regime' (2008) 14(8) *CTLR* 213–19.

[158] See links at http://ec.europa.eu/comm/competition/antitrust/art82/index.html (including consultation submissions and economic analysis—http://ec.europa.eu/comm/competition/publications/studies/eagcp_july_21_05.pdf). See more generally J Drexl, 'Abuse of Dominance in Licensing and Refusal to License: "A More Economic Approach" to Competition by Imitation and to Competition by Substitution', in Ehlermann and Atanasui (eds), above n 11, 647–64.

[159] DG Competition Staff Discussion Paper on the application of Article 82 of the Treaty to exclusionary abuses http://ec.europa.eu/comm/competition/antitrust/others/discpaper2005.pdf. Relevant paragraphs in respect of issues addressed here are 77, 225ff (esp 238ff). See also McCann, above n 144.

the CFI in *Microsoft*, are rigid—and as a result, refusal to license can be abusive only in limited cases.[160] The emerging alternative (if any) from the European Commission involves a complex analysis of market behaviour and innovation prospects that makes it difficult to predict the outcome—rather like the TTBE.

IV. CONCLUSION

Competition law can enable an informed and balanced analysis of the impact and proper place of IP rights in relation to the Internet. It should also curb the use that IP owners make of the power they acquire, both on their own and in conjunction with others, without criticising and restricting unnecessarily those who have been successful and innovative.

But competition law, even more than IP law, operates at national and regional levels. It could be argued, given the global nature of the Internet, that any activity in relation to the Internet, even from one non-EU Member State in relation to another, still has an impact on trade between Member States.[161] This could enable the European Commission and courts to impose their competition law in respect of all Internet-related activities. This would in turn avoid the issues considered above in respect of the lack of an international (and transworld) competition law, subject of course to the more practical question of enforcement. It should be borne in mind, however, that US competition or antitrust law applies if the conduct has an effect in the US. This has not prevented parallel investigations by the EU and US regulators in respect of the international activities of multinational businesses, such as those in relation to Microsoft.[162]

Whichever competition law is applied, the extent to which conduct is consistent with competition law must be assessed in each case, with careful regard for the facts, consumer and competitor activity and the theories of economics and innovation that are considered relevant by the decision-maker applying the appropriate law. These theories, and perspectives on the relevance of IP to innovation, have changed over time. While there is a growing openness to IP and competition being consistent (or not necessarily inconsistent), there is also a scepticism as to the place of IP in encouraging innovation in software and in the Web 2.0 and beyond.

In summary, IP owners should be aware of the potential might of

---

[160] This is consistent with the conclusion reached after the US Department of Justice and Federal Trade Commission Hearings on Antitrust and Intellectual Property Law and Policy in the Knowledge-Based Economy (2002). See http://www.ftc.gov/reports/innovation/P040101 PromotingInnovationandCompetitionrpt0704.pdf, 5–6 and 15–22, 23, 27–32. Note that in 2009 in the FTC established a fresh round of hearings, 'The Evolving IP Marketplace', http://www.ftc.gov/bc/workshops/ipmarketplace/.

[161] *Dow Jones v Gutnick* [2002] HCA 56; 210 CLR 575. See generally ch 3.

[162] See eg Garrod and Keane, above n 44, and Korah, above n 61, ch 9, for further consideration of the national and international question.

competition law; and competition advocates must recognise the power held by IP owners. There is no easy answer to the relationship between IP and competition; it is best described as an uneasy truce, seeking to accommodate the evolving norms and practices of the Internet world.

Part IV
Privacy, Data Protection and Cybercrime

14

Privacy and Data Protection Online: The Laws Don't Work?

LILIAN EDWARDS[1]

PRIVACY IS NOT a simple subject, especially online privacy. What kind of value is privacy? How far should the law protect it? What balance should be struck between the individual's right to privacy and the duty of the society to protect its people from terrorism and crime? Is privacy an objective concept, important in the same way to all persons, or is it an inherently subjective value, in which case how should or can a balance be struck against other values, not restricted to security, but including freedom of expression and the promotion of the market? Is privacy solely an individual right, or does society as a whole have a stake in the preservation of privacy as a common good?

If we decide (as historically, we have) that privacy is a value worthy of protection by *law*, how should this be done, and who should enforce such rules, both against the state, and against commercial and private interests? And, of particular significance in this chapter, can rules protecting 'data privacy' be practically enforced in the transnational, borderless, information-dense world the Internet has now created?

Questions like these have long been contested both in law and in society,

[1] My grateful thanks to Rowena Rodrigues, PhD student, University of Edinburgh for substantial research assistance; to Judith Rauhofer, Lecturer, UCLAN, for many helpful insights and arguments as to the nature of privacy as a value and a right; to Ian Brown, Research Fellow, Oxford Internet Institute; and Chris Marsden, Senior Lecturer, Essex University, for collaboration on research on the social networking site parts of this chapter, and general advice; and to Hector MacQueen for comments on the draft. Any errors are of course the author's alone.

Parts of this chapter appeared in earlier and considerably different forms in L Edwards and L Rodrigues, ' The Right to Privacy and Confidentiality for Children: The Law and Current Challenges', in C Clark and J McGhee (eds), *Private and Confidential?: Handling Personal Information in Social and Health Services* (London, Polity Press, 2008); L Edwards, 'Reconstructing Consumer Privacy Protection On-line: A Modest Proposal' (2004) *International Journal of Law, Computers and Technology* 314; and in L Edwards and I Brown, 'Data Control and Social Networking: Irreconcilable Ideas?', in A Matwyshyn (ed.) *Harboring Data: Information Security, Law and the Corporation* (Stanford, Stanford University Press, 2009, forthcoming). Available in draft version at SSRN: http://ssrn.com/abstract=1148732.
[2] See Edwards, ch 15.

and will recur throughout this and the following four chapters. They will not be solved in this brief introduction. Instead, this chapter attempts to give a very basic legal grounding on privacy and data protection law, which will be built upon in specific key instances such as spamming[2] and other forms of online marketing and data collection,[3] state surveillance[4] and data retention[5] in subsequent chapters.

First, we will briefly consider what the legal rules are which seek to protect the privacy and confidence rights of individuals in the UK and Europe and how they evolved; secondly, we will focus on how effectively (or not) these rules operate in the context of the Internet and the information society; thirdly, we will consider some key recent societal developments which suggest that privacy is declining in significance as a societal value, while 'openness' is in the ascendant; finally some brief conclusions will be reached on the purported 'death' of informational privacy, the future of data protection (DP) law and how technology as well as law can help protect personal data.

I. PRIVACY PROTECTION AND THE LAW

The two most important legal regimes to consider in privacy protection in the UK are DP law, and the law of confidence. DP law in the UK is to be found in the Data Protection Act 1998 (DPA), itself derived from the European Data Protection Directive (DPD) (see below p 452), which harmonises this legal area across the EU. The law of confidence, on the other hand, is a creature of the common law, and is idiosyncratic to English law (Scots law, however, sharing most of the same rules). Both regimes, have been informed, and, in the case of the law of confidence, almost transformed in recent years, by the guarantees of a human right to private life, derived from the European Convention of Human Rights (ECHR), Article 8; especially since the incorporation of this instrument into UK domestic law in the Human Rights Act 1998. Since the 1998 Act, the right to private life as a fundamental human right can now be plead in any court in the land, with no need to go to the European Court of Human Rights (ECtHR) in Strasbourg to raise the issue.[6] Public bodies (such as social work depart-

---

[3] See Edwards and Hatcher, ch 16.

[4] See Rauhofer, ch 17.

[5] See Rauhofer, ch 18.

[6] It is beyond the scope of this chapter to examine fully ECtHR case-law in this area but it is worth noting that there has been a clear growth in cases emanating from Strasbourg which have significant effects on the law of data protection: notably just in the last 12 months, *I v Finland*, Case 20511/03, 17 July 2008 (on how to strike a balance between journalistic freedom of expression and individual privacy); *K v Finland*, Application no 25702/94, 2 December 2008 (on the balance to be struck between disclosure of the identity of anonymous alleged offenders and privacy of said); *Reklos and Devourlis v Greece*, Application No 1234/05, 15 January 2009 (rights of parents not to have photographs of infant taken in hospital without consent); and *S and*

ments, courts and local authorities) must act in accordance with it, and (in theory at least) the government must certify that legislation passed is compliant with the ECHR. Breaches of, or failure to implement, the ECHR in state laws can still, however, be finally adjudicated by the ECtHR as a remedy of last resort.

DP protects what is known very generally as *informational privacy*: loosely, the right to control what is known about you. The type of information protected is differently defined in different countries and is not always clear (see further below) but typically includes 'personal data' such as name, address, date of birth, contact details, financial, medical and social work details, identifiable photos, relationship status, political allegiance, sexual, genetic, biometric, racial and ethnic details, school records, domestic situation, and so forth.

The law of confidence, by contrast, prevents a second party from disclosing information which should be kept private between that person and the data subject. Historically the law of confidence arose only in special well-known relationships of trust, or in a commercial 'trade secrets' context.[7] In the seminal case of *Douglas v Hello!*,[8] the law of confidence was significantly widened by the courts to create a near commercial right of personality. In that case, it was held that if (i) someone has information that is 'private or personal'; (ii) to which he or she could properly deny access to third parties; and (iii) he or she reasonably intended to profit commercially by using or publishing that information, then a third party who is, or ought to be, aware of these matters, and who has knowingly obtained the information without authority, will be in breach of duty if he uses or publishes that information to the detriment of the owner.

Since *Douglas*, a stream of cases has followed, and arguably the doctrine of confidence is now evolving into the nearest thing the legal systems of the UK have to a common law of 'privacy', albeit relating primarily to the control of the exploitation of one's personality or image. Yet the exact nature, and even the existence, of this right in UK law is much contested.[9] Indeed in *Campbell v MGN*, the tort was rechristened by Lord Nicholls as 'misuse of private information' and his Lordship commented that that it was time to recognise that 'the values enshrined in articles 8 and 10 are

Marper v UK Applications 30562/04 and 30566/04, 4 December 2008 (not legal to retain DNA samples of suspects on police database). It seems privacy and DP issues are now as likely to arise at Strasbourg as at the ECJ in Luxembourg.

[7] The law of confidence will not be explored in full in this chapter. See for a recent account of how the law of confidence has been extended in the UK to protect the privacy (and revenues) of, in the main, celebrities, see ch 18 of H MacQueen, C Waelde and G Laurie, *Contemporary Intellectual Property: Law and Policy* (Oxford, Oxford University Press, 2007).
[8] [2005] EWCA Civ 595.
[9] See in particular, *Campbell v MGN* [2002] EWCA Civ 1373 (Ct App); [2004] UKHL 22, (HL); *McGregor v Fraser* [2003] EWHC 2972; *Ash v McKennit* [2005] EWHC 3003 (QB); *Murray v Big Pictures* (UK) Ltd [2008] EWCA Civ 446.

now part of the cause of action for breach of confidence'.[10] The decision also formalised a new two-step test for an actionable tort of this kind depending on whether (i) the information disclosed was private and not public; and (ii) whether disclosure of the information about an individual ('A') would give substantial offence to A, assuming that A was placed in similar circumstances and was a person of ordinary sensibilities (paragraph 92).

One key problem is that privacy has traditionally been thought of as a right to protect one's personality and preserve one's autonomy, in the non-economic context of human rights. These modern confidence cases, however, seem often to involve invoking the law of privacy in a bid to commoditise one's image rather than to protect a right of seclusion. It remains unresolved if the English courts wish to provide celebrities with essentially a new intellectual property right over their 'image' or 'brand' with which a new revenue stream can be properly secured, as is the case in states such as New York where 'publicity rights' statutes exist;[11] or if they merely wish to correct egregious interferences into what is clearly some form of private life by an intrusive tabloid press[12]—which is already encouraged if not mandated by the ECtHR.[13] Is privacy just another commodity that should be bought and sold?[14]

Another problem is whether such a right of whatever purpose or scope is compatible both with the public's right to 'know', the media's right to report on news, and general rights of freedom of expression, eg of partners or friends.[15] Note also that an act of disclosure of private information may be a breach of both DP law, and the law of confidence; this was true, for example, in *Campbell v MGN*,[16] where photographs published of Naomi Campbell the supermodel, indicating that she was attending Narcotics Anonymous, gave rise to claims for infringement of both regimes.

Privacy may, of course, also involve *physical* or bodily privacy—the right not to be touched or in some way acted on against your will. This area of law is generally protected in the UK under existing laws such as the criminal law of assault or rape, or even under medico-legal laws such as the laws about abortion. In some cases where the law presents no obvious remedy, the ECHR has been invoked to provide one. In *Wainwright v United Kingdom*,[17] for example, the ECtHR held that an unduly intrusive

---

[10] *Campbell*, HL, above n 9, paras 14 and 17, respectively.

[11] See eg *Douglas v Hello!*, above n 8.; cf *Ash v McKennit*, above n 9.

[12] See for eg *Murray*, above n 9.

[13] See *Von Hannover v Germany*, App No 59320/00, European Court of Human Rights, 24 June 2004.

[14] On this commodification of privacy argument, see an excellent account by C Prins, 'When Personal Data, Behavior and Virtual Identities Become a Commodity: Would a Property Rights Approach Matter?' (2006) 3(4) *SCRIPT-ed* 270, available at: http://www.law.ed.ac.uk/ahrc/script-ed/vol3-4/prins.asp.

[15] See in particular *Campbell v MGN*, above n 8 and *Ash v McKennit*, above n 8.

[16] Above n 9.

[17] Application No 12350/04.

strip search of relatives visiting a prisoner in jail had been a violation of Article 8 ECHR, even although the searches had been carried out in accordance with UK law.

In this section we will concentrate on informational or data privacy through the lens of European and UK DP law. This is a highly complex area full of legal minutiae: in the space allowed, it is not possible to go into comprehensive detail and several excellent books aimed at either or both of students and practitioners can fulfil that task.[18] Instead this introduction has concentrated on key notions such as personal data, consent and the eight basic DP principles. In particular, the chapter does not describe the practical formalities of registration or 'notification' required of data controllers, nor does it deal in detail with exemptions from DP law or sanctions for breaches of DP law, important though both these areas are.

II. DATA PROTECTION LAW

Informational privacy as a concept has its origins in the combination of fear for individual privacy in the era of World War II, Nazism and the rise of Stalinism; and the emergence of widespread automated data processing. The pressing fear in Western states as the world rebuilt in the 1940s and 1950s was of the total surveillance 'Big Brother' state that had been glimpsed in Germany and the Soviet bloc. DP legislation thus began in Hesse in Germany in 1970[19]and was first harmonised as a model European regime by the Council of Europe Convention of 1981.[20] It has since been adopted as mandatory law in the EU in the shape of the European DPD.[21] Rooted in the ECHR's guarantee of a human right to private life in Article 8, DP law was clearly intended to protect the privacy of individual citizens against the state, and therefore, with some small exceptions, protects neither the deceased nor juristic persons (companies and similar unincorporated associations).

At the international legal level, as well as the ECHR and the 1981 Coun-

---

[18] See eg P Carey, *Data Protection: A Practical Guide to UK and EU Law*, 3rd edn (Oxford, Oxford University Press, 2009); R Jay and A Hamilton, *Data Protection Law and Practice*, 3rd edn (London, Sweet & Maxwell, 2007). Detailed student coverage of the area can be found in I Lloyd, *Information Technology Law*, 4th edn (London, Butterworths, 2004). LA Bygrave, *Data Protection Law: Approaching its Rationale, Logic and Limits* (Information Law Series 10, 2002) 116 is an excellent review of DP from a more critical academic angle, and C Kuner *European Data Protection Law*, 2nd rev edn (Oxford, Oxford University Press, 2007) is an excellent account from a European and corporate compliance perspective.

[19] See further the detailed history of DP law in Rauhofer, ch 17.

[20] EC: 108th Convention for the protection of individuals concerning automatic processing of personal data (1981). For a more detailed account of the historical origins of DP law, see Rauhofer, ibid.

[21] Directive 95/46/EC of the European Parliament and of the Council of 24 October 1995 on the protection of individuals with regard to the processing of personal data and on the free movement of such data.

cil of Europe treaty, the Universal Declaration of Human Rights (UDHR),[22] the International Covenant on Civil and Political Rights (ICCPR)[23] and the 1980 OECD Guidelines on the Protection of Privacy and Transborder Flows of Personal Data,[24] all enshrine the right to private life[25] and have all contributed to the creation of modern DP law.[26]

A. The Coming of the Information Society and the Post-9/11 World: Their Impact on DP Law

In the 1940s and 1950s, state collection and processing of personal information was achieved via pre-digital bureaucratic methods, such as census information gathering, monitoring of internal passports, organisation of data in paper files, and human surveillance (as in East Germany, where anecdotally during the Cold War one in three citizens was in the employ of the secret police as an informer). From the late 1960s on, however, a new factor emerged: the arrival of the modern digital computer. The rise to prominence of DP law in recent times is generally attributed to the increasing use of computers and electronic communication devices.[27] Works such as Garfinkel's *Database Nation*[28] and, more recently, Solove's *The Digital Person*[29] have publicised the idea that we are now, by virtue of information technology, especially data mining, ubiquitous electronic surveillance, and local and global data sharing, 'sleepwalking into a surveillance society'.[30]

Computerisation and digitisation allow collection, processing and storage of personal data on a scale unprecedented in the analogue era. Huge amounts of digitised data can be stored in principle for ever at relatively low cost, be searchable in minutes or seconds, not hours, by a vast number of criteria, and be further processed in limitless numbers of useful ways. Crucially, data collected from one source (or one 'database') can be combined with other databases, to generate new data revealing significant

[22] GA res 217A (III), UN Doc A/810 at 71 (1948).

[23] GA res 2200A (XXI), 21 UN GAOR Supp (No 16) at 52, UN Doc. A/6316 (1966), 999 UNTS 171, entered into force 23 March 1976.

[24] Available at http://www.oecd.org/document/18/0,2340,en_2649_34255_1815186_1_1_1_ 1,00.html.

[25] See respectively Art 12 UDHR, Art 17 ICCPR, Art 8 ECHR.

[26] See again further discussion in Rauhofer, ch DP4.

[27] Carey, 2nd edn, above n 18, 1.

[28] S Garfinkel, *Database Nation: the Death of Privacy in the 21st Century* (Sebastopol, CA, O'Reilly, 2000). See also J Rosen, *The Unwanted Gaze: the Destruction of Privacy in America* (Vintage Books, 2001).

[29] DJ Solove, *The Digital Person: Technology and Privacy in the Information Age* (New York, New York University Press, 2004).

[30] See the Surveillance Studies Network, 'Report on the Surveillance Society', ICO, September 2006, para 11.3.3, available at http://www.ico.gov.uk/upload/documents/library/data_protec tion/practical_application/surveillance_society_full_report_2006.pdf ('Surveillance Society'). The exact quote was uttered by Richard Thomas , UK Information Commisioner, at an official engagement.

connections and comparisons—the concept of 'data mining'. 'Profiling'—looking for patterns in the data collected or aggregated about a person, or group of persons—has become increasingly ubiquitous. (The issues of profiling are discussed extensively in the context of the online marketing sector in chapter 16.)

Data held in databases for indefinite periods may also be reused for functions quite different from the purposes for which they were originally collected: this is the concept of 'function' or 'scope creep'. Thus data collected about a person for medical purposes—eg a positive test for HIV—might theoretically later be used to categorise that person as a risk when he seeks life assurance, or permanent employment. DP law tries to combat these undesirable results (in terms of personal privacy) by introducing restrictions both on *how long* data can be retained, and crucially on 'fishing'—collecting data for no particular *purpose,* or for extremely wide purposes, and using it as and when desired. Given the technical scope of modern computer storage and database technology, and the flimsy enforcement of data protection in practice,[31] however, 'scope creep' may in practice be almost impossible to control. Indeed, Bennett and Raab[32] suggest that it is one of the key hallmarks of the modern bureaucratic society that information *will* be collected just because it can be—to serve as a valuable potential commodity for the unknown future and for risk management. Rauhofer has labelled this 'the dream of the risk-free society'[33] where the hope is that if enough data is collected, any future risk can be predicted and averted. Such trends are not only counterintuitive, but worrying for all data subjects, especially today's children, who may perhaps have to grow up with the weight of data collected when they were too young to know about it metaphorically hung round their neck.

Digitisation is of course only one step in the transformation of the personal data world. The Internet has created a world in which data can be accessed ubiquitously and flows untrammelled across political frontiers. This creates almost impossible problems of audit and control from a data privacy perspective. Since different laws govern rights of privacy and confidentiality in different countries, export and import of personal data may involve loss or gain of privacy rights. How to deal with the impact of different jurisdictions on DP rights remains an opaque and politically thorny issue, as seen in the US/EU 'safe harbour' dispute, which we discuss below.

These problems of digitisation and transglobal data flows have combined with recent historical events to create a climate of fear among privacy

---

[31] See below, p 467.

[32] C Bennett and C Raab, *The Governance of Privacy,* 2nd edn (Boston, MA, MIT Press, 2006) 19–20.

[33] J Rauhofer, 'Privacy is Dead—Get Over It: Art 8 and the Dream of a Risk-free Society', 2nd GikII Workshop, 2007, UCL, London.

activist groups that we are losing our privacy by degrees. Many civil society groups already argue that rights such as privacy and freedom of expression are simply not as well protected on the Internet as they were in conventional media.[34] The post-9/11 approach to dealing with the threat of global terror has arguably disrupted the traditional balance struck between state security and fundamental values of privacy, and that balance may have tipped unduly in the direction of security, especially online.[35] The UK of all of the EU states has in particular been accused of steamrollering privacy in the pursuit of law enforcement and risk management, as well as streamlining governmental functions. The drive towards 'joined up' government initiated by Tony Blair has created a culture of building large, multiple-access databases to solve every social problem; these databases have so far invariably proved to be expensive, insecure and of questionable efficacy.[36] As *The Independent* summarised its cover story of 18 April 2009, 'Internet Privacy: Britain in the Dock.'

This leads us to a final key consideration arising from digitisation and the 'database society', ie data security. It is reasonably obvious if data held in handwritten files has been amended, or if the physical data store (an office, a filing cabinet) has been broken into; it is less obvious when data lives intangibly on a hard disk, laptop or CD. In recent years, public interest in DP, commonly seen in the past as detailed, nerdish and obscure,[37] has been fuelled by a deluge of reports of data leakage on an extravagant scale. While in North America, the worst data leakage scandals have tended to come from the private sector, eg Choicepoint in 2005[38] and TJ Maxx in 2007, in the UK the greatest anxiety has followed the loss in October 2007 by Her Majesty's Revenue and Customs (HMRC) of data relating to 25 million people seeking child benefit—almost half the inhabitants of the country.[39] The data, which included names, addresses, dates of birth, bank account details and National Insurance numbers, was placed on

---

[34] Prominent civil society organisations include EPIC, the Electronic Privacy Information Centre in the US; and FIPR, the Federation for Internet Privacy Research in the UK. See on the Internet and its threat to freedom of expression elsewhere in this volume, Edwards, chs 1 (ISPs) and 20 (pornography).

[35] Again, see a more detailed discussion of the crisis in privacy vs security in Rauhofer, ch DP4 and DP5.

[36] See also the influential report, 'Database State' (Joseph Rowntree Trust, April 2009) available at http://www.jrrt.org.uk/ , which surveyed 46 public-sector databases and argues that a quarter of all government databases are breaking DP law.

[37] See C Pounder, editorial, [2007] *Out-Law* 26 November, at http://www.out-law.com/page-8663: 'Isn't it sexy to be a data protection officer now? The staggering revelations of security breaches at HMRC have propelled data protection out of shadowy domain of geeks and anoraks, and into the bright sunlight of public debate.'

[38] See the useful chronology of data breaches and losses at http://www.privacyrights.org/ar/ChronDataBreaches.htm.

[39] See data compiled at http://en.wikipedia.org/wiki/2007_UK_child_benefit_data_misplacement.

an unencrypted CD by a junior official, sent using an insecure courier, and simply 'lost in the post'.

Subsequent revelations that have emerged in the wake of a government inquiry[40] and press and Information Commissioner pressure have included the loss of details of 600,000 military personnel via a laptop stolen from a car in Birmingham, the admission by the Ministry of Defence that 420 such laptops have been lost since 2003, and the loss of the records of 3 million learner drivers.[41] The full fallout of 'ChildBenefitGate' has yet to be quantified, but immediate results in the UK are likely to include a renewed public concern for, and awareness of, privacy breaches; and new and more effective enforcement powers for the Information Commissioner.[42] In a brutally critical report, the Joint Committee on Human Rights concluded that 'The fundamental problem is a cultural one: there is insufficient respect for personal data in the public sector.'[43] The government's own Poynter Report, issued in June 2008, agreed that 'information security at the time of the incident, simply wasn't a management priority' and that the incident was 'completely avoidable'. The effect on public confidence is starkly visible: in the February 2008 Eurobarometer report on attitudes to DP across Europe,[44] 77 per cent of data subjects in the UK reported they were very or fairly concerned about how their personal data was handled. This was one of the highest votes of no confidence in data handling in any EU state.

As more and more data is collected, created, compiled and stored, both in the private and public sector, the ability of individuals to know *what* data is held about them, and to *control* it, recedes. DP law aims, as we shall see below, to empower the data subject by giving them rights to find out what data is held about them and how it is being processed, to correct it if it is wrong, and most importantly, to say yes or no to collection of data *ab initio*.

---

[40] See Poynter Review page at http://www.hm-treasury.gov.uk/independent_reviews/poynter_review/poynter_review_index.cfm.

[41] See 'MoD Admits it Has no Idea What Was on 400 Stolen Laptops', *The Independent* 20 January 2008.

[42] See below, p 468.

[43] See 'Government Must Take Data Protection More Seriously, Says Parliament Committee', *Out-law News* 18 March 2008.

[44] See Eurobarometer/European Commission Flash Report, February 2008, 'Data Protection in the EU: Citizen's Perceptions', http://ec.europa.eu/public_opinion/flash/fl_225_en.pdf; and 'Data Protection in the EU: Data Controller's Perceptions', at http://ec.europa.eu/public_opinion/flash/fl_226_en.pdf (Hereafter 'Eurobarometer').

III. KEY LEGISLATIVE INSTRUMENTS: INTERNATIONAL LEVEL

A. The Data Protection Directive

The DPD,[45] adopted in October 1995, is perhaps the most comprehensive and significant enactment on informational privacy in the world. The UK DPA, implementing the DPD, wholly replaces the previous 1984 Act. The DPD was extended to deal with technological challenges by the Privacy and Electronic Communications Directive (PECD)[46] as implemented in UK by the Privacy and Electronic Communications (EC Directive) Regulations (PECR)[47] in October 2003. The DPD aims at protecting the fundamental right to privacy but only where personal data is processed wholly or partly by automatic means or is included in a manual filing system .

Article 6 DPD lays down eight fundamental DP principles (implemented in Schedule 1 of the DPA):

1. Personal data shall be processed fairly and lawfully.
2. Personal data shall be obtained only for one or more specified and lawful purposes, and shall not be further processed in any manner incompatible with that purpose or those purposes.
3. Personal data shall be adequate, relevant and not excessive in relation to the purpose or purposes for which they are processed
4. Personal data shall be accurate and, where necessary, kept up to date.
5. Personal data processed for any purpose or purposes shall not be kept for longer than is necessary for that purpose or those purposes.
6. Personal data shall be processed in accordance with the rights of data subjects under the DPD.
7. Appropriate technical and organisational measures shall be taken against unauthorised or unlawful processing of personal data and against accidental loss or destruction of, or damage to, personal data.
8. Personal data shall not be transferred to a country or territory outside the European Economic Area, unless that country or territory ensures

---

[45] OJ L281, 23/11/1995, 0031–0050.

[46] 2002/58/EC. The PECD is currently going through a process of reform as part of the package of electronic communications laws known as the Telecoms Package. Reform is at time of writing deadlocked due to disagreement on one non-DP-related point but a final draft is expected to pass sometime in 2009. See Common Position adopted by the Council on 16 February 2009 with a view to the adoption of a Directive of the European Parliament and of the Council amending Directive 2002/22/EC on universal service and users' rights relating to electronic communications networks, Directive 2002/58/EC concerning the processing of personal data and the protection of privacy in the electronic communications sector and Regulation (EC) No 2006/2004 on consumer protection cooperation, Council document No 16497/1/08, available at http://register.consilium.europa.eu/pdf/en/08/st16/st16497-re01. en08.pdf.

[47] SI 2003 No 2426.

an adequate level of protection of the rights and freedoms of data subjects in relation to the processing of personal data.

In respect of Principle 1, the DPD sets out a number of conditions, only one of which need apply, before personal data can be processed.[48] The most significant of these threshold conditions is the consent of the data subject (see detailed discussion below). There is a stricter regime for specified categories of *sensitive personal data* wherein processing is only allowed by explicit consent of the data subject,[49] or, less frequently, under another exemption.[50]

The rights of data subjects alluded to in Principle 6 include:

(a) the right to access their own personal data without excessive delay or expense.[51] This subject access right is, however, subject to a large number of exceptions, and in practice is used mainly in specialised contexts such as employment tribunals.

(b) the right to control the *integrity* of data relating to them, including the right to rectify, erase or block the processing of data whose processing does not comply with the DPD;[52]

(c) the right to object[53] to the processing of their personal data,[54] but only in limited circumstances, eg where processing is likely to cause damage or distress and where personal data is used for direct marketing purposes;[55]

(d) the right not to be subject to a legally relevant decision based solely on the automated processing of data,[56] eg a decision to withdraw or refuse to extend financial credit must not be based solely on automated processing.

The transfer of personal data to third countries in conformity with Principle 8 is now provided for in Chapter IV of the Directive and was the most controversial part of the Directive during its passage. Article 25 states that transfers of personal data to third countries outside the EU may take place only if the third country in question ensures an 'adequate' level of protection, the adequacy of which must be assessed in the light of all the circumstances surrounding the data transfer.[57] Merely making a webpage accessible to anywhere in the world does not, however, constitute a transfer

---

[48] DPD Art 7.
[49] For exemptions and restrictions see DPD Art 13.
[50] DPD Art 8.
[51] DPD Art 12(a).
[52] DPD Art 12(b).
[53] DPD Art 14.
[54] DPD Art 14(a).
[55] See DPD Art 14(b), and Art 7(e) and (f). See full discussion of online marketing and consumer data privacy in Edwards, chs 15 and 16.
[56] DPD Art 15.
[57] DPD Art 25 (2).

of personal data to a third country, since a third party still needs to make the effort to seek access to that data; the data must be 'pulled' not just 'pushed'.[58] If this were not so, the special regime of Chapter IV would in effect expand to apply to all data processing on the Internet.[59] The aim of this provision is simple: to make sure that data exported outside the EU is not then processed in ways completely contrary to the DP laws of Europe, resulting in EU citizens suffering harm. The problem becomes obvious when one considers that data about EU data subjects might, for example, easily be collected by a website business based in the US, transferred to data-miners in China or sold to spammers operating in the Phillipines, while DP law does not operate in any of these countries nor is there likely to be any real local equivalent protection.[60]

At present, only a few non-EU countries, including Switzerland, Guernsey, Jersey, the Isle of Man and Argentina, have been accredited by the EU as providing 'adequate' protection. Canada has been accredited for certain categories of information. In the difficult case of the US, a special agreement was negotiated under which companies within the US can register to join what is known as 'safe harbour' if they agree to fulfil certain fair information practices, either by their own self-regulatory conduct, or by joining a privacy or trust seal association such as TrustE. Space precludes full discussion of the 'safe harbour' compromise in this chapter, but a full critique can be found in the second edition of this text in the chapter by Charlesworth.[61] Charlesworth argues forcefully that safe harbour represents a crucial watering-down of the protection given to personal data on its exit from the EU, in particular in relation to enforcement of safe harbour by trust seal bodies, an attitude espoused by many legal commentators, both European and North American.[62] It is noteworthy that the European Commission's review of safe harbour in 2004 also expressed considerable dissatisfaction with the privacy safeguards offered by safe harbour companies in practice.[63] Busch, a political scientist, however, inter-

---

[58] See *Lindqvist*, discussed below n 87, at paras 56–72.

[59] Above, para 69.

[60] Note DPD Art 4 which provides that EU DP law is asserted to apply, regardless of the nationality of the data controller, where processing is carried out in an 'establishment' in an EU country, or where there is no such establishment but 'equipment' is used for processing which is situated in a Member State. Leaving aside the vagueness of the key terms above (is a telephone line equipment? Is a cookie placed on a user's hard disk?) in effect enforcement of these rules against non compliant extra-EU data controllers is mainly theoretical.

[61] A Charlesworth, 'Data Privacy in Cyberspace', in L Edwards and C Waelde (eds) *Law and the Internet*, 2nd edn (Oxford, Hart Publishing, 2000). The latest safe harbour rules and other information, including which companies have signed up, can be found at http://www.export.gov/safeharbor/.

[62] See eg testimony of Joel Reidenberg at Hearing on the EU Data Protection Directive: Implications for the US Privacy Debate, 8 March 2001, at http://reidenberg.home.sprynet.com/Reidenberg_Testimony_03-08-01.htm.

[63] Noting that, for example, less than a quarter of the companies signed up to safe harbour had privacy policies on their site expressly containing all seven safe harbour principles—a crucial requirement. See Commission Staff Working Document, 20 October 2004.

estingly prefers to view 'safe harbour' as a successful and pragmatic political compromise.[64]

In all other cases, transfer of personal data outside the EU is in principle banned, but in practice can be achieved lawfully by obtaining the consent of the data subject to the transfer, or by the use of special contractual clauses which have been vetted by the EU authorities.[65] In practice, the number of companies signed up to 'safe harbour' declined after the glory days of the dotcom boom around the turn of the millennium, and the number now accredited is, though not negligible, so few compared to the total number of US companies as to make safe harbour look increasingly like a dead letter.[66] Instead, now the EU has approved model contractual conditions for 'private export' of personal data, it seems this is the preferred route for legitimate data export to the US and elsewhere, notwithstanding the questionable protection this gives European consumers post-export.[67] Some companies are now also exploring the use of Binding Corporate Rules to satisfy Article 26.[68]

IV. NATIONAL LEVEL

A. The Data Protection Act 1998

The UK DPA came into force on 1 March 2000. The UK system is policed by the Information Commissioner's Office (ICO), which has issued

---

[64] See A Busch, 'From Safe Harbour to the Rough Sea? Privacy Disputes across the Atlantic' (2006) 3(4) *SCRIPT-ed* 304, at http://www.law.ed.ac.uk/ahrc/script-ed/vol3-4/busch.asp.

[65] See DPD Art 26, and the European Commission Decision of 27 December 2004, amending Decision 2001/497/EC as regards the introduction of an alternative set of standard contractual clauses for the transfer of personal data to third countries (notified under document number C(2004) 5271). See OJ L 385, 29/12/2004, 0074–0084. Those model clauses can be found at http://www.privacydataprotection.co.uk/documents.

[66] In 2004, 493 members were listed. In 2008, this number does seem to have roughly quadrupled but it is still remarkably low compared to the total number of US companies dealing in personal data. This rise can probably be related to the revival in fortune of the IT sector and Web 2.0. Notable safe harbour members include Facebook and Google. See, however, J Cline, 'Roadmap for an International Safe Harbor Framework' (2006) *International Review of Law Computers & Technology* 361, who, while acknowledging the criticisms of the safe harbour EU–US model, attempts to reform the basic concept as a model generally for international data flows out of the EU. Interestingly, his suggestion is that this model be negotiated within the WTO and include a dispute-resolution mechanism run by the WTO.

[67] 'Safe harbour' has if anything more explicit post-transfer safeguards for data subjects built in to the regime than does transfer of data by contractual conditions; yet safe harbour itself was trenchantly criticised on its compliance record, eg repeated scandals relating to misuse of personal data by prominent TrustE members such as Microsoft, Yahoo! and GeoCities. See Charlesworth, above n 61.

[68] See for the UK, ICO guidance at http://dataprotectionthinker.blogspot.com/2005/12/binding-corporate-rules-scheme-ge.html.

extensive legal guidance on the interpretation of the DPA,[69] the principles and related issues.[70] Data protection is a UK-wide matter reserved to Westminster. However, a Scottish Information Commissioner also exists who has a role in relation to Scottish DP interests as well as policing the separate Scottish Freedom of Information (FOI) scheme.

The DPA, like the DPD, uses certain specific and important terminology, most of which is defined in section 1(1) of the Act and is paraphrased here.

- *'Data'* means information which is processed wholly or partly by means of equipment operating automatically, *or* is recorded with the intent that it should be processed by this equipment, *or* is recorded as a part of a relevant manual filing system.[71]
- *'Data controller'* is the person, natural or juristic, who determines the purpose and manner of the data processing. Most duties in the DPA are placed on data controllers.
- *'Data processor'* is the person who processes the data on behalf of the data controller, eg a data warehouse or batch processing mainframe. Data processors in this technical sense are relatively unimportant in the DPA scheme of duties.[72]
- *'Data subject'* is the living person who is the subject of the personal data.
- *'Personal data'* is any information which relates to a natural person (the data subject) who can be identified or is identifiable from that data, directly or indirectly. The DPD definition in Article 2 gives examples of personal data as including an 'identification number' and 'one or more factors specific to [the data subject's] physical, physiological, mental, economic, cultural or social identity'. The DPA definition is slightly different in that it specifies in relation to 'indirectly' that this includes the case where the person cannot be identified by the information alone, but can be when it is combined with other data 'likely' to be held by data controller. This test of likeliness is not found in the original DPD definition.

What constitutes personal data is one of the central causes of doubt in the DP regime, both in the EU generally and in the UK specifically.[73]

---

69 See ICO, 'Data Protection Act 1998: Legal Guidance', available at http://www.ico.gov.uk/upload/documents/library/data_protection/detailed_specialist_guides/data_protection_act_legal_guidance.pdf.

70 See ICO, Data Protection document library, available at http://www.ico.gov.uk/tools_and_resources/document_library/data_protection.aspx.

71 See interpretation of 'relevant filing system' in *Durant v FSA* [2003] EWCA Civ 1746, Court of Appeal (Civil Division).

72 Note the Art 29 Working Party *Opinion in the SWIFT Case*, Opinion 10/2006 (WP 128), 6 December 2006, which determined that SWIFT, a Belgian-based clearing house for international bank transfers made at the instruction of various EU banks, was not a mere data processor but had sufficient independent capacity to be regarded as a data controller, and was thus subject to the full rigour of Belgian DP law.

73 The ICO issued new guidance for organisations on identifying personal data in February 2009: see http://www.ico.gov.uk/upload/documents/library/data_protection/detailed_specialist_guides/what_is_data_for_the_purposes_of_the_dpa.pdf.

The definition is crucial, because it is a threshold requirement to the application of any of the DP rules. Yet studies have shown in the past that there is a wide variation across the EU as to how the phrase is interpreted both in law and in practice.[74]

The definition of personal data in the UK was significantly limited by the case of *Durant v FSA* [75] in 2003. In that case, the court held that:

> Mere mention of the data subject in a document held by a data controller does not necessarily amount to his personal data. Whether it does so in any particular instance depends on where it falls in a 'continuum of relevance or proximity' to the data subject as distinct, say, from transactions or matters in which he may have been involved to a greater or lesser degree.

The court added that if the data was 'biographical in a significant sense, that is, going beyond the recording of the putative data subject's involvement in a matter or event that has no personal connotations', then it is likely to be regarded as 'personal data'.[76]

This definition has proved controversial and is currently, it appears, being challenged in the European Court of Justice by the European Commission itself. In some contexts, it might conceivably be highly restrictive—eg in a record of activities made by closed-circuit television (CCTV), pictures of A, a passer-by, might not be regarded as 'personal data' of A if the focus of the camera was not intentionally on A, but on, say, persons going into a shop nearby. This might mean that the rules of fair processing were not applied to those pictures from the moment they were captured, although such rules would cut in if the pictures of A were later specifically processed with intent to identify or otherwise affect A's rights.[77]

The Article 29 Working Committee, whose job is to deliver opinions on crucial and disputed areas of DP law in an attempt to secure European harmonisation, has reported recently on the definition of personal

---

[74] See the excellent pan-EU survey commissioned by the ICO, 'What Are Personal Data?', Sheffield University, 2004, available at http://www.ico.gov.uk/upload/documents/library/corporate/research_and_reports/final_report_21_06_04.pdf.

[75] Above n 71. The meaning of personal data in the context of anonymised medical data was also discussed in the Scottish FOI case, *Common Services Agency v Scottish Information Commissioner* [2006] CSIH 58 at http://www.scotcourts.gov.uk/opinions/2006CSIH58.html. The Scottish judgment was reversed by the House of Lords in [2008] UKHL 47 but their Lordships declined to comment on *Durant* as part of the binding opinion, regarding it as irrelevant to the issue of effective anonymisation at hand.

[76] *Durant v FSA*, above n 71, para 28.

[77] See discussion of this point in L Edwards, 'Taking the "Personal" Out of Personal Data: *Durant v FSA* and its Impact on the Legal Regulation of CCTV' (2004) 1(2) *SCRIPT-ed*, at http://www.law.ed.ac.uk/ahrb/script-ed/issue2/durant.asp. See also ICO, 'Data Protection Technical Guidance, Determining What is Personal Data' (21 August 2007), which in an apparent bid to limit the narrowing of the scope of personal data in *Durant*, suggests that the *Durant* test need only be consulted if data is not 'obviously about' or 'linked to' an individual. It is believed this guidance was a direct response to EU criticism in the Art 29 Opinion on Personal Data, cited in n 78 below.

data,[78] partly in response to the *Durant* controversy, but also to address the problem of whether DP law applies to certain data collected online which may not look like 'traditional' personal data, but the processing of which has the potential seriously to invade personal privacy. This could include information such as a user's web traffic collected by an advertiser, or search terms collected by an engine such as Google (see discussion of both these cases in chapter 16). The key issue in these kind of cases is whether an IP address is 'personal data'. IP addresses are simply a string of numbers which uniquely identify a computer, but only at a particular time; they do not in theory identify a person (many people in the household may use that machine) or even a particular machine on a permanent basis (most consumers sign up to domestic ISPs which dynamically assign and reassign IP addresses according to demand; thus an IP address can normally only identify even a household in conjunction with date and usage logs held by the ISP).

The controversy is important because information society service providers, including search engines, use IP addresses to connect the extensive data they collect and store about users—eg what search terms they enter, what results they click on—to a particular user or household. If IP addresses, held in conjunction with this search data, are defined as 'personal data', then Google (or business partners) are restricted in what they can do with it by the DP regime (so long as they operate in Europe[79]). In particular, until recently Google retained all such collected data for almost indefinite lengths of time. If DP law applied, however, it would suggest that such data should be retained only as long as necessary to fulfil the purposes for which it was collected. Under pressure from the EU authorities, in 2007 Google agreed to reduce the maximum length of retention to 18–24 months.[80] In DP terms, this is still controversially long.

Google argued, however, that 'the concept of personal data should be defined pragmatically, rather than upon the likelihood of identification'. Whether IP addresses were personal data should be dealt with on a case-by-case basis, depending on the context and the practicality of identification of a data subject.[81] The Article 29 Working Party report of

[78] Art 29 Working Committee *Opinion 4/2007 on the Concept of Personal Data*, 20 June 2007, WP 136.

[79] See Art 29 Working Party *Opinion on Data Protection Issues Related to Search Engines*, 4 April 2008, WP 148, which inter alia, discussed the obvious jurisdictional objection that Google is based in the US not Europe. However, the Report clearly asserted that the DPD *does* clearly apply to search engines which deposit cookies on the machines of EU-resident users, even if the search engine is based economically or physically outside the EU (see DPD Art 4(1)(a).) See also the earlier WP 56 of 2002, available at http://ec.europa.eu/justice_home/fsj/privacy/docs/wpdocs/2002/wp56_en.pdf

[80] See public letter from Schaar, chair of the Art 29 Working Committee to Peter Fleischer, Privacy Counsel of Google, 16 May 2007.

[81] See 'Are IP Addresses "Personal Data"?', Peter Fleischer's blog, 5 February 2007.

2007, however, drew attention to recital 26 of the DPD, which provides that 'to determine whether a person is identifiable account should be taken of *all the means likely reasonably to be* used either by the controller or any other person to identify the said person' (original italics). From this they concluded that the 'test is a dynamic one and should consider the state of the art in technology at the time of processing and the possibilities of development during the period for which the data will be processed'. In 2008, the Working Party went further and issued a dedicated report on search engines and DP, in which they reiterated that, in most cases, IP addresses have to be seen as person-related, and therefore to be safe data controllers must assume they fall within the DPD.[82]

Thus, the EU certainly seems to feel that Google (and other online data collectors using IP addresses or similar as unique identifiers) must respect European DP law when they capture data from EU-based citizens—and in particular must respect the limits DP law places on data retention.[83] How to enforce such an assertion is a more political matter, however.

- *'Sensitive personal data'* is a subset of personal data which is regarded as so intensely personal that special safeguards are needed to guard against abusive processing. As defined in the DPD Article 8 and subsequently incorporated into the DPA, section 2, sensitive personal data means data relating to race, political opinions, health and sex life, religious and other beliefs, trade union membership and criminal records. These categories betray their historical and cultural origins in Europe in the 1980s and arguably exclude some important and valued types of personal information in twenty-first century Britain, eg there is no mention of biometric information such as fingerprints, retinal scans or DNA profiles (or the samples themselves[84]), or of financial details such as credit card data. Nor is there any consideration of the subject of the data: it might be argued that *all* data disclosed by a child, for example, is 'sensitive'.[85] Wong[86] points out that following the ECJ decision in

---

[82] See comment by Shaar reported in *Out-law.com* at 26 February 2008 on the Art 29 Working Party Opinion, below n 83.

[83] See further Art 29 Working Party *Opinion on Data Protection Issues Related to Search Engines*, 4 April 2008, WP 148. Interestingly the WP did not declare that the Data Retention Directive (see further ch 18) applied to Google and other search engines—hence only the basic DP rules found in the DPD relating to length of storage apply. The WP did, however, recommend a maximum retention period of six months for search engines.

[84] See D Beyleveld and MJ Taylor, 'Patents for Biotechnology and the Data Protection of Biological Samples and Shared Genetic Data', in J Herveg (ed), *The Protection of Medical Data: Challenges of the 21st Century* (Anthemis, 2008) in which the authors argue interestingly if controversially that the physical DNA sample itself might be regarded as 'personal data' and hence subject to DP protection.

[85] Compare the US system, which lacks an omnibus regime such as DP law and has no general concept of 'sensitive personal data' but does have specific and highly regulated statutory privacy regimes for health, financial and children's data (HIPAA, Sarbanes–Oxley and COPPA).

Lindqvist[87] where a simple photograph of a woman with a note that she had had health problems was held to embody 'sensitive personal data', there is a danger that almost all personal images can be so categorised— eg a picture of a person must usually reveal their skin colour and thus something about race.[88] The special regime for sensitive personal data might thus be potentially extended to cover every picture on the World Wide Web, a consequence that was surely not intended. Arguably the concept of especially sensitive personal data is useful, but a more flexible or purposive system of classification might be desirable.

Certain conditions must be satisfied before sensitive personal data can be processed, on top of the conditions for processing of ordinary personal data: these are considered below, p 462.

- *'Processing'* is very widely defined to include obtaining, recording or holding the information or data on the data subject, or carrying out any set of operations on the data, *including* organising, adapting, altering, retrieving, combining, consulting, using, disclosing, transmitting or disseminating it. It also covers blocking, erasing and destroying information or data.[89] In the leading ECJ case of *Lindqvist*, a Swedish woman set up a personal 'home page' on which she posted pictures of fellow members of her church along with some identifying details. It was held that she was indeed 'processing personal data' within the meaning of the DPD, even though the process was only partly automated by the use of web-serving software. Importantly, a defence that her activities were in the course of a non-profit-making or leisure activity and so fell outside Article 3(2) of the DPD (or as the UK DPA puts it, were for 'domestic purposes'[90]) was rejected. The Court considered that Mrs Lindqvist's activities could clearly not be seen as carried out in private or in the course of her family life, since they involved publication of data on the

---

[86] R Wong, 'Data Protection Online: Alternative Approaches to Sensitive Data?' 2007(2) *Journal of International Commercial Law and Technology* 9, at www.jiclt.com/index.php/JICLT/article/view/28/15.

[87] *Lindqvist v Kammaraklagaren*, European Court of Justice, Case C-101/01, 6 November 2003.

[88] See further *Murray v Big Pictures (UK) Ltd* [2007] EWHC 1908 (Ch) where the first instance court noted *obiter* regarding a photo of JK Rowling's (white) baby taken while the infant was wheeled through a public street, that 'It seems to me that if a photograph and the information it contains constitutes personal data, then it is hard to escape from the conclusion that insofar as it indicates the racial or ethnic origin of the data subject it also consists of sensitive personal data.' However under the DPA, Sched 3, r 5, the photographer was exempt from the special rules regarding sensitive personal data, as the child's parents had exposed the child in public. The court, however, declined to consider that any image also necessarily conveyed *health* data as 'A photograph of an apparently healthy individual in fact tells one nothing about his actual state of health' (para 80).

[89] See, however, *Johnson v Medical Defence Union Ltd* [2007] EWCA Civ 26 for a case where an activity was *not* held to be 'processing' within the DPA scheme.

[90] See DPA s 36.

Internet to 'an indefinite number of people'.[91]

The implications of this case, which is often described as a 'highwater mark' of DP maximalism, have been much criticised. In principle it implies that every person who sets up a family photo page, every blogger who writes about her colleagues or friends online, every child or adult with a Facebook or MySpace page which displays friends' photos or details, every charity or civil society group which publishes a list of its members on a website, is processing personal data within the DPD and the UK DPA, and thus must abide by the complicated rules of the DP regime. These may (as in the UK) involve mandatory registration as a data processor, and potential criminal sanctions if this procedure is not followed. Many have argued this is an unnecessary incursion of bureaucracy into the quasi-domestic and certainly non-profit-making sphere,[92] yet it is difficult to see where the line could be drawn in the shifting sands of the Internet where 'free' services are decidedly not always private or non-economic activities. However this author would argue that a website that is password-protected or 'friends-locked' (as is possible on many blog or social networking sites (SNSs)) is not made available to 'the public' and thus should fall within the 'domestic purposes' exemption. A better solution would be, it is asserted, to reconsider the DPD exemption in this area to better fit the reality of the user-generated content world and overrule *Lindqvist*. Certainly the Article 29 Working Party's latest opinion on social networking sites appears to regard the users of SNSs as primarily 'data subjects' not 'data controllers', but importantly *only* so long as they restrict access to their pages to a selected list of friends and hide their profiles from search engines.[93] As discussed below, it is, however, precisely these acts of 'privatisation' that are almost never set as default by the software of the SNS provider and it is well known that few SNS users ever change the default settings.

B. Fair Processing and Consent

The DPA incorporates word for word the eight data protection principles in the DPD noted above into Part I of Schedule 1 of the Act. Interpretative provisions which expand on the Principles 1, 2, 6 and 6–8 are set out in Part II of Schedule 1.

'*Fair processing*', as required under DP Principle 1, is a crucial notion in

---

[91] *Lindqvist*, above n 87, para 47.

[92] See eg R Wong, 'Social Networking: Anybody is a Data Controller!', BILETA Conference 2007, Glasgow Caledonian University; R Wong and J Savarimuthu, 'All or Nothing: This Is the Question? The Application of Art 3(2) Data Protection Directive 95/46/EC to the Internet' (2008) 25 *John Marshall Journal of Computer & Information Law* available at http://papers.ssrn.com/sol3/papers.cfm?abstract_id=1003025.

[93] See Art 29 WP Opinion 5/2009 on online social networking, 12 June 2009, WP 163.

giving teeth to rights of privacy for data subjects. The best-known ground (though given no precedence in strict law) for rendering processing 'fair' is that the data subject has given their consent.[94] As we shall also see below, however, in the discussion of social networking sites such as Facebook, consent is increasingly failing to be an effective threshold condition in a world where users regularly accept standard term contracts to access online services, and effectively give away their personal data without consideration or safeguards.

Other important grounds than consent do exist to render processing 'fair',[95] eg that the processing is necessary for the performance of a contract to which the data subject is a party,[96] for the administration of justice,[97] to fulfil various legal obligations of the data controller,[98] and that it is necessary to protect the data subject's 'vital interests.[99] One ground which is commercially relevant but sometimes controversial is that of DPA, Schedule 2, paragraph 6, which says that processing may be carried out if in the data processor's 'legitimate interests', so long as there is not 'prejudice to the rights and freedoms or legitimate interests' of the data subject. The terminal subclause is essential here, or any business person (eg an advertiser) could ride rough-shod over the privacy rights of individuals on the grounds that to do so was essential to his business. Traditionally this provision has been seen as setting up a balance between the interests of the business and the rights of the data subjects affected; however, the recent ECJ case of *Bavarian Lager*[100] interestingly suggests instead that where there is any incursion which truly affects the privacy of the individual data subject, rather than a balance, the business interest must give way.

In the case of sensitive personal data, the requirement of fair and lawful processing must be satisfied, but, in addition, at least one of a number of additional conditions must be satisfied.[101] These include: that the data subject has given *explicit consent*; that processing is necessary to protect the vital interests of the data subject; that processing relates to data deliberately made public by the data subject;[102] that processing is necessary for legal reasons (including obligations under employment law) or for the adminis-

---

[94] DPA Sched 2, para 1.
[95] DPD Sched 2.
[96] DPA Sched 2, para 2(a).
[97] DPA Shed 2, para 5(a).
[98] DPA Sched 2, para 3.
[99] DPA Sched 2, para 4.

[100] *Bavarian Lager v Commission of the EC*, 8 November 2007, Judgment of the Court of First Instance in Case T-194/04.

[101] DPA Sched 3.

[102] See further *Murray*, above n 88. This would interestingly seem to allow processing without *explicit* consent of sensitive data made available on social networking sites (SNSs), such as Facebook—good news both for SNS operators and for third parties such as direct marketers who often collect personal data from SNS pages. Note that *non* explicit consent (which might be collected via, eg, a privacy policy agreed to as part of registration with the site) would still be necessary, however, under ordinary Sched 1 rules. See further p 476.

tration of justice; that processing is necessary for medical purposes; that racial or ethnic data needs to be processed for equal opportunities monitoring. It can be seen that except in unusual circumstances such as litigation, the principal requirement for processing of sensitive data is likely to be 'explicit consent'.

So what is 'consent' and how does it differ from 'explicit consent'? Consent is one of the key concepts of DP law, yet, oddly, it remains undefined in the UK DPA (on the supposition that the nature of consent was well understood in our law). Within the DPD, Article 2 it is defined as 'any freely given specific and informed indication of his wishes by which the data subject signifies his agreement to personal data relating to him being processed'. This definition was not transposed into UK law. The ICO has, however, indicated in guidance that consent should be 'informed' and 'unambiguous'. The DPD definition of 'ordinary' consent should also be contrasted as something implicitly less rigorous than the (sometimes equally uncertain) requirement for 'explicit consent' for the processing of *sensitive* personal data.[103]

Clearly, consent to the processing of 'ordinary' data can be *implicit*—eg drawn from facts and circumstances or actions. Consent can also be defined as '*opt out*' rather than '*opt in*'. In opt out, a person is asked only to make an indication if they do *not* consent or have decided to withdraw consent, eg 'Tick here if you do not wish your personal data to be shared with carefully selected third parties' (a formulation often seen on consumer websites). In opt in, however, the subject is asked to give prior consent before processing is undertaken. Opt in is usually seen as more protective of user privacy. In practice the distinction may not be so clear: on a website where a data controller seeks consent, there might alternatively be an opt-out box which is blank, or an opt-in box which is pre-ticked. Which of these, if either, gives the user the most practical protection? The law, meanwhile, mandates neither and the result is mainly public confusion.

In many situations, furthermore, consent will be given without any semblance of a 'freely given specific and informed indication of his wishes'. For example, many standard form employment contracts require employers to consent to employer surveillance of their workplace, their e-mails and their telephone calls from work. Few employees will actually read and understand such clauses, and even fewer will turn a job down rather than give consent, there being effectively no possibility of negotiating on such standard terms.[104] When one turns to children, the power differential be-

---

[103] Which requirement *is* explicitly implemented in UK law: see DPA Sched 3, para 1.

[104] Note, however, that Part 4 of the Employment Practices Data Protection Code issued by the ICO states that there must be no penalty imposed on the employee for saying no to the processing of sensitive personal data, and that if consent is provided, the employee must be able to withdraw that consent in the future. Part 4 of the Code also states that blanket consent, obtained at the outset of employment, 'cannot always be relied upon'.

tween a school demanding fingerprints as price of access to the library, or the canteen, and a child is obvious. Given the increased surveillance of children by parents, schools, the law and the state (see below), this is a crucial point.

Another problem with consent is: how *long* does it last? ICO guidance makes it clear that consent once given may not last forever. Combined with the rules restricting data retention, in most cases it seems reasonable to assume that both consent and data should last only as long as necessary for the processing, given the stated purposes of processing.[105] On the Internet, however (as we have already seen in the example of the Google cookie), indefinite retention often seems to be the norm; and as we discuss further in chapter 16 there are of course strong economic incentives to retain as much personal data as possible in commercial contexts where it can be monetised.

Guidance about how consent should be obtained can also be drawn from the other requirements in the DPA for 'fair processing'. First, when considering if processing is 'fair', regard must be had to the method by which consent is obtained, eg it will not be 'fair' if the data subject was deceived or mislead.[106] Secondly, the data subject giving consent must be given information as far as is practicable at the appropriate time about the identity of the data controller, and the *purposes* for which the data is being collected. In general, those purposes should be made public and specific in the register where UK data controllers are required to make an entry and which is available via the Information Commissioner's website. However, these purposes are often specified in very broad terms, and do little to inform the public, or restrain unfettered data collection. For example, it is legitimate to say little more than that that data is being collected or processed for reasons such as 'research' or 'education'.[107] Among private-sector data collectors, it is common to register so many categories of reasons for data collection that few, if any, categories of data will be left out whatever is collected. 'Scope creep'—the use of data collected for one purpose for another purpose—is thus in reality rather easy.

Capacity to consent under the DPA is also related to age. In Scotland, the Act specifies that consent can be given by a child under 16 as soon as they have a 'general understanding' of what it means to exercise the right to give consent. A person aged 12 or over is presumed to be of sufficient age and maturity to have that capacity.[108] Below that age, consent should in

---

[105] See ICO Guidance, above n 69, para 3.1.5, 29–30.

[106] DPA Sched 1, Pt II, para 1(1).

[107] See R Anderson, I Brown et al, 'FIPR: Children's Databases–Safety and Privacy: A Report for the Information Commissioner' (March 2006) available at http://www.ico.gov.uk/upload/documents/library/data_protection/detailed_specialist_guides/ico_issues_paper_protecting_chi drens_personal_information.pdf ('FIPR Report').

[108] DPA s 66.

principle be given by the person or persons with parental responsibilities and rights.[109]

In England, the situation is less clear. The ICO has not provided specific guidance and the Act is silent. In principle, drawing on the seminal child capacity case of *Gillick v West Norfolk and Wisbeck AHA*,[110] it would appear that a child should have the ability to give consent to data collection or processing when they are of an age and maturity to understand the nature and consequences of exercising that capacity. This is the standard test for the giving of medical consent by a child without the consent (and in some cases, the knowledge) of their parent or guardian and has become known as '*Gillick*-competence'. However as the writers of the FIPR Report on the Children's ID Database ('ContactPoint') have observed, the interpretation of *Gillick* is also not entirely straightforward, and there is a danger that a young child might be asked to consent against their best interests without the protective guidance of their parent(s). Again, if a child is not '*Gillick*-competent', it seems DP consent should be given for the child by those with parental responsibilities and rights. The issue of who consents is germane because the UK is currently engaged in putting the details of millions of its children into databases, for purposes such as proactive social work involvement, youth justice and joined-up agency co-operation. Laudable though these purposes are, the net effect for children may be that they become the next 'database generation' without fully understanding what they (or their parents) have given away in terms of personal privacy.[111]

C. Exemptions[112]

A number of important exemptions from and modifications to the DPA exist, either in the Act itself or in separate SIs. The exemptions in the DPA can be found in Part IV (sections 28–36) and Schedule 7. Some exemptions merely allow data controllers to ignore the fair processing and subject

---

[109] This arises from the general law relating to parental responsibilities and rights: see in Scotland the Children (Sc) Act 1995 ss 1 and 2. This rule is modified by specific rules in statutory instruments—eg the DP (Subject Access Modification) (Social Work) Order 2000/415 provides that a parent cannot make a subject access request on behalf of a child if it would be likely to prejudice the carrying on of social work by virtue of resultant serious harm to the child or another person. Similar rules exist in relation to health data (SI 2000/413) and education data (SI 2000/414).

[110] [1985] 3 All ER 402.

[111] See general discussion in FIPR Report, above n 107. The ContactPoint children's database discussed in the report, and subject to repeated criticism since, nonetheless finally went live on 18 May 2009—see http://news.bbc.co.uk/1/hi/education/8052512.stm.

[112] The exact rules here are complex and too lengthy for this chapter—see further Carey, 2nd edn, ch 9.

access rights provisions,[113] while others exempt the data controller from almost all DPA obligations.[114]

Most notably, not only law enforcement agencies, but anyone, even a private householder, who claims they are processing personal data in the 'prevention or detection of crime' is exempt from the fair processing and subject access rules.[115] Thus a private shop-owner who sets up a CCTV camera to watch shoppers in case they are shoplifters or robbers need not obtain consent of data subjects but need merely give notice that there is a camera on premises. It is arguably for this reason that CCTV is so prevalent in the UK, and that cameras can be found not just in public but increasingly in residential areas where they are potentially highly intrusive of private life. National security is also an important exemption:[116] in this case, however, a ministerial certificate must be obtained certifying that processing is for purposes of safeguarding national security.

The other principle exemptions are processing in the case of:

- regulatory activity;[117]
- journalism[118], literature and art;[119]
- research, history and statistics;[120]
- information made available to the public by or under enactment;[121]
- disclosures required by law and in connection with legal proceedings;[122]
- domestic purposes;[123]
- miscellaneous exemptions;[124]
- armed forces;

[113] Paras 2 and 3 of Part II of Schedule I of the Act (fair processing of information) and s 7, subject access.

[114] The First Data Protection Principle, except where it requires compliance with the conditions in Sched 2 and 3 of the Act (the conditions for processing and conditions for processing sensitive data); the Second, Third, Fourth and Fifth Data Protection Principles; s 10 (right to prevent processing likely to cause damage or distress); and s 14(1)–(3) (rectification, blocking, erasure and destruction).

[115] DPA s 29. Note that the EC has introduced a Framework Decision on the protection of personal data processed in the framework of police and judicial co-operation (Council Framework Decision 2008/977/JHA), 30 December 2008. However, the main point of this instrument is to enable greater data sharing between national EU police forces, not to increase the stringency of the treatment of data collected pursuant to the crime prevention exemption.

[116] DPA s 28.

[117] DPA s 31.

[118] See discussion of the extent of the 'public interest' aspect of the journalism exemption in *Campbell v MGN* [2002] EWCA Civ 1373, cf *Douglas v Hello!* [2003] EWHC 786 (Ch) where the journalism exemption was not made available as publication was found not to be in the public interest, in the belief of the data controllers. Note also that the Art 29 WP 87 (above n 93) has indicated that the 'journalism' exemption may be open to amateur bloggers just as much as professional reporters.

[119] DPA s 32.

[120] DPA s 33.

[121] DPA s 34.

[122] DPA s 35(1).

[123] DPA s 36. See discussion in relation to *Lindqvist*, above n 87.

[124] Sched 7, eg confidential references given by or to data controllers for specified purposes.

- exemptions contained within the Data Protection (Miscellaneous Subject Access Exemptions) Order 2000;[125]
- orders made in relation to health, education and social work[126]
  - Health (The Data Protection (Subject Access Modification) (Health) Order 2000;[127]
  - Education (The Data Protection (Subject Access Modifications) (Education) Order 2000;[128]
  - Social Work (The Data Protection (Subject Access Modifications) (Social Work) Order 2000.[129]

In the Coroners and Justice Bill 2009, the UK government attempted to introduce a 'data sharing' provision which would have effectively allowed all public-sector departments to share personal data both between themselves and in certain circumstances with the private sector. Such a sweeping power would have effectively exempted much of the public sector from crucial DP safeguards, with particular fears as to disclosure of patient health data which might have breached the usual guarantees of medical confidentiality. In the face of severe public and professional criticism, the proposals were dropped in March 2009. They may, however, yet reappear.

D. Enforcement and Compensation

Enforcement is part of the role of the ICO. The policy of the UK DP regime has, however, historically been to encourage compliance from data controllers rather than simply to impose penalties. Data subjects are encouraged to complain of breaches to data controllers in the first instance, and data controllers themselves are encouraged to consult with the ICO and seek advice, with prosecution seen as a last resort if agreement cannot be reached as to compliance. Where it suspects a breach, the ICO is not allowed to immediately bring a prosecution, but must first serve either an information notice (asking the data controller to provide details of their processing activities), a 'special' information notice, or an enforcement notice (requiring the data controller to comply with specified DP principles). Only if these are insufficient to procure compliance can the ICO proceed to the courts. Failure to comply with any of these notices is a criminal offence. The ICO can also seek a warrant to exercise powers of entry, seizure of documents and equipment, etc.

As may be imagined from the above, prosecutions have been rare in the

---

[125] SI No 419. SI 2000 No 419 (as amended by The Data Protection (Miscellaneous Subject Access Exemptions) (Amendment) Order, SI No 1865.

[126] DPA s 30.

[127] SI 2000 No 413, also called the 'Health Order'.

[128] SI No 414, the 'Education Order'.

[129] SI No 415, the 'Social Work Order'.

past, and even if successful, sanctions are usually low. In theory, DP breaches in the UK can be punished by a maximum £5,000 fine on summary prosecution or an unlimited fine on indictment (section 60), but more commonly the results have been low fines or conditional discharges. Most prosecutions are for the relatively minor offences of failing to register (section 17) or notify changes as a data controller to the ICO (section 21) or, more seriously, for unlawfully selling or obtaining personal data (section 55). The ICO, hampered by significant underfunding as its workload has increased (despite being the largest privacy watchdog in Europe), has done little to pursue prosecutions as a rhetorical or symbolic gesture, generally taking on only small to medium-sized achievable targets, eg a recent offensive against the trade in personal information, bought by the likes of journalists and private detectives,[130] and against solicitors in particular[131] for failing to register.

This 'softly softly' approach has entirely failed to make visible inroads against either the vast number of small-scale privacy breaches associated with the Internet, or the large-scale data breaches that have become prevalent in the last few years, especially in the public sector. Indeed the ICO stated in 2008[132] that broadly it would focus its limited resources not on enforcement, but on reducing the risk to UK residents of misuse of personal information about them. The ICO also noted its intention to target the increasing surveillance of UK citizens. While laudable goals, these policy statements showed that DP enforcement was intended to be neither comprehensive nor generally deterrent in the same way as ordinary criminal prosecution.

Since these announcements, however, there has been a change of Information Commissioner and a public backlash against the enormous public sector data breaches mentioned earlier—both of which may now lead to increasingly punitive powers for the ICO. Notably, the ICO has already received the power to serve an assessment notice on a data controller, effectively allowing it to intervene ahead of a potential breach as an 'audit' body, and investigate whether DP principles are being adhered to.[133] Furthermore the Criminal Justice and Immigration Act 2008 introduced the power for the Information Commissioner to impose civil monetary penalties on data controllers who knowingly or recklessly commit serious contravention of the DP principles (including security)[134]—ie fine those in breach without having to go to court, as regulators such as ICSTIS already can. Note, however, that negligent data breach remains excluded. Penalties

---

130 See *What Price Privacy Now?* (ICO, May 2006) available at http://www.ico.gov.uk/upload/documents/library/corporate/research_and_reports/ico-wppnow-0602.pdf.

131 See 'Lawyers Penalized for Data Protection Breach', *OUT-LAW News* 21 February 2008.

132 ICO *Data Protection—Protecting People* (2008) available at http://www.ico.gov.uk/upload/documents/library/data_protection/detailed_specialist_guides/ico_dps_final.pdf.

133 DPA 98 s 41A.

134 S 144, inserting new s 55A into the DPA.

were also increased for the section 55 crime of unlawfully obtaining or trading in personal data by virtue of the Criminal Justice and Immigration Act 2008, section 77—including the possibility of a two-year jail sentence.

E. Mandatory Security Breach Disclosure

It is often suggested that in the corporate sector the bad PR caused by a disclosed data breach is a far more effective sanction than any given by the ICO or the courts. For this reason, among others, the EC is likely to regulate as part of the proposed reforms to the PECD that data breaches in some industry sectors should be subject to rules of mandatory public disclosure.[135] Data breach disclosure rules are already common in the US and in some other systems such as Japan. Their effectiveness, however, remains controversial, with some evidence of 'notification fatigue', and much of the devil is in the detail, eg how major must a security breach be before it needs to be notified? Who should it be notified to? What details should be notified? Who should determine the seriousness of the breach? Should notification go to every potential victim of a data breach, or just to a regulator or law enforcement agency? And what remedies should the public have in response to such a breach notification?

The draft European proposals at the time of writing propose that notification should be made, without 'undue delay', to the competent national authority (in the UK, the ICO) where the data breach 'is likely to adversely affect the personal data and privacy of a subscriber as an individual'. A requirement of 'severity' may yet be also imposed, further restricting the scope of the provisions. It is then for the national regulator to decide whether to mandate disclosure to individuals affected (data controllers may voluntarily disclose more widely if they so please). No notification need be made if the data breached is encrypted and so 'unintelligible' to persons unauthorised to access it. The national regulator is to be empowered to audit the data controllers in breach to check they have met their obligations under the data breach notification regime, and impose sanctions if there is failure. ENISA, the European security agency, as well as the Article 29 Working Party will have a role in trying to impose some degree of harmonisation as these proposals are implemented across Europe.

These proposals, though still provisional, have already received severe criticism from both the Article 29 Working Party and the European Data Protection Supervisor.[136] Criticism has particularly focused on the limited

---

[135] See the revised PECD draft rules, above, n 46, draft revised Art 4, 'Security of processing'.
[136] See Art 29 WP Opinion 1/2009 on proposals amending Directive 2002/58/EC, WP 159, 10 February 2009; Second Opinion of the EDPS on the review of Directive 2002/58/EC concerning the processing of personal data and the protection of privacy in the electronic communications sector, available at www.edps.europa.eu.

scope of the data breach proposals, which at present apply only to 'publicly available electronic communication services'. This would include ISPs and telecoms companies such as BT and Orange, but not obvious sources of concern such as banks or financial institutions. The European Commission has provisionally agreed that there is no reason to limit the regime just because it has been introduced via telecoms reform; and has indicated it will extend the debate to general information society service providers, with a view to proposing legislation by the end of 2011. Commentators have also noted, however, that if regulators such as the ICO are already struggling to deal with their caseload, an avalanche of data breach notices will probably stretch their resources to breaking point; and that similar legislation in the US has failed to restrict the growth of identity theft and other data breach frauds.[137] Overall it seems unlikely that breach notification, though a positive step, will be any kind of panacea.

Data subjects who suffer loss as a result of breaches of DP law can seek compensation in a civil action in the UK courts under section 13(1) of the DPA. Damage must have occurred 'by reason of' a data controller's contravention of a DPA requirement[138] and can be awarded for economic loss or distress (section 13(2)). Such claims are in practice extremely rare. This seems unsurprising given the general impediments to consumer litigation combined with widespread consumer ignorance as to DP rights and remedies.[139] The current lack of viable civil class action procedures in the UK is another key reason why security breach notification may still not lead to better redress for notified users whose privacy rights have been infringed.[140]

V. DATA PROTECTION LAW AND THE FREEDOM OF INFORMATION ACT 2000[141]

The Freedom of Information Act 2000 (FOI) seeks to encourage open government and greater public accountability by facilitating access to infor-

---

[137] See S Romanosky, R Telang and A Acquisti, 'Do Data Breach Disclosure Laws Reduce Identity Theft?', 16 September 2008, draft available at http://papers.ssrn.com/sol3/papers.cfm?abstract_id=1268926, which found, comparing US states with a security breach disclosure law to those without, that such a law seemed only to reduce identity theft by 2 per cent on average.

[138] See *Johnson v Medical Defence Union* [2006] EWHC 321 (Ch) where the claim was not upheld.

[139] Eg a personal information survey instructed by the ICO in February 2008 revealed that around 40 per cent of UK users either were unaware of the DPA or had only recently learnt of its existence. See http://www.ico.gov.uk/upload/documents/library/data_protection/detailed_specialist_guides/icm_research_into_personal_information_feb08.pdf.

[140] Even in the US, where class actions by consumers are common, courts have on the whole failed to allow them in relation to data breaches, thus making effective claims by consumers for damages almost impossible—see A Matwyshwn 'Behavioural Targeting of Online Advertisements and the Future of Data Protection' [2009] Journal of Computers and Law, available at www.scl.org.

[141] Scotland has its own legislation, the Freedom of Information (Sc) Act 2002.

mation held by public authorities. The Act provides that any person, legal or natural, has a right to know whether information, either about oneself or a third party, of a particular kind is held by a public authority, and to have that information communicated, and the public authority concerned has to reasonably accommodate the applicant. The request for information has to be in writing, and the applicant has to sufficiently identify himself and pay the fees prescribed. The FOI Act interacts with the DPA in that a FOI request can be refused if it relates to 'personal data or if disclosure of the information would contravene any of the data protection principles'.[142] The reasoning behind this is that the data subject already has subject access rights to his own data, and access by others should depend on the data subject's consent. Thus personal data is exempted from FOI requests.[143] This interaction raises again the difficulty of exactly ring-fencing what is 'personal data', as already seen in the case of *Common Services Agency v Scottish Information Commissioner*[144] where the issue was whether health data anonymised by an algorithm that could easily be broken might not yet in some circumstances be 'personal data'.[145] The definition of personal data looks set to be driven by courts in the FOI field just as much as DP in future.[146]

VI. DOES DATA PROTECTION LAW WORK IN CYBERSPACE?

The scheme described above is generally regarded as a careful and comprehensive approach to the protection of personal data and online privacy, applying internationally recognised fair information principles. The practice has, however, been less satisfactory, and the rise of the Internet as a marketing medium has in particular revealed dismaying gaps in the tapestry of DP law. The EU has tried to patch over the difficulties with the PECD,

[142] FOI Act 2002 s 40.

[143] On the general policy issues involved in the clash between FOI and data protection rights, see a European perspective from P Kleve and RV De Mulder, 'Privacy Protection and the Right to Information: In Search of a New Symbiosis in the Information Age', in S Kierkegaard (ed), *Cyberlaw, Security & Privacy* (International Association of IT Lawyers, 2007) 201–12, available at http://ssrn.com/abstract=1138287.

[144] Above n 75.

[145] See also *Mr C P England and London Borough of Bexley v Information Commissioner*, 10 May 2007; *Lancashire County Council v Information Commissioner*, 27 March 2007; , The Corporate Officer of the House of Commons v Information Commissioner, and Norman Baker MP (as an additional party), 16 January 2007; *A v The Information Commissioner*, EA/2006/0012, 11 July 2006.

[146] See also the EC law case of *Bavarian Lager*, above n 100 , which, while not directly about FOI legislation in the UK sense, deals with the same clash between principles of open access to public bodies and their documents, and the protection of personal privacy. In that case, the Court of First Instance held that public disclosure of the personal names of representatives at a public-sector body meeting making a certain critical decision *should* be allowed, since although the names were technically 'personal data', disclosure was not capable of actually and specifically affecting protection of the privacy and integrity of the persons concerned.

both before and during its current reform process, but as we shall see in the next two chapters, that Directive is still being outstripped by new technologies. What are the challenges that have arisen to make DP so problematic when applied to the new digitised and networked world? And does the DPD still operate to protect personal data in this new world in a more than formal manner or do we need a new Directive?

A. History and Focus of Data Protection Legislation: From Mainframes to Client–Server

As discussed above, historically, the European DP regime derived from the fear of a Stalinist-type 'Big Brother' state and was thus tailored mainly to restrict the surveillance activities of the state. Where control of private data gathering was envisaged, the model was that prominent in the 1970s and 1980s, ie mainframe technology. The cost and size of such machines was such that in the main only large and law-compliant organisations had the ability to collect, hold and process huge amounts of data about consumers. Such prominent commercial actors—helpfully described by Swire as 'elephants'[147]—were easy targets for the law and law enforcement agencies and privacy officials. Not only were they visible with established headquarters and attachable assets, but they also had a brand to consider and customer perceptions to worry about, and thus were likely to comply on notice or warning rather than require aggressive legal action. As a result, DP laws in the UK at least were generally designed to encourage negotiation-based settlement rather than actual prosecutions, and sanctions were set laughably low.[148] If 'elephants' are the main target of the legislation, DP is a practical privacy protection regime: bureaucratic, but enforceable.

The situation now is, however, very different. The trend since the dawn of the personal computer has been away from the mainframe model and towards a much larger number of smaller, more decentralised computers processing and collecting personal data. Computing power is ever cheaper, and chips have become small enough to fit intelligent processing of data into smartphones, digital televisions, etc. The client–server model has to a great extent displaced the mainframe/dumb terminal model: the Web, of course, is predicated on this paradigm. Servers, unlike mainframes, are easily moveable to wherever the legal, social and financial climate is most amenable.

The Internet, meanwhile, has opened up transnational selling and buying to a world that would never have had the resources in the pre-Internet world to transact across national borders. Data about European citizens, as

---

[147] See P Swire, 'Of Elephants, Mice and Privacy: International Choice of Law and the Internet' (1998) 32 *International Lawyer* 991.
[148] See discussion at p 467 above.

noted above, is now just as likely to be processed in India or the US as in the EU. Web publishing, blogging and related data-processing activities have become available to almost everyone, especially in the 'Web 2.0' world of user-generated content (UGC). Thus the number of potential 'data controllers' is suddenly in the millions, rather than thousands, and most are not subject to EU law enforcement. 'Data controllers' of this new kind— who fit the category Swire terms 'mice', since they are numerous, fast moving, fast increasing in numbers, easily able to run away and hide, and generally likely to be lacking in resources—will tend to be entirely untutored in DP, may not even know they have obligations under it, and usually lack legal expertise or advice. They will be less inclined towards legal compliance as they will in all likelihood lack a long-standing public profile and customer base, or internal bureaucracies to deal with the 'paperwork' of DP. They may even disappear, possibly to 'data havens', if realistic sanctions (or the threat thereof) are imposed on them.

The effect of all this was accurately predicted in 1998 by Peter Swire, the father of safe harbour:

> Even within Europe, it is far from clear that a DP regime conceived for a limited number of mainframes can assure compliance in a world of pervasive personal computers. Outside of Europe, US and other website operators are even less likely to comply with the Directive, and many of these operators may remain beyond the jurisdiction of European law. Web sites will also likely be established outside of Europe to process data in ways that are forbidden by the Directive.[149]

B. The Sheer Size and Scope of Cyberspace: Compliance, Oversight, Awareness and Resources

The trends that have been outlined so far–decentralised data control, trans-national data flows, and millions of data controllers—have clearly created problems for DP laws. These are further aggravated by the sheer size of the World Wide Web, the enormous volume of personal data it contains, and the huge number of people involved in donating and collecting personal data. Awareness of DP is low: as noted above, it is dull, fiddly and bureaucratic. Both data controllers and data subjects tend to report near ignorance of DP law and duties. In the February 2008 Eurobarometer survey, only 56 per cent of data controllers polled (selected from a sample which spanned from companies of over 20 employees to giant corporations, and did not include one-man businesses) said they were familiar with DP, and only 13 per cent were very familiar. Only 4 out of 10 respondents said their company had a privacy policy. Almost none reported familiarity with privacy enhancing technologies (PETs). Of data subjects, only a quarter

---

[149] P Swire and R Litan, *None of Your Business: World Data Flows, E-Commerce and the European Privacy Directive* (New York, Brookings Institution Press, 1998) 69–70.

reported knowing all their rights under DP law, and only 28 per cent knew of the existence of their state data protection commissioner. Pressure to implement and comply with DP law comes thus largely not from the public, nor from shareholders who see DP purely as an overhead. Knowledge is sparse and most DP implementation is by internal human resources staff rather than lawyers. European consumer organisations concerned with online privacy, such as the Online Rights Group (ORG) and the Foundation for Internet Privacy Research (FIPR), have also yet to acquire the same high profile that organisations such as the Electronic Freedom Foundation (EFF) and the American Civil Liberties Union (ACLU) arguably have in the US.

Privacy commissioners, who cannot be funded by commerce and remain independent, and are the poor man of state support, also have few resources with which to fight the giant battle of DP compliance. In the UK, the HMRC scandal of October 2007 may have, if temporarily, changed the playing field (see above) and awoken the public to the risks and harms associated with negligent data security—but in general, there are few votes to be got from putting money into privacy, and much backing to be gained from liberalisation of the market from 'red tape'. This takes us to consideration of why DP is not only out of touch with the reality of the modern data-saturated world, but also unpopular with the commercial world.

C. The Globalised Nature of the Internet and Modern Corporate Business Models

One of the key problems with meaningfully enforcing EU DP law, as noted already above, is the problem of applying EU rules to a distributed globalised virtual world of data exchange. The US is still the driving force of the Internet and e-commerce world, and most personal information about UK consumers will probably still be collected by US-based businesses, websites or servers, or their subsidiaries in Europe.[150] But the US protects data exported from the EU, if at all, by means only of the much-criticised 'safe harbour' compromise,[151] and has shown little or no interest in moving further towards a European-style omnibus legal data privacy regime. (Indeed such tentative moves as there were in that direction after the 1998 negotiations seem to have retreated in the wake of the obsession with national security at the expense of privacy since 9/11.) Meanwhile small US web-based businesses, and especially the 'mice' who operate on the grey legal fringes, such as pornography sites, gambling sites and spammers, will probably continue simply to ignore EU DP law even where they interact

---

150 It might be argued that the US might be displaced in time by Japan, Korea, China and other Asian-Pacific countries as IT and e-commerce leader. Since most of these still have no equivalent to EU-style data protection regimes, however, the problem persists.

151 See n 57 above.

with European consumers. And even compliant US businesses, as we have already seen, are increasingly abandoning what safeguards safe harbour offers in favour of the private standard terms legitimised by Article 26.

Jurisdictional rules do of course theoretically exist to try to deal with the problem of transglobal corporate data flows,[152] but arguably the resources and the political will to enforce European rules effectively outside Europe simply do not. US industry has shown little desire to take on the financial burden of full DP compliance, nor does DP fit with the model of national and international data sharing between affiliate and subsidiary companies which has evolved in a competitive and increasingly merger-and-acquisition fixated market.[153] Tellingly, the same points have been echoed in European industry itself,[154] which has always struggled to catch up with the natural advantage the US has had as the first nation into the e-commerce market. Kuner, writing in a text oriented towards European business practice, notes: 'There have been increasing complaints by companies that European DP law is based on outmoded regulatory models and does not sufficiently take the requirements of electronic commerce into account', and then goes on to list seven factors underlying this statement.[155]

D. Conceptual and Harmonisation Problems

Finally a problem unconnected directly to the rise of the Internet, but again, probably aggravated by it, has been a growing dissatisfaction at the degree of vagueness in the DP Directive and the consequent diversity of interpretation of key words and phrases throughout the EU Member States. One of the strengths of the DP regime, given that it deals with trans-national data flows, should be that at least it harmonises the law in Europe;

---

[152] See Art 4 of the DP Directive 1995, para 4(1)(c) of which states that a Member State may apply its national laws to a data controller if 'the controller is not established on Community territory, and for the purposes of processing personal data makes use of equipment, automated or otherwise, situated on the territory of the said member state, unless such equipment is used only for the purposes of transit through the territory of the Community'. Such a definition appears to catch the typical US based e-commerce website (eg Amazon.com) which sells goods or services to UK consumers and collects personal data about UK consumers using 'equipment' here. 'Equipment' is not defined, but is usually deemed to include conduits necessary for the 'processing' such as UK ISP wires, cables, routers, etc. See also discussion of Google cookies in Art 29 WP 148 (see n 79 above) which makes it clear EU jurisdiction applies even where 'equipment' consists only of software such as cookies.

[153] See P Drahos and J Braithwaite, *Information Feudalism: Who Owns the Knowledge Economy?* (London, Earthscan Publications, 2002); M Castells, *The Rise of the Network Society*, 2nd edn (Oxford, Blackwells, 2000).

[154] Regan notes that in the negotiations surrounding the 1995 DP Directive, many EU-based companies lobbied alongside US business for laxer laws: P Regan, 'American Business and the European Data Protection Directive: Lobbying Strategies and Tactics', in C Bennett and R Grant (eds), *Visions of Privacy: Policy Choices for the Digital Age* (Toronto, University of Toronto Press, 1999).

[155] Kuner, above n 18, 45–48.

but even this claim, it seems, is no longer really true. Debates have broken out about basic notions in the Directive such as 'personal data',[156] 'equipment' and 'domestic purposes';[157] some rules are so broad that their interpretation is wholly unpredictable; enforcement policies vary hugely from Member State to Member State, to the extent that multinational companies operate in a sort of 'regulatory limbo';[158] and in particular, the lynchpin of the Directive, the notion of 'consent', is increasingly deconstructed by the realities of commercial standard-form contracts, web click-through forms and browse-wrap contracts,[159] and consumer ignorance and lack of time.

VII. FROM PRIVACY TO DISCLOSURE: THE NORMS DON'T WORK?

We have tried to demonstrate above that the DP laws devised in the 1970s and 1980s are failing to protect personal data in a world of digitised data and global networks. Another issue, though, is whether a societal will still exists to protect privacy as a fundamental value, in the way that came naturally to the survivors of World War II and the next generation. An important cultural shift is happening; a 'value gap' seems to be opening up at the time of writing between those aged under 30 or so, who have grown up familiar with an Internet world, and the rest of the populace. We live now in a world where conversations that would once have been private are habitually conducted in public on mobile phones; where young (and even sometimes older) people are willing to display their worst character traits, their poor business sense and their sex lives on live public television if it brings them a brief dose of D-list celebrity stardom; and where, arguably, openness rather than seclusion has become the more admirable character trait among the young(er). It is amusing that *Big Brother*, used at the beginning of the chapter in the Orwellian sense of a society where total surveillance is used to maintain tyranny and terror, has become to a younger generation associated with the idea that public visibility is desirable and a chance to show off and grab the limelight. Britain was traditionally a rather discrete and private society; it now seems to be following the US towards more of a culture of openness.

What effect might this perceived shift of values, or norms, have on the regulation of privacy and its enforcement? And if members of society, perhaps the younger and less experienced members, are willing to give up their own privacy (or trade it for perceived advantages), then what will the consequences be, both for each individually and for society as a whole?

---

[156] See discussion earlier at n 73 and surrounding text.
[157] See discussion earlier at n 152, and of *Lindqvist*, above n 87.
[158] Kuner, above n 18, 37ff.
[159] See further Riefa and Hornle, ch 2.

An important case study here can be drawn from the world of social networking sites (SNSs). Sites such as MySpace, Facebook, Orkut, Linked-In, Bebo and Flickr have attracted students and seniors, business users and entertainment seekers, Americans and Europeans in ever-increasing numbers. SNSs[160] can be characterised as 'online social networks for communities of people who share interests and activities, or who are interested in exploring the interests and activities of others, and which necessitates the use of software'.

A. The Case of the Oxford Proctors and the Philosophy Student

In July 2007, Oxford proctors in charge of university discipline used Facebook to find evidence of students breaking university rules. Students, who, in post-exam hilarity, had held wild parties, sprayed each other with champagne or shaving foam, or thrown flour bombs at each other, often posted photos of these incidents on Facebook. Proctors combed Facebook for evidence of such incidents and caught a number of students *in flagrante*. As a result, some of these students received disciplinary e-mails or more vigorous sanctions. The response from students was dismay and shock. The student union claimed that the incident was a 'disgraceful' intrusion into the privacy of the students concerned. One caught perpetrator complained that she was 'outraged':

> Alex Hill, 21, a maths and philosophy student, received an e-mail stating that three of her photos provided evidence that she had engaged in 'disorderly' conduct. 'I don't know how the proctors got access to it,' the St Hugh's College student said. 'I thought my privacy settings were such that only students could see my pictures . . . I'm outraged.'[161]

A key point raised by the Oxford case is whether Facebook and similar SNSs are indeed a 'private' space where the user has reasonable expectations of privacy, or a 'public' space where such expectations do not or should not exist.[162] Ms Hill's 'outrage' at being stalked in an 'underhand' fashion by Oxford proctors seems to show an honest (if unreasonable?) belief that she was operating in a friendly private space. Should such attitudes be taken into account and reified by the law? Livingstone, researching attitudes of young persons in the UK to privacy on Facebook in 2006, found that young people had both a conflicted attitude to privacy and often were either ignorant or confused as to how far they could protect

---

160 http://en.wikipedia.org/wiki/Social_network_service.

161 See 'Caught on Camera—and Found on Facebook', *The Times* 17 July 2007, at http://technology.timesonline.co.uk/tol/news/tech_and_web/the_web/article2087306.ece.

162 Interestingly, a recent UK Internet libel case asserts that blog sites are a public space and thus there is no reasonable expectation of privacy or anonymity there: see *The Author of a Blog v Times Newspapers Ltd* [2009] EWHC 1358 (QB).

themselves by altering privacy settings.[163] Barnes, working in the US, noted that there was also an apparent disconnect—which she named the 'privacy paradox'—between 'the way users say they feel about the privacy settings of their blogs and how they react once the they experience unanticipated consequences from a breach of privacy'.[164] Put simply this means that users usually say they wish to protect their personal data but rarely do anything about it—at least until after harmful consequences have transpired. Students and young persons also clearly want to keep information private from *some* if not all persons, eg parents and teachers, but do not seem to realise Facebook is a public space. Such pervasive assumptions seem to go beyond mere ignorance to actually perverse perceptions of social network and virtual community spaces, especially odd given so many students of today are tech-savvy and (by definition?) well educated and familiar with information technology.

Privacy jurisprudence itself is conflicted about whether 'privacy in public' exists and should be protected. The ECtHR has been in the process for some years of recognising that privacy rights do exist even in public spaces, even where celebrities, the archetypal 'public property', make themselves accessible to press attention in public—most noticeably in the celebrated recent ECtHR case of *von Hannover.*[165] In the UK, the courts and the Press Complaints Commission have given spectacularly contradictory decisions concerning celebrity privacy in quasi-public spaces such as beaches.[166] On SNSs, where the whole purpose for users is to network and to expose parts of themselves so as to engender trust and communication, the discourse is hopelessly confused.

[163] See S Livingstone, 'Taking Risky Opportunities in Youthful Content Creation', Poke 1.0, London, November 2007, abstract accessible at http://nms.sagepub.com/cgi/content/abstract/10/3/393.

[164] S Barnes, 'A Privacy Paradox: Social Networking in the US' [2006] *First Monday* issue 11/9, September, available at http://www.firstmonday.org/ISSUES/issue11_9/barnes/, citing FB Viegas, 'Blogger's Expectations of Privacy and Accountability; An Initial Survey' (2005) 10(3) *Journal of Computer-Mediated Communications* at http://jcmc.indiana.edu/vol10/issue3/viegas.html.

[165] Above n 13.

[166] See Anna Ford's complaint about paparazzi taking photos of family beach holiday, not upheld, at http://www.pcc.org.uk/news/index.html?article=MjAyNA, and Gail Sheridan, complaint over use of long lens to photograph her in her own back garden, at http://www.pcc.org.uk/news/iondex.html?article=NDUzNw—both privacy complaints not upheld; cf JK Rowling, complaining of press photos taken while on a Mauritius beach as family holiday, upheld, at http://www.pcc.org.uk/news/index.html?article=MjA0NQ, despite very similar circumstances to Ford. (See also Rowling's sympathetic treatment in the courts in *Murray v Big Picture*, above n 8.) The PPC is not a court and asserted in the Rowling complaint that it did not have to follow its prior decisions, especially Ford, though it would have regard to them. See also apology to Sara Cox, equivalent of 'settlement', at http://www.pcc.org.uk/news/index.html?article=Mjg2MQ==. Interestingly, following a number of complaints, the PCC has recently commissioned a report into whether use by newspapers of information found on SNSs is abusive of privacy and should be a breach of the PCC Code: see http://blogs.guardian.co.uk/greenslade/2008/02/pcc_faces_up_to_facebook_intru.html. Complaints about media treatment of privacy can also be directed to Ofcom where broadcasters are involved: see eg complaint by Mr Gareth Nixon at http://www.ofcom.org.uk/tv/obb/prog_cb/obb112/issue112.pdf (unsuccessfully) complaining of being filmed binge-drinking in public.

B. Social Networking Sites and Data Protection Law

Social networking site operators are of course data controllers, and so under DP law they must, in pursuit of 'fair processing', gain the consent of their users to process their personal data—and indeed, 'explicit consent' in the case of sensitive personal data[167] (which abounds on SNS—in almost every Facebook profile a user reveals his or her race, politics, sexuality or religious beliefs, since these are predetermined fields in the user profile, which most users fill in without much thought). However, this consent is invariably obtained, since it is required as part of registration before 'admission' to the site is granted. In the SNS world, consent is usually obtained by displaying a privacy policy (or terms and conditions) on the site and asking the user to accede to them by ticking a box. As there is no chance to negotiate, and little or no evidence that users either read or understand these conditions, it is hard to see how this consent is 'free and informed' (see earlier discussion)—yet business practice for the entire sector seems to regard this consent is satisfactory. A further problem arises where SNS *users* display facts or images about other users—eg commonly, photographs featuring multiple persons. Such users rarely seek prior consent and such software tools as are made available usually only facilitate *post factum* removal, for example, of 'tags' on Facebook. As in the discussion of *Lindqvist* above, the question again arises as to whether ordinary users should be subject to the full panoply of DP obligations vis-à-vis their peers, and if they are not, how invasions of privacy by users rather than the site itself should be controlled. One suggestion has been that sites should be subject to liability for invasion of privacy if they do not take down expediently on complaint.

Many SNS users give away their personal data with alacrity because they feel they have nothing to hide, and many more make the same choice (if it is to be called a 'choice') simply because social networking is fun and trendy. Personal choices deserve respect, but inertia is something different; and the autonomy to make choices should also be balanced against the risks users are not fully equipped or informed to consider, especially the young and vulnerable. SNSs can aptly be described as a stalker's[168]—and a voyeur's—paradise. People and companies collect the apparently harmless data disclosed by SNS users—including birthdates, house addresses, e-mail addresses, telephone numbers, friends, relatives, and pet names or nicknames (often used as clues to passwords for the likes of online banking)—for a variety of dubious purposes. These range from legitimate

---

[167] Although note the earlier comment that processing of sensitive data may not require explicit consent where users have made it public themselves—see n 102.

[168] The first UK prosecution for harassment explicitly involving Facebook was initiated in March 2008. See http://www.out-law.com/page-8913.

law or norm enforcement purposes (as in the Oxford case itself[169]), to stalking by friends, strangers or perhaps ex-partners, to surreptitious mining of data without consent for economic exploitation by inter alia spammers, fraudsters, direct marketers, data miners and identity thieves;[170] to government surveillance when looking for terrorists or threats to national security. There are also worries about the use of data disclosed on Facebook etc by the media and press.[171]

Data disclosed on SNSs may persist for unknown lengths of time and acquire significance later that it did not have at the time of disclosure. The harmless pranks of today's youth, rather than disappearing into obscurity, may instead remain enshrined on an SNS and become a reason to be labelled as delinquent, denied admission to university or even employment, promotion or insurance, at some indefinite future time. One of the most worrying aspects of the SNS phenomenon is the generally acknowledged surge in their use by employers and other institutions as a means to screen applicants.[172] Social network profiles also have a bad habit of persisting, even when the site appears to offer means of deletion.[173] Even where the site does provide effective deletion mechanisms, disclosed data may still be available via Google cache[174] or archiving sites such as the Way Back Machine. Such concerns about persistence, yet again, do not seem to have communicated themselves to younger users. A study by the UK Information Commissioner's office (ICO) in 2007 found that almost 60 per cent of UK 14–21 year olds did not realise the data they were putting online could be

---

[169] See also the news that Scotland Yard specifically patrols Facebook for crooks, at http://www.theregister.co.uk/2008/04/25/met_police_social_networking/ and the use of sites like Bebo and Facebook to crack down on anti-social youths in central Scotland, reported at http://news.bbc.co.uk/1/hi/scotland/tayside_and_central/7430993.stm.

[170] See 'Cyber Thieves Target Social Sites', BBC News, 3 January 2008, suggesting that in 2008 SNSs would become 'an attack vector for the hi-tech gangs who are behind the vast majority of cybercrime', available at http://news.bbc.co.uk/1/hi/technology/7156541.stm.

[171] See n 166 above and 'Facebook Profiles Need Shielding from Media Intrusion', *OUT-Law News*, 9 June 2008. In a survey commissioned by the Press Complaints Commission, 78 per cent of users said they would change what they post about themselves online if they thought the media might use it.

[172] See eg 'Would Be Students Checked on Facebook', *Guardian* 11 January 2008 (Cambridge University tutor admits to screening students via Facebook), available at http://education.guardian.co.uk/universityaccess/story/0,,2238962,00.html ; 'Caught on Camera', *The Times*, above n 150 (survey of 600 UK companies revealed that one in five employers had used Facebook and other SNSs to screen applicants).

[173] Facebook, for example, were warned by the ICO when deleted profiles were still found to be accessible. They bowed to ICO and other pressure and guaranteed that total deletion of profiles would in future be possible—see http://www.out-law.com/default.aspx?page=8882. Facebook's terms and conditions were also subsequently changed after public disquiet so that Facebook was not entitled to continue to use data on a deleted profile after deletion.

[174] Facebook profiles were originally not made available to Google spiders. However, Facebook took a decision to make profiles available to Google and other search engines in September 2007. Interestingly, users were given an opportunity to opt-out of (rather than the more privacy-protective option to opt *in* to) having their profiles indexed. See discussion in this writer's blog, 'Facebook and Privacy Returns', *Pangloss* 5 September 2007, available at http://blogscript.blogspot.com/2007/09/facebook-and-privacy-returns.html.

permanently linked to them, and were generally horrified when this was suggested.[175]

Dissemination to hostile third parties and persistence of disclosed data are by no means the only threats. Social networking sites also often allow third-party software programmes (sometimes called 'apps') access to user data. Facebook, the leading UK SNS, has built much of its appeal on these services. Again, user consent is usually sought in the most formal sense (ie give consent or you cannot use the app), but typically the user must give away *all* their personal data on the SNS or not be able to access the software at all—even if all the app does is something as simple as send a friend a 'virtual' bunch of flowers, requiring almost no data. Once data has been divulged to third parties via an app, that data is effectively beyond the control of both user and the SNS site itself. It is possible that the SNS may contractually require the third-party app developer to take reasonable security precautions and accord with local privacy laws—but the user will not usually see that contract before agreeing to install the app, nor be party to it, nor have title to enforce it.

To make matters worse, many apps are 'viral', in the sense that a user cannot sign up to them, or get results out of them, unless they pass the app on to 10 or 15 other friends on the same SNS first. What this boils down to is that the price of entry is not only giving away your own details but also those of your friends. Being viral, such apps spread rapidly. And being, on the whole, trivial applications, users rarely stop to think whether sharing data with unknown third parties is wise or in their best interests. All in all, it might be suggested that the easiest way to become an identity thief in the SNS world is to simply write a popular app, sit back, and gather all the personal information you want. Interestingly, the June 2009 Article 29 Working Party Opinion on SNSs[176] takes especial note of the threat to privacy of third-party apps, and suggests, first, that the SNS operator should 'have means to ensure that third party applications comply with the DPD' and secondly, that the APIs which allow the app access to user data held by the SNS should be written in a way that provides for granularity—so that users need *not* be asked for all their data just to send a virtual bunch of flowers.

Are there ways in which the users can still have fun and interact on SNSs, while protecting the, shall we say, naïve user from the consequences of their actions? The conventional answer is consumer education:[177] persuade

---

[175] See full report at http://www.ico.gov.uk/upload/documents/library/data_protection/detailed_specialist_guides/research_results_topline_report.pdf. One respondent to the survey (female, age 14) replied 'Initial thoughts – who cares? Subsequent thoughts – omg!'

[176] Opinion WP 5/2009, above n 93.

[177] See *Home Office Good Practice Guidance for the Providers of Social Networks etc* (2008), available at http://police.homeoffice.gov.uk/publications/operational-policing/social-networking-guidance?view=Binary.

consumers to read privacy policies and think about the dangers, perhaps compare different sites on the market, teach them to use the privacy tools the sites make available, and everything will be alright. This author is, however, rather dubious of this solution.[178] Consumers, especially the young, the elderly, the less well educated and the technophobic are not good judges of the risks of disclosure of personal data on the Internet, especially when the advantages—popularity, networking—are so much more tangible and present. Nor are they likely to put effort into learning how to use often well-hidden privacy features or read legalistic privacy policies: these are not entertaining activities. Common sense as well as scientific evidence say that people prefer jam today and disregard risk tomorrow. SNS users are particularly unlikely to worry about the privacy of *other* users, and at present one common problem is how easy many SNS platforms make it to 'tag' photos of third parties (who may or may not be members of the SNS too) without their knowledge or prior consent.

SNS operators themselves, for all the prevalent rhetoric of being alert to the safety and needs of their users, have little economic reason to respond to fairly non-existent customer pressure to produce more privacy-protective terms and conditions or defaults—for the simple reason that their business model is usually entirely based on collecting data from users and selling it directly or indirectly to advertisers. Since the sites themselves do not generally charge an entry fee, what they are really selling to stay in business is, in the main, their user's data—in other words, their privacy.

The law is, however, used to dealing with consent as a faulty risk management process in the context of consumer law. Many laws require provision of pre-contractual information to consumers, and prejudicial terms in standard term contracts, which indicate a significant imbalance in bargaining power, can be struck down as unfair terms under UK and EU law.[179] There are no cases in the UK as yet of such clauses in SNS privacy policies or terms and conditions being attacked, though in the US an arbitration clause that was part of the 'rules' of an online virtual world has been successfully struck down.[180] Such victories are rare, however, and in any case most users have neither the knowledge nor the desire to take court

---

[178] Fascinatingly, a recent Cambridge survey of 45 SNSs showed that sites rarely made efforts to promote privacy as a selling point, and in fact that the sites which made the biggest efforts to promote and implement privacy tools tended to do badly in terms of audience growth. This does not reassure that the market will respond positively to forefront privacy, and does explain why privacy settings are so often metaphorically printed in grey on grey. See J Bonneau and S Preibusch, 'The Privacy Jungle: On the Market for Data Protection in Social Networks', Workshop on the Economics of Information Security, 2009, UCL, London, at http://weis09.infosecon.net/files/156/index.html.

[179] See further discussion in Riefa and Hornle, ch 2. See in the UK, the Unfair Contract Terms Act 1976 as amended, and the Unfair Terms in Consumer Contract Regulations 1999 SI No 2083, and at EU level, EC Unfair Terms Directive 1993 93/13/EEC: L 95/29.

[180] *Bragg v Linden Labs*, 30 May 2007, District Court for E, Pennsylvania, Civil Action No 06-4925.

action against their favourite social network (and run the risk of being thrown off it and losing contact with their friends).

A better and far more effective approach than private parties taking contractual challenges to SNSs might be for the *state* to regulate SNSs by legally requiring them to amend their software—their 'code'—to protect the average user's personal data from obvious threats. In SNSs, for example, it is very often possible to restrict sight of a user's profile to the people who have been defined as that user's 'friends' or 'buddy list', but in general profiles are public by default, and user have to take positive efforts to restrict their profile in this way. If the site itself made 'friends-only' the default—which the user could then choose to 'opt-out' of—then users would be far better protected against the likes of spammers and identity thieves, etc. Instead, however, privacy-enhancing tools of this kind are frequently unobvious or difficult to use. The cynical might imagine that this is because, as noted above, the revenue stream from the SNS *comes* from third parties—advertisers—having access to as much data, on as many profiles, as possible. The UK Home Office code of conduct for SNSs released in 2008 suggests that the profiles of minor users at least should by default be locked to friends-only[181] while the Article 29 Working Party Opinion on SNSs recommends not only 'privacy-friendly default settings' for all users, but also that restricted access profiles should not be found using internal search engines. This seems the beginning of the right way forward.[182]

A practical approach, might be for users, when they join an SNS or similar site, to be automatically taken through an 'install routine' as is the norm when installing a piece of software. This routine could ask the user in simple language what data they want to disclose, who they want to be able to see it, and perhaps how long they want it to exist for. This would be far more effective than expecting the user to learn proactively to use well-hidden privacy preferences. There is also no reason, for example, why users could not be prompted to decide if they want to keep their profile going, say every six months, which might at least partially overcome the problem of the 'leftover' persistence of the records of youthful folly. Third-party apps might be required to implement code (as the Article 29 Working Party suggested) so as to obtain only the data necessary to fulfil their function.

These are all 'code' solutions that could be implemented fairly easily if imposed by law or mandatory industry code of practice. Finally, SNS sites

---

[181] Above n 177.

[182] See also discussion of future regulation of SNSs in the UK in the Byron Report, 'Safer Children in a Digital World' (2008), at http://www.dfes.gov.uk/byronreview/pdfs/Final%20 Report%20 Bookmarked.pdf. In Europe, ENISA, the European security agency, has also called for regulation: see ENISA Position Paper No 1, 'Security Issues and Regulation for Online Social Networks' (October 2007), at http://www.enisa.europa.eu/doc/pdf/deliverables/enisa_pp_ social_networks.pdf.

could be forced to allow interoperability between their sites and other proprietary venues. In simple terms, this would mean that if a user was unhappy with the protection they received on site A, they could pick up their profile along with their 'friends list' and move it to another site. Such data portability would engender real competition between sites to attract users, which might lead to more concern for user rights, and less for advertisers.

VIII. THE DEATH OF PRIVACY?

Does the social networking phenomenon described above really indicate a sea change in attitudes to privacy? And if so, is this yet another reason why DP law needs to be amended or wholly rejected? We have already shown that corporations view DP as a business impediment, that DP deals badly with global data flows, that oversight authorities are underfunded and underpowered, and that consumers either know little about DP or have little faith in it. If consumers are furthermore rejecting privacy as a fundamental value, then the future for DP is bleak.

But this is not the true, or at least the complete, story. Conceptions of privacy are certainly changing, but the need on the one hand for private space, where people can make choices and enjoy intimacy without intrusion, and on the other for protection from 'privacy harms'[183]—fraud, spam, misuse of personal data, identity theft—has not disappeared. The SNS phenomenon shows that perceptions of 'private space', and of risk, are flawed—not necessarily that the young have no interest in privacy. It also shows that much of personal privacy is about granular control: I may want to share all my data with X, some with Y and absolutely none with Z. The HMRC scandal meanwhile shows viscerally that when the state loses our data, and the risks and consequences of that loss are obvious, the public is still visibly appalled. Furthermore, even after the blip that 9/11 has caused, the public is beginning to reassert in poll after poll that it is not keen on unrestricted public surveillance by both the state and commercial entities.[184]

What happens next? The European Commission is due to review the DPD in the near future and has already nearly completed the process of amending the PECD (as discussed at points above). There will almost certainly be further changes of detail to come to deal with phenomena like radio frequency identification (RFID) (discussed in chapter 16), mobile

---

[183] The concept of 'privacy harms' is expanded on in L Edwards, 'Reconstructing Consumer Privacy', above n 1, 317–18.

[184] In the February 2008 Eurobarometer poll, only 16 per cent of the sample approved of unrestricted state monitoring of phone calls, and only 25 per cent were happy to have their Internet use monitored.

computing, distributed processing,[185] and perhaps social networking. But will there be serious changes of principle? As Hustinx, the European Data Protection Supervisor, said in November 2007:

> The Internet . . . is the most fundamental revolution in data collection and data transfer since the printing press. If the most fundamental revolution in the last 500 years is not going to present some challenges to traditional notions of DP, then I do not think we are challenging ourselves to think things through.[186]

At the international human rights level, change is clearly afoot, and the accumulation of threats to privacy in a digital world is being rebutted in a variety of interesting contexts. We have already noted the increasing presence of the ECtHR in what might generally be regarded as DP areas, from the perspective of Article 8 of the ECHR. In EU courts, the ECJ recently asserted in the *Promusicae* case that the rights of the entertainment industry to find out who is illegally downloading music and movies do not necessarily trump the privacy rights of Internet users. Instead they opined that Member States and their courts 'must take care to rely on an interpretation of [the DPD and the Copyright Directives] which allows a fair balance to be struck between the various fundamental rights protected by the Community legal order'.[187] In Germany, the Constitutional Court has radically declared a new fundamental right of privacy, confidentiality and integrity in computer systems.[188] The EU Charter of Rights, which may or may not become a mandatory part of EU law at the time of writing under the Lisbon Treaty, declares as well as the familiar right to a private life, the right to protection of personal data.[189] Even in the US, not historically a privacy-protective jurisdiction, the Supreme Court of New Jersey has recently declared for the first time that US citizens have a 'reasonable expectation of privacy' in personal data they supply to Internet service providers.[190]

---

[185] On both of these, see A Charlesworth, 'The Future of UK Data Protection Regulation' (2006) 11 *Information Security Technical Report* 46—sadly, space precludes further discussion of these important topics here. See also on future reform of EC DP law, Y Poullet and J-M Dinant, 'Towards New Data Protection Principles in a New ICT Environment' (IDP, 2007), available at http://www.uoc.edu/idp/5/dt/eng/poullet_dinant.pdf.

[186] See report of Hustinx debate with Google Privacy head, Peter Fleischer, at *OUT-Law News* 9 November 2007 at http://www.theregister.co.uk/2007/11/12/privacy_law_debate/.

[187] *Promusicae v Telefonica*, European Court of Justice, 29 January 2008, Case C-275/06, para 68.

[188] 27 February 2008. Judgment available in German at http://www.bverfg.de/entscheidungen/rs20080227_1bvr037007.html. See discussion at http://www.tjmcintyre.com/2008/02/german-constitutional-court-recognises.html.

[189] Art 8; 2000/C 364/01.

[190] *New Jersey v Reid*, Supreme Court of New Jersey (A-105-06) 21 April 2008.

A. Code and Privacy

As indicated above, though, law is not the only solution, or at least traditional law of the current DP variety. Legislators must increasingly think about how 'code' can be manipulated to protect privacy, rather than legislating as is traditional at a principled level, to regulate *people* rather than technologies. The European Commission has repeatedly declared its support for privacy-enhancing technologies (PETs),[191] though it does not yet seem to have found a way to convince the general public of their value, or indeed, existence.[192] Above, we have given several examples of how regulated code might protect the users of SNSs rather better than mere abstract DP laws. The associated concept of 'privacy by design', as discussed further in subsequent chapters, is also receiving serious attention, in the UK[193] and globally.[194] This is, in essence, the idea that privacy should be 'engineered in' early in the process of designing systems, especially large multi-user databases, rather than strapped on after the main design is complete as a half-hearted add on. The emphasis here is on *data minimisation*—collecting less data ab initio, by code means and also by reliance on legal principles such as the Australian rule that systems must be designed to allow an anonymity option if practical. This idea of privacy built in *ex ante* rather than *post factum* may yet transform the field.[195]

Turning back to law, it may be that we have to abandon the idea of DP law as a one-size-fits-all regime. Different legal and non-legal solutions may fit different sectors of activity. In the traditional heartland of DP, the protection of the citizen from state surveillance, DP clearly still has an outstandingly important role to play, simply because the state has such power to affect the everyday life and privacy of citizens, and so *must* be seen to be law compliant. The problems here seem in essence political and organisational rather than conceptual: political will for compliance, enforcement powers, training of public officials, resourcing issues, education of citizens, etc.

In the commercial world, however, there do seem to be real issues about whether the principles of a regime created for a world of relatively small numbers of non-networked mainframe computers still work in a world of

---

[191] See most recently *Communication from the Commission to the European Parliament and Council, Promoting Data Protection by PETs*, Brussels, 2 May 2007 COM(2007) 228 final.

[192] Eurobarometer reported that only 39 per cent of UK data subjects had ever even heard of let alone used PETs—the fourth lowest score in the EU.

[193] See eg the ICO report, 'Privacy by Design' (26 November 2008) available at http://www.ico.gov.uk/about_us/news_and_views/current_topics/privacy_by_design.aspx.

[194] See eg in Canada, A Cavoukian, *Privacy by Design.. Take the Challenge* (Information and Privacy Commissioner of Canada, 2009).

[195] Interestingly, the first British Standard (BS 10012:2009) on the management of personal data was published in June 2009 (*OUT-LAW News* 3 June 2009). This raises the interesting question of whether technical and organisational standards might be a better medium than law for setting standards in a field like DP.

multiple data controllers, distributed global data flows and mobile ubiquitous data usage. It is possible that regulators should be directed here to apply one set of rules and sanctions to large database operators, and another to small to medium-sized operators. One key problem, which will be discussed at length in the following two chapters, is whether consent has any meaningful role left to play as a safeguard for consumers giving away personal data online to information society service providers.

In the personal world of social networking and the like, the problem of meaningful consent recurs but other factors are different again. One key problem is that created by the *Lindqvist* case; the idea that every domestic Internet user who contributes content to Web 2.0 sites like Facebook or Twitter is a data controller with the same set of obligations in principle as Virgin or HSBC is clearly absurd. As noted earlier, this is an area ripe for reform.

One argument, in which this author has increasingly little faith, however, is that the problem of disclosure of personal data on SNSs may be a 'blip' problem. The youth of today may be currently enthusiastically giving away their personal data on the Internet, this argument goes, but the next generation will be very well versed in how to manipulate the Internet and have no problem locating and using privacy defaults and similar controls. This seems to ignore the point that consumers as a herd tend to be reactive and not take safeguards until the worst has already happened. An even more hopeful suggestion is that in time we will turn into a more forgiving, sympathetic society; if the eternal memory of Google remembers everyone's faults equally, we will perhaps have to, in turn, employers and lovers, colleagues and referees, forgive each other's sins for fear of being equally castigated. As the employment appeal tribunals fill with Internet-related cases, this also seems somewhat far off.

Finally some suggest simply that privacy is becoming an outmoded concept: disclosure is in, privacy is out. On this, only time will tell. What is certainly true is that as the next generation of 'digital natives'[196] grows up to become adult consumers of the information society, their privacy needs, in the public, private and cultural sectors, are going to be no less but very different than those of current users. Multiple online identities, distributed and federal identity management, aggregate or group profiled data, and users who ascribe their loyalty to no particular territorial jurisdiction as respects their online life, are all going to be challenges for the next iteration of DP.[197]

---

[196] See J Palfrey and U Gasser, *Born Digital: Understanding the First Generation of Digital Natives* (New York, Basic Books, 2008).

[197] Note that as this book went to press, the European Commission finally formally launched a consultation towards reforming the DPD; see Consultation on the legal framework for the fundamental right to protection of personal data, 9 July 2009.

In the next four chapters we examine in detail emerging problems for DP and privacy in first, the commercial world, and secondly, the world of state surveillance.

15

Consumer Privacy Law 1: Online Direct Marketing

LILIAN EDWARDS[1]

I. INTRODUCTION

AS WE DISCUSSED in the previous chapter, consumer privacy online, in theory protected by the European data protection (DP) regime, is under an unprecedented assault in a world where personal data has become an increasingly valuable business commodity. Marketers and enterprises ubiquitously collect, analyse, combine and mine personal data in the pursuit of the perfect one-to-one business-to-consumer (B2C) advertising market. Combined with a similar spurt of data collection and processing activity from the law enforcement agencies of the state, we have collectively become what is sometimes called a 'surveillance society' or a 'database nation'.[2] The implications of this for the relationship between state and citizen are primarily examined in Rauhofer's chapters in this volume. Here we will look at the commercial and consumer world.

Digital marketing is a long-standing phenomenon: the first spam was sent 30 years ago on 3 May 1978 to 400 people on Arpanet, by DEC—a now-defunct computer-manufacturer. Spam is best defined as unsolicited bulk e-mail (though see below). From one spam in 1978, we have now reached a place where around 80–90 per cent of e-mail is spam and it is choking the Internet's pipes to a standstill. Spam is thus not just a privacy problem but also a public and economic blight. Policymakers need to look at ways to preserve the Internet as a whole from collapsing under the deluge of spam, rather than merely attempting to protect individual privacy and consumer rights.[3] However, to date spam has been regulated incre-

---

[1] Much earlier versions of parts of this chapter appeared in L Edwards (ed), *The Legal Framework for European Electronic Commerce* (Oxford, Hart Publishing, 2005) and L Edwards and C Waelde (eds), *Law and the Internet: A Framework for Electronic Commerce* (Oxford, Hart Publishing, 2000).

[2] See discussion in Edwards, ch 14.

[3] A good example of this is the US Can-Spam Act Pub L No 108-187, 117 Stat 2699 (2003)

mentally in Europe primarily as a privacy issue, and through a perplexing multiplicity of instruments. We examine these below, and also look to see if the US and Australia have been any more successful at dealing with the real threat of spam.

To complicate matters further, spam is now not just a carrier for unwanted and sometimes fraudulent content but also for malware and electronic infection; as such it is but one aspect of the general insecurity of the Internet. In this sense, spam is also indirectly regulated by the criminal law which seeks to control the dissemination of malware: we examine this part of the puzzle in greater detail in chapter 21.

After spam, came cookies—small text file 'bugs' placed on the hard disk of a computer, used extensively on e-commerce sites to store data records about the user's transactions for purposes of profiling and marketing.[4] Cookies in the commercial world are essentially legitimised 'spyware', in that they allow businesses to spy on consumers online; but unlike spyware, cookies enable the provision of useful not malevolent services—eg allowing websites we commonly visit to recall our names, user logins, passwords, home addresses, frequent flyer numbers, previous purchases, credit card details, etc. Cookies also, however, enable data collection for purposes such as advertising and profiling both by the site itself and third parties—a service that shades into the realms of privacy invasion. It is interesting therefore that in Europe spyware and cookies are now regulated by the same instrument, the Privacy and Electronic Communications Directive 2002 (PECD),[5] which is currently under reform as part of the European reform of the entire telecoms regulatory framework.[6] We examine these rules in detail below.

Spam and cookies were only the first tentative investigations into the true potential of the Internet and digital technology for selling and data collection. For a start, cookies only let advertisers collect data about

(codified at 15 USC ss 7701–7713 and 18 USC s 1037), which combines traditional rules protecting the privacy of recipients of spam with rules aimed at merely reducing the amount of spam in the world, eg forbidding the use of third-party computers as 'zombie drones' to send out spam. See further below.

[4] See further http://www.allaboutcookies.org.

[5] Directive (2002/58/EC) on privacy and electronic communications (also known as the e-Privacy Directive).

[6] A common position on the draft reformed package bar one key issue was finalised in May 2009. At time of writing it appears the package is heading for a conciliation process which should result in a final law passed in 2009. Issues relating to spam in this chapter are, however, probably settled into their final form. See Common position adopted by the Council on 16 February 2009 with a view to the adoption of a Directive of the European Parliament and of the Council amending Directive 2002/22/EC on universal service and users' rights relating to electronic communications networks; Directive 2002/58/EC concerning the processing of personal data and the protection of privacy in the electronic communications sector; and Regulation (EC) No 2006/2004 on consumer protection cooperation, Council document No 16497/1/08, available at http://register.consilium.europa.eu/pdf/en/08/st16/st16497-re01.en08.pdf.

consumers when they are online. Why not collect data about potential buyers when they are in the real world also? As we discuss below, data about us can now be extracted while we talk on our mobile phones or e-mail from our smartphones and Blackberries. Even when we are far from our terminals and desks, and perhaps unaware of having any 'electronic presence'—when we go shopping on the high street, use passports to leave the country, travel by Tube in London or go to hospital or go clubbing—it is now possible for data to be gathered about us. Radiofrequency identification (RFID) chips have turned the offline world into a place where digital data relating to the activity of living persons can still be collected—the so-called 'Internet of Things'. Locational data, generated by our ubiquitous mobiles and other e-paraphernalia, can tell businesses where we are, so that local or relevant services can be sold to us there and then. Social networking sites (SNSs), such as Facebook, MySpace and Bebo, also tell the world copious amounts about what we like to do, read, hear or say. In the future, more 'sensor data' may be collected by tiny chips embedded in roads, cars or fabrics, creating a world of 'ubiquitous computing' or 'ubicomp'.

Once data can be collected about us wherever we go, online or offline, the next step for marketing is to investigate what all that data, combined, profiled and mined, might tell us about the target consumer—and what exactly that particular consumer might want to buy or do. This dream of perfect 'targeted' or 'behavioural' advertising is currently both the Next Big Thing for commerce and for funding of 'Web 2.0' businesses, but also one of the greatest potential threats we currently have to individual privacy. Google, the world's leading search engine, the self-declared aim of which is to 'organize the world's information', has explicitly announced that its ultimate goal is to know so much about everyone that the most appropriate advert will eventually be deliverable to the perfectly targeted consumer. This exemplifies the paradoxical problem of regulating ubiquitous data collection for commercial purposes. Google is essentially funded by the provision of ever more targeted ads, in the form of its successful AdWords and AdSense programmes, and without that revenue, would clearly not supply for free the sophisticated search facilities that make the Internet manageable. Yet to do this, Google is essentially managing a campaign of night and day surveillance of 90 per cent or so of the Internet users on the planet, albeit benevolently and with certain safeguards. We discuss these themes in this and the next chapter.

Finally in these two chapters we will consider the idea most often attributed to Lawrence Lessig[7] that law is not the only regulatory mechanism available in relation to Internet activities. As we will see below, spam, for example, has proven impervious to legal interventions for a variety of

---

[7] See L Lessig, *Code 2.0* (New York, Basic Books, 2006) and available at http://codev2.cc/.

reasons. Could *technology* (or as Lessig calls it, 'code') succeed in protecting individual privacy where law seems to be failing? We will return to this point in our conclusions.

II. SPAM

Few Internet users will not at some point have received an e-mail message of the following kind:
Subject: you forgot the attachment

> From: 'ExtremePriceCuts.net' <extremepricecuts@extremepricecuts.net>
> Reply-to: zebedee@hotmail.com
>
> ---
>
> From nothing to rich in 90 hours!! I cracked the Code! I made over $94,000!!!!
> You May Be Closer (Maybe Hours Away)
> To Financial Freedom
> If YOU Needed $24,000 In 24 Hours
> And your life depended on it...
> How Would YOU Do It?
> http://www.esioffers.com/track_link.html?link=3664

Such unsolicited or 'junk' e-mails are colloquially known as spam.[8] They are usually sent out to thousands if not millions of electronic mailboxes simultaneously, most often for dubious commercial purposes, though some are also sent by private individuals for non-commercial purposes, eg to spread racist or homophobic hate views or for political or religious campaigns. Spam was once easily spotted by its 'enticing' subject lines such as 'get rich quick' but recent iterations of spam tend to disguise their true nature as far as possible both to avoid e-mail filters and to increase the 'click-through' rate (ie to induce the reader to open it and follow a hyperlink). The ultimate development in this line takes the form of 'phishing' e-mails[9]—spam that fraudulently pretends to come from a bank or other legitimate institution and encourages users to unwittingly give away personal data such as bank account details, passwords and credit card numbers (or even just university login details). Although most often found in the context of email, websites (such as the very popular SNSs[10] and

[8] The name 'spam' is, as a matter of Internet urban myth, supposed to derive from a well-known Monty Python television comedy sketch involving the chanting of 'spam, spam, spam' over and over again. Spam is of course, originally a trade-marked term for a form of canned luncheon meat.
[9] The top 10 spam origin countries as of June 2009 included the US, China, Russia, the UK, Brazil, Japan and India. See Spamhaus at http://www.spamhaus.org/statistics/countries.lasso. In all cases it is highly likely most the spam is being sent not from local spammers, but merely via zombie machines situated in the country in question. Compare the Spamhaus top 10 list to the top 10 countries by 'zombie population' at Cipher Trust: http://www.ciphertrust.com/resources/statistics/zombie.php. The resemblance is obvious.
[10] The SNS MySpace, for example, has been very active in defending its site from spam in the

'blog' sites[11]) and mobile phones[12] can also be spammed, and for this reason some leading spam-blocking sites,[13] have suggested the best description would be 'unsolicited bulk material' or UBM. This nomenclature also places the emphasis on the *bulk* in which the spam is sent, not its *contents*, fraudulent or otherwise, which as we shall see below, is a crucial point for would-be regulators of spam.

But classification of messages as spam may also depend on their content, even though spam is far easier to spot simply by bulk. However, 10,000 e-mails promoting a Nigerian bank fraud scheme are considered to be spam, while 10,000 emails encouraging alumni of a major university to make tax-deductible gifts to that university might not. In the US, political spam is exempted from the CAN-SPAM Act for fear of stifling freedom of speech.[14] 'Classic spam' typically advertises goods or services such as pornography, get-rich-quick schemes, pyramid-selling schemes, dating agencies or software with which to become a spammer yourself. These communications are often misleading or outright fraudulent; and they are very often offensive, obscene or illegal in content. Although these categories often raise legal issues of fraud as well as privacy, in the main tailored spam legislation has not touched this area as it is already well regulated in most criminal codes.[15]

Crucially, spam arrives without the consent of the recipient—hence the European usage, 'unsolicited commercial communications'.[16] The leading

US. In a May 2008 action, they secured a default judgment for a record $234 million against the so-called 'Spam King' Sanford Wallace and another defender. See http://news.bbc.co.uk/1/hi/technology/7399868.stm. The judgment is thought to be the largest ever given against senders of unsolicited commercial e-mail.

[11] The UK Advertising Standards Agency dealt in 2006 with a complaint that a radio station, TALK-SPORT, was leaving deceptive 'comment spam' on football 'blog' sites (see http://www.out-law.com/page-7556). The comments praising TALK-SPORT appeared to come from genuine sports fans, but were really disguised ads. The ASA held the ads broke ASA rules that adverts must be clearly labelled as such. This practice, sometimes known as 'astro-turfing' (http://en.wikipedia.org/wiki/Astroturfing), probably also falls within the 'hard' anti-spam laws law of Reg 22 of the UK PECD Regulations—see Reg 2, definition of 'electronic mail', and below.

[12] EB Cleff, 'Privacy Issues in Mobile Advertising', 2007 Bileta Conference, Hertfordshire (available at http://www.bileta2007.co.uk/papers/images/stream_9/CleffE.pdf), points out that mobile advertising is a very effective way to market products and brands, as mobile phones, unlike home and work computers, are typically used only by a single person. Hence personalisation and targeting can be very precise.

[13] Spamhaus, the UK-based private spam filtering organisation, notes that: 'The word Spam means 'Unsolicited Bulk Email'. Unsolicited means that the recipient has not granted verifiable permission for the message to be sent. Bulk means that the message is sent as part of a larger collection of messages, all having substantively identical content. . . . Spam is an issue about consent, not content. Whether the UBE message is an advert, a scam, porn, a begging letter or an offer of a free lunch, the content is irrelevant—if the message was sent unsolicited and in bulk then the message is spam.' See http://www.spamhaus.org/definition.html.

[14] Commercial speech in the US can have more restrictions than political speech under Constitutional law.

[15] Although see the UK Fraud Act 2006 which is explicitly designed to combat phishing.

[16] As used, eg, in the EC E-Commerce Directive 2000/31/EC.

spam country of origin is usually the US, though it is hotly pursued by the former Soviet Union and by East Asian countries such as China and South Korea. Significantly, EU countries tend to be low in the ranking. It is therefore a major problem for law enforcement, further discussed below, that the majority of spam that circulates in EU countries comes from spammers outside Europe.

Prior to 2000 or so, there was very little *legal* debate on how spam could, or should, be controlled in Europe. By contrast, argument raged among 'techies' as to the best technological methods for controlling spam. The US, always ahead in Internet litigation, became home to running battles in the courts between spammers and those who longed to stamp out the practice—notably Internet service providers (ISPs)—in the mid to late 1990s, and a flood of individual state statutes subsequently attempted to grapple with the problem in various ways.[17] Eventually, a Federal statute, was, after many attempts, passed which prescribes a uniform approach to spam regulation for the entirety of the US—the CAN-SPAM Act of 2003.[18] In the US the legal background to regulating spam is very different from the approach in Europe; since not only is there no omnibus DP regime, but it has also long been accepted, albeit with some reluctance, that direct marketing is a form of speech and as such protected by First Amendments rights, although the protection given is much less than that which would be accorded non-commercial speech.[19]

UK and European regulatory interest has increased in direct proportion to the increasing amount of e-mail that is spam—spam in Europe has grown from only 7 per cent of global e-mail traffic in April 2001 to at least 50 per cent of EU e-mail traffic at January 2004 to an estimated 80–90 per cent of all in 2008 depending on time and location.[20] In the US, estimates vary, but 90 per cent or more of all e-mail traffic may be spam. The *New York Times* reported in 2007 that 'more than a hundred billion unsolicited messages [are] clogging the arterial passages of the world's computer networks every day'.[21] At these levels, spam is not just an

---

[17] See D Sorkin's useful inventory of spam laws at http://www.spamlaws.com/state/summary.shtml.

[18] This is the informal title of the Controlling the Assault of Non-Solicited Pornography and Marketing Act of 2003. The Act passed on 25 November 2003 and came into force on 1 January 2004. See n 3 above.

[19] See eg *Virginia State Board of Pharmacy v Virginia Citizen's Consumer Council Inc* 425 US 748 (1976) and subsequent cases and commentary. See also most recently the failure of telemarketers to have the 'Do Not Call' register set up by the Federal Trade Commission declared a breach of the First Amendment: see decision of the 10th US Circuit Court of Appeals in *Mainstream Marketing Service v FTC* at http://www.ca10.uscourts.gov/opinions/03-1429.pdf.

[20] See EU press release, IP/o4/103, 27 January 2004. A variety of industry-based pressure group in Europe are dedicated to the fight against spam, including E-CAUCE, the European Coalition against Unsolicited Commercial Email, website at http://www.euro.cauce.org/en/index.html. A useful US and Europe based anti-spam site is Junkbusters at http://www.junkbusters.com. Spamhaus, above n 13, are a useful source of technical information and statistics.

[21] See M Specter 'Damn Spam', *New York Times* 6 August 2007 at http://www.newyorker.com/reporting/2007/08/06/070806fa_fact_specter.

annoyance to users and service providers, but is on the way to making the entire Internet effectively unusable for those without highly effective filters in place. Since spam is also now frequently used as a delivery device for viruses, worms and distributed denial of service (DDOS) attacks,[22] it is not uncommon to view every spam e-mail nowadays as a 'ticking bomb'.

III. WHY IS SPAM A PROBLEM, AND WHOSE PROBLEM IS IT?

A. 'Living Persons' as Victims of Spam: Offence, Annoyance and Invasion of Privacy

Most obviously, much spam is annoying, distasteful, and in some cases deeply offensive, to its recipients. Furthermore, traditional direct marketing was usually only directed at solvent adults, while spammers will indiscriminately spam children and other vulnerable groups so long as they have an e-mail address. Spam also now appears in so many media that it is omnipresent: in the brave new world of the twenty-first century, unsolicited marketing also arrives as texts to mobile phones, executable attachments delivered by e-mail, comment spam on blogs, and, perhaps worst of all, 'pop-ups' and 'pop unders', windowed advertisements that can obscure the user's desktop, incessantly harass users unskilled in adblocking-ware, and are difficult to close, endlessly repetitive and sufficient to incite 'spam rage'[23] in the meekest of users.[24]

From a traditional European legal perspective, therefore, spam's main offence is to be an invasion of the privacy of the individual. Looked at this way, spam is not a dissimilar problem to traditional, non-electronic direct marketing, although it is important to note that the costs of marketing by spam are shifted almost wholly from the spammer, to either the recipient or the ISP. For the spammer, each spam costs less than 0.025¢ to send. Given this view, it was natural that the main[25] legal response in Europe was to cite the protection offered by DP law.[26]

---

[22] See discussion in ch 21 (Brown, Edwards and Marsden).

[23] 'Spam rage' was plead in defence in the case of a Silicon Valley computer programmer, who was arrested for threatening to torture and kill employees of the company he blamed for bombarding his computer with web ads that offered to enlarge his penis: see 'Man Arrested Over "Spam Rage"', *WIRED* 21 November 2003, at http://www.wired.com/news/culture/0,1284, 61339,00.html.

[24] Or as the judge at first instance in the US District Court case of *U-Haul International v WhenU.com Inc*, 279 F Supp.2d 723 (ED Va, 5 September 2003) plaintively puts it: 'Computer users, like this trial judge, may wonder what we have done to warrant the punishment of seizure of our computer screens by pop-up advertisements that require us to click, click and click again in order to return to our Internet work.'

[25] Spam of course may also involve fraud. However, such is usually covered by one or more existing laws relating to fraud in general, to mail fraud, credit card fraud or to abuse of phone lines or telecommunication rather than special legislation (though see the background to the UK Fraud Act 2006 which as already noted is designed to combat phishing.)

DP law does indeed in general forbid the processing, which includes collection and transmission, of 'personal data' which identifiably describes a 'living individual'[27] without the consent of that individual. It also bans in particular the use of personal data by direct marketers if the individual whom those details describe refuses to allow them use.[28] Such protection, however, is not available to corporations, which are not living persons and thus incapable of being regarded as data subjects.[29] Since small to medium-sized enterprises (SMEs) and sole traders suffer just as much, or more, economically from spam as individuals this is a major flaw in a DP-centric approach to spam regulation. The UK PECD regulations, as we shall see, do offer some limited extension of protection to juristic persons.

B. Economic Impacts of Spam: The Internet, the ISPs and Employers

If offence and annoyance to individuals, plus some significant economic loss to a few gullible souls,[30] was all the damage spam caused, there would be good reason to leave it solely regulated by DP law, or indeed, to leave it unregulated by law at all and solely dealt with by technologies such as filtering. But spam can also be seen as a problem that is economic, not emotional, in impact; which impacts disproportionately on certain industry groups; and affects the public interest in general, more than private individuals. DP laws are mainly intended to encourage administrative compliance by responsible businesses (see discussion in previous chapter), and are ill suited either to punishing those who flagrantly disrespect the law, nor are they aimed at compensating those who suffer financially as a result. As noted earlier, fines for DP violations in the UK have recently been raised,[31] but jail sentences have only very recently become available.[32] Individual

---

[26] See EC Data Protection Directive (95/46/EC), implemented in the UK by the DPA, and PECD, above.

[27] See DPA s 1(1) and discussion in Edwards, ch 14.

[28] See DPA s 11.

[29] This point is taken up interestingly by L Bygrave, *Data Protection Law: Approaching its Rationale, Logic and Limits* (Dordrecht, Kluwer, 2002).

[30] It is often incredulously asked: 'But who actually responds to spam? How *do* spammers make money?' A number of explanations are put forward in the literature. One is that most spammers make money from selling other spammers software and mailing lists of spammable addresses. A variation on this is that spammers are only trying to obtain personal details, not actual customers, so as to perpetrate further frauds and identity thefts. Another view is that the costs of spam are so low and billions of messages so easy to send, that a tiny return rate will still turn a profit. Victims are also often unlikely to complain and reveal their own gullibility so, as frauds go, it is a very safe one. See further J Sauver, 'The Economics of Spam: The Spam Business Isn't Always What You'd Think' at http://cc.uoregon.edu/cnews/summer2003/spameconomics.html.

[31] See the Criminal Justice and Immigration Act 2008.

[32] See ch 14, 467. Compare Italy, where jail sentences of up to three years are possible; and Virginia, where a spammer was recently jailed under the state spam statute for nine years (see 'US Duo in First Spam Conviction', BBC News, at http://news.bbc.co.uk/1/hi/technology/3981099.stm).

compensation for victims of breaches of DP law is possible,[33] but in the two UK cases where a spammer was successfully sued by an individual Internet user, the damages were a mere £300 including costs, and £750.[34] One problem is that although spam *en masse* is highly annoying, it is difficult to blame one particular spammer for significant economic loss.[35]

(i) ISPs and the Economic Effects of Spam

ISPs, especially the largest ones such as AOL, Comcast, BT Internet, etc, suffer the brunt of the immediate economic damage caused by spam. The sheer bulk of traffic sent out by spammers uses up bandwidth and slows Internet traffic down, not just e-mail but also web-based services. ISP servers from which spam is sent, or to which or through which it is transmitted, may crash, not just as a result of the initial volume of mail sent out but because of a deluge of 'mail undeliverable' messages returned to it from inaccurate e-mail addresses used by the spammer. Spam surges (and anti-spam measures taken in reponse) may also delay delivery of legitimate mail. This represents a major problem to ISPs who to retain customer confidence need to provide 24-hour access to users and workplaces.[36] In *AOL v Prime Data Systems Inc*,[37] the court estimated that the real costs to AOL of dealing with each spam message were 0.078¢ per message. Since in that case 130 million junk e-mails were sent, the court awarded US$4,000,000 against the spammer (including a punitive triple multiplier on the estimated damages). In another case it was estimated that handling spam had so degraded the performance of the server afflicted by spamming that e-mails that should have been delivered in minutes were taking three days to arrive.[38]

Another major cost for ISPs is filtering and its associated problems. Most major ISPs filter spam aggressively in an attempt to service their customer base. However, the downside of such proactive filtering is dealing with

---

[33] DPA s 13.

[34] Respectively, *Roberts v Media Logistics (UK) Ltd*, 2005, noted at http://www.theregister.co.uk/2005/12/29/uk_spam_win/ and *Dick v Transcom Internet Services*, 2008, noted at http://www.out-law.com/default.aspx?page=7831. In both cases, the award was settled out of court and is thus not a precedent; and in any case, both were brought as small claims actions which effectively limited the possible damages awardable to these levels.

[35] Even Naomi Campbell, a global celebrity, was merely awarded nominal damages for the breach of her data privacy rights at the first stage of her battle with the press in the UK courts—see *Campbell v MGN* [2002] EWCA Civ 1373. (At the Court of Appeal, her DP claim was rejected—and although this decision was itself reversed in the House of Lords, the DP point was not pursued.)

[36] Compare the international furore caused, when Microsoft were forced in 2004 by hackers to shut down the free web-based e-mail system Hotmail for a few hours as a result of its compromise by hackers.

[37] No 97-1652A (ED Va, 20 November 1998).

[38] *Compuserve Inc v Cyber Promotion Inc* 962 F Supp 1015 (SD Ohio 1997).

complaints from customers whose e-mails are wrongly blocked as spam *and* from recipients who fail to receive e-mail which was falsely identified as spam. Blocking of such 'false positives' may lead to valuable transactions falling through and important appointments being missed; although the issues of tort or delict law here are uncharted, it is clear that costs accrue to ISPs whichever way they decide to 'play safe'. Less directly, large ISPs (and webmail services such as Gmail and Hotmail) suffer brand tarnishing if they are associated with spam. Customer loyalty is seriously diminished by spam, and ISPs such as AOL have seen their capital value reduced as a consequence.

The EU has long espoused the view that development of consumer confidence in the Internet is dependent on trust in retailers and the medium, and both spam and cookies are key problems in persistently reminding users that the Internet is not yet a wholly safe and lawful environment. Yet it is quite possible to argue that, for *consumers*, the battle against spam has in fact been won: most ISPs now filter out almost all spam with ever-improving algorithms, and most users are desensitised enough by familiarity to ignore whatever gets past. The battle over spam is therefore arguably really not one involving ordinary users, but a conflict between spammers and ISPs, webmail services, SNSs (who spend vast amounts filtering out spam), and banks and other financial bodies, who are in a constant battle to close down phishing sites. Given this context, is DP law, which aims to protect personal privacy and does not generally give rights to corporations, really still the best way to regulate spam?

It is noticeable that of the mere three cases brought to court in the UK under the PECD Regulations so far, one was brought not by an individual but by Microsoft's Hotmail, and against not an ordinary spammer but against a certain BizAds, who provided e-mail address lists for spammers to use.[39] Two interesting legal points were held. One, the court agreed that the PECD Regulations did not only give a right of action to individuals affected by spam but also to networks, such as Hotmail, which had clearly suffered loss of reputation and money as a result of spam. This seems, in advance of projected changes in EU law,[40] to give both networks and ISPs title to sue under the UK regulations in general. Secondly, the PECD Regulations also cover not just spammers but those who 'instigate the transmission' of spam, which might potentially include as well as spam list sellers , the writers and even distributors of spamming software.

---

[39] See *Microsoft v MacDonald (trading as Bizads)* [2006] EWHC 3410 (Ch) at http://www.juriscom.net/documents/highcourtjce20061212.pdf.

[40] Above n 6.

(ii) Employers

The other group who bear the cost of spam, it is often claimed, are employers. Spam wastes employee time, both when they examine and delete spam, or, worst still, become frustrated (or intrigued) and try to reply to it. Reports (usually commissioned by the writers of spam-blocking software, and so to be taken with a pinch of salt) repeatedly show that companies lose large amounts of money through spam, with some claiming that employees waste up to 10 per cent of their day opening and discarding spam e-mail. The EU based its original legislative attack on spam on the claim—however this was calculated—that it was costing European businesses, even in 2003, more than €2.25 billion a year.[41]

(iii) Spam as Part of the 'Botnet' Problem: The Public Interest in Regulation

Spam is, finally and perhaps most importantly, a threat to the public interest in a safe, secure and reliable Internet. Once this was because it threatened to clog the Internet pipes of the world, bringing electronic communication to a standstill. The European Commissioner for the Information Society, Erik Likannen, put it thus in a speech in 2003:

> Combating spam has become a matter for us all and has become one of the most significant issues facing the Internet today. It is a fight over many fronts. . . *We must act before users of e-mails or SMS stop using the Internet or mobile services* [emphasis added], or refrain from using it to the extent that they otherwise would.[42]

High-speed broadband has meant that death of the Internet by spam has possibly been averted, though as seen above, it still costs network providers a great deal to manage. But spam is now also a mere facet of the general problem of Internet cyber-insecurity and 'zombies' or 'botnets'. The botnet problem is discussed in depth in chapter 21. Briefly, spam is almost never now sent from a spammer's own e-mail address or e-mail server. If an ISP sees a subscriber sending out millions of e-mails, he or she will be swiftly dumped for breaking the ISP's terms and conditions. (Some ISPs remain known 'spam havens'—catalogued on the Spamhaus website—but they number only a few these days.) Similarly, if spammers use their own e-mail server, they will be easily traced (notwithstanding use of a fake reply address, their Internet Protocol (IP) address will be trackable) and thus closed down (and possibly prosecuted).

Instead, spam is now primarily sent from 'zombies' or 'bots'—individual

41 Cited by P Bartlett, 'EU Businesses Count Spam Costs' BBC News, 15 July 2003, at http://news.bbc.co.uk/1/hi/business/3068627.stm
42 Speech of 25 July 2003, quoted in DG Information Society Working Paper, 'Issue Paper for EU Workshop on Unsolicited Commercial Communications or Spam' (16 October 2003).

computers, usually belonging to home users or small businesses, which have been taken control of by remote third parties by means of computer virus infestation. A 100,000 home computers which have become 'zombies' might be joined into a 'botnet' run by a 'zombie master'. If such a botnet is covertly used to send out spam, each individual bot need only send a few e-mails each—remaining invisible to the ISP and infected user—and it will be extremely difficult to track the spam back to the true spammers. And botnets are no longer difficult for even technologically incompetent spammers to use. Spammers need not create their own, but can buy, or even rent them by the hour, via the Web, at almost ridiculously low prices.

Botnets are not, however, just used to send spam. Once a botnet has been created, it can be used for many other covert criminal purposes, eg sending phishing emails, sending out further viruses or worms, creating DDOS attacks (discussed further again in chapter 21) and facilitating 'click fraud'. These are all growing legal problems and in the UK have been variously addressed by the Computer Misuse Act 1990 as amended, the House of Lords Report on Personal Internet Security[43] and fraud legislation. As a result, it is important to keep in mind that laws to crack down on spam are really best seen now as laws to deal with the consequences of botnets, which are themselves the consequences of failure to regulate for and create a secure virus-resistant Internet.

IV. SPAM LAW IN EUROPE AND THE UK

A. The Data Protection Directive and the Data Protection Act 1998

The Data Protection Directive (DPD), and its UK implementation in the Data Protection Act 1998 (DPA), impose duties on 'data controllers' broadly: (i) to comply with the Data Protection Principles;[44] and (ii) to notify the Information Commissioner if they are processing personal data[45] If these duties are breached, then the data controller may be liable to compensate any individual adversely affected, even if the Commissioner does not serve an enforcement notice,[46] and criminal liability may also be incurred.[47]

To determine if DP law regulates spam, it was first necessary to decide if spammers were 'data controllers'. A data controller is defined as 'a person who . . . determines the purposes for which and the manner in which personal data are, or are to be, processed'.[48] This begs the question: do

---

[43] See further discussion in ch 21 (Brown, Edwards and Marsden), 690.
[44] DPA s 4(4).
[45] DPA s 17(1).
[46] DPA s 13.
[47] DPA s 21.
[48] DPA s 1(1)).

spammers process 'personal data'? Typically, spammers harvest from newsgroups, websites or ISPs, or buy, or generate, long lists of personal e-mail addresses, to which a spam e-mail is then sent by special software. Under section 1(1) DPA, 'Processing' includes 'carrying out any operation on the information or data', which seems to fit these activities satisfactorily. 'Personal data' itself is defined in section 1(1) as 'data which relates to a living individual who can be identified (a) from those data, or (b) from those data and other information which is in the possession of, or likely to come into the possession of, the data controller'. Does an e-mail address, without any other added information, identify an individual, in the same way that a name and physical address would? There has been doubt on this matter in the past.[49] However, the PECD appears clearly to assume that e-mail addresses. if they do belong to a living person. are to be regarded as 'personal data' and this is also the approach taken, with some caveats, in guidance supplied by the UK Information Commissioner.[50]

Assuming the DPA does apply to spammers, it was clear that on most occasions, the act of spamming would be prima facie in breach of the Act in multiple ways. For example, spammers typically fail to register with the Data Commissioner as required, and also fail to respect requirements such as data security and use only for stated purposes. Most importantly, however, spammers invariably failed to meet the most significant DP rule, deriving from the First Data Protection Principle, that the consent of data subjects to the processing of their data must be obtained. Admittedly, such consent is not required if one of the other exemptions in Schedule 2 is applicable, but the only one that seems relevant to spam is that the processing is 'necessary for the purposes of legitimate interests pursued by the data controller' which interests must be balanced against the data subject's rights, especially to privacy.[51] If the processing is detrimental to the interests of the data subject, as it arguably will always be in the case of spam, then the exemption is highly unlikely to exculpate the data controller.

B. From Opt-out to Opt-in?

The DPA furthermore gives the data subject the specific right under section 11 to demand to cease receiving—or to *'opt out'* from—the processing of his personal data for the purposes of direct marketing[52] by a data controller.

---

[49] See Edwards, above n 1.

[50] See Information Commissioner's Office, *DPA 1998: Legal Guidance*, 12, available at http://www.informationcommissioner.gov.uk/.

[51] DAP, Sched 2, para 6(1).

[52] 'Direct marketing' is defined for these purposes as 'the communication (by whatever means) of any advertising or marketing material which is directed to particular individuals' (s 11(3)) and so includes spam as well as traditional junk mail.

This right was seen as important for consumer protection, even though anecdotal evidence showed that consumers rarely had either the knowledge or the impetus to seek out data controllers and express their desire to opt out. 'Opt-out' from traditional direct marketing is facilitated by the Mailing Preference Service, a voluntary 'opt-out register' run by the Direct Marketing Association,[53] where consumers can register their preference not to receive direct marketing. Direct marketers then come by virtue of section 11 under an effective obligation to check the names on the register and remove 'opt-out' names before they send out a mailshot. Similar voluntary preference services exist for fax and telephone 'cold calling'. No such voluntary register, however, exists specifically for e-mail spam, unsurprisingly as, as noted above, spam comes overwhelmingly from spammers who are outside the EU, anonymous and uninterested in complying with EU or UK law. Spammers nearly always fail in any case to respect opt-out requests even where they ostensibly provide an opportunity to opt out within their own e-mails or websites (usually of the 'click here if you don't want to receive any more messages of this kind' type). Indeed, best practice is never to reply to such an invitation as it will generally be used only to verify that the spammed e-mail address is still valid.

From 1997 on, the leading policy question became whether spam should be regulated by an 'opt-in' regime rather than an 'opt-out' one. 'Opt in' would mean that consumers would actually have to express a *prior preference* to receive unsolicited communications from the business in question before it would be legal for them to be sent such communications. In effect, spam would be banned without prior permission. 'Opt out' meant consumers would be deluged with spam until they asked the sender to stop, please. It is easy to see which is more effective, given that very few people are equipped to find out that opt-out registers exist and are in any case likely to be discouraged when 'opt outs' offered turn out to be fraudulent. Most independent non-industry commentators agreed that an opt-in scheme for spam would be more appropriate. Online, opt in is actually easier for legitimate businesses to implement than opt out. Any consumer who buys something from a website can be offered a box to click if they want to 'receive further information'. It can even be pre-ticked , though this is of dubious legality. By contrast, opt out requires overhead in time and fees for checking a mailing list off against an opt-out register.

Over a number of years, opportunities to move to an opt-in regime in the UK were nonetheless avoided, mainly due to opposition from the domestic direct marketing industry. Consumers were, for example, only

---

[53] See further http://www.informationcommissioner.gov.uk/cms/DocumentUploads/The per cent20Mailing per cent20Telephone per cent20and per cent20Fax per cent20Prerence per cent 20Services.pdf.

guaranteed opt-out rights[54] under the EC Distance Selling Directive 1997[55] in relation to spam[56] even though the parent Directive gave Member States the choice of implementing via opt in or opt out.[57] This Directive, being of later vintage than the DPD, was nevertheless an advance as it was the first time a Directive had been clearly drafted to cover to cover e-mail as well as conventional mail and phone communications.[58] Similarly, the Department for Trade and Industry (DTI), when implementing the Telecommunications (Data Protection and Privacy) (Direct Marketing) Regulations 1998,[59] introduced to deal with 'cold calling', chose an opt-out rather than opt-in regime, with the Telephone Preference Service established as an opt-out register.

Attempts were made in the European Parliament during the passage of the E-Commerce Directive to ban both spam and cookies outright, but these were in the end thwarted. Instead only some rather feeble transparency provisions were introduced in Articles 6 and 7. First, Article 6 required that (all, not just unsolicited) 'commercial communications'[60] had to be 'transparent' in the sense that certain information had to be made available which identified the sender, adequately disclosed the nature and conditions of promotional offers made by the communication, etc.[61] These requirements largely duplicated work already done in the Distance Selling Directive. Secondly, *unsolicited* commercial communications had to be 'identifiable clearly and unambiguously' as such to the recipient as soon as they arrived.[62] The obvious way to implement such is by labelling, ie putting a word such as 'advertising' in the subject line of any spam e-mail. Spam filters can then in theory read the label and filter out the message. The UK Electronic Commerce (EC Directive) Regulations 2002 imple-

---

[54] Interestingly, the Distance Selling Directive of 1997 Art 12(1) did prescribe a very limited mandatory 'opt-in' regime but only for junk faxes and automated calling machines. These were distinguished from ordinary distance selling, in the case of faxes, because the costs of marketing were transferred from seller to recipient, and in the case of automated calling machines, because of the extreme aggravation they caused. Both reasons arguably applied just as strongly to spam.

[55] Directive 97/7/EC ('DSD').

[56] DSD Art 10(1).

[57] The consultation paper issued by the DTI in November 1999 included draft regulations which contained alternate opt-out and opt-in schemes—however, an opt-out scheme was in the end chosen.

[58] See DSD Art 2 and Annex 1, which specifically refers to 'electronic mail'.

[59] SI 1998 No 3170.

[60] Defined in the UK Regulations (see n 62 below), Reg 2 as (with exceptions) 'a communication, in any form designed to promote, directly or indirectly, the goods, services or image of any person pursuing a commercial, industrial or craft activity, or exercising a regulated profession'. The exceptions are a communication which contains merely an address, domain name or e-mail address; and a communication promoting A but sent by an independent person B.

[61] The Commission has suggested that such information might satisfactorily be provided by a hyperlink in the case of a webpage making a commercial communication; such a link could also be placed in an e-mail or advertising message delivered by text to mobile phones (where space precludes full spelling out of such information).

[62] Art 7(1).

menting the ECD did not go into that degree of detail, however, merely demanding that any promotional offer or promotional competition or game be clearly identified (along with its qualifying or participation conditions).[63]

Even if labelling is adopted by legitimate sellers, it is not much of a solution to the real problems caused by spam, namely bulk and time wasting. It may spare the sensibilities of recipients if a message is labelled (say) 'Advertising: red hot porn', but this achieves little else. Even spam filtering is not that much assisted by labelling: it may interfere with users forwarding spam to ISP postmasters or abuse teams. In any case, the practical evidence since the ECD was implemented in 2002 is that, again, spam coming from outside the EU (and probably from within it as well) has resolutely ignored these rules. Finally, on the great 'opt-in' debate, Article 7 of the ECD provided only that states must 'respect the opt-out registers', a provision not transposed in the UK Regulations as redundant.

C. The Privacy in Electronic Communications Directive

It was thus left to the PECD 2002 to finally adopt an opt-in rule. Factors pushing legal reform were not only EU harmonisation—for many businesses, clarity on what they have to do throughout Europe is more important than the actual shape of the rule—but also the direct marketing industry itself, which admitted that spam in its current form had rendered the industry untrustworthy. Article 13(1) of the PECD demands that all EU Member States require prior consent—'opt in'—for the use of personal data to send unsolicited electronic mail.[64] 'Electronic mail' is widely defined to include 'any text, voice, sound or image message sent over a public communications network which can be stored in the network or in the recipient's terminal equipment until it is collected by the recipient'.[65] The clear intention here was to make the Directive 'technology neutral' and less prone to immediate obsolescence as new forms of communications were invented. At present, this definition clearly includes not just e-mail, but voicemail, video messaging to 3G smartphones, and mobile text messages.[66]

There are, however, significant exceptions to the 'opt-in to spam' rule. Prior consent is *not* required if the details of the recipient were previously obtained 'in the context of a sale of a product or service', so long as:

---

[63] SI 2002/1931, Regs 7 and 8.

[64] Implemented in the UK PECR Reg 22.

[65] PECD Art 2(h).

[66] Use of automated calling machines to 'cold call' by phone, and of fax machines to send unsolicited faxes to consumers, also clearly requires opt-in: see UK PECR Regs 19 and 20. Businesses, however, have to choose to opt out from faxes (Reg 20(1)(b)). Ordinary cold calling by phone to both categories remains legal unless the subscriber has opted out (Reg 21).

- the recipient is given a clear, simple and free opportunity to opt out of receiving spam each time a new communication is sent; and
- the goods or services were 'similar' to those now being marketed.[67]

Does this exception operate only where an *actual* prior sale had occurred or does 'in the context of a sale or service' include scenarios where, say, a user had gone so far to place an order but then pulled out, or even merely browsed a site, perhaps comparing prices? The UK PECD Regulations, Regulation 22, take the latter approach. So long as the business has legitimately obtained the contact details (in terms of the requirements of DP law concerning fair collection and processing), details can be used if they have been obtained in the course of the 'sale *or negotiations*' (emphasis added). Guidance from the Information Commissioner suggests that 'negotiations' require some kind of active expression of interest by the data subject in the company's products and do not include the case where all that has happened has been the browsing of a site and depositing of a cookie.[68] It remains to be seen how courts or regulators will interpret this clause when or if a dispute arises.

And what are 'similar' goods or services? No elaboration is given in the UK Regulations but, again, according to the government during the consultation period, 'similarity' should be established with reference to the reasonable expectations of the buyer at the time she gives her contact details. To give an illustrative example of this approach, if a consumer buys baked beans online from Tesco, it would be reasonable for Tesco then to market television and DVDs (say) to that consumer without prior consent, because the consumer could reasonably have known that Tesco sold all these types of goods at the time she first gave away her personal information. However, if Tesco, *subsequent* to the baked bean purchase, acquired, say, a life assurance business, it would *not* be reasonable for them then to market life assurance to the consumer, as she could not have reasonably expected Tesco to offer that service.[69] This seems a somewhat technical interpretation, which is unlikely to instil the trust in consumers which is the whole object of the exercise.

What else does the PECD do to prevent spam? Article 12 (implemented in UK Regulation 18) strengthens the right of an online subscriber to withdraw their name from an online public directory of subscribers—eg a BTInternet customer could ask for their e-mail address not to be visible on

---

[67] PECD Art 13(2) and PECR Reg 22(3). The wording remains the same in the draft reform PECD rules.

[68] *Guidance to the Privacy and Electronic Communications (EC Directive) Regulations 2003, Part 1: Marketing by Electronic Means*, at http://www.informationcommissioner.gov.uk/.

[69] Interestingly, the Art 29 Working Party Opinion on Art 13 of Directive 2002/58/EC also emphasises that 'only the same natural or legal person that collected the data may send marketing emails . . . subsidiaries or mother companies are not the same company' (para 3.5, 11601/EN WP 90, 27 February 2004).

a publicly accessible list of BTInternet subscribers. Spam mailing lists were often culled in the past from easily harvestable open directories of ISP customers, but this is less true nowadays so this provision may have already lost significance.

Finally, as noted above, the UK PECD regulations are significant in going some small way towards extending the protection of DP law to juristic persons as well as living individuals. Regulation 22, as discussed above, extends *only* to individual users, not to 'corporate subscribers' as defined in the Regulations. As Carey notes,[70] this is not that crucial an omission, as most spam e-mails sent to businesses will still go to a named individual's e-mail inbox and fall within the rules; only spam e-mails addressed explicitly to the business name only would remain legal. But Regulation 23,[71] which makes it unlawful to send a marketing e-mail with no valid return address, or with the identity of the sender disguised or concealed, *does* apply to e-mails received by corporate subscribers as well as to individuals, thus providing UK companies *as such* with their first real remedy in the fight against spam.

V. ASSESSMENT OF LEGAL SOLUTIONS TO SPAM, AND ALTERNATIVE SOLUTIONS TO SPAM

The PECD brought the 'opt-in' wars to a close. But was it all worth it? Spam volumes continue to rise inexorably. Spammers mostly operate outside Europe and pay little attention to European law; they are generally very hard to trace; they work through botnets distributed across the world; even if found, the work needed to bring them within European enforcement jurisdiction will be enormous; and the resources to fight spam in this way simply do not exist in most European countries where spam law enforcement is primarily the remit of underfunded data protection authorities. Even in the UK, almost a third of companies are reportedly still not complying with the PECD rules for e-mail marketing.[72]

One partial solution may be to give ISPs and similar bodies title to go out and actively sue spammers, and to give DP commissioners wider powers to investigate and sue, thus taking the onus off individual users, for whom court action is difficult and rarely cost effective in the UK, as we saw above.[73] But in general the obvious message emerges that there has to be a better way to fight spam than trying to impose domestic law on probably

---

[70] P Carey, *Data Protection*, 2nd edn (Oxford, Oxford University Press, 2004) ch 12.

[71] Implementing Art 13(4) of the PECD.

[72] See January 2007 report by CDMS, noted at http://www.out-law.com/default.aspx?page =7647.

[73] The draft reforms for the PECD rules propose that title to sue should exixts for any person 'adversely affected by infringements . . . and therefore having a legitimate interest in the cessation or prohibition of such infringements'.

foreign, anonymous and untraceable spammers using geographically distributed botnets.[74]

The Americans, with more years of experience at fighting spam via the law than we Europeans, are faring no better. The recent US Federal CAN-SPAM Act of 2003 is widely regarded as a damp squib and even a retrograde step since it pre-empts some more radical state spam laws. The main planks of the CAN-SPAM Act are in essence akin to a weaker version of the PECD, incuding (i) mandatory opt-*out* (*not* opt-in), (ii) prohibition of false or deceptive subject lines to spam e-mail and (iii) mandatory labelling of 'sexually oriented' spam. The CAN-SPAM Act does, however, provide for far more draconian fines than the EU legislation and up to five years in prison. In the Australian Spam Act 2003, similar enforcement measures have been implemented with possible fines for a repeat spammer of up to AU$1.1 million per day.[75] Just as in Europe, however, spam volumes in the US have continued to rise inexorably, even since the CAN-SPAM Act came into force on 1 January 2004.[76]

While it is essential to criminalise the activities that enable spamming, passing laws is really only a first step in the process of reducing spam activity and/or blocking its detrimental effects. Technical solutions and standards may well be more effective than laws and also have the key advantage that they largely operate on a global basis, unlike law. A third point is that although the EU has attempted to draft 'technology-neutral' laws to fight spam and more generally protect consumer privacy, law has inevitably and continually lagged behind in the spam 'arms race'. Technical standards by their nature would have at least a better chance of keeping up.

Other non-legal approaches have been canvassed. In the 2005 version of this chapter, we discussed in detail the economic solutions to spam that were popular at the time.[77] In brief, these were based on the idea that spam is ubiquitous because the costs of sending it are so low and hardly increase even for great volumes. Make sending each e-mail costly, the argument

---

[74] The EU has continually attempted for the last decade to broker *international* co-operation on spam, particularly between the EU and US, as has the UN organisation, the International Telecommunications Union (ITU), but the process remains slow despite mutual good intentions. Even intra-EU co-operation on spam law enforcement has been difficult to achieve. See eg Communication on Fighting spam, spyware and malicious software, COM(2006) 688 final.

[75] Unlike the US legislation, however, the Australian Act adopts 'opt-in'. It is thus regarded as probably the best current model for spam legislation in the world, combining the best of the EU and US solutions. See further D Vaile, 'Spam Canned—New Laws for Australia' (2004) 6(9) *Internet Law Bulletin* 113.

[76] The FTC report, 'Effectiveness and Enforcement of the CAN-SPAM Act' (2005) did reveal that spam accounted for 67 per cent of all emails sent in the past year, down 9 per cent on the previous year. However it was doubted this drop was related to Can-Spam as opposed to, for example, better policing of open relays by ISPs and hosts. See also J Soma, P Singer and J Hurd, 'Spam Still Pays: The Failure of the Can-Spam Act of 2003 and Proposed Legal Solutions' (2008) 45 *Harvard Journal of Legislation* 165.

[77] L Edwards (ed) *The Legal Framework for European Electronic Commerce* (Oxford, Hart Publishing, 2005) 52–55.

goes, and spammers will be pushed out of business. If the cost per e-mail is kept sufficiently tiny, normal users of e-mail will not be affected—only spammers who send thousands or millions of messages. Bill Gates, for example, proposed an e-mail 'postage stamp' of perhaps 0.01¢ an item. These ideas seem to have came to nothing: partly because people have an instinctive revulsion to paying for e-mail after so many years of sending it for free; partly because several difficult issues emerged about who would take, use and administer the micropayments; but mainly because now spam is sent almost exclusively by botnets, it would be nearly impossible to impose the charge on the actual spammers. Only the innocent victims whose computers have been turned into 'zombies' would suffer, and that would do nothing to deter spammers.

A. Technical Solutions—The Answer?

Within the knowledgeable Internet community itself, there has been consensus for many years that the best results will come not from legal regulation, but from 'self-regulation' by technical strategies.[78] ISPs, local network managers and individual users have long used filtering software to winnow out e-mails sent from the addresses (IP addresses and/or Uniform Resource Locators (URLs)) of known spammers. There is, however, a constant 'arms race' between filtering technologies—now using advanced techniques such as Bayesian probabilities not just keyword and URL checking—and spamming technology. For example in 2007, the world was blitzed with 'image spam', spam sent not as text but as a digitised picture, which completely evaded filters for some while until these were updated.

Another approach is co-operative 'blacklisting' of sites and ISPs known to harbour spammers. Such services are provided by organisations such as Spamhaus, based in Europe, and the Real Time Black Hole List.[79] Traffic coming from a blacklisted site will not be transmitted on via other networks or ISPs where administrators have consulted the blacklist, with the effect that the blacklisted site becomes isolated from the rest of the Internet, effectively 'sent to Coventry'. However, no such system is foolproof, and a site that is being unknowingly made use of by spammers against its own policies (a 'zombie' perhaps), or one that is sending out multiple copies of an e-mail for a legitimate reason (eg an alumni e-mailing from a university) may find itself blacklisted alongside the 'guilty' sites. A key problem is the risk that mistaken placing of a site on the list might be

[78] See overview of technologies by the OECD at Anti-Spam Toolkit of Recommended Policies and Measures, at http://www.oecd-antispam.org.
[79] This list is one of a number of DNS blacklists run by the Mail Abuse Protection System (MAPS, which is incidentally SPAM backwards) and now a service of Trend Micro. See http://www.mail-abuse.com/.

seen as libellous or as a restraint of trade (Spamhaus is currently fighting such a suit[80]), which not only affects the list organisation itself, but disencourages co-operation in providing information to the list or republishing the list. An interesting recent Australian approach to the blacklist concept is to offer every computer user free software which allows automated reporting of spam mail they receive to the Australian regulator.[81]

Lawrence Lessig, the highly respected Internet law guru, has lead a movement against blacklists on the ground that they represent undemocratic, unaccountable, vigilante justice.[82] An extreme solution is to use a 'whitelist', ie *only* accept e-mail from a list of prior approved senders: this has obvious difficulties for agencies such as the government and universities, which constantly receive enquiries from strangers, as well as for most individuals.

The most currently promising technical solutions involve variations on configuring e-mail servers, or more radically, redesigning the e-mail standard format itself, to make it possible to spot any attempt to falsify or disguise the true origin of an e-mail message. Filtering out all mail with fake reply addresses or falsified header information will effectively filter out almost all spam. Initiatives to create e-mail that can always be authenticated as coming from a verifiable, and traceable, source have been launched in the past notably by the Internet Engineering Task Force (IETF) and a loose confederation of major industry players (the Anti-Spam Alliance[83]); the latest great white hope is known as Domain Keys Identified Mail (DKIM), which uses digital signatures to guarantee the true origin of an e-mail.[84] There are many obstacles still in the way of developing a trusted e-mail system acceptable to all players—technological interoperability, proprietary standards and patents, trade secrets, industry rivalry and privacy concerns about the possible loss of anonymised e-mail—but in the end this is likely to be the most promising route to stamping out spam.

Spammers are, however, fighting back, in the usual technological arms race. Public websites which are incessantly spammed, such as SNSs, blog sites and comment forums, have evolved their own ingenious technical solution in the form of CAPTCHA barriers—CAPTCHA being an acronym for 'completely automated public Turing test to tell computers and humans apart'. Basically, human commenters are asked to repeat displayed letters,

[80] See update at J Leyden, 'Court Junks $11m Judgment against Spamhaus', 5 September 2007, http://www.out-law.com/default.aspx?page=8444.
[81] See the SpamMATTERS reporting software, on the Australian Communications and Media Authority site at http://www.acma.gov.au/.
[82] See L Lessig, 'The Spam Wars', 31 December 1998, http://www.lessig.org/content/standard/0,1902,3006,00.html. Lessig's attitude may have been coloured by the fact that his former employer, Harvard University, was at one time blacklisted on the Real Time Black Hole List.
[83] The group includes Yahoo!, Microsoft, EarthLink and America Online.
[84] See eg 'New Anti-phishing Technology Could Battle Spam Too', *OUT-LAW News*, 8 June 2007, http://www.out-law.com/default.aspx?page=8129.

which are too distorted for automated spamming software to decipher. However, recent reports indicate that it is only a matter of time before spamware catches up with this, using artificial intelligence techniques to overcome the recognition hurdle.[85]

VI. WHAT NEXT?

In the next chapter, we go on to consider how online marketing has evolved since that first spam in 1988, and how the law has struggled to keep up. In particular we look at the change in emphasis from the regulation of online advertising per se, to the prior data collection and profiling exercises. At the end of that chapter we will offer some overall conclusions on the future of user privacy in a world of commercial and ubiquitous surveillance of location, image, habits and identity.

[85] See 'Spammers Use of AI Only Just Begun', *Infoword* 31 May, 2007, http://www.infoworld.com/article/07/05/31/Spammers-use-of-AI-only-just-begun_1.html?APPLICATION per cent20 SECURITY. CAPTCHAS are also sometimes solved by humans in return for rewards such as free porn: see BBC, 'PC Stripper Helps Spam to Spread', 30 October 2007, http://news.bbc.co.uk/1/hi/technology/7067962.stm.

16

Consumer Privacy Law 2: Data Collection, Profiling and Targeting

LILIAN EDWARDS AND JORDAN HATCHER[1]

IN THE LAST chapter we looked at the challenge to consumer privacy posed by the phenomenon of unsolicited online direct marketing, or 'spam'. In this chapter, we turn from this relatively simple example of direct marketing online to looking at how consumers are more subtly tracked, profiled and targeted by advertisers, online and increasingly offline too, using digital technologies. Tracking technologies have evolved from simple 'cookies', first regulated in the Privacy and Electronic Communications Directive (PECD)[2] in 2002, to far more complex technologies of commercial surveillance. These are currently perplexing privacy advocates, privacy commissioners and the European Commission alike, while users are still largely ignorant of their existence. Will our individual and collective privacy suffer from this new type of scrutiny, and can data protection (DP) law still adequately manage to protect us? In particular, this chapter takes the debate around the Phorm 'Webwise' system as a case study to illustrate how difficult it is for the law to tackle these issues.

I. THE PRIVACY AND ELECTRONIC COMMUNICATIONS DIRECTIVE

The PECD deals with a variety of challenges to consumer online privacy. The explicit intention of the PECD when it passed in 2002 was to update the DPD for the Internet era. Recital 5 states that:

> New advanced digital technologies are currently being introduced in public com-
> munications networks in the Community, which give rise to specific requirements
> concerning the protection of personal data and the privacy of the user. . . . The

---

[1] Much earlier versions of parts of this chapter appeared in L Edwards (ed), *The Legal Framework for European Electronic Commerce* (Oxford, Hart Publishing, 2005) and L Edwards and C Waelde (eds), *Law and the Internet: A Framework for Electronic Commerce* (Oxford, Hart Publishing, 2000).
[2] 2002/58/EC.

successful cross-border development of [digital network] services is partly dependent on the confidence of users that their privacy will not be at risk.

The PECD thus attempted to regulate not just spam and emerging issues such as cookies and spyware, but also to 'futureproof' the DPD against threats to consumer privacy not yet on the market. This intent to target all possible technologies, not just specific ones, is sometimes known as the aim of 'technological neutrality'. Many commentators would argue that the PECD has, however, failed in this aim. For this, among other reasons, it is currently under review as part of the wholesale revision of all EU laws relating to electronic communications.[3] Throughout this chapter we will note significant changes made to the PECD as of end June 2009, but these remain only in draft, and may be reversed before the final version emerges.

II. COOKIES

Cookies are small text files (usually less than 1 kbyte in size) which reside on the local hard disk of the computer, or terminal equipment of, a user, and contain a limited amount of profile information about that user.[4] Cookies are usually visible to users who know where to look,[5] but the information in the cookie, even if located, will usually be apparent gibberish to the user; this is because it merely acts as a unique identifier connecting the computer where it has been deposited, to information held server-side by the business which deposited the cookie.

Typically, cookies are used on businee-to-consumer (B2C) e-commerce sites such as Amazon, eBay, etc. When a user browses such a site, personal information is collected—what pages she views, what search terms she types in, what images she clicks on, what items she selects—and stored in the website's server-side database. That information is then connected to the user on subsequent repeat visits to that site via the cookie which acts to identify the user. (Sites cannot simply use Internet Protocol (IP) address to recognise the user, as many users access the Internet via consumer Internet service providers (ISPs) such as AOL which typically dynamically assign different IP addresses to users each time they log in.)

'Persistent' cookies[6] of this kind are very useful to users: they enable

---

[3] The review of the EC Telecoms Package embraces Directives 2002/21/EC, 2002/19/EC, 2002/20/EC, 2002/22/EC and Regulation (EC) No 2006/2004 as well as the PECD. It commenced in 2007 and the latest Common Position at time of writing was reached in May 2009. For full citation, see n 6 in the previous chapter.

[4] See A Sharpe, 'The Way the Cookie Crumbles' (2002) 2 *Privacy & Data Protection* 6.

[5] The directories they are stored in depend on the configuration of the system, eg C:/Windows/Cookies.

[6] 'Persistent' cookies are cookies that are not deleted at the end of a website session but remain on the hard disk of the user more or less indefinitely. These should be distinguished from 'session cookies' which are used as a technical device to maintain continuity during one Internet website browsing session. Session cookies are deleted at the end of the visit to a particular website and do not normally involve the processing of personal data or any possible invasion of personal privacy.

sites to know who you are, in essence, and are sometimes said to give the site a 'memory'; there is no need to log in every time, and data such as delivery addresses and credit card details can usefully be remembered and filled in automatically for the user. Cookies are also very useful to e-commerce businesses—and to online advertisers—as they enable a profile of the user's shopping habits and preferences to be built up. User X, for example, may be revealed by cookies to be repeatedly surfing a particular website for vintage Nike as opposed to Adidas brand trainers. This is valuable information, which can be used by the business itself, sold to competing businesses or to advertisers or used in combination with other information for data mining purposes.[7]

More worryingly though (from a privacy perspective), web advertising companies such as, DoubleClick have expanded this model using 'third-party cookies'. If you surf Amazon.co.uk, say, Amazon deposits a cookie so it can 'remember' what you did and bought—this is a second-party cookie. However, what DoubleClick does is strike deals with *numerous* website businesses. If DoubleClick and Amazon become advertising partners, now when you surf Amazon, not only is an Amazon cookie deposited *but also* a DoubleClick ('third-party') cookie. This way Double-Click may learn what you do when you visit not only Amazon, but maybe also other online book stores such as Waterstones and Borders sites (assuming they are also DoubleClick partners). If at all three, you search for books on fly-fishing, it is then fairly easy to work out what adverts (eg for not only fishing books but fishing holidays, fishing tackle) may be usefully served to you when you next visit a Doubleclick partner website. Such multi-site information provided an early route towards better profiling of the overall activity of a user, and opened up the possibility of serving more relevant or 'targeted' ads.

Cookies became an object of contention during the debates over the EC Electronic Commerce Directive (ECD),[8] when the European Parliament became aware that personal information about consumers browsing the Internet was being collected using second- and, especially, third-party cookies, usually without the consumers' explicit consent, or knowledge. So horrified were the Parliament that they proposed the total banning of cookies without prior consent ('opt-in'), to the utter consternation of European industry.[9] The matter was not resolved within the ECD, and instead, the PECD introduced in 2002 in Article 5(3) (on 'confidentiality of communications') the relatively lukewarm requirement that cookies might only be set if the consumer was 'supplied with *clear and comprehensive*

---

[7] See, for history of such uses, L Edwards and G Howells, 'Anonymity, Consumers and the Internet: Where Everyone Knows You're A Dog', in C Nicoll, J Prins and MJM van Dellen (eds), *Digital Anonymity and the Law* (The Hague, Asser Press, 2003).

[8] 2000/31/EC.

[9] See G Mackay and M Lomas, 'The Cookie Monster' (2002) 12(6) *Computers and Law* 14.

information . . . about the purposes of the processing, and is offered the right to *refuse* such processing by the data controller' (emphasis added).

This 'informed opt-out' requirement was a rather watered-down version of the original desire of the European Parliament to introduce opt-in and it is dubious if the information requirement adds much to the basic opt-out. Many sites merely offer a hyperlink to a privacy policy elsewhere on the Web. Such privacy policies may themselves be unintelligible; and in any case it is well known that consumers rarely read privacy policies anyway. The issue of how opt-out should be indicated—are small-print, pre-ticked tick boxes saying 'I agree to share information with third party advertisers' acceptable for example?—has already been raised in chapter 14 above. The PECD, recital 25 provides that 'Information and the right to refuse may be offered once . . . also covering any further use.' So 'opt-out' information need in any case be offered only the first time a user arrives at a website. On the other hand, the recital does go on to require that 'the method for giving information, offering a right to refuse or requesting consent should be made as user friendly as possible'.[10]

Setting cookies is also allowed without any consent where '*strictly necessary* in order to provide an information society service *explicitly requested* by the subscriber or user'.[11] Many websites at present, whether by intent or laziness, are not designed to work without persistent as well as session cookies. Some *will* work, but not as well; the Amazon site is a good example of this, as it (unusually) provides fairly good functionality without cookies, but popular features such as the 'shopping cart' and 'your preferences' do disappear. Many sites, however, simply fall over if the user chooses to 'turn off' or delete the persistent cookies for that site. So depending on the interpretation of 'strictly necessary', this provision may well be an open invitation to bypass the requirement of consent completely.

The draft revisions to the PECD are likely to replace the current consent requirement with a slightly reworded provision which requires that the user 'has given . . . consent, having been provided with clear and comprehensive information'. However, the current exception for 'strictly necessary' cookies will be retained.[12] Although this is opt-in, not opt-out, it will not necessarily create many changes in practice given the width of the

---

[10] The NCC survey, 'Consumer Privacy in the Information Age' (December 1999, PD65/L/99) spoke to focus groups of consumers about privacy, and one of their strongest findings was that consumers did not like the current variation in how consent is sought by tick boxes, and felt opt-in was much more in the best interests of consumers than opt-out. The report attaches a model standardised tick-box format.

[11] Art 5(3) PECD and recital 25 (italics added).

[12] The Art 29 Working Committee, reviewing the proposed draft reforms to the PECD in 2006 argued that it was unacceptable to make accepting cookies the price of admission to a site, and asked for the PECD to be clarified on this point: see Opinion 8/2006 on the review of the regulatory Framework for Electronic Communications and Services, with focus on the PECD, WP 126. However, as of the Common Position agreed in May 2009, the exception for 'necessary' cookies was still in place in the revised draft PECD.

exception for 'necessary' cookies. In fact, the majority of Internet adverts are now served without the use of third-party cookies at all, as popular browsers, such as later versions of Microsoft's Internet Explorer, are usually now set by default to block third-party persistent cookies. Many more experienced users also use free software such as AdAware or Flashblock, or limit Java scripting to block the serving of adverts. The most pressing need to regulate cookies in the interests of consumer privacy may in fact thus have already been met by code not law.

A. UK Regulations

On the question of how consumers should be offered the right to refuse cookies, the UK Regulations implementing the PECD[13] are silent, except for reasserting that the offer to refuse cookies need not be made more than once. The Information Commisioner's guidance suggests that the require-ment to offer a way of refusing cookies can be met simply by offering guidance on how consumers might use the facilities of their browser program to reject cookies.[14] This may cease to be adequate for 'consent' if the EU law changes as discussed above. The position in the UK Regulations is also unclear when the consumer is using a computer while at work; here it seems the person with the right to refuse cookies may well be the employer *or* the employee/consumer—and whose wishes should prevail in the case of conflict is not entirely clear.[15]

On the question of what is 'strictly necessary', likely to become even more important under the proposed rule change, the Regulations again say nothing, although the guidance notes do specify that '*such storage of or access to information should be essential as opposed to reasonably necessary*' and most importantly, cookies must be set 'for the provision of the service requested by the user, *rather than what might be essential for any other uses the service provider might wish to make of that data*' (italics added).[16] This seems clearly intended to exclude the collecting of data to pass to third-party ad servers, as that is *not* usually the service the user was requesting.

---

[13] See Privacy and Electronic Communications (EC Directive) Regulations 2003, SI 2003/2426 (the 'PECR') and *Implementation of the Directive on Privacy and Electronic Communi-cations* (DTI, March 2003, URN 03/762) at http://www.berr.gov.uk/files/file15097.pdf.

[14] *Guidance to the Privacy and Electronic Communications (EC Directive) Regulations 2003, Part 2: Security, Confidentiality, Traffic and Location Data, Itemised Billing, CLI and Directories,* para 2.4.

[15] Ibid, para 2.6.

[16] Ibid, para 2.5.

III. LOCATION AND TRAFFIC DATA

The PECD also introduced for the first time in 2002 specific rules restricting collection of location and traffic data by the private sector. Note, however, that these types of data may be classed as 'personal data', if they identify living persons, and so might have already been covered by the DPD before 2002.[17] As we will see in the discussion of RFID chips below, though, it is not always clear if these types of data *are* always 'personal'.

- *Location data* is data 'indicating the geographic position of the terminal equipment of a user of a publicly available electronic communications service'. Broadly it refers to information that reveals the whereabouts of the user of a mobile phone or similar telecommunications device. It includes the longitude, latitude and altitude of a user at time of communication, direction of travel, and timestamp information as to *when* a user was using a mobile device at a particular location.[18]
- *Traffic data* is data processed by the provider of an electronic communications network (such as a phone or cable company or ISP) 'for the purpose of the conveyance of a communication' on such a network, or for billing purposes. Such data includes the routing, duration, volume of and time taken for a communication.[19]

Traffic data has long been collected by telcos and ISPs for the purposes of billing, capacity management, and other internal procedures. It is basically all the data *about* a communication (often called 'meta-data')—when the user dials or logs on, when she terminates the communication, who is called or e-mailed, for how long, and so forth. Such data will be automatically generated when a user communicates. However, in an age of always-on, flat-rate broadband, many ISPs and telcos have less operational reasons to retain this traffic data in detail than before, at least in relation to non-voice traffic. However, as discussed by Rauhofer in chapter 18, they may now be forced to retain such data by national law enforcement agencies who wish to use this data to fight crime and terrorism, and may also seek to monetise this collected data as an additional revenue stream. The EU therefore sought to clarify the privacy safeguards concerning its processing in the PECD, so that (for example) traffic data could not be sold simply to enable surveillance of a user against their will by private interests.

Collecting *location* data as potentially valuable is a newer concept. A market for mobile e-commerce ('m-commerce') is developing in which

---

[17] Whether some traffic data is 'always' personal data is particularly controversial: see discussion of IP addresses as personal data in Edwards, ch 14, 458.

[18] PECD Art 2(c) and recital 14.

[19] See PECD Art 2(b) and recital 15. Full definitions of both terms for UK purposes can be found at Reg 2 of the UK PECR. Interestingly the UK definition of 'location data' is wider than that stipulated by the PECD itself.

location data is crucial.[20] Location data is typically sold by the telco originally collecting the data to third parties who then in their turn use it to sell services to mobile users on a basis of location or proximity, eg taxis, nearest fast food, weather forecasts, or even tracking children via their mobile phone for worried parents.[21] Location data can also be used to serve relevant adverts to mobile consumers direct to their phone, or even to direct tailored adverts at computer-equipped billboards as the consumer passes by—the 'intelligent billboard' concept.[22] These services, which the user accesses on top of simple communications, are known as 'value-added services'.

The type of location data collected by mobile phone operators is typically cellular data—revealing where a user is within certain 'cells' (areas of square yards or possibly miles across), this information being vital to deliver mobile communications access. The PECD seems to have been mainly drafted with cellular data in mind, and although it should in principle apply to other types of location data, it is again not at present very technology neutral in this respect. As we will see later, there are already clear difficulties about fitting RFID chips into the location data legal regime and other technologies such as GPS (General Positioning System) may also raise similar issues. GPS chips, which utilise highly pinpointed satellite directional technology, are becoming a major source of user location data. These chips were once prohibitively expensive for consumer applications, but they are now widely found in both satellite navigation systems used in cars, and in many smartphones, where they enable use of mapping services such as Google and Nokia Maps.[23] No legal issues with use and resale of consumer GPS information have arisen yet, it seems, but the technology may yet produce some. GPS devices have in fact the potential to be notably more privacy invading than 'ordinary' mobile phones, since they pin-point a user's location far more accurately than cellular data does.

In principle, therefore, both traffic data and location data have quite proper commercial reasons to be collected. But they can also be privacy-threatening technologies. It hardly needs to be said how useful it might be to a government, or a terrorist, or a commercial competitor, to know the exact location of mobile device users; or who exactly a telephone

---

[20] See eg companies such as Placeast (http://www.1020.com)/ and NAVTEQ's LocationPoint (http://developer.navteq.com/site/global/zones/advertising/p_advertising.jsp).

[21] See 'Tracking Down Your Child', http://news.bbc.co.uk/1/hi/technology/3218473.stm, and Child Locate at http://www.childlocate.co.uk/. Some mobile operators (and third parties such as Facebook) have also begun trialling consent-based services services which show you where your friends are if they are physically near you, have their mobiles on, and have also signed up to the service.

[22] See eg SuiPo http://www.poster.suica.jp/ (Japanese interactive poster from Japanese version of London's Oyster Card).

[23] Indeed GPS in smartphones has become so popular that the geek sport of 'geo-caching' has developed—looking for objects hidden in locations found by GPS. See http://www.geocaching.com.

subscriber has rung in the last month; or what websites they visited via their ISP, or to whom they sent e-mail. All this information can fall under location and traffic data. When such data is stored and archived for long periods, rather than deleted relatively quickly once its billing or initial commercial purposes are complete, the potential privacy violation implications become even more obvious.

Yet in the post 9/11 and 7/7 world, as already noted, enormous pressure is being put on telcos and ISPs, both by law and by voluntary codes, to store and retain exactly this kind of data for periods well beyond existing commercial good practice, in the interests of the future possibility (however remote) of criminal or national security investigations. The data retention regime for data collection, access and retention for security and law enforcement purposes in the EU is currently prescribed in the Data Retention Directive[24] and in the UK principally in the Anti-terrorism, Crime and Security Act 2001[25] and the Regulation of Investigatory Powers Act 2000 (RIPA) and its subsidiary regulations. A full discussion can be found in chapter 18 below but the main point to note here is that even though the PECD attempts to protect user privacy and confidentiality of communications (Article 5) and the DPD generally discourages long-term data retention, both laws may be overridden by national security and law enforcement objectives.[26] Despite this, the PECD claims it has nothing to do with the relationship between citizen and state but is restricted to regulating the private sector.[27]

A. The PECD Rules

(i) Location Data

Article 9 of the PECD provides that location data can only be processed with the consent of the user or subscriber, and only where it is necessary to provide 'value-added' services. A 'value-added' service is defined as any service which requires the processing of traffic data or location data beyond that which is necessary for the transmission of a communication or the billing in respect of that communication.[28] So Orange (say) cannot simply sell the locations of its users to private detectives, or obtain a blanket consent to sell this data for any purpose in their subscriber contract. Users

---

24 Directive 2006/24/EC of the European Parliament and of the Council of 15 March 2006 on the retention of data generated or processed in connection with the provision of publicly available electronic communications services or of public communications networks and amending Directive 2002/58/EC.
25 See full discussion of the data retention rules in Rauhofer, ch 18.
26 See UK PECR, Regs 28 and 29.
27 See PECD rec 11.
28 UK PECR Reg 2(1).

must give consent to release the data only to receive a named service, and the consent is restricted to lasting only as long as necessary for that service to be provided.

The service provider processing the location data must inform the user or subscriber *prior* to obtaining consent of what the location data may be used for and for how long. So Orange users exiting St Pancras station in London might receive a message saying that they can receive details about the nearest restaurants or cinemas, but only if they give consent for their location to be shared for that particular purpose. Users must also have the option to 'opt out' of releasing location data to a service provider at any particular time, even if they have previously given this consent.

If location data is anonymised, however, no consent is required. So Orange might legally tell a local pub (for consideration) that 40 Orange users are within 500 yards between 5 and 6 pm one night, without obtaining their consent, so long as their names (and numbers) are not released. There are already instances of companies trying some interesting workarounds to make commercial use of anonymised mobile phone location data without user consent. Gunswharf shopping centre in Portsmouth, for example, operates a system which allows shops which have units there to track when customers enter their store, and how long they stay there, by tracking the chips in the customer's mobile phones (which also reveal nationality).[29] The tracking is de facto anonymous, as the system has no access to the mobile phone numbers associated with the chips (or the names of users) but it is not impossible that identifying data *could* be produced by associating the phone locations tracked with another source of data—eg closed-circuit television (CCTV) images taken at the entry to each shop, combined with a timestamp on the cell data, and processed using image recognition software. Such systems do not currently appear to process personal data (says the ICO), but they definitely make some users feel uneasy. Note that Article 9(3) does clearly say that *processing* of location data must be restricted to persons acting as agents of telcos *or* providers of 'value-added services'. Thus if Gunswharf did at some point collect personal identifying data rather than simply anonymised location data, it would seem they would breach this provision as no extra 'value-added' service is provided to the user.

(ii) Traffic Data

Traffic data processing is also restricted, though not as thoroughly as with location data. Traffic data, according to section 8 of the PECR, can only be collected for limited purposes defined as:

---

[29] See 'Shops track customers via mobile phone', *Times Online* 16 May 2008, http://technology.timesonline.co.uk/tol/news/tech_and_web/article3945496.ece.

- management of traffic or billing;
- customer enquiries;
- prevention of detection of fraud;
- the marketing of electronic communications services;[30] or
- the provision of a value added service.

Even when traffic data falls within one of these permissible processing categories, further restrictions apply.[31] First, the user or subscriber to whom the data relates must give their consent. This consent may be withdrawn at any time. Even then, the data must be processed and stored only for the duration necessary for the relevant purpose. Aside from these particular exceptions, the general principle is restated from DP law that when traffic data has fulfilled its function—ie aided the transmission of a communication—it should be either deleted or anonymised.[32]

This last point raises the interesting detail that the PECD rules clearly only legitimise the situation where location or traffic data is collected by the mobile or telecoms service provider and sold on with the consent of the user, for the provision of third-party services beneficial to the user. What if traffic or location data is collected by persons *other* than an ISP, fixed or mobile telecoms operator? The PECD explicitly says that it is not about state surveillance[33] (a matter dealt with in other laws) but this leaves the issue of interception of data so it can be collected by a third party and used for commercial or surveillance purposes. Here it seems the relevant rules become the criminal law rules on interception or wire-tapping[34] and computer hacking.[35] As we shall see later, these rules are very relevant to considering if sophisticated targeted advertising systems like Phorm 'Webwise' meet legal requirements.

IV. LOCATION DATA AND THE 'INTERNET OF THINGS':
RFID AND BEYOND

A. The Technology and the Commercial Uses

RFID (radiofrequency identity) chips are tiny microchips attached to an antenna (internal or external) which receive and transmit information by means of radio waves. They are very small, cheap, come in many varieties,

---

[30] As defined by s 32 of the Communications Act 2003.
[31] Ibid, Reg 7(2)–(4).
[32] Ibid, Reg 7(1).
[33] PECD rec 11.
[34] On interception, see the discussion below about Phorm, RIPA 2000 and Art 5 of the PECD. See also Rauhofer, ch 17.
[35] Regulated in the UK as 'unauthorised access' by s 1 of the Computer Misuse Act 1990.

and are currently used for a multiplicity of commercial purposes.[36] The price of such cheapness is that RFID chips are usually passive, ie they do not broadcast their location as such, but need to be *detected* by readers, at a range that varies with the system, from a few millimeters to 100 meters or more (the latter only for active RFID tags).[37] RFID should not be confused, as it sometimes is, with GPS, which uses satellite technology to enable pinpointing of locations of persons or objects from very great distances. RFID chips are far cheaper than GPS systems and thus far more suitable to the inventory and stock control of many millions of manufactured items. Even so, it is still commercially impractical due to the number of readers needed for RFID tags to be used by private operators except within a relatively small area like a shop, school or hospital, or a tightly controlled area such as a subway transport system or 'gated' campus, where readers can be placed at strategic chokepoints.

The most common commercial uses of RFID are for product tracking, inventory control, access control to sealed areas ('smart doors'), contact-less stored-value transport cards (e.g. the Oyster card used by Transport for London commuters) and animal tagging. Other applications include using RFID to tag banknotes (fraud and crime prevention), adding scannable biometric data to passports via RFID chips, hands-free payment mechanisms[38] and people-tagging.[39] Importantly, RFID chips when read, typically disclose their location; they are thus technologies involving processing of location data, as discussed above.

Most consumer concern around RFID has centred to date on their use in high street stores as a more advanced form of Universal Product Code (UPC) or barcode. But unlike UPC codes, which only carry information on the class of object (make and model information), RFID tags provide a unique identifier for that specific object (eg make, model, unique ID #5679, shelf 6, row 13). Thus if an invisibly small RFID tag is attached to, say, every shirt sold in Marks and Spencers, and not removed or deactivated at point of sale, whether deliberately or by accident, then the unique

---

[36] See useful overview in Annex of the Art 29 DP Working Party, 'Working Document on Data Protection Issues Related to RFID Technology' (19 January 2005) 6–7; also A Brown, 'RFID: An Unlawful or Just Unwanted Invasion of Privacy?' [2003–04 December/January] *Computers and Law* 27.

[37] Active RFID chips, which have their own power supply and can broadcast over a wider range, do exist, but tend to be too large and expensive to be used in most commercial applications.

[38] For a rather unusual example of this, see S Morton 'Barcelona Clubbers Get Chipped', 29 September 2004, at http://news.bbc.co.uk/1/hi/technology/3697940.stm (subdermal implanted RFID chips for clubbers wearing only swimwear to pay for drinks). More significantly, see n 63 below on the growth of contactless credit cards.

[39] See description of tagging of school children in Tokyo to reassure parents, reported widely October 2004, eg http://www.cbsnews.com/stories/2004/10/11/tech/main648681.shtml. See also A Savvas, 'Doncaster School Tracks Pupils with RFID Chips' *Computer Weekly* 26 October 2007, http://www.computerweekly.com/Articles/2007/10/26/227753/doncaster-school-tracks-pupils-with-rfid-chips.htm (school using RFID tagged uniforms in trial).

RFID chip may by disclosing its location, if read, also disclose the location of its wearer. The fear commonly expressed is that RFID chips will operate as a sort of micro-bug, unknown to users for an indefinite time after sale.

In fact, not only does the low range of RFID readers make this implausible but RFID chips themselves (in the ordinary high street scenario) usually carry no information except the inventory code and description for the particular item to which they were attached, and thus taken by themselves do not identify the buyer, nor disclose personal data to the controller of the RFID system. In the example above, even if active after point of sale, they would merely disclose eg 'I am shirt #5679 and here I am, at timestamp now'. The identity (and thus location) of the buyer *might*, however, be discovered if the RFID tag data was associated at the point of sale with personal data derived from a credit card, smart card or store loyalty card. In stores such as Marks and Spencers, the obvious solution to this problem is to make sure RFID chips are deactivated at point of sale so that no data can be collected after association has become possible. This is generally now adopted as best practice in most stores using RFID in retail operations.

In other scenarios, however, such solutions are not as easily found. One much discussed example involves the Oyster smart card (RFID) system operated by Transport for London. Users of such cards access London's public transport via their card, with their card effectively collecting details of where and when they go. So long as such a card is anonymous—as it is when simply bought via pay-as-you-go—it does not disclose the identity of the user. However, registering an Oyster card as yours on the Transport for London website (so unspent credit could be refunded if the card was lost, for example) or refilling the card using your credit or debit card, would associate the card with your personal details, thus turning the RFID-held data into 'personal data' for the purposes of the DPD and PECD.[40] In such cases, deactivation of the chip is clearly not an option. There is evidence that Oyster card location and personal data is indeed being used extensively by both police and private detectives, so that a technology designed to make commuting more efficient, has almost by accident become an unexpected means of privacy invasion.[41]

B. RFID chips and Data Protection Law

How DP law relates to RFID has caused substantial confusion.[42] The Art-

[40] See further discussion in Rauhofer, ch 17.

[41] Eg 'Oyster Data is "New Police Tool"' 13 March 2006, at http://news.bbc.co.uk/1/hi/england/london/4800490.stm. Note that this problem arises from the way the Oyster card system has been designed and is not necessarily inherent to the idea of contactless smart cards. It is claimed, for example, that Singapore's Octopus card system is better designed to allow and preserve anonymity than London's Oyster equivalent.

[42] There is a growing legal literature on RFID. See Brown above n 36; E Ustaran, 'Data

icle 29 Data Protection Working Party ('Article 29 WP') issued a working document on RFID and DP law in 2005, which dealt only with the DPD not the PECD for reasons discussed below to do with the restriction on scope of the PECD to publicly available networks. As already noted, RFID chips themselves do not necessarily contain 'personal data', ie information identifying a living person.[43] However, if the RFID chip data when associated with other data in the hands of the RFID operator, identify, or are likely to identify, a living individual, then the DPD becomes relevant, and imposes duties on the RFID operator as a person processing personal data. As the Article 29 WP put it, 'the use of RFID technology to track individual movements which, given the massive data aggregation and computer memory and processing capacity, are if not identified, identifiable, also triggers the application of the data protection directive'.[44]

Unhelpfully, this means that data controllers using RFID chips in their shops or warehouses will sometimes be treated in law as processing personal data, and at other times not. This may commonly depend, as discussed above, on something as random as whether a consumer pays for RFID-chipped goods with cash or credit card, or whether a tag is accidentally left on without deactivation. Other particular circumstances may affect the duties of the RFID operator under DP law.[45] In an early notorious RFID trial, Tesco attached RFID chips to small, high-value, and thus much stolen, packets of razor blades they sold, in order to monitor and prevent shoplifting. Anonymisation was put in place by the good practice of deactivating tags at point of sale. However, those who shoplifted the razor blades were caught on CCTV as they left the shop so they could be identified to police later, and a timestamp on the CCTV image was matched to the RFID chip read at the same time of exit. Those who stole razor blades did not have the attached chips deactivated, as they did not go through point-of-sale procedures. Thus the RFID chips on the shoplifted razor blades continued to collect personally identifying data (as the chip could now be associated with the image on CCTV at the time when the RFID passed the camera).[46] In this case only, Tesco, it seemed,

Protection and RFID Systems' (2003) 3(6) *Privacy and Data Protection* 6; the Ontario Privacy Commisioner has published legal guidelines on using RFID tags in libraries at http://www.ipc.on.ca/docs/rfid-lib.pdf; S De Schrijver and J Schraeyen, 'Radio Frequency Identification (RFID) and Privacy: 1984 anno 2007?', (2008) 14 *Computer and Telecommunications Law Review* 1. In Europe, the EU Art 29 Working Party published 'Working Document on RFID', 10107/05/EN WP 105, 19 January 2005 ('Art 29 Working Document').

[43] See in the UK s 1 of the DPA.

[44] Art 29 Working Document, above n 42, 8. See further discussion of the 'identifiable' element of defining personal data in the Art 29 Working Party 'Opinion 4/2007 on the Concept of Personal Data', Section III, 3, 01248/07/EN WP 136, 20 June 2007.

[45] See 'Big Brother at the Supermarket Till?', BBC News, 27 January 2005, http://news.bbc.co.uk/1/hi/business/4211591.stm.

[46] See further 'Tesco Using RFID Tags to Track Shoppers; MP Wants Regulation', *OUT-LAW News*, 31 July 2003.

fell under DPD duties,[47] including the duty to process data fairly[48] but only to those customers who had stolen from their store, not legitimate users.

C. RFID, the PECD and Location Data

A further complicating factor is whether RFID tags fall under the 'location data' regime in the PECD described above. Location data is currently technically defined as 'any data processed in an electronic communications network *indicating the geographic location of the terminal equipment of the user* of a public electronic communications service'.[49] There are two main problems of interpretation here.

(i) 'Terminal Equipment'

First, as Brown notes, it is hard to say in natural language that RFID tags—or even the goods to which they are attached or embedded—are 'terminal equipment of the user'.[50] Undefined in the PECD and UK PECR, the obvious natural language interpretation would be that what is meant is a mobile phone handset, a personal computer, PDA (personal digital assistant), or the like. Yet if RFID chips fall within the DP regime, it would seem only sensible that they also should fall within the PECD location data regime, given their locating functionality and the PECD's prime goal of updating DP law. This purposive interpretation,[51] if accepted, would be significant, since it would imply the application of the stringent consent rules required for processing of location data applied, rather than just the considerably looser rules of 'fair processing' in the DP regime. Under those rules, as we have already noted, consent is not necessarily required at all,

---

[47] Fuller consideration of how the DP Principles apply to operators using RFID chips can be found in the Art 29 Working Document. It is possible in the scenario above that Tesco might claim exemption from some (though not all) obligations under DPD Principles because they were processing data for the purposes of preventing or detecting crime (see Data Protection Act 1998 s 29).

[48] Note, however, that this does not necessarily mean that Tesco would be unable to process the data collected on the RFID chip without the consent of the shoplifter (clearly this would be difficult), since the First Data Protection Principle allows as alternate ground for processing personal data that 'legitimate interests' can justify processing, although not at prejudice to the user's privacy (see further ch 14). In practice, many RFID operations may consider they rely on this ground, particularly in occasional accidents where chips are not deactivated after sale, since consent is rarely requested of purchasers of chipped goods, either before or at point of sale.

[49] PECD, Art 2(c) and rec 14 (italics added).

[50] Above, n 36. Ustaran (also above n 36), however, seems to take the view that locations of identifiable users disclosed via RFID chip do not constitute 'location data'.

[51] It is worth noting also in favour of this interpretation that new draft rec 40a of the revised PECD provides: 'Where measures aiming to ensure that *terminal equipment* is constructed so as to safeguard the protection of personal data and privacy are adopted pursuant to Directive 1999/5/EC or Council Decision 87/95/EEC, *such measures should respect the principle of technology neutrality*' (italics added).

since other grounds for 'fair' processing exist, notably the justification of 'legitimate business purposes'.[52]

Interestingly, the draft revised Article 5(3) of the PECD (as of the Common Position of May 2009) would provide also (as we have already seen in the context of cookies) that consent is required for 'the storing of information, or *the gaining of* access to information already stored, in the terminal equipment of a subscriber or user', and that clear information about processing must be given prior to asking for consent. If RFID chips are regarded as 'terminal equipment', this too would imply a duty to put in place an 'informed opt-in' consent regime for RFID, something not commonly in place in consumer operations currently.[53]

This problem of definition was considered during the revision of the PECD. At one point, the draft revised definitions Article of the PECD referred instead of 'terminal equipment' to 'data collection and identification devices', a phrase specifically designed to include RFID chips. However, in February 2009,[54] this new wording was dropped and the latest draft version, the common position of May 2009, has sadly failed to reinstate this wording. However, importantly, draft revised recital 44 still firmly asserts:

> When [RFID chips] are connected to publicly available electronic communications networks or make use of electronic communications services as a basic infrastructure, the relevant provisions of [the PECD] including those on security, traffic and location data and on confidentiality, should apply.

If this survives to the final version of the revised PECD, it seems to conclusively settle this debate.

(ii) Public and Private Networks

Secondly, the PECD currently only applies to RFID systems where personal or location data is processed over publicly available electronic communications networks. The European DP Supervisor has criticised this scope restriction as 'one of the most worrisome issues that the Proposal [the draft reforms] has failed to address'.[55] This criticism is centred on the growth of

---

[52] See n 48 above.

[53] Note, however, the exception to this rule, also discussed earlier in the context of cookies, that consent is not required if the use of RFID chips is 'strictly necessary in order *for the provider of* an information society service explicitly requested by the subscriber or user *to provide the service'*. (The reference to an ISSP—which would not, it seems, include a non-online retailer such as, say, Tesco in the previous examples—shows again how badly this provision maps on to the world of RFID and the Internet of Things, even despite assertions of technology neutrality.)

[54] See Common position, Brussels, 9 February 2009 (OR en): Interinstitutional File: 2007/0248 (COD) 16497/08.

[55] See the European Data Protection Supervisor's Second Opinion on the Review of the PECD, 9 January 2009, available at http://www.edps.europa.eu/. See also criticism from the European commission in 'Radio Frequency Identification (RFID) in Europe: Steps Towards a Policy Framework', P6 COM(2007) 96 final 15 March 2007.

private networks run by corporate bodies, and the increasingly blurred distinction between use of private networks *by the public*, and public networks. The worry is that although users may have guarantees of data privacy under the PECD when using publicly accessible networks like those provided by ISPs and telecoms companies such as BT or Vodafone, they do not when using, as is increasingly the case, private communications networks—eg those provided at work, in hotels, cybercafés, airports or on trains. Similar concerns could apply to networks in shops such as Tesco, to which RFID chips report back data. During the revision of the PECD it was suggested that its scope should be extended to cover 'publicly accessible private networks', which might include the kind of networks mentioned above (although perhaps not private shop networks, to which shoppers rarely get access). However, in the Common Position of May 2009, this seems also to have been dropped (and justified by draft revised recital 43). This apparent exclusion from the PECD of many RFID operators using private networks, such as supermarkets and high street stores, may go a long way to explaining the relative complacency as to any need to ask consent from purchasers of RFID chipped goods.

D. RFID-specific Laws?

Finally, quite separately from the PECD reform process, in May 2009 the Commission issued a Recommendation on RFID[56] which proposes a model regime for RFID operators. This is however a 'soft law' instrument only, chosen as such for speed of implementation and cost effectiveness.[57] Under the Recommendation, RFID operators, in addition to existing obligations under the DPD and the PECD, are asked to produce 'Privacy and Data Protection Impact Assessments' and make these available to their national regulatory authority.[58] In addition, they should produce and publish a plain-language policy on the use of RFID, as well as use a common mark to indicate the presence of RFID readers (similar to the ubiquitous CCTV camera notices seen throughout the UK).

For the retail industry specifically, the Recommendation strongly recommends deactivation of chips at point of sale, but this is not required where there is either consent of the customer[59] or an assessment by the retailer that there is no detrimental privacy impact or that they can mitigate this risk.[60] It is not clear this assessment is best left to the retailers who will

---

[56] Commission Recommendation of 12 May 2009 on the implementation of privacy and data protection principles in applications supported by radio-frequency identification (SEC(2009) 585) (SEC(2009) 586).
[57] Ibid, para 4.2 (4) of the Impact Statement.
[58] Paras 4–5 of the Recommendation.
[59] Para 11 of the Recommendation.
[60] Para 12 of the Recommendation.

have commercial reasons to wish tags left on—to enable after-service, customer returns, etc. The Commission will report by the end of 2012 on how the Recommendation is being implemented by Member States and industry.

E. Future Threats from Location Tracking: The Ubicomp World

The high street trials of RFID technology in the mid-2000s stirred up adverse publicity in both the US[61] and Europe, but as we have seen, the privacy concerns were actually fairly limited by the short-range and passive nature of the technology. In practice, high street retailers using RFID have mostly seemed happy to self-regulate to minimise privacy violations, and bad press, by accepting deactivation at point of sale as standard practice.

The EU continues to look at RFID regulation[62] but real worries now lie beyond the high street stores in the newer applications. Transport system RFID-chipped smart cards, RFID-tagged banknotes, debit/credit contactless payment cards,[63] location tracking chips for employees and schoolchildren, all add up to a world in which ubiquitous tracking is enabled as much offline as online. Historically, surveillance in the real world has of course always been possible—but the cost has made it the exception rather than the norm, and mainly the preserve of the law enforcement rather than private/commercial sector. RFID and its successors may change all this. Even more novel applications of RFID touched on above, such as tagging of hospital patients,[64] will add to this array of surveillance. Soon elderly people in nursing homes may even find their kettles chipped, so that faraway relatives can check they are still active and making cups of tea without having to visit.[65] In all these scenarios, RFID chips—or, probably, more advanced forms of sensor data technology—stay active and associated

---

[61] See CASPIAN, Consumers Against Supermarket Privacy Invasion and Numbering, at http://www.nocards.org/.

[62] See 2007 Report, Comm(2007) 96 final , which looked at surrounding issues such as spectrum allocation and research support, and the Commission's site on RFID at http://ec.europa.eu/information_society/policy/rfid/index_en.htm.

[63] Visa, Mastercard and American Express are all offering contactless versions of their credit cards. See http://www.creditcards.com/credit-card-news/contactless-credit-cards-data-privacy-1273.php. Security experts suggest there may indeed be dangers of data being intercepted by 'pirate' close-range RFID readers.

[64] *OUT-Law News* reported on 14 October 2004 that the US Food and Drug Administration had approved the subdermal implant of RFID chips into patients so they could be used to identify what drugs the particular patient needed, with less chance of human error. They could also record data about allergies. Several US states (such as Wisconsin) have since banned 'forced' RFID chip implantation (mainly by employers), with legislation proposed in others. See eg N Anderson, 'California Outlaws the Forced Subdermal RFID Tagging of Humans', *Ars technica* 4 September 2007, at http://arstechnica.com/news.ars/post/20070904-california-outlaws-forced-rfid-tagging-of-humans.html.

[65] The Ipot, which sends tea kettle usage data to relatives via email, is reported at 'i-Pot Helps Elders Feel Less Lonely', *Endgadget* 15 April 2005, at http://www.engadget.com/2005/04/15/i-pot-helps-elders-feel-less-lonely/.

with the card-holder, wearer or user for the duration of ownership, and the privacy risks seem thus much higher. This is especially true for those whose autonomy is already limited—such as the young, old and sick—and for whom this kind of tagging may be imposed not consensual (or traded for benefits such as lower premiums on health insurance, or safer jobs).

We are at the beginning, it seems, of a slow shift to a world of ubiquitous computing (or 'ubicomp'), sometimes known as the Internet of Things. This is the world where we connect to both private networks and the public Internet, not necessarily via a familiar terminal such as a computer, mobile phone, digital television or even games console, but merely by interacting with chip-enabled objects in our real-world environment. In a much-cited science fictional dream, this is the world where everyone will have a 'smart fridge' which notes itself via sensor chips that the milk section is empty, and automatically orders more online. This world may be a joy for busy homemakers and excited geeks, but it also opens up thrilling and terrifying new ways to invade privacy—and will be a holy grail for marketers, providing them with detailed information on consumer habits both 'at home' and in the marketplace. It is hard to see how this ubicomp world, if and when it arrives, cannot have an impact on the wider concept of 'private life' if not on narrower informational privacy and data protection legislation. How the law should prepare for the coming of the ubicomp world is something we will return to in the conclusion. First, however, we will move on from looking primarily at data collection technologies, to seeing how data collected is being used to profile and target users in ever more sophisticated, and potentially privacy-invasive, ways.

V. PROFILING AND TARGETED ADVERTISING: FROM GOOGLE TO PHORM AND BEYOND?

A. Google

Everyone knows nowadays that the easiest way to find out about a new employer, a new lover or a commercial competitor is to 'Google' them. The Web is chock full of, in DP terminology, personal data—and sensitive personal data. Google itself can thus be seen as a wonderful aid to navigating the Internet or a possible source of privacy invasion. However, Google does nothing illegal in terms at least of EC DP law in its basic search function, since it merely provides links to material that others have foolishly or otherwise let the public access. (Copyright may be another story—see chapter 7 above.) However, some of Google's other innovations raise more complicated worries.

Search terms themselves (input into Google or other engines) are a fertile source of data about the searcher. Even if this data is anonymised so that the name of the searcher is not directly available, identification may be possible via the terms themselves—for example, many users search for their own name (so-called 'vanity searching'). AOL vividly brought the sensitivity of search information to the world's attention in August 2006 when they made public three months worth of search data for 657,000 of their users, albeit in anonymised form.[66] Although AOL quickly took the search data back down, this was not before the *New York Times* had managed to identify from internal evidence AOL searcher No 4417749 as an over-60 widow in Lilburn, Georgia, USA.

Search engines have straightforward business reasons to collect (and retain) search data—mainly to improve their own search algorithms which will in turn benefit the user (and advertisers) by providing better more tailored searches—but that data is also usable for purposes other than immediate searches. A great deal can be learnt about a person from their web searches over time. Google has used this insight to create a business model which has been the great success story of the Internet in the last decade.

B. The AdWords System

Google, across all its sites and services, collects enormous amounts of data about its users. This data includes not only search terms, but also data such as browser and language used by user, IP address of user (which often provides location), time of searching, frequency of search, etc. Google also keep records of previous user search history (connected to the user via the cookie Google places on the user's machine) and information drawn from other Google sites such as the social networking site (SNS) Orkut, blog service Blogger, stats services Google Analytics, IM service Google Talk, Google Mail, Google Docs, and others, as well as through their contro- versial acquisition of DoubleClick. Google uses all this data acquired to help determine which contextual or targeted ads can be best served to users as they use Google's services.[67] Advertisers pay a premium for such con- textual adverts for the simple reason that users are more likely to click on them (known as a higher 'click-through' rate). This is known as 'behav- ioural advertising', 'targeted online advertising' or even (unfortunately) 'ehaviorial advertising'.[68] We consider the legal and privacy implications of targeted advertising models in the rest of this chapter.

[66] M Barbaro and T Zeller Jr, 'A Face Is Exposed for AOL Searcher No 4417749', *New York Times* 9 August 2006, at http://www.nytimes.com/2006/08/09/technology/09aol.html?_r= 1&oref=slogin.

[67] Reportedly, however, not all data from across all Google sites and services is shared, and some data is kept in various silos.

[68] This last is a creation of the US Federal Trade Commission. See http://www.ftc.gov/bcp/ workshops/ehavioral/.

Google transformed the search and online advertising markets in 2000 with the introduction of their twin programmes, AdWords and AdSense. AdWords, with brilliant simplicity, displays adverts on the Google family of sites which are relevant to the search terms a searcher used.[69] So if X searches for 'Spanish holidays' on google.co.uk, adverts are displayed to the right of the generated search results for (say) flights, package holidays and hotels in Spain which would appeal to a UK-based, English-speaking user. The Google model can in principle be rolled out across all its services (mail, maps, Docs, etc) and even to other platforms than the Web: so targeted adverts may already be served in-game via connected consoles[70] and even offline entirely with AdSense for Audio (for radio)[71] and Internet television advert trials ongoing.

AdWords makes money by allowing advertisers to bid to have their ads associated with a particular keyword or set of keywords (eg Nike might bid for the search word 'trainers', as might Converse) and Google ranks the prominence (first in the list, say) and frequency of adverts from a particular business according to how much they bid. As multiple advertisements can appear next to one search, and there are millions of searches per second, the system is very lucrative for Google. The adjunct programme, AdSense, also gives any website the chance to display Google ads on their own site.

The success of Google's targeted adverts model expanded further in 2004 with Google's introduction of Gmail (or Googlemail, as it is sometimes known). Gmail is a free web-based e-mail service that brings in revenue by applying the AdWords model to webmail. Gmail users see adverts that relate to the content of their email text alongside their email. These ads were, interestingly, greeted with more suspicion in the 'private' world of e-mail than the more public one of search, but were largely accepted by users in return for the benefits of Gmail such as excellent search and storage facilities.

When Gmail was released in the UK and EU, privacy activists complained[72] that Google were processing the text of the e-mails, both sent *and* received, without proper regard for 'fair processing' under DP law. Some of the text of these e-mails might well contain personal or indeed sensitive personal data according to the DPD, the latter requiring explicit consent from the data subject for processing. Gmail *users* would invariably

---

[69] The adverts served are also now targeted using other factors personal to the searcher and their history with Google, as well as geo-targeting and language, bringing the AdWords programme much nearer to the type of full behavioural targeting discussed below. See further http://www.google.com/privacy_ads.html.

[70] 'Google has acquired AdScape media', http://www.google.com/press/annc/annc_adscape. html. In-game adverts are placed within video games, eg on graphics of walls or billboards.

[71] See http://www.google.com/adsense/audio/; Google has, however, subsequently left the radio field: see 'Google Exits Radio but Will Explore Online Streaming Audio', 12 February 2009, at http://google-tmads.blogspot.com/2009/02/google-exits-radio-but-will-explore.html.

[72] See 'Google's Gmail Sparks Privacy Row', BBC News, 5 April 2004, http://news.bbc.co.uk/1/hi/business/3602745.stm.

have consented to the processing of their data to enable the serving of contextual adverts, as part of the standard term contract they agreed to when they opened the account. However, anyone *emailing* a Gmail account would not have given such a consent. Gmail, it was thus argued, were in breach of DP law. Google, however, deny this, apparently on the rather debatable ground that only machines, not humans, ever 'see' (ie process) the e-mail data, whoever has written it.[73] In the event, the controversy over Gmail seems fairly minor when compared to greater privacy invasions possible in later services.

After the success of Google Adwords, AdSense and Gmail, it became apparent that online targeted advertising was a commercial pot of gold. Other industry players, such as websites which had access to personal data, especially SNSs like Facebook, and intermediaries such as ISPs, began to wonder if there was some way they could claw back a part of this valuable revenue opportunity. Google has, of course, the natural advantage of having monopoly access to search terms entered into the most popular search engine in the world. But search terms are but a tiny fragment of all the information users generate and access while online. What if a site or an ISP could give advertisers comprehensive access to the contents, website addresses and traffic data of all the sites a particular user visits over time? If this could be achieved, users could be profiled in detail and extremely targeted adverts could be developed. Advertisers would very likely pay a large premium for such adverts if they lead to a higher 'click-through' rate, making the concept rather appealing.

Mere tracking of traffic data can be done through the use of conventional third-party cookies placed with the help of members of an advertising network—the 'DoubleClick' model already discussed. However, this model is restricted to tracking only traffic data as opposed to content, and technologically minded users can easily block some or all cookies using freely available software. Indeed, as noted earlier, many browsers already automatically block third-party cookies. More sophisticated ways of enabling a complete pattern of a user's Internet activity to be built up were, it seems, needed.

C. Phorm 'Webwise'

One such more sophisticated model is Phorm's 'WebWise' system,[74] which was announced as ready to launch in the UK in early 2008, and fast became embroiled in controversy which has delayed it going 'live' thus far as of end

[73] See Googlemail Privacy Policy at http://mail.google.com/mail/help/intl/en-GB/privacy.html, accessed 24 April 2008. Cf Privacy International complaint against Gmail filed in 17 countries, available at http://www.privacyinternational.org/issues/internet/gmail-complaint.pdf.
[74] See http://www.phorm.com/.

June 2009. Phorm offers to advertisers the ability to send targeted adverts based on the websites a user visits, with the assistance of the user's ISP. In essence, traffic between a user and a website is intercepted so that the Phorm system is then able to examine what requests have been made to websites by the user, and what content has come back. Phorm 'sees' what the user sees, and knows where the user has visited and what requests they made there. This information is then used to generate detailed profiles of the user, which are in turn used to deliver highly targeted ads to websites which are also partners to Phorm. So, for example:

> If you read a lot of pages about photography, you'll see ads for cameras when you visit a partner site like FT.com. An advertiser can be very specific about what will be displayed. . . . For instance, Canon could instruct Phorm to deliver adverts for its latest digital camera to anyone who visited a web page identified by Canon as giving a glowing review the previous week. It can narrow that request even further: Canon can tell Phorm only to deliver the ad to anyone who read that review and also visited more than two other pages that mentioned the model name eg IXUS 970, within the past three days.[75]

The user is typically unaware of such interception, although crucially Phorm claim that one of the strengths of their system is that the real-world identity of the user is protected far more rigorously than it is in most data-profiling systems. Information collected is allegedly anonymised, not linked to the IP or real-world address of the user, and thus no personal identifying data about the user is stored, passed to the advertisers or to sites where adverts are placed. This makes both privacy and commercial sense: the saleable information here is that a 40 year old man who is interested in buying a new digital camera also reads the FT website; not that he is named James Smith. Information about sensitive topics is not collected (eg drugs, alcohol, medicines) and children are not targeted.[76]

The user's ISP is a necessary contracting party to the scheme, but the websites *visited* by the user are not asked for consent, nor given a share of the advertising revenue (unless they are also sites where adverts are placed). Phorm were originally reported to have struck a deal to deliver targeted adverts in conjunction with several of the leading ISPs in the UK, including TalkTalk, BT and Virgin, but although trials have run, none have so far implemented live services as of end June 2009, due apparently to legal uncertainty and bad press. Involvement of the ISP is crucial, as we will see, not just because they offer Phorm a 'back door' into the user's machine, but also because they are the party with a direct relationship with the user

---

[75] 'The Law of Phorm' *OUT-LAW News*, 1 May 2008, at http://www.out-law.com/page-9090. Note, Phorm indicate that other privacy safeguards will operate in such examples.
[76] Ibid, reported comments of Phorm CEO Kent Ertugrul at public meeting, April 2008.

who can extract a consent to the interception and profiling activity of Phorm.

Following considerable public concern about privacy implications,[77] the matter was investigated by (inter alia) digital rights groups Foundation for Information Policy Research (FIPR) and the Online Rights Group (ORG), and the Information Commissioner's Office, resulting in an ICO statement in April 2008[78] that in their view, 'opt-in' consent was required from the user before use of Phorm was legal. (We will examine below in more detail what laws potentially come into play here.) The Phorm controversy has rumbled on since, with Phorm continuing to reject any claims it has acted illegally, either in principle or in how it has actually implemented trials, the ICO failing to bring any proceedings against it, and the EU taking legal action in the absence of any steps by the UK.[79] Many large players, including Amazon, eBay and Google, have also informally barred Phorm from intercepting communications by users with their website.

It is the European Commission that is likely to finally bring the Phorm debate into the courts. The European Parliament as well as the European Data Protection Supervisor and the Article 29 Working Committee have also long been concerned over online advertising of the targeted variety, and the privacy implications have worried them ever since DoubleClick came under scrutiny as the ECD went through the legislative process (see previous chapter). Concern has grown through the DoubleClick/Abacus merger in 1999, the Gmail launch in 2004 and the Google/DoubleClick merger in 2007/08. What, then, are the laws that Phorm may have broken?

D. The Law and Phorm

Although Phorm is merely an example and not the whole of the targeted advertising industry,[80] it makes a good case study through which to examine the multiple and complex legal issues that arise in this domain.[81] Relevant laws include, in the UK, the general framework of DP law (see ch

[77] The Phorm publicity resulted in an immediate response from privacy groups and users, including an anti-Phorm Firefox plugin, a number of anti-Phorm websites and blogs, a 10 Downing Street e-petition, and several anti-Phorm Facebook groups.

[78] See http://www.ico.gov.uk/upload/documents/pressreleases/2008/new_phorm_statement_040408.pdf

[79] See 'EC Takes Legal Action over Phorm', BBC News, 14 April 2009, at http://news.bbc.co.uk/1/hi/technology/7998009.stm.

[80] Several ISPs in the US, such as Front Porch and NebuAd, have also adopted Phorm-like approaches. See 'American ISPs Already Sharing Data with Outside Ad Firms', *The Register* 10 April 2008, at http://www.theregister.co.uk/2008/04/10/american_isps_embrace_behavioral_ad_targeting/. NebuAd has endured similar controversy to Phorm and now seems to have been withdrawn from the market, at least for the moment.

[81] Helpful analyses of Phorm from respectively the technical and legal viewpoint can be found at R Clayton's overview at http://www.cl.cam.ac.uk/~rnc1/080404phorm.pdf; and Nicholas Bohm's brief at http://www.fipr.org/080423phormlegal.pdf.

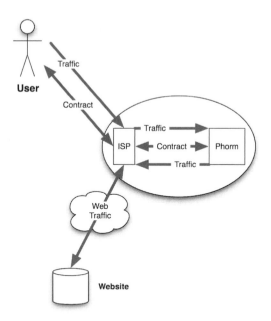

Figure 16.1 How Phorm works

14), the PECR rules examined earlier and the anti-interception rules of the RIPA.

An initial diagram may help the reader follow the complex analysis below (Figure 16.1).

Phorm WebWise works by collecting and processing three types of data:

1. Traffic data about what websites a user has been to, eg URLs of sites visited. This seems to fall into what is termed 'traffic data' in terms of the PECD (and UK PECR), and may even hypothetically include 'location data'.[82]

2. The text (and images) of webpages downloaded, or search terms input by a user into engines such as Google. This is what most people call the content of the communication: substantive information, not just traffic data.

3. This substantive data may *also* in some cases be regarded as 'personal data' under DP law, if it identifies or is likely to identify a living person; it may also quite possible include sensitive personal data.

---

[82] Eg if an Internet user accessed the Web via their mobile phone. Phorm themselves deny they collect 'traffic data' within the technical meaning of the PECR. One justification may be that traffic data as regulated by the PECD is impliedly only relevant if it is also personal data. It is unclear if the data Phorm collects does identify a living person, roughly the criteria for 'personal data', due to the internal technologies of anonymisation employed. See discussion of DPA s 1 in ch 14 above.

These three categories of data raise two important and interlocking legal issues.

(i) Consent to Processing

According to the PECR, rule 7(3)(b), traffic data can only be collected and processed for marketing or value-added services if the user has given his consent. This consent need not be explicit but the substantive data collected raises further issues of consent. If such data includes sensitive personal data, explicit consent *will*, it seems, be needed (as none of the other grounds for 'fair processing' of such data seem applicable). This seems to be the basis of the ICO's assertion that 'opt in' is required for Phorm—and accordingly Phorm have made it clear they do intend to collect explicit positive consent from the user, via his or her ISP. This would be a one-time query when Phorm first went live, but the user would be given opportunities, having consented, subsequently to opt out. This would also meet the similar requirement for consent if location data was also processed.

So far, so good, as long as the purposes for which the data is to be used are specified adequately. A remaining problem, though, is *who* is entitled to give this consent: the data subject whose traffic data is collected during a particular session, or the person whose name is on the account with the ISP? For example, Mrs Thomson, a householder, might be the account-holder on Virgin Broadband and say 'yes' when Phorm is first rolled out to Virgin customers; but Mr Thomson, her partner, might subsequently use the machine and have his web traffic collected by Phorm. Home computers are usually used by more than one person, so the problem is not easily resolved. Regulation 7 of the PECR says that the consent of the user *or* subscriber may be obtained to processing but does not specify which in particular circumstances. Schedule 3 of the Data Protection Act 1998, meanwhile, refers only to the data subject in terms of processing of sensitive personal data.

(ii) Interception of Communications

The second and perhaps crucial question is whether Phorm is illegally intercepting communications between users and the websites they visit. As noted above, what it does can seem rather like old-fashioned telephone wiretapping, except that pages are seen by third parties, rather than conversations overheard. Should such activity not be illegal, just as private (non-police) telephone wiretapping is illegal without the consent of the interceptee? This matter is covered in the UK by the RIPA.

[83] RIPA s 3(1).

Section 1 of the RIPA makes it an offence to intercept communications transmitted through a public telecommunications system without lawful authority. Consent to interception provides lawful authority.[83] But consent must be obtained from both the user and the 'intended recipient' of the communication sent by the user.[84] In the case of Phorm, there is ongoing debate as to whether it is just the user whose data is processed who has consented, or whether the website also needs to supply such consent in explicit fashion or whether consent can be presumed.[85] If the former is true, then the system is likely to be legally if not commercially unworkable.

Phorm's argument is that websites that make their content publicly available give their implied consent to having their content intercepted. This is not such an unlikely argument on first sight: websites are generally seen as giving a standing consent (or 'implied license') for copies of pages served to be made by users, and similar suggestions are often made about websites which have their content copied by Google 'spiders' (see further chapter 7 above).[86] However, there is an obvious benefit to sites in being spidered by Google bots—users can then find them—while there is no obvious benefit for websites not Phorm partner sites to be intercepted by Phorm. In any case, it is quite possible for websites if they so wish to *explicitly* indicate their refusal of consent to such interception, possibly using the robots.text standard format, or by using an actual notice on their homepage. If any site does this, then in practice implied consent from *all* websites cannot be assumed. This would mean that Phorm would need to individually check consent was available from every website a user visited— a task which might not be automatable, and thus would be economically unviable. In the wake of the Phorm furore, several websites, including major players like Amazon, have adopted 'anti-Phorm' notices, or publicly declared they do not consent to be intercepted by Phorm,[87] and some digital rights organisations have produced boilerplate 'anti-Phorm' notices for sites to adopt.[88]

As Struan Robertson of OUT-Law cogently notes,[89] the issues bedevilling Phorm, both around processing of personal data, and interception to communication, boil down to obtaining appropriate consent, from the appropriate person, As Phorm claim they will always collect overt opt-in

---

[84] Ibid.

[85] See above n 81.

[86] In fact, if sites do *not* give consent to interception by Phorm, an interesting argument can also be made that Phorm violates the *copyright* of websites visited by users: see N Boem and N Harrison, 'Profiling Web Users—Some Intellectual Property Problems' (2008) 19(4) *Computers and Law*, available at http://www.scl.org/.

[87] See R Wray, 'Amazon Opts Out of Phorm's Targeted Internet Advertising System after Privacy Fears', 16 April 2009, http://www.guardian.co.uk/technology/2009/apr/16/amazon-phorm-targeted-advertising.

[88] See eg http://www.antiphorm.co.uk/ ('No permission is given for this site to be intercepted or processed by Phorm').

[89] Above, n 75.

consent (via the ISP) when the system goes live for an ISP's subscribers, the legal problems around DP (and PECD) law connected to collection of traffic, location and personal data do seem mainly to have been met. However, the RIPA argument, that both user and website need to consent to interception, remains unsolved.

This is not just a problem for Phorm in the UK but in Europe generally. Earlier in this chapter furthermore (in the context of cookies) we noted Article 5 of the PECD which protects the security of electronic communication by obliging Member States to 'prohibit listening, tapping, storage or other kinds of interception or surveillance of communications and the related traffic data'. There are only limited exceptions: the defence most relevant to Phorm is that of consent by the intercepted party in Article 5(2) but as with the RIPA, consent to interception requires the consent of *both* ends of a communication, ie the user and the website. For this reason, Viviane Reding, the EC Commissioner, announced on 14 April 2009 that the Commission was suing the UK for failing to implement DP law properly by refusing to declare Phorm illegal. She stated firmly: 'I call on the UK authorities to change their national laws and ensure that national authorities are duly empowered . . . to enforce EC legislation.'[90]

Some might feel that this debate is about mere technicalities of interpretation of legislation that was never designed for systems such as Phorm. Others argue that Phorm is distinctly infringing privacy by collecting data as a private company which might contribute to substantial uncontrolled profiling and categorising of users. The question, as Struan Robertson of *OUT-Law* frames it,[91] is whether any real harm is done here to user's interests, which the law should step in to control. Is Phorm merely providing slightly more wanted advertisements, or is it really dangerous Internet wiretapping? We return to this dilemma below.

E. Social Networking Sites and Targeted Adverts

The above clearly suggests that behavioural advertising will be an ever more significant issue for online privacy, growing even more as RFID and the Internet of Things take hold. Building profiles of users that can then be used for tailored marketing depends on access to as much data about the user as possible. As we have seen, Google initially acquired this data from searches and later on other data collected by their family of services; Phorm acquires it from multiple websites visited. In future, operators are

---

[90] R Wray, 'Phorm: UK Faces Court for Failing to Enforce EU Privacy laws', *Guardian* 14 April 2009, at http://www.guardian.co.uk/business/2009/apr/14/phorm-privacy-data-protection-eu.
[91] Above, n 75.
[92] See further L Edwards and I Brown, 'Social Networking and Privacy: Irreconcilable Ideas?' in A Matwyshwn (ed), *Harbouring Data* (Stanford, Stanford University Press, 2009, forthcoming).

likely to also add in data collected in the 'real world' as well as online, eg data collected by RFID indicating movements on transport systems. SNS operators are also in a strategic position here[92] given the enormous amount of personal data disclosed by their users, generally without privacy protection.

SNS owners currently make their money by collecting and selling this data to advertisers and third-party marketers, in anonymised or aggregate form, obtaining consent unobtrusively via the standard site terms and conditions which must be assented to before access is allowed (compare Phorms's explicit proposed 'opt-in'). Adverts on SNSs have generally a lower click-through rate than on many other sites, so a new targeted adverts model would be attractive. Behavioural advertising is thus fast arriving in the SNS world.

In late 2007, both MySpace and Facebook announced plans to target adverts (or rather to allow advertisers to do so) at users of their sites, using information gleaned from their user profiles together with other sources of data. One early product of this programme was 'Facebook Beacon', which combined data collected from partner websites, together with Facebook user profile data. Since Amazon was a partner, for example, a sudden announcement might appear on User A's Facebook profile (and friend's newsfeed) that 'User A went to Amazon and bought *Law and the Internet*'. The idea was that friends of User A might be more likely to consider buying the same book if A 'recommended' it than if they merely saw an advert from the publishers. This might have worked had the privacy consequences been properly considered. No one apparently contemplated what might happen if the book bought was not *Law and the Internet,* but (say) *The Guide to Gay Sex*. Unsurprisingly, there was a serious public backlash at reports of privacy intrusion, even if it was (as is likely) strictly legal (even under EC DP law) since user consent would have been collected (albeit in standard term online contracts) by both Amazon and Facebook. Facebook capitulated after 50,000 users signed an online petition against Beacon, and changed consent to Beacon to explicit 'opt-in', enshrined in their privacy policy, effectively killing the service.[93]

Despite this blip of bad PR, it is clear that roll-outs of targeted advertising on various Web 2.0 user-generated content sites are proceeding apace.[94] An industry privacy norm does seem to be emerging (interestingly in both the US and the EU, despite their very different privacy heritages) that 'opt-in' consent is more appropriate than 'opt-out' in respect of

---

93 See privacy policy at http://www.facebook.com/policy.php.

94 Google announced a behavior-tracking advert system in March 2008 (see *OUT-Law News*, 11 March 2008) and eBay have also launched their AdCommerce service (see https://adcommerce.ebaypartnernetwork.com/adnetfiles/home/en-US/index.html).

95 See http://www.iabuk.net. The rules do, however, forbid the targeting of children under 13. Note that the US advertising industry is also under pressure to produce an internal code of

targeted advertising, whatever laws theoretically apply. Interestingly, though, the UK Internet Advertising Bureau, perhaps attempting to forestall regulation, recently released a set of guidelines for interactive advertising.[95] These recommended only 'opt-out' consent and received a rather poor press. In any case they have no mandatory force and their compliance cannot be easily checked by the average user. Self and co-regulatory codes of practice for behavioural advertising have also been issued or proposed recently by the Federal Trade Commission (FTC) in the US[96] and Microsoft in their submission to the FTC. Clearly the industry is keen to make targeting and profiling acceptable to the general public and regulators. Why is this?

F. Web 2.0: Revenue vs Privacy?

Web 2.0 businesses, particularly user-generated content host sites such as YouTube, Flickr and SNSs, are dependent on advertising revenue, given user reluctance in the large to pay subscription fees, except occasionally for 'value-added' or 'premium' services.[97] Advertising has always been spread unevenly among online sites, with the cake overwhelmingly swallowed by Google; and although the online advertising sector grew massively around 2006–08, the ongoing recession will not make it easy for Web 2.0 sites to stay afloat. Google's great commercial success with AdWords (and as later applied to Gmail, GoogleDocs, Google Street View, etc) combined with the recession, has made the growth of targeted advertising, if not restricted by regulation, inevitable. For the sites that stand to gain, DP laws and anti-interception laws are probably seen largely as unfortunate obstacles to the commercial success of their site.

Users, however, also have an interest in the financial solvency of their favourite sites. Advertising revenues mean that vast amounts of exciting content and functionality in the Web 2.0 world are made available to users for free which might otherwise wither on the vine in a subscription-based economy. The question must therefore be asked: where should the line be drawn between protecting user privacy, and restricting new forms of commercial and technological innovation? Does targeting really invade privacy? Or in Robertson's sense above, is there any real harm done? Targeted advertising, it is often argued, is in fact a pro-privacy move—it means users receive fewer adverts, more relevant adverts and in the

---

practice in this area: see 'FTC Gives Behavioral Ad Punters One Last Chance', *OUT-LAW News*, 13 February 2009.

[96] See http://www.ftc.gov/os/2009/02/P085400behavadreport.pdf.

[97] See eg LiveJournal the blog site, which currently offers two types of account; a 'free' account where the user must submit to receiving ads, and a 'paid' account which is ad-free (and has extra features). Unsurprisingly, the former predominates but the latter attracts the older, more privacy conscious or more irritable user.

contexts where a response can most usefully be made. They may even receive actually wanted adverts. Should the law do anything, then, to place barriers in the way of an exciting new business model for financing web-based services?

On the other hand, some experts, such as Richard Clayton of Cambridge, see Phorm as presenting a disproportionate threat to privacy, given the minor if any benefit the user receives in return. As he put it at a Phorm public meeting: 'It's like the Post Office opening all my letters to see what I'm interested in, merely so that I can be sent a better class of junk mail.'[98] Following this argument through, it might be suggested that Phorm (or its partner ISPs) should offer users benefits such as cheaper broadband in return for taking their data. Although this once seemed unlikely given the lack of any norm of paying users for data collected online, Phorm have in fact indicated they may be thinking along these lines.[99]

Returning to the debate on whether Phorm et al actually cause 'harm', many users, perhaps often of an older generation than the 18–24s who dominate the social networking and Web 2.0 scenes, understandably do feel that even if 'legal', Phorm and its ilk 'still violate many consumer's sense of ethical privacy practices'.[100] They see the relatively trivial issue of targeted advertising as merely the visible part of the iceberg of universal collection of personal data on line (as described in this chapter) and in the 'real world' (by mobile phones, RFID, smart cards, credit card payments, e-cash and perhaps GPS). That world, in which everyone is profiled and dossiered by such ubiquitous data collection, mining and profiling, is to many a terrifying one. It is perhaps finally for this reason rather than issues of UK or European law that BT, the UK's leading telco, decided in July 2009 not to roll out Phorm after all despite committed investment in trials.[101]

Three crucial questions emerge: do users have the chance to give an informed and explicit consent to the collection of data about them? Who should be allowed to collect such data? And how should those collectors be allowed to use it? These are the basic questions of DP law, but resurrected in a very different world than that where DP developed. We may not worry that much if Google or Phorm or Virgin or Tesco or Facebook collects data about us, and the results appear to be slightly more interesting adverts which we mostly do not read anyway; but we are perhaps more worried if they sell that data to credit brokers or insurance companies or employers, or if the government demands that data under national security legislation

---

[98] See 'Phorm "Illegal" Says Policy Group' BBC News, 9 April 2008 at http://news.bbc.co.uk/1/hi/technology/7301379.stm.

[99] C Williams, 'Phorm Mulls Incentives for Ad Targeting Wiretaps', *The Register* 26 September 2008, at http://www.theregister.co.uk/2008/09/26/phorm_webwise_incentives_survey/.

[100] A Matwyshyn, 'Behavioural Targeting of Online Advertisements and the Future of Data Protection' (2009) 19(6) *Computers and Law* 24.

[101] See *The Guardian*, 6 July 2009, at http://www.guardian.co.uk/business/2009/jul/06/btgroup-privacy-and-the-net.

or civil subpoena. Do we know how reliable the data is that is held about us, and how reliable it remains after it has been combined, mined and turned into profiles? Do we feel we have control over it? Do we believe that data we are assured is anonymised using current technologies will stay anonymised, or can it be reconstructed as personal data using evolving analytical techniques? Recent technical stories would seem to indicate the answers to the last is increasingly, yes.[102]

Maglena Kuneva, the Commissioner for Consumer Affairs of the EU, has recently expressed strong worries about this area. In a recent much-quoted speech,[103] she made it clear that ISPs, websites and advertisers were violating 'basic consumer rights in terms of transparency, control and risk' through data collection and behavioral targeting. She threatened regulation if the online advertising sector did not clean up its act. In particular though, and most radically, she noted that the application of DP law to 'personally identifying' data alone might not be enough.

As we noted above, targeted advert systems such as Phorm often deal in anonymised (or allegedly anonymised) profiles, as the name itself is of almost no value. This excludes them from much of DP regulation. Yet the identity of users so profiled can increasingly now be identified with enough data and the right algorithms, given the degree of specificity they now entail. De-anonymisation is a real possibility. Kuneva thus asserted that:

> Consumer policy needs to go beyond [DPlaw] and address the fact that users have a profile and can be commercially targeted based on that profile, even if no one knows their actual name.

Yet the public have accepted some degree of targeted advertising. While Phorm and Facebook Beacon have aroused the ire of the public, Gmail has been a huge success—primarily it seems because the public got in return something they wanted, namely an excellent webmail service with huge amounts of storage and unparalleled search facilities, for 'free'. Users go on using SNSs and eBay because they are both free and useful despite the arrival of targeted adverts. Is this market acceptance, and return, enough to offset any nagging worries as to privacy?[104] As Edwards has commented before, privacy is often balanced in legal debate against security—but in the commercial and consumer world, the balance is more often of convenience, or economic return, against privacy. On the whole, in that competition,

---

[102] See eg A Narayanan and V Shmatikov, 'De-anonymizing Social Networks', at http://www.cs.utexas.edu/~shmat/shmat_oak09.pdf;

[103] See 'EU Issues Ultimatum on Internet Privacy', *The Register* 31 March 2009, at http://www.theregister.co.uk/2009/03/31/kuneva_behavioural/.

[104] See http://news.bbc.co.uk/2/hi/business/3602745.stm for a useful comparison of the market advantage Gmail had over competitors in 2004 (time of launch) in terms of storage capacity offered free to users.

[105] There is a fascinating emerging body of work on the economics of information privacy, lead by researchers such as Schneier, Acquisti, de Camp, Clayton and Anderson, which deserves

privacy seems very often to be valued at a fairly low price, by both advertisers *and* users.[105] As a worst scenario, we might envisage, through apathy, lack of information and inertia, a future world where everyone is non-transparently categorised, not just as a middle-class, white, above-average income consumer (say), but perhaps also as anti-authoritarian, left-wing, green, Islamic, etc, etc. This kind of privacy threat goes beyond the commercial sector since such evidence would clearly be useful to the state. Yet such data would have been gathered not by experienced policemen or intelligence services, but on the basis of acontextual, and possibly erroneous or misattributed, evidence, collected by a variety of database and profile compilers over an indeterminate period of time. For policymakers, the question now therefore is whether the law should intervene to prevent market failure in the world of consumer—and citizen—privacy.

VI. CONCLUSION

The terrain we have surveyed in this chapter is a confusing one for lawyers and legislators. Few lawyers can even understand how Phorm works let alone start to apply the rules of the DPD and PECD to it. Matwyshwn[106] crystallises three problems which afflict law in this domain. First, the legality of targeted advertising and behavioural data collection is currently predicated on consumer consent. Yet that consent is usually neither informed, freely given or negotiable. As a result it is now conspicuously failing to be a gatekeeper for privacy. Second, law is in conceptual confusion in this area. As we saw with Phorm, we are no longer sure if the relevant laws are of DP or of criminal computer interception and intrusion. Thirdly, law will always be running behind technology in this area. To these we can add Kuneva's fourth point, that law generally only protects personal identifying data right now, not anonymised data, and this is ceasing to be sufficient.

In the previous two chapters we canvassed the idea that where law fails, code may find some solutions to problems of technological privacy invasion. Real control may come not just from reform of DP law, nor from new codes of practice in the commercial sector (who are unlikely, like turkeys, to vote for Christmas) but from so-called 'privacy-enhancing technologies' (PETS) which users can embrace. These might at simplest level block or deactivate RFID chips, delete selected cookies or disable targeted ads.

But instead of putting the responsibility to use PETS on consumers, why not demand that systems be built in privacy-protective ways from the start?

---

close attention. See as a starting point, the collected papers of the Workshops on the Economics of Information Security, available online.

[106] Above n 100.

The current great white hope for privacy advocates is 'privacy by design', basically the idea that systems should be designed so that collection and/or disclosure of data is minimised ab initio.[107] (Phorm, paradoxically, was actually intended to be a contribution to this movement; its architecture is specifically designed to complicatedly hide the identity of the user whose web traffic data is collected.[108]) In 2008, the UK Information Comissioner endorsed this approach, producing a report on 'Privacy by Design'.[109]

But the movement towards privacy by design must also be informed by a general framework of human rights protection of privacy as a fundamental right. The European Parliament has been active in starting a process towards an 'Internet Bill of Rights' and some of the proposals in the associated Lambrinidis Report[110] provide a valuable final focus for this chapter. Lambridinis writes:

> We must ask ourselves 'What are the limits of consent? This question applies both to what a company can ask a user to disclose, and to what extent an individual should be allowed to cede of his privacy and other fundamental rights in order to receive certain Internet services or privileges.

The report goes on to draw an analogy between the nascent Internet market and established practice in labour contracts, where it is universally acknowledged within the EU that there are limits to how far employees can be asked to agree to bad bargains by pure consent. Given the inequality of power, workers are limited in how far they can consent to working hours exceeding certain limits, wages beneath certain levels and other labour rights. Given this, Lambridinis asserts that the debate about 'the limits of consent' will be the next great Internet battle.

The Report and its recommendations, which include not only limits on user consent but also limits on how far governments can ask private companies to disclose data, eg by subpoena, has now become an EP Recommendation, effectively EU 'soft law'.[111] It may yet even become hard law. The pace of progress we have observed in this chapter makes the development of a principled constitutional approach to protecting privacy rights in a technocratic world more than pressing.

107 See discussion of this concept in Edwards, ch 14, 486.

108 This privacy-enhancing perspective on Phorm was interestingly provisionally guaranteed after audit by 80:20, a software firm run by Simon Davies, chair of privacy rights group Privacy International. In this sense Phorm can be seen as an improvement on the 'DoubleClick model', where the identity of the user whose data is collected can be made available to the ad-provider via cookies and connected databases, whereas Phorm claimed such data was hidden from the advertisers (though of course not the ISP).

109 Available at http://www.ico.gov.uk/upload/documents/pdb_report_html/index.html

110 Report with a proposal for a European Parliament recommendation to the Council on strengthening security and fundamental freedoms on the Internet (2008/2160(INI)) 25 February 2009 http://www.europarl.europa.eu/sides/getDoc.do?pubRef=-//EP//TEXT+REPORT+A6-2009-0103+0+DOC+XML+V0//EN

111 The report was adopted by the Committee on 17 February 2009.

17

Privacy and Surveillance: Legal and Socioeconomic Aspects of State Intrusion into Electronic Communications

JUDITH RAUHOFER

RECENT HISTORY HAS been dominated by the intersection of two concurrent developments: the rise of information and communications technology and the global threat of terrorism. Sophisticated information technology systems permeate almost every aspect of modern life. While enhancing citizens' participation in the social, commercial and political arena, their use by the perpetrators of terrorism and organised crime represents a threat—whether actual or perceived—to democratic systems of government. Modern communications systems, in particular, can be used to plan and commit criminal offences, but also to investigate, prosecute and, ultimately, prevent the commission of such offences.

Since the events in New York, Washington DC and Pennsylvania in September 2001 and the attacks in Madrid in 2003 and in London in 2005 the threat of terrorism has been omnipresent in Western societies. Those events have changed the way many people feel about liberty, security and the interaction between the two. Law both influences and reacts to events which have changed the prevailing order or which have the potential to do so in the future. Consequently, a re-evaluation of the existing legislative regime has taken place, where the need to protect individual human and civil rights jostles for position with the need to protect a public right to security. The verdict seems to be that individual liberty is—for the time being—required to take a back seat.

The right to privacy is one of the most prominent sacrifices that has been made on the altar of terrorism prevention. Governments the world over are introducing increasingly intrusive surveillance measures to gain information about their own population in the name of public and national security. The zeal with which such intrusions take place belittles the achievements made by democratic societies in relation to the protection of individuals' right to privacy and control over their personal information. At worst, privacy protection itself is blamed for the state's inability to provide absolute protection to its citizens.

There are those who question this dichotomy, who argue that no real tension exists between privacy and security, that those rights are not elements in a zero-sum game where the value of one must necessarily be diminished to ensure the continued existence of the other. For example, security expert Bruce Schneier argues that security affects privacy only when it is based on identity:[1] the increased use of identification checks at airports, the gathering of intelligence about identified individuals through surveillance, and the use of biometric information and sophisticated profiling systems, to name but a few.

This 'identity approach' is based on the assumption that, if law enforcement agencies only had enough information about individuals, they could somehow divine which of those individuals is likely to commit criminal or terrorist offences in the future. However, identity-based security systems, particularly where they are based on biometrics, frequently include the seed of their own destruction as they are often based on large, centralised databases that include all the data against which individuals' identity is checked. If one of these databases is compromised—as large databases are wont to be—the damage to the security system tends to be irreversible. This possibility is also emphasised by Schneier, who argues that, while biometrics are hard to forge, the electronically stored data that ultimately enables identification is easy to steal. As a result, those systems 'don't handle failure well':

> Imagine that Alice is using her thumbprint as a biometric, and someone steals the digital file. Now what? This isn't a digital certificate, where some trusted third party can issue her another one. This is her thumb. She has only two. Once someone steals your biometric, it remains stolen for life; there's no getting back to a secure situation.[2]

In addition, Schneier claims that the 'identity approach' is misplaced, because rather than providing security in real terms, it often constitutes nothing more than 'security theatre' that does little to improve, and in some case actually harms, security.[3]

> Sometimes it seems those in charge—of governments, of companies—need to do

---

[1] B Schneier, 'Security v Privacy', *Schneier on Security: A Blog Covering Security and Security Technology*, 29 January 2008, available at http://www.schneier.com/blog/archives/2008/01/security_vs_pri.html, last accessed 15 June 2008.
[2] B Schneier, 'Biometrics: Uses and Abuses' (1998) 42(8) *Communications of the ACM*.
[3] Ibid.

something in reaction to a security problem. Most people are comforted by action, whether good or bad.[4]

Schneier explains that security theatre can actively compromise real security when it uses up valuable resources, both human and financial. For instance, police and security personnel employed to secure a high-profile but low-risk event will be sorely missed if a real emergency occurs elsewhere. Money spent on the implementation of a national identity card system could be better spent, as Tony Blair himself pointed out in his 1995 Labour Party conference speech, on putting 'extra police officers on the beat'. Schneier views such liberty-depriving security measures as 'band-aids' and evidence of 'bad security planning', which are most often found when system designers failed to take security into account from the beginning.[5]

At the same time, he argues that measures likely to provide real security, such as reinforcing airliner cockpit doors, better authentication of airport maintenance workers, or dead-man switches that force planes to automatically land at the closest airport have no effect on individual privacy at all.[6]

Where state surveillance measures nonetheless intrude on individuals' rights to privacy, a debate is ongoing about the best way to safeguard individual freedoms from the excessive and arbitrary use of those measures by the executive. The importance of a system of checks and balances which ensures adequate oversight of the acting authority has become more apparent as the ability for ever-greater intrusions has increased. There exists a notable difference in the approach to oversight in the UK and the countries of continental Europe. While the UK largely insists on allowing the executive to retain control both over the right to authorise and to oversee surveillance measures, continental European jurisdictions rely to a much greater extend on judicial oversight. Advocates of the latter approach point out that because of the very nature and logic of secret surveillance individuals will rarely be aware of the fact they are being observed. They argue that this necessitates strong and effective supervisory controls by an independent third party. In contrast, the UK government has generally claimed that judicial oversight would require the disclosure of sensitive information about the working methods of the intelligence services and that this would harm the effectiveness of those measures.[7]

This chapter will examine the relationship between the right to privacy and the right to security embodied in the most recent use of electronic surveillance techniques by law enforcement and intelligence agencies. In

---

[4] B Schneier, *Beyond Fear—Thinking Sensibly about Security in an Uncertain World* (New York, Copernicus Books, 2003) 38.

[5] Ibid.

[6] B Schneier, 'Protecting Privacy and Liberty', *Crypto-Gram Newsletter* 30 September 2001, available at http://www.schneier.com/crypto-gram-0109a.html#8, last accessed 15 June 2008.

[7] See eg the UK government's submission to the ECtHR in the case of *Malone v UK* [1984] 7 EHRR 14.

particular, it will look at the right to privacy as embodied in Article 8 of the European Convention of Human Rights (ECHR), focusing on the protection of information privacy as a concept arising from the increased use of information processing technology. The chapter will explore the legal framework for the interception of (electronic) communications and the disclosure of encryption keys by trusted providers. It will outline the conflict between judicial and executive oversight of surveillance measures exemplified in the different approaches used in the UK and continental European jurisdictions, and it will consider the changes the UK was required to make to its approach as a consequence of European human rights legislation.

I. PRIVACY

Warren and Brandeis famously described privacy as 'the right to be let alone'[8] which right included an individual's right to control the communication of his 'thoughts, sentiments, and emotions'[9] to others. They based the need for privacy not only on existing concepts of property, contract and trust, but also on a notion that was only just developing at the time: the right to the protection of an individual's personality. A similar approach was taken in other countries during the twentieth century, most notably Germany whose Constitutional Court views privacy as an aspect of Germany's constitutional guarantee of individual self-determination.[10] A degree of self-determination is needed, it is claimed, to enable individuals to develop their own personality, to interact with other members of society on an equal footing, and to participate freely and without fear of prosecution in the democratic political process. Minor differences in interpretation notwithstanding, the 'privacy paradigm', as understood in most liberal democratic societies, seems to rest on an understanding of privacy as a necessary demarcation line between different individuals and between an individual and the state. This demarcation line, which 'ensures strong citadels of individual and group privacy'[11] and 'limits both disclosure and surveillance',[12] is seen as a prerequisite for liberal democratic societies. As Westin argues, democratic life 'relies on publicity as a control over government, and on privacy as a shield for group and individual life'.[13]

---

8 SD Warren and LD Brandeis, 'The Right to Privacy' (1890) 4 *Harvard Law Review* 193–220. In fact, the phrase 'right to be let alone' had been coined by Judge Cooley several years earlier. See TM Cooley, *A Treatise on the Law of Torts, Or the Wrongs Which Arise Independent of Contract*, 2nd edn (Chicago, Callaghan & Company, 1880) 29.

9 Ibid, 198.

10 BverfGE 65, 1.

11 AF Westin, *Privacy and Freedom* (New York, Atheneum, 1967) 24.

12 Ibid.

13 Ibid.

A. The Human Rights Approach

This view is reflected in the way in which the legal protection of privacy has been constructed across the world as part of the edifice of fundamental human and civil rights. Article 12 of the Universal Declaration of Human Rights of 1948 restricts the 'arbitrary interference' with a person's privacy, family, home or correspondence; the Fourth Amendment of the US Constitution includes the 'right of the people to be secure in their persons, houses, papers, and effects against unreasonable searches and seizures'; and numerous other national constitutions include similar protections and guarantees.

At a European level, Article 8(1) ECHR protects an individual's right to 'respect for his private and family life, his home and his correspondence'. The ECHR was opened for signature in Rome on 4 November 1950 and entered into force in September 1953. It requires Contracting States to adopt legislative and other measures to give effect to the Convention rights both in relation to interference by public authorities and (in a more limited way) by private organisations. Complaints under the ECHR can be brought against Contracting States either by other Contracting States or by individual applicants (individuals, groups of individuals or non-governmental organisations) resident in a Contracting State and affected by a violation by that State of a Convention right. It is interpreted and enforced by the European Court of Human Rights (ECtHR) in Strasbourg.

Much of the ECtHR's case-law in relation to privacy intrusions was developed in connection with a number of cases dealing with the interception of telephone conversations by law enforcement agencies. The court established in *Klass v Germany* that the use of covert surveillance technologies invariably engages Article 8 ECHR. It held that although telephone conversations are not expressly mentioned in Article 8(1) ECHR, 'such conversations were nonetheless covered by the notions of 'private life' and 'correspondence' referred to in that provision'.[14]

At the same time, Article 8(1) ECHR is not an absolute right. It is restricted by Article 8(2) ECHR, which provides that a public authority may interfere with the exercise of this right if such interference is

> necessary in a democratic society in the interests of national security, public safety or the economic well-being of the country, for the prevention of disorder or crime, for the protection of health or morals, or for the protection of the rights and freedoms of others.

Although the ECtHR accepts that the domestic legislature enjoys a 'margin of appreciation' concerning the fixing of the conditions under which a measure with the potential to interfere with Article 8(1) ECHR can be

---

[14] [1978] 2 EHRR 214. See also *Amann v Switzerland* (2000), 30 EHRR 843.

employed, it insists in *Klass* that the exception in Article 8(2) ECHR is to be narrowly interpreted.[15]

(i) *'In Accordance with the Law'*

In order for the interference by the public authority not to infringe Article 8(1) ECHR, it must be 'in accordance with the law'. In this context, 'law' is interpreted as covering not only written law but also unwritten law,[16] including case-law. However, in *Malone v UK* the ECtHR expressed the view that the phrase 'in accordance with the law' does not 'merely refer back to the existence of domestic law, but also relates to the quality of that law, requiring it to be compatible with the rule of law, which is expressly mentioned in the preamble to the Convention'.[17] In particular, the law in question must be 'adequately accessible' to the citizen and must be formulated with sufficient precision to enable the citizen to 'foresee, to a degree that is reasonable in the circumstances, the consequences which a given action may entail'.[18] Over the past 25 years, the UK 'has been found wanting in this area in a number of cases'.[19] In *Malone*, the ECtHR concluded that the UK government's tendency to use executive guidelines and conventions rather than primary legislation[20] to regulate measures interfering with citizens' right to privacy made it difficult for those citizens to distinguish with any certainty 'what elements of the power . . . are incorporated in legal rules and what elements remain within the discretion of the executive'.[21] To that extent, 'the minimum degree of legal protection to which citizens are entitled'[22] was found lacking in the UK.

(ii) *'Necessary in a Democratic Society'*

The law must also at all times remain 'within the bounds of what is necessary in a democratic society'.[23] In particular, the ECtHR must be satisfied that in relation to any interference with the right to privacy there 'exist adequate and effective guarantees against abuse'.[24] In this context, the

---

[15] Above n 14, para 42.

[16] *Malone v UK* [1984] 7 EHRR 14, para 66.

[17] Ibid, para 67.

[18] *Sunday Times v United Kingdom* [1983], 2 EHRR 245. The ECtHR took a similar line in *Kruslin v France* [1990] 12 EHRR 547 and *Kopp v Switzerland* [1997] 4 BHRC 277, concluding that in both cases the national law on which the restrictive measure was based did not meet the 'foreseeability' requirement.

[19] N Taylor, 'Policing, Privacy and Proportionality' (2003) *European Human Rights Law Review (EHRLR)* Suppl (Special issue: privacy) 86, 87.

[20] See 'Interception' below.

[21] Above n 16, para 79. The court took a similar view in *Leander v Sweden* [1987] 9 EHRR 433.

[22] Ibid.

[23] *Klass v Germany*, para 46.

[24] Ibid, para 50.

court observed in *Klass* that it has to take account of two important facts in its appreciation of the scope of protection offered by Article 8:

> The first consist of the technical advances made in the means of espionage and, correspondingly, of surveillance; the second is the development of terrorism in Europe in recent years. Democratic societies nowadays find themselves threatened by highly sophisticated forms of espionage and by terrorism, with the result that the State must be able, in order effectively to counter such threats, to undertake the secret surveillance of subversive elements operating within its jurisdiction.[25]

The court therefore accepted that the existence of some legislation granting powers of secret surveillance over, among others, telecommunications, was, 'under exceptional conditions, necessary in a democratic society in the interest of national security and/or for the prevention of disorder or crime'.[26]

(iii) Proportionality

Taylor argues that the principle of proportionality is in fact a 'vital factor'[27] in the ECtHR's jurisprudence that attempts 'to find a balance between the interests of the individual and the interest of the wider community',[28] despite the fact that it does not explicitly appear within the text of the ECHR itself. This is confirmed by the ECtHR in *Jersild v Denmark* where it held that it 'will look at the interference complained of . . . and determine whether the reasons adduced by the national authorities to justify it are relevant and sufficient and whether the means employed were proportionate to the legitimate aim pursued'.[29]

The ECtHR will also consider if there is a less restrictive alternative to the measure employed. For example, in *Campbell v United Kingdom*, the ECtHR found that a blanket rule on the opening of prisoners' mail was a disproportionate response to the problem of ensuring that prohibited material was not contained in the mail.[30] The court found that the same objective could have been met by opening the mail in the presence of the prisoner without actually reading it.

Measures interfering with a Convention right must also be subject to effective supervisory control. In relation to the interception of communications, the ECtHR stated in *Klass* that 'it is *in principle* desirable to entrust [such control] to a judge'.[31] Judicial review of surveillance measures, in

---

25 Ibid, para 48.
26 Ibid.
27 Above n 19, 88.
28 Ibid.
29 *Jersild v Denmark* [1995] 19 EHRR 1.
30 [1993] 15 EHRR 137.
31 Above n 23, 56 (emphasis added).

particular, may intervene at three stages: when the surveillance is first ordered, while it is being carried out, or after it has been terminated. The ECtHR held:

> As regards the first two stages, the very nature and logic of secret surveillance dictate that not only the surveillance itself but also the accompanying review should be effected without the individual's knowledge. Consequently, since the individual will necessarily be prevented from seeking an effective remedy of his own accord or from taking a direct part in any review proceedings, it is essential that the procedures established should themselves provide adequate and equivalent guarantees safeguarding the individual's rights.[32]

However, in the case of *Klass* the court accepted that extra-judicial supervisory authorities established by the German government to oversee interceptions[33] were sufficiently independent of the authorities carrying out the surveillance, and were vested with the necessary powers and competence to exercise effective and continuous control. In *Malone*, where the court did not address the issue of supervisory control because it had already decided that the UK system of authorising an interception was not 'in accordance with the law', Pettiti J criticised that approach in his concurring opinion and called for a distinction to be drawn between the dangers of a crisis situation caused by terrorism (as was the case in *Klass*) and the dangers of ordinary criminality (as in *Malone*). He argued that '[i]n so far as the prevention of crime under the ordinary law is concerned, it is difficult to see a reason for ousting judicial control', particularly if, as the British government suggested, only suspected criminals were placed under surveillance.

Over the past 25 years, the ECtHR has developed a framework for the way in which Article 8 ECHR should be applied to the question of surveillance and intereception that subjects governments' assertions about the need to restrict individual rights for the purpose of national security to greater scrutiny. In this context, the UK has been at the receiving end of the Strasbourg court's judgments rather more frequently than other signatory states. Much of this is likely to be due to the deferential attitude of the English courts to legislative decisions taken by the British Parliament—an attitude that arises from the doctrine of parliamentary and legislative supremacy, which forms the basis of English constitutional law and which

---

[32] Ibid, para 55.

[33] In 1967, the German government had adopted an amendment to Art 10 of the German Basic Law (the German Constitution) permitting the restriction of the general right to the secrecy of telecommunications on the basis of statutory law. Where the restriction is intended to protect 'the free democratic constitutional order or the existence or security of the Federation or a Land', that statute may replace the individual's general right to be notified of any interception and his normal legal remedies through the courts by a system of scrutiny by agencies and auxiliary agencies appointed by Parliament. The German Parliament appointed the G10 Commission, which is responsible for the supervision of the ordering of interception measures. It consists of three members, of which the Chairman must be legally qualified.

provides that Parliament is free, at every moment of its existence as a continuing body, not only from its own prior legislation but also from 'legal limitations imposed *ab extra*'.[34] In relation to the protection of human rights, this attitude has been criticised by many commentators who have argued that the Convention should 'set a floor and not a ceiling to the protection of individual rights':[35]

> The concept of a 'margin of appreciation' recognises the role of national institutions (including national courts) to insist on higher standards. For the English courts merely to adopt a 'Strasbourg' approach would risk creating a lacuna where, by default, it is the Government which claims the benefit of the flexible margin.[36]

With the incorporation of the Convention into domestic UK law by virtue of the Human Rights Act 1998 (HRA), which came into force on 2 October 2000, the importance of the ECtHR's interpretation of Article 8 ECHR has, if anything, increased. Despite their continued reluctance to overturn legislative measures adopted by Parliament, the UK courts are now required, so far as it is possible, to read and give effect to domestic legislation 'in a way which is compatible with the Convention rights'.[37] Furthermore, it is unlawful for public authorities to act in a way that is incompatible with Convention rights.[38] Individuals or companies can therefore enforce their Convention rights against public authorities under section 6 HRA.

Although the HRA provides that the House of Lords does not have the power to declare void laws passed by the UK Parliament if they violate any of the provisions of the HRA, section 4(2) HRA grants a right to the courts to make a 'declaration of incompatibility' where they conclude that a piece of legislation has been passed in contravention of any Convention right. While there is an expectation that Parliament will then amend the Act in question, it is under no legal—merely a moral—obligation to do this. Although the HRA has undoubtedly contributed to changing the attitude of British society as a whole, and of the legal profession in particular, towards the need for a constitutional framework protecting citizens from state interference, it is likely that the ECtHR will continue to take the lead in relation to the interpretation of Article 8 as applicable to electronic intrusions for some time to come.

---

[34] HLA Hart, *The Concept of Law* (Oxford, Clarendon Press, 1961) 145.
[35] See eg A Nicol, 'National Security Considerations and the Limits of European Supervision' (1996) 1 *EHRLR* 37, 44.
[36] Ibid.
[37] HRA s 3.
[38] HRA s 6(1).

II. SURVEILLANCE

The balance between the right to privacy and the need to preserve national security and fight crime is 'now perceived to have shifted in favour of law enforcement'.[39] Much of the anti-terrorism legislation adopted in the wake of the attacks in the US, London and Madrid relies heavily on surveillance techniques that amount to severe privacy intrusions. At the same time a paradigm shift seems to have taken place in the way the state and the public perceive the role of law enforcement and intelligence services (collectively referred to hereafter as law enforcement agencies (LEAs)). Rather than investigating and prosecuting crimes already committed, LEAs in their new role will focus, rather in the way depicted in the movie *Minority Report*,[40] on the prevention of crimes that may be committed in the future. Easy access to information about all citizens (rather than just those under concrete suspicion) is deemed to be necessary for the 'profiling' and categorising that underpin this preventative approach, and the facilitation of that access constitutes one of the cornerstones of the new policy. Benett and Raab have pointed out that while the problems arising from privacy intrusion often tend to be seen in terms of a combination of human and technological fallibility (non-observance of organisational procedures combined with inaccuracies, security failures, etc), in a situation where 'technologies and humans combine perfectly to pursue organisational goals . . . there is not necessarily a concomitant lowering of the risk to privacy'.[41]

> Indeed the fear of the 'surveillance society' in which our personal data can be matched, profiled, mined, warehoused and manipulated for a range of social and economic ends is premised exactly on the fear that human agents and new technologies will combine as *intended* to reach new levels of intrusiveness, and from which there is no escape.[42]

Although governments do not routinely reveal the functionalities of the surveillance techniques they employ, the switch from reactive to proactive policing was accompanied by a noticeable trend towards the increased use by LEAs of technical surveillance devices. The development of the Internet as a major communications technology has supported that switch by re-defining the traditional telephone wiretap and offering LEAs new methods of surveillance. From the interception of electronic communications and the disclosure of encryption keys to the retention of communications

---

[39] VO Benjamin, 'Interceptions of Internet Communications and the Right to Privacy: An Evaluation of Some Provisions of the Regulation of Investigatory Powers Act against the Jurisprudence of the European Court of Human Rights' (2007) 6 *EHRLR* 637, 637.

[40] Steven Spielberg (2002).

[41] CJ Benett and CD Raab, *The Governance of Privacy*, 2nd edn (Cambridge, MA, MIT Press, 2006) 26.

[42] Ibid.

data[43] and 'online searches' through the installation of spyware on citizens' personal communications devices, LEAs have strived to adapt their policing techniques to the changing technological environment. The warnings of privacy advocates are commonly set aside on the basis that the use of modern technology now enables us to distinguish between measures that are 'truly' privacy intrusive (which are to be avoided) and measures taken in the interest of the 'common good' whose benefits outweigh their negative implications.

> We are now in a position where we can approach these problems in a differentiated way because we have an arsenal of possible regulatory instruments at our disposal. . . . There is therefore no need for us to say either 'Yes' or 'No'. Instead, we can distinguish as appropriate when, for example, defining the factual circumstances on which a statutory authorisation must be based, when determining who may legitimately be the subject of regulation and the perimeters of the various uses of information. In each case we can respond to the specific requirements of the situation.[44]

However, in the same way as the categorisation and profiling of consumers' habits and preferences allows the exploitation of those habits and preferences by the burgeoning direct-marketing industry, the availability to LEAs of highly specific and increasingly extensive knowledge about citizens' behaviour, and the risk of abuse of that knowledge, raises serious issues for the right to privacy and for the democratic polity.

In view of the increased use of modern information and communications technology for everyday activities, this applies especially in relation to the monitoring of people's online communications. While such monitoring does not necessarily imply the existence of a 'surveillance society', one could argue that it calls for highly effective organisational, technical and regulatory security features to protect citizens from the virtual equivalent of Jeremy Bentham's 'panopticon' (the fictional prison whose inmates could all be watched from a central point without them being able to establish when and to what extent such observation would take place). This is confirmed by the ECtHR which confirmed that a reasonable expectation of privacy also applies in the case of e-mail and Internet usage,[45] so that the principles developed in relation to telephone tapping are likely to be transferable to electronic intrusions. The legislative and policy instruments employed in the move from offline to online surveillance and from 'investigative prosecuting' towards 'proactive preventative' policing therefore deserve particular attention.

---

[43] See Rauhofer, ch 18.
[44] HP Bull, 'Zweifelsfragen um die informationelle Selbstbestimmung—Datenschutz als Datenaskese', [2006] *Neue Juristische Wochenschrift* 1617, 1619, translation by the author.
[45] See eg *Copland v United Kingdom* [2007] ECHR 62617/00.

A. Interception

Historically, it has been argued that in the UK there has been a repeated failure to provide adequate legislative control of the interception of communications which extends back into the nineteenth century.[46] At the time, Sir James Graham, the Secretary of State, had opened the letters of Italian revolutionary Guiseppe Mazzini and had communicated some of their contents to the Neapolitan government. The affair caused a stir in Britain as it raised a fear among the population that the practice of opening letters was widespread and that letters of ordinary citizens were not immune from interception.

In 1957, the Birkett Report,[47] which enquired into the interception of communications by public authorities, concluded that, despite the fact that the power was not regulated by legislation, the executive's right to intercept both postal and (later) telephone communications was widely acknowledged 'from early times' and that 'its exercise has been publicly known'.[48] At the time of the report, the grounds on which any authority to intercept should be based were included in a letter sent by the Home Office to the Metropolitan Police and Customs in 1951 (the '1951 Letter'). It stated that to justify an interception (i) the offence under investigation had to be really serious; (ii) normal methods of investigation must have been tried and failed, or must, from their nature, be unlikely to succeed; and (iii) there had to be good reason to think that the interception would result in a conviction.[49]

(i) The Interception of Communications Act 1985

In the mid-1980s, the ECtHR's decision in *Malone* forced the UK government to 'delineate more precisely, by way of statutory provisions, the circumstances and mechanisms which would allow for the lawful interception of communications'.[50] As a result, the Interception of Communications Act 1985 (ICA) received Royal Assent on 25 July 1985. The purpose of the Act, in the words of the then Home Secretary, was to provide 'a clear and comprehensive statutory framework for the interception of communications' as well as a 'means of redress and an effective one, for those wishing to complain that interception has been improperly authorised'[51].

---

[46] D Ormerod and S McKay, 'Telephone Intercepts and their Admissibility' [2004] *Criminal Law Review* Jan 15, 18.

[47] Cmnd 283 'Report of Privy Councillors appointed to inquire into the interception of communications' (1967) (Birkett Report), para 11.

[48] Ibid.

[49] Ibid, para 64.

[50] SA Price, 'The Interception of Communications Act 1985: An Examination of the Government's Proposals for Reform' (1999) 5(6) *Computer and Telecommunications Law Review (CTLR)* 163, 164.

[51] Rt Hon Leon Britten MP, HC Debs, Vol 75, col 151, 12 March 1985.

Section 2(2) ICA granted power to the Home Secretary to issue an interception warrant if he considered that it was in the interest of national security or for the purpose of preventing or detecting serious crime or safeguarding the economic wellbeing of the UK. 'Serious crime' included any offence which 'involves the use of violence, results in substantial financial gain or is conducted by a large number of persons in pursuit of a common purpose' as well as any offence for which a person over the age of 21 who has no previous convictions could reasonably be expected to be sentenced to imprisonment for three years or more.[52] Section 7 ICA established a Tribunal responsible for investigating complaints by individuals who believed that their communications had been intercepted without a proper warrant.[53] The decisions of the Tribunal were not subject to judicial review by the courts.

(ii) The Regulation of Investigatory Powers Act 2000

The framework established by the ICA was frequently criticised for being too vague, particularly in relation to the grounds for interception. For example, when deciding whether a warrant was necessary in the interest of national security, the Home Secretary was merely required to consider whether the information that was the subject of the warrant 'could reasonably be acquired by other means'.[54] This requirement was noticeably less stringent than even the guidelines set out in the 1951 Letter.[55]

The restrictions the ICA imposed on the work of the Tribunal were also condemned for continuing to prevent judicial or parliamentary scrutiny of the interception activities of the executive.[56] Finally, it was argued that a list of 'serious arrestable offences', as it was contained, for example, in section 116 of the Police and Criminal Evidence Act 1984, would have provided greater legal certainty than the definition of 'serious crime' on section 10(3) ICA[57], notwithstanding the fact that this would in some respects have widened the scope of the offences covered.

Lord Mustill summed up the general feeling about the ICA in *R v Preston,* when he called it a 'short but difficult statute'.[58] However, in the end it was the rapid development of new information and communications technology, together with the introduction of the HRA and the defeat of the government in *Halford v United Kingdom*[59] where the ECtHR held that

---

[52] ICA s 10(3).
[53] ICA s 7(9).
[54] ICA s 2(3).
[55] Above n 49.
[56] See eg I Leigh, 'A Tapper's Charter?' [1986] *Public Law (PL)* 8, 18; and IJ Lloyd, 'The Interception of Communications Act 1985' (1986) 49(1) *Modern Law Review* 86–95.
[57] See eg B Vaughan 'Is Anybody There' [1980] *PL* 431.
[58] [1994] 2 AC 130 (148).
[59] [1997] 24 EHRR 523.

the ICA did not apply to interceptions of calls made on private telecommunications networks,[60] that prompted calls for a renewal of the regulation of surveillance measures.

In June 1999, the government published a consultation paper[61] proposing considerable reforms of the existing statutory regime and extending the application of the existing legislation to new areas. In particular, the government aimed to 'provide a single legal framework which deals with all interception of communications in the United Kingdom, regardless of the means of communication, how it is licensed or at which point on the route of communication it is intercepted'.[62] This was not only intended to address the issues raised in *Halford*; it also aimed to extend the scope of the ICA to providers of new communications services such as Internet service providers (ISPs) particularly in relation to the interception of electronic mail.

Following much controversy in both Houses of Parliament, the Regulation of Investigatory Powers Act 2000 (RIPA) received Royal Assent on 28 July 2000. It came into force in stages under a number of Commencement Orders over the following six years. Part I, Chapter I of RIPA, which deals with the interception of communications, came into force on 2 October 2000.[63] RIPA includes a general offence of unauthorised interception of 'any communication in the course of its transmission' whether by means of, among other things, a public[64] or a private[65] telecommunications system. Interceptions are lawful where they take place with the consent of both the sender and the recipient of the communication[66] or where they are carried out by the communications service provider for purposes connected with the provision or operation of that service or for the purpose of the provider's compliance with his legal and regulatory obligations.[67]

(a) Interception Warrants

Section 4 RIPA provides a defence to the section 1 tort of unlawful interception if interceptions are carried out on the basis of a warrant issued by the Secretary of State. The Secretary of State may issue a warrant, if he believes that it is necessary for certain purposes specified in section 5(3) RIPA ('RIPA purposes') and that the interception authorised by the warrant

[60] Accordingly, such interceptions were found not to be 'in accordance with the law'.
[61] Cmnd 4368, 'Interception of Communications in the United Kingdom: A Consultation Paper' (1999).
[62] Ibid, para 4.1.
[63] The Regulation of Investigator Powers Act 2000 (Commencement No 1 and Transitional Provisions) Order 2000 (SI2000/2543).
[64] RIPA s 1(1)(a).
[65] RIPA s 1(2).
[66] RIPA s 3(1).
[67] RIPA s 3(3).

is proportionate[68] to its aim.[69] The RIPA purposes are identical to the purposes previously included in section 2(2) ICA. In addition, the Secretary of State now has the power to issue a serious crime warrant in response to a request for assistance under an international mutual assistance agreement. Despite the criticism aimed at it by commentators and observers,[70] the definition of 'serious crime' first included in the ICA is retained in section 81(3) RIPA.

Interceptions under Part I, Chapter I RIPA are governed by the Interception Code of Practice (ICP) issued by the Home Office in 2002,[71] which is designed to underpin the warrant provisions. It provides guidance on the procedures that must be followed before interception of communications can take place under those provisions. In April 2009, the Home Office published a consultation paper on existing RIPA powers, including a review of which public authorities can use those powers, and proposals to issue consolidating orders listing all the public authorities able to grant authorisations under RIPA.[72] As part of the consultation, the government proposed to make a small number of changes to the ICP. However, as the changes to the ICP are intended to be minor, the government did not include the revised ICP in that consultation exercise. Instead, it announced that the revised ICP would be published (and any representations made on the code would be considered) before being subject to debate in Parliament and replacing the existing code.[73]

(b) Confidential Information and Legal Privilege

RIPA does not provide any special protection for 'confidential information'. Nevertheless, the government advises intercepting authorities to take particular care in cases where the subject of the investigation or operation might reasonably expect a high degree of privacy, or where confidential information is involved.[74] Confidential information consists of communications between a Member of Parliament and another person on constituency matters, confidential personal information, confidential journalistic material or matters subject to legal privilege.

Under paragraph 3.4 of the ICP, 'legal privilege does not apply to communications made with the intention of furthering a criminal purpose (whether the lawyer is acting unwittingly or culpably)'. If a warrant is

[68] The proportionality requirement was included in order to make RIPA compliant with the HRA and in light of the increased relevance of the concept in ECtHR case-law.

[69] RIPA s 5(2)(b).

[70] See n 56 above.

[71] The Code of Practice was adopted under s 71 RIPA through The Regulation of Investigatory Powers (Interception of Communications: Code of Practice) Order 2002 (SI 2002/1693).

[72] Home Office consultation, 'Regulation of Investigatory Powers Act 2000: Consolidating Orders and Codes of Practice', 17 April 2009, available at http://www.homeoffice.gov.uk/documents/cons-2009-ripa?view=Binary. Last accessed 29 June 2009.

[73] Ibid, 7–8.

[74] ICP para 3.2.

likely to result in the interception of legally privileged communications, the application should include 'an assessment of how likely it is that communications which are subject to legal privilege will be intercepted'.[75] If communications which include legally privileged communications have been intercepted and retained, the matter 'should be reported to the Interception of Communications Commissioner during his inspections and the material be made available to him if requested'.[76] In *Re Mc E (Appellant) (Northern Ireland) (and other joined cases)*,[77] the House of Lords, by majority decision, held that, although legal privilege has been held by the ECtHR to be part of the right of privacy guaranteed by Article 8 ECHR,[78] Article 8 does not impose an absolute prohibition on surveillance, provided it is authorised by law and is proportionate. Although the decision related to covert human surveillance rather than the interception of communications, the court's findings are a useful aid to the way in which the relationship between RIPA and the ECHR should be viewed in the area of legal privilege.

The court argued that although, in general, privileged consultations are inviolable, there is a need for exceptions, as recognised in *R v Cox and Railton*,[79] where Stephen J identified the reasons why communications in furtherance of crime should not be covered by the rule of legal professional privilege. The law would confer an 'unjustified immunity on dishonest lawyers'[80] if covert surveillance of legal consultations was not permitted even where there were strong grounds for suspecting that the privilege was being abused. In addition, the ICP includes detailed provisions on how to obtain authorisation for monitoring consultations subject to legal privilege. The court therefore concluded that it would be surprising that no objections were voiced about the inclusion of these provisions in the Code, if Parliament had not intended such consultations to be covered by RIPA.

(c) Interception Capability

Section 12 RIPA allows the Secretary of State to impose an obligation on public telecommunications providers to maintain an 'interception capability'. This provision was the subject of substantial controversy when the RIP Bill was first discussed, as ISPs, in particular, feared that the cost of installing such capabilities (which cost, at the time, they were expected to bear) would stifle development of their fledgling industry. In the face of threats by many of the larger providers that they would move their services to more business-friendly jurisdictions, the government eventually agreed

---

[75] ICP para 3.4.
[76] ICP para 3.6.
[77] [2009] UKHL 15.
[78] See eg *Campbell v United Kingdom* (1992) 15 EHRR 137 and *Foxley v United Kingdom* (2000) 31 EHRR 637.
[79] [1884] 14 QBD 153.
[80] *Re Mc E (Appellant) (Northern Ireland) (and other joined cases)*, para. 102.

to make the requirement subject to a specific notice by the Home Secretary. It also guaranteed that providers would receive 'a fair contribution towards the costs incurred'.[81]

In view of the technical difficulties involved in maintaining intercept capability, particularly in relation to electronic communications, the government also agreed to establish a Technical Advisory Board, comprising six representatives from the security services and six from industry, which the Home Secretary must consult before making an order to install intercept capabilities.[82]

(d) Oversight

Oversight of RIPA activities falls to a judicially qualified Commissioner and a Tribunal.[83] The Interception of Communications Commissioner is responsible for reviewing the granting and exercise of interception warrants although not all authorisations will be subject to scrutiny. Instead, the Commissioner will randomly select a number of warrants each year and report any errors found in an annual report. Complementing the activities of the Commissioners, Part IV of RIPA establishes the Investigatory Powers Tribunal as a means of receiving complaints under section 7(1)(a) HRA and providing redress to individuals. However, these oversight arrangements provide only a minimal standard of compliance with the requirements of Article 8 ECHR, particularly as regards the focus on retrospective review and the lack of independent judicial authorisation of activities. As Ferguson and Wadham argue:

> Retrospective review is likely to be less rigorous than prior scrutiny and it may well be easier to satisfy the requirements of necessity and proportionality when armed with the incriminating results of the surveillance. This creates the risk that although the statutory authorisation regime may comply with Article 8, individual exercises of the investigatory powers could be unnecessary or disproportionate.[84]

While the Tribunal's jurisdiction looks, at first glance, comprehensive, its efficacy as a check and balance on an overzealous surveillance apparatus has repeatedly been called into question. The absence of any obligation of the intercepting agency to disclose the interception to the subject of the surveillance even after it has taken place means that, in the majority of cases, the individual will not be aware of being monitored and will therefore be unlikely to lodge a complaint. The secrecy surrounding the Tribunal proceedings and the lack of an appeals process denies the

---

81 RIPA s 14(1).

82 RIPA ss 13 and 12(9)(b). An almost identical approach was used in 2009 in the context of the introduction of mandatory data retention requirements for communications service providers, see Rauhofer, ch DP5.

83 RIPA ss 57 and 65.

84 G Ferguson and J Wadham, 'Privacy and Surveillance: A Review of the Regulation of Investigatory Powers Act 2000' [2003] *EHRLR* Suppl (Special issue: privacy) 101, 105.

individual an opportunity to have deficiencies in the initial hearing remedied at a later stage. Ferguson and Wadham argue that 'the impact of these limitations is perhaps reflected in the fact that neither the Tribunal nor its predecessors have upheld a single complaint'.[85]

Overall the interception provisions contained in Part I, Chapter I RIPA have been condemned by human rights campaigners not only for their lack of judicial authorisation or oversight, but also for the expansiveness of the grounds on which a warrant may be based, the lack of protection of legally privileged material and the broadness of the exceptions to the warrant requirement.[86]

In particular, the requirement—as a condition precedent to the issuance of a warrant—of the 'belief' of the Secretary of State that an interception is necessary is overly subjective, especially in the light of the constraint— emphasised by the ECtHR in *Klass*—that covert surveillance measures should only be permitted to the extend that they are 'strictly necessary for safeguarding the democratic institutions'.[87] Arguably, the effect of RIPA on individual privacy is disproportionately high in relation to the interception of electronic communications as 'Internet usage is transforming more into a way of life than a way of communicating and, in this regard, . . . goes beyond the traditional post and telecommunication'.[88] Interception of those communications may thus 'amount to an unprecedented intrusion on a person's seclusion not dissimilar to interference with a person's very thoughts'.[89] This sentiment has been given some credence in a recent decision by the German Constitutional Court, which granted special protection to a 'right to the confidentiality and integrity of information technology systems'.[90] However, to date the argument has not been adopted by the ECtHR.

(e) Circumvention of RIPA Safeguards in Practice

The safeguards in RIPA, such as they are, have been rendered still less protective by the High Court decision, *R (on the application of NTL Group Ltd) v Ipswich Crown Court*.[91] Here, the court confirmed the right of the

---

85 Ibid, 106.

86 See eg Y Akdeniz, 'Regulation of Investigatory Powers Act 2000: Part 1: BigBrother. gov.uk:state Surveillance in the Age of Information and Rights' (2000) *Criminal Law Review* 73, 79; G Crossman with H Kitchin, R Kuna, M Skrein and J Russell, 'Overlooked: Surveillance and Personal privacy in Modern Britain' (Liberty Report, 2007).

87 Above n 25.

88 V Okechukwu Benjamin, 'Interception of Internet Communications and the Right to Privacy: An Evaluation of some Provisions of the Regulation of Investigatory Powers Act against the Jurisprudence of the European Court of Human Rights' (2007) 6 *EHRLR* 637–48, 645.

89 Ibid.

90 BVerfG, 1 BvR 370/07 of 27 February 2008, German version available at http://www. bundesverfassungsgericht.de/entscheidungen/rs20080227_1bvr037007.html?Suchbegriff=onli ne, last visited on 9 April 2008.

91 [2003] QB 131 (QBD (Admin)). This decision has also been confirmed in *R v Allsopp* [2005] EWCA Crim 703, [2005] All ER (D) 310 (Mar).

police to require telecommunications provider NTL to take steps to intercept e-mail not on the basis of a warrant under section 5 RIPA but under wider police powers to obtain evidence in a criminal investigation contained in section 9 of the Police and Criminal Evidence Act 1984 (PACE). Woolf LCJ and Curtis J held that section 1(5)(c) RIPA, which states that interception is lawful if it is employed under any statutory power that is exercised 'for the purpose of obtaining information or of taking possession of any document or other property', means that LEAs can continue to exercise existing police powers. Lord Woolf commented:

> I find it impossible to accept that it was the intention of Parliament in legislating in the terms that it did in section 1 of the RIP Act for all practical purposes to defeat the powers of the police under section 9 in this area.[92]

The decision has been criticised,[93] however, on the grounds that the carve-out in section 1 RIPA on which the Court relied specifically refers to 'any stored communication'. Lundie argues that this suggests that the information should already be in existence at the time of the exercise of the statutory power. In the case in question, however, NTL routinely overwrote e-mails and had to put in place specific technical provisions enabling it to copy the e-mails to a different system for later use, in order to comply with the PACE order. It is at least questionable if this procedure would stand up to scrutiny by the ECtHR as it is likely to allow LEAs to circumvent what little safeguards are included in RIPA.

III. ENCRYPTION AND ACCESS TO ENCRYPTED INFORMATION

In the wake of the exponential growth in the use of the Internet in the mid-1990s, questions were raised about the security of communications transmitted via the new network. The use of cryptography and cryptographic techniques to ensure the integrity of messages and data packets and to authenticate the sender of such messages became increasingly common. Encrypting messages implies, in short, 'the use of algorithms to encrypt data in order to render it unintelligible to third parties who do not have the secret information necessary to decrypt the message'.[94] This 'cryptographic key' must be used both for encrypting the message and decrypting it. Two common techniques for encrypting electronic data are private key encryption and public key encryption. Private key encryption involves parties using identical (symmetrical) keys to communicate with one another. Each party is in possession of the same secret key and uses it to decrypt messages

---

[92] Ibid.

[93] See eg A Lundie, 'High Court Confirms Police Powers to Intercept Emails (Case Comment)' (2003) 9(1) *CTLR* 10, 11.

[94] P Gerard and G Broze, 'Encryption: An Overview of European Policies: IT, Telecoms and Broadcasting' (1997) 3(4) *CTLR* 168.

received from the other party. Public key encryption, or public key infrastructure (PKI), avoids the need for sharing (and thereby putting at risk of disclosure) a single, secret key by using a pair of non-identical (asymmetrical) keys—a public and a private key—that are deployed in combination. A party (A) will share or even publish its public key while keeping its private key secret. To send messages to A using PKI, the sender (B) needs to use A's public key to encrypt the message he is sending. A will then use his private key to decrypt the message. The public keys of businesses or individuals will usually be stored by 'trusted third parties' (TTPs) providing PKI services.

A. Historical Background

Until the early 1970, cryptographic techniques were mainly used by military and intelligence services to ensure secure communications. Although no legal restrictions existed on the 'importation, possession or use of encryption technology' within the EU, its export to non-EU Member States was subject to export controls for dual-use goods.[95] In the UK, cryptographic systems were included in a list of controlled technologies produced by the Co-ordinating Committee for Multilateral Export Control (COCOM) until it was disbanded in 1994.[96]

However, with the increased use of computer networks by businesses, particularly in the financial sector, encryption became of growing importance to commerce and industry.[97] At the same time, governments became increasingly concerned about the impact that the use of strong encryption techniques would have on law enforcement and national security. In the US, the Clinton administration proposed an Escrowed Encryption Standard (EES) which used a classified symetrical algorithm developed by the National Securicy Agency (NSA). Escrowed encryption meant that two government agencies, the National Institute of Standards and Technology and the Department of Treasury, each held one half of the encryption key. The US government's initial plan was to demand the installation of the technology, which became known as the 'Clipper Chip', in all telecommunications equipment in order to enforce it as a national standard. This would have meant that the above agencies would have been able to decrypt all communications sent using chipped equipment. The proposal was highly controversial, however, so that, in May 1996, the US government revised

[95] Cryptographic hardware and software were listed in Annex 1 (Part 2 of Category 5) of Council Regulations 3381/94 OJ L367/1 which provided that information security equipment and software which uses digital encryption techniques could not be exported without a licence.

[96] For an excellent description of the regulatory regime in the UK in the mid-1990s, see C Ward, 'Regulation of the Use of Cryptographic Systems in the United Kingdom: The Policy and Practice' (1997) 3(3) *CTLR* 105, 108.

[97] See further on the commercial significance of encryption, Riefa and Hornle, ch 2.

its position in a document titled 'Achieving Privacy, Commerce, Security and Public Safety in the Global Information Infrastructure'.[98] Instead, it proposed the establishment of a PKI which would allow the use (including the export) of cryptographic software provided it was escrowed with an approved agent. Implied in these plans was the assumption that those agents would disclose an escrowed key to LEAs if it was needed to decrypt a message in the context of a criminal or national security investigation.

The UK government followed this concept of 'approved agencies' when it published its own White Paper on 'Regulatory Intent Concerning Use of Encryption on Open Networks' in June 1996,[99] including plans to bring forward proposals for the licensing and regulation of TTPs. In March 1997, the outgoing Conservative government issued a public consultation paper entitled 'Licensing of Trusted Third Parties for the Provision of Encryption Services' which included detailed proposals on the regulation of TTPs.[100] Organisations providing encryption services would be required to be licensed. Law enforcement, security and intelligence agencies would be given the right to obtain access to encryption keys held in escrow by TTPs.

Around the same time, the OECD Council published a set of guidelines for cryptography policy. Interestingly, these guidelines did not refer directly to PKI and TTP structures, but instead included a number of principles that emphasised the importance of the use of cryptographic techniques for the establishment of an information society and a functioning e-commerce market. Principle 5 of the guidelines provided that 'fundamental rights of individuals to privacy, including secrecy of communications and protection of personal data, should be respected in national cryptography policies and in the implementation and use of cryptographic methods'.[101]

New Labour's victory in the General Election in May 1997 originally delayed the introduction of a bill dealing with encryption technologies. However, although Labour, in its pre-election manifesto document 'Communicating Britain's Future', had rejected a 'Clipper'Chip' style use of PKI, once in government, it adjusted to the idea and in April 1998, it issued a Statement on secure electronic commerce. Although the mandatory licensing requirement was dropped, the legislation proposed a voluntary licensing system for TTPs providing encryption and key recovery services. In response to concerns that '[e]ncryption might be used to prevent law

[98] Available at http://epic.org/crypto/key_escrow/white_paper.html, last accessed 12 April 2008.

[99] Paper on Regulatory Intent Concerning Use of Encryption on Public Networks, DTI, June 10 1996.

[100] Public Consultation Paper, March 1997, available at http://www.cl.cam.ac.uk/~rja14/dti.html, last accessed 15 June 2008.

[101] OECD Cryptography Policy Guidelines: Recommendation of the Council Concerning Guidelines for Cryptography Policy, 27 March 1997, available at http://www.oecd.org/document/11/0,3343,de_2649_34255_1814731_1_1_1_1,00.html, last accessed 12 April 2008.

enforcement agencies from understanding electronic data seized as the result of a search warrant or communications intercepted under a warrant issued by a Secretary of State',[102] the government signaled its intention to enable LEAs to obtain a warrant for lawful access to the encryption key.

In March 1999, it published a consultation document entitled 'Building Confidence In Electronic Commerce',[103] followed by a further consultation paper in July 1999 called 'Promoting Electronic Commerce'.[104] The latter included a draft Electronic Communications Bill (ECB).[105]

The encryption provisions of the ECB were hugely controversial and attracted widespread criticism not only from human rights campaigners but also from the business community. Civil liberties groups felt that 'demanding decryption keys was an over-aggressive invasion of privacy and security'.[106] Businesses argued that any disclosure of an encryption key, including disclosure to LEAs, could compromise the security of that key. This, in turn, was likely to undermine public trust in the encryption infrastructure designed to underpin secure e-commerce. Consequently, such provisions had no place in legislation with the purported objective of 'Promoting Electronic Commerce'.[107] It was also suggested that the introduction of a PKI system could have a negative impact on the competitiveness of the UK e-economy. If key escrow was introduced in the UK, then firms would turn to foreign TTPs for their cryptographic requirements.

This condemnation eventually forced the government's hand and it announced, on the day of the Queen's Speech in 1999, that it had dropped Part III of the Bill. Instead, it was included with very minor changes as Part III of the Regulation of Investigatory Powers Bill that was adopted by Parliament, despite an equally high level of controversy, in July 2000.[108]

---

[102] Secure electronic commerce statement made by Parlimentary Under-Secretary Barbara Roche in April 1998, available at http://fipr.org/polarch/secst.html (last accessed 23 July 2009).

[103] Building Confidence in Electronic Commerce—A Consultation Document, URN 99/642, 5th March 1999, available at http://www.cyber-rights.org/crypto/consfn1.pdf, last accessed 12 April 2008.

[104] Cm 4417.

[105] For an in-depth analysis and critique of the Bill, see eg C Wardle, 'The draft Electronic Communications Bill' (1999) 5(8) *CTLR* 235, and H Rowe 'Promoting Electronic Commerce: Consultation on draft UK Legislation and the UK Government's Response to the Trade and Industry Committee's Report on Electronic Commerce' (1999) 1(7) *Journal of International Financial Markets* 289.

[106] Ibid, para 6.2. See also the Legal Opinion, jointly commissioned by FIPR and JUSTICE, on the human rights aspects of the draft ECB, available at http://www.fipr.org/ecomm99/ecommaud.html, last accessed on 15 June 2008.

[107] See The House of Commons Select Committee on Trade and Industry, 'Report on Building Confidence in Electronic Commerce: The Government's Proposals', HC 187, Seventh Report of session 1998–99, 19 May 1999.

[108] See 'Interception' above.

B. Part III of RIPA

Section 49(2) RIPA grants certain persons listed in Schedule 2 to RIPA the right to serve notice ('section 49 notice') on any person believed, on reasonable grounds, to be in possession of an encryption key to disclose that key. The key must be capable of decrypting 'protected information' obtained through seizure or interception.[109] The imposition of a disclosure requirement must be necessary in the interests of national security, for the purpose of preventing or detecting crime or in the interests of the economic well-being of the UK.[110] As with the conditions for obtaining an interception warrant under Part I, Chapter I RIPA, the imposition of the disclosure requirement must be proportionate to the aim it seeks to achieve and it must not be reasonably practicable to gain access to the protected information in an intelligible form without imposing such a disclosure requirement.

While section 49 mainly deals with notices served on TTPs in possession of public keys, section 50 deals with the effects of a notice that has been served on a person in possession of a private key who is also in possession of the information to be decrypted. In this case, the disclosure requirement consists, in the first instance, of an obligation to use the key to decrypt the information and to disclose it to the requester in 'intelligible form'.[111] Alternatively, the recipient of the notice may also disclose the key itself.[112] However, under section 50(3), the person serving the section 49 notice can still request the disclosure of the key, if the notice states that it can only be complied with by the disclosure of the key itself. Section 50 could therefore be said to drive a coach and horses through the safeguards provided by the ability to substitute key disclosure with disclosure of the protected information itself.[113] That risk has only partially been addressed through the introduction of section 51 RIPA, which provides that only senior officers of the relevant agency have the right to give a direction under section 50(3) RIPA. They must believe that the purposes for which key disclosure is imposed would be defeated if the direction were not given, and that the giving of the direction is proportionate to the aim that is sought to be achieved by requiring disclosure of the key itself rather than the protected information in intelligible form. Whether these safeguards will be sufficient to uphold the substance of section 50 (1) and (2) remains to be seen.

A person who fails to comply with a section 49 notice is liable to a fine or imprisonment of up to two years.[114] Controversially, section 53(2)

---

[109] RIPA s 49(1).
[110] RIPA s S 49(3).
[111] RIPA s S 50(1).
[112] RIPA s S 50(2).
[113] ECB s 10.
[114] RIPA s 53(5).

includes a reversal of the burden of proof. Where the requester can show that the recipient of the notice was in possession of the requested key at any time before the notice was served, it will be assumed that he is still in possession of that key unless he can prove 'that the key was not in his possession after the giving of the notice and before the time by which he was required to disclose it'.

Although section 53(3) provides that the recipient of a notice shall be taken to have shown that he was not in possession of a key at a particular time 'if sufficient evidence of that fact is adduced to raise an issue with respect to it, and the contrary is not proved beyond a reasonable doubt', it has been argued that this presumption of continued ownership may be in breach of rights concerning the burden of proof. At the same time, the requirement to disclose a key that may later be used to decrypt information potentially incriminating the key holder may also violate the privilege from self-incrimination under Article 6 ECHR.[115] No ECtHR case-law exists to date, but in *R v S and A*[116] the Court of Appeal held that although an individual's knowledge of the encryption keys might engage the privilege against self-incrimination if the information itself contained incriminating material, even in that case, the appellants' privilege would not be violated as the mere disclosure of the encryption key would not affect the trial judge's powers under section 78 PACE to exclude evidence including the underlying material (ie the protected information), the encryption key and an individual defendant's knowledge of the encryption key, if he felt that the admission of the evidence would have an adverse effect on the fairness of the proceedings.

Finally, section 54 RIPA imposes an obligation of secrecy on any recipient of a section 49 notice and any person who becomes aware of it or its contents. Failure to comply with this tipping-off ban is an offence carrying a maximum penalty of five years' imprisonment. The peculiar discrepancy between the penalties for failure to comply with a section 49 notice (up to two years' imprisonment) and a violation of the tipping-off offence (up to five years' imprisonment) can be interpreted as a sign for the importance the security services attach to the secrecy of their methods and operations. It is on a par with another peculiarity of English surveillance law, namely the prohibition on the use of intercept evidence in criminal proceedings.[117] This need for secrecy has prompted fears by many civil liberties campaigners about the accountability of police forces and security services in the area of covert surveillance.

Part III of RIPA came into force on 1 October 2007[118] together with a

---

115 See eg Akdeniz, above n 86, 87.
116 *R v S and A* [2008] EWCA 2177.
117 RIPA s 17.
118 The Regulation of Investigatory Powers Act 2000 (Commencement No 4) Order 2007 (SI 2007/2196).

Code of Practice[119] that provides guidance on the scope of the powers of investigating agencies, the rules on giving notice, the rules on the effect of imposing disclosure requirements, the keeping of records and the offences. Among other things, the Code sets out detailed requirements for the use and storage of, and access to, disclosed material with particular safeguards required for encryption keys. Failure to comply with these requirements may entitle the owner of disclosed information or an encryption key to recover damages. Where a disclosure requirement is imposed upon a business or service provider in order to assist an investigation, appropriate consideration must be given to minimising any actual or possible disruption to the business or service.

Nevertheless, the provisions have been widely condemned for damaging public trust and confidence in the use of key cryptography[120] and for violating individuals' rights under the ECHR. Ramsbottom warned in an article published in 2000 that

> [f]rom a human rights point of view [the disclosure of a key] is a massive intrusion for an individual, but from a commercial point of view there is potential for disaster. The corporate key of a large multi-national company which manages the networks of a cluster of banks and other financial institutions is immediately vulnerable to anybody who has had the corporate keys disclosed to them.[121]

In light of the recent data security breaches by government departments[122] and the sale of confidential financial data of customers of a major Liechtenstein bank by an internal whistleblower, this warning may only now be fully appreciated.

IV. CONCLUSION

It is not in doubt that the work of LEAs in detecting, prosecuting and preventing serious crime and terrorism may be greatly aided by the surveillance powers described in this chapter. However, any morphing of a reactive force into a proactive, intelligence-led force must be accompanied

---

[119] The Regulation of Investigatory Powers (Investigation of Protected Electronic Information: Code of Practice) Order 2007 (SI 2007/2200).

[120] See eg Akedeniz, above n 86, 86.

[121] D Ramsbottom, 'Regulation of Investigatory Powers Act—Updating or Snoopers Charter?' (2000) 6(8) *Computer and Telecommunications Law Review* 207.

[122] This includes the loss of two disks containing personal details from 7.25 million families claiming child benefit by HM Revenue and Customs (see 'Lost in the Post—25 Million at Risk after Data Discs Go Missing', *The Guardian* 21 November 2007, available at http://www.guardian.co.uk/politics/2007/nov/21/immigrationpolicy.economy3, last accessed 15 June 2008). A few months previously, a computer hard drive which belonged to a contractor working for the Driving Standards Agency and which contained details of three million candidates for the driving theory test had gone missing in the US (see 'Millions of L-driver Details Lost', BBC News Online, 17 December 2007, available at http://news.bbc.co.uk/1/hi/uk_politics/7147715.stm, last accessed on 15 June 2007.

by stringent safeguards and oversight if the pendulum is not to swing too far in the other direction, replacing the citizens' right to presumed innocence with a presumption of guilt instead.

Although IT opens up avenues of communication, it also opens up avenues of government control. In 2000, an editorial in *The Observer* made the point that the British, with 'a tradition of an unwritten constitution, executive power and few automatic rights',[123] may be 'the most exposed of all'.[124]

> British common law makes no presumption that the individual has the right to privacy and this has generated an extraordinary culture in British officialdom, which presumes a right to investigate. . . . We must presume innocence until there is proof of guilt, and the collection of evidence to prove guilt must be at the direction of a court with clear lines of accountability.[125]

However, while the British with their lack of historical experience in 'surveillance gone wrong' may be more vulnerable than most to a surveillance apparatus outgrowing its purpose, plans for the use of even more intrusive online surveillance techniques that are currently being discussed in Germany—a country with rather a lot of historical experience in this area—are equally worrying.

In 2006, the Government of the German State of North Rhine–Westphalia adopted an Act that would have enabled security and intelligence agencies to carry out 'online searches' of citizens' computers via the remote installation of spyware and trojans. Although these attempts have, for the time being, been declared void by the German Constitutional Court for violating a 'right to the confidentiality and integrity of information technology systems' arising from Articles 1 and 2(2) of the German Constitution[126], both the North Rhine-Westphalian State Government and the Federal Government are expected to adopt new laws with the same aim, albeit that those laws are bound to be compliant with the stringent conditions suggested by the Constitutional Court in its decision. Other countries considering similar legislation, eg Austria, will observe these developments with interest.

The use of a wide variety of surveillance systems by security and LEAs, including interception of communications, the retention of communications data[127] and access to encryption keys, combined with the appropriation by these authorities of other technologies not originally designed for the

---

[123] *The Observer*, 3 December 2000, 'Spied on from Cradle to Grave—Bugging Is Not the Answer to Crime', available at http://www.guardian.co.uk/uk/2000/dec/03/ukcrime.leaders, last accessed on 21 April 2008.
[124] Ibid.
[125] Ibid.
[126] Cases 1 BvR 370/07 and 1 BvR 595/07.
[127] See Rauhofer, ch 18.

purposes of surveillance, form part of what social scientists call a 'surveillant assemblage'.[128] Lyon defines this as 'a set of loosely linked systems' that 'operates across state institutions and others that have nothing (directly) to do with the state'.[129] A good example of this is the Metropolitan Police's use of personal data collected by Transport for London through its Oyster card system. A rechargeable smart card ticket designed for customers of the London transport system, Oyster was originally introduced to simplify ticket controls, eliminate queues and cut down on travel times. However, its surveillance potential, namely the fact that it becomes a personalised[130] record of users' movements through London, makes it attractive for LEAs who now routinely request that location data in respect of individuals under observation as part of a criminal investigation.[131] Lyon concludes that the surveillant assemblage is being 'co-opted for conventional "strong state" purposes'[132] and that 'panic responses' that 'both silence critical discussion and impose restrictions on civil liberties through policing and security crackdowns, are likely to have long-term and possibly irreversible consequences'.[133]

Bennett and Raab have argued[134] that the assumption underlying much of current public policy, namely that privacy conflicts with public or community values like internal security or government efficiency, ignores the fact that privacy itself should be seen as a social or public value. State-sanctioned privacy intrusions facilitated through the excessive use of surveillance, are therefore bad not only for individuals but also for society. The German Constitutional Court agreed with this argument when it described a right to informational self-determination[135] as an essential condition for the functioning of a democratic society. This means that a loss of informational self-determination or information privacy will also always constitute a loss of 'democratic substance'.[136]

In this context, Regan observed that 'privacy is becoming less an

---

[128] See eg K Haggerty and R Ericson, 'The Surveillant Assemblage' (2000) 51(4) *British Journal of Sociology* 605–22.

[129] D Lyon, *Surveillance after September 11* (Cambridge, Polity Press, 2003) 31.

[130] This is only the case where the card is charged through the use of a credit card or by direct debit, when the card's identity is connected with the personal data of the credit card or bank account holder. The Oyster card can in fact be used anonymously, if it is only ever charged using cash.

[131] See eg 'Oyster Data is "New Police Tool"', BBC News Online, 13 March 2006, available at http://news.bbc.co.uk/1/hi/england/london/4800490.stm, last accessed 15 June 2008; and 'Oyster Data Use Rises in Crime Clampdown', *The Guardian* 13 March 2006, available at http://www.guardian.co.uk/technology/2006/mar/13/news.freedomofinformation, last accessed on 15 June 2008.

[132] See above n 129, 34.

[133] Ibid.

[134] See above n 41, 23.

[135] Developed in its decision on a national census, see above n 10.

[136] S Simitis, 'Die informationelle Selbstbestimmung—Grundbedingung einer verfassungskonformen Informationsordnung' [1984] *Neue Juristische Wochenschrift* 394 399.

attribute of individuals and records and more an attribute of social relationships and information systems or communication systems'.[137] At the same time a commodification[138] of the right to privacy that is supported by a view of privacy as merely an individual right has made it easier for governments to convince individuals of the intrinsic value and legitimacy of the privacy–security trade-off. To the extent that privacy has turned into a tradeable object under the control of the rights holder, the 'privacy risk' of any measure—whether taken by private or public organisations—is now routinely viewed as only one of a number of competing risks such as threats to public or national security, loss of convenience[139] or loss of material gain. A prime example for the latter is the ease with which retail loyalty cards schemes manage to extract substantial amounts of personal data from customers in exchange for the opportunity to earn 'points' or cashback. The chance of having 'jam today' seems to make many consumers forget that they may well pay for this tendency towards instant gratification by being mined, measured and profiled for retailers' marketing activities tomorrow. As a result, it has become easier to justify privacy intrusions on the basis of the overriding interests of other individuals or the community. However, as Regan argues, there is a risk that '[i]f one individual or a group of individuals waives privacy rights, the level of privacy for all individuals decreases because the value of privacy decreases'.[140]

To avoid the negative effects of 'surveillant assemblage systems', protection is needed 'not just to guard against unwanted observation, but to guard against the possibility of observation itself'.[141] Individuals who are uncertain whether or not and when they are being watched are likely to behave as if they are being watched constantly. The German Constitutional Court acknowledged that this permanent threat of being observed is a powerful tool of social control in the hands of the observer.[142] The ECtHR has taken a similar view in its case-law on wiretapping and other forms of surveillance.[143]

One could argue that citizens of information societies are currently prone to substituting trust in the state for trust in each other. Their resistance to the 'hijacking' of their privacy for the purpose of security has largely been minimal. This seems to reaffirm Leigh's and Lustgarten's contention back in 1994 that '[f]ar too often, the cry of "security"

---

137 P Regan, *Legislating Privacy: Technology, Social Values and Public Policy* (Chapel Hill, University of North Carolina Press, 1995).

138 C Prins, 'When Personal Data, Behavior and Virtual Identities Become a Commodity: Would a Property Rights Approach Matter?' (2006) 3(4) *SCRIPT-ed* 270.

139 L Edwards, 'Introduction to the Special issue on Privacy' (2006) 3(4) *SCRIPT-ed* 265.

140 See above n 135, 233.

141 P Ganley, 'Access to the Individual: Digital Rights Management Systems and the Intersection of Informational and Decisional Privacy Interests' (2002) *International Journal of Law and Information Technology* 241.

142 See above n 10.

143 See above n 14.

functions in the political world as a sort of intellectual curare, inducing instant paralysis of thought'.[144] However, measures that undermine social trust also undermine, through their emphasis on individual behaviour, social solidarity.[145] Where we trust an all-seeing, all-knowing state (however benevolent it may be in its intentions) more than we trust our fellow citizen, the state's panoptic gaze may already have succeeded in damaging not only the political but also the 'social fabric' of our society.

[144] I Leigh and L Lustgarten, *In From the Cold: National Security and Parliamentary Democracy* (Oxford, Oxford University Press, 1994).

[145] For an exploration of the effect of surveillance on social trust and social cohesion, see Rauhofer, ch 18.

18

The Retention of Communications Data in Europe and the UK

JUDITH RAUHOFER

I. INTRODUCTION

IN THE PREVIOUS chapter we looked at how, historically, the efforts of law enforcement agencies (LEAs) in relation to the surveillance of personal communications have concentrated on the interception (opening of letters, tapping of phone calls, etc) of communications by suspected individuals.[1] The focus has been on what can be learned from the *content* of those communications. In the previous chapter we also discussed the legal regime in relation to interception of the content of communications, as formulated for the UK in the Regulation of Investigatory Powers Act 2000 (RIPA) and noted the safeguards provided by law to strike a balance between the privacy of individuals and the need to protect the state and its citizens.

However, with the increased use of electronic communication, LEAs have turned their attention to a new form of data which, in their opinion, is equally likely to assist them in the detection, prosecution, and even prevention of crime and terrorist attacks. Instead of concentrating solely on the content of a message, LEAs now increasingly want to use collateral information that is generated automatically whenever a communication is transmitted via telephone or computer. This collateral information is commonly known as 'communications data' and includes data such as when or where the communication is made, rather than what the message itself is about.

Communications data is generated automatically as a by-product of modern communications systems. It not only allows LEAs to track individual suspects but also, it is argued, to trace the associates of criminals and terrorists and to draw conclusions in relation to the methods they use

---

[1] For a description of the UK legislative framework relating to the interception of electronic communications, see Rauhofer, ch 17.

and the level of organisation they employ. It also allows the identification of behavioural patterns for the purpose of profiling individuals. This is now seen as one of the most important weapons in the armory of public and private organisations.[2] It is not only used for the purpose of criminal investigations, but also in the context of a range of other public and private sector decision-making processes, including, among others, border controls, fraud prevention and financial risk assessment. As we have also seen in previous chapters by Edwards, very similar techniques of 'traffic data' detection also have extensive commercial uses, eg in marketing.

Historically, the laws restricting interception of content have been far more privacy-protective than those restricting collection of communications data, as it was seen as less personal and sensitive than actual content. Yet it is almost impossible to decide not to generate communications data in the modern information society. Because information technology (IT) systems have now become an intrinsic part of everyday life, most people hardly even register their use. Living without them is almost unimaginable and would, in any case, be difficult to achieve in practice. In its February 2008 decision on online searches, the German Constitutional Court acknowledged this major shift in the role that IT plays in the life of ordinary citizens (and the impact this has on privacy) when it found that, these days, individuals depend

> on the use of information technology systems for the development of their personality and therefore entrust to those systems—are even forced to populate those systems—with personal data. A third party with access to such a system, is able to procure a substantial amount of crucial data and will no longer need to rely on further data retrieving or data processing measures. The impact of such access on the individual's personality exceeds by far that of specific data collection.[3]

A similar argument could be made in relation to communications data. Although many see its collection and use as less intrusive than interception of 'content', if enough communications data is retained for a sufficiently lengthy period of time, it is possible to gain a complete picture of the individuals to whom it relates, their actions and their beliefs. Indeed,

---

[2] See eg AJ McClurg, 'A Thousand Words Are Worth a Picture: A Privacy Tort Response to Consumer Data Profiling' (2003) 98 *North Western University Law Review* 63; TS Raghu, PK Kannan, HR Rao and AB Whinston, 'Dynamic Profiling of Consumers for Customised Offerings Over the Internet: A Model and Analysis' (2001) 32/2 *Decision Support Systems* 117; L Lessig, *Code and Other Laws of Cyberspace* (New York, Basic Books, 1999); KA Taipale, 'Data Mining and Domestic Security: Connecting the Dots to Make Sense of Data' (2003) *Columbia Science and Technology Law Review* 1; A Bartow, 'Our Data Ourselves: Privacy, Propertization and Gender' (2000) 34 *University of San Francisco Law Review* 633; DJ Solove, 'Privacy and Power: Computer Databases and Metaphors for Information Privacy' (2001) 53 *Stanford Law Review* 1393.

[3] *BvR* 370/07 and *1 BvR* 595/07, available at: http://www.bverfg.de/entscheidungen/rs2008 0227_1bvr037007.html.

Caspar Bowden, former Director of the Foundation for Information Policy Research (FIPR), concludes that communications data 'constitutes a near complete map of private life: everyone one talks to (by e-mail and phone), everywhere one goes (mobile phone location co-ordinates), and everything one reads online (websites browsed)'.[4] The claim that a lower threshold of protection in law should apply when deciding if the retention and use of communications data restricts individuals' fundamental rights is therefore at least questionable. In this chapter we will examine and assess what safeguards the law does provide in relation to collection and retention of, and access to, retained communications data.

In addition, advances in communications technology have encouraged citizens to conduct even more of their daily activities over the telephone and on the computer than was previously the case, thereby creating yet more electronic data[5] to be stored and profiled. It is therefore likely that the importance of communications data will increase rather than diminish.

It has often been argued that the focus of LEAs on the use of communications data began in the wake of the terrorist attacks on 11 September 2001 when they realised that much of the planning of those attacks was carried out using e-mail and mobile phone communications. However, it can be shown that the authorities' love affair with communications data goes back much further. Provisions allowing LEAs *access* to communications data retained by communications service providers (CSPs) in the normal course of business were already in place in Part 1 of Chapter II RIPA before 9/11 (see further below); and attempts to persuade the UK government to require the mandatory retention of that data for up to seven years date back to the late 1990s.[6] One of the earliest efforts by the UK LEA community to persuade the government to introduce data retention legislation was made in a submission on communications data retention law by the National Crime and Intelligence Service (NCIS)[7] to the Home Office in August 2000. Allegedly prepared after consultation with 'a number of leading UK Communications Service Providers'[8] with details on what data should be retained for how long and whom by, the submission reflects a sea-change in modern policing and the role of LEAs from reactive to intelligence-led preventative law enforcement.[9] Communications data was seen

---

[4] C Bowden, 'Closed Circuit Television for Inside your Head: Blanket Traffic Data Retention and the Emergency Anti-terrorism Legislation' (2002) *Duke Law & Technology Review* 5.

[5] S Freiwald, 'Uncertain Privacy: Communication Attributes After the Digital Telephony Act' (1996) 69 *Southern California Law Review* 949–1020.

[6] See J Rauhofer, 'Just Because You're Paranoid, Doesn't Mean They're Not After You: Legislative Developments in Relation to the Mandatory Retention of Communications Data in the UK and the European Union' (2006) 3(4) *SCRIPT-ed* 322, http://www.law.ed.ac.uk/ahrc/script-ed/vol3-4/rauhofer.asp.

[7] NCIS Submission on Data Retention Law, *Looking to the Future—Clarity on Communications Data Retention Law*, 21 August 2000.

[8] Ibid, para 1.1.2.

[9] Ibid, para 2.2.1.

as part of the intelligence which would enable LEAs to detect criminal activities and criminal networks prior to any actual crime being committed.

One of the key assertions of this chapter, therefore, is that the human rights relevance of data retention as well as its socioeconomic effect is much greater than LEAs would have us believe, and that the law as it stands fails to respect this view by providing proper privacy safeguards. It is both necessary and appropriate to examine these issues at a time when the storage and use of such collateral information is increasing the world over.

II. COMUNICATIONS DATA

Three types of communications data can be distinguished:[10] traffic data, location data and subscriber data.

- *Traffic data* includes any data that identifies the person transmitting the communication, the person to whom it is transmitted and the circumstances under which it is transmitted. In the case of e-mail, the data may include the time the e-mail was sent, the sender and the addressee as well as the size of the file. In the case of telephone calls, it includes the number called and the number from which the call was made as well as the length of the call. ISPs providing access to the Internet will keep a log of the time access was initiated and terminated,[11] and, in the case of access to the World Wide Web, the Uniform Resource Locators (URLs) of websites visited and the order in which they were accessed (server logs).
- *Location* data is a subset of traffic data, and includes the geographical coordinates (cell-site information) used by telecommunications providers to track a mobile phone to within a few hundred meters.
- *Subscriber* data includes personal information relating to the identity of the person making a telephone call or accessing the Internet—name, billing address, etc.

It is generally accepted that communications data constitutes 'personal data' within the meaning of the Data Protection Directive (DPD)[12] and the UK Data Protection Act 1998 (DPA) as, unless anonymised, it allows people with access to it to identify the subjects of such data, either from

[10] In the UK, RIPA s 21 includes a definition of communications and traffic data for the purpose of access to such data under RIPA Part I, ch 2, see below.

[11] However, it has been argued that, in practice, these types of data are no longer relevant as they are linked to 'technologies and systems of the late 20th and very early 21st centuries'. They suggest an experience of dial-up access (log-in and log-out on a regular basis) that has been superseded by a transition to 'always-on' broadband where log-in and log-out may be separated by several months, see P Milford, 'The Retention of Communications Data: A View from Industry' (2008) available from http://ww.practicallaw.com.

[12] EC Directive 95/46/EC on the protection of individuals with regard to the processing of personal data and on the free movement of such data, [1995] OJ L281/31.

that data alone (eg as with subscriber data) or from it and other data (eg as with traffic or location data when it is linked to subscriber data). Like telephone metering data in previous decades, it is also covered by the definition of 'private life'[13] contained in Article 8 of the European Convention on Human Rights (ECHR). To fully understand the extent to which the use of communications data can affect an individual's right under Article 8 ECHR, a distinction must be made between the conditions under which such data can or must be *retained* and the grounds on which it can be *accessed*.

III. RETENTION OF COMMUNICATIONS DATA

A. Voluntary Retention of Communications Data

At the European level, the DPD requires Member States to ensure that data controllers only collect personal data for specified, explicit and legitimate purposes and do not further process this in a way incompatible with those purposes.[14] Under Article 6(1)(d), data controllers must also take every reasonable step to ensure that data which is inaccurate or incomplete is erased or rectified.

In addition, the Privacy in Electronic Communications Directive (PECD)[15] requires Member States to ensure the confidentiality of communications and related traffic data in public telecommunications networks and publicly available electronic communication services.[16] It also stipulates that CSPs must erase or make anonymous any traffic or billing data they generated upon termination of the communication in question, unless they require such data for their own billing or marketing purposes (the latter use being subject to the subscriber's consent).[17] CSPs which continue to retain communications data beyond the requisite period are likely to face civil and criminal liability. Article 15(1) of the PECD only permits a derogation from that principle in very limited circumstances 'when such restriction constitutes a necessary, appropriate and proportionate measure to safeguard national security, defence, public security, the prevention, investigation, detection and prosecution of criminal offences or of unauthorised use of the electronic communication system'.

These provisions mean that, in effect, data retention is thoroughly discouraged by data privacy law. This also accords with industry practice

[13] See *Malone v UK* [1984] 7 EHRR 14.
[14] DPD Art 6(1)(a).
[15] EC Directive 2002/58/EC concerning the processing of personal data and the protection of privacy in the electronic communications sector, [2002] OJ L201/37, 31 July.
[16] PECD Art 5(1).
[17] PECD Art 6.

among CSPs, which tend for obvious economic and storage reasons to retain communications data only as long as necessary for billing, fault identification and customer services. However, as LEAs sought to depend on communications data for policing and investigation, longer periods of retention than the business case dictated for CSPs became, from their perspective, crucial. Accordingly, Article 15(1) of the PECD also explicitly allowed Member States to adopt legislative measures providing for the retention of data for a limited period, provided it was justified on the grounds listed above. This enabling provision is in stark contrast to the Directive's predecessor, the Telecommunications Privacy Directive,[18] which was generally seen as prohibiting the introduction by Member States of blanket data retention.

In the UK, Part 11 of the Anti-Terrorism Crime and Securities Act 2001 (ATCSA) provided for the introduction of a Voluntary Code of practice on data retention by CSPs. The Act was adopted in the wake of the 9/11 attacks and came into force on 14 December 2001. The Voluntary Code itself was eventually adopted, after consultation with CSPs,[19] in December 2003.[20] It stipulates a voluntary retention period of six months for most Internet- and e-mail-related data with the exception of server logs which need only be retained for a maximum of four days.[21] If the Voluntary Code were to prove ineffective at any time, the Secretary of State had the right to impose mandatory data retention requirements[22] by order.[23] Although the Home Secretary's power to impose mandatory retention requirements was originally subject to a sunset clause providing that his authority would lapse in December 2003,[24] this period was subsequently extended twice,[25] and eventually expired in December 2007. In the light of recent legislative developments in the area of mandatory data retention[26] the fate of the Voluntary Code is currently unclear.

B. Mandatory Retention of Communications Data

Article 15(1) of the PECD was the first step in a shift towards the mandatory retention of communications data. In April 2004, the governments

---

18 EC Directive 97/66/EC concerning the processing of personal data and the protection of privacy in the telecommunications sector, [1998] OJ L24/1, 30 January.

19 ATCSA s 102(1).

20 The Retention of Communications Data (Code of Practice Order 2003 (SI 2003/3175).

21 See Annex A of the Code.

22 ATCSA s 104(1).

23 ATCSA s 104(8).

24 ATCSA s 105.

25 By the Retention of Communications Data (Extension of Initial Period) Order 2003 (SI 2003/3173) and the Retention of Communications Data (Further Extension of Initial Period) Order 2005 (SI 2005/3335).

26 See 'Transposition in the UK' below.

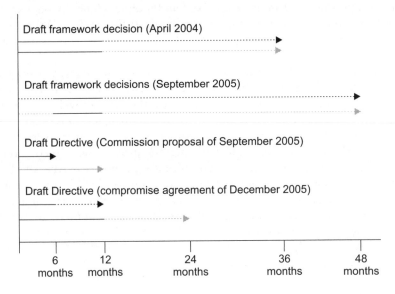

Figure 18.1

of the UK, France, Ireland and Sweden submitted a joint proposal for a draft Framework Decision intended to put in place a pan-European framework. The proposal as drafted would have required the retention, for a minimum of 12 months and a maximum of 36 months,[27] of all communications data generated by CSPs within the EU. The proposal was widely criticised[28] for lacking a correct legal basis.[29]

As a result, the European Commission adopted a proposal for a Directive on the retention of telecommunications data on 21 September 2005.[30] In its original form, the draft Directive intended to introduce a harmonised

[27] See Draft Framework Decision on the retention of data processed and stored in connection with the provision of publicly available electronic communications services or data on public communications networks for the purpose of prevention, investigation, detection and prosecution of crime and criminal offences including terrorism, 28 April 2004, Council document 8958/04. In later versions of the draft framework decision, the retention period was extended to a maximum 48 months for Member States that entered a derogation 'when such retention constitutes a necessary, appropriate and proportionate measure within a democratic society', see Report from the Working Party on Cooperation in Criminal Matters, 12 September 2005, Council document 12236/05.

[28] See eg European Parliament Report, A6-1074/2005, 31 May 2005 and Opinion of the Council Legal Service of 5 April 2005 on the Draft Framework Decision on the retention of data processed and stored in connection with the provision of publicly available electronic communications services or data on public communications networks for the purpose of prevention, investigation, detection and prosecution of crime and criminal offences including terrorism—Legal basis, Document No 7688/05.

[29] See discussion later under 'Legal Challenges'.

[30] COM/2005/438/FINAL. Hereafter the Data Retention Directive (DRD).

retention period of 12 months for fixed and mobile telephony data and six months for Internet data. In contrast to the draft Framework Decision, the proposed Directive did not permit individual Member States to adopt longer retention periods.

The adoption of the proposal by the Commission sparked a brief but intense period of discussion between the Council, the European Parliament and the EU Presidency, held at the time by the UK, as well as intensive lobbying of all institutions by human rights campaigners, LEAs and CSPs alike. Eventually, after one of the shortest legislative procedures in the history of the EU, the European Parliament approved the Directive on 14 December 2005 in the form of a compromise proposed by the UK Presidency, which reintroduced many of the provisions included in the original proposal for a Framework Decision. The success of that compromise was largely due to a backroom deal between the representatives of the UK Presidency and the leaders of the two biggest parliamentary parties. The DRD was eventually adopted by the European Council in February 2006 and came into force on 3 May 2006.

(i) The Data Retention Directive

The DRD provides for a retention period of 6–24 months,[31] with an option for individual Member States to introduce longer periods where they face 'particular circumstances warranting an extension for a limited period'.[32] Retained data will be available for the purposes of the investigation, detection and prosecution of serious crime.[33] The definition of 'serious crime' is left to the national law of the Member States.[34]

Member States must require CSPs to retain a wide range of data, including:

- data necessary to trace and identify the source of a communication (telephone number, name and address of subscriber, sender's IP address, etc);
- data necessary to identify the recipient of a communication (number dialled, name and address of recipient, IP address of recipient, etc);
- data necessary to identify the date, time and duration of a communication (date of the communication, start and end time of a telephone conversation, logon and logoff time of Internet access service);
- data necessary to identify the type of communication;
- data necessary to identify users' communication equipment or what purports to be their equipment;

---

[31] DRD Art 6.
[32] DRD Art 12(1).
[33] DRD Art 1(1).
[34] See discussion below under 'Assessment'.

- cell site data necessary to identify the location of mobile communication equipment.[35]

In contrast to the provisions of the proposed Framework Decision, CSPs will not be required to retain server log data (ie evidence of webpages visited), as this was seen as too intrusive a measure which might fall foul of the proportionality requirement set out in Article 8 ECHR.[36] Data relating to unsuccessful call attempts need only be retained if this is already done by the provider for its own business purposes.[37] CSPs, in particular, had objected to this requirement as it would have substantially increased the amount of data to be retained and with it the storage cost.

As a result of the compromise deal, the DRD does not require Member States to reimburse CSPs for the costs of retention. Such a requirement had been included in the original Commission proposal, but was dropped after it proved to be a major obstruction to reaching agreement. Instead, Member States are free to decide whether or not they will compensate providers. The costs of setting up and administrating data retention facilities in the UK alone have been estimated to be well over £100 million,[38] while a legal, technical and economic study on the evaluation of the economic impacts of the data retention obligations relating to electronic communications commissioned by the French Internet Service Providers Association (AFA) calculated a total investment cost of €224 million for a CSP with 1 million subscribers.[39] Two other studies, commissioned by the Dutch government[40] and by the Austrian Internet Service Providers Association[41] respectively, put the cost of implementation at between €133 million and €155 million over five years for the entire Dutch market and at €972,400 (in the first year) and €465,000 (for every subsequent year) for an average-sized ISP serving approximately 500,000 customers.

Notably, the DRD also does not regulate the gaining of *access* to, and *use of*, the retained data by public authorities and LEAs of the Member States. Member States have the right to regulate access under their national laws (subject to their international legal obligations). As we will see below, in the UK access is regulated by RIPA, Chapter II, Part 1.

[35] DRD Art 5.
[36] For a detailed description of the proportionality requirement under Art 8 ECHR, see Rauhofer, ch 17.
[37] DRD Art 3(2).
[38] Report of an Inquiry by the All Party Internet Group on Communications Data, January 2003, para 145.
[39] AFA Summary document, 'Aid to Evaluation of the Economic Impacts of the Data Retention Obligations Relating to Electronic Communications' (7 December 2006). The AFA concluded that in relation to the 20 million French Internet subscribers, this would represent an investment cost greater than €2 billion.
[40] Verdonck, Klooster, and Associates, 'Study into the National Implementation of the European Data Retention Directive' (2006).
[41] G Stampfel, W Gansterer and M Ilger, *Data Retention—The EU Directive 2006/24/EC from a Technological Perspective* (Wien and München, Medien und Recht Publishing, 2008).

(ii) Transposition in the UK

The UK initially implemented the Directive for fixed-line and mobile telephony services through the Data Retention (EC Directive) Regulations 2007,[42] which were adopted on 26 July 2007 and came into force on 1 October 2007. In recognition of the fact that retention of communications data relating to the Internet constituted 'a more complex issue, involving much larger volumes of data and a considerably broader set of stakeholders within the industry',[43] the UK government decided to make a declaration in accordance with Article 15(3) of the Directive, postponing its application to the retention of communications data relating to Internet access, Internet telephony and Internet e-mail to 15 March 2009.[44]

In August 2008, the Home Office launched a consultation on draft regulations designed to enable the transposition of the DRD with respect to Internet-related data.[45] In February 2009, the Home Office published its response to the consultation together with a revised version of the draft regulations, an explanatory memorandum, the final impact assessment and a transposition notice.[46] The Data Retention (EC Directive) Regulations 2009 (2009 Regulations), which replace the 2007 Regulations, were eventually approved in March 2009 and came into force on 6 April 2009.

Regulation 10 of the 2009 Regulations provides that the Regulations do not apply to a CSP unless it is given notice in writing by the Secretary of State. The Secretary of State must, however, issue such a notice unless the relevant data is already retained in the UK by another provider in accordance with the 2009 Regulations. In its impact assessment, the government contended that Recital 13 of the Directive (which provides that data should be retained in such a way as to avoid it being retained more than once) allows Member States to limit its application to avoid duplication of retained data. Regulation 10 is therefore intended to reduce the number of CSPs required to retain communications data, while continuing to aim for full retention of all data generated by UK CSPs. In practice, this is likely to mean that where CSPs provide services across networks operated by other CSPs, only one of them will be required to retain the resulting communications data.

The data to be retained under the 2009 Regulations is set out in the Schedule to the Regulations and mirrors the list of data contained in the

---

[42] SI 2007/2199

[43] Home Office, 'The initial transposition of Directive 2006/24/EC on the retention of data generated or processed in connection with the provision of publicly available electronic communications services or of public communications networks and amending Directive 2002/58/EC, A consultation paper', 27 March 2007, 5.

[44] Reg 4(5) of the Regulations.

[45] Home Office, Consultation: Transposition of Directive 2006/24/EC, 12 August 2008.

[46] Government Response to the Public Consultation on the Transposition of Directive 2006/24/EC, 11 February 2009.

Directive.[47] Data in respect of calls that are connected but not answered must also be retained. However, unconnected calls are specifically excluded.[48] Data revealing the content of a communication is also excluded.[49]

CSPs must retain all communications data for a period of 12 months.[50] In relation to Internet-related data, this is twice as long as in the Voluntary Code, which only required retention for six months.

Regulation 11(1) of the 2009 Regulations allows (but does not require) the Home Secretary to reimburse any expenses incurred by CSPs in complying with the 2009 Regulations. However, such reimbursement is conditional on the expenses having been notified to the Home Secretary and agreed in advance.[51] The Home Secretary may also require providers to comply with any audit that may be reasonably required to monitor any claim for reimbursement.[52]

In response to concerns expressed by many respondents to the consultation about how the Regulations ought to be interpreted in practice, the government decided to establish an 'Implementation Group' to support the Home Office's implementation strategy.[53] This group will:

- support bilateral consultation and specific agreements with individual public communications providers;
- develop guidance to assist in the implementation of the Regulations so that the new obligations which they impose are fully understood and complied with;
- assist in undertaking an evaluation of the application of the Directive with a view to determining whether it is necessary to amend the provisions.

The government has not provided information about the proposed status and membership of the Implementation Group.

(iii) Interception Modernisation Programme

In May 2008, the government proposed a 'Bill on communications data retention for the prevention and detection of crime and the protection of national security' as part of its draft legislative programme for 2008/09.[54]

---

[47] DRD Art 5.
[48] Reg 4(2)–(3), 2009 Regulations.
[49] Reg 4(5), 2009 Regulations.
[50] Reg 5, 2009 Regulations.
[51] Reg 11(2), 2009 Regulations.
[52] Reg 11(3), 2009 Regulations.
[53] Government Response to the Public Consultation on the Transposition of Directive 2006/24/EC.
[54] 'Preparing Britain for the Future: The Government's Draft Legislative Programme 2008/09', Cm 7372, May 2008, available at http://www.official-documents.gov.uk/document/cm73/7372/7372.pdf, last accessed on 15 July 2008.

The Bill was originally intended to modify the procedures for acquiring and retaining communications data, and was initially seen as part of the transposition process in relation to Internet data. The announcement prompted fears that the government might intend to set up a national database 'holding details of every phone call, e-mail and time spent on the internet',[55] meaning that rather than individual CSPs storing their own data and granting access to them to public authorities, CSPs would have to hand over that data to the government for it to be stored and accessed centrally.

One of the arguments put forward in favour of the plan is that it would make it simpler and swifter for LEAs to retrieve the information instead of having to approach hundreds of different service providers. However, the scope for data breach will undoubtedly be greater if the data is held on one centralised database, particularly in light of the government's less than exemplary record at maintaining the integrity of such databases.[56] Mirroring those fears, the UK Information Commissioner's Office (ICO) issued a statement:

> If the intention is to bring all mobile and internet records together under one system, this would give us serious concerns and may well be a step too far. We are not aware of any justification for the state to hold every UK citizen's phone and internet records. We have real doubts that such a measure can be justified, or is proportionate or desirable. Such a measure would require wider public discussion. Proper safeguards would be needed to ensure that the data is only used for the proper purpose of detecting crime.[57]

The ICO pointed out that 'holding large collections of data is always risky'[58] and that 'the more data that is collected and stored, the bigger the problem when the data is lost, traded or stolen'.[59] Rather than creating a new additional system to house all communications data, the ICO offered to advise how existing systems could be improved, should they indeed be found wanting.[60]

In response to the public outcry following its announcement, the government initially decided to withdraw the plans for a Communications Data Bill which, accordingly, was not included in the 2008 Queen's Speech. Instead it promised that plans for the storage of and access to retained communications data would be discussed as part of its 'Interception

---

[55] '"Big Brother" Database for Phones and E-mails', *Times Online* 20 May 2008, available at http://business.timesonline.co.uk/tol/business/industry_sectors/telecoms/article3965033.ece, last accessed on 15 July 2008.

[56] For a more detailed description of recent scandals involving the handling of personal data by government agencies, see Edwards, ch 14.

[57] Statement by Jonathan Bamford, Assistant Information Commissioner, on the proposed Government database, 19 May 2008, available at http://www.ico.gov.uk/upload/documents/pressreleases/2008/proposed_government_database.pdf, last accessed on 15 July 2008.

[58] Ibid.

[59] Ibid.

[60] Ibid.

Modernisation Programme' (IMP), a cross-governmental programme designed, 'to maintain the UK's lawful intercept and communications data capabilities in the changing communications environment'[61] and to ensure the continued ability of LEAs to intercept and monitor communications in the face of changes in communications technology. The consultation was eventually published on 27 April 2009.[62] Among other things, it includes proposals[63] to include new forms of communication, eg networking sites and instant messaging (IM), which are not covered by the retention requirement under the DRD. Although the government appears to have retrenched—albeit reluctantly—on the question of a central super-database,[64] the consultation does, however, signal its plans still to move ahead with deep packet inspection (DPI), a form of computer network packet filtering that examines the data (content) part of a packet as it passes an inspection point, which may represent a serious change in the accepted balance between citizen privacy and state security. Indeed if DPI is to come into regular use, it is hard to see how any difference can be meaningfully maintained between the regulatory regime for content and that for communications data.

IV. ACCESS TO RETAINED COMMUNICATIONS DATA

In the UK, access to communications data retained by CSPs, whether for their own business purposes or in accordance with the Voluntary Code, is regulated by Part I of Chapter II RIPA.

A. Relevant Public Authorities and Designated Persons

Section 25(2) RIPA provides that individuals holding certain offices, ranks or positions with relevant public authorities have the right to obtain and disclose communications data retained by CSPs. They may also grant authorisation to access that data to others within the same public authority.

A 'public authority' includes any body or office which is listed in section 25(1) RIPA. Initially, the relevant public authorities specified by RIPA included the police, the National Criminal Intelligence Services, the National Crime Squad, Customs and Excise, the Inland Revenue and the

---

[61] Written answer submitted to the Earl of Northesk by Lord West of Spithead, the Parliamentary Under-Secretary (Security and Counter-terrorism), Home Office on 8 July 2008.

[62] Home Office consultation, 'Protecting the Public in a Changing Communications Environment', 27 April 2009, available at http://www.homeoffice.gov.uk/documents/cons-2009-communications-data, last accessed on 1 June 2009.

[63] Meeting of the Fourth Delegated Legislation Committee, Hansard, Monday 16 March 2009, available at http://www.publications.parliament.uk/pa/cm/cmtoday/cmstand/output/deleg/dg04090316-01.htm, last accessed on 1 April 2009.

[64] See the Consultation Paper, above n 62, 4, 25.

intelligence services. RIPA provides that persons permitted to access communications data will be authorised ('designated') by order.[65] RIPA also allows the government to specify further public authorities which may be entitled to obtain communications data under these provisions.[66]

Like the other parts of the Act, Chapter II of Part I RIPA has been the subject of considerable controversy. A draft order laid before Parliament in 2002, which added numerous public authorities to the list of organisations under section 25(1) RIPA, was dubbed a 'snoopers' charter' by critics and had to be withdrawn under pressure.[67] This was optimistically seen as a government U-turn, but led only to the launch, in March 2003, of a public consultation.[68] The Order made following the consultation reinstated, with only very minor changes, the list of authorities originally put forward by the Home Office.[69] Although only a small number of bodies have unfettered access to data, the list of additional public authorities includes a substantial number of authorities which seem remarkably unconnected to the investigation, detection and prosecution of serious crimes. Among others, access has been granted to the Financial Services Authority, the Department of Trade and Industry (now the Deparment for Business, Innovation and Skills), the National Health Service, the Department of Health, the Home Office, local authorities, the Charity Commission and the Gaming Board for Great Britain. Restricted access is provided to certain individuals working for, among others, the Foods Standards Agency, the Environment Agency and the Health and Safety Executive.[70] The scope and length of this list can perhaps only be understood when compared with the equally wide purposes for which access may be granted (the 'RIPA purposes') discussed below.

The controversy about the fact that wide-ranging RIPA powers were given to such a large number of public authorities erupted again in the wake of reports that local authorities were using their powers for purposes not entirely envisaged when the legislation was first drafted (eg to check if

[65] RIPA s 25(2).
[66] RIPA s 25(1)(g).
[67] See eg B Brogan '"Snooper's Charter" Dropped' *Daily Telegraph* 19 June 2002, available at http://www.telegraph.co.uk/news/main.jhtml?xml=/news/2002/06/19/nsnoop19.xml, last accessed on 13 April 2008.
[68] Home Office Consultation, 'Access to Communications Data: Respecting Privacy and Protecting the Public from Crime', March 2003, available at http://www.statewatch.org/news/2003/mar/ripa.pdf, last accessed on 13 April 2008. The responses were published in February 2004: *Responses to the Access to Communications Data Consultation Paper: 'Respecting Privacy and Protecting the Public from Crime'*, January 2004, available at http://www.homeoffice.gov.uk/documents/comms-data-2003/sw144-consultation-responses.pdf?view=Binary, last accessed 13 April 2008.
[69] The Regulation of Investigatory Powers (Communications Data) Order 2003 (SI 2003/3172) which came into force on 5 January 2004.
[70] In July 2006, the Home Office added even more public authorities to the list through the Regulation of Investigatory Powers (Communications Data) (Additional Functions and Amendment) Order 2006 (2006 Order), SI 2006/1878.

parents were truly residing within school catchment areas, or to detect whether people were putting their bins out for collection on the wrong day, or allowing their dogs to foul the pavement[71]). As a result, the Home Secretary promised a consultation on the use of RIPA powers in December 2008[72] which was published in April 2009.[73] It includes a review of the powers of public authorities under RIPA to grant authorisations in respect of direct surveillance,[74] covert human intelligence and access to communications data. The review contains proposals to issue consolidating orders and revised codes of practice which are likely to be implemented by SI.

B. RIPA Purposes

Section 22(2) RIPA lists a number of purposes which justify those persons and authorities designated under the Act obtaining access to communications data held by CSPs. Originally, access could be obtained:

- in the interests of national security;
- for the purpose of preventing or detecting crime or of preventing disorder;
- in the interests of the economic well-being of the UK;
- in the interests of public safety for the purpose of protecting public health;
- for the purpose of assessing or collecting any tax, duty or levy;
- for the purpose, in an emergency, of preventing death or of preventing or mitigating injury or damage to a person's physical or mental health.

Section 22(2)(h) RIPA permits the Home Secretary to add further purposes to this already extensive list and—perhaps unsurprisingly—the government quickly exercised that power[75] and added two more RIPA purposes. Designated persons may now obtain and disclose communications data:

- to assist investigations into alleged miscarriages of justice; and
- for the purpose of:
  — assisting in identifying any person who has died otherwise than as a result of crime or who is unable to identify himself because of a physical or mental condition, other than one resulting from crime; or

---

71 See eg BBC News Online, '"Spy Law" Used in Dog Fouling War', 27 April 2008, http://news. bbc.co.uk/1/hi/uk/7369543.stm.

72 See Home Secretary's speech, 'Protecting Rights, Protecting Society', available at http://press.homeoffice.gov.uk/Speeches/home-sec-protecting-rights, last accessed on 1 June 2009.

73 Home Office, 'Regulation of Investigatory Powers Act 2000: Consolidating Orders and Codes of Practice, A Public Consultation Paper', available at http://www.homeoffice.gov.uk/documents/cons-2009-ripa?view=Binary, last accessed on 1 June 2009.

74 See Rauhofer, ch 17.

75 See Reg 2 of the 2006 Order.

— obtaining information about the next of kin or other connected persons of such a person or about the reason for his death or condition.

Is the length and detail of this list of purposes compatible with the rather more limited exceptions to the fundamental right of privacy in Article 8 ECHR? To some extent this question is defensively anticipated by the accompanying Code of Practice which provided guidance on this point.

C. Code of Practice on Access to Retained Communications Data

As with the other parts of the Act, section 71 RIPA requires the Secretary of State to prepare and publish a draft code of practice in relation to Chapter 2 of Part I RIPA. In July 2007, Parliament accordingly adopted the Regulation of Investigatory Powers (Acquisition and Disclosure of Communications Data: Code of Practice) Order 2007.[76]

Among other things, the Code deals with the scope of the powers of those with access to retained communications data, including the *necessity* and *proportionality* of such access. It makes it clear that the acquisition of communications data under RIPA will only be a justifiable interference with an individual's human rights under Article 8 ECHR if the conduct being authorised or required to take place is both necessary and proportionate and in accordance with law.[77] It also provides that a person 'designated' under RIPA to access communications data must have a current working knowledge of human rights principles.[78] Finally, the Code sets out various data protection safeguards regarding communications data acquired or obtained under RIPA.[79] These were inserted as additions into the Code following controversy over the original draft and constitute a small level of success on the part of privacy and civil liberties campaigners.

D. Oversight

The Interception of Communications Commissioner is responsible for keeping under review the implementation and practical application of Chapter II of Part I, RIPA in relation to the acquisition and disclosure of communications data.[80] All public authorities have a duty to report any errors that occur when they are acquiring communications data under paragraph 5 of the Code of Practice. They are obliged to provide an explanation for the errors and, most importantly, they must also describe the

[76] SI 2007/2197. The order and the Code of Practice came into force on 1 October 2007.
[77] Ibid, para. 2.1.
[78] Para 3 of the Code of Practice.
[79] Para 7 of the Code of Practice.
[80] RIPA s 57(2)(b).

action that they have taken to prevent similar errors occurring again. The Commissioner's 2007 Annual Report discloses 1,182 errors resulting from 519,260 requests made by LEAs and other public authorities.[81] Despite this fairly high number of errors, no explanation is given of individual errors. This makes it difficult to evaluate both the level of misconduct by public authorities and the effectiveness of the oversight system.

V. CONSTITUTIONALITY, HUMAN RIGHTS AND THE RETENTION REGIME: ASSESSMENT[82]

The UK government's approach to regulating access to retained communications data raises a number of constitutional and human rights questions. The very wide list of public authorities that were granted access to communications data under section 25 RIPA combined with the extensive list of RIPA purposes for which such access may be sought, has prompted claims that the legislation may indeed not be compatible with the individual's right to privacy under Article 8 ECHR.

Article 8(1) ECHR protects an individual's right to 'respect for his private and family life, his home and his correspondence'. This right may be restricted under Article 8(2) ECHR if such a restriction is 'in accordance with the law' and is

> necessary in a democratic society in the interests of national security, public safety or the economic well-being of the country, for the prevention of disorder or crime, for the protection of health or morals, or for the protection of the rights and freedoms of others.

Any restrictive measure must be appropriate and proportionate. This means that it must balance the interests pursued by it against its detrimental effects on individuals.[83]

If one accepts that the use of communications data does indeed engage an individual's right under Article 8(1), it is at least questionable whether all of the RIPA purposes can be justified on the basis of Article 8(2) ECHR. Doubts exist, for example, in relation to the purpose of assessing taxes, duties or levies and where data is accessed to identify dead persons or their next of kin. The wide grounds for access set out in section 25 RIPA also

---

[81] Report of the Interception of Communications Commissioner for 2007, HC 947 SG/2008/127, July 2008, available at http://www.official-documents.gov.uk/document/hc0708/hc09/0947/0947.pdf , last accessed on 1 April 2009.

[82] For a detailed discussion of the compatibility of blanket data retention with human rights legislation, see P Breyer, 'Telecommunication Data Retention and Human Rights: The Compatibility of Blanket Traffic Data Retention with the ECHR' (2005) *European Law Journal* 365.

[83] B Hofstötter 'The Retention of Telecommunications Data in Europe—A Paradigm Shift in European Data Protection Law?' (2006) *Proceedings of KnowRight 2006*, Schriftenreihe der Osterreichischen Computer Gesellschaft, Wien.

exceed by far the grounds for which communications data can be retained under the DRD in the first place. Article 1(1) of that Directive clearly states that retained data should only 'be available for the purposes of the investigation, detection and prosecution of serious crime'.[84]

In addition, one could argue that in order to ensure the proportionality of the legislation, the circle of persons that are granted access to the retained data should be kept as small as possible. This clearly contradicts the UK government's apparent 'kitchen sink' strategy which seems to be starting from the point of view that access should generally be granted to almost all public authorities before considering what limitations on that access may be appropriate in individual cases.

Any interference with an individual's right under Article 8 ECHR must be 'in accordance with the law'.[85] The law in question must be 'adequately accessible' to the citizen and must be formulated with sufficient precision to enable the citizen to 'foresee, to a degree that is reasonable in the circumstances, the consequences which a given action may entail'.[86] Although the Code of Practice goes some way in fulfilling these requirements, some doubt remains over whether its provisions are sufficiently clear to ensure compatibility with Article 8 ECHR.

In *Weber and Saravia v Germany*[87] the European Court of Human Rights summarised its case-law on the requirement of legal 'foreseeability' in the field of electronic surveillance. It found that although 'foreseeability' could not mean that 'an individual should be able to foresee when the authorities are likely to intercept his communications so that he can adapt his conduct accordingly',[88] the 'domestic law must be sufficiently clear in its terms to give citizens an adequate indication as to the circumstances in which and the conditions on which public authorities are empowered to resort to any such measures'.[89] The Court went on to explain the minimum safeguards that should be set out in statute law in order to avoid abuses of power. Despite the fact that these safeguards refer to the interception of communications—ie the 'content' of communications rather than the collateral communications data—they give a clear indication of the extent of the information the Court expects the public to be given in order to ensure compliance with Article 8 ECHR. Most importantly, the safeguards include a description of the nature of the offences that may give rise to an

---

[84] In practice, local authorities have already been widely criticised for using their RIPA powers for the purpose of detecting and prosecuting individuals for minor offences such as fly-tipping and dog fouling; see discussion above.

[85] For more detailed information on this requirement, see Rauhofer, ch 17.

[86] *Sunday Times v United Kingdom* [1983], 2 EHRR 245. The European Court of Human Rights (ECtHR) took a similar line in *Kruslin v France* [1990] 12 EHRR 547 and *Kopp v Switzerland* [1997] 4 BHRC 277, concluding that in both cases the national law on which the restrictive measure was based did not meet the 'foreseeability' requirement.

[87] Admissibility decision, No 54934/00, 29 June 2006.

[88] Ibid, para 93.

[89] Ibid.

interception order; a definition of the categories of people liable to be the subject of such an order; the procedure to be followed for examining, using and storing the data obtained; the precautions to be taken when communicating the data to other parties; and the circumstances in which the information obtained may or must be erased or destroyed. One could argue that neither RIPA nor the Code of Practice include sufficient equivalent information to satisfy at least the first two requirements. In particular, the mere listing of the—very general—RIPA purposes as grounds for an authorisation for access to retained data is unlikely to be sufficiently specific.

It is also questionable whether the oversight provisions contained in RIPA are sufficient. It is generally accepted that measures interfering with an ECHR right must be subject to effective supervisory control. In *Klass v Germany*,[90] the European Court of Human Rights stated that it was in principle desirable to entrust that control to a judge, although it accepted that other non-judicial oversight authorities could substitute. However, even if the Interception of Communications Commissioner's supervision of access requests under RIPA could be seen as an acceptable alternative to judicial review, questions do arise over whether the mere publication in an annual report of the number of errors uncovered, without any further information about the circumstances of the individual cases, can be sufficient to satisfy the public interest in exposing abuses of power by public authorities. If, as the government argues, the use of communications data is less privacy-intrusive than the interception of the communications concerned, then surely the body responsible for overseeing such use can afford to be more open about failures to meet legislative requirements without jeopardising ongoing inquiries or the position of those requesting the information. This is particularly true, given that many of the requests are made by public authorities, and for purposes unconnected to criminal activity. Under the circumstances, the data protection safeguards contained in the Code of Practice are arguably little more than window dressing designed to disguise the more substantial shortcomings of the legislation.

VI. LEGAL CHALLENGES TO DATA RETENTION

Already, the DRD has come under considerable fire from both supporters and opponents of data retention. In February 2009, the European Court of Justice (ECJ) dismissed[91] an action filed by the Irish government[92] which had challenged the legal basis for the Directive, arguing that it was a matter

---

[90] [1978] 2 EHRR 214.
[91] *Ireland v European Parliament and Council of the European Union*, Case C-301/06, 10 February 2009.
[92] Action brought on 6 July 2006—*Ireland v Council of the European Union, European Parliament* (Case C-301/06), OJ C 237/5.

relating to criminal justice rather than the internal market. As such, the appropriate measure would have been a framework decision under the third pillar.[93] The Irish government claimed that measures adopted under Article 95 EC Treaty ('first pillar') must have as their 'centre of gravity' the approximation of the laws of the Member States. The Directive, it argued, was concerned with combating serious crime and was not intended to address any defects in the internal market. However, the ECJ largely followed the opinion of the Advocate General,[94] published in October 2008, in which he had found that the Directive was constitutionally adopted on the correct legal basis. The Court did not, however, examine any possible infringement of fundamental rights of privacy under Article 8 ECHR. Indeed, it very clearly stated that the action brought by Ireland—and consequently the final decision—related solely to the choice of legal basis and not to any possible infringement of fundamental rights. This is likely to leave the door open for future challenges to the Directive in relation to its compatibility with the ECHR.

Judicial or constitutional reviews relating to the compatibility with the right to privacy of national laws implementing the Directive are also already pending in the domestic courts of a number of Member States. In Germany, a writ for judicial review of the German Act implementing the Directive was filed before the German Constitutional Court in January 2008 in the form of a class action backed by more than 30,000 complainants, mainly privacy advocates involved in the campaign against data retention.[95] These complainants claimed that the blanket retention of communications data of all citizens violates the right to the secrecy of telecommunications[96] as well as the right to informational self-determination.[97] The Constitutional Court restricted, in a preliminary decision in March 2008, the use of data retention by German LEAs[98] until further notice. Notably, it criticised section 113a of the German Telecommunications Act, which implements the Directive in Germany, for permitting access to the retained data for *all* crimes and not just 'serious crimes' as specified in the Directive. Accordingly, where German LEAs seek to access retained data for less serious crimes, the Constitutional Court stipulated that such access should only be granted where there is real evidence that the data subject in question was involved in the crime being investigated. This development is particularly interesting from a UK point of view, given

[93] Title VI TEU, in particular Arts 30, 31(1)(c) and 34(2)(b).
[94] Opinion of the Advocate General, *Ireland v European Parliament and Council of the European Union*, Case C-301/06, 14 October 2008.
[95] The German language version of the writ is available at http://wiki.vorratsdatenspeicherung. de/images/Verfassungsbeschwerde_Vorratsdatenspeicherung.pdf, last accessed on 18 February 2008.
[96] Art 10(1), third indent of the German Consitution (GG).
[97] Art 2(1) in conjunction with Art 1(1) GG.
[98] Interim decision of the German Constitutional Court of 20 March 2008, 1 BvR 256/08.

that the grounds for access listed in section 25 RIPA are substantially wider than those in the German Act. The Constitutional Court now has the option to decide whether or not to rule on the case itself or whether to refer the issue for preliminary decision to the ECJ.

In February 2009, the Administrative Court in Wiesbaden suspended a case relating to the data retention obligation of an agricultural Internet portal.[99] It concluded that

> data retention violates the fundamental right to privacy. It is not necessary in a democratic society. The individual does not provoke the interference but can be intimidated by the risks of abuse and the feeling of being under surveillance. . . . The directive [on data retention] does not respect the principle of proportionality guaranteed in Article 8 ECHR, which is why it is invalid.[100]

As a result, the Wiesbaden court decided to refer a number of questions to the ECJ for preliminary decision, including the question whether the DRD is generally valid. It remains to be seen whether the ECJ will use this opportunity to review the compatibility of the Directive with the individual's right to privacy, if indeed it sees itself as competent to do so. The ECJ has shown itself willing to protect fundamental rights as general principles of EU law in the past, but the demarcation line between its competence in this area and that of the European Court of Human Rights has been far from clear. In its decision on the Ireland challenge, the ECJ emphasised that the Directive merely relates to activities of CSPs (involved in the *retention* of communications data) and not to the activities of LEAs and other public authorities (who gain *access* to the retained data). While factually correct, this could suggest that the ECJ may limit its own jurisdiction to a review of the question of whether the mere retention of data infringes fundamental rights, rather than taking into account the effect that law enforcement's access to—and use of—that data will have on those rights.

VII. ASSESSMENT

At the European level, it could be said that the DRD constitutes a victory of 'subsidiarity' over 'harmonisation'. Many contentious issues had to be left for determination by the Member States in order to achieve the final compromise and this has inevitably lead to differences in the implementation of the Directive by the Member States. Crucially while retention is

---

[99] Administrative Court Wiesbaden, Decision of 27 February 2009, Az 6 K 1045/08.WI. In an earlier decision the Administrative Court Berlin had already decided that in view of the fact that under German law CSPs are not reimbursed for additional costs they incur in retaining communications data, the retention obligation was unconstitutional, Decision of the Administrative Court Berlin, Az VG 27 A 321.08. These decisions are currently under review.

[100] Ibid.

harmonised, the issue of access has been left to national control—yet it is the combination of retention and access that has actually invaded individual privacy.

Lack of harmony on definitions will inevitably create disharmony across Europe. For example, it is the right of Member States to define what constitutes a 'serious crime'. While in the UK, 'serious crime' is defined widely as any offence for which a person without any previous convictions could reasonably be expected to be sentenced to imprisonment for a term of three years or more, or which 'involves the use of violence, results in substantial financial gain or is conducted by a large number of persons in pursuit of a common purpose',[101] the German Telecommunications Act dispensed with the requirement of 'seriousness' altogether and allowed providers to disclose retained communications data to LEAs where this is necessary for the prosecution of any criminal offence.[102]

The lack of harmonisation in relation to cost reimbursement by Member States is also an issue. Although the European Commission confirmed that it does not view compensation of providers as illegal state aid,[103] it is clear that the reimbursement of providers in some Member States, but not others, may distort the Single Market and ultimately lead to a migration of providers to those Member States where authorities are obliged to reimburse costs.

Scope creep is another obvious problem. Data retained for one purpose—law enforcement—can also be used for other attractive purposes. Should this be allowed? Member States' freedom to legislate in this area also leaves them open to lobbying by industry, and notably, the content industry in its fight against online 'piracy'. For example, the UK Creative and Business Media Association (CMBA), representing the digital content industry, has already demanded that access to retained data should also be granted for the purpose of investigating other crimes, such as intellectual property infringement. This could lead to a situation where an instrument brought in as an anti-terrorist measure may in the future be used to prosecute illegal file-sharers. Interestingly, in the case of *Promusicae v Telefónica de España SAU*,[104] the ECJ declared that EU Member States are not under an obligation to enact provisions allowing the use of personal data for civil procedure purposes. It did not, however, specifically *prohibit* the enactment of such legislation. Thus in the UK, for example, there seems no reason why rights-holders might not obtain access to such data on the basis of an ordinary *Norwich Pharmacal* order.[105]

---

101 RIPA s 81(2) and (3).

102 S 113b Nr 1 Telecommunications Act 2004—although see judicial criticism of this above.

103 Note from Vice-President Franco Frattini to the Commission, Proposal for the Directive on data retention, 7 December 2005, SP (2005) 4782/2.

104 Judgment of the Court (Grand Chamber) of 29 January 2008 (Reference for a preliminary ruling from the Juzgado de lo Mercantil No 5 de Madrid—Spain)—*Productores de Música de España (Promusicae) v Telefónica de España SAU*, C-275/06, OJ C 64/9.

105 See eg *Totalise PLC v The Motley Fool Limited* [2001] EMLR 750.

Scope creep might also arise via other, supposedly unconnected legislative activity.[106] The EC Telecoms Framework reforms, commented on elsewhere in this volume, at one point included a proposal that CSPs should be allowed, and indeed encouraged, to process traffic data 'for the purpose of implementing technical measures to ensure the security' of their network.[107] These proposals seem to have been removed at time of writing; however, their appearance in a draft Directive just over two years after the DRD was adopted is a good example of the danger of 'function creep', ie the expansion of the uses to which personal data can be put once it has been collected, even if not anticipated at the time of retention. By following this approach, Member States leave themselves open to a gradual erosion of the right to privacy. Experience has shown that the mere existence of 'data pools', once generated, quickly creates 'unwholesome desires' in those who could, but for the original purpose restriction, derive benefit from using that data.[108] From that realisation, it is a short way to the adoption of additional legislation which expands the purposes for which that data may be used. However, such 'function creep' will inevitably lead to a gradual loss of control by individuals over their own personal data, all the more dangerous because the process is a creeping and incremental one.

Considering both this chapter and the previous one, the almost unlimited collection of data about citizens' online behaviour and the use of that information by public authorities for the purpose of creating profiles of potential offenders may well lead to serious and worrying social changes in the form of 'social categorising'.[109] This may privilege some citizens and disadvantage others by including them in 'suspected categories' in advance of any crime committed by them. Members of such 'suspected' categories (eg members of Muslim communities) may perceive themselves as under unwanted observation and forced into avoiding activities and associations that might be misconstrued.[110] This could ultimately lead to a loss of political participation by specific minority groups, which, in turn, could damage the political fabric of the democratic society.[111] Bennett and Raab

---

[106] See the European Parliament's Committee on Civil Liberties, Justice and Home Affairs (LIBE) opinion on a draft Directive, COM(2007) 698 final.

[107] Opinion of the Committee on Civil Liberties, Justice and Home Affairs, 26 June 2008, 2007/0248(COD), Amendment 27 inserting a new Art 6(6a). The justification here was the popular idea of giving network providers every tool to take steps to fight off malware, etc, but some commentators feared the result would be negation of data retention and data protection safeguards.

[108] See eg the discussion in the previous chapter of how the Transport for London Oyster card has transmuted quietly from neutral smart card technology into a useful tool for surveillance by both private and public interests—see p 571 of this volume.

[109] See eg D Lyon *Surveillance after September 11* (Cambridge, Polity Press, 2003) 27.

[110] Ibid, 142.

[111] So eg P Regan, *Legislating Privacy: Technology, Social Values and Public Policy* (Chapel Hill, University of North Carolina Press, 1995) 227. See also E Blaustein, 'Privacy as an Aspect of Human Dignity: An Answer to Dean Prosser' (1964) 39 *New York University Law Review* 1000.

point out that social categorising may lead to privacy inequities where the 'political public realm is harmed if restraint on arbitrary power can only be exercised by certain, perhaps privacy-privileged, persons or categories'.[112] The future existence of 'privacy haves' and 'have-nots' may be seriously damaging to the social fabric of society.

Equally worrying is the shift in the role of LEAs from reactive to intelligence-led preventative policing.[113] Rather than investigating and prosecuting crimes that have already been committed, LEAs in their new role focus, rather in the way depicted in the film *Minority Report*,[114] on the prevention of crimes that may be committed in the future.[115] This shift is informed to a large extent by the 'dream of a risk-free society',[116] a feeling now seemingly prevailing that the state should be able to prevent hazards from occurring that were previously viewed as outside our control.[117] Sunstein argues that in a democracy, officials, including lawmakers, are particularly quick to respond to public alarm.[118] If citizens are worried about terrorism, we might well expect that politicians, adamant that they will not be blamed for inactivity, will dedicate substantial resources to showing that everything is being done to minimise or even prevent another terrorist attack from occurring. However, this role can only be fulfilled through access to information about all citizens (rather than just suspects in a particular case) and through detailed profiling of those citizens on the basis of that information. This can ultimately lead to a presumption of 'guilty until proven innocent'. Consequently, any morphing of a reactive force into a proactive, intelligence-led force must be accompanied by stringent safeguards and oversight of that force to avoid the sacrifice of the presumption of innocence, a fundamental tenet which underpins every democratic system based on the rule of law.

At the time of writing, many EU Member States have yet to transpose the Directive even though the implementation period[119] for both telephony and Internet data has now expired. In view of the cases pending in several

---

112 CJ Benett and CD Raab, *The Governance of Privacy*, 2nd edn (Cambridge, MA, MIT Press, 2006) 41.

113 See n 9 above.

114 Steven Spielberg, 2002, which forecast the detection and prosecution of 'pre-crime', albeit with the use of precognitive ability.

115 A prime example for this approach is the creation by the government of the ONSET database, a profiling tool which examines a child's behaviour and social background to predict potential child offenders.

116 For further discussion of the effect that this dream has on data collection and processing practices, see J Rauhofer, '"Privacy Is Dead, Get Over It!" Information Privacy and the Dream of a Risk-free Society' (2008) 17(3) *Information & Communications Technology Law* 185–97.

117 See eg PL Berstein, *Against the Gods: The Remarkable Story of Risk* (New York, John Wiley, 1998).

118 CR Sunstein, 'The Laws of Fear' (2002) *Harvard Law Review* 1119, 1127.

119 The German news agency DPA reported in January 2008 that the EU Commission sent official letters of complaint to 19 Member States because they have not yet transposed the Data Retention Directive. See eg http://www.heise.de/newsticker/meldung/101268.

Member States and the increasing possibility of a referral of the human rights question to either the ECJ or the European Court of Human Rights (or both), CSPs and privacy campaigners may hope that implementation will, in the end, not be necessary. However, by the time the legal issues have finally been resolved, it is likely the technical infrastructure required to facilitate both data retention and access to retained data will be firmly in place. And as we have seen, governments like the UK's have already shown a desire in any case to exceed the requirements of the DRD in home regulation. Regardless of the outcome of the current legal challenges to the DRD, it is therefore likely that governments will find a way to make use of that infrastructure in the medium to long term, unless their constituents react forcibly.

The fact remains that no business case has yet been made that electronic intrusion on the scale envisaged by the DRD is necessary for the purpose cited. Even a study commissioned in 2005 by the UK EU Presidency,[120] one of the strongest supporters of blanket data retention, found that the majority of the data requested by LEAs were generated less than three months prior to the request. This roughly equates to the period for which communications data is retained by CSPs for their own business purposes in any case. Mandatory retention in excess of that three-month period therefore seems neither appropriate nor proportionate to the stated objective. To date, LEAs have been remarkably reluctant to publish any empirical data about actual cases where communications data retained longer than six months (say) has been useful, and indeed necessary, for the successful conclusion of a criminal investigation.

Given the problems addressed of scope creep, economic distortions, legal disharmony and severe potential for future threats to privacy, equality and democracy, it is hard to see how the current and emerging retention and access regimes can be justified, even in the name of security and crime prevention—or at least not without much clearer evidence. It can only be hoped that governments will eventually agree to adopt more stringent safeguards, driven by popular disquiet, before the maximum surveillance society has been achieved to the maximum deficit of its citizens.

---

[120] *Liberty and Security—Striking the Right Balance*, paper by the UK Presidency of the European Union available at http://www.edri.org/docs/UKpresidencypaper.pdf.

19

Cybercrime and Internet Security: A Criminological Introduction

RICHARD JONES

I. INTRODUCTION: CRIMINOLOGY AND THE STUDY OF CYBERCRIME

BROADLY SPEAKING, CRIMINOLOGY may be said to be the academic study of anything to do with crime or deviance,[1] or of society's responses to these. Criminology may therefore study crime's causes, patterns or trends; or of society's various responses to crime (be these preventive, criminal legal, prosecutorial, punitive, or representational). While few criminologists at present come from a computing background, among the strengths that criminology can already bring to an understanding of cybercrime are a repertoire of explanations of the causes of crime; of policing and crime prevention; research methodologies; and the study of crime within its wider social and political contexts.

In this chapter, it will be argued that criminology offers various existing resources—in the form of theories, concepts and research findings—of potential value to the study of cybercrime, including to those working outside criminology. The aims of the criminological study of cybercrime might be said to be to identify, model and theorise patterns or regularities in the commission of cybercrime or cyber-deviant (that is, sub-criminal) activity, in order to understand, explain, prevent or detect that activity. The quest for understanding the activity may also extend to questioning its 'common-sense', academic or media representations.

II. CYBERCRIME AS CRIME IN A NEW SOCIAL SPACE

In the 1990s and early 2000s, initial criminological research on cybercrime

---

[1] Deviance may loosely be defined as subcriminal behaviour, of an anti-social or socially stigmatised kind. The concept does not withstand close examination (C Sumner, *The Sociology of Deviance: An Obituary* (Buckingham: Open University Press, 1994), but is useful in escaping a strict reliance on criminal law.

included some discussion as to the 'novelty' or otherwise of cybercrime.[2] Rather than pursue this debate any further directly here, I wish in this chapter to frame my discussion by reference to, and by development of, an argument put forward by Manning, namely that within criminology, traditional understandings of policing seem inadequate to account for contemporary developments in that area.[3] The policing of 'new social spaces', Manning argues, requires rethinking of conventional assumptions that policing occurs within national territorial borders, that police or the state have distinctive claims to the use of force, and that insofar as policing involves the protection of property that this is of the real kind.[4] Manning argues, effectively, that the contentions of those who point to transnational policing as representing a new development in policing can be extended further: 'Transnational policing', he writes, 'is partly about the regulation of a new, growing and resonant kind of social space. Communicational policing, the ordering of "cyberspace", is a growing facet of policing':

> What is needed is a conception of policing in the information age, an age in which national boundaries are less marked and clear, where information is a commodity, and secrecy and security concerns are located, in large part, in transnational information networks.[5]

Manning's argument is of interest here not merely because of its early and far-sighted identification of the significance that the new social space of the Internet is likely to hold for the police in years to come (even if in the past decade the advances have so far been slower than Manning perhaps expected), but additionally because his discussion of the nature of this social space is not restricted to policing concerns alone, and is instead of wider applicability within the study of cybercrime. More particularly, Manning correctly argues that the emergence of the Internet is part of contemporary 'fundamental changes in social embeddedness', or in other words, and drawing from the social theorist Anthony Giddens,[6] that electronic communication systems such as the Internet facilitate the creation and maintenance of 'social relations across vast spaces', which in turn may be to wider transformative social effect. 'Increasingly', Manning maintains, 'interpersonal processes are mediated and produced by the mass media and aspects of modern experience are derived from electronically represented images rather than exclusively from direct, sensate personal experience', and 'New social realities (definitions of the real and the signif-

---

[2] See eg W Capeller, 'Not Such a Neat Net: Some Comments on Virtual Criminality' (2001) 10 *Social and Legal Studies* 229–42.

[3] P Manning, 'Policing New Social Spaces', in J Sheptycki (ed), *Issues in Transnational Policing* (London, Routledge, 2000).

[4] Ibid, 177–79.

[5] Ibid, 180.

[6] A Giddens, *Modernity and Self-identity* (Cambridge, Polity Press, 1991).

icant) are framed by media, and by computer screens which create ersatz social realities.'[7]

This seems a useful way of framing the study of cybercrime, because instead of arguing about the novelty of cybercrime, the analysis instead posits an emerging new social space, and asks: what is the nature of the criminal activity that takes place in this space, what are its mechanisms and motivations, and what can or indeed should be done about it? In turn, this analysis seems to echo earlier discussions within criminology in the light of 'some changes that appear to be taking place in prevailing understandings of public and private spaces, and of their functions'—a debate that took place within the context of the ethical implications of installing situational crime prevention measures within 'semi-public' spaces such as shopping malls,[8] but which also appears relevant to understanding the use, policing and control of the Internet. The public social migration into these new social spaces may have begun in the real world but is now also virtual in form.

III. CRIMINOLOGICAL THEORIES OF CRIME CAUSATION AND THEIR APPLICATION TO CYBERCRIME

If we accept the proposition that there are some continuities between cyberspace and the physical world, then for criminology one way of proceeding is to explore the extent to which existing criminological theories appear to offer insights into known details about cybercrime. Indeed, several criminologists have already identified possible theories, and suggested how they might be applied. McQuade, for example, offers a simple and brief overview of a wide range of criminological theories, before suggesting aspects of cybercrime those theories may help explain.[9] Elsewhere, Williams has suggested how 'control theory' might help account for online deviance, and Yar has reflected on the relevance of 'routine activities theory'.[10] Many other works discuss cybercrime within the context of criminological scholarship in general.[11] In this section, I will introduce just a few different criminological theories, sketching their potential applicability to cybercrime. Whether or to what extent these theories *actually*

[7] Manning, above n 3, 188.

[8] A von Hirsch and C Shearing, 'Exclusion from Public Space', in A von Hirsch, D Garland and A Wakefield (eds), *Ethical and Social Perspectives on Situational Crime Prevention* (Oxford, Hart Publishing, 2000) 79.

[9] S McQuade, *Understanding and Managing Cybercrime* (Boston, Pearson Education, Inc (Allyn and Bacon), 2006) ch 5.

[10] M Williams, *Virtually Criminal* (London, Routledge, 2006); M Yar, 'The Novelty of "Cybercrime": An Assessment in the Light of Routine Activities Theory' (2005) 2(4) *European Journal of Criminology* 407–27.

[11] M Yar, *Cybercrime and Society* (London, Sage, 2006); D Wall, *Cybercrime* (Cambridge, Polity Press, 2007); G Newman and RV Clarke, *Superhighway Robbery: Preventing E-commerce Crime* (Cullompton, Willan Publishing, 2003).

explain cybercrime is a matter for subsequent empirical research. Nevertheless, considering how the theories might be applied is a necessary first step to testing their validity—and by setting out their main claims, also serves as a way of introducing them.

A. Techniques of Neutralisation

In a brief but justly famous article, the American criminologists Sykes and Matza argued that far from achieving an 'inversion' of mainstream cultural norms and values, as earlier 'subcultural' theory had maintained, delinquents typically retained an underlying belief in mainstream values.[12] Delinquent behaviour could nevertheless still occur, as a result of a temporary 'neutralisation' of the sense of doing wrong that the moral infractions otherwise tended to create. Delinquents invoke specific neutralisation 'techniques', typically through expressing spurious justifications for what they had done. These could feature a denial of responsibility, of causing harm, or of the existence of a victim; of condemning the law-abiding condemners; or of appealing to 'higher' social loyalties. Examples include phrases such as, "'I didn't mean it." "I didn't really hurt anybody." "They had it coming to them." "Everyone's picking on me."'[13] In a subsequent article, the same two authors argue that delinquents' values actually often echo society's very own 'subterranean values', and hence are not as far removed from mainstream society as we and they may think.[14]

Matza maintains that subcultural theories overpredict delinquents' commitment to deviance, arguing instead that delinquency is more intermittent and is often time-limited to adolescence.[15] Most delinquents, he contends, 'drift' into (and later out of) delinquency, lacking a true commitment to delinquency even during their delinquent phase. Their delinquency is enabled by the prior and temporary neutralisation of a deeper and lasting belief as to what is morally right. Insofar as the delinquent harbours a 'sense of injustice' when confronted with their wrongdoing, this indicates that the alleged 'inversion' of societal norms has not truly taken place (because otherwise they would happily admit and affirm their deviance).[16] Delinquents collectively play-out a subculture of delinquency, but individually lack the commitment to delinquent subcultures predicted by the original subcultural theory.

There are various possible applications of the theory to cybercrime. Yar

---

[12] G Sykes and D Matza, 'Techniques of Neutralization: A Theory of Delinquency' (1957) 22(6) *American Sociological Review* 664–70.

[13] Ibid, 669.

[14] D Matza and G Sykes, 'Juvenile Delinquency and Subterranean Values' (1961) 26(5) *American Sociological Review* 712–19.

[15] D Matza, *Delinquency and Drift* (New York, John Wiley, 1964).

[16] Ibid, ch 4.

suggests it could be used interpret hackers' justifications for what they do.[17] Another application is in relation to file-sharing.[18] Matza's theory would maintain that deep down, (most) file-sharers know that what they are doing is wrong. Techniques of neutralisation could include claims along the lines that, 'The music industry only has itself to blame', 'DVDs are too expensive', 'Everyone does it', 'I'm not hurting anybody', or 'The real "villains" are the recording and movie industries.' The claims of industry bodies such as the UK's Federation Against Copyright Theft (FACT) have been much ridiculed, yet it is possible that the moral argument they are advancing is actually accepted by many of those downloading or sharing material. Techniques of neutralisation may also be used by other types of cybercriminal, such as those circulating child pornography, or by spammers or cybervandals.

B. 'Edgework'

Lyng has suggested that the study of the pleasures of 'voluntary risk taking', or 'edgework', is important for understanding some people's otherwise mysterious penchant for risky behaviour.[19] The notion of 'edgework' has informed the 'cultural criminology' school, among others, but here I will focus on Lyng's original article. While archetypal edgework involves the risk of serious physical danger, such as in skydiving, rock-climbing or downhill skiing, Lyng suggests that edgework requires the individual to have particular skill, namely in 'the ability to maintain control over a situation that verges on complete chaos, a situation most people would regard as entirely uncontrollable', including 'business entrepreneurship', drug-taking, and crime.[20] Lyng reports that 'most edgeworkers regard this general skill as essentially cognitive in nature, and they often refer to it as a special form of "mental toughness"'.[21] This leads to a certain 'elitist orientation among some edgeworkers' who believe they are one of 'a select few and who often feel a powerful solidarity with one another based on their perceived elite status'.[22] Among the subjective sensations experienced by edgeworkers is heightened focus, slow down or speed up in time, 'a feeling of "oneness" with the object or environment'. Lyng notes that some edgeworkers even actually 'artificially' increase the risks, which he regards as indicative of their more general 'commitment to get as close as possible

[17] Yar, above n 11, 34.

[18] R Moore and EC McMullan, 'Perceptions of Peer-to-Peer File Sharing Among University Students' (2004) 11(1) *Journal of Criminal Justice and Popular Culture* 1–19.

[19] S Lyng, 'Edgework: A Social Psychological Analysis of Voluntary Risk Taking' (1990) 95(4) *American Journal of Sociology* 851–86.

[20] Ibid, 857, 859, 856.

[21] Ibid, 859.

[22] Ibid, 860.

to the edge without going over it'.[23] As Lyng recognises, his concept bears 'some resemblance' both to Goffman's concept of 'action', and to Csikszentmihalyi's 'notion of "flow"'—indeed the relation between them may be closer than he is inclined to acknowledge.[24] Whilst edgework need not entail actions that are criminal, both Lyng and Goffman offer crime as an example of a particular kind of thrill-seeking activity.

The notion of 'edgework' has various applications to cybercrime. Lyng's exploration of the more risk-seeking, action-like, type of behaviour leads us closer to the study of what Katz recognises as the 'seductive thrills' of illicit behaviour.[25] Doing something illegal on the Internet would seem to require a certain 'voluntary risk taking', the would-be offender deciding to risk detection and possible arrest and prosecution. Doing something prohibited on the Internet is likely to require a degree of computing proficiency (eg in how to set up an anonymous e-mail account in order to send abusive e-mails). Edgework may usefully help draw attention to the 'sneaky thrills' users may experience in seeking out illicit pornographic materials, in 'hacking' into protected servers or in 'cracking' data encryption systems. In each case, part of the subjective attraction of 'doing' the crime may lie in the adrenaline rush in doing wrong, but also in thereafter using computing skills in order to finesse the offence and evade detection. Just as it is reported that in the real world some offenders report feeling drawn to certain venues, pursuits or parts of town, in their search of the 'action', some of which may be criminal, so too some users online may migrate towards more dubious communities and forums, and the illicit and exciting activities they open up.[26] Just as some robbers may be motivated by 'the buzz or excitement that it generated', including 'overpowering the victim and obtaining dominance over the situation',[27] so too may computer 'hackers' be attracted to what Hayward and Young refer to elsewhere as 'the adrenaline rush of crime'.[28]

C. Routine Activities Theory

As both Yar and Grabosky have noted, routine activities theory (RAT) might usefully be applied to cybercrime.[29] In Cohen and Felson's classic formu-

---

23 Ibid, 862.

24 Ibid, 862–63; E Goffman, 'Where the Action Is', in E Goffman (ed), *Interaction Ritual* (Harmondsworth, Penguin, 1972); M Csikszentmihalyi, *Flow* (London, Random House, 2002).

25 J Katz, *Seductions of Crime* (New York, Basic Books, 1988).

26 Goffman, above n 24.

27 T Bennett and F Brookman, 'Violent Street Crime: Making Sense of Seemingly Senseless Acts' (2008) 22(1–2) *International Review of Law Computers & Technology* 171–80, 174.

28 K Hayward and J Young (2004) 'Cultural Criminology: Some Notes on the Script' (2004) 8(3) *Theoretical Criminology* 259–73, 264.

29 Yar, above n 11; P Grabosky, 'Virtual Criminality: Old Wine in New Bottles?' (2001) 10 *Social and Legal Studies* 243–49.

lation of this theory, 'criminal acts' are said to 'require the convergence in space and time of *likely offenders*, *suitable targets* and the *absence of capable guardians* against crime'.[30] By means of this simple formulation, RAT attempts to capture the essential elements of any crime. If correct, crime could be prevented by negating any one of these elements. The theory's name derives from the claim that the routine activities of people's lives inadvertently throw up confluences of the three elements. This pragmatic account emphasises crime 'situations' rather than criminals' individual dispositions, and as such is related to other situational approaches such as situational crime prevention (see below).[31] RAT's emphasis on the 'organization of time and space' in 'explain[ing] how crime occurs and what to do about it'[32] raises interesting questions in terms of its applicability to cybercrime.[33] Specifically, Yar argues that 'the transposability of RAT to virtual environments requires that cyberspace exhibit a *spatio-temporal ontology* congruent with that if the "physical world", ie that place, proximity, distance and temporal order be identifiable features of cyberspace'.[34]

Yar argues that if in cyberspace everything is always 'just a click away', and its places at 'zero distance' from one another, then a different spatiality is present.[35] However, he then argues, unequal access to cyberspace by different socioeconomic groups, as well as the role that hyperlinks play in establishing virtual linkages between related sites, establish some spatial continuities with the real world. He maintains that there are fewer continuities in respect of temporality (the Internet 'is populated "24/7"').[36] The element of 'suitable targets' partially transposes, though the quality and accessibility of online targets may be different to those in the real world.[37] Lastly, he concludes that while formal guardianship by police is minimal, cyberspace does indeed possess a range of 'private and informal social guardians' (eg computing officers, forum administrators and other users), as well as numerous 'physical' guardians such as 'intrusion detection systems'.[38]

RAT is perhaps surprisingly well placed to offer a useful analysis of cybercrime. For example, far from undermining its emphasis on temporality, it could be argued that cybercrime reveals the impact of globalisation, '24/7' culture and time zones on such offending. Similarly, the problems

---

[30] L Cohen and M Felson, 'Social Change and Crime Rate Trends: A Routine Activity Approach' (1979) 44(4) *American Sociological Review* 588–608, 588 (emphases in original).

[31] M Yar, 'The Novelty of "Cybercrime": An Assessment in the Light of Routine Activities Theory' (2005) 2(4) *European Journal of Criminology* 407–27, 411–12.

[32] M Felson, *Crime and Everyday Life*, 3rd edn. (London, Sage, 2002) 123.

[33] See Yar, above n 31, 414, passim.

[34] Ibid, 414, emphasis in original.

[35] Ibid, 415.

[36] Ibid, 418.

[37] Ibid, 419–22.

[38] Ibid, 423.

that police encounter in maintaining a visible presence online do not diminish the importance of guardianship, but instead highlight its role; a central factor in the continuing widespread use of peer-to-peer (P2P) file-sharing, for instance, might precisely be that such technology escapes the gaze of guardians. Indeed, the theory might usefully be applied to all manner of unlawful activities online, which could be seen to remain rife partly as a consequence of communities or environments lacking capable guardians. The theory does, of course, raise an interesting question as to the aims, intentions and moral values of a guardian (if one is present): file-sharing and pornographic forums may be conspicuous by their lack of capable guardians guarding against such activities, yet feature forum administrators who guard against breaking of the forum's *own* rules—and who thus capably guard with the aim of perpetuating, not preventing, the forum's activities.

The sheer scale of 'likely offenders' and 'suitable targets' online may generate its own amplifying, 'network effect'. Felson has specifically examined the way in which '[o]ne crime can feed into another', including through the 'interplay of illegal markets', 'of victimization as a cause of crime' and the significance of 'repeat victimization', and of seeing 'crime as an ecosystem',[39] and such dynamics may prove useful for the study certain types of cybercrime and deviance.

IV. POLICING THE INTERNET

The police would seem to be one of the bodies best placed to enforce criminal law relating to cybercrime (though as we shall see, they are by no means the only body so involved). Policing has long been a topic of interest within criminology, and recently, interest has expanded to the study of private policing, and of policing functions carried out by various agencies at local, national and international levels. Within criminology, the term 'policing' is now often used to refer to a general role or function, and not just to the activities of police officers alone.

While not especially quick to become involved in policing cybercrime, both the police and other policing agencies typically now have some staff dedicated to this area, though arguably cybercrime remains a niche area in the eyes of many police forces and officers. The reasons for this may include that it does not easily fit with officers' notions of 'real' police work; that it is often relatively low-visibility work; lack of funding; or that it requires specialist technical skills.[40] Furthermore, institutional politics may

---

[39] Felson, above n 32, ch 8.
[40] Y Jewkes and M Yar, 'Policing Cybercrime', in T Newburn (ed), *Handbook of Policing*, 2nd edn (Cullompton, Willan Publishing, 2008), 580–605, 595–97.

inhibit police uptake of technology; and while key individuals within the police may promote early adoption of certain new technologies, this often happens against an institutional backdrop favouring late adoption.[41] Perhaps the single greatest difference between policing the Internet and policing the real world is that the virtual world does not appear to lend itself to being patrolled in quite the same way as is common in the real world: it is harder to reassure with your presence if you are invisible, and may also fail to engage with police cultural values relating to patrols, police presence and arrests. This may be less of a crime prevention problem than it first appears, however, since there is little evidence that real-world policing patrols have much effect on reducing crime rates; instead, they may be a form of 'reassurance policing' or 'security theatre'.[42]

In other aspects of policing of cybercrime, however, there appear to be a number of roles the police can more naturally play. One is surveillance (achieved by 'lurking', monitoring Internet traffic, etc). Another is the detective role. It is in this area that specialist police units (along with specialist private companies) would seem to have the most natural claim to expertise. Indeed, the sophistication of the tasks involved may quite possibly lead specialist police units increasingly to recruit staff (officers or civilians) with technical backgrounds. As Casey explains, considerable care, and today also specialist software, may be required in obtaining electronic evidence.[43] There is now a considerable body of law regulating the admissibility of this evidence, though, as with real-world crime, police investigators' awareness of the law of evidence is likely to vary considerably, and investigating officers may often choose to seek expert legal guidance during an investigation.[44]

If we expand the notion of 'policing' to its wider meaning (above) it becomes clearer that it is already fairly extensive. Jewkes argues that, '[j]ust as the policing of terrestrial space has demanded a "joined-up approach" between individual citizens, private sector agencies and the police, so too has the policing of cyberspace become a pluralistic endeavour'.[45] Both Wall, and Nhan and Huey, have suggested that notions developed within criminology (eg by Johnson and Shearing) to account for apparent networks of policing ranging across organisations, or that conceive of diverse

[42] See P Manning, *The Technology of Policing* (New York, New York University Press, 2008).

[42] On the idea of 'reassurance policing', see M Innes, 'Reinventing Tradition? Reassurance, Neighbourhood Security and Policing' (2004) 4(2) *Criminal Justice* 151–71; see also J Wood and C Shearing, *Imagining Security* (Cullompton, Willan Publishing, 2006) 58; Wall, above n 11, 178. On 'security theatre', see B Schneier, *Beyond Fear* (New York, Copernicus/Springer, 2006) 38–40; B Schneier, *Schneier on Security* (Indianapolis, IN, Wiley Publishing, 2008) 173–75.

[43] E Casey, *Digital Evidence and Computer Crime*, 2nd edn (New York, Academic Press, 2004).

[44] See S Mason, *Electronic Evidence: Disclosure, Discovery and Admissibility* (London, Butterworths, 2007); S Mason (ed), *International Electronic Evidence* (London, British Institute of International and Comparative Law, 2008).

[45] Jewkes and Yar, above n 40, 608; see also I Loader, 'Plural Policing and Democratic Governance' (2000) 9(3) *Social & Legal Studies* 323–45.

entities carrying out policing as 'nodes' within a wider security 'assem-blage', can also be used to model policing of the Internet.[46] In any case, as Wall shows, Internet policing activities today appear to be carried out not only by state police (and by various units and agencies therein) but also by individuals (eg forum moderators), Internet service providers (ISPs), computing and administrative staff, computer security consultants, state security services or private companies (eg in financial services or telecom-munications sectors).[47] More generally, whereas public police in the real world have been said to differ from private police partly by dint of their 'monopoly' on the use of force, it remains to be seen how far this holds true online.[48]

Lastly, it is worth considering whether it may be possible to automate certain policing practice in the years ahead, and in particular whether 'autonomous agents' could be used in criminal investigations.[49] Auton-omous software agents are computer programs that can set about tasks, learning as they go along, interacting with data or even other computing systems as they encounter them. A central attraction of such programs for law enforcement is that they may be able intelligently to search and scan a far greater number of sites, and for far longer time periods, than can humans. Schafer suggests they could be used, for example, to scan financial transactions for irregularities, or to monitor forums or chatrooms. Moreover, agents could potentially be taught to impersonate humans online—though this raises interesting legal questions in relation to privacy and to admissibility of evidence, for example.[50] As Schafer notes, one intriguing solution would be to design legally compliant behaviour into the agents' own code, such that they intelligently followed key legal rules in context-specific ways.[51] It is possible that other developments, such as of the 'semantic web', in which information on the Internet is tagged so as to make it easier for computers to analyse the data, will facilitate the use of autonomous agents. On the other hand, such agents could be thwarted by

[46] Wall, above n 11, 167; J Nhan and L Huey, 'Policing Through Nodes, Clusters and Bandwidth', in S Leman-Langlois (ed), *Technocrime: Technology, Crime and Social Control* (Cullompton, Willan Publishing, 2008); L Johnson and C Shearing, *Governing Security: Explorations in Policing and Justice* (London, Routledge, 2003); on the notion of 'surveillant assemblage', see K Haggerty and R Ericson, 'The Surveillant Assemblage' (2000) 51(4) *British Journal of Sociology* 605–22.

[47] Wall, above n 11, ch 8, esp 168; see also M Yar, 'Computer Crime Control as Industry: Virtual Insecurity and the Market for Private Policing', in K Franco Aas et al (eds), *Technologies of Insecurity* (London, Routledge Cavendish, 2008).

[48] For the classic discussion of public police use of force, see E Bittner, *The Functions of the Police in Modern Society* (Cambridge, MA: Oelgeschlager, Gunn & Hain, Publishers, Inc, 1980 [1970]).

[49] See B Schafer, 'The Taming of the Sleuth: Problems and Potential of Autonomous Agents in Crime Investigation and Prosecution' (2006) 20(1) *International Review of Law, Computers & Technology* 63–76.

[50] Ibid, 66–73.

[51] Ibid, 74–75.

the use of secure private networks. Whilst such sophisticated systems remain largely theoretical at present, they are useful reminders as to possible new ways of policing the Internet.

V. INTERNET SECURITY AND CYBERCRIME PREVENTION

A. Crime Prevention

Brantingham and Faust suggest that, as with public health, crime prevention approaches tend to take the form of one of three types: primary (across the population as a whole); secondary (targeting those apparently particularly 'at risk'); or tertiary (targeting 'known offenders, victims or places that are already part of the crime pattern').[52] Crime prevention approaches are also often described as being either 'social' (targeting wider social processes) or 'situational' (targeting the specific locale in which the crime is committed); the latter is of particular interest in relation to cybercrime.

Situational crime prevention (SCP) was developed by RV Clarke and others during the 1980s. It argues that crime can most effectively be prevented by intervening in the specific situations in which it is committed.[53] By studying the mechanisms by which crime is actually committed, we can work out how to make it harder to commit. (This principle has been adopted by 'ethical hacking'—essentially weakness-testing computer and network security—though SCP purists might argue that ethical hacking promotes a never-ending patching stance, and that a better approach is to design in good security from the outset.) According to the approach, the study of 'criminality' or of the supposed wider 'causes of crime' is both unnecessary and fruitless. (Clarke believes, indeed, that criminology must either embrace such 'crime science' or become irrelevant and wither away.[54]) SCP classically seeks to increase the effort required to commit crime, to increase the risks of being detected or to reduce the rewards gained. SCP maintains that although carried out for self-gain, much offending is opportunistic, and that sufficient increases or reductions effectively prevent (or at least reduce) offending. This approach, seeking to 'design out' crime, is reminiscent of Lessig's 'architectural regulation'; and indeed some of Lessig's examples, such as in relation to car radio theft, are

---

[52] A Crawford, 'Crime Prevention and Community Safety', in M Maguire et al (eds), *The Oxford Handbook of Criminology*, 4th edn (Oxford, Oxford University Press, 2007) 870; P Brantingham and L Faust, 'A Conceptual Model of Crime Prevention' (1976) 22 *Crime and Delinquency* 284–96.

[53] RV Clarke, '"Situational" Crime Prevention: Theory and Practice' (1980) 20 *British Journal of Criminology* 136–47.

[54] RV Clarke, 'Technology, Criminology and Crime Science' (2004) 10 *European Journal on Criminal Policy and Research* 55–63.

recognisable as SCP measures.[55] SCP today contends that additional strategies can involve reducing (situational) provocations and removing
excuses.[56] Crime reduction measures based on such mechanisms will have
to overcome offender 'techniques of neutralisation' (see above) if they are
to prove effective, yet this recognition of the possible role of social psychological and normative mechanisms in reducing offending is of considerable
potential import.

Newman and Clarke have argued that SCP principles can usefully be
applied to e-commerce crime. Information, they argue, is often a 'hot
product', attractive to criminals, and the information age unwittingly
generates a raft of attractive targets for criminals— including information
that is intellectual property, contained in protected financial or government
systems, or that can be used to obtain goods or services.[57] Hot products are
attractive to criminals because they are 'CRAVED' (concealable, removable,
available, valuable, enjoyable, and disposable), which, they suggest,
describes 'information in e-commerce almost perfectly'.[58] They argue that
many of the systems already found in computer security can be seen to
follow SCP principles, and that greater awareness of these principles could
be used more systematically to improve e-commerce security. Anderson
agrees, suggesting that its methods 'are not far from what security engineers
do'.[59] For example, intrusion detection systems increase the perceived risks
of detection; copy protection systems using digital rights management
(DRM) aim to reduce the rewards; and public campaigns by intellectual
property (IP) rights-holders or their industry groups ('Copying software is
stealing') are an example of trying to remove excuses.[60]

The approach is not without its critics. Hayward suggests that SCP rests
on a 'sociologically hollow' account of offenders and offending.[61] Ferrell,
Hayward and Young have argued that SCP, along with related rational choice
theories, reduce 'crime and crime control to a managerial problem . . .
[and] forfeit . . . any understanding of *internal* psychic-emotive processes'
of the sort described above in the section on 'Edgework'. The 'cultural
criminology' approach developed by these authors instead maintains that

[55] L Lessig, *Code Version 2.0* (New York, Basic Books, 2006) 125–26.

[56] DB Cornish and RV Clarke, 'Opportunities, Precipitators and Criminal Decisions: A Reply
to Wortley's Critique of Situational Crime Prevention', in MJ Smith and DB Cornish (eds),
Theory for Practice in Situational Crime Prevention (Crime Prevention Studies Volume 16)
(Cullompton, Willan, 2003) 41–96; cf. Lessig'sdiscussion of the potential role of 'social norms'
in regulation (above n 55).

[57] G Newman and RV Clarke, *Superhighway Robbery: Preventing E-commerce Crime*
(Cullompton, Willan, 2003), chs 3 and 4.

[58] Ibid, 70.

[59] R Anderson, *Security Engineering*, 2nd edn (Indianapolis, IN, Wiley Publishing, 2008) 370.

[60] Newman and Clarke, above n 57, 114–15.

[61] K Hayward, 'Situational Crime Prevention and its Discontents: Rational Choice Theory
versus the "Culture of Now"' (2007) 41(3) *Social Policy & Administration* 232-250.

subjective emotions and textured socio-cultural dynamics animate many crimes, *and increasingly so under late modern conditions*. . . . The actual, lived *experience* of committing crime, of concluding a criminal act, of being victimized by crime, bears little relationship to the arid world envisioned by [rational choice] theorists.[62]

This appears a strong critique of SCP's conception of offending and offenders—and yet, despite all their (considerable) differences the two theories are not necessarily entirely incompatible. Cultural criminology posits that certain internal emotional processes are at work, and emotions can (sometimes, at least) be managed or contained. It is not impossible to conceive of forms of SCP that seek to incorporate emotional factors into their accounts, and to try to intervene in emotional processes. Indeed, SCP's incorporation of the role of 'reducing provocations' may be interpreted as just this.[63]

Its proponents remain unswayed, however, and Newman and Clarke argue that critics are wrong to dismiss SCP as simply part of a 'society of control', and maintain instead that its social benefits outweigh its costs.[64] However, SCP necessarily remains judged against its own measure, namely crime reduction effectiveness. Clarke and others have documented numerous studies indicating it is indeed effective, to a greater or lesser degree.[65] An argument sometimes made by proponents of SCP is that to the extent that it fails to be effective, this is because it has not yet correctly identified the mechanisms of offending. The logical response, it is argued, is a redoubling of its efforts, not its abandonment. By itself, however, this appears an unfalsifiable argument, and therefore suspect. SCP's stronger claims appear to derive from evaluative evidence confirming its empirical effectiveness in certain applications.

Ekblom notes that a potential challenge facing SCP may be the 'arms race' or 'predator–prey' problem, namely that some offenders may not easily be dissuaded, as SCP usually assumes, and may instead be motivated to overcome attempts at stopping them.[66] In relation to cybercrime, examples might include those involved in 'cracking' of encryption used in DRM systems; spammers, developing ever-changing spam-filter bypass strategies; or writers of malware, requiring the never-ending deployment of 'security patches'. This problem, of the determined cybercriminal, may thus represent an interesting fundamental limit to the applicability to specialised

---

[62] J Ferrell, K Hayward and J Young, *Cultural Criminology* (London, Sage, 2008) 67 (emphases in original).

[63] On the role of provocation reduction in situational crime prevention, see Cornish and Clarke, above n 56, 41–96.

[64] Newman and Clarke, above n 57, ch 8.

[65] See RV Clarke (ed), *Situational Crime Prevention: Successful Case Studies*, 2nd edn (Guilderland, NY, Harrow and Heston, 1997).

[66] P Ekblom, 'Can We Make Crime Prevention Adaptive by Learning from Other Evolutionary Struggles' (2000) 8(1) *Studies on Crime and Crime Prevention* 27–51.

forms of cybercrime, such as computer hacking, of classic formulations of SCP. However, a revised, 'dynamic' form of SCP approach, of the kind suggested by Ekblom and Tilley, which acknowledges and focuses on 'the more intelligent, entrepreneurial end of the range of criminals' might possibly be better placed to tackle sophisticated forms of cybercrime.[67] Despite this, a further problem is that, because of the ease with which information and tools can be disseminated online, even if only one person takes the trouble to crack a particular form of encryption, if that person shares this knowledge, the 'effort' subsequently required to defeat the preventive measure may be so low as to render the measure ineffectual. Indeed, paradoxically, it may be that the *harder* the preventive measure is to beat, the *more* it attracts the attention of those skilled enough potentially to defeat it. There may thus be something CRAVED about solutions and software that overcome legitimate restrictions; cracking or spamming tools may themselves be CRAVED. Another way of looking at this is to suggest that the Internet offers a new way for individuals to combine their efforts; and that whether this is done for good (eg open-source collaborations) or ill, the magnitude of the combined effort may mean that the target-hardening ('increasing the effort') strand of SCP cannot in isolation be relied upon online.

B. Internet Security and Security Engineering

Concerns regarding the security of the Internet appear to have given new impetus to consideration of security and its principles in general. Schneier has drawn from his experience in computer security, distinguishing between the security principles of authentication, authorisation and identification.[68] Identification is the process of establishing a person's identity, typically retrieving this from a local or remote data store. Authentication is a process of checking whether a person is the permitted user he claims to be, such as by requiring him to present a valid token or ticket, or to supply (confirm) a password or number code. Authorisation is instead the process of deter-mining *what* each authenticated person is allowed to do. Authentication and identification are in some ways quite similar, and may be linked or otherwise jumbled together, but the difference between them remains important.[69] For example, I may set up an anonymous e-mail account (without identification), yet the account will almost certainly be secured by authentication (a username and matching password). In relation to cyber-crime we can see, then, that 'hacking', for example, may involve attacks on

---

[67] P Ekblom and N Tilley, 'Going Equipped: Criminology, Situational Crime Prevention and the Resourceful Offender' (2000) 40(3) *British Journal of Criminology* 376–98, 390–91.

[68] Schneier, *Beyond Fear*, above n 42, 182–83.

[69] Ibid, 182.

one of more of these processes: discovering a user's password, eg by means of a 'dictionary attack' (to defeat the authentication system); or of tricking a computer system into granting the higher privileges of an administrator account (thus defeating initial authorisation restrictions). The two could both conceivably be prohibited under a general concept of 'unauthorised access', yet remain quite different in their manner and consequence.

Schneier contends that greater attentiveness to such distinctions is helpful when designing and improving security systems. Yet things can still go wrong. In relation to software, McGraw distinguishes between bugs, flaws and defects. A defect is an aspect of a programme that does not work as it should (in terms of its (inadequate) security), typically as a result of a bug or flaw. A 'bug' is 'an implementation-level software problem', such as a coding mistake, whereas a 'flaw' is a deeper shortcoming deriving from the software design or architecture.[70] Such distinctions seem useful in distinguishing between relatively readily fixable mere coding mistakes, on the one hand, and the more intrinsic security limitations of certain software architecture on the other. McGraw explains how various attacks on software can be achieved, such as in a 'buffer overflow' attack exploiting a coding bug, but also takes care to explain to programmers how to fix and avoid such bugs. In this respect, his approach is very much one of prevention and of designing out (cyber)crime wherever possible, and is thus similar to SCP. A third leading expert on computer security, Ross Anderson, has been instrumental in helping develop security engineering as an academic discipline, and in his wide-ranging introduction to the area combines technical discussion of security practices and common flaws with an awareness of the wider social and human factors involved, including their social and political context.[71] By showing the breadth of topics involved, and through combining technical knowledge with discussion of more general principles, Anderson's work appears in many respects to overlap with various areas of criminology.

The relevance of all this to the study of cybercrime prevention is that it offers pre-existing concepts and principles for creating better security or for analysing the weaknesses of existing security online. The approach is not a crude advocate of incessant target-hardening, and instead is often guided by pragmatism. For example, this approach recognises that while requiring users to use very strong passwords may protect them against 'dictionary' or even 'brute strength' attacks, it is also likely to make them harder to remember, and hence more likely that they will be written down and compromised in another way. As such, at its best, security engineering appears to suggest how within security subtle distinctions and decisions can

---

[70] G McGraw, *Software Security: Building Security In* (Boston, Pearson Education, Inc (Addison Wesley), 2006) 14–16 and ch 1 generally.
[71] Anderson, above n 59.

and should be made, and is alive to the wider social and political implications of these. Security engineering focuses our attention on the mechanics, practical operation and aims of security. Security is not simply something present or absent, or even somewhere in between; it operates in a certain way, a way that may or may not be socially desirable, and that may or may not fulfil its stated goal. As such, security engineering offers a resource for understanding possible mechanisms of cybercrime prevention; may in time find productive points of convergence with the criminological study of crime prevention; and may offer theoretical and technical understandings of real-world security, especially (as is frequently the case today) where that security involves computers, networks or electronic devices.

C. 'Social Engineering', 'Digital Deception' and Security

The use of deception in crime commission is not itself new, and its real-world forms have been documented over the years. Laurie Taylor offers a colourful account of London villains, explaining 'The Beauty of a Good Con'.[72] Polsky famously sketched an ethnography of the lives of American poolroom 'hustlers' of the late 1960s, noting that the 'hustler is a certain kind of con man. And conning, by definition, involves extraordinary manipulation of other people's impressions of reality and especially of one's self, creating "false impressions"'.[73] Edwin Lemert noted that '[t]he confidence man manipulates his victims so that they often remain unaware they have been duped, or so that they fear to go to the police', while the cheque forger, not like today's phishing websites, employs a more mobile approach, recognising the need continually to strike and quickly 'move on'.[74] Earlier still, Maurer documented the ways of 1940s' confidence men and their confidence tricks.[75] Indeed, tricksters of one sort or another have no doubt been operating not just for centuries but for millennia. However, the new online spaces of the Internet appear to have presented the deceitful with new opportunities. Attention to the human element in persuading people to part with things of value (including information) is useful in drawing attention to the limits of technological systems by themselves in preventing crime.

Anderson suggests that '[m]any real attacks exploit psychology at least as much as technology', and quotes Schneier as maintaining that '[o]nly amateurs attack machines; professionals target people'.[76] Such 'social

---

[72] L Taylor, *In the Underworld* (London, Unwin Paperbacks, 1985).

[73] N Polsky, *Hustlers, Beats and Others* [Pelican Books; Anchor rev edn] (Harmondsworth, Penguin Books, 1971) 63.

[74] E Lemert, *Human Deviance, Social Problems, and Social Control* (Englewood Cliffs, NJ, Prentice-Hall, 1967) 122.

[75] M Maurer, *The Big Con* (London, Arrow Books (Random House), 2000).

[76] Anderson, above n 59, 17.

engineering', as Mitnick and Simon term this form of attack, involves tricking people into doing or saying something to the attacker's advantage. As such, these attacks usefully draw our attention to the 'human element of security', to how it can be exploited, and how it can be made more secure.[77]

Mitnick famously provides numerous examples of 'social engineering'. The scams he recounts use a variety of techniques, many involving 'pretexting'. Pretexting involves pretending to be someone else—especially someone from within the same company, or an official, expert, customer or client—with an apparently legitimate reason (pretext) for getting in touch, and apparently trustworthy. Many of the examples Mitnick offers involve multiple telephone calls and multiple pretexts, with information progressively obtained, reused and exploited by the caller. Pretexting can be used to obtain financial data, valuable information (such as passwords, salary or tax records), or to persuade someone to do something one wants them to do; the method can be used by criminals, private investigators or others.[78] Telephone pretexting can be used to gather information to help commit a crime online; but pretexting can instead use e-mail or websites as the medium of deception. Pretexting appears to exploit various aspects of social psychology, including the inclination to trust fellow insiders, and a desire to help others, as well as gratitude, conformity, obedience to authority, sympathy, guilt or intimidation.[79]

Many 'scam'-type cybercrimes such as 'phishing' involve e-mail pretexting, often on an industrial scale—though the generality and crudity of the bulk e-mails sent out probably means they are far less likely to deceive.[80] The lesson from all this is that however technically secure computer systems appear, this may all be undone if key personnel are insufficiently careful as to whom they disclose information.

Deception online has been termed 'digital deception', and defined as 'the intentional control of information in a technologically mediated message to create a false belief in the receiver of the message'.[81] Not all deception online will be criminal. Online deception may nevertheless be of criminological interest even where an offence may not yet have been committed,

---

[77] K Mitnick and W Simon, *The Art of Deception* (Indianapolis, IN, Wiley Publishing, Inc, 2002).

[78] Ibid, 28–32, 40–42; on workplace deception more generally, see D Shulman, *From Hire to Liar: The Role of Deception in the Workplace* (Ithaca, NY: Cornell University Press, 2006).

[79] Mitnick and Simon, above n 77. For an excellent yet accessible social psychological discussion of many of these same processes, and their study and role in several disturbing experiments and incidents including the famous Stanford Prison Experiment, see P Zimbardo, *The Lucifer Effect: How Good People Turn Evil* (London, Rider Publishing, 2007).

[80] See eg T Holt and D Graves, 'A Qualitative Analysis of Advance Fee Fraud E-mail Schemes' (2007) 1(1) *International Journal of Cyber Criminology* 137–54.

[81] J Hancock, 'Digital Deception: Why, When and How People Lie Online', in A Joinson et al (eds), *The Oxford Handbook of Internet Psychology* (Oxford, Oxford University Press, 2007) 290, original emphasis removed.

such as where an adult masquerades as a child in an online chatroom. Hancock usefully distinguishes between 'identity-based digital deception' (pretending to be someone else, as for example is routinely done by spammers in advance fee fraud e-mails), and 'message-based digital deception' (where the identity of the message-sender is genuine, but the message contains deceptive content, eg promising that the sender of an advance fee will in return subsequently receive a huge payment). Textual online communication and graphical 'avatars' offer obvious opportunities for deception regarding one's identity including one's age, race and gender.[82] Grazioli and Jarvenpaa studied a range of online deceptions and 'identified seven common deception tactics' including 'masking' (hiding important information), 'decoying' ('distracting the victim's attention' from what is really happening) and 'double play' ('convincing a victim they are taking advantage of the deceiver').[83] Phishing e-mails or their accompanying fake banking websites, for example, seek to mislead victims as to what is really happening (that they are disclosing crucial login information), through a combination of story pretext, disguised Uniform Resource Locators (URLs), and familiar brand logos and website designs.

Technological responses to deceptive offending may nevertheless be possible. Graham argues that Bayesian statistical analysis of spam offers an effective way of filtering it; spammers 'have to deliver their message' and '[i]f we can write software that recognizes their messages, there is no way they can get around that'.[84] An emerging response to phishing is for banks to issue a unique hardware 'dongle' to each customer, which the customer must plug in to their computer in order to access their online account. In this way, even if a customer inadvertently discloses their username and password to a third party, there is no easy way for that party to access the individual's bank account. Of course, it might still be possible for a deceiver to obtain the dongle by deception ('Please mail it to this address for repair/replacement') but a certain type of rapid online deception will have been closed off. In addition to technological prevention strategies are strategies seeking to educate the public into being more cautious before disclosing information to unknown third parties, or of being alive to the wiles of deceivers in general.[85]

It seems plausible to suppose that part of the attraction of deceiving others comes from the 'sneaky thrills'; from the excitement of balancing on the edge of success (deception) and failure (apprehension); or from the pleasure of dominating or 'getting one over' the victims.[86] If this is the

[82] Ibid, 290–91.

[83] Ibid, 292, citing S Grazioli and S Jarvenpaa, 'Consumer and Business Deception on the Internet' (2003) 7(4) *International Journal of Electronic Commerce* 93–118, 96–98.

[84] P Graham, *Hackers & Painters* (Sebastopol, CA, O'Reilly Media, Inc, 2004) 121.

[85] See Mitnick and Simon, above n 77.

[86] See, respectively, Katz, above n 25; Lyng, above n 19; and Bennett and Brookman, above n 27.

case, it suggests a way of understanding the commission of such deception (from the edgework/cultural criminology perspective) but also to suggest ways in which it could be prevented (by technological/SCP means; or by public education and individual alertness).

VI. SOME FUTURES OF CYBERCRIME AND INTERNET SECURITY

In this final section I shall very briefly sketch two areas that may become increasingly important over the next few years.

A. Crime and Deviance in Online Worlds

One area likely to become increasingly important is the study of crime and deviance in online worlds, where 'world' means a persistent, extensive, massively multi-user, virtual environment. Such worlds appear a logical extension and development of most of the ephemeral or visually or textually persistent Internet worlds of the present. A world may be designed for one or more purpose, including gaming, recreation, commerce, education or communication. Worlds may be navigated in first or third person, and may feature an avatar seen by other users. It seems likely that such worlds will become more common and more widely used over the years ahead, because they offer a richer and more immersive user experience, and one which will become ever more so as the technology develops. Crime or deviance (the latter including subcriminal antisocial behaviour) are an issue for such worlds because users will 'visit' such worlds for particular purposes, and if these are frustrated will express anger or simply leave. As Williams has shown, symbolically hurtful activities online (eg virtual vandalism, hate speech or avatar virtual violence) can have real psychological effects on the victims.[87]

A challenge for those running these worlds will be how to prevent or police harmful or undesirable activities. It may be possible to 'code out' certain behaviours.[88] Users are, however, imaginative, and may be able to circumvent limitations imposed on them by means of 'cheats', 'patches' or simply by exploiting existing features of the virtual world. Some deviance may alternatively be at the level of social norms, in which established conventions are deliberately flouted. In these cases, and especially among established communities of users, it may be that informal social control and sanctioning offer powerful control mechanisms. Among the more anonymous interactions, however, these may be less successful. Alternatively,

---

[87] Williams, above n 10; see also S Turkle, *Life on the Screen: Identity in the Age of the Internet* (New York, Touchstone/Simon & Schuster, 1997).
[88] See Lessig, above n 55.

some larger communities may seek to establish their own internal systems of governance, 'law'-making and virtual justice.[89]

B. Private Networks and Underground Communities

Whereas the virtual worlds described above are typically expansive and relatively open to newcomers to join, other communities may seek to remain hidden and closed to outsiders. Password-protected forums requiring invitations to join are one such technology that facilitate and support closed communities. Encrypted or stealthy P2P networking such as offered by Justin Frankel's WASTE software[90] offer a more advanced solution. Private networks may be used to link friends (friend-to-friend, or F2F), or small to medium-sized groups of trusted individuals. Clearly these 'darknets'[91] could be used for a variety of purposes, but would seem particularly attractive to file-sharers, criminal subcultures (such as paedophile groups or football hooligans, in order privately to discuss their real-world criminality), political subversives and organised crime. Subcultural theory may indeed offer a useful way of understanding such groups. Private network technologies present challenges for law enforcement because of their hidden nature. However, law enforcement and government are not necessarily powerless to act. As with political subversive groups, one strategy may be to try to infiltrate them. Closed groups bind together among trusted insiders, and exclude outsiders,[92] but once infiltrated are vulnerable. Other strategies may be to monitor networks for suspicious encrypted traffic; or to use legal measures to demand encrypted material be decrypted.

VII. CONCLUSION

In this chapter, I have offered a criminological introduction to the study of cybercrime, and to its policing and prevention. Following Manning, recognising today's Internet as a new form of social space,[93] I have attempted to show how cybercrime should be understood within this context: cybercrime involves symbolic communication and manipulation, in respect both of electronic information but also in many cases too of human actors, where these may be very local or instead potentially physically distant from one another across time and space. The Internet is the latest in a historical

---

[89] See essays in J Balkin and BS Noveck (eds), *The State of Play: Law, Games, and Virtual Worlds* (London, New York University Press, 2006).

[90] The name is said to be drawn from the Thomas Pynchon novel *The Crying of Lot 49* (1996), in which a shadowy network called 'WASTE' uses hidden mailboxes to communicate.

[91] See P Biddle et al, 'The Darknet and the Future of Content Distribution' (2002) paper presented at the 2002 ACM Workshop on Digital Rights Management.

[92] See also J Coleman, 'Social Capital in the Creation of Human Capital' (1988) 94 *American Journal of Sociology* S95–S120; H Becker, *Outsiders* (New York: The Free Press, 1963).

series of electronic technologies that have furthered 'time-space distan-ciation', in which social relationships have tended to become 'disembedded' from being exclusively based on face-to-face exchanges, and instead can be supported, in whole or part, across temporal and geographical divides.[94] Cybercrime can be understood, at least in part, in terms of the illicit oppor-tunities and rewards it potentially offers, the Internet conjuring up this world of attractions and making it remotely available. This is a social space, though, of human creation, a world potentially rich in social communi-cation between real human beings. Its regulation and control, then, are never merely technical issues, but always and already matters of social and political import.

[93] Manning, above n 3.

[94] For a wider social theoretical discussion of the transformative effects of such processes in modernity, and in 'late modernity' in particular, see Giddens, above n 6.

20

Pornography, Censorship and the Internet

LILIAN EDWARDS[1]

I. INTRODUCTION

OVER A DECADE since the Internet became an acknowledged main-stream commercial medium, it still retains its less than savoury reputation as a happy hunting ground for pornography and other types of distasteful content. Reports appear daily in the press scaremongering about the presence of paedophilia and porn not only on the Web, but in chat-rooms, in peer-to-peer (P2P) 'darknets', on social networking sites and even in virtual worlds such as Second Life.[2] The unhappy image of the Internet as a repository of sleaze has been fixed in the UK ever since *The Times* and *Sunday Times* reported in 1996 on the problem of hardcore porn and paedophilia on Internet newsgroups, and arose even earlier in the US: the *Time* magazine cover story on 'Cyberporn' of 3 July 1995 is generally acknowledged as the trigger which led to the US Communication Decency Act 1996 (CDA), a notoriously unsuccessful attempt to make the Internet safe for children, discussed further below.[3]

From 1996 on, pornography on the Internet fast became the 'new moral panic'[4] and the online paedophile the folk devil of the information super-highway. Unsurprisingly, national control of obscene and pornographic text, images and video on the Internet has become a major regulatory concern.[5] The problem of how to deal with illegal or harmful content on the

[1] My thanks to Jordan Hatcher for research assistance, and to John Ozimek, Richard Jones (Edinburgh) and Ian Walden (in a personal capacity only) for helpful comments. The usual disclaimer applies.

[2] See Reuters report, 'UK to Investigate Pedophilia in Virtual Worlds', 30 October 2007, at http://secondlife.reuters.com/stories/2007/10/30/uk-to-investigate-pedophilia-in-virtual-worlds/.

[3] See W Grossman, *Net.Wars* (New York, New York University Press, 1997) ch 9, 'Unsafe Sex in the Red Page District', 120.

[4] For a critique of the mythology around the net and pornography, see A Hamilton, 'The Net Out of Control: A New Moral Panic: Cansorship and Sexuality', in Liberty (ed), *Liberating Cyberspace* (Pluto Press, 1999).

[5] Control of video and images in computer games, whether played on proprietary consoles or

Internet is, of course, not restricted to pornography alone. In earlier chapters we have examined the problem of defamatory content (chapter 1) and copyright infringing content (chapter 5) as well as the general problem of the liability of online intermediaries for hosting or distributing content originated by others. Some of the themes from those chapters will be continued here. This chapter will, however, concentrate on content that is deemed *criminal* in most jurisdictions, rather than as a norm merely civilly actionable. Child pornography is the major topic here, but many of the issues canvassed herein, particularly in relation to filtering and censorship, can also be applied *mutatis mutandem* to other areas such as anti-religious statements (the law of blasphemy, or incitement to religious hatred), racist or inflammatory statements (incitement to racial hatred or 'hate speech'), and the making of politically subversive statements such as speech inciting or 'glorifying' terrorism.[6] In both the UK and the US, for example, considerable moral panic has been whipped up from time to time over the availability of 'bomb-making' recipes on the Web, and not just since 9/11.[7]

Rules dealing with illegal or harmful content vary a great deal from country to country depending on their social, ethical, legal and religious history. For example, in France and Germany, strict rules exist forbidding the sale of Nazi memorabilia and the publication of material that denies the occurrence of the Holocaust; in England, the law of criminal blasphemy and blasphemous libel has been abolished,[8] while in Scotland it persists, at least for now, in common law; in China and other East Asian countries, rules restricting political speech exist which tend to be regarded as unduly restrictive by Western standards; in the kingdom of Thailand it is a crime to insult the monarch. The fact that standards as to what material is criminally offensive vary so much across jurisdictions complicates still further the issue of control of Internet content, given the fact Internet content is freely distributed across physical national boundaries.

Some of the basic issues in this area that this chapter will try to address are the following:[9]

accessed via the Internet, is a subset area of problems which has traditionally been the subject of voluntary rating systems in a manner akin to film classification, unlike most 'ordinary' web-based Internet content. See further below.

[6] See Terrorism Act 2000; Terrorism Act 2006.

[7] Eg the BBC reported on 30 June 2000 that Copeland, the notorious nail-bomber of a gay pub in London, had discovered how to make bombs from the Internet. See http://news6.thdo. bbc.co.uk/hi/english/uk/newsid%5F808000/808745.stm.

[8] See Criminal Justice and Immigration Act 2008, s 79.

[9] Up-to-date information on the whole area of cyberspace and freedom of expression can best be gathered from websites: in the UK, Cyber-Rights and Cyber-Liberties run by Yaman Akdeniz at http://www.cyber-rights.org specializes in opposition to web censorship, and the matter also falls under the remit of the Online Rights Group (http://www.openrightsgroup.org/)/; in the US, numerous good sites exist, including the Electronic Frontier Foundation (http://www.eff.org/); in Australia the main site is Electronic Frontiers Australia (http://www.efa.org.au/). See also for general overview M Godwin, *Cyber Rights: Defending Free Speech in the Digital Age* (London, Times Books, 1998).

- What laws already exist which can be applied to regulate criminal pornographic content distributed or accessed via the Internet or tele-communications?
- Has the Internet created novel problems in this area that *cannot* be adequately regulated by the existing legal and regulatory framework?
- Can such laws be *enforced* successfully in the environment of the Inter-net, and, if not, what steps should be taken?
- Should control of content be undertaken only by state law enforcement agencies and courts, or by private bodies such as Internet service pro-viders (ISPs) and search engines?
- Should states and private institutions seek to control access to prohibited or unwelcome Internet content by technological ('code') means such as filtering, rather than by legal means? What are the implications for free speech of such online filtering?

A. Nation-state Control and the Cyber-censorship Debate

In the earliest days of the Internet, the debate about illegal online content was arguably dominated by 'cyber-libertarians', who viewed any attempt by the state or law to regulate Internet content as inappropriate censorship.[10] Contrarily, those who might be dubbed 'cyber-paternalists', usually repre-senting state, industry or conservative concerns, took the view that the new medium offered special and extensive risks which justified special restric-tions, legal or extralegal. For cyber-libertarians, the clarion call was 'What is legal offline, should be legal online'; for cyber-paternalists, the cry is still more often than not 'Will no one think of the children?' In order to protect the interests of parties such as, most notably children, but sometimes also women, minority races and religious groups, as well as the general moral fibre of society, they argued that a certain degree of regulation—or, to call a spade a spade, censorship—was justified. As we will see below, this attitude is now (understandably) almost universally adopted by most of the world's governments, at least in relation to child pornography. Indeed the unanimous rejection of the pervasiveness of child pornography online can be observed in the fact that the Cybercrime Convention adopted in 2001 has only one provision on content-related online crimes: a provision requiring all signatories to criminalise in their national law the possession, making and distributing of images of child pornography via computers and the Internet.[11]

---

[10] See eg John Perry Barlow's 'A Cyberspace Independence Declaration', issued on the Web the day after the CDA was signed into operation and archived at http://www.eff.org/~barlow; ACLU White Paper, 'Fahrenheit 451.2: Is Cyberspace Burning? How Rating and Blocking Proposals May Torch Free Speech on the Internet' (1996).

[11] Cybercrime Convention, Budapest, 23 November 2001, available at http://conventions. coe.int/Treaty/EN/Treaties/Html/185.htm. See Art 9. Child pornography is defined in the Con-vention as material which depicts a minor, or someone who appears to be minor, engaged in

By the time of the dotcom boom in 2000, the cyber-libertarian tendency had retreated and it had become well established that nation states had both the right to regulate, and an interest in regulating, the Internet, and in particular, an interest in protecting children—as the Internet ceased to be the plaything only of academics, researchers and geeks, and became part of daily social and family life. An often-cited turning point in the assertion of national state sovereignty over content, even on the Internet, was the *France v Yahoo!* case of 2000,[12] which attracted global attention. French groups working against anti-Semitism protested at the existence of Nazi memorabilia in listings for sale on the Yahoo! auction sites in both France and the US. France has strict laws forbidding the glorification of the Holocaust and these extend to a criminal ban on displaying for sale or buying Nazi-associated items (such as Iron Crosses and swastikas). The US, having wide constitutional protection of freedom of expression, has no such rules. Yahoo! France obeyed the French rules and did not allow Nazi items to be listed on its site (yahoo.fr). However, French citizens could, either by linking to Yahoo! US (yahoo.com) via Yahoo.fr, or directly, buy such items from the Yahoo.com site, which was physically hosted in the US and obeyed US rather than French law. The French groups sought an order to stop Yahoo! US supplying such items to French citizens.

The French court, perhaps unsurprisingly, found against both Yahoo.fr and Yahoo.com, and ordered Yahoo! to restrict access to listings involving Nazi memorabilia to any and all French citizens. The decision would have been extremely difficult for Yahoo! US to implement technically at the time, although the French court had ordered, prepared and drawn on an opinion prepared by a panel of technical experts, which had claimed that a reasonable majority of French citizens accessing Yahoo.com could be identified and blocked as desired, using a combination of registration information provided by users, Internet Protocol (IP) address and other cues such as the language of the browser.

In fact, however, the decision was never implemented, as the US courts fairly quickly decided not to enforce the French judgment, on the grounds it impinged on US rights of freedom of expression under the First Amendment.[13] The result was thus legal stalemate, though Yahoo! US subsequently closed down its Nazi-related listings voluntarily, in a bid to stave off any bad publicity.

As Penfold noted in 2001: '[T]he French decision, while practically

---

sexually explicit conduct, or 'realistic images' representing a minor engaged in such conduct. A minor is defined as someone under 18.

12 *LICRA et UEJF v Yahoo! Inc and Yahoo France*, Tribunal de Grande Instance de Paris (Superior Court of Paris), 22 May 2000.

13 See *Yahoo! v La Ligue Contre le racisme et L'Antisemitisme*, US District Court for N Dist of Ca, Nov 7 2001, available at http://www.cdt.org/jurisdiction/011107judgement.pdf. A later US appeal in fact held that this jurisdictional decision had exceeded its reach but by then the issue had gone cold.

ineffective, may not be meaningless. [It] may rather be indicative of an increasing willingness to attempt to assert some kind of sovereign control over internet content.'[14] Whether and why the *Yahoo!* decision in the French court was 'ineffective' is an important issue we will return to below in the general content of blocking and filtering of Internet content. What it does illustrate very vividly here is both the desire to uphold national content laws, and the difficulty of doing so in a medium where content is as likely to be accessed from abroad as from servers at home.

The EU has taken the view ever since the mid-1990s that it is its job to protect minors and vulnerable groups online, while attempting not to overregulate the Internet and throttle speech, enterprise and innovation. As the European Commission said in 1996:

> The vast majority of Internet content is for purposes of information for totally legitimate (and often highly productive) business or private usage. However like any other communications technology, particularly in the initial stages of their development, the Internet carries an amount of potentially harmful or illegal content or can be misused as a vehicle for criminal activities. . . . As in any other sector of activities, the Internet may be used for legitimate purposes or misused by some elements of society. The framework for the Internet should, therefore, *foster economic development*, while taking account of *justified social and societal concerns*. Consumers and businesses must be reassured that the Internet is a safe and secure place to work, learn and play.[15]

The *Yahoo!* case flags the issue of whether international harmonisation of Internet content laws is desirable or even possible. If France could not enforce its idiosyncratic laws in the US, should all countries agree on a core of Internet content crimes which would be enforceable in each and all of them? In some ways, this is what the Cybercrime Convention does try to do. However, the disparity of national laws in this area, and the strong national sentimental attachment to them, as already noted, makes such a task almost impossible—and in the end, as already noted, the Cybercrime Convention drafters managed to agree only one such crime, namely the possession and distribution of child pornography images.

B. The Role of ISPs and Search Engines

A final important question to consider in this area, then, is how are national laws criminalising Internet pornography to be enforced? If child pornography can be easily downloaded from law havens such as Russia, or

---

[14] See C Penfold, 'Nazis, Porn and Politics: Asserting Control over Internet Content' (2001) 2 *Journal of Information, Law & Technology (JILT)*, at http://www2.warwick.ac.uk/fac/soc/law/elj/jilt/2001_2/penfold/.

[15] Communication of 16 October 1996 on Illegal and Harmful Content on the Internet, COM(1996) 487.

inconspicuous servers in the US (the home of most child pornographic images according to the Internet Watch Foundation (IWF)[16]), then what can the police in countries such as the UK and France really do? The most obvious way forward here is to enrol the help of the ISPs who give access to the Internet and are thus the natural 'gatekeepers' to the Internet. If ISPs can be persuaded to block access to illegal content such as child pornography, by whatever means, then the problem becomes a much simpler one for governments to solve. The most obvious way to do this is to place liability on ISPs if they are found to be hosting or distributing the illegal content in question.

Attempts to enrol ISPs as 'Internet porn cops' thus go hand in hand with rules which put liability on ISPs in respect of obscene content authored or published by others. However, this runs squarely against the principle of ISP immunity from liability as a mere carrier or distributor which we explored in depth in chapter 1 and which was enshrined in Europe in the Electronic Commerce Directive, Articles 12–15. The issue of ISP liability in relation to content, and particularly their duties, if any, to monitor and filter out illegal content, has thus become a very controversial area.

Current international trends, as we discuss at the end of this chapter, are indeed moving towards compelling ISPs to block or 'censor' undesirable content, but opponents are still arguing strongly that this kind of 'privatised censorship' not only unduly restricts freedom of expression but does so in a non-transparent, non-democratic and non-accountable way. Most recently, the debate has expanded to include the place of search engines such as Google and Yahoo! since removing a site from search results effectively dispatches it to obscurity for most users, given an Internet of several billion pages. Should private actors such as Google take on a task of censorship which is usually regarded as the prerogative of the state? If not, how should they be regulated?

It is useful overall to consider if it is ethically 'better', or practically more efficient, in terms of maintaining the balance between free speech and protection of the public, for the state to turn its enforcement efforts towards those who *originate* potentially harmful content (authors); those who *read or access* it (Internet users); or those who participate in *publishing and distributing* it (ISPs, hosts, aggregators and search engines).

In this chapter we will make specific reference to the laws of the UK (which differ significantly in criminal matters between England and Scotland) but will also take account of developments in the US, Australia and Europe. One important distinction to note right from the start is that two types of pornography are under discussion herein. First, there is pornography aimed at adults which is illegal for adults to read or view according to the rules of a particular legal system. The material most universally

---

[16] See detailed discussion below, p 651.

accepted as falling into this category is child pornography, ie material featuring actual or simulated sex acts involving children (usually but not always defined as persons under 18[17]). The IWF prefers the use of the term 'images of child sexual abuse' for such material; the older term is, however, retained herein as arguably more inclusive, eg of 'virtual' computer-generated or animated pornographic scenes.

Secondly, there is pornography or other sexual material which is not illegal for adults to access, but may be considered harmful or upsetting for *children* to see. As we shall see, on the Internet it is not easy to set aside separate zones where adults can indulge in adult erotica without fear of child access, and this issue cannot be addressed, as it is in the non-virtual world, by criminalising the sale of pornography where children can buy it, or its display where they can can see or gain access to it (eg 'top shelf' laws). The issues raised by the two types of pornography are separable but overlapping. Should attempts to control Internet content concentrate only on what is incontrovertibly *illegal* for all—mainly child pornography—or also attempt to facilitate parent, families, minority groups and other citizens who wish to protect their children and families from *harmful* content, ie not per se illegal but offensive?

II. CONTROL OF INTERNET CONTENT BY LAW

A. National Criminal Laws; Effectiveness

There is more anecdotal evidence than hard statistics as to the nature and prevalence of Internet pornography. The once authoritative survey was the Carnegie-Mellon study of 1995[18] but this has been repeatedly attacked as methodologically flawed[19] and is of course now out of date. Pornography can undoubtedly be found on many thousands if not millions of websites and is a multibillion-dollar business for numerous countries.[20] What is less well noted is that as restrictions on what can be accessed on the World Wide Web have tightened, other less noticeable to entirely impenetrable conduits for distribution of illegal material have emerged: limited–access

---

[17] A child is so defined in the UN Convention on the Rights of the Child. UK law often defines a young person over 16 as having mature capacity, eg to marry, to give consent to sexual intercourse. However, even in the UK, child pornography legislation tends to recognize a grey area between 16 and 18 where 'childhood' persists. For definition of child in the Cybercrime Convention, see n 10 above.

[18] Reported in M Rimm, 'Marketing Pornography on the Information Superhighway' (1995) 83 *Georgetown Law Journal* 1849.

[19] See Grossman, above n 3, 120.

[20] See some interesting statistics at http://familysafemedia.com/pornography_statistics.html. They claim 'The pornography industry is larger than the revenues of the top technology companies combined: Microsoft, Google, Amazon, eBay, Yahoo!, Apple, Netflix and EarthLink.'

P2P networks ('darknets') are one route, and pornographic images are also swapped via direct conduits such as instant messaging (IM).

Pornographic images swapped these ways can now also be encrypted, so that even if intercepted they would be non-identifiable as such. It is well known that anonymising P2P systems such as Freenet and Tor, which were originally designed to allow users to preserve their freedom of expression in the face of state censorship, are now regularly used by paedophile rings to pass round their wares. While the prevalence of pornography on websites is at least visible, the volume of such material swapped via P2P, IM and even older protocols such as FTP remains unquantifiable. These technological changes have considerable implications for current national and EU-level strategies for stopping access to child pornography, which are still on the whole focused on a web-based model of child porn, which in the words of Harvard cyberlaw scholar Jonathan Zittrain, is 'so last millennium'.[21]

The lack of a baseline for the exact amount and whereabouts of pornographic material on the Internet makes it difficult to assess in any empirical way how effective, if at all, national laws are in controlling illegal or offensive Internet content. Nonetheless, being seen to be 'doing something' about child pornography on the Internet remains a political imperative for most governments. As we already saw in the *Yahoo!* case, states have often been driven towards symbolic regulation of the Internet even where they knew the practical effect was likely to be low. Internet pornography continues to command inches of comment in the more dramatic reaches of the tabloid press, and the claim that regulation will do something to protect children tends to be a vote winner, even if there are, as is often the case, other more subtle reasons why that legislation might be seen as desirable. Thus in the past decade or so, the combined spectre of the paedophile and the terrorist have been pressed into use repeatedly to ensure the passing of laws that might otherwise in calmer times be seen as unreasonable intrusions into freedom of expression, privacy and autonomy.[22]

Why is Internet pornography a particularly tough nut to crack for the law? In the past, both adult erotica (now barely restrained by law enforcement agencies at all) and child pornogrpahy have both been limited in circulation by the sheer limitations of hard copy. By contrast, electronic

---

21 Comment at the Cyber-Rights and Cyber-Safety Conference, Oxford, 2005.

22 Note an interesting article from 1995, L Miller, 'Women and Children First: Gender and the Settling of the Electronic Frontier', in J Brook and I Boal (eds), *Resisting the Virtual Life : The Culture and Politics of Information* (City Lights, San Francisco, 1995). Miller, writing at the very beginning of the opening up of the Internet, suggested that the prevalent metaphor then of the Internet as a 'Wild West frontier', and the effect this might have on vulnerable women (eg harassament online, stalking), was being used to justify regulation of the Internet—so as to protect women. In fact, however, the state interests might have been in regulating the Internet in general. Such a theory seems prescient in an era when we have seen censorship, and surveillance both justified by respectively, protection of children and the fear of terrorism when the state may gain advantages other than protection of the vulnerable from such laws.

pornography can be indefinitely copied at marginal cost; the quality of the image does not degrade on multiple copying; material is childishly easy to circulate, both within states and across national boundaries; it is difficult for law enforcement authorities to detect material because of the vast size of cyberspace and the availability of encryption; even if Internet pornography is located, 'seizure' is not a major restricting loss as it is with stocks of (for example) glossy hardcore magazines; it is easy to 'restock' with electronic pornography, or to copy the material from one site or one country to another.[23] And, as we have already mentioned, perhaps the key problem for the law to address is the difficulty of enforcing local laws in a world where content is distributed globally in digital fashion.

While child pornography used by adults is the main current subject of legislation, with some concern also about other forms of extreme adult pornography such as 'snuff videos', there is also serious public concern over how easy it is for children to access inappropriate material (which may encompass violent, racist, pro-terrorist and homophobic content as well as pornographic material) on the Internet and via mobile phones. As access to the Internet has become ubiquitous (and essential) for children in schools and the home, so has the ability of children to access dubious material without adult supervision grown. It is well known that in many households, children are more adept at surfing the Web than their parents (and at disguising their tracks, eg by deleting history files or circumventing parental supervision software).

Broadband access to the Internet has removed any hope of supervision by amount of data downloaded, or restriction on speed of download. Internet content is always available, not limited to a 'post-watershed' time period, and not limited to channels that can be 'locked' by parents (as was briefly popular for television) or to particular .xxx domains (as has often been hopefully suggested). Wireless networks mean access is often available throughout the house and in streets and cafés, via a widening number of gadgets (eg game consoles), thus effectively nullifying the possibility of meaningful personal supervision. Most children now have mobile phones, many of them already 'smart phones' which can access the Web and e-mail.[24] Mobile broadband dongles for laptops are plunging in price. Despite this, Canute-style, the number one advice to parents from governments remains the repeated injunction to sit next to children as they access the Internet from the home desktop.

---

[23] See T Gibbons, 'Computer Generated Pornography' (1995) 9 *International Yearbook of Law, Computers and Technology* 83.

[24] According to Flash Eurobarometer 248, 'Towards a Safer Use of the Internet for Children in the EU—A Parents' Perspective' (2008), around two-thirds of children aged between 6 and 17 across the EU have mobile phones although around a half of these did not give Internet access. In the UK, around 60 per cent of this age group had mobile phones.

B. UK Law

As a general principle of UK law and most legal systems, state jurisdiction in criminal matters is territorial.[25] Thus, in theory at least, there is no legal vacuum in relation to criminal activities online. Each state's laws on pornography, hate speech, blasphemy, etc, apply within its own territory, and will apply to criminal acts perpetrated there or which affect state citizens (the 'effects' doctrine), just as they do in respect of communications distributed via conventional media. Most states already have in place rules extensively prohibiting the distribution, sale, import and use of child pornography; many have also criminalised hate speech, and speech which aids terrorists, or glorifies 'terrorism'.[26] Internet content is not under-regulated; if anything it is overregulated as the content laws of various countries compete to tell users and ISPs what (not) to do.

Indeed in the UK, there is already a considerable amount of legal regulation of obscene material, both from before and after the arrival of the Internet. In England and Wales, the main pieces of general obscenity legislation are the Obscene Publications Acts 1959 and 1964, which make it an offence to publish an obscene article, or to have an obscene article for publication for gain.[27] These Acts, it should be noted, did not criminalise the mere private *possession* of obscene material, merely its *distribution*. An 'article' is defined to include matter which may be looked at as well as read, as well as sound records and any film or other record of a picture or pictures.[28] An article is 'obscene' if its effect is 'such as to tend to deprave and corrupt persons who are likely . . . to read, see or hear' it.[29] In practice, ever since the Williams Committee[30] reported on the operation of the Acts in 1976 following the unsuccessful prosecution of the paperback *Inside Linda Lovelace*, the 1959 Act has almost never been used to prosecute books or textual matter. Its substantial use is to restrain the circulation of obscene pictures, films and videos rather than the written word, and more particularly, the circulation of hardcore pornography.[31]

---

[25] Note, however, that states may sometimes assert jurisdiction over extraterritorial events if those events are initiated elsewhere but affect their territory or their residents. Statutes (such as, in the UK, the Computer Misuse Act 1990) may also include extraterritorial jurisdiction clauses, although of course they may be externally viewed as in breach of international law.

[26] See references nn 5 and 7 above.

[27] 1959 Act, s 2(1) and 1964 Act, s 1(2).

[28] 1959 Act, s 1(2)

[29] 1959 Act, s 1(1).

[30] Committee on Obscenity and Film Censorship, HMSO, 1979, Cmnd 7772.

[31] See G Robertson and A Nicol, *Media Law*, 3rd edn (1992), ch 3. But see prosecution raised of obscene textual story posted online about the pop band Girls Aloud, reported 6 October 2008—this was the first prosecution in the UK under the Obscene Publications act since an unsuccessful case in 1991: http://www.theregister.co.uk/2008/10/06/obscene_publication_girls_aloud/. The case was however dismissed at trial in June 2009 as the prosecution did not lead any evidence.

In terms of computer pornography, the 1959 Act was amended so that an 'article' included a computer disk, and 'publication' clearly included the electronic transmission of material from one computer to another.[32] Thus the downloading of pornography from the Internet to, say, a laptop, without any physical medium as intermediary such as a disk or a printout is clearly caught. In Scotland, similar prosecutions can be brought under the Civic Government (Sc) Act 1982, section 51, which broadly covers the publication, sale or distribution of 'obscene material', which is defined to include inter alia a computer disk and any kind of recording of a visual image.[33] Prosecutions can also be brought in Scotland under certain common law offences.

The 1959 Act embodies the traditional liberal approach that it is acceptable to possess obscene material in *private*, so long as there is no attempt to publish, distribute or show it to others, particularly for gain. However, in the case of *child* pornography, which by its nature features images of the sexual abuse of children, Parliament has taken the view since 1988 that the phenomenon is so heinous that possession *as well as* circulation should be criminalised. Indeed child pornography has become such a key problem that a special body, the Child Exploitation and Online Protection Centre, has been created to lead law enforcement efforts in this area.[34] The primary Acts here are the Protection of Children Act 1978 (POCA) (which does not apply in Scotland or Northern Ireland), and more recently, the Criminal Justice Act 1988 (CJA 1988—which in various provisions has effect throughout the UK[35]), the latter of which makes it an offence for a person to have any indecent photograph of a child in his *possession*,[36] on top of the pre-existing offences of taking, distributing, showing or publishing such a photograph.[37] A child is defined as a person under 18.[38] The POCA was also amended to encompass new technologies of digital manipulation in 1994 so that a new offence was added of 'making' an indecent photograph or 'pseudo-photograph' (discussed further below).

In 1995, the UK police used these new possession offences to organise their first major crackdown on international Internet paedophile rings, in an operation known as Operation Starburst. Nine UK men were arrested (other arrests being made abroad of foreign nationals) and at least two convicted of possession offences under section 160 of the 1988 Act. Subsequent operations have followed, such as Operation Cathedral in 1998,

[32] See Criminal Justice and Public Order Act 1994, Sched 9, para 3.
[33] 1982 Act, s 51(8).
[34] See CEOP website at http://www.ceop.gov.uk/.
[35] In Scotland, the Criminal Justice Act 1988 inserted a s 52A into the Civic Government (Sc) Act 1982 which provides the simple possession offence for Scotland in s 52A (1). Other offences relating to child pornography are found in s 52 of the 1982 Act.
[36] 1988 Act, s 160 (England) and 161 (Scotland).
[37] Protection of Children Act 1984, s 1.
[38] Sexual Offences Act 2003, s 45, amending the POCA 1978 , s 7(6)

which resulted in nine people being charged with various offences,[39] and Operation Ore, a huge international operation carried out alongside the FBI from 2003 on, which involved the investigation of around 6,500 British suspects. As of June 2005 it was reported that the investigation had thus far resulted in 1,670 prosecutions, 1,451 convictions and 500 cautions. Akdeniz notes that this was the biggest Internet child pornography operation of recent times, producing a huge spike in the UK statistics.[40]

III. PROBLEMS WITH ADAPTING NATIONAL CRIMINAL LAWS TO INTERNET PORNOGRAPHY

A. Adaptability of Existing Legislation to the Internet: Pseudo-photographs and 'Making'

In theory, therefore, UK authorities seeking to regulate Internet pornography appear to have adequate existing legislation and case-law to apply. Questions have arisen, however, as to whether these existing rules are sufficiently flexible when applied to the novel environment of the Internet and electronic publishing. A good recent example of the problems that can arise can be taken from English case-law relating to the POCA. In *R v Fellows and Arnold*[41] the Court of Appeal had to consider whether the Act applied in a case involving the use of a computer by two paedophiles. Images of child pornography were maintained on an electronic database and access was allowed to other paedophiles by issue of a password which allowed the images to be viewed and downloaded. The main issue for the court was whether the images stored in the computer memory could be defined as 'photographs' in terms of the 1978 Act. At the time of the alleged offences, the Act merely defined a photograph as 'including' an indecent film, a copy of an indecent photograph or filmm and an indecent photograph comprised in a film.[42] The photographs in this case had never been printed out by the accused, but merely stored on the computer hard disk and shown on the monitor screen, and similarly made available to others. Taking a purposive approach to the statute, the court found that a visual image stored electronically on disk was not a photograph itself, but *was* a 'copy of a photograph', which fell within the definition quoted above. Furthermore, the court went on to find that knowingly holding such

---

[39] See NCIS report, 'Project Trawler: Crime on the Information Highways' (June 1999) 16–17. Contact details can be found at http://www.ncis.co.uk.

[40] See Y Akdeniz, 'Possession and Dispossession: A Critical Assessment of Defences in Possession of Indecent Photographs of Children Cases' [2007] *Crimimal Law Review* 274.

[41] [1997] 2 All ER 548. See also C Cobley, 'Child Pornography on the Internet' (1997) 2 *Communications Law* 30.

[42] See 1978 Act, s 7(2).

images on computer disk where they could be found and accessed by others had elements of 'active participation' such that the offence of distributing or showing such photographs to others could be held to have been committed by the maintainers of the database.

The 1978 Act was in fact amended subsequent to the events of the *Fellows* case by the Criminal Justice and Public Order Act 1994, which extended the definition of a 'photograph' to include 'pseudo-photographs' which are defined as any 'image, whether made by computer graphics or otherwise howsoever, which appears to be a photograph'.[43] As we shall see below, the concept of a criminally indecent image may yet be extended further.

B. Possession, Caching and Mens Rea

In *Atkins v DPP; Goodland v DPP*,[44] the Queen's Bench Division found itself asked to consider two interesting questions relating to Internet pornography. First, did having indecent photographs stored on the *cache* of a computer system belonging to a certain person constitute 'possession' by that person for the purpose of section 160(1) of the CJA 1988? And secondly, did the downloading (saving) of indecent photographs to a particular *drive* on that computer system, from the Internet, constitute the separate offence of the 'making'[45] of an indecent photograph under section 1(1) of the POCA?

At first instance, the magistrate's court found the answer to the first question to be yes, even though an image browsed on a webpage can be saved to a computer's cache without either the knowledge or intent of the browser. Few people know that the default setup of most home machines causes an image that is clicked on to be automatically stored (or 'cached') on the machine's hard disk. Possession in the magistrate's view was, however, an offence of strict liability, and so since the image was there, the offence had been committed (unless one of the specific statutory defences was proved). On the other hand, the magistrate took the view that simply saving existing digital images to a particular drive on a computer was not

---

[43] 1994 Act, s 84(7). The 1994 Act also amended the definition of a photograph in the Civic Government (Sc) Act ss 52 and 52A (see n 32 above). Note that despite the apparent width of the definition, it is limited by context—in *Atkins v DPP: Goodland v DPP* (2000) 2 Cr App R 248 (discussed further below) the court held that an image which obviously consisted of pieces of two photographs physically joined together could not be said to 'appear to be' a photograph, and so did not qualify as a 'pseudo-photograph'.

[44] [2000] All ER 425.

[45] The offence of 'making' an indecent photograph was added both to the 1978 Act and the equivalent Scottish legislation by the Criminal Justice and Public Order Act 1994, at the same time that the concept of a 'pseudo-photograph' was also introduced to the legislation. The argument that the offence of 'making' was thus referrable *only* to 'pseudo-photographs' and not to other types of indecent photographs was, however, explicitly rejected in *Atkins*.

'*making*' a new photograph.[46] This was storage, reservation or some concept of that kind; there was no creative, new, act of manufacture, which he felt to be a requisite.

The Queen's Bench, however, reversed the magistrate on both points. Possession was not an offence of strict liability; rather it did involve the need for some kind of knowledge of the existence and effect of the cache. '[T]here was no intention to criminalize unknowing possession of photographs.' An analogy was suggested with the case of *R v Steele*,[47] where a man charged with the offence of possession of a firearm was held guilty, despite his plea that he did not know that what he had in a holdall of which he had possession was a firearm. However, the correct analogy here, the court held, was of the cache to the holdall, not the firearm. Thus a person who knows that computers are usually set up to automatically cache images browsed may reasonably expect consequences if he looks at indecent photos on the Internet, whereas a person who knows nothing of caches or that his computer has one will not. Accordingly in this case the possession offence was struck down.[48]

In contrast, however, the Queen's Bench found that the accused *had* 'made' indecent photos by saving images *deliberately* to a particular drive of the computer. The natural and ordinary meaning of the word 'to make' was 'to cause to exist; to produce by action, to bring about'; so this was sufficient to include both the saving and the printing off of an image from the Internet. However, the court emphasised that if an image was automatically and inadvertently saved to a cache, this would not be 'making', since it, along with other offences under section 1(1) of the 1978 Act such as taking or permitting to be taken an indecent photograph of a child, were serious offences (commanding higher sentences than mere possession), which could not be committed unintentionally. Similarly it has been agreed that if someone opens an attachment not knowing it contains an image of child abuse, then there is no *mens rea* for either a possession or 'making' offence.[49] There is also no liability where an attachment containing illegal images is sent unsolicited to a party so long as having opened it they do not retain it for longer than a reasonable time.[50]

The interesting result of *Atkins* and subsequent decisions is that both the 'possession' and the 'making' offences discussed above end up with

[46] The distinction is important because 'making' commands heavier sentences than mere possession.

[47] [1993] Crim LR 298.

[48] Similarly in *Collier* [2004] EWCA Crim 1411, it was held that if a man knows he has indecent photographs in his possession (in this case on tangible media such as CD-ROMs), but he proves he did *not* know there were indecent sexual images of *children* amongst them, then again he is not knowingly in possession of child pornography and should be acquitted.

[49] *Smith and Jayson* [2002] EWCA Crim 683.

[50] See Criminal Justice Act 1988, s 160(2)(c) and discussion in *Humphreys* [2006] EWCA Crim 640; see also discussion in Akdeniz, above n 40.

judicially supplied requirements of intention, rather than being interpreted as offences of strict liability. This is not the conservative response to the policy goal of restricting the ownership and transmission of child pornography that might have been anticipated by cyber-cynics.

C. Deleted Images and Legitimate Reason Defence

A key problem for investigations is that a person knowingly in possession of illegal images of child abuse is very likely to delete them from his hard disk before the police get there if he possibly can. Can an offence of 'possession' then still be charged? The matter is complicated by the fact that modern forensics can frequently retrieve deleted images, to a greater or lesser extent, even where an 'ordinary' non-expert user could not himself still gain access. Are these retrieved images still in 'possession'? In the Court of Appeal case of *Porter*,[51] the defendant's home was raided and two computers seized, which were later found to contain 3,575 still images and 40 movie files of child pornography. However, 875 of the images had been placed in the 'recycle bin' which had then been emptied; nonetheless officers were able to retrieve these images using special forensic software. The other 2,700 images had been deleted beyond ordinary retrieval but thumbnail images of them could still be viewed using a program ACDSee the defendant had on his computer plus special forensics provided by the US Federal government. At first instance the judge held Porter possessed all the files regardless of whether they were in a 'deleted' state or not. The main issue was whether he had ever had knowledge of being in possession of illegal images. On appeal, however, the court held that possession in the context of photographs referred to a defendant's 'control or custody' of the images. If images had been deleted, then possession would depend on whether he had the specialist knowledge and software to be able to retrieve them, ie it was a question of fact whether he had actual control over them. This is apparently a subjective test, not a question of what knowledge or facilities the reasonable man (or the reasonable pornographer?) would have.[52] In this particular case, Porter's appeal was successful.

A final and rather desperate defence open to the accused pornographer is to plead that he had a legitimate reason for having the images in his possession.[53] While the courts are likely to be sceptical of such claims,[54] they can exceptionally succeed.[55]

---

[51] [2006] EWCA Crim 560.

[52] See Akdeniz, above n 40.

[53] See Criminal Justice Act 1988, s 160(2)(a); there is an equivalent defence in Scottish law, see the successful plea in *R v Whitelaw*, Paisley Sheriff Court, reported in *The Scotsman*, 6 February 2003.

[54] See *Wrigley*, CA, Case No 99/01497/Z5, 26 May 2000. The defendant, a graduate of Keele University, claimed he was conducting genuine academic research which required him to pose as

D. How Far Do You Go?

As we saw above, in 1996 the burning question to answer was whether it was reasonable to regulate the Internet in the same way as hardcopy media or broadcasting. Over a decade later, the question has apparently been turned around: the issue now is perhaps how far may restrictions on content be imposed which would be regarded as contravening civil liberties if applied to traditional media like newspapers and television, where long-standing public and journalistic concerns still exist about preserving freedom of expression. Three recent developments show how, in the UK at least, it is increasingly easy to justify measures against the Internet, given the 'moral panic' it arouses, which may nonetheless not be consistent with our past stance on freedom of expression in the media.

(i) Extreme Pornography[56]

As noted above, the classic liberal position on pornographic and obscene material has been that it is legitimate to possess such materials for one's own private use, but not to distribute or sell them where they may harm or offend others. Child pornography is acknowledged to represent a different class of threat since its very existence means (bar the issue of 'virtual' pornography) that a criminal offence has already been perpetrated, as children cannot legally give consent to sexual activity.

In 2006,[57] however, the UK government pushed this clear dividing line further by consulting on the prohibition of what is grouped together as 'extreme pornography'—images depicting material that is 'extremely offensive to the vast majority of people and . . . should have no place in our society'.[58] Although some of this material will, like child pornography, intrinsically involve illegal acts, eg genuine 'snuff' movies, some will not (eg simulated 'snuff' movies). A futher motivation for introduction of a possession offence is apparent in Home Office statements, namely that these images are so appalling they should simply not be allowed to be owned in our society, as well as circulated. Since distributors and publishers will usually be based abroad, possession offences are arguably the only way to clamp down on circulation in the UK. The proposals, now enshrined in

---

a paedophile online; however, the court pointed out that he had not discussed this research with any of his tutors nor had he revealed the items in his possession on his initial arrest.

55 See *Whitelaw*, above n 53.

56 The extreme pornography rules described below apply only in England and Wales. However, Scotland unveiled proposals in September 2008 for an even more stringent regime of their own: see http://www.theregister.co.uk/2008/09/30/scotland_extreme_pr0n_law/.

57 *Consultation on the Possession of Extreme Pornographic Material* (Home Office, 2006), at http://www.homeoffice.gov.uk/documents/cons-extreme-porn-3008051/.

58 Statement by Home Office minister Paul Goggins, reported by *OUT-Law*, 30 August 2005.

the Criminal Justice and Immigration Act 2008, sections 63–67, thus represent a considerable conservative shift in UK policy on censorship.

Under the 2008 rules, it is an offence to be in possession of an 'extreme pornographic image'.[59] 'Pornographic' means that the image must reasonably have been assumed to have been produced solely or principally for the purpose of sexual arousal.[60] An image includes a still or moving image, and also data that is capable of conversion into an image.[61]

'Extreme' means that an image[62]

(a) portrays in an explicit and realistic way an act threatening a person's life or resulting in serious injury to the anus, breast or genitals ('snuff' or violent sexual pornography); or an act involving sexual intercourse with a human corpse (necrophiliac pornography); or sex with an animal (bestial pornography); and

(b) the image is also grossly offensive, disgusting or otherwise of an obscene character.

In relation to (a), a reasonable person must think the person or animal was real. So in the example above of a simulated snuff movie, unless the reasonable person would think it was a genuine snuff movie—ie that a real woman was actually killed—it would not qualify as 'extreme pornography'. This provides a defence for ordinary entertainment films (and animations, and games) which commonly depict simulated killings and violence.

What of a realistic torture scene within a normally distributed movie such as the famous torture scene in the Bond film *Casino Royale*? Would the reasonable person think a real person was actually being tortured? Probably not, but section 64 of the 2008 Act also adds a special exclusionary rule excluding images that have passed normal classification censorship checks from being caught under the new 'extreme pornography' rules.

Are the new rules objectionable in a free speech society, as the likes of Amnesty International, Justice and Backlash have argued? Most ordinary folk, to be honest, probably welcome these rules unreservedly. Government advocates have pointed out that the Internet has provided easy distribution to children and adults alike of material that would never have 'cleared customs' in the past or even been made available via licensed sex shops, and therefore exceptional laws are necessary. More worryingly, several tabloids have pursued the line that laws are required because real-world crimes can be inspired by consumption of extreme Internet content. The UK law itself is well known to have been inspired by the 2003 rape and murder of Jane Longhurst, whose killer was reportedly surfing the Web for necrophiliac and similar sex images hours before the murder. There is no

---

[59] Criminal Justice and Immigration Act 2008, s 63(1).
[60] Ibid, s 63(3).
[61] Ibid, s 63(8).
[62] Ibid, s 63(6) and (7).

real empirical proof, though, that Internet violence generally inspires real life violence, and the argument that what you read or see directly inspires criminal behaviour has on the whole been regarded as 'not proven' for decades in UK censorship of 'offline' materials.[63]

Thus the questions asked by free speech advocates are, first, are we are seeing an unjustified erosion of civil liberties on the Internet compared to the 'real world', and one driven by moral panic rather than real research? And secondly, is this the beginning of one of the much-cited 'slippery slopes' of excessive censorship which may eventually engulf both online and offline worlds? Members of the bondage, domination, sadism and masochism (BDSM) community have in particular protested that their private sexual choices, which are not generally illegal (although *pace* the well-known *Spanner*[64] case in the European Court of Human Rights) are being treated as a crime since they often involve possession of extreme pornography, or taping of their own 'role-playing' activities to create videos which may be defined as such.[65]

In particular they object that the definitions of what is 'extreme' are unhelpfully vague for non-lawyers, and have been backed in this by the Joint Human Rights Committee of Parliament. However, as with possession of child pornography, defences do exist for the accused who unknowingly comes into possession of extreme porn.[66] (Note, however, that everyone is presumed to know the *law*.) A defence is also available where the 'extreme image' depicts what is in reality consensual sexual behaviour, and the act is one to which consent can be given (so not under-age sex).[67] This should protect those making the 'home tapes' mentioned above, as evidence of consent should be readily available from the involved parties. Penalties of up to three years' imprisonment can be imposed if a prosecution is successful.[68]

(ii) Cartoon or Computer-generated Pornography

The free speech arguments may seem abstract and pious when compared to the reality reported by hardened police officers of video streaming unstoppably into the UK from abroad via P2P and IM servers, depicting (in reality or simulation) the rape and murder of women for male sexual gratification. Few would argue that stopping distribution of such material is not a good thing. On the other hand it might be said that we have already slid a yard

---

[63] See the explicit admission in the 2007 consultation on cartoon depictions of child sex (see below n 70 at para 72) that there is no known evidence that links fantasy images of child sexual abuse and the commission of offences against children.
[64] *Laskey, Jaggard, and Brown v UK* (1997) 24 Eur HR Rep 39.
[65] See eg advice on the Backlash site: http://www.backlash-uk.org.uk/.
[66] Criminal Justice and Immigration Act 2008, s 65.
[67] Ibid, s 66.
[68] Ibid, 67.

or two down that much-predicted slippery slope since the law proscribing extreme pornography was passed in 2008.[69] The government's latest proposal, announced in 2007, is that possession of drawings and computer-generated images of child sexual abuse should be criminalised.[70]

These proposals seem partly inspired by claims that paedophiles are circumventing the law by using computer technology to manipulate real photos or videos of abuse into drawings or cartoons, and partly by fears of the rising popularity of Japanese *manga* and *anime* cartoons and films which often depict extreme sex and violence, and perhaps crucially, also often involve young women of indeterminate age. In either case, it is quite possible that the law already allows many such materials to be deemed criminal images of child abuse (see the discussion above of 'pseudo-photographs' in *Fellows and Arnold* and the subsequent legislation[71]) and that adequate distribution (if not possession) laws already exist. Questions must then arise as to whether the creation of yet more laws is only window dressing. Advocates of the new laws will, however, respond that 'virtual' pornography feeds a criminal need for child pornography which may lead on to actual abuse, even if no actual children are harmed in the making of the materials; and that circulation of such materials implies a general societal acceptability of such images which must be contradicted.

Alternatively, if these laws do truly set out to create a new domain of content illegal to possess, does it encroach beyond images into the hitherto largely untouched world of text? Cartoons, after all, contain words as well as pictures, and comic books regularly win literary awards these days as well as being 'for kids'. If *manga* are criminalised today, will ultraviolent but artistically well-regarded graphic novels such as Frank Miller's *Sin City* be next? The Home Office 2007 consultation mentioned possible defences for works of art and works of historic interest but these do not seem to appear in the Bill. However, an image will not be caught under the Bill unless it is 'grossly offensive, disgusting or otherwise of an obscene character'. Whether this excludes all works of art is a matter of opinion. As with 'extreme pornography', images or stills from classified films are excluded. Most controversial of all is the question of how a cartoon image of a 'child' is to be identified as an under-age sexual image. The Bill currently provides that an image is to be treated as one of a child where the

---

[69] See *The Register's* comment of 28 May 2008 at http://www.theregister.co.uk/2008/05/28/ government_outlaws_pictures/: 'First they came for the child pornographers. . . . It may not have quite the same resonance as Pastor Niemuller's oft-quoted aphorism. But the reality behind this particular slippery slope is just as sinister.'

[70] See *Consultation on the Possession of Non-photographic Visual Depictions of Child Sexual Abuse* (Home Office, 2007), at http://www.homeoffice.gov.uk/documents/cons-2007-depiction-sex-abuse?view=Binary and Ministry of Justice press release, 28 May 2008. Proposed legislation was introduced in the Coroners and Justice Bill 2009, s 49, which was still in progress as this book went to press.

[71] Above n 45 and text surrounding.

'impression conveyed by the image is that the person shown is a child'. In the sexualised world of *anime* which frequently features sexual images of young and age-indistinct schoolgirls, this provision clearly has civil liberties implications. It may be particularly worrying in virtual worlds like Second Life where 'age play' is common in certain well-marked off domains. Should graphic (sic) images of simulated sexual behaviour between two child-like avatars operated by two adult players really be criminalised? Or is this more like adult role-playing in a quasi-private space than sharing of child pornography?

It is interesting to contrast the US position, where the Supreme Court specifically ruled some while back that rules prohibiting computer-generated or 'virtual' pornography were impermissibly wide according to the First Amendment,[72] and the global hilarity which greeted an Australian judge's conclusion in late 2008 that cartoons showing sex acts involving children modelled on characters from *The Simpsons* were examples of child pornography.[73] Is this the model the UK government wishes to follow, without good empirical research to back its concerns?

Given the above, the overall trajectory seems to be away from a clear bright line that only Internet child pornography should be illegal, towards a greyer cloud of illegality which seeks to spread its shadow over parts of the previously legal territory of 'unwelcome' material. As well as the extreme pornography and virtual pornography rules already noted, the Bill introducing the 'virtual pornography' laws also carries proposals to make it clear that setting up suicide websites, a current media fixation, is illegal;[74] and we have already noted earlier the arrival of laws in the Terrorism Act 2006 which would outlaw websites that 'glorify terrorism'.[75] Still more content rules may follow: a crackdown on extremist but non-terrorist Islamic sites has also been floated.[76] More significantly, the Byron Review, commissioned by the government as a high-profile examination of the safety of children online which reported in 2008,[77] clearly contemplates a more interventionist approach if necessary. One of its concerns is user-

---

[72] See *Ashcroft v Free Speech Coalition* 534 US 234, 122 SCt 1389.

[73] See 'Children Sex Acts Based on The Simpsons Are Ruled Pornographic', heraldsun.com. au, 8 December 2008, at http://www.news.com.au/heraldsun/story/0,21985,24767204-5006022,00.html.

[74] Coroners and Justice Bill 2009, ss 46ff; note that ISPs or hosts of suicide sites benefit from the usual immunities of the E-Commerce Directive Arts 12-15 as reproduced in Sched 10 to the Bill, ie will not be liable under any part of the Bill if they take a site down on notice.

[75] Note also the Electronic Commerce (Terrorism Act 2006) Regulations 2007 No 1550 which creates a new detailed statutory regime of take-down (with, for the first time, clear time limits) for terrorist material hosted by ISPs, etc.

[76] L Page, 'Home Sec in Anti-terror Plan to Control Entire Web', *The Register* 17 January 2008, at http://www.theregister.co.uk/2008/01/17/home_office_smith_speech_web_terror_crack down_insanity/

[77] T Byron, *Safer Children in a Digital World: The Report of the Byron Review* (London, 2008).

generated adult content—so-called 'YouPorn', sexting,[78] etc. Their recommendations include codes of practice for user-generated content sites (eg Facebook, YouTube), making them undertake to take down such 'inappropriate' content within a given time.[79] The Byron Review also hinted that if current self-regulation proves unable solve the problems of child access to 'adult' but non-illegal harmful content, then full regulation may be necessary. Finally, it is worth noting that a recent review of computer game content in the UK (strongly associated with the Internet and young users[80]) also noted that the existing self-regulatory regime for the games industry appears to be failing and that regulation might be necessary if self-regulation reforms did not work.

This trend may be justifiable, but it is a development which should be observed and debated, rather than allowed to happen unnoticeably by degrees, and driven by tabloid pressure rather than evidence of harm. McIntyre describes a shift from what he calls 'legislative forbearance' concerning Internet content (as opposed to television, radio and other traditional audio-visual content[81]) towards a greater willingness to regulate: a move from industry self-regulation, to sector-specific laws or binding codes of practice. It also involves, McIntyre notes, a move from offences involving possession of 'self-evidently' illegal content—most child sexual images—to offences that require assessment of *intention*—'glorifying terrorism' and its ilk. Given that the main restriction on Internet content may be take-down or blocking by non-legal bodies such as ISPs, not courts, this may be more than unfortunate (see further discussion below).

(iii) Grooming and Moderation

An increasing worry in recent years for law enforcement agencies has been 'cyber-solicitation' or 'grooming': the use of Internet chatrooms and social networking sites such as Facebook and Bebo by paedophiles to lure children into a relationship which may progress to extensive correspondence and the creation of trust, meetings in person, cyber-sex and actual sexual abuse. The anonymity of the Internet lends itself to paedophiles disguising their identity, age and sex in order to entice children to sexual

---

[78] 'Sexting' is the sending of adult pictures of videos of yourself to another user by text of similar, using your mobile phone. Where under-age teenagers send pictures of themselves, they are arguably sharing images of child sexual abuse. In the US a number of prosecutions have resulted.

[79] Noted by TJ McIntyre, 'Content, Control and Cyberspace: The End of Internet Regulatory Forebearance in the UK?' unpublished paper circulated at 1st SCRIPT-ed Conference, Edinburgh, March 2009; and see J Ozimek, 'UK Minister Looks for Delete Key on User Generated Content', *The Register* 2 October 2008, at http://www.theregister.co.uk/2008/10/02/web_regulation_byron/.

[80] See Select Committee on Culture, Media and Sport, 'Report on Harmful Content on the Internet and in Video Games' (2008) para 77.

[81] McIntyre, above n 79.

encounters, and the matter is complicated further in law by the fact that the child may be located in one jurisdiction and the potential abuser or 'groomer' in another. For UK law enforcement agencies, particular difficulties arose as to whether a person arrested at the 'grooming' stage prior to any actual attempted physical abuse could be charged with an offence. Although 'grooming' acts might be regarded as acts preparatory to an actual act of child abuse, and thus chargeable under the law of attempts, this would be by no means certain. The Sexual Offences Act 2003 thus created a number of new offences designed to cover this lacuna, including arranging or facilitating the commission of a child sex offence (section 15) and meeting a child following sexual grooming (section 17). Again, as with the other new offences described above, although the intent is clearly honourable, questions arise as to whether the new laws exceed the boundaries of civil liberties. Grooming involves in essence meeting a child with the intent to commit a sexual offence; but no offence might ever be in fact committed. It is conceivable that an attempted offence might be charged even where no actual meeting had taken place so the *actus reus* would simply be online conversations. In the worst-case scenario, the conversations might not even be with a real child but with a police investigator posing as a child. The advantages of enabling police intervention as early as possible to protect the children involved are obvious, but again where should the line be drawn?[82]

Finally, as of January 2009, it is illegal to moderate a 'public interactive communication service which is likely to be used wholly or mainly by children'—eg a kid's chatroom, or perhaps a service like Bebo—without being vetted as fit to work with children and registered with the Independent Safeguarding Authority.[83]

IV. THE INTERNATIONAL LEGAL SCENE

A. The US and the Communication Decency Act 1996 Debacle

In the US, the history of attempted state control of Internet content took a rather different path than that followed in the UK and the rest of Europe, although starting from a common point of public outrage at the discovery of the prevalence of Internet pornography around 1996. In the US, still to

---

[82] Another government proposal on the table is to proactively ban convicted sex offenders from joining social networking sites (see 'Sex Offenders Face Website Bans', BBC News, 4 April 2008.) Such a law seems eminently pointless since it would be near impossible to stop such a person obtaining new unknown e-mail addresses and, hence, identities. It is, however, also implemented in Facebook's new Statement of Rights and Responsibilities, para 4.4 (available at http://www.facebook.com/terms.php, as of 1 May 2009).

[83] See Safeguarding Vulnerable Groups Act 2006, Sched 3.

some extent the home of the 'moral majority', the legal battle has historically raged around the grander ambition of protecting children from all
'bad content' online, rather than the limited goal of merely criminalising
child pornography. The CDA, introduced in the wake of the *Time* magazine
cover story of 1996, broadly imposed criminal sanctions on anyone who
placed 'obscene or indecent' content on the Internet, knowing that it might
be read or seen by a minor (a person under 18). The Act was immediately
attacked by civil society groups as over-broad, since it is generally impossible without overt technical measures such as age verification to know if a
child 'might' be reading a website or other public communication. Effectively, therefore, the CDA criminalised all adult content on the Web, even
material which was never intended for the eyes of children. Moreover the
CDA was badly drafted since it criminalised not just 'obscene content' such
as child pornography, which was already, uncontroversially, illegal for all,
but also 'indecent' material, which was ill defined, and included material
that had been acknowledged in the US as having some degree of First
Amendment protection. At a more symbolic level, the Act was seen as a
declaration of war on the 'traditional' free-speechers of the Internet, and as
demonstrating flagrant disregard for the right of freedom of expression
online.[84]

The legality of the CDA was challenged by a variety of civil liberties
groups and, to the great delight of much of the emergent Internet
community, the Supreme Court quashed the offending provisions on 25
June 1997.[85] Their argument was effectively that the CDA would turn the
whole of the Internet into a 'children's reading room'. Since it was not yet
possible technically to guarantee that adult speech would only be accessed
by adults, no 'zoning' was possible as it was with, for example, adult films
in cinemas, and sex shops. The rationale that the CDA was a necessary
infringement on the freedom of speech of adults to protect the interests of
children was robustly rejected. Forty years earlier in the *Butler v Michigan*[86]
case, the Supreme Court had overturned a state law banning the sale of
books unfit for children on the oft-quoted grounds that such legislation
burns down the house to roast the pig. In *Reno v ACLU*,[87] the Court now
reasserted that while protection of children was an important goal, it could
not be legitimately achieved by interfering with the constitutional rights of
adults. The Internet was not as invasive a medium as radio or television:
pornographic websites, for example, were usually well signposted and often
password protected and were unlikely to be stumbled upon by accident.
Accordingly censorship of the Internet to bring its content down to the

---

84 See, most famously, Barlow, above n 10.
85 *Reno v ACLU*, 521 US 844 (1997), at http://www.aclu.org/court/renovacludec.html
86 353 US 380, 97 SCt 524 (1957).
87 Cited at n 49.

'lowest common denominator' that should be exposed to children would be even *less* acceptable in relation to the Internet than broadcast media.

While it was true that sites could make efforts to restrict access by children to adult-oriented material by putting in place requirements for adult verification passwords such as AdultCheck,[88] or credit card details, these would present a formidable financial overhead to small website operators, some of whom might be providing socially useful information such as help on sexual abuse, homosexuality or AIDS. Some would cease to publish this information as a result, or close down altogether. The restrictions on these sites were not justifiable given the impact on the free speech rights of adults. The CDA was accordingly overturned.[89]

In the aftermath of the *Reno v ACLU (No 1)* decision, Congress had a second go with the Child Online Protection Act (COPA). Section 1403(a) of this Act provided that any *commercial* Web publisher who knowingly makes available to minors material that is 'harmful to minors' was to be subject to penalties including jail time and large fines. COPA was tailored to be more robust under constitutional inspection than the CDA in that it (i) only applied to commercial websites; (ii) gave a fuller definition of what material was 'harmful to minors' (but which still included material not illegal for adults to access, such as some types of adult pornography); and (iii) gave more evidence about the possible harm to children of Internet content. These distinctions were not enough, however, to save it from meeting the same fate as the CDA. The statute was overturned as unconstitutional first by the District Court,[90] subsequently by the US Court of Appeals[91] and eventually, like the CDA, by the Supreme Court.[92] The main issue this time was whether a more effective and less speech-restrictive means existed to protect children *other* than by general criminalisation of Internet content for all adults.[93] Over a decade later, although COPA-

---

[88] AdultCheck (http://www.adultcheck.com/) is currently the most popular adult verification site. Clients give the site information, including credit card details, and it provides an AdultCheck ID which can then be used to gain access to 'adult' sites. AdultCheck (according to its own publicity) is currently used on around 125,000 adult sites.

[89] See a detailed analysis of the judgment in J Wallace, 'Extinguishing the CDA Fire' (1997) 3 *JILT*, at http://elj.warwick.ac.uk/jilt/cases/97_3cda/.

[90] *ACLU v Reno II* 31 F Supp 2d 473 (ED Pa1999).

[91] *ACLU v Reno II* 22 June 2000, US Court of Appeal for the 3rd Circuit, available at http://www.epic.org/free_speech/copa/3d_cir_opinion.html.

[92] *Ashcroft v ACLU* 535 US 564 (2002). Because the Internet had changed dramatically in the five years since the district court gathered factual evidence, however, the justices returned the case to the district court for a full trial on whether there are effective ways to keep children safe online that burdened speech less than COPA's criminal penalties (see note below). Note that COPA never come into operation; its existence was challenged by ACLU and its operation suspended one day after it was passed by Congress.

[93] See *ACLU v Alberto Gonzales* No 98-5591 (ED Penn, 22 March 2007) in which a lower court found as a matter of fact that user-side filters were reasonably effective as a means to protect children, and hence COPA should not be constitutionally tolerated.

related litigation continues,[94] it seems unlikely that a US Federal statute can be drafted which censors the Internet as a whole without falling foul of the First Amendment. Effectively, like Europe, the US seems to have given up the attempt to prosecute anything other than child pornography on the Internet; indeed Krause claims there have been only 10 prosecutions for non child sexual pornography since 2005,[95] remarkable in a country containing the substantial 'Bible Belt'.

B. The EU

In Europe, although there is a greater history of protection of minors in relation to content in the media, and less emphasis on protection of free speech, the US CDA and COPA debacles have nonetheless left a legacy. First, it became clear that legislation could not get away with protecting children by abnegating adult rights of freedom of expression on the Internet. Secondly, the widespread public opposition to both CDA and COPA showed that, in general, the state would do well to avoid directly and bluntly being seen as a censor of the Internet, except in respect of the most universally despised material, ie child pornography.[96]

In Europe, this lead to a clear distinction being drawn between material that is *illegal* for all to possess, which can be directly censored, and merely *harmful or undesirable* content, which should generally be subject to user or parental, rather than state, control.[97] This shift can ideologically be seen as a move from direct state regulation, to a mixture of state regulation and 'self'-regulation.[98] In this philosophy, users should be empowered to block

[94] See further http://usgovinfo.about.com/od/rightsandfreedoms/a/copastruck.htm. The latest defeat for COPA was in June 2008 in the Philadelphia Federal Court of Appeals. Interestingly, the leading opinion stated 'Perhaps we do the minors of this country harm if First Amendment protections, which they will with age inherit, are chipped away in the name of their protection.'

[95] See the fascinating article by J Krause, 'The End of the Net Porn Wars' [February 2008] *ABA Journal*, available at http://abajournal.com/magazine/the_end_of_the_net_porn_wars/. According to the author, there have been less than 10 prosecutions for obscenity (ie non-child porn) since 2005, and meanwhile in the 10 years since the CDA, Internet porn has become a huge financial business in the US, with 2006 US revenues from Internet porn estimated at $2.84 billion, up 13 per cent over 2005.

[96] A useful comparison of EU and US approaches to regulating Internet porn in the interests of children can be found in MD Birnhack and JH Rowbottom, 'Shielding Children the European Way' [2003] *Chicago-Kent Law Review* 101.

[97] See European Parliament Communication of 16 October 1996 on Illegal and Harmful Content on the Internet (above n 12) ch 3: 'In terms of illegal and harmful content it is crucial to differentiate betwen content which is illegal and other harmful content. *These different categories of content pose radically different issues of principle, and call for very different legal and technological responses.* It would be dangerous to amalgamate *separate issues such as children accessing pornographic content for adults, and adults accessing pornography about children.* Priorities should be clearly set and resources mobilised to tackle the most important issues, that is the fight against criminal content.'

[98] See further Marsden et al, 'Options for and Effectiveness of Internet Self and Co-Regulation Phase 1 Report' (RAND Europe, 27 June 2007).

access to such material for themselves and their children by the provision of appropriate filtering and rating software, tailored to the cultural and linguistic diversity of Europe's heterogeneous population. This is intended to avoid both the threat of US-based ratings systems imposing US cultural sensibilities on European users, and the CDA-like threat of direct state censorship prejudicing the rights of adult citizens.

This model was adopted in a series of copiously funded European projects known originally as the European Action Plan,[99] and later as the Safer Internet Plan, which have run consecutively from 1999 to date, with indefinite continuation expected.[100] These action plans focus on enabling self-regulation by users (including parents), ISPs and hosts such as schools and libraries rather than on top-down criminal law. Thus the EU programme has funded (and continues to fund) research into, for example, development and use of technical tools such as filtering and rating systems (see below), the fostering of international co-operation, research and policing, and the creation of a network of European hotlines. Finally, the EU project looks to the future with a plan to raise awareness among parents and children of the opportunities and risks of the Internet by public education schemes.

Currently research seems to be focusing on, inter alia, the creation of a pan-European alert line to report child pornography and other offensive material, the benchmarking of filtering software products as effective (SIP-BENCH[101]), the production of filters for dealing with child pornography distributed via P2P networks (MAPAP[102]) and the safe use of mobile phones by children.

Having noted the shift in UK governance politics towards top-down control of harmful as well as illegal content, it is more than possible that Europe may follow more slowly in this direction: the proposed 2009 EU Framework Decision on 'combating the sexual abuse, sexual exploitation of children and child pornography' would certainly seem to indicate this.[103]

V. ENFORCEMENT PROBLEMS AND THE MOVE FROM LAW TO CODE SOLUTIONS

The key problem with enforcement of national pornography laws, of course, is that Internet pornography is a global phenomenon. Pornography

---

[99] For more details, see this chapter in the 2000 (2nd) edition of this book.

[100] The scheme which ran 2005–08 was known as Safer Internet Plus. A new scheme has been prposed for funding for 2009–13.

[101] See project home page at http://ec.europa.eu/information_society/activities/sip/projects/targeted/filtering/sip_bench/index_en.htm

[102] See project home page at http://ec.europa.eu/information_society/activities/sip/projects/targeted/filtering/mapap/index_en.htm.

[103] See C Williams, 'UK.gov to Get Power to Force ISPs to Block Child Porn', *The Register* 2 April 2009.

is as likely to be accessed by a UK citizen sitting at a terminal in Edinburgh from a server or website physically located in Russia, or Japan, or the US, as from one within UK criminal jurisdiction. In fact due to the efforts of the IWF, discussed below, very little child pornography is now actually hosted within the UK: according to IWF reports of complaints about Internet content,[104] less than 1 per cent of potentially illegal content has been hosted in the UK since 2003, down from 18 per cent in 1997.[105] Thus almost all child pornography accessed over the Web by UK residents comes from abroad, with most material downloaded from the US (62 per cent), followed by Russia (28 per cent).[106]

As we have seen, it is legally possible (although much may depend on the exact wording of the criminal laws in question) for national authorities to prosecute and punish the *recipients* of pornography, even if the material itself is hosted on a foreign server,[107] and also to punish parties who store illicit material on foreign located servers, or supply it by uploading it to such servers, so long as *they themselves* are personally located within the jurisdiction. In *R v Waddon*, a businessman running a large Internet pornography operation in the UK from websites physically located in the US was found guilty of publishing obscene articles in the UK under the Obscene Publications Act 1959. The court held that 'publication' took place both when the defendant transmitted the data constituting the images to the US websites and continued when the material was received in the UK by a client of those websites (using a site password).[108]

In the main, though, the problem of individuals undetectably making private use of child pornography accessed from sites abroad (and perhaps then swapping it in person or via encrypted P2P) remains and is extremely hard to police, except in occasional large and resource-intensive co-operative policing operations such as Operation Ore. Clearly a more efficient solution in terms of access would be for such material to be blocked by the relevant ISP when a UK user seeks to access it. We turn now to looking at developments in this area.

---

[104] The Internet Watch Foundation (IWF) is a private non-governmental body, established by representatives of the ISP industry to meet law enforcement concerns about Internet pornography in September 1996. See further below.

[105] See IWF site at http://www.iwf.org.uk/. The latest available 2007 Trends figures on the IWF site do not contain information about percentage of porn hosted in the UK but the implication is it is very little.

[106] Latest figures on IWF website for year end 2006.

[107] See eg the discussion of 'making' in *Atkins*, above n 43.

[108] See report at http://www.cyber-rights.org/documents/rvgraham.htm.

VI. CONTROL OF ILLEGAL AND HARMFUL CONTENT BY ISPs

A. ISP Liability

In one of the most infamous incidents in Internet legal history, in May 1998, a court in Bavaria, Germany, found Felix Somm, the Chief Executive Officer of CompuServe Europe, guilty of distributing child pornography and other adult content.[109] This rested on the fact that CompuServe, like most ISPs, had routinely circulated within Bavaria Usenet newsgroups, including some that were deemed to contain content illegal under Bavarian law. Pleas that CompuServe had neither originated this content nor could exercise effective monitoring of it, or control over it (newsgroup feeds taken by ISPs usually run to millions of individual news items) failed to prevent the original prosecution succeeding; however, an appeal in November 1999 (after Germany had enacted new legislation in the area) did eventually reverse the decision, to somewhat less publicity.[110]

The EU attempted to address the understandable fears of the ISP community subsequent to the *Somm* affair by introducing as part of the Electronic Commerce Directive[111] provisions relating generally to ISP liability in relation to all kinds of illegal and actionable content. These are discussed in some detail in chapter 1, and also in chapter 6 in relation to copyright. Broadly, ISPs are absolved from liability where they act as a 'mere conduit'—akin to the idea of a common carrier—ie where they merely transmit and do not in any way alter material provided by, and intended for, a third party. Similarly, an ISP is not liable for the 'automatic, intermediary or temporary storage' of content provided by a third party where that storage is done for the sole purpose of speeding up the transmission of Internet content. This refers to the practice of caching, which is generally implemented automatically so that calls for the same piece of content by other users can be fulfilled without the need to retrieve that content again from the original site. This speeds up the Internet for all parties.

The most important provisions for ISPs and illegal content are in Article 14 of the Directive on 'hosting', which deals with where ISPs host or store content more than transiently. Article 14(1)(a) provides that ISPs are

---

[109] Local Court, Munich, May 12 1998. An English-language version of the case is available at http://www.cyber-rights.org/isps/somm-dec.htm. See also Bender, 'Bavaria v Felix Somm: the Pornography Conviction of the Former CompuServe Manager' [1998] *International Journal of Communications Law and Policy* Web-Doc 14 January, at http://www.digital-law.net/papers/index.html.

[110] See 'Germany Clears Net Chief of Child Porn Charges', *The Independent* 18 November 1999.

[111] Electronic-Commerce Directive, Directive 2000/31/EC, OJ L178, 8 June 2000, available at http://www.europa.eu.int/eur-lex/en/dat/2000/l_178/l_17820000717en00010016.pdf.

exempt from *criminal* liability so long as they do not have 'actual knowledge' of illegal activity or information; and are exempt from *civil* liability so long as they do not have actual knowledge *and* are not 'aware of facts and circumstances from which the illegal activity or information is apparent'. The ISP is not required to actively seek this knowledge or awareness, nor can a general obligation to monitor all material hosted or transmitted be placed on the ISP.[112] However, if an ISP does obtain such knowledge or awareness—eg if the police, or a member of the public notifies them that they are hosting an illegal photograph as an item in a newsgroup they carry—then under Article 14(1)(b), they become liable again if they do not remove that item 'expeditiously'.

While there has to date been no case in the UK in which an ISP has been prosecuted for distributing or publishing pornography, as we have seen, laws such as the POCA could probably in theory be invoked against them as possessors, publishers or distributors of pornography, although some statutory defences might also be available.[113] ISPs are more vulnerable to prosecution than the actual pornographers, because they have a physical base of operations within the jurisdiction and are locatable, respectable, and susceptible to public pressure. In 1996 the London Metropolitan police, following the lead provided by the then Science and Technology Minister, threatened to prosecute a number of UK ISPs for distributing around 130 Usenet newsgroups to their subscribers which had been found in the past to contain illegal pornography or other types of sexual material, unless the ISPs moved towards 'self-regulation',[114] ie took steps themselves to remove these newsgroups from the service they provided to their subscribers.[115] This action lead directly to the creation in 1996 of the quasi-industry body, the IWF[116] (originally 'Safety-Net'),

---

[112] Ibid, Art 15.

[113] Eg the Protection of Children Act 1978, s 1 (4), provides that it shall be a defence to an offence under s 1(1)((b) or (c) (distribution or possession offences) that the defender had not himself seen the indecent photographs and did not know, nor had any cause to suspect them to be, indecent. See G Leong, 'Computer Child Pornography—The Liability of Distributors' [1998] *Criminal Law Review* Special Edition on Crime, Criminal Justice and the Internet 19; and T Palfrey, 'Pornography and the Possible Criminal Liability of Internet Service Providers under the Obscene Publication(s) and Protection of Children Act' (1997) 6 *Information and Communications Technology Law* 187.

[114] Akdeniz quotes Mike Hoskins, Commander of the Metropolitan Police Clubs and Vice Unit in 1996 as saying to ISPs at a public meeting 'either the industry takes it upon itself to clean up the Net or the police intervene'. See Y Akdeniz 'The Regulation of Pornography and Child Pornography on the Internet' (1997) 1 *JILT*, at http://elj.warwick.ac.uk/internet/97_1akdz/.

[115] It has been suggested that one of the purposes of this exercise was to put UK ISPs 'on notice' of what content they were carrying so that the defence outlined in n 113 would not be available to them in any subsequent prosecution.

[116] The original Board of the IWF was composed exclusively of representatives from ISPs. The current Board has a wider representation comprising members selected from ISPs, and non-industry members selected from, for example, charities concerned with child welfare, the National Union of Students and the Campaign against Censorship of the Internet in Britain. See http://www.iwf.org.uk.

which has become the 'quasi-public face of Internet regulation in the United Kingdom'.[117]

B. The IWF: From Hotline to 'Cleanfeed'

The IWF's main role was originally to provide a free hotline channel via which the public could report, by telephone, e-mail or fax, material they encountered on the Internet which fell within the IWF's remit. The IWF advertises its remit as to receive reports of 'content [the public] have been inadvertently exposed to or seen on the internet, which they believe to be potentially illegal'. As stated policy, the IWF accepts complaints about child pornography (or 'images of child sexual abuse' as their preferred terminology) worldwide; obscene material in the UK; and race hate material in the UK. The IWF vets these reports of objectionable content to see if they truly concern illegal content, and takes action if appropriate, which can consist of

- making a report to the UK police (if the item appears to have originated within the UK);
- reporting to the Serious and Organised Crime Agency (SOCA) who organise liaison with foreign police forces in the case of foreign content);
- recommending removal of the item from the servers of UK ISPs;
- adding the item complained of to the IWF 'blacklist' (see below). Notably only child pornography Uniform Resource Locators (URLs) are at present added, not the two other categories of material within the remit.

Advice to remove an item is given by the IWF to UK ISPs, whose decision it then is whether to comply. From 1996 to 2002, the IWF's role was solely to recommend take-down to UK ISPs by notice. The reason ISPs fell into place with IWF notice and take-down was, primarily, to protect their own backs. So long as an ISP acted to take-down on notice it could satisfactorily claim immunity as a host from liability under the EU E-commerce Directive Rules discussed above. From 2002 the IWF agreed with ISPs that they would not provide a feed of newsgroups which regularly contained child sexual abuse images or advertised such.

The sea-change came in 2004 when the IWF blocklist (or, as it is often inaccurately known, its 'cleanfeed'—a term that is actually trademarked by Thus plc) was created. Items that are hosted abroad and deemed illegal child sexual images of abuse are added to a URL 'blocklist' which is maintained by the IWF and updated around twice a day. Almost all UK ISPs

---

[117] See D Wall, 'Policing and the Regulation of the Internet' (1998) *Criminal Law Review* Special Edition on Crime, Criminal Justice and the Internet 79. See a recent journalistic assessment of the IWF by CJ Davies, 'The Hidden Censors of Your Internet', *UK Wired* June 2009, 40.

voluntarily agreed from 2004, when BT made appropriate software available, to take the 'blocklist' feed and implement it by means of automated blocking filters.[118] (The list itself is sent out in encrypted form, to avoid illicit use thereof, but it can be edited by the receiving ISP, so they can add their own URLs to it.)

Some ISPs, however, refused or simply failed to implement the IWF blocklist, for a mixture of resources and freedom-of-speech reasons. However, in 2007, the Home Office took the decision to massively increase the significance and influence of the IWF. Home Office minister Vernon Coaker issued a press release that all UK ISPs were to agree to sign up to the IWF blocklist by the end 2007, or the government would be forced to legislate. Most fell into place , although a few smaller ISPs (such as Zen Internet) refused to comply. In 2009, the National Society for the Prevention of Cruelty to Children (NSPCC) called for these ISPs to come into line, but although no positive response came from the ISPs themselves, in the process it emerged that only around 700,000 UK users had non-filtered Internet access, a tiny proportion.[119]

Effectively, therefore, the UK has put in place, without public debate, new laws or a system of public accountability, a universal non-transparent scheme of online censorship that is in theory capable of blocking any particular piece of Internet content, whether illegal or not. The IWF, of course, claim quite correctly that it is not and never would be their policy for this to happen. But the IWF blocklist system is now a good example of what Lessig, in his influential book *Code and Other Laws of Cyberspace*, termed 'upstream filtering':[120] filtering imposed from above without the knowledge or often the consent of the users whose access it affects. Such filtering is, of course, justifiable as the best or perhaps the only way to successfully prevent the dissemination of child pornpgraphy, but it can also indubitably be abused. 'Cleanfeed' is not dissimilar in essence to the system by which Google, Yahoo! and other search engines currently allow the Chinese government to dictate to them what pages can be included, and which excluded, in the search results they return to Chinese citizens.[121] Such manipulation of what can be found on the Internet by private censors has been widely disparaged in the West, yet until the Wikipedia incident in 2008 (see below) the role of the IWF was largely unknown except by a few industry and civil society commentators and public approval was 100 per

---

[118] However, the IWF and ISPs did agree a policy from 2002 that the ISPs would not provide a feed of newsgroups which regularly contained child sexual abuse images or advertised such. From 1996 to 2002, the IWF's role was solely to recommend take down to UK ISPs by notice.

[119] See Williams, above n 103. The article notes that EU supranational legislation might require the government to finally pass hard legislation in this area.

[120] See now the revised edition, *Code 2.0* (New York, Basic Books, 2006) ch 12.

[121] Indeed Google in the UK voluntarily filters its search results via the IWF Cleanfeed (not being an ISP, it is not required to do so). See further discussion of Google's position below.

cent.[122] As we shall discuss below, such a system, however benevolent in creation and intention, does raise considerable free speech worries.[123]

What content does the IWF block? Around 85 per cent of reports to the IWF are about child pornography, 10 per cent about general obscenity, and 5 per cent about racial hatred.[124] Material actioned is overwhelmingly of foreign origin. In 2008, 1,536 unique domains were blocked, a 21 per cent decrease since 2006. The number of reports of illegal material has climbed inexorably every year since 1996, from 615 reports processed in 1996 to 33,947 reports in 2008. It is possible, however, that this reflects more of a growth in public access to, and awareness of, the Internet, than in the quantity of illegal material itself. In fact the 2008 figure represents a 3 per cent decline on the year previous.

Notably, although the IWF has successfully reduced the amount of child pornography hosted in the UK to almost zero, it can take only a very limited role in persuading authorities *abroad* to take down, that being the responsibility of the authorities abroad. A recognised problem is that even if sites are closed down, they hop servers and jurisdictions and change URL to stay open, making removing them an ongoing game of 'whack a mole'. In 2008, the average life of an identified child pornography host was 100 days or less in the year, although 19 per cent stayed up for longer than this. Many of these will have been in the US, the main source of child pornography reported to the IWF. The IWF admits that 'the longevity of some domains . . . continues to pose an international challenge'.[125] Since the IWF is not empowered to obtain take-down abroad, it is thus thrown back on reliance on maintenance of the blocklist as its key tool for reducing total access to child pornography in the UK.[126] However, the 21 per cent decrease in blocked unique domains since 2006 does, it is claimed, show some overall success in reducing the number of 'live' hosting sites abroad.

Should we worry about this system of blocklisting? Removing access to child pornography is clearly a societal good. Bambauer argues, however,

122 See J Ozimek, 'Scorpions Tale Leaves IWF Exposed: "Look, That Regulator Isn't Wearing Any Clothes"', *The Register* 9 December 2008, at http://www.theregister.co.uk/2008/12/09/iwf/.

123 See further L Edwards, 'From Child Porn to China, in One Cleanfeed' (2008) 4(1) *SCRIPT-ed*, at http://www.law.ed.ac.uk/ahrc/SCRIPT-ed/vol3-3/editorial.asp.

124 Statistics here and below from the IWF homepage, www.iwg.org,uk, as of July 2008, and where updated, *2008 Annual Report*. In particular note the trends page collected from reports over 10 years, 1996–2006, at http://www.iwf.org.uk/media/news.archive-2006.179.htm. The percentages by content in the 2008 Annual Report are not given, only raw figures, but appear of roughly the same proportions.

125 *Annual Report 2008*, at Fig. 6.

126 See fascinating discussion in T Moore and R Clayton, 'The Impact of Incentives on Notice and Take-down', available at http://www.cl.cam.ac.uk/~rnc1/takedown.pdf. They compared take-down times for 'phishing' sites abroad requested by banks, and child pornography sites where requests were made by police. On average a site hosting child pornography stayed up a median time of 11 days and the mean lifetime was 30 days. By contrast, phishing sites measured their lives in hours, with some removed in only 4.3 hours and the median life 47.6 hours (far longer than the mean). This seems to show room for improvement in the former case.

that 'legitimate filtering is open, transparent, narrowly focused, and accountable to citizens and users'.[127] The IWF fails on most, if not all, of these counts. It has been indubitably successful at clearing child pornography off UK servers, and has made a fair stab at blocking it when it is hosted abroad, but its constitutional foundations as a law enforcement body are dubious. Civil society groups note that it performs a quasi-judicial function—assessing if material reported by the public is illegal—when it is not a court; and performs a public function—deciding if material should be censored—when it is a private and self-appointed body. Unlike Parliament or the courts, it thus has no obligations of public reporting or auditing (though see below) and until the Wikipedia fracas described below, its presence was generally unknown to most ordinary citizens and its methods of deliberation remain non-transparent. Its scope is currently narrow but capable of expanding (as discussed above), although this is against the expressed wishes of the IWF itself. Yaman Akdeniz, the Director of Cyber Rights UK, encapsulates these criticisms by asserting that 'the formation of the IWF sets a dangerous precedent for privatised censorship'.[128]

The IWF partially attempted to meet these criticisms early in its existence by reconstituting its executive board to embrace a wider representation of interested parties,[129] but it is still basically true that it is more an industry body than a public one, and that it is not accountable to the public through any kind of parliamentary or other scrutiny (although to be fair it does publish both annual reports and minutes of meetings). However, as Wall noted in 1998, if 'the IWF [were] to canvass public opinion over the issues such as child pornography, then such public support would be considerable'.[130] The self-regulatory nature of the IWF enabled it to be set up quickly, and to command the co-operation of almost all of the industry. There is also a long history of industry self-regulation in the UK media as exemplified by the Advertising Standards Authority and the Press Complaints Commission, although the success of at least the latter can be questioned.

In late 2008, however, the IWF came to mainstream public attention in the UK as an online censor with reports that it had blocked access to Wikipedia, the popular online peer-edited encyclopedia site. The reason for this blocking was that one page contained an image of an apparently pre-pubescent girl, on a well-known classic rock album cover, which had been deemed sexual by the IWF.[131] Due to complications caused by Wikipedia being a high-traffic site, the effect was not just to block that image, but to

---

[127] See above n 45 at 18.
[128] See Akdeniz, above n 114, 235.
[129] See http://www.iwf.org.uk/public/page.103.htm.
[130] See Wall, above n 117, 86.
[131] See further Ozimek, above n 122.

bar the whole of the UK from editing Wikipedia, leading to considerable public attention.

The Wikipedia affair vividly illustrated the basic problems of universal online content blocking by a non-judicial and non-state body: namely (i) the IWF had no legal authority to decide this dubious image was actually illegal (especially given it was widely available elsewhere on the Internet, and indeed had been on sale in UK record stores for over 30 years); (ii) no appeal process existed to the courts (although the IWF did invoke its own internal appeals procedure[132]); and (iii) no explicit notice was given to either the public or Wikipedia that blocking had been imposed, or, more importantly, why. Indeed, every UK ISP that implemented the IWF blocklist except Demon returned a '404 page Not Found' error in respect of Wikipedia, which implies technical problems have prevented the page loading, rather than intended prohibition of the site. Thus IWF-initiated blocking was notified to neither users nor target, the IWF's argument being that it is for the service provider hosting the blocked site to notify the site owner. In the end, in the face of a violent public reaction at discovering the existence of previously unknown tools of censorship online, the IWF reversed its decision for rather hazy legal and practical reasons.[133]

Notwithstanding the Wikipedia affair, the IWF's work has been regularly held up as a model of effective control to the rest of the world, and the 'voluntary hotline' model has become popular in Europe, and is supported financially by the various EU action plans discussed above. There is now an association of European hotlines, INHOPE,[134] whose membership is steadily growing. It is certainly true that the IWF filter is a quicker, cheaper and more practicable method of removing child pornography from UK public view than the more conventional police or court-based route, and that child pornography is a pernicious and hard to attack problem on the Internet. Furthermore, by mediating, and providing a central hotline for, complaints about Internet content, the IWF effectively protects ISPs from having to deal with complaints from the public about pornography and hate speech (though not other topics such as spam) as part of daily business, and from being distracted by frivolous or unfounded ones. In this context the IWF may well actually act in defence of free speech, since the IWF will (one hopes) have the sense and experience to throw out complaints about entirely legal Internet images or content, where a small ISP, lacking legal advice and as best-practice risk management, might simply give in and remove the item in question.[135]

---

132 Whether the IWF is susceptible to judicial review as a 'public body', or indeed to private actions for libel for mistaken placement of a site on the blocklist, remain open legal questions.

133 See the IWF own's statement at http://www.iwf.org.uk/media/news.251.htm.

134 See https://www.inhope.org/.

135 See further the discussion around *Godfrey v Demon Internet* [1999] 4 All ER 342 in Edwards, ch 1.

The key problems with the future of the IWF are of function creep and independence. When the IWF's vetting was confined almost exclusively to child pornography, this presented relatively little difficulty in identification or legal nuance. However, the IWF has since expanded its remit as a complaints hotline (as the statistics above show) to cover the rather more complicated offence of incitement to racial hatred. There have also been repeated rumours of governmental pressure to add pro-terrorist material to its complaints remit and perhaps even its blocklist.[136] In a widely reported speech in January 2008, the Home Secretary, Jacqui Smith, suggested that ISPs should be prepared to block terrorist websites in the same way that they currently block child pornography sites.[137] The question of whether an unappointed, non-legally trained body might end up censoring this wider range of content, without executive or judicial supervision, is rather more worrying, especially in the post-9/11 terrain of new and sometimes vague laws on 'glorifying terrorism', and increasing ethnic and religious tensions. The IWF's own worries about taking over adjudication of legal grey areas can be seen in its very public refusal thus far to add either racist or 'extreme pornography' material to its blocklist. It has also clearly rejected suggestions that it might 'pre-vet' sites as legal in respect of extreme pornography.[138]

In summary the IWF undoubtedly does an important and difficult job to the best of its abilities, but its remit and quasi-public status (which have both arisen by historical incident rather than forward planning) need to be reconsidered as soon as possible, given the powers it now potentially possesses to exclude any kind of online content from the UK, without the notice of either the public or the courts. As an absolute worst-case scenario, for example, a future government might instruct the IWF to add to its blocklist any number of anti-government websites. If the Wikipedia precedent was followed, all the public might see is a '404' error message. Perhaps even more worryingly, any ISP which takes the IWF blocklist can also in theory *add* whatever URLs it pleases to it, again without public scrutiny.

Although these may both seem unlikely events, it is high time that the IWF was reconstituted as a public body, ideally comprised of a majority of

---

[136] The legal framework for this is already in force in the form of the Electronic Commerce Directive (Terrorism Act 2006) Regulation 2007, which implements the Electronic Commerce Directive in relation to the Terrorism Act 2006. These provide that where a host has actual knowledge that it is hosting unlawful terrorism-related material and it has failed to take-down the material expeditiously on acquiring such knowledge, it may be liable under the Terrorism Act. However the IWF FAQ continues as of July 2008 to state that terrorist sites are not part of their remit and such activities should instead by reported to the Police Anti-Terrorist Hotline.

[137] See speech reported at http://press.homeoffice.gov.uk/Speeches/sp-hs-terrorism-keynote-jan-08. See also cogent analysis in G Goth, 'Terror on the Internet: A Complex Issue, and Getting Harder' (2008) 9(3) IEEE Distributed Systems Online art no 0803-3003.

[138] See Ozimek 'IWF Rethinks its Role', *The Register* 12 December 2008, at http://www.theregister.co.uk/2008/12/12/iwf_investigates_itself/.

legal professional members alongside industry and charity representatives, and chaired by an independent member of the judiciary who could resist the kind of governmental pressure hypothesised above. Statistics as to type of content blocked, and *justifications* for decisions taken, should also be regularly and publicly compiled to inform democratic debate. In particular, when IWF blocking is applied, a '403 prohibited page' rather then a '404 technical error page' should be returned to the searching user. Finally, the need for an apparatus with the potential for unsupervised covert censorship should be minimised by the IWF seeking powers to work with authorities abroad to facilitate take-down of illegal content overseas wherever possible,[139] rather than simply expanding the blocklist.

C. The Global Rise of Automated Censorship of Internet Content

The IWF/'cleanfeed' story of how a voluntary self-regulatory scheme evolved to a fully fledged system of top-down national censorship of the Internet is not an isolated one. Worldwide, censorship of online content is on the increase as technical expertise develops and filtering gets cheaper. The Open Net Initiative (ONI),[140] a major anti-censorship watchdog backed by Harvard, Toronto, Cambridge and Oxford universities, has undertaken a global survey of Internet censorship in over 40 countries and found that it has developed rapidly in recent years, not just in countries where suppression of speech might be expected, such as China (famous for its 'Great Firewall'[141]), Vietnam, Saudi Arabia, Myanmar, etc, but also in numerous Western and Asian democracies such as not only the UK but also Australia, Canada, Germany[142], France, Sweden and Norway, Thailand and many others.[143] In Western countries, however, filtering tends to be tightly focused rather than generic, and is more often taken on as a voluntary role rather than imposed. Notably, even in the US, home of the First

[139] The IWF view on this is that take-down may not always be desirable if it prevents authorities abroad catching the culprits. This author's view, however, is that the interest in free speech here outweighs the public interest in retribution, so long as the images are successfully and permanently removed. The balance is admittedly a difficult one.

[140] See http://opennet.net/. Useful maps of global online censorship can be found at http://map.opennet.net/filtering-IT.html. See also the book based on their research by RJ Deibert, J Palfrey et al (eds), *Access Denied: The Practice and Policy of Global Internet Filtering* (Cambridge, MA, MIT Press, 2008).

[141] See an interesting discussion of how the Chinese firewall works at http://news.bbc.co.uk/1/hi/technology/7312746.stm.

[142] See discussion of French and German deletion of Google search results below. See also 'Germany Pushes IWF-style Blocklist', *The Register* 16 January 2009, reporting that the German Minister for Families was considering an IWF-style filtering system, and hoping to reach an agreement with major ISPs. As of July 2009, steps were being taken towards such a system.

[143] See also TJ Mcintyre and C Scott, 'Internet Filtering: Rhetoric, Legitimacy, Accountability and Responsibility', in R Brownsword and K Yeung (eds), *Regulating Technologies* (Oxford, Hart Publishing, 2008).

Amendment, Mayor Cuomo of New York has recently persuaded three major ISPs to block sites alleged to provide child pornography.[144] Since this action is voluntary, it is probably constitutional. (Interestingly sub-Saharan Africa currently has the lowest level of regulatory filtering—probably due to lack of resources rather than lack of political desire to censor.)

The ONI has identified four major means of content filtering online: technical blocking (eg by IP address or by the URL of a site, or by Domain Name System (DNS) tampering); search result removals; take-down; and induced self-censorship (eg by making known the presence of constant surveillance). Censorship also occurs at at least four distinct 'upstream' levels: Internet backbones, ISPs, institutions (eg schools and universities) and individual computers (eg user-installed filters such as Net Nanny).

It is important, of course, to draw a distinction between systems such as the IWF blocklist, which still only block illegal rather than harmful content (to use the European Commission's terminology), and systems such as the Chinese Great Firewall where content is blocked for a wide variety of reasons, including politics, religion, propaganda and current events (censorship was carefully considered during and in the run up to the Beijing Olympics in 2008), other than the pure removal of illegal content.

An interesting Western example of online censorship which straddles the two categories and is worth detailed examination[145] is currently being fought over in Australia. In the last edition of this book, I described in detail the controversial Internet censorship scheme ushered in by the Australian Broadcasting Services Amendment (On-Line Services) Act 1999.[146] The Act ambitiously attempted to regulate both Internet content hosted and physically held in Australia, and content physically held abroad but accessible in Australia via Australian ISPs. Furthermore, it did not restrict itself to the lowest common denominator of child pornography but attempted to control legal but 'adult' material as well, in the alleged interests of child safety. When originally introduced, the shape of the scheme was broadly that Australian ISPs were required either to *remove* 'prohibited content'[147] if they physically hosted the offending material within Australia (by order of a 'take-down' notice); or to *block access* to it

[144] See http://news.bbc.co.uk/1/hi/world/americas/7446637.stm.
[145] See also D Bambauer, 'Filtering in Oz: Australia's Foray into Internet Censorship', Brooklyn Law School Legal Studies Research Paper No 125 (December 2008), at http://papers.ssrn.com/sol3/papers.cfm?abstract_id=1319466.
[146] See at http://scaleplus.law.gov.au/html/comact/10/6005/0/CM000060.htm. The 1997 Australian scheme is a complex one and is described in rather condensed style here. A more detailed description can be found in in C Kendall, 'Australia's New Internet Censorship Regime: Is This Progress?' (1999) 1 *Digital Technology Law Journal*, at http://wwwlaw.murdoch.edu.au/dtlj/articles/vol1_3/kendallDTLJ1_3.html.
[147] 'Prohibited content' is that classified as Refused Classification (RC) or X by the National Classification Board, or R when not in a restricted access system. See further Kendall, above n 146, paras 37–45.

if it was physically held abroad (by order of an 'access-prevention' notice). The sanctions for failing to do so were heavy daily fees.

In the event, public and industry hostility to this scheme was such that foreign content access prevention was effectively abandoned during the progress of the Bill. ISP administrators insisted that, given the technologies of the time, access prevention would in practice be impossible. Proscribed sites could still easily be accessed using proxy servers, or by changing URL or IP addresses. These arguments succeeded, and ISPs were eventually compelled only to make available to their subscribers filtering software, updated with banned URLs at regular intervals, which they could voluntarily choose whether or nor to use. In the end only a third of families opted to take the free filter software, and it cannot really be known if or how they use it. The scheme was described as having turned Australia into the 'village idiot' of the world,[148] and was largely regarded as a wholly ineffective political gesture, since even when domestic Australian content was removed by take-down, it often reappeared later unscathed on foreign severs in more hospitable countries such as the US.[149] The scheme was, however, extended in 2007 to apply to mobile Internet content, and is still in force.[150]

Ten years later, this happenstance softening of the Australian pro-censorship tendency is being reversed. Stephen Conroy, the incoming Labour Communications Minister, has proposed an extensive new censorship scheme which will rebuild the 1999 reforms in a form similar to the UK's IWF compulsory 'cleanfeed' scheme, as well as extending it to mobile and P2P traffic and sites. Under this plan, all ISPs will have to provide a 'clean feed' to households and schools, free of pornography and other 'inappropriate' material. Adult subscribers who wish to gain access to legal but adult material will be allowed to 'opt out' of these filters.[151] Opt out will, however, only be allowed in respect of material which is not defined as 'level one', which comprises all illegal material. However, what has particularly aroused cyber-libertarian ire is that it is not yet clear what other ('level two') material will be deemed 'inappropriate'.[152] The minister has so far

---

[148] See Penfold, above n 14.

[149] In the first three months of the Act coming into operation, out of 45 foreign sites which were deemed 'prohibited content', 17 were originally Australian hosted. Clearly Australian content had simply noved abroad. See also 'Down Under Smut Goes Up and Over', *Wired* 2 February 2000, at http://www.wired.com/news/politics/0,1283,34043,00.html, which describes the move of www.teenager.com.au (an Australian teen sex site) to a US server (without change of URL) after a take-down notice was issued.

[150] See Restricted Access Decleration 2007 available at ACMA home page http://www.acma.gov.au.

[151] See details of the announced plans at the Electronic Frontiers Australia site, http://www.efa.org.au/censorship/mandatory-isp-bocking/.

[152] In fact in 2009, the draft Australian blocklist was leaked to the Internet to government consternation. See J Oates, 'Secret Aussie Blacklist Leaked', *The Register* 19 March 2009, at http://www.theregister.co.uk/2009/03/19/australia_list_leaked/. A similar leak of a proposed

announced that around 10,000 websites may be blocked[153] (by comparison the IWF tracks only around 1,200 child pornography websites) and that material transferred by the popular P2P BitTorrent protocol will also be targeted.[154] Technical experts have expressed severe doubts that even web-page filtering, let alone P2P filtering, will actually be feasible and effective (just as in 1999), and note that, if installed, such filters would probably severely slow the Internet for all Australians, with social and commercial costs.[155]

The Australian experience, if it moves on to implementation from its current feasibility trials, will be a valuable case study of whether compulsory upstream Internet content filtering systems of harmful as well as illegal content can truly be both effective and acceptable in democratic transparent societies. In the meantime, it seems important to conclude with some general assessment of what the risks of such systems are. In his 2009 analysis of the Australian system, Bambauer notes perceptively that

> the debate over filtering has shifted, from whether it should occur to how it should work. Cyberlibertarianism is alive and well, as the discussions in Austra-lia's press and Parliament prove, but it is no longer ascendant. This shift disguises an important change in focus for regulating information. Filtering looks easy and cheap, and calls to block access to material that is almost universally con-demned—such as child pornography, extreme violence, or incitements to terrorism—are hard to resist. But this focus confuses means with ends. The key question is what set of measures best achieve the end, or combat the evil, at issue—and how tolerable their countervailing drawbacks will be.[156]

Without wishing to fall into the trap of turning to consider methods of filtering before deciding if filtering itself is the best way to proceed, here are some concluding points which must be considered, it is asserted, before any national filtering scheme is initiated.

VII. FILTERING SYSTEMS: KEY ISSUES

A. Purpose of Scheme and Audience Restricted

Schemes must be created with a particular purpose in mind if they are to avoid scope creep and overblocking. Does the scheme wish to block only material that is illegal for all to view, eg child pornography, or seek also to protect the interests of families and children (allegedly) by blocking legal

voluntary German pornography blocklist lead to a raid on Wikileaks German offices by police— see http://www.theregister.co.uk/2009/03/26/german_police_raid_wikileaks/.
[153] See http://news.bbc.co.uk/1/hi/technology/7760996.stm.
[154] See http://www.news.com.au/technology/story/0,28348,24833959-5014239,00.html.
[155] See Ovum, 'Internet Content Filtering—A Report to DCITA', 4 April 2003.
[156] Above, n 145.

but adult content, as the proposed Australian system would? Is it intended also to reduce the prevalence of hate speech or anti-government speech? Is it truly intended to be as near 100 per cent effective as possible, or is it merely a rhetorical gesture?

Cyber-libertarians would generally argue that only the first motivation is proper. And as we have seen, EU policy since the US CDA debacle has been to follow the line of banning only illegal content, leaving control of 'harmful' content to users, who can in theory empower themselves by employing self-installed filters or picking a filter-using ISP. In reality, however, Europe's citizens have made little use of filtering technology, despite much spending of EU cash, and this has by and large been put down to either apathy or lack of technical understanding. A market for 'family friendly ISPs' has also failed to materialize except perhaps in the US, where a number of Christian ISPs do operate successfully. PICS,[157] the 'neutral' filtering standard espoused by the EU as the answer for private filtering (and discussed at length in the last edition), has fallen into effective disuse, even though it is available in most standard browsers.[158] Arguably, then, there is a role for national governments to step in to protect children where parents are failing.

In Australia itself, however, research has shown that although only a third of families have adopted filters voluntarily, it is not at all clear that those who have not adopted them have failed to do so through inertia, fear or ignorance. In a survey commissioned by the government in 2005,[159] 50 per cent of the parents who had not installed filters reported that this was because they trusted their children, and 17 per cent said they had alternative ways to supervise their children. Only 5 per cent said they were unsure how to use filters and 3 per cent that they did not know where to get them. Hence, it may be that many families are quite happy to deal themselves with what their children read and watch. More empirical evidence of this sort should be collected before we assume this is a problem needing top-down solutions with free speech put at risk.[160]

Whichever option is selected, however, it is important to marry up the purpose with the methods used to achieve it. If the purpose is to censor illegal material, then as with the IWF cleanfeed, extending it to the whole

---

[157] See http://www.w3.org/PICS/.

[158] PICS is incorporated into current versions of Internet Explorer, but its webpage (above) reports no new developments dated later than 2000. New filtering standards based on XML and the Semantic Web are now under development. However, there seems no reason why they should become any more popular than PICS, which is available for free in the world's most popular browser.

[159] See ACMA report 'kidsonline@home: Internet Use in Australian Homes', April 2005.

[160] Interestingly, not dissimilar results were found in the European Commission survey, Flash Eurobarometer 248, above n 24. Around half of parents across the EU had installed filtering software, but of those who had not, 64 per cent said they did not use it because they trusted their child and only 14 per cent said they did not use them because they did not know how to get them or use them.

population seems justifiable (though the effectiveness of the method chosen must also be considered—see below). If the system intends primarily to safeguard children, perhaps it should be applied only to schools or children's libraries, or left as an option for parents by the provision of free filtering software (as in Australia at present). It should also be remembered that children themselves have rights of freedom of speech and expression as they mature, and that filtering everything unpleasant out of the Internet while they are of school age (assuming for a minute that this is possible) and then waiting for it to hit them when they leave school or home may not be the most productive solution.

B. Judges

A second key issue is who judges what content is to be banned and classifies the content accordingly. As argued above, censorship of content by non-elected, non-independent and non-judicial authorities such as the IWF is in principle unacceptable. As noted, though, the IWF is something of a historical accident: most systems of the future will presumably be designed, like the Australian system, with a state body in charge.

But censorship can be achieved as effectively by suppression of search results, as the ONI noted above, as by actual filtering. Search engines are private profit-making bodies, and the leading search engine in the world, Google, is a private body with legal responsibilities to its shareholders, not to the public interest in freedom of speech, despite its much-quoted public motto, 'Do no evil'. Research by Zittrain and Edelman[161] has shown that Google, generally without publicity, censors its search results to avoid legal problems in a variety of countries, including Western nations such as the UK, France and Germany, as well as non-democratic states such as China. In their 2002 study, they found over 100 sites which would be returned to searchers as legal in the US but were excluded in France and Germany, often because they parlayed Holocaust denial or white supremacy.

Thompson[162] argues that the problem here is not censorship per se, but the fact that Google is appointing itself as the arbiter of what is the law, rather than submitting disputes in such controversial areas to the national courts in question. He suggests a legal obligation for search engines to return results to the fullest of their technical capacity. It is hard to agree, however, that the risk of losing in a criminal law trial should be passed on to Google (or another search engine) every time. Thompson's second suggestion, an obligation of transparency whereby search providers must inform searchers where areas of content have been removed from their

---

161 See their report issued 2002 at http://cyber.law.harvard.edu/filtering/; reported on at *New York Times*, 'TECHNOLOGY: Study Tallies Sites Blocked by Google', 25 October 2002.
162 B Thompson, 'Google Censoring Web Content', BBC News website, 25 October 2002.

index on legal grounds, seems more possible, and would have illuminated matters in the UK Wikipedia dispute discussed above. In general, to avoid scope creep and provide for democratic debate, it seems essential that notice of blocking along with reasons for blocking must be made public, whether it is carried out by a private body such as Google, or a public agency such as the ACMA.[163]

C. Effectiveness

Web filtering can be easily avoided by those who really want to, and any government wishing to install it must consider the impact of this on effectiveness. Depending on how filtering is achieved, blocking can often be evaded by a proscribed site changing its URL, or merely its underlying IP address. Users in turn can simply use a foreign proxy server site to anonymise their surfing destinations.[164] Steps can be taken to inhibit avoidance, but they are likely to result in serious overblocking—the EFA paper on the Australian scheme, for example, notes that a serious Web-filtering system would also need to block the Google cache, the Way Back Machine,[165] and numerous other Internet archive sites where content is mirrored. It can be argued that child pornography Web-filtering systems merely inhibit the ignorant or lazy or those who stumble on illegal material by accident,[166] and do not stop for a minute those who are ostensibly the real targets of the efforts involved—namely serious paedophiles who may go on to commit actual abuse.

A key anti-avoidance issue is whether filtering is only to be imposed on websites or on other types of digital content, such as Internet news-groups,[167] P2P filesharing systems, IM and e-mail, as well as mobile phone

---

163 It is becomingly increasingly common in fact for blocklists to be leaked to sites like Wiki-leaks. See above n 152. Computer scientists are also working on hacking or reverse-engineering such encrypted blocklists, partly to defeat blocking by, for example, China—see eg work of Richard Clayton, Cambridge Computer Lab at http://www.cl.cam.ac.uk/~rnc1/080129- cms.pdf.

164 The author personally observed students in Beijing in 2008 routinely using proxy servers to access sites such as Wikipedia sometimes banned in China.

165 Interestingly, *The Register* has also reported that the IWF had added images on the Wayback Machine to its blocklist, which had lead to some ISPs banning the entire 85 million webpage archive. Details were not given as to what images had been banned and ISPs involved gave 404 'page not found errors'. See 'IWF Confirms Wayback Machine Porn Blacklisting', *The Register* 14 January 2009.

166 Mike Galvin of BT, one of the creators of the IWF 'Cleanfeed' system, admitted in an interview with *The Guardian* on 26 May 2005 that Cleanfeed 'won't stop the hardened paedophile' and went on to say that its main aim was to stop accidental access by users following links such as those in spam emails.

167 Internet newsgroups have largely fallen out of common use but are still extensively used for porn trafficking: see January 2009 report of USA conviction of seven paedophiles following the bust of a well-organised network that used Internet newsgroups to distribute illegal items to its members over a two-year period. See 'Child Porn in the Age of Teenage "Sexting"', *The Register* 16 January 2009.

traffic. As we have discussed above, illegal content is now known to be more commonly swapped in encrypted P2P 'darknets' than on the open Web, which begs the question: why bother to filter the Web at all? In response to such criticisms, the Australians have claimed they intend to extend their reach to cover material traded via the P2P protocol BitTorrent and the European Commission has initiated research into P2P content blocking.[168] Such research is still likely to prove useless in the face of modern evolving encrypted P2P systems. At present such systems (eg Tor and Freenet) are rarely used by the average EU or US citizen because they are user-unfriendly and slow, but in go-ahead Japan, the leading P2P systems, enabled by their fast next-generation consumer broadband networks, are both encrypted and popular with consumers. It will not be long before such systems make the leap to Europe and the US as home broadband networks are upgraded there too. At that point only the most foolish paedophile would attempt to access child pornography using the open Web.

A slightly easier target is mobile content. In Europe, many mobile operators already provide filtering software and filtered content for children, and UK operators have since 2004 voluntarily signed up to Ofcom-brokered codes of conduct requiring filtering of content to under 18s and labelling of over-18 content on their servers.[169] Reliably imposing these restrictions on *children* given the existence of cheap, anonymous pay-as-you-go phones may, however, be a harder task than foreseen.

D. Resources

Even if we only look at filtering the Web, classifying the ever-expanding billions of Internet pages manually as 'illegal', 'inappropriate' or whatever will realistically cost billions of dollars and be an ever-moving target.[170] (This has not, however, stopped the Culture Minister Andy Burnham recently suggesting exactly this for the UK.[171]) The IWF avoids this problem by being complaint-driven—which means its list is, of course, very partial[172] and thus of questionable success. In reality, blocklists in commercial filters are usually generated partly by automated and partly by

---

[168] See n 102 above

[169] See http://www.computerweekly.com/Articles/2004/01/20/199686/uk-mobile-operators-agree-to-censor-adult-content-on-3g.htm.

[170] The EFA pages (above n 151) estimate that even if a 1,000 people were employed full time for a year, they would fail to categorise more than 0.1 per cent of all the pages on the Web, and at the end of that year the list would be hopelessly out of date.

[171] See BBC report, 27 December 2008, at http://news.bbc.co.uk/1/hi/uk/7800846.stm.

[172] Testing of the IWF Cleanfeed system for use in New Zealand found that their list contains probably only about 10–15 per cent of offending websites (statistic cited in EFA pages, above n 151).

manual means, which as the ONI note, means they are inevitably prone to both over- and underblocking.

> Many blacklists are generated through a combination of manually designated web sites as well as automated searches and, thus, often contain websites that have been incorrectly classified. In addition, blunt filtering methods such as IP blocking can knock out large swaths of acceptable websites simply because they are hosted on the same IP address as a site with restricted content.[173]

Over- and underblocking have been constant problems throughout the history of automated filter systems (public or commercial) which have depended on keyword, URL or IP address blocking, and it is difficult to imagine what advances in artificial intelligence might improve the current situation, where content analysis engines are known derisively as 'guessing engines'.[174] Without spending imponderable amounts of money, it has to be acknowledged that any filtering system set up will both miss some illegal content and block some legitimate content.

E. Trade-offs

The above analysis provides some kind of framework within which reasoned decisions can be made about decisions to filter, rather than as Bambauer says, their cheapness (compared to conventional law enforcement), speed of implementation and opportunity for political capital providing reason enough to storm ahead.

In privacy circles, it is now often recommended, before introducing a system of electronic monitoring in the workplace, that a privacy impact assessment (PIA) exercise be carried out which balances the harm done to rights of privacy of employees against the gains made by the employer introducing surveillance. The author proposes a similar 'free speech impact assessment' (FSIA) exercise which could measure the likely effectiveness of the filtering system to achieve its named purpose(s) against the harm done potentially to freedom of expression, consider the financial costs likely and assess possible alternatives.

Such an exercise would be interesting as a tool for analysis. Take the IWF's cleanfeed system, for example. It is intended to crack down on access to child pornography, and yet its blocklist probably carries only some

---

[173] See http://opennet.net/about-filtering.

[174] It is sometimes asked why it is so difficult to automate recognition of obscene images (say) when such high rates of detection are now quoted for spam emails (Symantec, for example, reports a 95 per cent effectiveness rate of capture with minimal false positives). The reason is that most modern spam blocking does not depend on analysing the content of the e-mail but looks instead at the bulk factor (how many people was it sent to) and other indicia such as mismatch between elements of header information (eg 'received from' is falsified). See further EFA paper, above, n 151.

20 per cent of child pornography websites,[175] and the majority of serious paedophiles access child pornography via P2P darknets (an anecdotal but likely assumption) rather than the Web. Thus the gains of the system in relation to its purpose seem more limited than usually portrayed. On the other hand, the current potential for scope creep, and the non-transparency of the system, could have a serious impact on the free speech rights of 100 per cent of the law-abiding UK population.

Another element the assessment should take into account should be the possible use of alternatives to filtering, which might achieve the same purpose but in a way less harmful to free speech rights. One answer here, already trailed above, might be for the IWF, assisted by the UK government, to work towards take-down of child pornography sites abroad (and prosecution of site owners) rather than merely adding them to the blocklist. As Richard Clayton has suggested, if phishing sites abroad (where money, not harm to children, is the issue) can be taken down in hours not days, then why can the same not be true of child pornography sites abroad?[176]

In future, international human rights bodies may also wish to intervene in the growth of domestic Web filtering. It is worth noting that the Council of Europe, the sponsors of the European Convention on Human Rights, have already made a recommendation that freedom of expression rights must be fully considered when implementing Internet filtering systems, both in the public and private sectors.[177] It suggests that users must be notified of filtering, that filters should be regularly reviewed and be proportionate and legitimate in relation to their intended purpose, and that awareness be raised as to their possible dangers. The Council of Europe has also, in consultation with EuroISPA, produced a set of human rights guidelines for ISPs,[178] which recognize the risks to children of illegal and harmful content, but still require that any filtering or blocking carried out should be legitimate, proportional and transparent. Most recently, the European Parliament has made a more general Recommendation on 26 March 2009 to the Council on strengthening security and fundamental freedoms on the Internet, which may be of lasting consequence.[179] A proposed EU framework decision on combating the sexual abuse and sexual exploitation of children, and child pornography, was also launched

---

[175] See above n 148.

[176] See ORG Blog, 15 December 2008 , 'Lesons and Questions for the IWF' at http://www.openrightsgroup.org/2008/12/15/lessons-and-questions-for-the-iwf/, and Moore and Clayton, above n 126.

[177] See Council of Europe Recommendation CM/Rec (2008) 6 on measures to promote the respect for freedom of expression and information with regard to Internet filters.

[178] Council of Europe, *Human Rights Guidelines for ISPs* (2008). See at http://www.coe.int/t/dghl/standardsetting/media/Doc/H-Inf(2008)009_en.pdf.

[179] See http://www.europarl.europa.eu/sides/getDoc.do?pubRef=-//EP//TEXT+TA+P6-TA-2009-0194+0+DOC+XML+V0//EN&language=EN.

on 25 March 2009.[180] The proposal recommends prior blocking of illegal content, but only under judicial or law enforcement supervision. Certainly there is no lack of international concern for, on the one hand, human rights, and on the other, children; the problems may come when well-meaning strategies for protecting both conflict.

VIII. FINAL THOUGHTS

As the above discussion has made plain, adopting a regime for regulating Internet content is fraught with difficulty. On the one hand, cyber-libertarians still resist any attempts to apply special restraints to Internet access on the apparently reasonable grounds that freedom of expression applies as strongly in the new media as in traditional media. On the other hand, governments recognise correctly that the Internet is a place where special risks arise which have no parallel in traditional media. These circumstances include the difficulty of applying existing law to a new and challenging environment; the ease and cheapness both of access to, and publication on, the Internet; the consequent risks to children of accessing adult content online; and, above all, the difficulty of enforcing national criminal laws given the transjurisdictional nature of the net.

However, the filtering solutions currently being promoted as an answer to the last issue, in countries such as the UK, Australia and elsewhere, have an inherent risk of curtailing freedom of expression without adequate transparency or accountability, and are rather blunt instruments with which to protect children and other vulnerable groups (eg racial minorities) given the current state of filtering technology and its inherent tendency to under- and overblock as well as the ease of avoidance. A final point to consider is that, heretical as it may sound, confronting obscene material may not be the most important threat children face on the Internet: studies have shown that children are caused more, or at least as much, harm by online and offline bullying, Internet grooming and disclosure of personal data[181] as exposure to adult material. Nothing, however, gets column inches like being seen to do something about Internet porn.

The less-visible threat to adult freedom of speech, of private censorship

---

180 See Proposal for a Council Framework Decision on combating the sexual abuse, sexual exploitation of children and child pornography, repealing Framework Decision 2004/68/JHA, MEMO/09/130, 25/03/2009, at http://europa.eu/rapid/pressReleasesAction.do?reference= MEMO/09/130.

181 See eg EU KidsOnline project, 4th alert, Safer Internet Day 2008, which found that giving out personal information by mistake was the most common threat to children in the EU. See also the interesting pan-EC study carried out by the European Commission in 2008 (Flash Eurobarometer 248, above n 24) which found that *parents* of 6–17 year old children across the EU were almost equally scared of their children's exposure to obscene material, and of Internet grooming, with fears as to bullying online very close behind.

by search engines, is also a matter needing international attention, especially given the difficult balance to be struck between allowing these private companies the right to run their own business affairs and remain profitable, and the almost-public function that search engines now perform, especially the market leader, Google. Consideration may even need to be given to whether, in the interests of human rights, a dominant player like Google may need to be regarded as a public body and so apt for human rights scrutiny, at least until competition provides a more evenly matched market.

Perhaps Lessig, whose notions of code foresaw how much more effective software filtering would be than law enforcement in regulating Internet speech, should still have the last word, even with words written way back in 1999 and quoted here in the last edition in 2000.

> We should not design for the most efficient system of censoring—or at least we should not do this in a way that allows invisible upstream filtering. Nor should we opt for perfect filtering so long as the tendency worldwide is to over-filter speech. If there is speech the government has an interest in controlling, then let that control be obvious to the users. Only when regulation is transparent is a political response possible.[182]

Such words are still valuable advice in 2009.[183]

---

[182] L Lessig, *Code and Other Laws of Cyberspace* (New York, Basic Books, 1999) 179–81, revised as *Code 2.0* (New York, Basic Books, 2006) 260.

[183] Lessig's 'heir apparent' Zittrain has also interestingly developed the idea of 'perfect enforcement' in his chapter of that name in Brownsword and Yeung (eds), above n 43. Zittrain points out that 'perfect' code enforcement (as in filters) may be less desirable than more 'leaky' or flexible legal enforcement, even where the underlying substantive law is to be respected. This can be because code enforcement is pre-emptive rather than imposing penalties after the fact; and can fail to respect procedural due process; but also because over-strict filters developed in less democratic regimes are easily ported to supposedly freer societies. A key point in respect of speech is that tolerated 'fair uses' easy to assert in the real world, become rights which must be affirmatively claimed online. This can be fascinatingly compared to the Australian opt-in system described above, where it has already been claimed that adults will hesitate to assert their right to see 'adult' content, for fear they may be embarrassed or penalised as a result.

21

Information Security and Cybercrime

IAN BROWN, LILIAN EDWARDS and CHRIS MARSDEN

I. INTRODUCTION

INFORMATION SYSTEMS ARE increasingly important to the efficient operation of government, corporations and society in general. With that importance has come an increasing risk of information security breaches, compounded by the increasingly networked nature of systems. That makes effective information security a public policy issue of far broader impact than technical information technology (IT) policy.

Network and information security (NIS) policymaking and investment have evolved rapidly, especially since 1999. This evolution has been punctuated at certain points where the necessity of adequate or mature NIS policy has been sharply emphasised by vulnerability to attack or shocks:

- the 'Millennium Bug' or Y2K programme of 1997–99, which led to a complete inventory of computing inside large organisations, often for the first time since the deployment of the personal computer (PC) in the mid-1980s;
- denial of service (DoS) attacks, beginning in 2001 against Yahoo! and eBay;
- business continuity planning in the wake of the 9/11 attacks in 2001;
- corporate responses to the increasing financial returns for attackers (eg the growth of 'phishing' and the 2004–05 cyber-extortion cases against gambling websites).
- the continued tendency towards government action to directly confront cybercrime, 'cyber-terrorism' and 'cyberwar', as for instance with the appointment of a 'cybersecurity czar' in the US in 2009.

Legislation, policy, government spending and corporate response in the field of information security have been examined by, for instance, the Organisation for Economic Co-operation and Development (OECD)[1] and

---

[1] See OECD, *The Promotion of a Culture of Security for Information Systems and Networks in OECD Countries*, DSTI/ICCP/REG(2005)1/FINAL of 16 December 2005, at http://www.oecd.org/dataoecd/16/27/35884541.pdf.

the European Commission, and the latter has identified three key risks for Internet security:

1. Attackers are increasingly motivated by profit rather than the technical interest that drove earlier 'hackers' – with growing interest from organised crime and a sophisticated underground economy in stolen information and hacking tools.
2. Mobile devices and networks present a significant new threat landscape, where security is so far less developed than on the PC.
3. Ubiquitous computing will move computation and networking into the fabric of buildings and everyday things (eg through radio frequency identification and sensor networks), presenting new vulnerabilities.[2]

II. MALWARE, BOTNETS AND OTHER TOOLS FOR CRIME

The production of malicious software or 'malware' used to attack systems and defraud individuals has soared in recent years. In 2008 security software firm Symantec identified 1,656,227 distinct new malicious programs, an increase of 165 per cent since 2007.[3] This growth has resulted from increasing opportunities for fraud, the vulnerability of online services to attacks by 'botnets' made up of huge numbers of compromised PCs, and an underground economy driven by interest from organised crime.

The authors of this software, those using it to control networks of compromised computers and acquire and sell-on sensitive information, and their targets are located around the globe. The Honeynet Project found in 2006/2007 that Brazil had the highest number of observed 'bots' or compromised machines, followed by China, Malaysia, Taiwan, Korea and Mexico. The controlling servers were located principally in the US, followed by China, Korea, Germany and the Netherlands.[4]

However, the distributed criminal networks that have grown up around these tools often include participants close to victims where they can (for example) more easily transfer funds. As the UK Police Central e-Crime Unit's Sgt Bob Burls has commented:

> It's a myth that hackers are 15-year olds in darkened rooms and similarly that all cybercriminals are overseas. As with drugs, you have major traffickers but also

---

[2] Communication on a strategy for a Secure Information Society—'Dialogue, Partnership and Empowerment' COM(2006) 251.

[3] Symantec, *Global Internet Security Threat Report: Trends for 2008* (2009) vol XIV, available at http://eval.symantec.com/mktginfo/enterprise/white_papers/b-whitepaper_internet_security_threat_report_xiv_04-2009.en-us.pdf.

[4] J Zhuge, T Holz, X Han, J Guo and W Zou, 'Characterizing the IRC-based Botnet Phenomenon', Informatik Tech Report TR-2007-010 (2007), available at http://honeyblog.org/junkyard/reports/botnet-china-TR.pdf.

street dealers. Wherever there is criminality there are criminal hierarchies, there will also be local pockets of criminality.[5]

A. Conduits for Attacks

(ii) Software: Operating Systems, Browsers and Other Applications

Viruses, Trojan horses and other types of malware typically exploit weaknesses in installed software to gain control of an Internet-connected machine and access data entered by and available to users.

This code spreads mainly through e-mail attachments, websites and by directly connecting to vulnerable machines. IT security company ScanSafe found in June 2008 that the number of legitimate websites being compromised and used to infect visitors' machines accounted for 66 per cent of all malware blocked,[6] but distribution channels vary in significance as vulnerable software is patched, security software is updated and new weaknesses are found. Just one recent attack on Microsoft Internet Information Services web servers hit around half a million websites.[7]

Software companies are in a constant arms race with hackers to fix vulnerabilities before they are exploited. Microsoft, for example, claimed to have disinfected more than 526,000 PCs in the Storm botnet in the last quarter of 2007, but accepts that Storm botnet controllers are 'probably out there still making money with some other botnet'.[8]

The frequency with which security problems continue to be discovered in widely used operating system and application software makes it extremely difficult for any adequate level of Internet security to be achieved. Microsoft and other large software companies have made many improvements in their security development processes, but the software market does not seem to be driving the use of well-understood but little deployed security engineering techniques—such as dramatic decreases in complexity of the security core of operating systems and much more careful isolation of the potentially malicious code present in webpages and e-mails. Until software companies are properly incentivised to make a step-change in the quality of their products, law enforcement agencies will be unlikely to have the resources to deal with the resulting flood of e-crime.

The use of open-source software[9] is not a security panacea. While many

---

[5] I Brown and L Edwards, 'McAfee Virtual Criminology Report' (2008), available at http://resources.mcafee.com/content/NAMcAfeeCriminologyReport.

[6] Scansafe, 'Annual Global Threat Report 2008' (2009), available at http://www.scansafe.com/resources/global_threat_reports2.

[7] G Keizer, 'Huge Web Hack Attack Infects 500,000 pages', *Computerworld* 25 April 2008.

[8] G Keizer, 'Microsoft: We Took Out Storm Botnet', *Computerworld* 22 April 2008.

[9] See further discussion in Guadamuz, ch 11.

programmers may be examining source code for flaws, not all open-source projects have the resources available to patch vulnerabilities in a timely way once discovered. Attackers are also more easily able to find flaws given the availability of source code.[10]

(ii) Networks

Botnets, networks of computers compromised by malicious software, are one of the key vectors for online attacks and criminality. During 2008 Symantec identified 9,437,536 distinct machines in such networks. The largest networks contain hundreds of thousands of machines and are capable of flooding the Internet with more than 100 billion spam messages per day.[11] These networks are also used to launch distributed denial of service (DDoS) attacks, where thousands of compromised machines send traffic to a target machine, overwhelming it and sometimes its network connectivity.

DDoS attacks continue to be conducted against companies and governments, sometimes as part of nationalist political campaigns. The FBI/Computer Security Institute Report 2007 report estimated that up to 10,000 DDoS attacks occur each day worldwide, with the hourly cost of these attacks reckoned between US$90,000 for a sales catalogue company to US$6.45 million for a retail brokerage. Attackers commonly extort money from targets by threatening attacks when they would be most costly—eg at gambling sites just before a major sports event.

Presentation sharing site SlideShare was hit in April 2008 in apparent reprisal against users' presentations on corruption in China.[12] Several tools were released early in 2008 to enable attacks by disgruntled Chinese computer users against CNN in retaliation for its coverage of issues in Tibet.[13] During the conflict between Russia and Georgia, DDoS attacks were observed against government and media sites in both countries.[14] Attacks were also observed at the end of 2007 between Russian and Ukrainian groups, and against Russian political activist Gary Kasparov.[15] We have even seen attacks on the Church of Scientology by the 'Anonymous' activist group.[16]

---

[10] R Anderson, *Security in Open versus Closed Systems—The Dance of Boltzmann, Coase and Moore* (Toulouse, Open Source Software Economics, 2002).

[11] J Stewart, 'Top Spam Botnets Exposed' (SecureWorks, 2008), available at http://www.secure works.com/research/threats/topbotnets/?threat=topbotnets.

[12] M Hendrickson, 'SlideShare Slammed with DDOS Attacks from China', *TechCrunch* 23 April 2008.

[13] J Nazario, 'NetBot Attackers Anti-CNN Tool', Arbor Networks Security, 23 April 2008.

[14] J Nazario, 'Georgia DDoS Attacks—A Quick Summary of Observations', Arbor Networks Security, 12 August 2008.

[15] J Nazario, 'Political DDoS? Ukraine, Kasparov', Arbor Networks Security, 13 December 2007.

[16] J Nazario, 'Church of Scientology DDoS Statistics', Arbor Networks Security, 25 January 2008.

(iii) Payment Services

Payment services are the route that almost all cybercriminals use to transfer fraudulent gains. These include traditional bank transfers and direct debits; money services such as Western Union; and new payment systems such as PayPal. Financial regulation has not kept up with innovations in payments systems, which makes the old policing mantra 'follow the money' increasingly less effective in the cybercrime era.

London's Metropolitan Police have identified four key types of fraud facilitated by payment services:

1. *Online auction site frauds.* Money is transferred in payment for goods that are never delivered, sometimes to fake escrow sites that do not provide the service claimed of holding payments until delivery.
2. *419/advance fee frauds.* Victims receive e-mails promising money in return for helping a fraudster transfer money, upon the payment of a 'small' fee that will later be repaid. Once entrapped, victims have been persuaded to pay large fees that are never reimbursed.
3. *Lottery fraud.* E-mail and letters are sent to victims claiming they have won a lottery. Winnings can be claimed upon payment of a fee— sometimes substantial. Victims, often elderly, are commonly further persuaded using telephone calls.
4. *Criminal cashback.* Goods plus fees to a 'shipping agent' are paid for using a stolen bank draft or cheque. Once the seller has transferred these fees back to the 'shipping agent', they commonly find the issuing bank recovers the draft or cheque, having being duped out of both the goods and the 'shipping fees'.[17]

Dupes ('mules') are commonly used as a middleman to transfer money from victim to fraudster. Recruited as an 'international sales representative', 'shipping manager' or other fake job, they are asked by fraudsters to receive 'payments' that they then transfer internationally after deducting a small 'commission'. When apprehended by police, the money has long since vanished through a payment system and cannot be retrieved—often leaving both the mule and victim out of pocket.

A key concern of law enforcement agencies is services that do not allow payments that are the proceeds of crime to be recovered. In a report for the US Federal Reserve, Ross Anderson concluded:

> Online fraudsters use a variety of nonbank payment services to launder the proceeds of crime. People had assumed that traceability was the key. However, investigation reveals that revocability is more important. Fraudulent payments within the banking system can be pursued and recovered with a reasonable prob-

---

[17] Metropolitan Police Service, 'Money Transfer Fraud' (2008), available at http://www.met. police.uk/fraudalert/money_transfer.htm.

ability of success; but once stolen funds are used to buy transferable financial assets such as eGold, recovery becomes much harder. This suggests that much of the benefit that could be obtained from regulating nonbanks more closely can be got by greater transparency about counterparty risks. . . . The current [Financial Action Task Force] rules impose unnecessary burdens, particularly on the poor, while not doing enough to facilitate rapid recovery of stolen assets.[18]

Impersonation ('identity fraud') is the other main route by which cyber-criminals have committed fraud. By gaining access to the passwords required to login to online banking services, fraudsters are able directly to withdraw funds from target accounts, or undertake more sophisticated fraud such as 'pump and dump' stock scams. By accessing information such as individuals' account details, dates of birth, social security and passport numbers, and addresses, fraudsters are able to gain access to funds in existing accounts and create new loan and credit facilities.

The US Federal Trade Commission in 2007 received 221,226 Internet-related fraud complaints totalling $525,743,643.[19] Javelin Strategy and Research have predicted that identity fraud will decline between 2007 and 2013, but individual victims' costs will rise from $860 to $1,271 due to growing sophistication in criminal fraud techniques that use elaborate social engineering schemes and multiple channels to evade detection for longer periods of time.[20]

III. LEGAL RESPONSES

A. UK Law: Computer Misuse Act 1990 Amendments

Existing UK law specifically tailored to deal with computer crime is largely to be found in the Computer Misuse Act 1990 (CMA). As one of the earliest legislative attempts to deal with computer crime, it was self-evidently not drafted for the Internet era. As a result, although the Act deals fairly effectively with hacking and dissemination of viruses, doubts have arisen as to whether the CMA adequately covers DoS.[21]

Two obvious routes existed within the CMA as originally drafted, which might be explored by those seeking to criminalize DoS. The first was section 1, originally designed to punish hacking, which prohibits 'unauthorised' access to 'any program or data'. The other was section 3, designed to

---

[18] R Anderson, 'Closing the Phishing Hole—Fraud, Risk and Nonbanks' (US Federal Reserve, 2007), available at http://www.cl.cam.ac.uk/~rja14/Papers/nonbanks.pdf.

[19] Federal Trade Commission, 'Consumer Fraud and Identity Theft Complaint Data January–December 2007' (2008) 10.

[20] Javelin Strategy and Research, 'Consumer Identity Fraud Report' (2008).

[21] See APIG report (discussed below), 5 (regarding hacking and viruses); 59–75 at 11–12 (discussing the efficacy of the CMA in prosecutions of DoS and DDOS attacks).

counteract the spreading of viruses, which originally prohibited any 'unauthorised modification of the contents of any computer' which was intended 'to impair the operation of any computer.' While section 3 was generally seen as most appropriate to the offence, there was doubt as to whether an actual 'modification' was made since a server that is brought down by a DoS attack suffers only temporary damage with usually no loss or corruption of data after the attack.

In 2004, Members of Parliament in the All-Party Internet Group (APIG) began a review of the CMA, on the basis that this legislation was created before the emergence of the Internet and therefore required updating. The Act was seen to focus too much on standalone computers, and not enough on computer networks. In addition, some of the definitions used in the 1990 Act need updating. The final report outlined several recommendations to the government for changes to the CMA. In March 2005, the APIG called for amendments to the CMA to address the threat from DoS attacks. An updated version of the CMA could be of greater benefit if it combined security regulations relevant for standalone and network situations.

The Police and Justice Bill 2005 thus amended section 3 by replacing the word 'modification' with 'act', which word is undefined save for including 'a series of acts'. In addition, section 3(2) of the CMA, as amended, specifies that the intent necessary to commit the crime exists whether the intention is to produce temporary or permanent impairment, or hindering or prevention of access to a computer, program or data.

Meanwhile DoS had finally arrived at the courts. In the unsatisfactory first UK prosecution for DoS, *R v Caffey*,[22] the charge was 'unauthorised modification' under section 3 of the CMA, but there was no opportunity for argument as to the applicability as the case fell on a dubious 'Trojan virus' defence.[23] The second reported prosecution was of greater significance. In *R v Lennon*,[24] a teenage hacker was accused of sending five million e-mails to cause a DoS attack against his former employer. At first instance, the judge refused to find there was an offence under section 3, not because of any doubts about the applicability of the word 'modification' but because

> In this case, the individual emails caused to be sent each caused a modification which was in each case an 'authorised' modification. Although they were sent in bulk resulting in the overwhelming of the server, the effect on the server is not a modification addressed by [the Act].

[22] Southwark Crown Court, 17 October 2003 (unreported).

[23] The acused claimed that although his server had indeed launched the DoS attack, this had only been because it had been taken over as a 'zombie' by malicious code. Forensic experts, however, failed to fail any evidence of such code. Remarkably, the court still accepted the defence and acquitted.

[24] Wimbledon Magistrate's Court, December 2005 (unreported).

In other words, the judge accepted the argument that an unsecured website impliedly authorises the sending of e-mails to itself. DoS was merely different in volume but not in essential character to the sending of e-mail in the ordinary way.

On appeal, perhaps unsurprisingly the decision was reversed.[25] The Queen's Bench held that:

> the owner of a computer which is able to receive emails is ordinarily to be taken as consenting to the sending of emails to the computer. His consent is to be implied from his conduct in relation to the computer. Some analogy can be drawn with consent by a householder to members of the public to walk up the path to his door when they have a legitimate reason for doing so, and also with the use of a private letter box. But that implied consent given by a computer owner is not without limit. The point can be illustrated by the same analogies. The householder does not consent to a burglar coming up his path. Nor does he consent to having his letter box choked with rubbish. . . . It is enough to say that it plainly does not cover emails which are not sent for the purpose of communication with the owner, but are sent for the purpose of interrupting the proper operation and use of his system.

Note that although the Court of Appeal thus solved the particular problem of DoS, the question of how 'authorised' was to be interpreted was never raised in the CMA amendments. Thus the CMA still leaves unresolved the *scope* of the standing implied consent given by web servers to receive e-mail and page requests. If five million e-mails sent to a server are outside the bounds of implied consent, surely millions or even thousands of spam e-mails face the same challenge? Does any reasonable user impliedly consent to the receipt of even one spam e-mail? It seems possible, therefore, that in future spammers might also find themselves charged effectively with DoS under section 3—a result neither the judiciary nor the reformers probably intended.

On other problems with the CMA as originally drafted, the maximum penalty for some offences has also been increased to ten years. The Police and Justice Bill doubles the maximum jail sentence for hacking into computer systems from five years to ten years, a provision that will classify hacking as a more serious offence and make it easier to extradite computer crime suspects from overseas. Furthermore a new section 3A contains provisions to ban the development, ownership and distribution of hacker tools. Some industry commentators considered the language used to be worryingly ambiguous, possibly criminalising the use and sale of crucial security tools such as anti-DoS intrusion detection software. In particular, section 3A provides that it is an offence to 'supply or offer to supply [such a tool], believing that it is likely to be used to commit, or to assist in the commission of [a Computer Misuse Act section 1/section 3 offence]'.

---

[25] *DPP v Lennon* [2006] EWHC 1201 (Admin).

Security experts have questioned how they cannot believe it is likely security tools they create will be abused by hackers and cybercriminals given the prevalence of the black market economy. The Crown Prosecution Service has, however, issued guidance on section 3A which seeks to reassure the security community.[26]

B. European Law

The EU is the world's largest free trade area, and all 27 Member States must implement European law. Failing implementation, European law can in certain circumstances take direct effect despite the lack of national law. Therefore much overarching NIS legislation and policy takes place at the European level (see Table 21.1).

There has been harmonisation among countries based on both common European legislation and co-operation in, for instance, police and computer emergency response team (CERT) activities. The extent to which this harmonisation resulted in convergence of national policies depended critically on:

- whether national political responses to specific NIS problems[27] produced strong national legal and policy differences; and
- whether pan-European policy preceded national response.

National responses to cybercrime date from the period around 1990 and also show significant legislative and policing developments that pre-date the European response (ENISA, the European Network and Information Security Agency, was only founded in 2004[28]). In criminal law, pre-existing national legislation combined with a European co-operative police force (Europol) led to harmonisation rather than convergence. In all these cases, European legislation came after national legislative and institutional arrangements, and national lawmakers had substantial initial room for independent policy formation. In telecoms legislation, an area of long-standing European convergence, the Data Retention Directive of 2006 signalled a greater convergence between national regimes. The very late establishment of ENISA as the central NIS co-ordination mechanism indicated a desire by Member States to maintain existing national institutional arrangements in their current form. From 2010, Europol formally becomes an agency of the European Union.[29]

---

[26] Although with mixed success—see Richard Clayton's response at http://www.lightblue touchpaper.org/2007/12/31/hacking-tool-guidance-finally-appears/.

[27] Including data protection failures and prevalence of viruses and other computer crimes.

[28] Regulation (EC) No 460/2004 of the European Parliament and of the Council of 10 March 2004 establishing the European Network and Information Security Agency, OJ L77, 13.3.2004.

[29] See IP/08/610 (2008) Europol to become EU agency in 2010, Brussels, 18 April 2008, at http://europa.eu/rapid/pressReleasesAction.do?reference=IP/08/610. Note also the discussion of the Data Retention Directive in ch 18.

Table 21.1 Summary of national legislation and European law implementing NIS[a]

Jurisdiction	Privacy law	Electronic privacy law	Electronic commerce law[b]	Cybercrime law[c]
EU	Data Protection Directive 95/46 of 24 November 1995	Directive 2002/58/EC repeals Directive 97/66/EC of 15 December 1997, Data Retention Directive 2006 of 21 February	Electronic Signatures: Directive 99/93 of 13 December 1999 Electronic Commerce: Directive 2000/31 of 8 June 2000	Framework Decisions and Communications;[d] 2001 Council of Europe Convention on Cybercrime is harder law
UK	Data Protection Act 1998	Regulation of Investigatory Powers Act 2000, Data Retention Regulations 2007 No 2199[e] and 2009 No 859[f]	Electronic Communications Act 2000, Electronic Signature Regulations 2002, E-Commerce Regulations 2003	Computer Misuse Act 1990
Germany	Federal Data Protection Law (BDSG) last amended 2001; G-10 law applies to communications secrecy	Information and Communication Services Act 1997, Telecommunications Act 2004 (Tele kommunikationsgesetz-TKG) last amended 14 March 2005	Digital Signature Law 2001	Penal Code Sections: 202a: Data Espionage 303a: Alteration of Data 303b: Computer Sabotage

| France | Information Technology and Liberty Act (Loi Informatique et Libertés) 1978 | Law 2004-801 of 6 August 2004 relating to the Protection of Data Subjects as Regards the Processing of Personal Data | E-Signature Law: Decree No 2001-272 of 30 March 2001 in accordance with Article 1316-4 of the civil code and related to electronic signatures Law No 2004-575 of 21 June 2004 of Confidence in the Digital Economy | Godfrain Act 1988. Penal Code Chapter 3, Articles 323-1 through 323-4: Attacks on Systems for Automated Data Processing |

[a] For a recent survey, see A Mitrakas, 'Information Security and Law in Europe: Risks Checked?' (2006) 15:1 *Information Communications Technology Law March* 33–53; also ITU, Global Cybersecurity Agenda High Level Expert Group, Global Strategic Report (2008), at http://www.cybersecurity-gateway.org/pdf/global_strategic_report.pdf.

[b] A useful source of e-banking legislation in English is http://rechtsinformatik.jura.uni-sb.de/cbl/cbl-statutes.php.

[c] All countries in the table have signed the Council of Europe Cyber Crime Convention.

[d] See particularly Communication on Cyber-crime, COM (2007) 267 and S Peers, Strengthening Security and Fundamental Freedoms on the Internet—An EU Policy on the Fight Against Cyber Crime, Report for the European Parliament, Policy Department C: Citizens' Rights and Constitutional Affairs (2009) PE408.335.

[e] http://www.opsi.gov.uk/si/si2007/uksi_20072199_en_1.

[f] http://www.opsi.gov.uk/si/si2009/uksi_20090859_en_1.

The European Council Framework Decision on Attacks against Information Systems[30] was adopted on 24 February 2005. Its objective is 'to improve cooperation between judicial and other competent authorities, through approximating rules on criminal law in the Member States in the area of attacks against information systems'. The Framework Decision indicates that attacks against information and computer systems are a tangible and dangerous threat that requires an effective response. The Framework Decision and the Cybercrime Convention have synchronised definitions of the relevant offences.

IV. COUNCIL OF EUROPE CONVENTION ON CYBERCRIME

One of the main international legislative instruments relevant to both global and European regulation of cybercrime and security is the Council of Europe Convention on Cybercrime. The final text of this was agreed on 23 November 2001 and it entered into force on 1 July 2004.[31] A further Protocol on racist and xenophobic acts in cyberspace was signed on 28 January 2003 and entered into force on 1 March 2006.[32] The Convention is open for signature by both Council of Europe Member States (EU Member States plus 15 other countries) and those non-Member States that participated in its drafting (including the US). It is also open for accession by other non-Member States.

The Convention is regarded as one of the most comprehensive documents on cybercrime available. Substantively, it focuses on efforts to outline common definitions for crimes relating to computers and also measures to encourage international co-operation. It is the only international agreement that covers all relevant aspects of cybercrime policing (substantive criminal law, procedural law and international co-operation). Since much cybercrime is by its nature cross-jurisdictional, the most valuable contribution of the Convention is to harmonise definitions of offences across states so that extradition and co-operative policing are made much easier. Although the Convention is applicable only to state governments and not to the private actors who de facto control many important parts of the Internet infrastructure, guidelines for law enforcement by service providers were issued in April 2008.[33]

---

[30] Council Framework Decision 2005/222/JHA on attacks against information systems.

[31] Due to its Art 36, which contains the conditions for entry into force. It specifies that the Convention should first be ratified by five states, including three Member States of the Council of Europe. The Convention would then enter into force on the first day of the month following the expiration of a three-month period after the fifth ratification. This condition was fulfilled with Lithuania's ratification on 18 March 2004, triggering the entry into force on 1 July 2004.

[32] Additional Protocol to the Convention on cybercrime, concerning the criminalisation of acts of a racist and xenophobic nature committed through computer systems CETS No 189 at http://conventions.coe.int/Treaty/en/Treaties/Html/189.htm.

[33] See http://www.coe.int/t/DG1/LEGALCOOPERATION/ECONOMICCRIME/cybercrime/ cy_activity_Interface2008/567_prov-d-guidelines_provisional2_3April2008_en.pdf.

How effective is the Cybercrime Convention? Some argue that the number of nations who have signed up is not impressive.[34] All 27 EU Member States have joined, but six years on only 12 have ratified, leaving 15 to go. Outside the EU, the Convention is seen as Western dominated, both in development and at the current time. Of the few non-EU nations that have acceded, only the US and Ukraine have ratified. On the other hand the Convention is often held up as a model law, even for countries unwilling to accede because the treaty is seen as too Western, or too demanding of resources. Marco Gerke, a cybercrime expert, states that 'the impact of the Convention is going beyond the number of countries that formally signed it. At least a couple of dozen countries have used the Convention while updating their legislation to bring themselves in line with international standards.'[35]

The key question for the success of the Cybercrime Convention is perhaps whether it can entice into membership those countries known to harbour the ringleaders of organised cybercrime—such as countries in the former Soviet Union bloc. Even where developing world and Eastern European countries have the political will to take a stance against cybercrime, it is often difficult to justify allocating resources for the fight when the beneficiaries will be not that state's own citizens but those of other countries. Despite this, the ongoing success of the Cybercrime Convention can be seen at a micro as well as a macro level. Many countries, including various Latin American states, are in the process of harmonising their law to meet Cybercrime Convention standards whether or not they plan to join. In other regions, such as the Arab states, there may be a preference to put together their own regional instruments rather than accede, but in most cases these are very similar to the Convention. The Convention is thus arguably a very successful instrument for international harmonisation.

The Council of Europe, who sponsor the treaty, also provide training in how to operate against cybercrime and use the Convention, for both judiciary and police, as well as assisting regions to move towards accession or to develope their own instruments. To this end, for example, workshops were held in 2007/2008 for West Africa and the Caribbean, and Cybex in Spain organised a programme for the training of judges.

Despite having only been in force since 2004, the Convention is already showing signs of needing an update. Specific problem areas such as phishing, identity theft and crime in 'virtual worlds'—eg fraud on virtual banks—are not covered as nominate crimes, though they may be subsumed beneath broader categories, such as phishing beneath online forgery and

---

[34] See R Anderson et al, 'Security Economics and European policy', Proceedings of the Workshop on Economics and Information Security, 2008, at http://weis2008.econinfosec.org/papers/MooreSecurity.pdf.

[35] Private conversation with Edwards during the research for the 'McAfee Virtual Criminology Report 2008', above n 5.

fraud (Articles 7 and 8). New investigation instruments such as key-loggers (eg the FBI's Magic Lantern) and identification instruments (eg CIPAV, the FBI's Computer and Internet Protocol Address Verifier) are already in use but the Convention does not mention these, and their permissibility is questionable. Renegotiating the treaty would be a Herculean task, so future additions are likely to be made by ways of optional protocols, as with the existing example relating to hate speech.

Will the Cybercrime Convention ever develop into a standing cyber-crime police force, much as NATO has developed a standing capacity to combat hostilities in its region? It is clear that national police forces, whether standard operations or specially trained 'cybercops', struggle to make any meaningful impact on cybercrime when so much of it is directed from countries outside their jurisdictional competence. One-time co-oper-ative international policing operations have had some striking successes, notably in relation to international paedophile rings, but these are very expensive, and extremely difficult and time-consuming to mount. An argument for a standing international cyber security force clearly exists, particularly as Interpol seems to have little or no profile in the field of cybercrime. The political will (and funding) for such a force seem at the moment, however, to be absent, and as noted at the start of this chapter, we seem instead to be entering a phase of distinctly national cyber-security initiatives[36] as states realise the full potential impact of a cyber-infra-structure attack.

V. SPECIFIC LEGAL PROBLEM AREAS

A. Phishing

Phishing is the use of social engineering and hacking techniques to gain information such as financial or other personal data. 'Phishermen' send e-mails that by some means or other extract login and password details from recipients, and can then be used to gain access to bank and similar accounts. Phishing is a fast rising crime and has accelerated in particular since the current recession began. Figures released in October 2008 in the UK by APACS, the UK clearing banks association,[37] showed that from January to June 2008 phishing attacks rose by 186 per cent on the same period in 2007. In total there were more than 20,682 phishing incidents during that six-month period compared to 7,224 the previous year.

---

36 See eg the announcement of the UK's first national Cyber Security Strategy launched in June 2009, reported at http://news.bbc.co.uk/1/hi/uk_politics/8118348.stm. For the US equivalent, see below n 66.

37 See http://www.apacs.org.uk/APACSannounceslatestfraudfigures.htm.

Similarly the Federal Trade Commission (FTC) issued a special phishing warning for the US, also in October 2008.[38]

There are two key reasons why phishing is a particularly growing threat at the current time. First, as credit facilities become restricted and subject to detailed checking, procuring personal data to open new accounts and acquire new credit cards loses appeal, while using phishing data to clean out existing accounts becomes more attractive. Secondly, the recession has brought in its midst vast confusion and loss of trust in the consumer sector.[39] As confusion around financial bust and merger (perhaps) clears, phishing is likely to diversify into public sector websites (eg television and motor licensing sites) with deleterious consequences for public confidence in e-government;[40] and into phishing of virtual currencies from virtual worlds[41]—where law enforcement will have, one suspects, not the first idea of where to start.[42]

In the following section we discuss what role (if any) law can play in preventing the kind of cyber insecurity that engenders phishing. A key issue for the law, however, is how to regulate the losses of users in this sphere, and in particular if banks should be obliged to reimburse customers for phishing losses. It is a common myth in the UK that banks are required to reimburse phishing losses where bank accounts are drained by phishers. It seems that most consumers draw an analogy with the well-known rights in respect of misuse of credit card details under the Consumer Credit Act (CCA) sections 83 and 84. In fact, UK law here is unclear and antiquated.[43] The CCA provides only that banks issuing credit cards must reimburse cardholders where the card data is fraudulently misused by a third party. In relation to debit fraud, remedies are conferred purely by the voluntary Banking Code, and there have been disputes in the past even over 'conventional' misuse of debit card details, eg re 'phantom' cashline/cash machine withdrawals, where banks have refused to reimburse, claiming the customer is at fault or lying.

Thus the commonest case of phishing, where a bank account is drained, is *not* covered by hard law since no consumer credit arrangement is involved. Historically, as Bohm et al have pointed out,[44] under the Bills of Exchange Act 1882, a bank that honoured a forged cheque was bound

---

[38] See http://www.ftc.gov/bcp/edu/pubs/consumer/alerts/alt089.shtm.

[39] BBC News, 10 October 2008, 'Bank Turmoil Fuels Phishing Boom', at http://news.bbc.co.uk/1/hi/technology/7663055.stm.

[40] See http://blogscript.blogspot.com/search/label/phishing.

[41] See ENISA Report, 'Virtual Worlds, Real Money' (November 2008), at http://www.enisa.europa.eu/doc/pdf/deliverables/enisa_pp_security_privacy_virtualworlds.pdf.

[42] See amusing fictional account in C Stross, *Halting State* (New York, Ace, 2007).

[43] See N Bohm, I Brown and B Gladman, 'Electronic Commerce: Who Carries the Risk of Fraud?' (2000) (3) *Journal of Information, Law & Technology*, at http://www2.warwick.ac.uk/fac/soc/law/elj/jilt/2000_3/bohm/; R Anderson, 'Closing the Phishing Hole—Fraud, Risk and Nonbanks', available at http://www.cl.cam.ac.uk/~rja14/Papers/nonbanks.pdf.

[44] See Bohm et al, above n 43.

repay the amount debited to the customer's account. By analogy, a bank that allowed a phisherman to withdraw the contents of an account using 'forged' credentials should surely be equally liable. Yet the latest edition of the Banking Code makes customers liable for unauthorised online banking transactions unless they have taken 'reasonable care'—defined as the use of 'up-to-date anti-virus and spyware software and a personal firewall' and that customers keep passwords and personal identification numbers (PINs) secret.[45] In practice, to date banks have usually paid up, but it may be questioned if financial cutbacks combined with a rise in claims will not put pressure on this gentlemen's agreement.

In other countries, a mishmash of legal and paralegal remedies has emerged, with little harmonisation across borders. For example:

- In the US, claims by customers that they have suffered loss due to card fraud of some kind are repaid under the Electronic Fund Transfer Act (EFTA), subject only to the customer reporting the fraud properly. Fault on the part of the consumer is not a relevant consideration.
- In Canada, losses are usually indemnified by banks but only according to voluntary banking codes. Furthermore fault removes customer rights, and in Canada, 'fault' on the part of the customer to exclude bank liability has reportedly been defined very widely, eg if 'shoulder skimming' has occurred, this might be construed as 'fault', similarly dropping a card on the floor revealing data, or having the PIN stuck to the back of the card.[46]
- In Costa Rica, the customer is left to carry the losses of bank frauds and identity fraud on his own.[47]

This lack of harmonisation is a problem given the increasing ability of consumers to bank outside their home jurisdictions, especially using Internet banks. In the event of consumer losses due to phishing, difficult issues may arise concerning identifying both the relevant legal system and the legal remedies available. There also appears to be a rise in a culture that presumes consumers to be at fault if losses occur due to phishing, and requires consumers to prove their innocence to get their money back. This seems disturbing, given that it is the banks, not the consumers, who are in the best place both to identify and warn against phishing entreaties, and to improve banking security thereby safeguarding consumers against foolhardy decisions—eg by implementing two-factor authentication for consumer withdrawals. Accordingly, as discussed below, the House of Lords Report on Personal Internet Security recommended in 2007, and again in

---

[45] British Bankers' Assocation, 'The Banking Code' (March 2008) s 12.9, available at http://www.bankingcode.org.uk/pdfdocs/PERSONAL_CODE_2008.PDF.

[46] Personal conversation by Edwards with Mary Kirwan, Canadian security expert, while conducting research for the 'McAfee Virtual Criminology Report 2008', above n 5.

[47] With thanks to Andres Guadamuz for this information.

2008, that banks should be presumptively held liable for phishing losses as a matter of law.[48]

B. Buying Zero Day Exploits

Exploits or 'zero day exploits' are software vulnerabilities that allow a particular piece of software to be hacked or in some way compromised. They are, basically, 'bugs' that arise inevitably in the creation of software as it goes through its development lifecycle. Exploits which compromise widely used programmes such as Internet Explorer, Word, Excel, Linux kernel programs, etc, can be extremely valuable. They can be used to cripple a commercial competitor or to open 'back doors' in programmes allowing theft of personal data, eg bank account details. They can even in theory inflict significant damage on the infrastructure of a nation state. They can also be used *indirectly* to blackmail the vendor of the affected software.

The market for exploits is cloaked in secrecy but some details have emerged in recent years:

- The *'white'* or legitimate market. Two main agencies exist which openly buy exploits at market prices, using contracts and non-disclosure agreements (NDAs): Tipping Point[49] and iDefense;[50] other players include Snosoft[51] and a number of small firms whose business model is to employ in-house vulnerability researchers.
- Occasional examples also exist of security researchers attempting to sell exploits on the open market by *'bug auctions'*. In 2005, a researcher, 'Fearwall', discovered a bug in Microsoft Excel that could potentially have caused enormous damage, and after first contacting Microsoft, went public by putting it up for sale on eBay. Bids reached $1,200 before the auction was pulled under pressure from the vendor. 'Fearwall' claimed he had really been seeking not money, but publicity to pressurise Microsoft into patching the vulnerability.
- The *'grey'* market: sales of exploits to government agencies. This market is a 'white hat' market but little is known about it. It is rumoured the US National Security Agency[52] has purchased exploits, and that various

---

[48] House of Lords Science and Technology Committee, Personal Internet Security, HL 165-I, 5th Report of Session 2006-07—Volume I: Report.

[49] http://www.tippingpoint.com/.

[50] http://labs.idefense.com/.

[51] See http://snosoft.blogspot.com/2007/01/exploit-acquisition-program.html for an example of their terms of purchase of exploits.

[52] See C Miller, 'The Legitimate Vulnerability Market', Proceedings of Workshop for Economics of Information Security, 2007, available at http://weis2007.econinfosec.org/papers/29.pdf and M Sutton and F Nagle, 'Emerging Economic Models for Vulnerability Research', Proceedings of Workshop for Economics of Information Security, 2006, available at http://weis2006.econinfosec.org/docs/17.pdf.

government agencies employ vulnerability experts to hunt for exploits as full-time staff or on freelance contracts.

- The *'black'* market: sales to criminals and corporations engaged in industrial sabotage or espionage. Again revenue can be gained directly by closing down a system, or indirectly by attempts to blackmail a vendor by threatening release of an exploit, resulting in bad public relations and possible loss of market share. This market is almost impenetrably difficult to research. However, one known example occurred in January 2006 when a Microsoft Windows Metafile (WMF) exploit was sold by auction for $4,000[53]—allegedly to more than one 'black hat' buyer. Investigations showed the exploit was later used by at least one buyer to capture machines to spread 'pump and dump' spam.

(i) Legal Issues around Exploit Sales

It might be surprising that there can be a white market in exploits at all. Discovered exploits are by their nature primarily intended to impede or cripple software, and, by extension, to hurt users and vendors who make money from that product. Arguably their sale should be illegal, or at least controlled, as the sales of weapons or dangerous goods are in most European countries. On the other hand it can be argued that exploits are, rather like encryption, a 'dual use' good. While their primary purpose is to cause damage, they can also be used by security experts to provide an early warning service of possible vulnerabilities (this is the business model of the likes of iDefense), and studied to build safer, less vulnerable software.

From a legal perspective it is not at all clear what is being 'bought' and 'sold' in the exploit market. A vulnerability is not a tangible object like a gun, so the first obvious argument would be that it is a piece of intellectual property (IP), and this seems anecdotally to be what some buyers and sellers claim. However, the only appropriate IP regime of protection would probably be copyright, and this analysis leads to severe problems. The programme code that the exploit relies on, and will often incorporate, will be the copyright of the vendor not the creator of the exploit—and the vendor will certainly not have licensed his code to the zero day exploiter to use (or abuse) in this way. Furthermore, sometimes what is sold may not be code as such, but merely a particular word or an idea—knowledge about how or when a vulnerability operates—in which case IP law will not be appropriate, although trade secrets law may be.

In fact, what is bought and sold mainly appears to be silence. Agreements in the exploit market are notoriously hard to broker because if the exploit seller demonstrates that the exploit works to the buyer, then he will often have given away the value of what was on sale—even more so if he

53 Cited in Miller, above n 52.

hands his code over to the buyers to test. As with all ideas, once it has been explained, what is left to sell? The market thus appears to reply mainly on NDAs rather than transfer of property per se. Since sales will normally be made under conditions of anonymity, there is also the problem of multiple sales. An exploit might be traded under three different names to three different markets. As a result the exploit market is de facto limited to a small group of experts who know and trust each other, with open auction sites partly filling the gap.

Finally, there remains a strong argument that an exploit market should not be valid in any form. Vendors tend to argue that any exploits that exist should 'belong' to them and thus in law not be saleable either back to them, or worse still, to someone else. 'It's my code and my mistake' said one unnamed programmer for a major software vendor. 'Shouldn't I be entitled to fix it? If Shakespeare had made a spelling mistake in one of his plays wouldn't he expect just to be told about it, not to have to pay for it before he could fix it?'[54]

Some security experts and economists argue, however, that a 'white market' should be allowed, for the following reasons:

- In a professionalised world of organised cybercrime, security experts, just like cybercriminals, increasingly work for financial reward not just glory. Discovering an exploit is hard work and researchers should be paid for it, since their work is for the public good.
- If a white market for vulnerabilities does not exist, researchers will sell to the black market, probably for greater reward.
- Discovering vulnerabilities should be encouraged as otherwise software remains insecure, adding to the instability of critical infrastructure and the growth of the zombie bot population. An exploit market increases potential scrutiny.

Nevertheless many commentators still feel uneasy about this covert 'arms trade', with a strong argument made that encouraging the discovery of software vulnerabilities simply encourages illegal activity and produces insecurity (of both software and the market).[55] Both the current major players on the white market respond that they engage in 'responsible disclosure', ie they disclose the vulnerability to the software vendor after they have made it available to their own customers. The vulnerability is thus eventually fixed ('patched'). They also claim to facilitate the procurement of exploit information by having a larger range of sources than any one company normally would. For example, iDefense reported in 2007 having a pool of about 400 contributors of vulnerability information over

[54] Conversation quoted during personal interviews by Edwards with a spokesman for iDefense for 'McAfee Virtual Criminology Report 2008', above n 5.
[55] K Kannan and R Telang, 'Markets for Vulnerabilities? Think Again' (2005) 51(5) *Management Science* 726.

the last four years.[56] Given an inevitable time gap between when a vulnerability has been found and when the vendor can patch it, the 'white market' business model is to provide advance disclosure to their own paying clientele who are thus protected before patching is implemented. The fault, if any, can then be said to lie with vendors for not patching sooner and more effectively.

Vendors, however, including major players such as Google and Microsoft, take the view that best practice is to disclose software vulnerabilities straight to them so they can be patched as fast as possible, and discourage an exploit market. Some vendors have been known to offer bounty programmes for amateur 'bug spotting' while discouraging the 'professional' approach.[57] Some support *mandatory* vulnerability disclosure. While delayed disclosure of bugs in traditional software products such as Word or Excel may be workable, and prevent collapse of confidence in a product, in relation to web services, immediate disclosure to the service provider so the vulnerability can be patched is regarded as vital, since silence leads to further infections being spread to multiple users.[58] A distributed non-commercial scheme in which all Internet users work voluntarily together to search and disclose exploits may also be a future model; a preliminary basis for such already exists in the StopBadWare list of infected websites, which appears as warnings against lists of Google search results.[59]

VI. FUTURE LEGAL DIRECTIONS

In August 2007 the House of Lords Science and Technology Committee published the results of their year-long inquiry into personal Internet security.[60] This investigation was particularly concerned with the nature and scale of the security threat to individuals; how these threats could best be tackled; what types of governance and regulation would be most appropriate in this area; and how well the government is responding to cybercrime. A wide range of individuals and organisations gave evidence to the inquiry, including academic lawyers and computer scientists, trade bodies such as the British Computer Society and Association of Payment and Clearing Services, Internet service providers (ISPs), law enforcement agencies and children's charities.

---

[56] See above n 54.

[57] Eg Netscape's Mozilla Foundation (http://www.mozilla.org/security/bug-bounty.html).

[58] See O Day, B Palmen and R Greenstadt, 'Reinterpreting the Disclosure Debate for Web Infection', Proceedings of the Workshop for Economics and Information Security, 2008, at http://weis2008.econinfosec.org/papers/Greenstadt.pdf.

[59] Project run by Harvard and Oxford universities plus others in collaboration with Google: see http://stopbadware.org/.

[60] Above n 48.

The Committee made recommendations in a number of areas, with the main aim being to better align the security incentives of organisations, ISPs and users. They found that end-users rarely have the time or technical background to shoulder the responsibility pushed onto them by the government for securing their own online activities. Financial services institutions, ISPs and software vendors in particular are in a better position to manage some security risks.[61] The best way to encourage them to do this would be to carefully reallocate to them some of the liability for fraudulent payments, traffic from infected machines and insecure software.

Banks have been encouraging customers to switch to online services (which are much cheaper to provide than branches and staff) while at the same time attempting to shift risk for fraudulent transactions onto those same customers, as discussed above. Given the continuing arms race between virus authors and antivirus software companies, and the ingenuity of those harvesting passwords from infected PCs and phishing sites, it will be difficult for the average user to assess the risk and veracity of a transaction. Banks have been slow to develop and deploy the type of hardware authentication tokens[62] that would protect users, because the costs of their failure to do so fall partly on their customers. Banks are also in a better position than their customers to profile and analyse transactions for suspicious events. The Lords Committee therefore recommended that banks be encouraged to take more responsibility for their customers' security by holding them liable for electronic fraud losses. They also suggested that banks and other businesses should be required to notify customers when security breaches occur, giving them advice on practical steps to reduce the resulting risks.[63]

The Committee similarly found that ISPs are in a better position than their customers to protect against certain types of attack. In particular, they are able to monitor outgoing traffic for and receive reports of spam, worm infections or DoS attacks. Once such traffic has been detected, ISPs are able to limit infected machines' network access to sites that will allow them to download the latest software patches and antivirus signatures and hence remove the infection. The Lords recommend that the E-Commerce Directive's Article 12 'mere conduit' defence[64] be removed once ISPs have detected or been notified of such traffic, making them liable for damage

---

[61] This argument was first made in Bohm, Brown and Gladman, above n 43.

[62] See eg details of Barclays Bank's new PINsentry device at https://www.barclays.co.uk/pinsentry/.

[63] Mandatory security breach disclosure is likely to be passed as part of the reform of the Privacy and Electronic Communications Directive 2002 in 2009, but only for the telecommunications industries and not for the likes of banks. See further, Edwards, ch 14, p 469.

[64] Directive 2000/31/EC of the European Parliament and of the Council of 8 June 2000 on certain legal aspects of information society services, in particular electronic commerce, in the Internal Market, OJ L178, 17.7.2000, 1–16.

done to third parties unless they take preventative measures within a limited time period.

Finally, the Committee noted that software companies have historically paid limited attention to the security of their products and that 'radical and rapid change' is needed. This is partly due to their ability to dump liability onto customers using restrictive licensing agreements that would be held void in many other markets (and partly due to the preference seemingly shown by consumers for flashy new features over security and stability in software). The Committee therefore recommended that, in the short term, liability waivers should be ignored when vendors have been negligent. In the long term, a framework for vendor liability and consumer protection should be developed. More specifically, the Committee suggested that users should receive better security advice when first setting up new software; that patches should automatically be downloaded when machines first go online; and that default security settings should be set as high as practicable to give users time to understand risks and tradeoffs of reducing those settings.

These recommendations broke new ground in the debate on Internet security in the UK. While they were almost completely rejected in the government's initial response to the report,[65] they have continued to generate discussion and further activity by the Lords Science and Technology Committee. They were also echoed in a recent cybersecurity review carried out by the US government, which further recommended attention to indemnification, tax incentives, and new regulatory requirements and compliance mechanisms.[66] While cybersecurity remains an enormous global problem, it does seem some consensus on a holistic strategy to combat it, taking into account law, business practice and technology or 'code', is finally beginning to emerge.

[65] The Government reply to the Fifth Report from the House of Lords Science and Technology Committee Session 2006-07 HL Paper 165, Cm 7234.

[66] US Government, 'Cyberspace Policy Review: Assuring a Trusted and Resilient Information and Communications Infrastructure' (2009), available at http://www.whitehouse.gov/assets/documents/Cyberspace_Policy_Review_final.pdf.

Index

693